ASCENT®
CENTER FOR TECHNICAL KNOWLEDGE

Autodesk® Navisworks® 2022 Fundamentals

Learning Guide

2nd Edition

AUTODESK.
Authorized Publisher

ASCENT - Center for Technical Knowledge®
Autodesk® Navisworks® 2022
Fundamentals

2nd Edition

Prepared and produced by:

ASCENT Center for Technical Knowledge
630 Peter Jefferson Parkway, Suite 175
Charlottesville, VA 22911

866-527-2368
www.ASCENTed.com

Lead Contributor: Jeff Morris

ASCENT - Center for Technical Knowledge (a division of Rand Worldwide Inc.) is a leading developer of professional learning materials and knowledge products for engineering software applications. ASCENT specializes in designing targeted content that facilitates application-based learning with hands-on software experience. For over 25 years, ASCENT has helped users become more productive through tailored custom learning solutions.

We welcome any comments you may have regarding this guide, or any of our products. To contact us please email: feedback@ASCENTed.com.

AS-NVW2201-BIM2IM-SG // IS-NVW2201-BIM2IM-SG

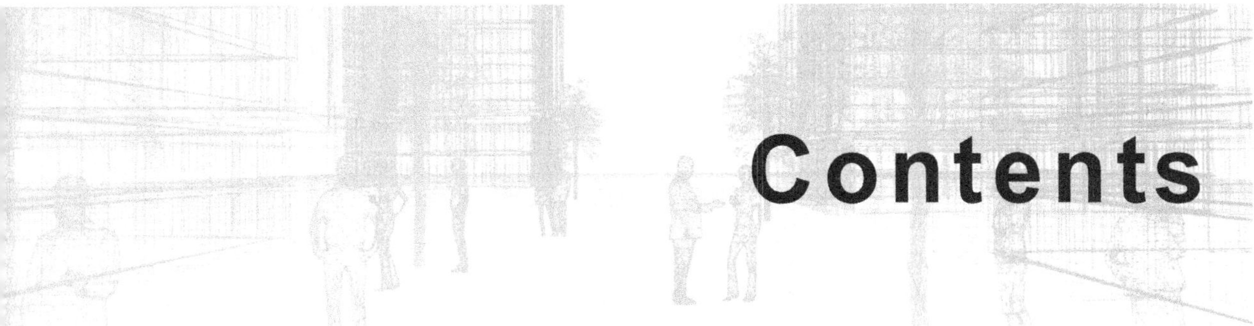

Contents

Preface

The *Autodesk® Navisworks® 2022: Fundamentals* guide shows you how to use the Autodesk® Navisworks® Manage software in a BIM workflow to better predict project outcomes, reduce conflicts, minimize changes, and lower project risks.

The guide provides instructions on how to consolidate civil, architectural, structural, and MEP models into a single BIM model and check for conflicts. It also discusses how to use the Review and Markup tools to communicate issues across disciplines, the Quantification module to create estimates for building material, and the TimeLiner, Animator, and Clash Detective to simulate construction and to identify any constructibility issues and on-site clashes. Finally, it describes how to use the Rendering feature of the software to better communicate design intent to the project team and other stakeholders.

This guide is designed for new and experienced users of the Autodesk Navisworks software in multiple disciplines.

Topics Covered

- Understanding the purpose of Building Information Modeling (BIM) and how it is applied in the Autodesk Navisworks software.
- Consolidate Models
    - Navigating the Autodesk Navisworks workspace and interface.
    - Creating a composite model.
    - Transforming models for proper alignment.

- Review and Analyze Models
  - Using basic viewing tools.
  - Saving and retrieving views.
  - Sectioning a model.
  - Investigating properties.
  - Searching for items.
  - Hiding and unhiding items.
- Communication
  - Measuring a model.
  - Adding tags and comments to model components.
  - Marking up and redlining the model.
  - Animate a model.
  - Writing scripts for interacting with the model.
  - Creating photorealistic images.
- Collaboration
  - Reviewing a model for clashes.
  - Consolidating redlines from other team members.
  - Performing quantification calculations and material take-offs.
- Construction
  - Creating a construction timeline.
  - Animating a construction timeline.

Prerequisites

- Access to the 2022.0 version of the software, to ensure compatibility with this guide. Future software updates that are released by Autodesk may include changes that are not reflected in this guide. The practices and files included with this guide might not be compatible with prior versions (e.g., 2021).
- The 2022 Civil 3D Object Enabler must be installed on the computer running Navisworks.
- A working knowledge of 3D design and task-scheduling software is recommended.

Note on Software Setup

This guide assumes a standard installation of the software using the default preferences during installation. Lectures and practices use the standard software templates and default options for the Content Libraries.

Students and Educators Can Access Free Autodesk Software and Resources

Autodesk challenges you to get started with free educational licenses for professional software and creativity apps used by millions of architects, engineers, designers, and hobbyists today. Bring Autodesk software into your classroom, studio, or workshop to learn, teach, and explore real-world design challenges the way professionals do.

Get started today - register at the Autodesk Education Community and download one of the many Autodesk software applications available.

Visit www.autodesk.com/education/home/

Note: Free products are subject to the terms and conditions of the end-user license and services agreement that accompanies the software. The software is for personal use for education purposes and is not intended for classroom or lab use.

Lead Contributor: Jeff Morris

Specializing in the civil engineering industry, Jeff authors training guides and provides instruction, support, and implementation on all Autodesk infrastructure solutions.

Jeff brings to bear over 20 years of diverse work experience in the civil engineering industry. He has played multiple roles, including Sales, Trainer, Application Specialist, Implementation and Customization Consultant, CAD Coordinator, and CAD/BIM Manager, in civil engineering and architecture firms, and Autodesk reseller organizations. He has worked for government organizations and private firms, small companies and large multinational corporations and in multiple geographies across the globe. Through his extensive experience in Building and Infrastructure design, Jeff has acquired a thorough understanding of CAD Standards and Procedures and an in-depth knowledge of CAD and BIM.

Jeff studied Architecture and a diploma in Systems Analysis and Programming. He is an Autodesk Certified Instructor (ACI) and holds the Autodesk Certified Professional certification for Civil 3D and Revit.

Jeff Morris has been the Lead Contributor for *Autodesk Navisworks: Fundamentals* since 2019.

In This Guide

The following highlights the key features of this guide.

Feature	Description
Practice Files	The Practice Files page includes a link to the practice files and instructions on how to download and install them. The practice files are required to complete the practices in this guide.
Chapters	A chapter consists of the following - Learning Objectives, Instructional Content, Practices, Chapter Review Questions, and Command Summary. • **Learning Objectives** define the skills you can acquire by learning the content provided in the chapter. • **Instructional Content**, which begins right after Learning Objectives, refers to the descriptive and procedural information related to various topics. Each main topic introduces a product feature, discusses various aspects of that feature, and provides step-by-step procedures on how to use that feature. Where relevant, examples, figures, helpful hints, and notes are provided. • **Practice** for a topic follows the instructional content. Practices enable you to use the software to perform a hands-on review of a topic. It is required that you download the practice files (using the link found on the Practice Files page) prior to starting the first practice. • **Chapter Review Questions**, located close to the end of a chapter, enable you to test your knowledge of the key concepts discussed in the chapter. • **Command Summary** concludes a chapter. It contains a list of the software commands that are used throughout the chapter and provides information on where the command can be found in the software.
Appendices	Appendices provide additional information to the main course content. It could be in the form of instructional content, practices, tables, projects, or skills assessment.

Practice Files

To download the practice files for this guide, use the following steps:

1. Type the URL ***exactly as shown below*** into the address bar of your Internet browser, to access the Course File Download page.

   Note: If you are using the ebook, you do not have to type the URL. Instead, you can access the page simply by clicking the URL below.

   https://www.ascented.com/getfile/id/cyanthera

2. On the Course File Download page, click the **DOWNLOAD NOW** button, as shown below, to download the .ZIP file that contains the practice files.

3. Once the download is complete, unzip the file and extract its contents.

   The recommended practice files folder location is:
   C:\Navisworks BIM Practice Files

   Note: It is recommended that you do not change the location of the practice files folder. Doing so may cause errors when completing the practices.

Stay Informed!

To receive information about upcoming events, promotional offers, and complimentary webcasts, visit:

www.ASCENTed.com/updates

Chapter 1

Introduction to Autodesk Navisworks

The Autodesk® Navisworks® software is used in the Building Information Modeling (BIM) workflow to review 3D designs. The software enables you to review and mark up models from different disciplines. Navigating the model is a crucial part of efficiently reviewing a BIM model.

In this chapter, you will explore the user interface and then uncover constructibility issues using the standard viewing tools, orbiting, and camera settings.

Learning Objectives in This Chapter

- Discover how to use Autodesk Navisworks to manage a project.
- Examine the user interface and understand how to use the parts most effectively.
- Identify constructibility issues in a model using the standard viewing tools.
- Improve your ability to walk and orbit around a model.

1.1 What Is Navisworks?

The Autodesk Navisworks software is used in a Building Information Modeling (BIM) workflow for reviewing 3D designs. It enables you to consolidate 3D models from multiple sources and applications, which helps you to check for clashes between disciplines. As models are consolidated, the size of the model is drastically reduced to make it possible to review multiple large models at the same time. The Autodesk Navisworks software provides tools for reviewing and markup, construction simulation, and collaboration between multiple stakeholders.

BIM is a strategy for the entire building life cycle. It includes design, construction, and facilities management. The BIM process supports the ability to coordinate, update, and share design data with team members across disciplines. Using the Autodesk Navisworks software in a BIM workflow enables design teams to have a more holistic view of multiple, integrated models and data that make up the project, as shown in Figure 1–1. This enables them to:

- Better communicate design intent
- Ensure that everything fits together properly without clashes
- Set the construction time line and sequencing.

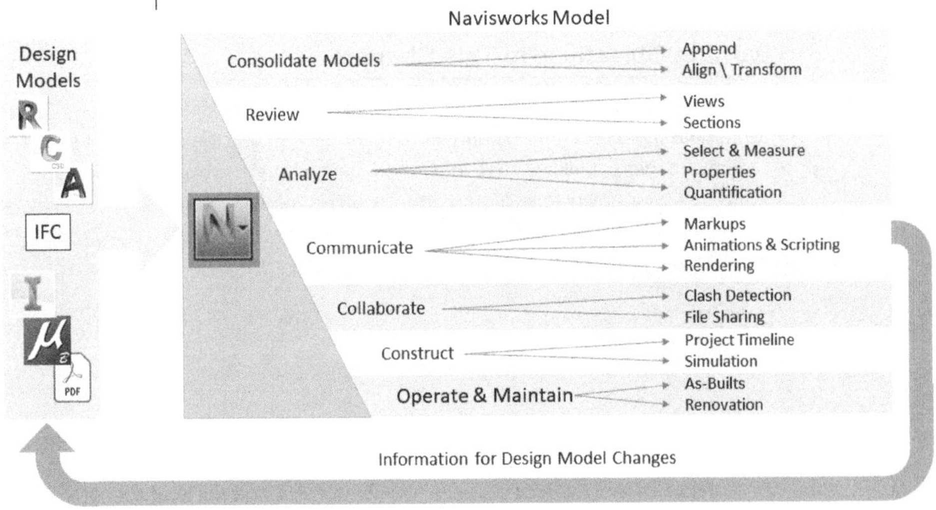

Figure 1–1

5D analysis includes 3D modeling plus time and cost.

There are several components in the Autodesk Navisworks software:

- Autodesk Navisworks Simulate provides review and communication tools for 5D analysis and coordination. It does not include Clash Detection.
- Autodesk Navisworks Manage provides tools for 5D analysis, advanced coordination (Clash Detection), and simulation.
- Autodesk Navisworks Freedom is a 3D viewer that enables stakeholders to review and explore a project model without needing the software that was used by the design team.

In this guide, you will focus on the Autodesk Navisworks Manage software, with an emphasis on how to:

- Consolidate models from different disciplines into one complete model.
- Review a model with viewing tools, including the use of walkthroughs, sections, and basic animations.
- Analyze a model by selecting and investigating items using the Selection Tree, shown in Figure 1–2.
- Communicate with all members of a project team by redlining views, as shown in Figure 1–2.

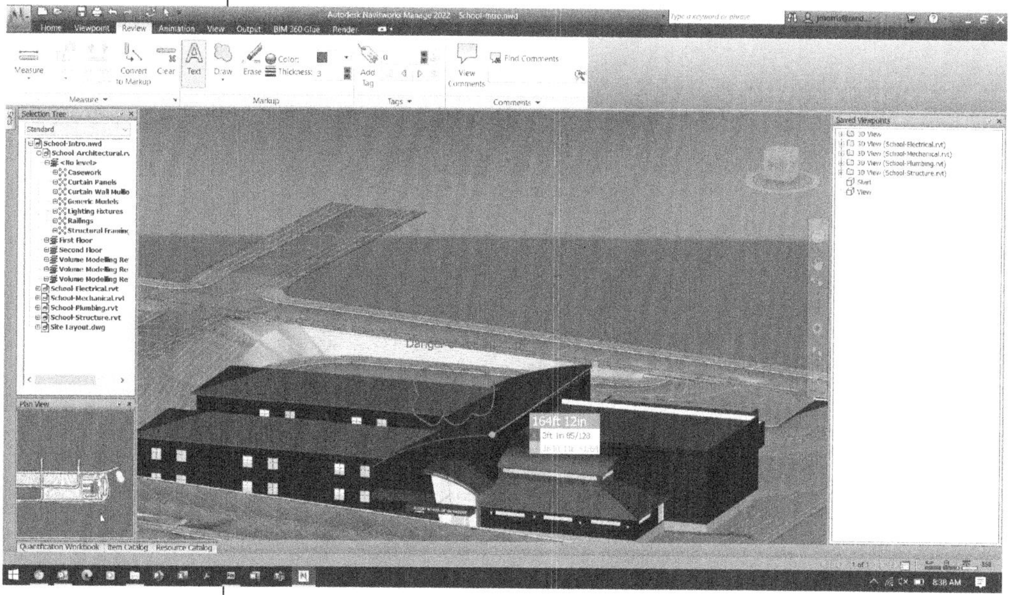

Figure 1–2

- Collaborate with all of the disciplines using clash detection tools that can be useful at all stages from early design development to construction.
- Construct the project virtually by visually reviewing the project schedule using TimeLiner.
- Operate and maintain the finished building by including links to as-builts and other information.

1.2 Overview of the Interface

The Autodesk Navisworks interface (shown in Figure 1–3) includes user interface tools that are common to most Autodesk® software, such as the application menu and ribbons. Knowing where to find the tools that you use most and how to maximize screen space by positioning various dockable windows helps you more easily view and review the model.

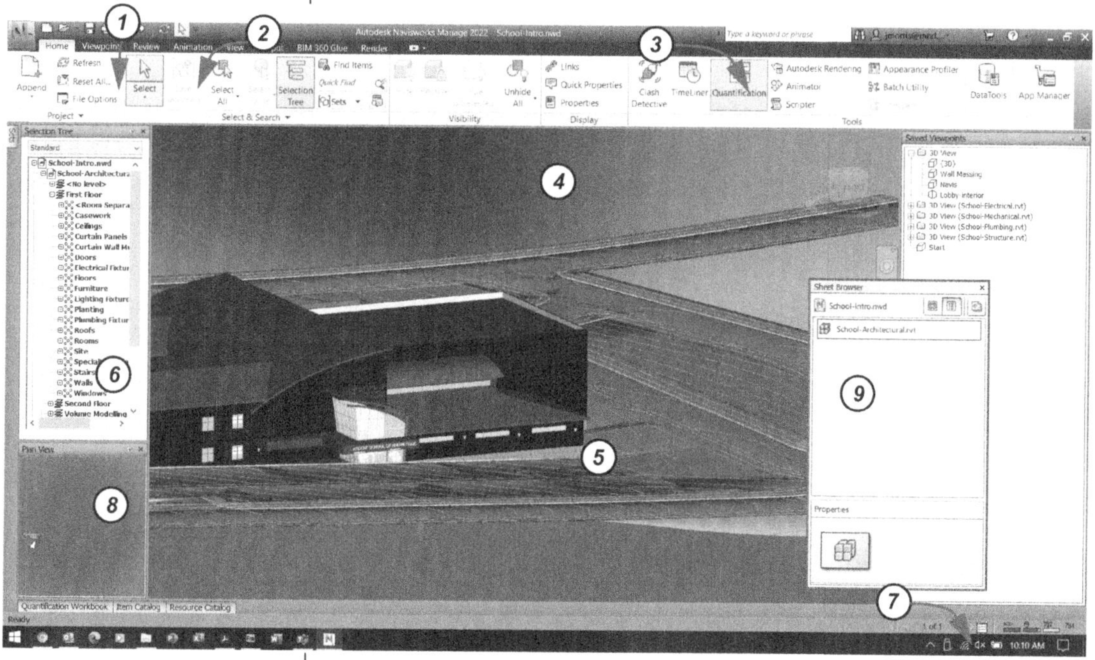

Figure 1–3

1. Application Menu	6. Dockable Windows
2. Quick Access Toolbar	7. Status Bar
3. InfoCenter	8. Plan View
4. Ribbon	9. Sheet Browser
5. Scene View	

1. Application Menu

The application menu provides access to file commands, settings, and documents. You can hover the cursor over a command to display a list of additional tools, as shown in Figure 1–4.

If you click on the primary icon, rather than the arrow, it starts the default command.

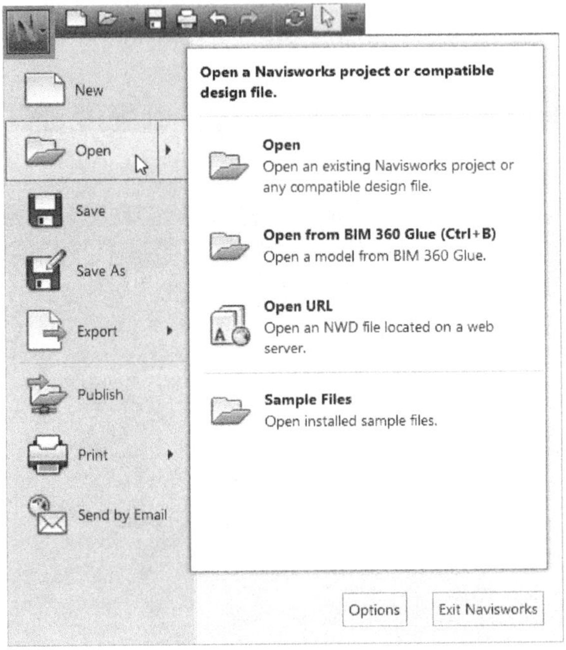

Figure 1–4

*Click **Options** to open the Options Editor where you can setup the user interface and other tools.*

- When no command is selected, a list of recently used documents displays. The documents can be reordered if required, as shown in Figure 1–5.

Click (Pin) next to a document name to keep it available.

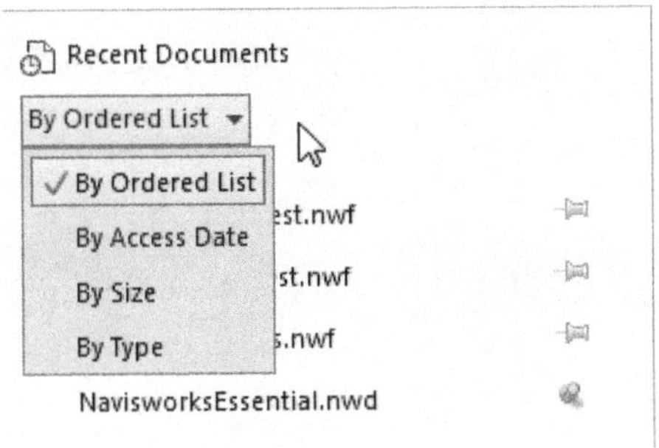

Figure 1–5

2. Quick Access Toolbar

The Quick Access Toolbar includes commonly used commands, such as **New**, **Open**, **Save**, **Print**, **Undo**, **Redo**, **Refresh**, and **Select**, as shown in Figure 1–6.

Figure 1–6

Hint: Customizing the Quick Access Toolbar

To change the docked location of the toolbar, or to add, relocate, or remove tools on the toolbar, right-click on the Quick Access Toolbar.

You can also right-click on a tool in the ribbon and select **Add to Quick Access Toolbar**, as shown in Figure 1–7.

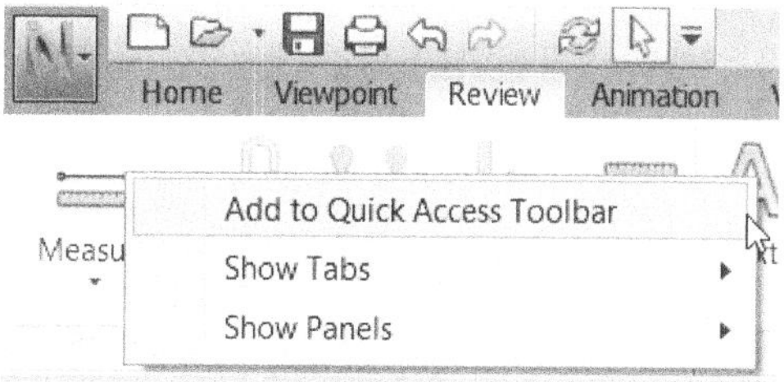

Figure 1–7

3. InfoCenter

The InfoCenter (shown in Figure 1–8) includes a search field to find help on the web, and also provides access to the Subscription Center, Communication Center, Autodesk360Services sign-in, and other help options.

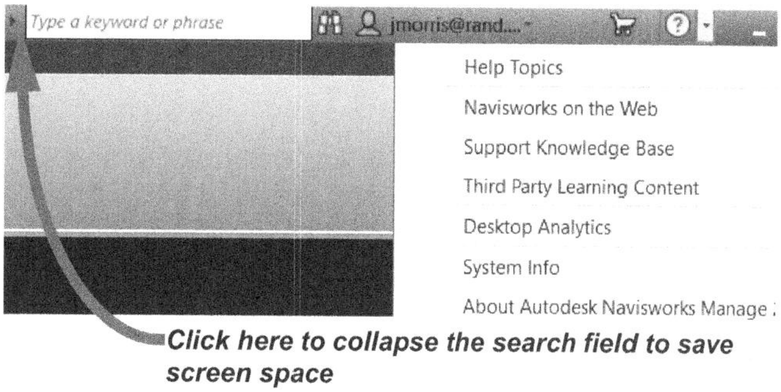

Figure 1–8

4. Ribbon

The ribbon contains tools in a series of tabs and panels, as shown in Figure 1–9. Selecting a tab displays a group of related panels. The panels contain a variety of tools, grouped by task.

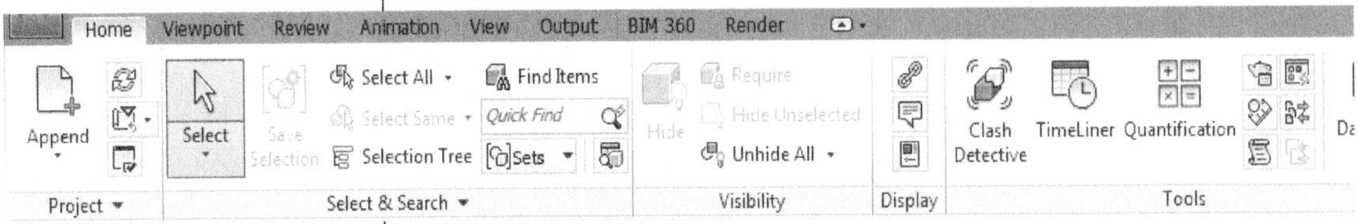

Figure 1–9

When you select an element in the scene view, the ribbon displays the *Item Tools* tab. This contains item specific tools, as shown in Figure 1–10.

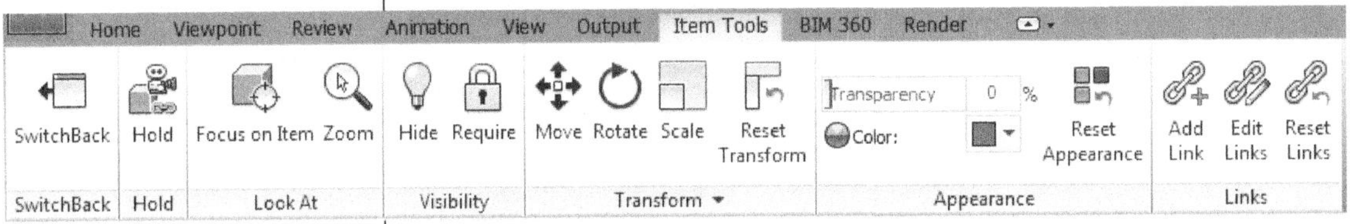

Figure 1–10

- When you hover the cursor over a tool on the ribbon, tooltips display the tool's name and a short description, as shown in Figure 1–11.

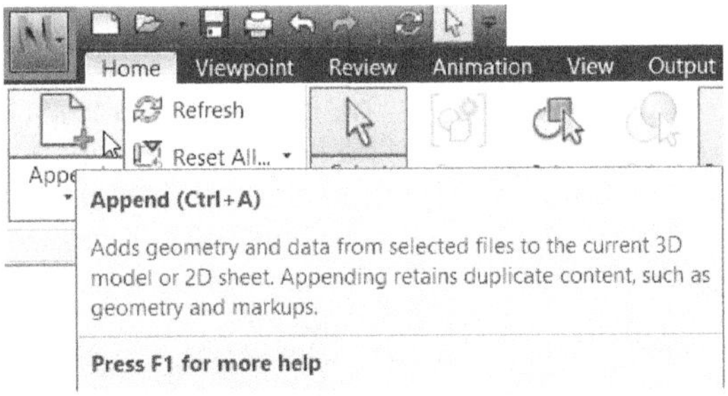

Figure 1–11

Do not press <Enter> when typing shortcuts.

- Many commands have keyboard shortcuts. For example, you can press <Ctrl>+<A> for **Append**, or <Ctrl>+<1> for **Select**. The keyboard shortcuts are listed next to the name of the command in the tooltips, as shown above in Figure 1–11.
- To rearrange the order in which the ribbon tabs display, select the tab, hold <Ctrl>, and drag the tab to a new location. The location is remembered when you restart the software.

- Any panel can be dragged by its title into the scene view area to become a floating panel. Click **Return Panels to Ribbon** (as shown in Figure 1–12) to return a panel to the ribbon.

Figure 1–12

5. Scene View

The scene view is where you view the model, as shown in Figure 1–13. You can reorient the view using viewing tools such as the ViewCube and navigation bar. You can also select items in the scene view.

Figure 1–13

- The background of the scene view varies depending on the type of view you are in. Figure 1–13 displays a perspective view with a horizon line with the *Render Style* set to **Full Render.**

6. Dockable Windows

Many of the tools in the Autodesk Navisworks software have windows that include information you can use while you are working. These windows can float in the scene view, or be docked to the top, bottom, or sides of the screen. They can be auto-hidden to display just a tab, as shown in Figure 1–14.

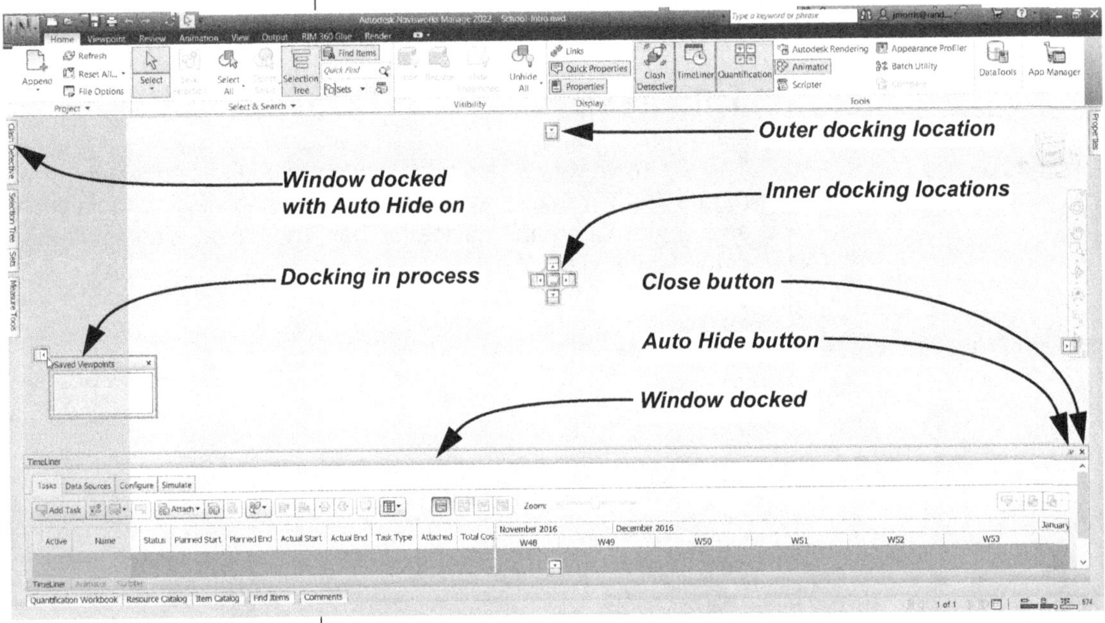

Figure 1–14

Holding <Ctrl> while moving a window prevents it from automatically docking.

- To dock a window, drag it by the title and hover over one of the location icons. A transparent blue box displays where the window can be docked. Release the cursor to place it.
- To undock a window, drag the title bar into the scene view.
- To hide a docked window, click (Auto Hide).
- To display a hidden window, hover over the tab.
- To close a window, click **Close**.
- You can toggle on or off any of the twenty-five dockable windows through the *View* tab>Workspace panel> (Windows) drop-down list.
- Windows can be tiled in the interface

Hint: Inner Docking Locations

Only the docking locations on the outer edges of the application interface enable you to pin/unpin windows. Inner docking locations cause windows to float over the scene view or tile on top of each other.

7. Status Bar

The status bar includes the Sheet Browser and File Performance information, as shown in Figure 1–15. The Sheet Browser enables you to access multi-sheet .DWF files (such as shop drawings) that might be attached to a project. The File Performance information displays information about the performance of the project file, such as the amount of memory being used by the software.

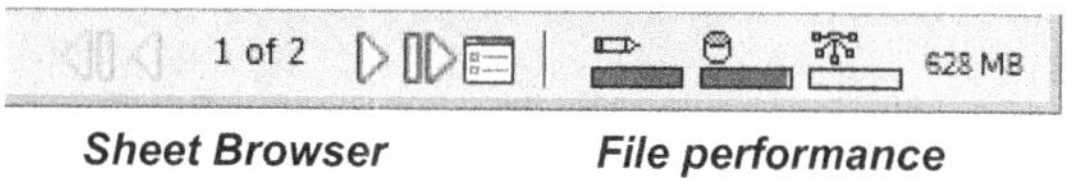

Figure 1–15

Hint: Right-Click Menus

Right-click menus enable you to quickly access required commands. These menus provide access to basic viewing commands, recently used commands, and all of the major Viewpoint commands, as shown in Figure 1–16. Additional options are available if you have an item selected.

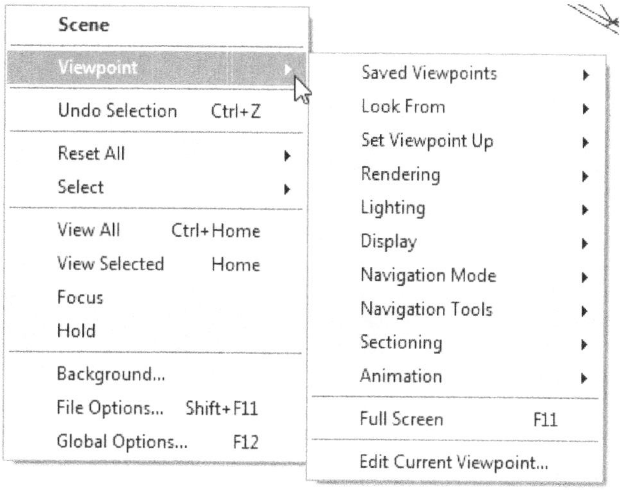

Figure 1–16

8. Plan View

A Plan View is a type of Reference view to aid in navigation in a 3D workspace. Like a bird's eye view, it gives an overall view of the model and shows where you are. You can quickly navigate to a location through the Plan View. The other type of Reference View is the Section View which aids in cutting sections through the model.

- Within the Reference View window, there are additional choices through the right-click menu, as shown in Figure 1–17.

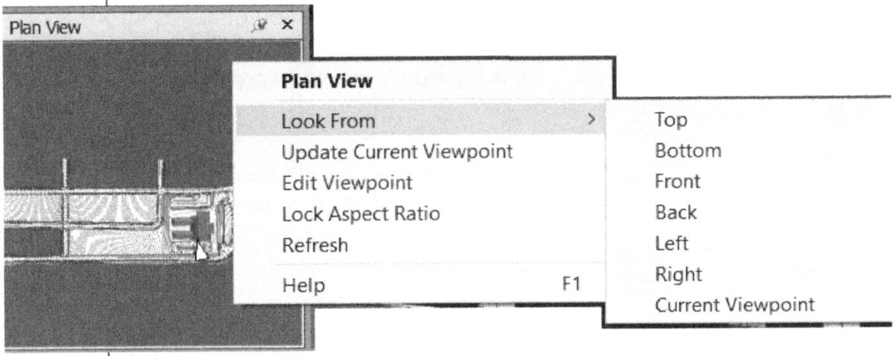

Figure 1–17

9. Sheet Browser

The Sheet Browser lists all the sheets and models in a multi-sheet file. Additional sheets can be contained within a file, such as 2D DWF files. When a particular sheet or model is selected in the Sheet Browser, a preview and thee properties of the sheet are displayed, as shown in Figure 1–18.

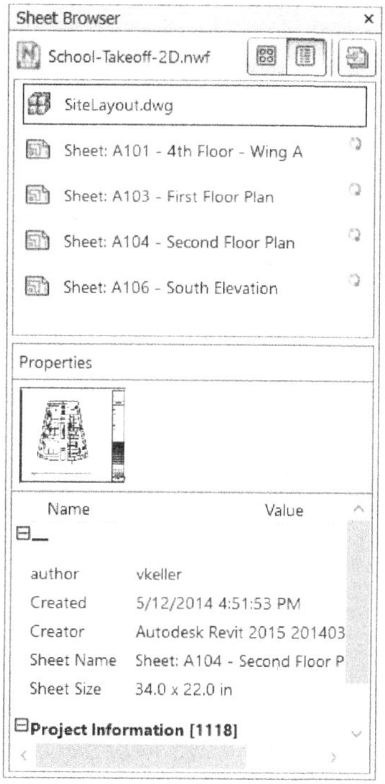

Figure 1–18

Customizing the Interface

You can customize and save the layout of the user interface for easy access to specific commands. This can help you switch between specific toolbars and windows that have the tools you require to perform certain jobs.

- When a workspace is saved, the location and size of each open window is captured.
- Changes to the ribbon or Quick Access Toolbar are not saved in the workspaces.
- Workspaces can then be shared with other users for more efficient access to corporate standards.

When the Autodesk Navisworks software is first loaded, four workspaces are available, as shown in Figure 1–19. The default workspace is the **Navisworks Standard** workspace.

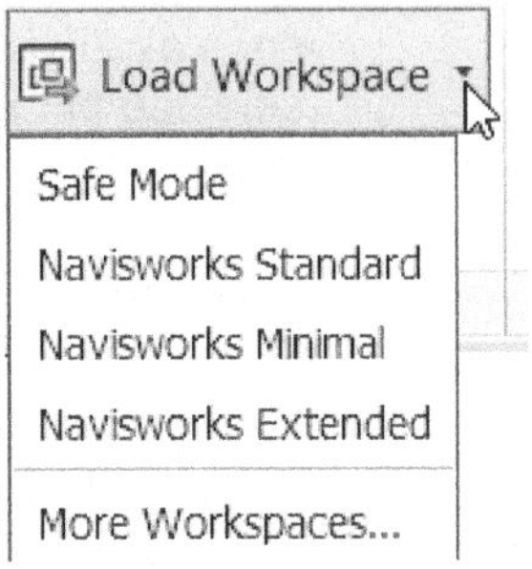

Figure 1–19

How To: Save a Workspace

1. Open, resize, and arrange windows as required.
2. In the *View* tab>Workspace panel, click (Save Workspace).
3. In the Save Current Workspace dialog box, type a name for the workspace to create a new workspace, or select the name of an existing workspace to overwrite it.
4. Click **Save**.

How To: Load a Workspace

In the *View* tab>Workspace panel, expand (Load Workspace) and select a saved workspace from the drop-down list.

Practice 1a Explore the User Interface

Practice Objective

- Configure the user interface layout.

In this practice, you will start by loading the Navisworks Standard workspace. Then, you will toggle windows on and off in the workspace to configure it to your needs.

You do not need to have a model open for this practice.

1. In the *View* tab>Workspace panel, expand (Load Workspace) and select **Navisworks Standard**, as shown in Figure 1–20.

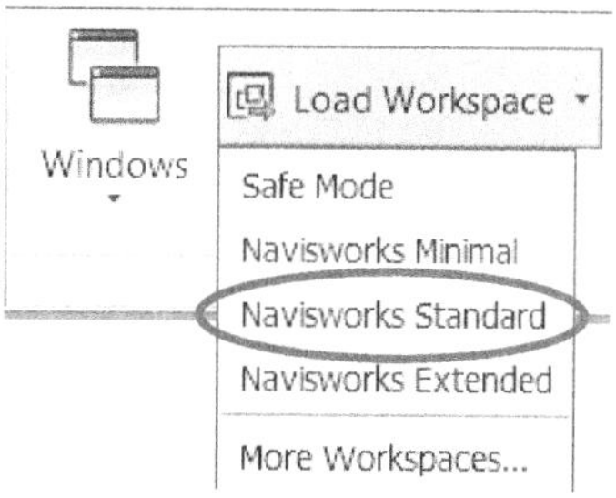

Figure 1–20

2. Review the user interface. Note the hidden, dockable windows to the left and right of the scene view.
3. In the *Home* tab>Select & Search panel, click (Selection Tree) or press <Ctrl>+<F12> to toggle off the Selection Tree window.
4. Click (Selection Tree) again to toggle the Selection Tree window back on.
5. In the Selection Tree window title bar, click (Auto Hide) to force the window to always display.
6. Click and drag the Selection Tree window title bar and move the window to the middle of the scene view to undock it.
7. Double-click on the Selection Tree window title bar to re-dock it to the left side of the screen.
8. In the Selection Tree window title bar, click (Auto Hide) to hide it.

1.3 Using Basic Viewing Tools

One of the most basic and powerful uses of the Autodesk Navisworks software is to navigate around and through a model. This enables you to present the model to others and locate any constructibility issues.

Because navigating is such a useful tool in the Autodesk Navisworks software, there are many different methods to navigate a model, including the mouse wheel, the ViewCube, the navigation bar, and the *Viewpoint* tab>Navigate panel, as shown in Figure 1–21.

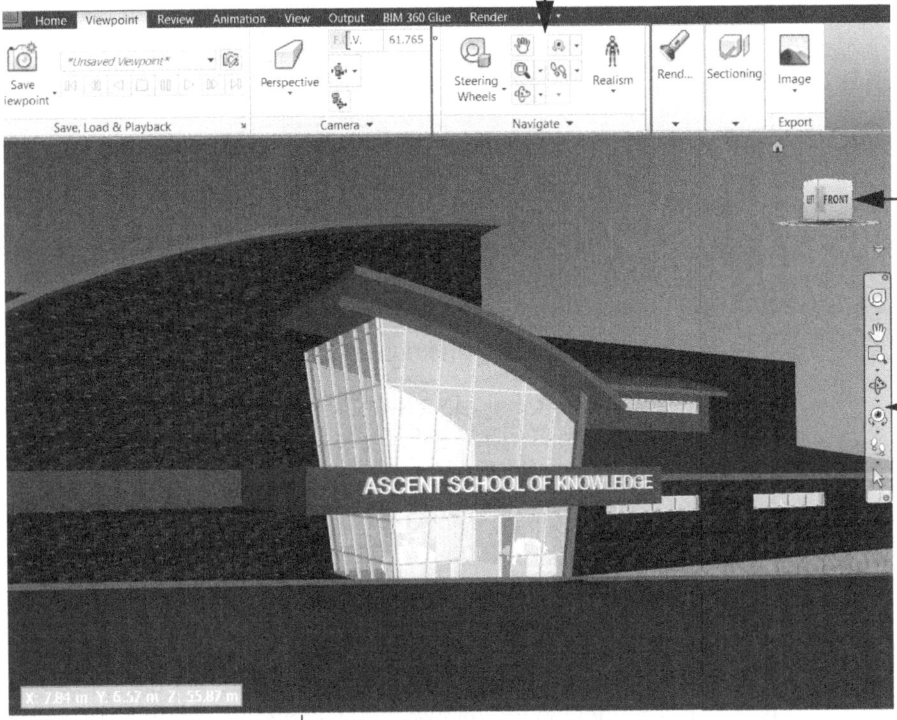

Figure 1–21

- Some of the navigation tools move the model within the view, while others are more like holding a camera.
- In the Autodesk Navisworks software, you can walk through walls.

- The camera position (x,y,z) displays at the bottom left of the main view to provide positional feedback, as shown in Figure 1–22.

Figure 1–22

Using the Mouse Wheel

You can use the mouse wheel to move around the scene. The movement is based on a pivot point, as shown in Figure 1–23.

Figure 1–23

- Note that the mouse wheel functionality changes depending on the command you are currently using. To **Zoom**, **Pan**, or **Orbit** a model, in the Quick Access Toolbar or navigation bar, click (Select), and then use the mouse wheel as follows:
  - **Zoom:** Scroll the mouse wheel up to zoom in and down to zoom out.
  - **Pan:** Hold the mouse wheel and then move the mouse to pan.
  - **Orbit:** Hold <Shift> and the mouse wheel, and then move the mouse to orbit around the scene.

- When you zoom, the current location of the cursor is the pivot point.
- Pan and Orbit use the pivot point defined by the most recent zoom.

Orbiting Around a Model

Viewing a model from all angles is an important part of using the Autodesk Navisworks software. While you can orbit a model using the mouse wheel, there are also several orbiting tools on the navigation bar and the *Viewpoint* tab>Navigate panel, as shown in Figure 1–24.

Figure 1–24

- The orbit commands all revolve around a pivot point. To specify the pivot point, hold <Ctrl> and click in the scene before orbiting.
- To use the orbit commands, select the command, click and hold the left mouse button, and then move the mouse:
    - (Orbit): Rotates in all directions while maintaining the "up" orientation.
    - (Constrained Orbit): Rotates with the model remaining on the original plane.
    - (Free Orbit): Rotates freely in any direction.

Using the ViewCube

The ViewCube provides visual clues as to where you are in a 3D view. It helps you move around the model with quick access to specific views (such as **Top**, **Front**, and **Right**), corner views, and directional views, as shown in Figure 1–25.

Figure 1–25

Hover the cursor over any face of the ViewCube to highlight it and then click to reorient the model. You can also click and drag the ViewCube to rotate it, which also rotates the model.

If you get lost in a model, use (Home) to return to a familiar view.

- (Home) displays when you hover the cursor over the ViewCube. Click to return to the view defined as **Home**.
- The right-click menu connected to the ViewCube includes options to:
  - Switch between **Perspective** and **Orthographic** mode.
  - Set the current view as the **Home** or **Front** view.
  - Open the Options Editor to access the ViewCube Options, including how the ViewCube looks and what happens when you switch views.
- In the *View* tab>Navigation Aids panel, click (ViewCube) to toggle the ViewCube on or off.

Hint: Perspective Views and Camera Options

You can switch between (Perspective) and (Orthographic) mode in the *Viewpoint* tab>Camera panel.

When in a perspective view, you can modify the **F.O.V.** (Field of View) using the slider bar. Alternatively, expand the *Camera* panel and specify the exact position and target of the camera, as shown in Figure 1–26.

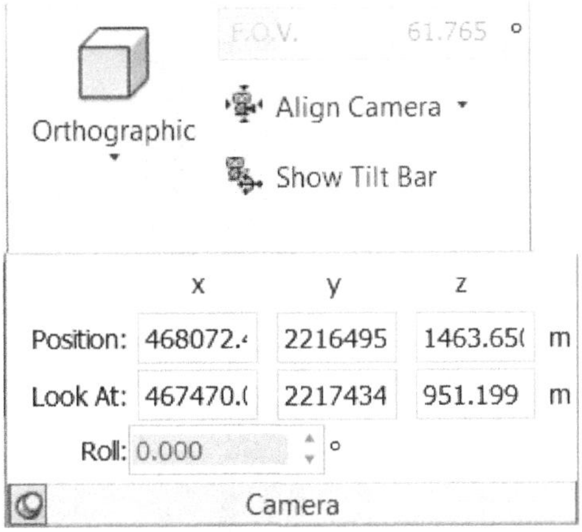

Figure 1–26

- (Align Camera) provides options to straighten the camera or focus on the X-, Y-, or Z-axes. These are similar to the faces of the ViewCube.
- (Show Tilt Bar) toggles a window with a slider bar where you can move the model up and down. This is similar to scrolling the mouse wheel up and down.

Zoom and Pan Commands

The navigation bar includes several standard viewing commands that are similar to those used in other Autodesk software, as shown in Figure 1–27. These options are also available in the *Viewpoint* tab>Navigate panel.

- In the *View* tab>Navigation Aids panel, click (Navigation Bar) to toggle it on and off.

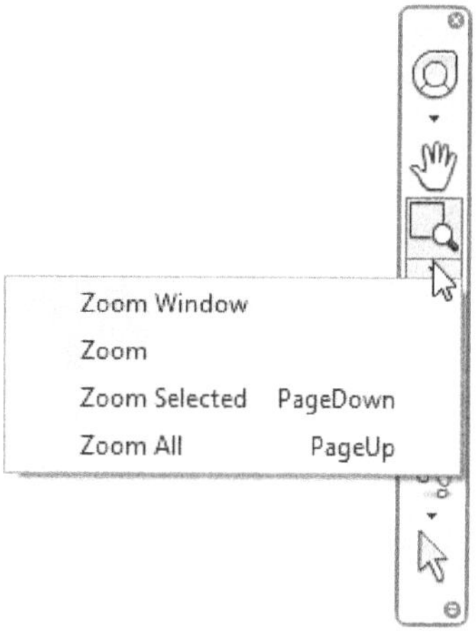

Figure 1–27

- (2D Wheel): Provides cursor-specific access to **Zoom** and **Pan**.
- (Pan): Move across a scene using the left mouse button.
- (Zoom Window): Zooms into a region that you define. To define the rectangular area you want to zoom in to, drag the cursor or select two points. This is the default command.
- (Zoom): Zoom in and out of a scene using the left mouse button.
- (Zoom Selected): Zooms in on any selected item in the scene.
- (Zoom All): Zooms in or out to fit the full model on the screen.

Walk

The (Walk) command works as if you are walking along with a camera. Drag the left mouse button to move forward or back as you walk around and through the model.

- To help you know where you are going, you can toggle on an avatar, such as the construction worker shown in Figure 1–28. In the navigation bar, expand the Walk drop-down list and select **Third Person** (or press <Ctrl>+<T>).

To change the avatar, in the Options Editor> Viewpoint Defaults> Collision pane, click ***Settings****.*

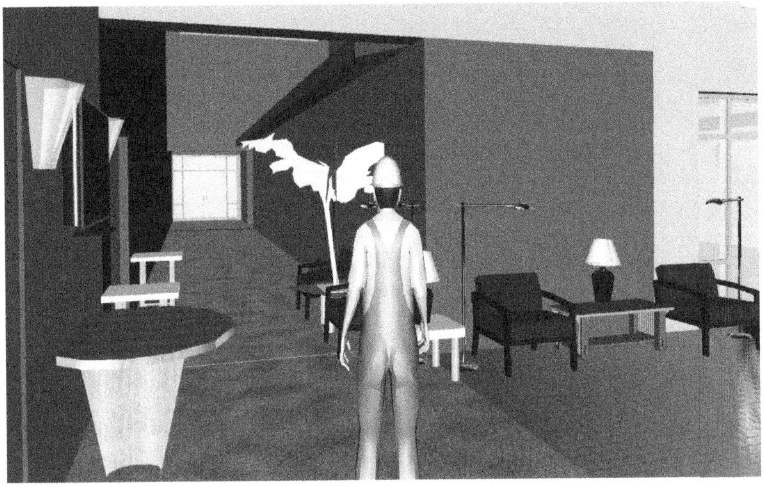

Figure 1–28

- Hold <Shift> as you drag to double the movement speed.
- Scroll the mouse wheel to move up and down, or press the wheel to move side to side. This changes the position of the camera.
- You can set the *F.O.V.* and camera *Position* (including the **Z**, which controls the height of the camera) in the *Viewpoint* tab>Camera panel.

Look Around

The (Look Around) command is a stationary camera that enables you to look right and left, up and down by dragging with the left mouse button.

Fly

The (Fly) command is similar to game navigation tools. The camera follows the direction of the mouse. Click the mouse and move it forward to start moving. Ascend or descend by moving the mouse up or down. Move left and right by moving the mouse in that direction.

Realism

The (Realism) command enables you to change how the camera interacts with the model. There are four settings you can turn on or off, as shown in Figure 1–29:

- **Collision:** Causes the camera to stop when it runs into a solid object in the model.
- **Gravity:** Causes the camera to remain a set distance from the top of objects to simulate walking on top of them.
- **Crouch:** Permits the camera to dip below objects in the model to get around them if there is enough room.
- **Third Person:** Toggles on an avatar to simulate a person being in the model.

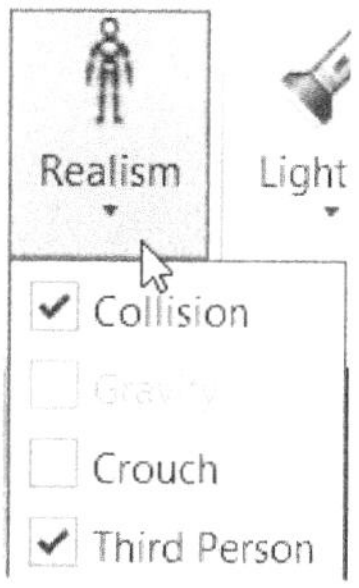

Figure 1–29

Hint: Controlling the Speed of Navigation Commands

In the *Viewpoint* tab, expand the Navigate panel to modify the *Linear Speed* and *Angular Speed*, as shown in Figure 1–30.

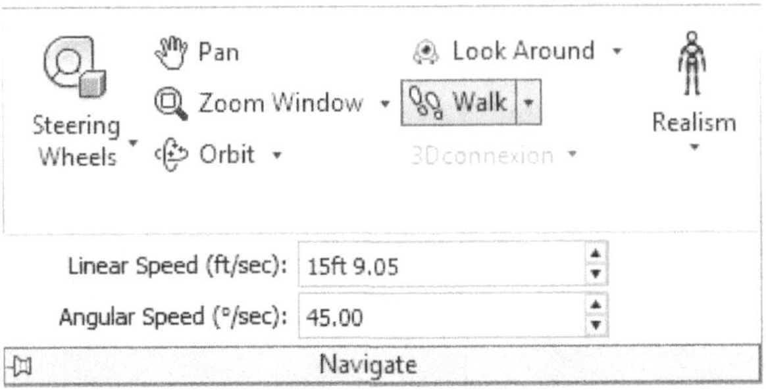

Figure 1–30

Viewpoints

In the Autodesk® Navisworks® software, you can save the position you are in the model and its vantage points. Such saved views are called viewpoints, which can be accessed through the Saved Viewpoints window, as shown in Figure 1–31.

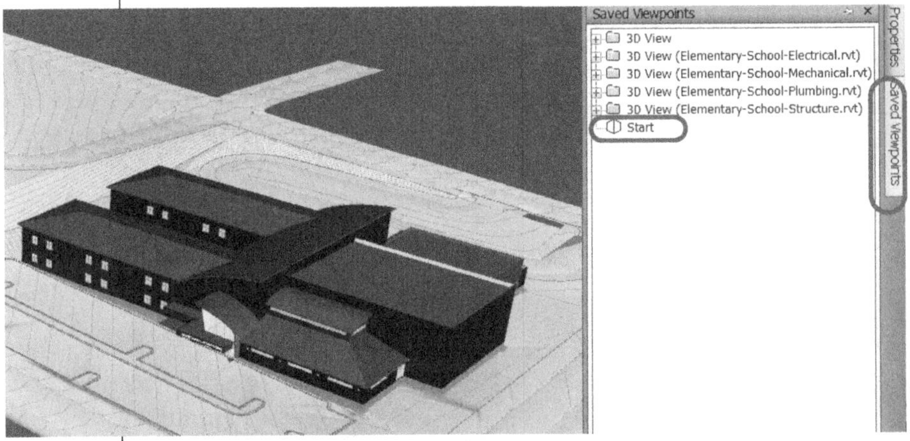

Figure 1–31

These viewpoints also save the conditions of the current scene, such as material variations, overrides, lighting conditions, objects that are hidden, etc. Viewpoints help you focus on specific conditions in a scene so that you can share information quickly with others.

Practice 1b Use Basic Viewing Tools

Practice Objectives

- Navigate the scene using the mouse.
- Navigate the scene using the ViewCube.
- Navigate the scene using the navigation bar.

In this practice, you will look around the model outside of the building and inside the building (shown in Figure 1–32) using various navigation tools.

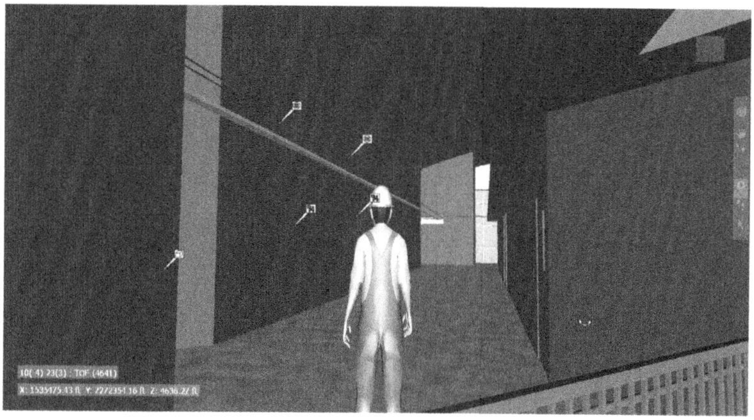

Figure 1–32

- The exact views you see might vary from the ones shown in this practice.

Task 1 - Navigate the model with the mouse and keyboard.

Note: Having project files stored in a common folder structure emulates proper BIM procedures. For training purposes, these folders reside on the local C drive, but in practice, these folders should be on a shared network drive so that the whole project team has access to them.

1. In the Quick Access Toolbar, click (Open).
2. In the Open dialog box, navigate to the *Navisworks BIM Practice Files* folder and review the list of subfolders used in these practices.
3. Open the *Intro* practice files folder.

4. In the Files of type drop-down list, select **Navisworks (*.nwd)**.

5. Select **School-Intro.nwd** and click **Open**.

6. If the drawing displays only boxes where the surfaces and roads should be (as shown in Figure 1–33), you will need to install the Autodesk Civil 3D Object Enabler. Consult *B.3 Autodesk Civil 3D Object Enabler* to install this prior to proceeding.

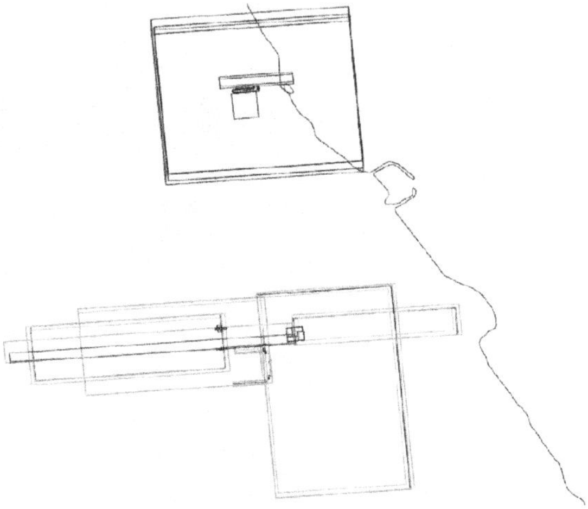

Figure 1–33

7. In the navigation bar, expand the zoom options and select **Zoom**, as shown in Figure 1–34.

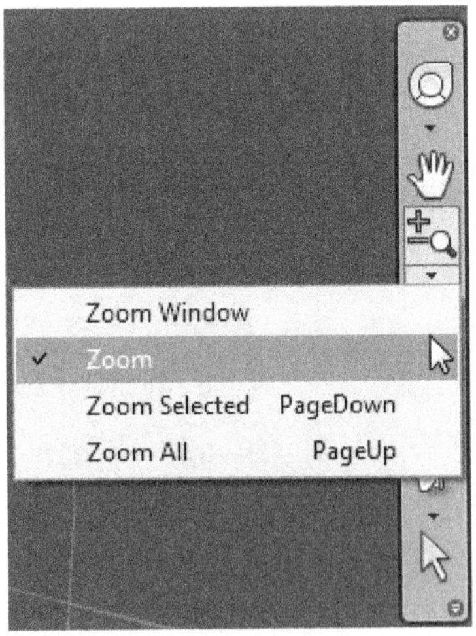

Figure 1–34

8. In the model, center the cursor over the building (as shown in Figure 1–35) and scroll with the mouse wheel to zoom in and out.

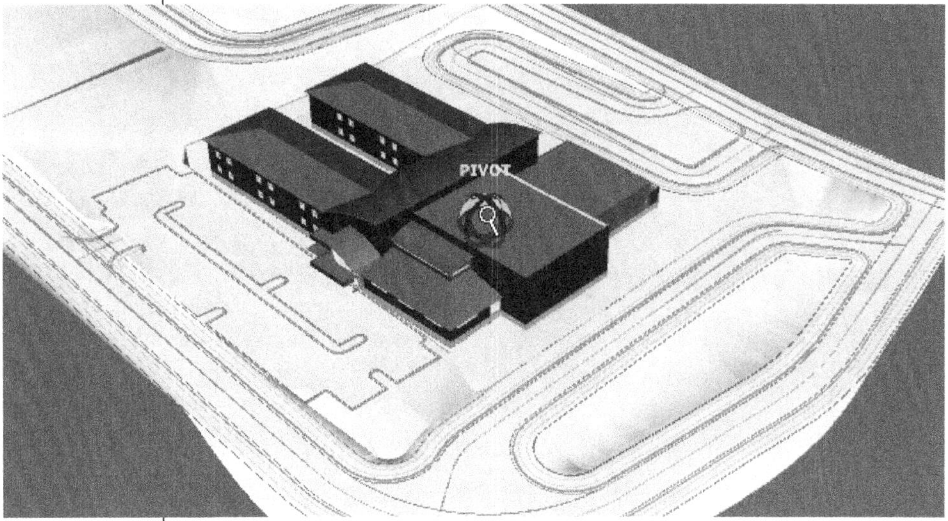

Figure 1–35

9. Hold <Shift> and the mouse wheel to orbit around the scene until the view of the model is similar to that shown in Figure 1–36.

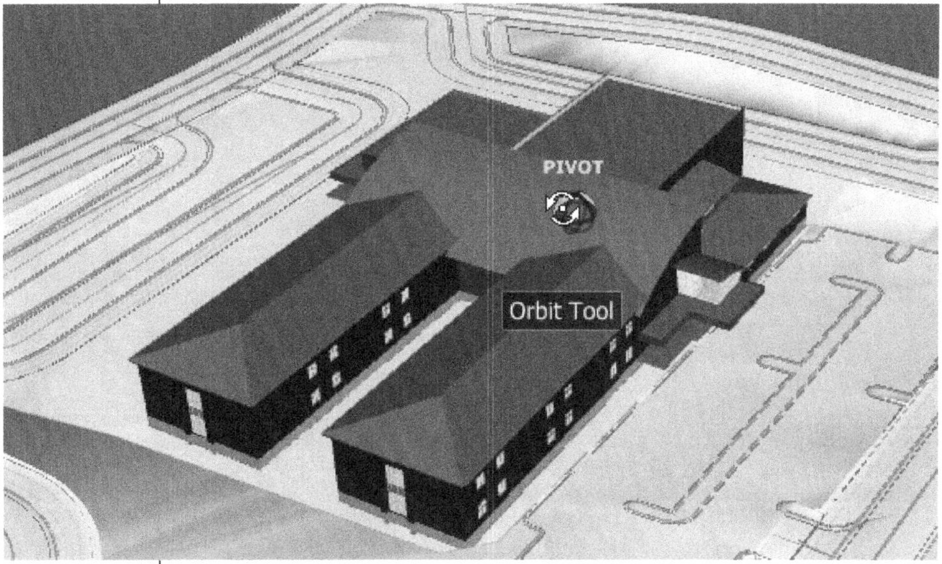

Figure 1–36

10. Hold the mouse wheel and move the mouse to the right to pan the scene and display the East side of the building, as shown in Figure 1–37.

Figure 1–37

11. Place the pivot point near the front entry, shown in Figure 1–37.

12. Use the mouse to zoom and pan the scene until you can see inside the building, such as the view shown in Figure 1–38.

Figure 1–38

13. In the *View* tab>Workspace panel, expand  (Windows) and select **Saved Viewpoints** to open the window (if not already visible; by default, it is usually in a hidden state in the top right corner of your screen).

*The **Start** saved viewpoint is not a default for Navisworks. Rather it has been created in each Navisworks file for this course's dataset.*

14. In the Saved Viewpoints window, select the saved viewpoint **Start.** This will get you back to the starting position of the model.

Task 2 - Navigate the model using the navigation bar and Navigation panel.

1. Continue working in the same model.

2. In the Selection Tree, expand **School-Intro.nwd> School-Architectural.rvt>Second Floor>Railings> Railing>Guardrail - Rectangular** and then select the second **Railing**, as shown in Figure 1–39.

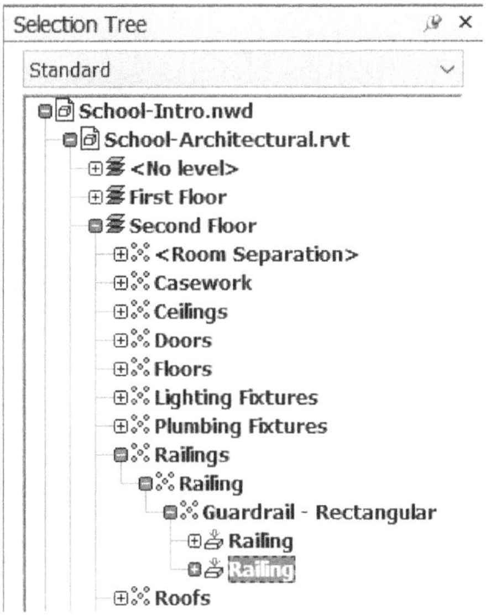

Figure 1–39

You might have to use the drop-down list to see the command.

3. In the navigation bar, click (Zoom Selected), as shown in Figure 1–40.

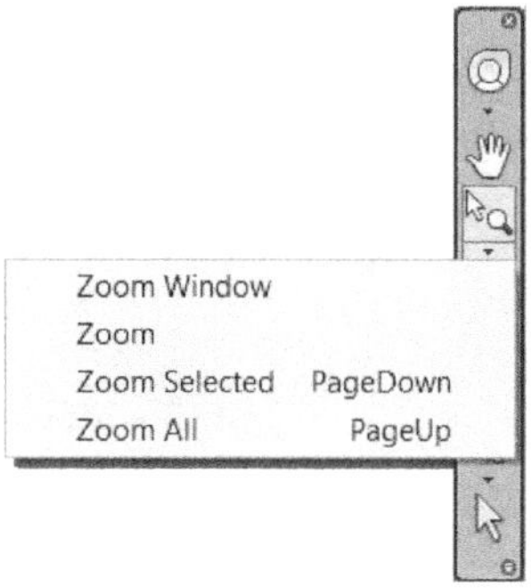

Figure 1–40

4. In the navigation bar, click (Look Around). Hold the left mouse button, move the cursor, and use the mouse wheel to zoom in and pan as required, until you are looking the other way down the hall, as shown in Figure 1–41.

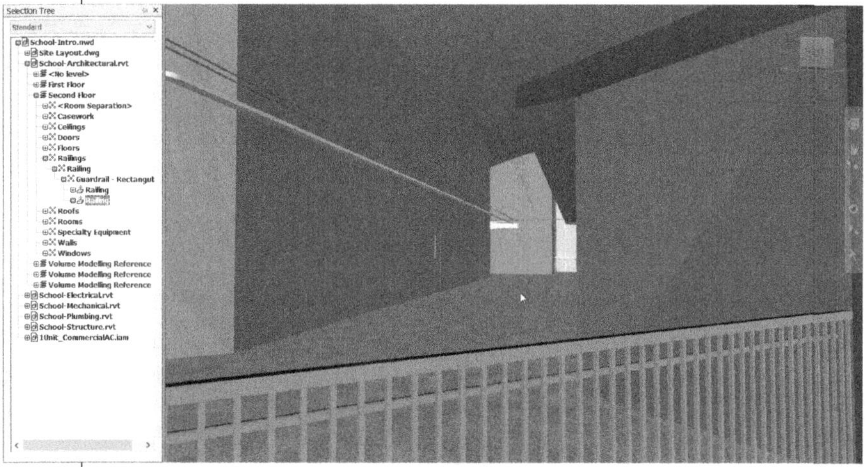

Figure 1–41

5. In the navigation bar, click (Walk).
6. Hold the left mouse button as you move the mouse slowly forward to simulate walking forward.
7. In the navigation bar, expand the Walk drop-down list and select **Third Person** to display the construction worker avatar, as shown in Figure 1–42.

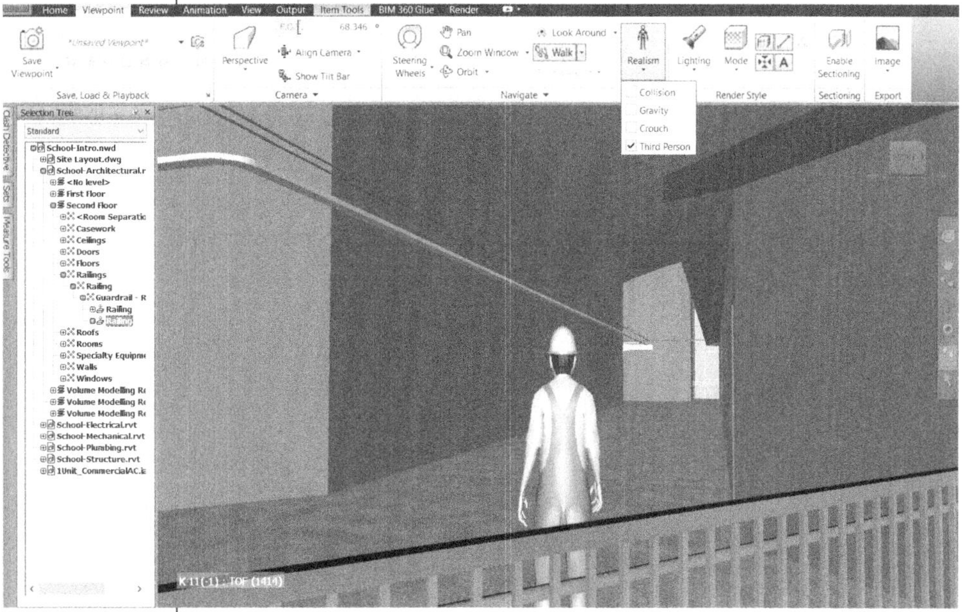

Figure 1–42

8. Continue dragging the mouse forward until you are half way down the hall. Then, pull the mouse backward slightly to simulate walking backward. Finally, move the cursor forward and to the right and watch as you walk through the wall into the bathroom.

9. Once in the bathroom, in the navigation bar, click (Look Around).

10. Hold the left mouse button as you move the mouse slowly forward to simulate looking up, then pull it back to look down. Next, move the mouse to the right to look around the room. Move it left to return to the original focus.

11. Hover the cursor over the ViewCube and click (Home).

12. In the ViewCube, click on the top south-east corner (as shown in Figure 1–43) to view the model in a perspective view.

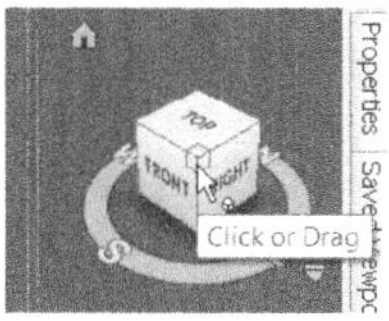

Figure 1–43

13. Press <Ctrl>+<T> to toggle off the **Third Person** view and in the navigation bar, click (Fly)
14. Click the left mouse button and then move the mouse forward to start moving. Ascend or descend by moving the mouse up or down. Move left and right by moving the mouse in that direction.
15. In the *Viewpoint* tab>Navigate panel, expand (Realism) and toggle on **Collision**.
16. Purposely move directly into the building and note how the camera stops as it collides.
17. Click (Home) on the ViewCube.
18. In the navigation bar, expand **Fly**, toggle off **Collision**, and then select **Walk**.
19. In the Quick Access Toolbar, click (New). This closes the file you were working in and opens a blank file.

Chapter Review Questions

1. If you have lost all of your dockable windows and tools, what is the fastest way to get them back?
   a. Use the Undo arrow in the Quick Access Toolbar.
   b. Close and restart the software.
   c. Select the required workspace.
2. In the following parts of the user interface, where are you most likely to find viewing tools?
   a. Quick Access Toolbar
   b. Dockable Window
   c. Scene View
   d. Status Bar
3. What do you do if you want a window available but not taking space from the scene view?
   a. Dock it to the side.
   b. Set it to Auto Hide.
   c. Move it off the screen.
   d. Open and close it.
4. How do you pan sideways in a model?
   a. Hold the mouse wheel and drag the mouse sideways.
   b. Hold the left mouse button and drag the mouse sideways.
   c. Hold the right mouse button and drag the mouse sideways.
5. How do you ensure that the camera cannot go through walls?
   a. Toggle on the **Collision** option.
   b. There is no way to prevent the camera from going through walls.
   c. Toggle on the **Background** option.
   d. Toggle on the **Gravity** option.

6. How do you quickly return to a default preset view of a model?
    a. Use the mouse wheel to zoom out.
    b. Hover the cursor over the ViewCube and click (Home).
    c. In the navigation bar, click (Zoom All).
    d. Click on the top south-east corner of the ViewCube.

Command Summary

Button	Command	Location
	**Constrained Orbit**	• Navigation Bar • **Ribbon:** *Viewpoint* tab>Navigate panel> expand Orbit
	**Fly**	• Navigation Bar>expand Walk • **Ribbon:** *Viewpoint* tab>Navigate panel> expand Walk
	**Free Orbit**	• Navigation Bar • **Ribbon:** *Viewpoint* tab>Navigate panel> expand Orbit
	**Load Workspace**	• **Ribbon:** *View* tab>Workspace panel
	**Look Around**	• Navigation Bar • **Ribbon:** *Viewpoint* tab>Navigate panel
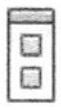	**Navigation Bar**	• **Ribbon:** *View* tab>Navigation Aids panel
	**Open**	• Application Menu • Quick Access Toolbar
	**Orbit**	• Navigation Bar • **Ribbon:** *Viewpoint* tab>Navigate panel
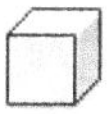	**Orthographic**	• Navigation Bar • **Ribbon:** *Viewpoint* tab>Camera panel
	**Pan**	• Navigation Bar • **Ribbon:** *Viewpoint* tab>Navigate panel
	**Perspective**	• Navigation Bar • **Ribbon:** *Viewpoint* tab>Camera panel
	**Save Workspace**	• **Ribbon:** *View* tab>Workspace panel
	**Steering Wheels**	• Navigation Bar • **Ribbon:** *Viewpoint* tab>Navigate panel
	**ViewCube**	• **Ribbon:** *View* tab>Navigation Aids panel
	**Walk**	• Navigation Bar • **Ribbon:** *Viewpoint* tab>Navigate panel
	**Windows**	• **Ribbon:** *View* tab>Workspace panel

	**Zoom**	• Navigation Bar>expand Zoom • **Ribbon:** *Viewpoint* tab>Navigate panel> expand Zoom
	**Zoom All**	• Navigation Bar>expand Zoom • **Ribbon:** *Viewpoint* tab>Navigate panel> expand Zoom
	**Zoom Selected**	• Navigation Bar>expand Zoom • **Ribbon:** *Viewpoint* tab>Navigate panel> expand Zoom
	**Zoom Window**	• Navigation Bar>expand Zoom • **Ribbon:** *Viewpoint* tab>Navigate panel> expand Zoom

Chapter 2

Consolidate Trade Models

The Autodesk® Navisworks® software is a complex Building Information Modeling (BIM) application that enables design teams to view project information independent of the software used to create the original design. Multiple models can be opened and stitched together inside the Autodesk Navisworks software to ensure all parts of the project work together. In this chapter, you will learn how to open a model and append additional models to it for steps to consolidate models in a BIM workflow.

Learning Objectives in This Chapter

- Open and save Autodesk Navisworks software-specific files.
- Consolidate a model using files from different types of software.
- Set the units for an appended model.
- Align models from different design team members.

BIM Workflow: Consolidate Models

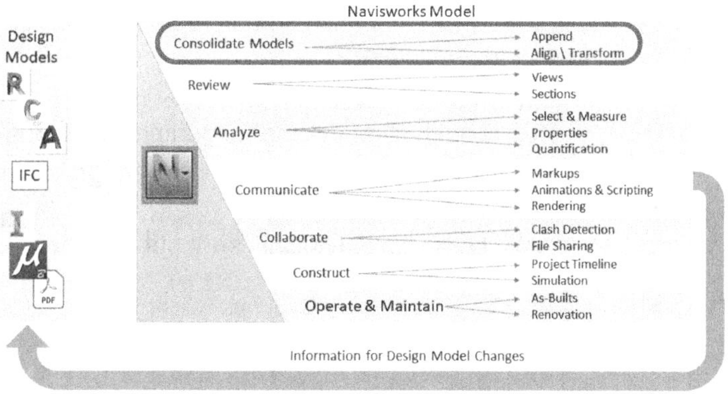

2.1 Consolidating the Model

The Autodesk Navisworks software is primarily used to combine CAD and BIM files from different disciplines into one composite model. These files can be 2D or 3D, and can be created in Autodesk® software (e.g., AutoCAD®, Autodesk® Civil 3D®, Autodesk® Revit®, etc.) or in software provided by other vendors. The advantage of using the Autodesk Navisworks software to combine models is the reduction in file sizes. For instance, if you have a 30 MB Autodesk Revit file, when you bring it into the Autodesk Navisworks software, it is reduced to 4 MB. The software simplifies the model to speed up visualization without losing details.

Many different file formats can be opened directly in the Autodesk Navisworks software or can be appended together into a single consolidated model. Figure 2–1 shows two appended models with the structural model selected.

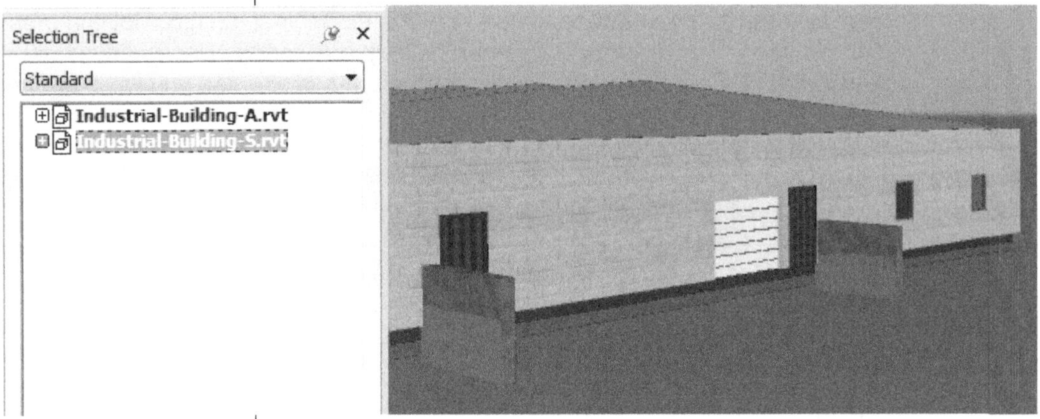

Figure 2–1

There are three main file types created by the Autodesk Navisworks software:

- **Navisworks (.NWD):** The current state (or "snapshot") of a project, with all of the model geometry and redlines included.
  - These files do not update if a change is made to the original linked files.
  - A .NWD file is typically sent out for others to review at set stages of the project.

- **Navisworks File Set (.NWF):** Includes links to the original files that form an Autodesk Navisworks model and redlines.
  - The model updates in these files when changes are made to the linked files.
  - The .NWF file is typically the file that you work in the most.

To refresh an updated model inside the .NWF file, you might need to delete the .NWC file.

- **Navisworks Cache (.NWC):** Snapshots of each original file that are created automatically when you open or append files from other software.
  - As long as the original file is not updated, the Autodesk Navisworks software uses these cache files as the data source when a file set is opened.
  - You typically do not work in cache files.

How To: Start a Navisworks Project

1. In the Quick Access Toolbar or Application Menu, click  (New). Alternatively, open a compatible file type.
2. In the *Home* Tab>Project panel, click  (Append). Alternatively, in the Quick Access Toolbar, expand  (Open) and click **Append**, or press <Ctrl>+<A>.

3. In the Append dialog box, expand the Files of type drop-down list and select the file format you want to use, as shown in Figure 2–2.
    - You can open or append many types of files, including Autodesk Navisworks, Autodesk Revit, AutoCAD, .DWG, and .DWF formats, as shown in Figure 2–2.

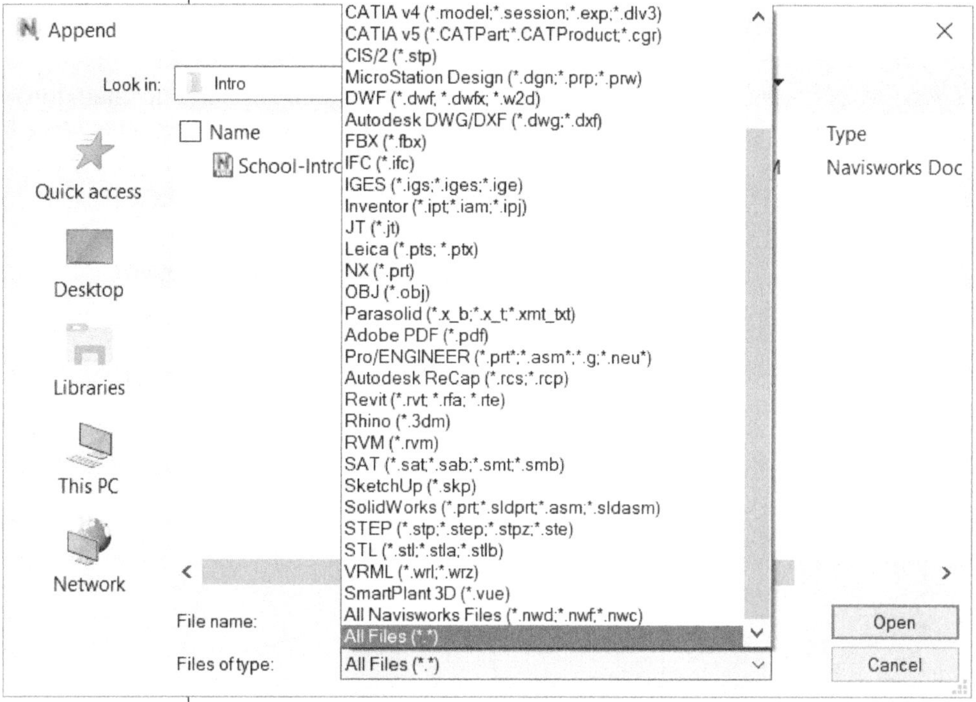

Figure 2–2

You can select multiple files to open or append by holding either <Shift> or <Ctrl>.

4. Navigate to the appropriate folder and select a file.
5. Click **Open**.
6. Continue appending other models as required.
7. In the Quick Access Toolbar or Application Menu, click (Save). The first time you save a file, the Save As dialog box opens. Select the type of Autodesk Navisworks file you want to save.

- Files can be saved as Navisworks File Set (.NWF) or Navisworks (.NWD). You can also save files so that they are compatible with previous versions of the Autodesk Navisworks software, as shown in Figure 2–3.

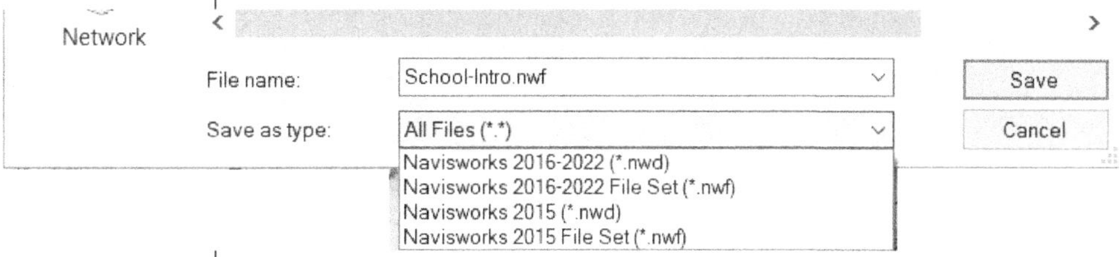

Figure 2–3

2.2 Aligning Models

When appending multiple models together, it is important to ensure that they are scaled properly and line up with each other correctly. By doing this, you can ensure that you get the correct measurements when you measure the model, and that clash detections are as accurate as possible.

Note that you are not asked for an insertion point or a scale factor during the Append process. These are set after the model is appended using the Units and Transform dialog box.

File Units

Each file has its own units. When you append files, they inherit the units of the base file and are scaled to match. If the units do not match as expected, you can modify each model's units, as shown in Figure 2–4.

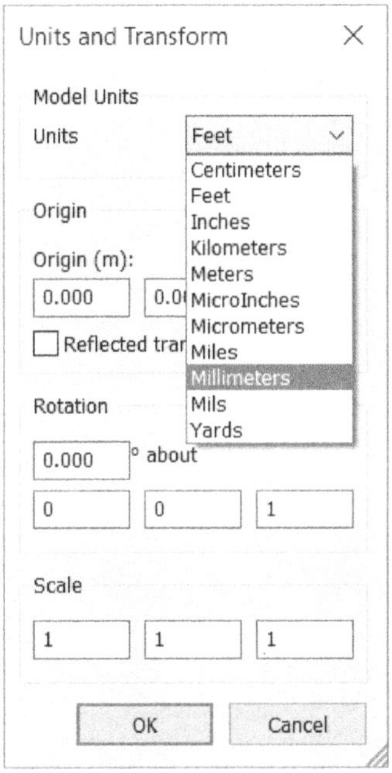

Figure 2–4

How To: Set the File Units

1. Confirm with the owner of the model which coordinate system they used to create their model.
2. Expand  (Application Menu) and select **Options**.

Select the units you want to use for your measurements in the Autodesk Navisworks model.

3. In the Options Editor dialog box, set the units for the base Navisworks model as follows, as shown in Figure 2–5:
   - In the left panel, expand **Interface** and select **Display Units**.
   - In the right panel, select the required units for *Linear Units* and *Angular Units*.
   - Set the *Decimal Places* precision for the units.
   - Click **OK**.

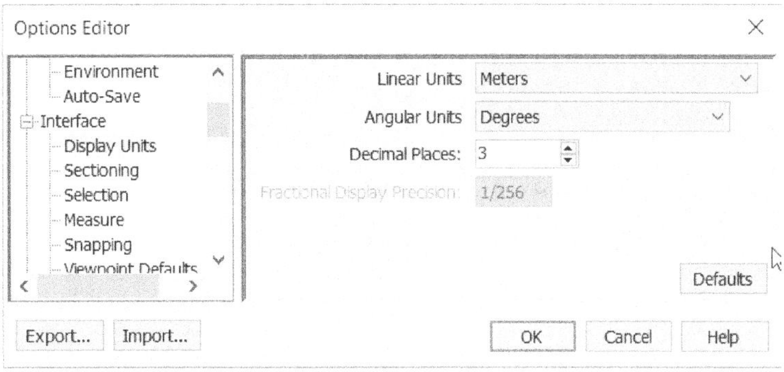

Figure 2–5

4. In the Selection Tree, select an appended model, right-click on it, and select **Units and Transform...** to set only that model's units.
5. In the Units and Transform dialog box, select the units that the file was created in, as shown in Figure 2–6. Click **OK**.

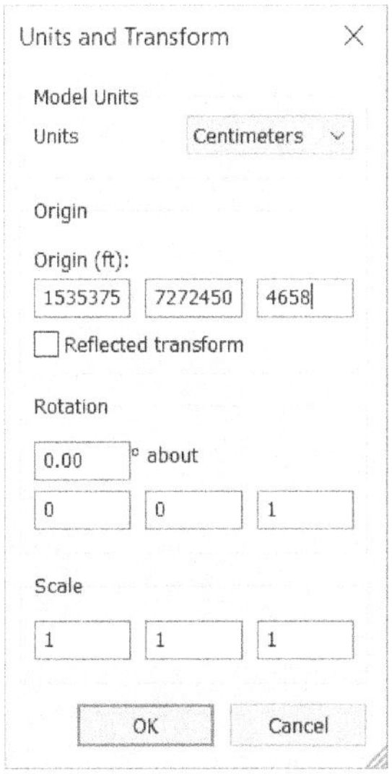

Figure 2–6

The appended model is scaled to match the base model's units.

File Transformation

Civil engineers typically work in real world coordinates, like state plane coordinate systems. Each of their models often have a different base point according to where their projects are located in the world. On the other hand, architects often have a model base point of 0,0,0, unless they input the project base point manually inside of the Autodesk Revit software.

You must perform a file transformation when the models from different design team members do not line up correctly. There are two ways to transform a file:

- **Using real world coordinates:** This setting uses the real world coordinates (as shown in Figure 2–7) located at the centroid of the appended model. Note that each model must be transformed individually when using this method.
- **Using a difference in coordinates:** This enables you to enter the distance you need the models to move in the X-,Y-, and Z-directions, as shown in Figure 2–8. This method can be used on multiple models simultaneously if they all need to move the same distance.

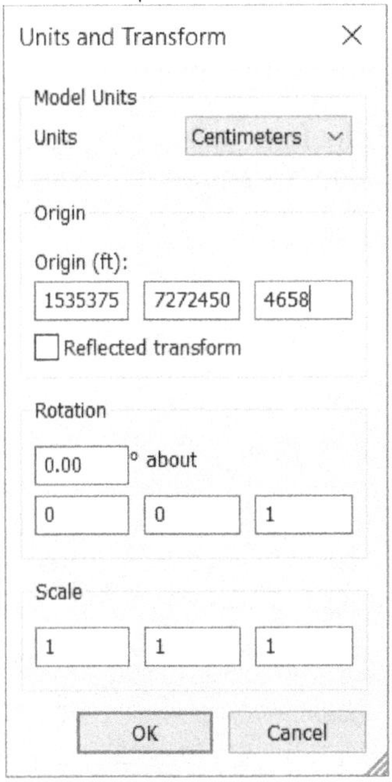

Figure 2–7

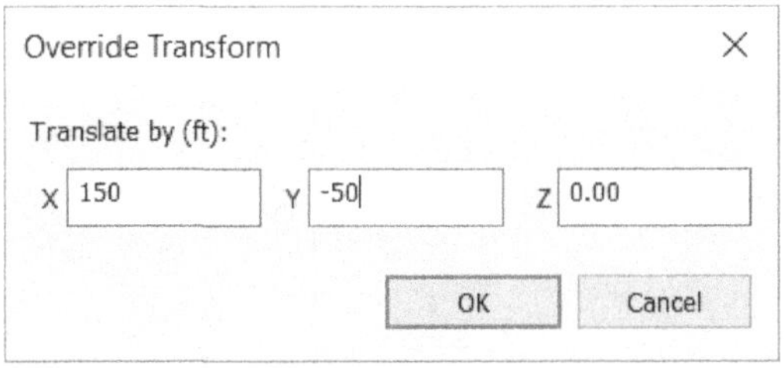

Figure 2–8

How To: Transform a File Using Real-World Coordinates

1. Confirm with the owner of the model which coordinate system they used to create their model.
2. In the Selection Tree, select an appended model, right-click on it, and select **Units and Transform** to set the model's units.
3. In the Units and Transform dialog box, enter the origin X-, Y-, and Z-coordinates, as shown in Figure 2–9.

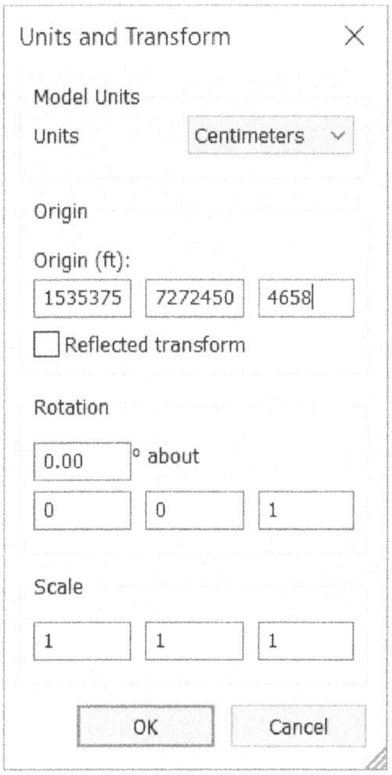

Figure 2–9

4. Click **OK**.

How To: Transform Models Using a Difference in Coordinates

1. In the Selection Tree window, select all of the files that need to be transformed.
2. Right-click on any one of the selected files and select **Override Item>Override Transform**, as shown in Figure 2–10.

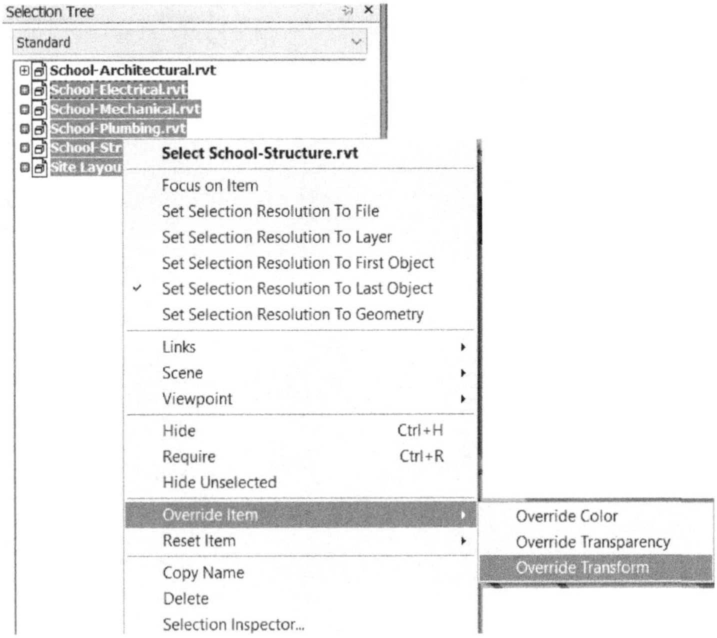

Figure 2–10

3. In the Override Transform dialog box, type the required X-, Y-, and Z-distances to move the models (as shown in Figure 2–11), and then click **OK**.

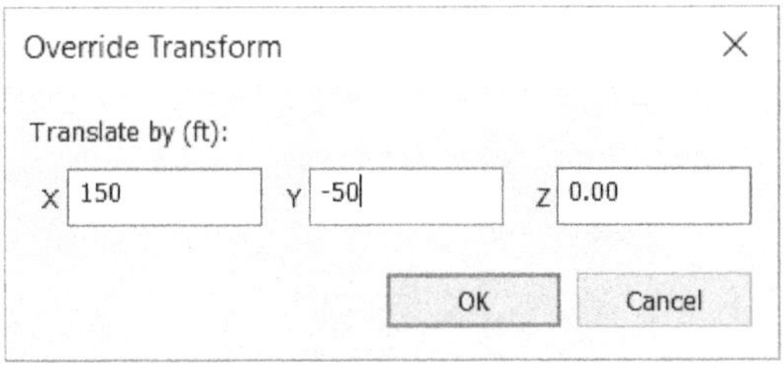

Figure 2–11

Hint: Heads Up Display (HUD)

You might need to determine where you are in a model before you can calculate the transformation coordinates to use. The Heads Up Display (HUD) information displays in the lower-left corner of the scene view, as shown in Figure 2–12.

- The location information that displays is the current camera location.
- Panning and zooming in the scene causes the coordinates in the HUD to change without moving the cursor.
- To toggle the display the various HUD elements, in the *View* tab>Navigation Aids panel, expand (HUD) and select **XYZ Axes**, **Position Readout**, or **Grid Location**.

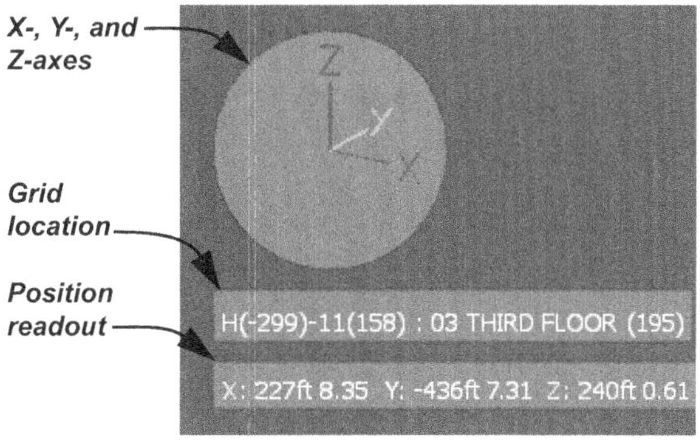

Figure 2–12

Civil 3D/Revit Coordination

Autodesk Civil 3D and Autodesk Revit are the two Autodesk "flagships" for civil engineering and building design respectively. There are many workflows to coordinate between these two applications, some of which involve BIM 360. These workflows may involve adding a site to the Revit model, where the Revit project basepoint is geo-referenced to coincide with the Civil 3D coordinate system.

If the authors of the Revit models that are being incorporated into a Navisworks model have access to these coordination tools, they should be encouraged to set a site in the Revit models that is geo-referenced and make it current prior to issuing the models.

Practice 2a Consolidate Models

Practice Objectives

- Consolidate models from multiple software sources.
- Align models with each other.

In this practice, you will open the preliminary planning phase to review the initial project layout, as designed in the Autodesk InfraWorks program and exported as an .FBX file, shown in Figure 2–13. Then, you will consolidate many of the design models into one Autodesk Navisworks file as the first step in the BIM workflow.

Figure 2–13

Task 1 - Open the preliminary design and review the project.

In this task, you will open an .FBX file that was created from an Autodesk InfraWorks model during the preliminary planning phase of the project. This enables you to review the early design of the project.

1. In the Quick Access Toolbar, click (Open).
2. In the Open dialog box, set the *Files of type* to **FBX (*.fbx)**.
3. Navigate to the *Navisworks BIM Practice Files/Project Files/InfraWorks Files* folder and select **SiteLayout.fbx**.

4. Click **Open**.

5. In the ViewCube, click on the SW corner to view the model in a South-West isometric view.

*If the Selection Tree is not displayed, go to the View tab>Workspace panel, expand **Windows** and select **Selection Tree**.*

6. Zoom and pan the model to become familiar with it.

7. In the Selection Tree, expand **SiteLayout.fbx>ID 0>ID -1** and select the first 7 **Mesh 1** items one at a time to view the items that are highlighted in the scene, as shown in Figure 2–14.

Figure 2–14

8. Press <Esc> to release the selection.

Task 2 - Consolidate multiple models into one file.

In this task, you will open an Autodesk Revit architectural model and append other Autodesk Revit models to it.

1. In the Quick Access Toolbar, click (Open).
   - Opening a file automatically closes any other open file.

2. In the Open dialog box, change the *Files of type* to **All Files (*.*)**.

3. In the open dialog box, expand the *Files of type* drop-down list and set the file format to **Revit (*.rvt; *.rfa; *.rte)**, as shown in Figure 2–15.

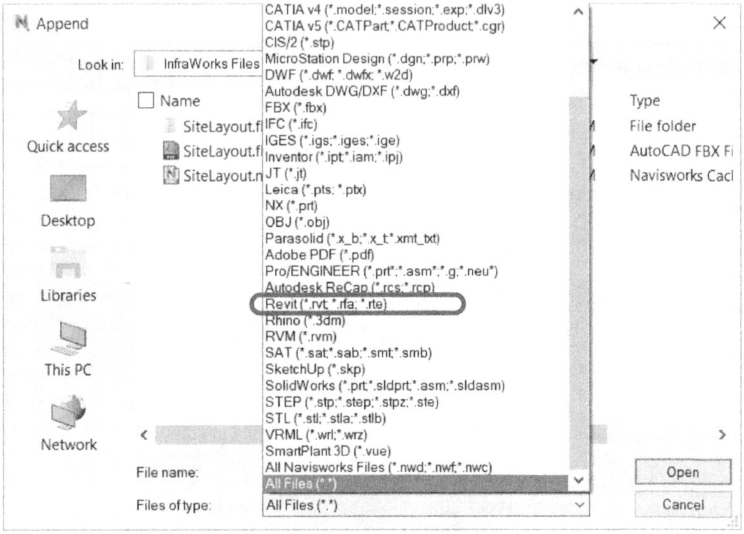

Figure 2–15

4. Navigate to the *Navisworks BIM Practice Files/Project Files/ Revit Files* folder and select **School-Architectural-Local.rvt**.

5. Click **Open**.

6. In the *View* tab>Navigation Aids panel, click (HUD), as shown in Figure 2–16. This is for Heads Up Display, which displays the coordinates in the lower left corner of the scene view.

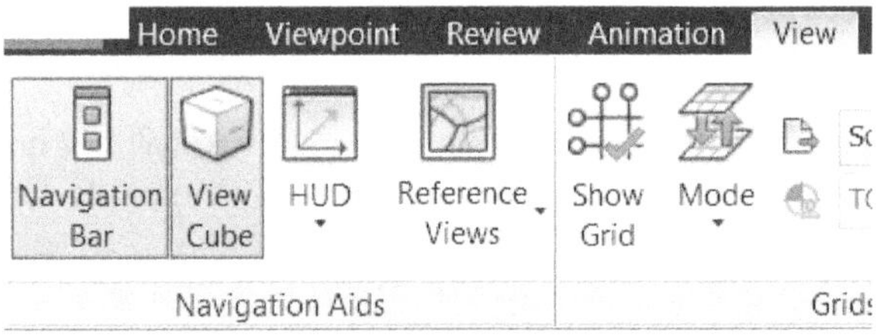

Figure 2–16

7. Note that the coordinates for this model are small, near 0,0,0.

8. In the *Home* Tab>Project panel, click (Append).

Hold <Ctrl> to select more than one.

9. Navigate to the *Project Files/Revit Files* practice files folder and select the **remaining** Revit files as follows:
   - **School-Electrical-Local.rvt**
   - **School-Mechanical-Local.rvt**
   - **School-Plumbing-Local.rvt**
   - **School-Structure-Local.rvt**

10. All models align. You can hide the architectural model to be able to see the other models by selecting a wall and using the <Ctrl>+<H> keystroke combination.

11. Press <Ctrl>+<H> again to unhide the school.

12. In the Quick Access Toolbar or Application Menu, click  (Save).

13. Save the file in the *Consolidate* practice files folder as **School-Local-<*your initials*>.nwf**.

Task 3 - Set units and transform the model.

In this task, you will open a file that was created in the Autodesk Civil 3D software, append an Inventor model and set any units and transformations, as required.

1. Expand  (Application Menu) and select **Options**.

2. In the Options Editor dialog box, ensure that the units for the base Autodesk Navisworks model are set as follows, as shown in Figure 2–17:
   - In the left pane, select **Interface>Display Units**.
   - In the right pane, set *Linear Units to* **Feet**.
   - Set *Angular Units* to **Degrees**.
   - Set *Decimal Places* to **2**.
   - Click **OK**.

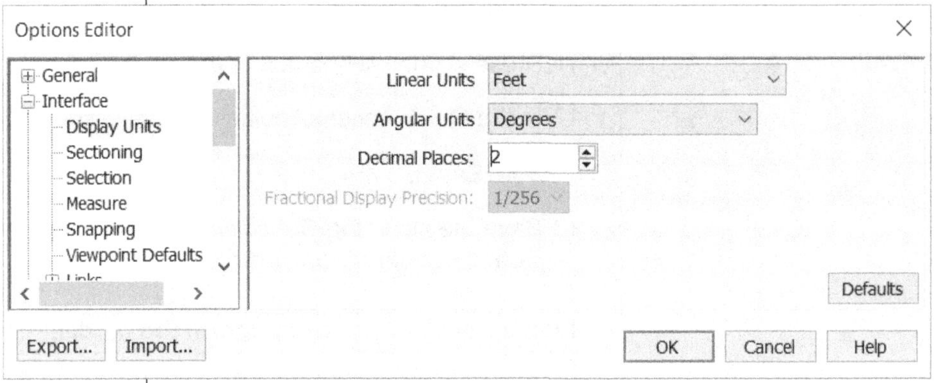

Figure 2–17

3. In the Quick Access Toolbar, click  (Open).

Opening a file automatically closes any other open file.

4. Navigate to the *Project Files/Civil Files* practice files folder, set the file format to **All Files (*.*)** and open **Site Layout.dwg**.

5. If a *Resolve* dialog box opens searching for missing external referenced graphic (*.png) files, click the **Ignore All** button, as shown in Figure 2–18.

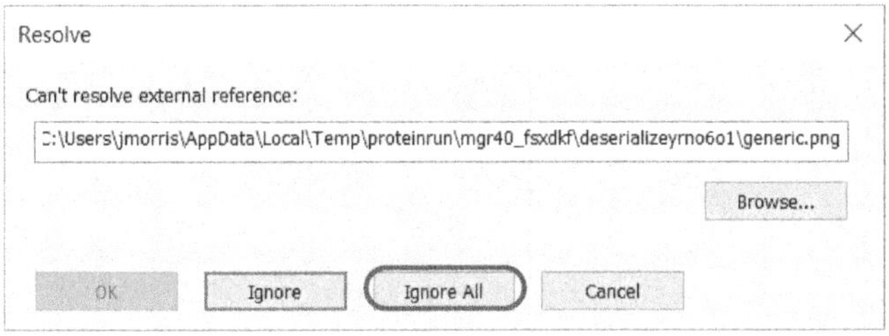

Figure 2–18

To view files created in Autodesk Civil 3D, you need to have the Civil 3D Object Enabler installed on your system.

6. If the drawing displays only boxes where the surfaces and roads should be (as shown in Figure 2–19), you will need to install the Autodesk Civil 3D Object Enabler. Consult *B.3 Autodesk Civil 3D Object Enabler* to install this prior to proceeding.

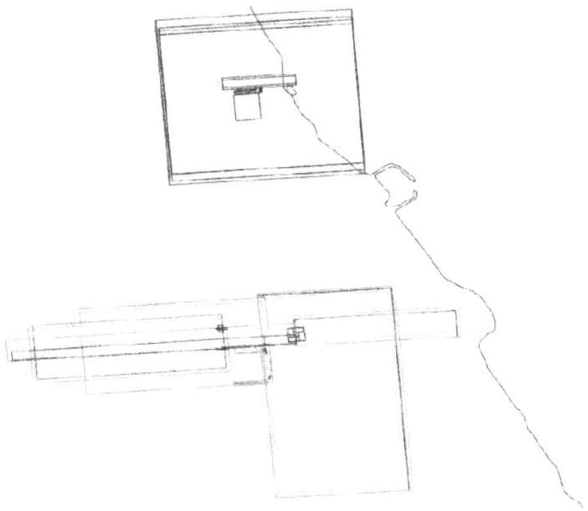

Figure 2–19

7. Notice the coordinates in the lower left corner. This is a Civil 3D file done in real-world coordinates and is properly geo-referenced, having very large values for X, Y and Z.

8. In the *Home* Tab>Project panel, click  (Append).

9. Navigate to the *Project Files/Revit Files* practice files folder, set the file format to **Revit (*.rvt; *.rfa; *.rte)**, and select **School-Architectural-Local.rvt**. This is the same file you opened last task and the location of the model is near 0,0,0. Therefore, you do not see it.

10. In the Home tab>Select & Search panel, if the (Selection Tree) button is white, click it to open the Selection Tree window. If the icon is blue, then the window is already open, usually as a tab on the upper left side of the screen, as shown in Figure 2–20.

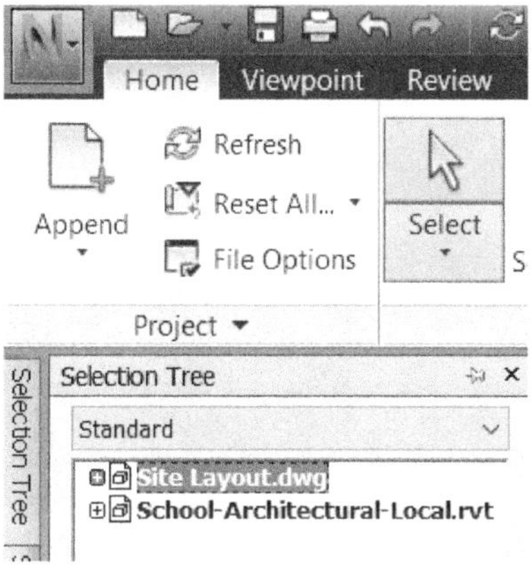

Figure 2–20

We will transform the school in a later step in this task.

11. In the Selection Tree window, select **School-Architectural-Local.rvt** and press <Page Down> on your keyboard. This will zoom to the selected file, the school. You see the school in blue (because it is selected), and the coordinates display near 0,0,0.

12. Press <Esc> to deselect the model

13. In the Selection Tree window, select **Site-Layout.dwg** and press <Page Down> on your keyboard. This will zoom to the Civil 3D site. The coordinates here are very high, since they represent the Northings, Eastings and Elevations of the geo-referenced site.

14. Press <Esc> to deselect the model.

15. In the *Home* Tab>Project panel, click (Append).

The file format should already be set to Revit from the last time you opened/appended files. Hold <Ctrl> to select more than one.

16. Navigate to the *Project Files/Revit Files* practice files folder and select the **remaining** Revit files as follows:
    - **School-Electrical.rvt**
    - **School-Mechanical.rvt**
    - **School-Plumbing.rvt**
    - **School-Structure.rvt**

17. Note that all of these Revit files (except for the architectural one) line up with the Autodesk Civil 3D drawing file. This is because a project base point was set in the Autodesk Revit files using a geo-referenced Revit site, and the site is set to current in the Revit file.

18. In the Quick Access Toolbar or Application Menu, click  (Save).

19. Save the file in the *Consolidate* practice files folder as **School-Georef-<*your initials*>.nwf**.

20. In the Selection Tree window, select **School-Architectural-Local.rvt** and select **Units and Transform**.

21. In the Units and Transform dialog box, set the following, as shown in Figure 2–21:

    - *Units:* **Feet**
    - *Origin (ft): X:* **1535369.9** *Y:* **7272458.4** *Z:* **4617.5**
    - *Rotation:* -**0.09** (Note the negative sign!)

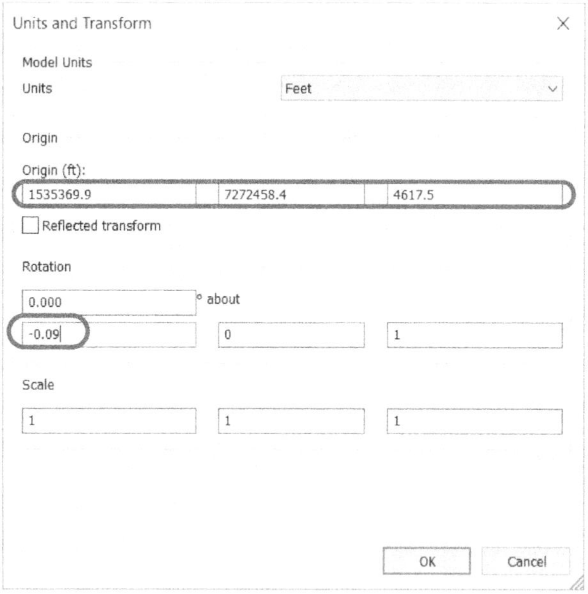

Figure 2–21

22. Click **OK**.

23. Use the ViewCube and other viewing tools to zoom in closer to the building on the site, as shown in Figure 2–22. Note that the Autodesk Civil 3D file includes both 2D and 3D elements. Ensure that you zoom in on the 3D elements.

Figure 2–22

24. In the *Home* Tab>Project panel, click (Append).

25. In the Append dialog box, expand the *Files of type* drop-down list and set the file type to **Inventor (*.ipt, *.iam, *.ipj)**.

26. Navigate to the *Project Files/HVAC Files* practice files folder and select **1Unit_CommercialAC.iam**. Click **Open**.

The AC unit might not display because it came in at the wrong location.

27. In the Selection Tree window, right-click on the newly appended Autodesk Inventor file and select **Units and Transform**.

28. In the Units and Transform dialog box, set the following, as shown in Figure 2–23:

- *Units:* **Centimeters**
- *Origin (ft):* (X) **1535375** (Y) **7272450** (Z) **4658**
- *Rotation:* **0**

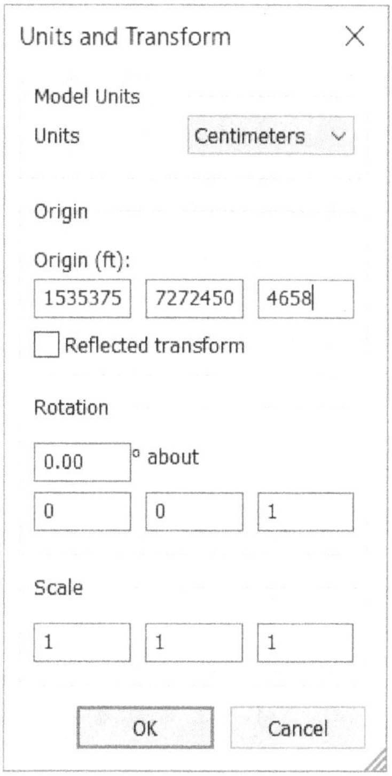

Figure 2–23

29. Click **OK**.

30. Note that the AC unit is still not in a useful spot. In the Selection Tree, right-click on **1Unit_Commercial AC.iam** and select **Override Item>Override Transform**, as shown in Figure 2–24.

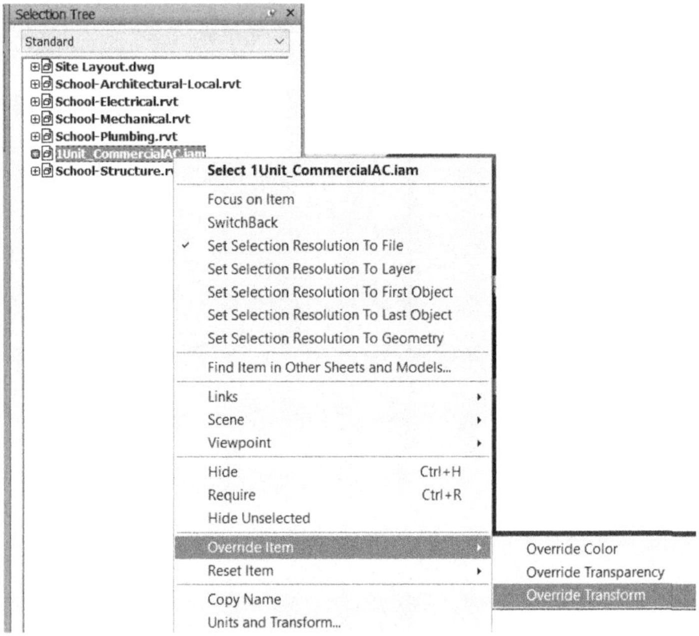

Figure 2–24

31. In the Override Transform dialog box, set *Translate by (ft)* to *X:* **150** *Y:* **-50** (as shown in Figure 2–25) and click **OK**.

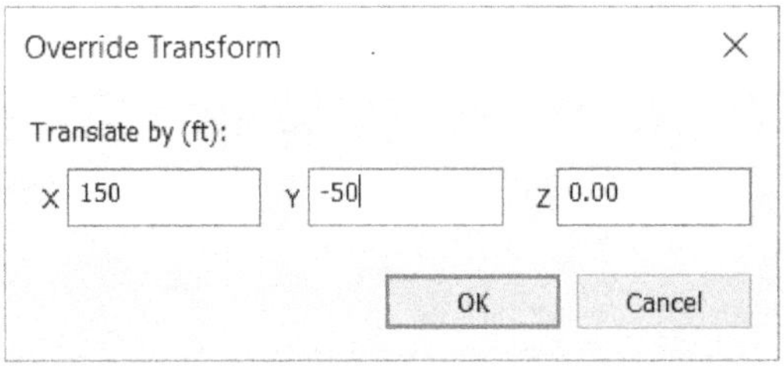

Figure 2–25

32. Note that the unit moves to the top of the flat roof, as shown in Figure 2–26.

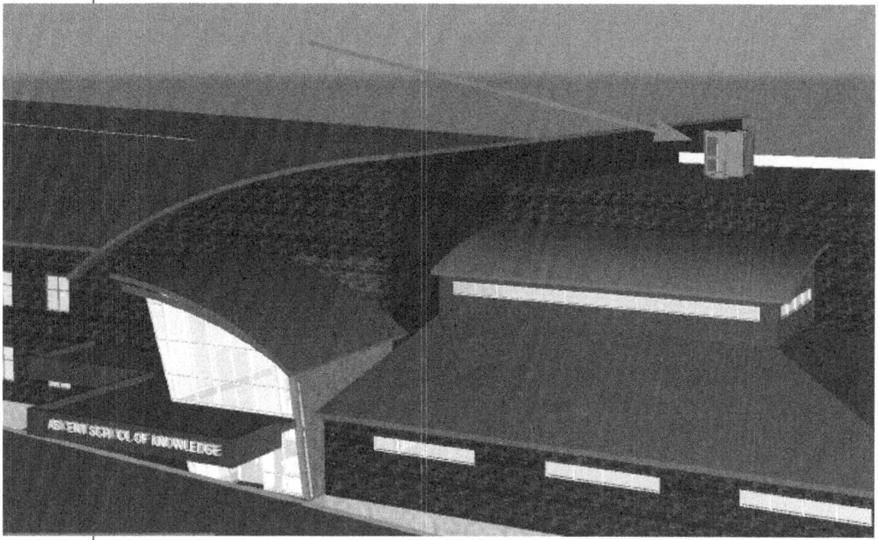

Figure 2–26

33. In the Quick Access Toolbar or Application Menu, click  (Save) to save the file.

Chapter Review Questions

1. In Autodesk Navisworks, if you open a file that was created in a different software program, can you append other types of files to it?
   a. Yes
   b. No
   c. It depends on the file type
2. Which file format is automatically created when you open or append a file into an Autodesk Navisworks project?
   a. .NWD
   b. .NWF
   c. .NWC
3. Which file format should you use if you want an Autodesk Navisworks project to stay linked to the original models and update as the original models update?
   a. .NWD
   b. .NWF
   c. .NWC
4. How do you change the measurement units for an Autodesk Navisworks model?
   a. You cannot change the units.
   b. In the Options dialog box, change the *Display Units*.
   c. You must start the project using the correct template at the beginning.
   d. The units must be changed in the original model.
5. How would you change the units for just one appended model?
   a. In the Options dialog box, change the *Display Units*.
   b. You cannot change one appended model independently, you must change them all at the same time.
   c. In the Selection Tree window, right-click on the model name and select **Override Item>Override Transform**.
   d. In the Selection Tree window, right-click on the model name and select **Units & Transform...**.

Command Summary

Button	Command	Location
	**Append**	• **Ribbon:** Home tab>Project Panel • **Quick Access Toolbar:** Expand Open
N/A	**File Units**	• **Right-click:** (with an item selected) **Units and Transform...**
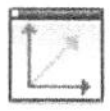	**HUD**	• **Ribbon:** *Views* tab>Navigation Aids panel
	**New**	• **Application Menu** • **Quick Access Toolbar**
	**Open**	• **Application Menu** • **Quick Access Toolbar**
N/A	**Options**	• **Application Menu**
	**Save**	• **Application Menu** • **Quick Access Toolbar**
	**Save As**	• **Application Menu** • **Quick Access Toolbar**

Chapter 3

Review Models

In a BIM workflow, once you have consolidated the models, you need to review them. Model review enables stakeholders to preview the project with all of the components included. In doing so, sight-lines, lighting, security, and many other criteria can be reviewed and verified. In this chapter, you will learn how to section the model and save views for easy reuse. You will also set up appearances and view options.

Learning Objectives in This Chapter

- Save scenes for later reuse.
- Section a model.
- Set up view options.

BIM Workflow: Review

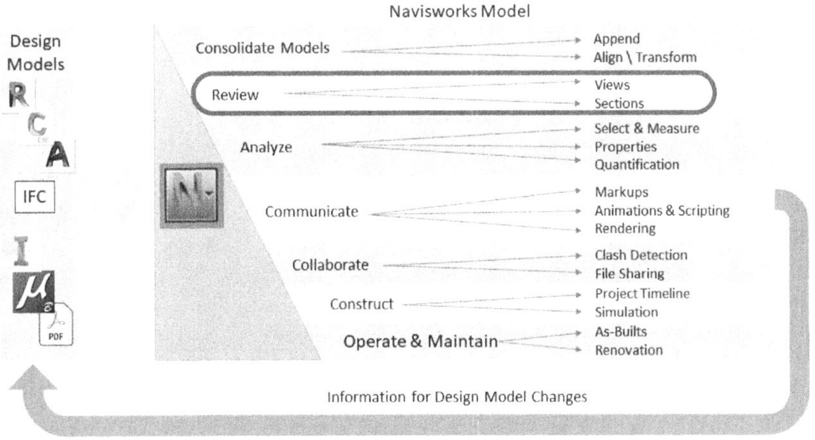

3.1 Saving and Retrieving Views

In the Autodesk® Navisworks® software, saved views are called viewpoints, which can be accessed through the Saved Viewpoints window, as shown in Figure 3–1. Viewpoints help you focus on specific conditions in a scene so that you can share information quickly with others. Viewpoints save the scene conditions, such as varying materials, lighting, or what is displayed or hidden. They can also include comments and redline tags.

Figure 3–1

- To open the Saved Viewpoints window, in the *View* tab> Workspace panel, expand  (Windows) and select **Saved Viewpoints**.
- In the Saved Viewpoints window, click on any view to make it current.

How To: Save a Viewpoint

1. Set up the view as required.
2. In the Saved Viewpoints window, right-click on a blank space and select **Save Viewpoint**, as shown in Figure 3–2.
   - Alternatively on the *Viewpoint* tab>Save, Load & Playback panel, click  (Save Viewpoint).

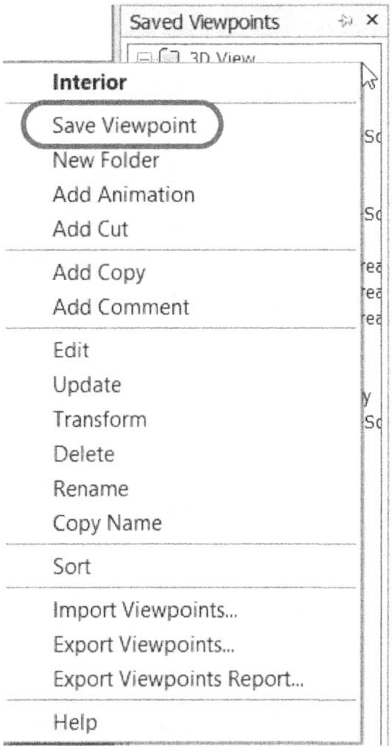

Figure 3–2

3. Type a name for the viewpoint and then press <Enter>.

Hint: Autodesk Revit Views

If a 3D view exists inside the Autodesk Revit software, it will be imported with the model. To ensure the view is recognized, you must ensure that you set the options shown in Figure 3–3 before appending the Revit model.

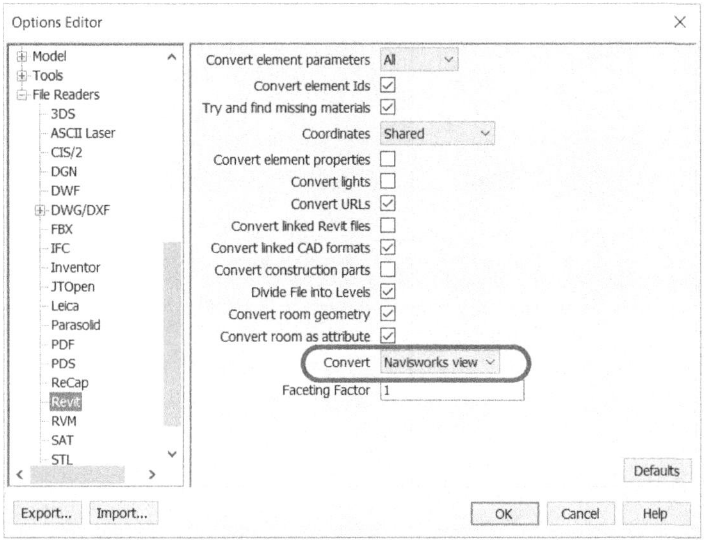

Figure 3–3

Editing Viewpoints

You might want to make a copy of a viewpoint before you start editing it. To do this, select ***Add Copy****.*

You can edit and update viewpoints. In the Saved Viewpoints window, select a view and right-click on it to display the menu shown in Figure 3–4.

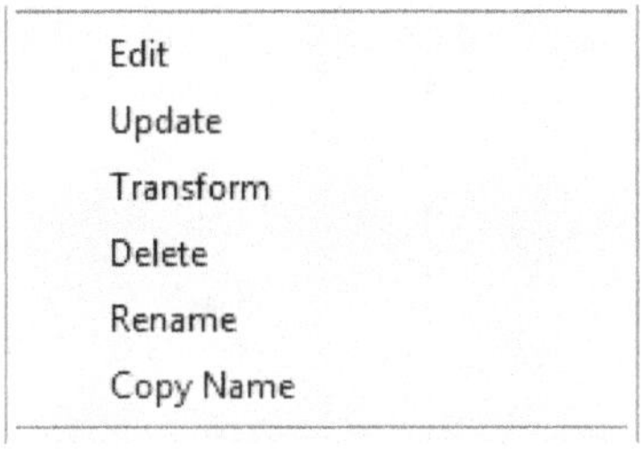

Figure 3–4

The viewpoint editing options are as follows:

- **Edit:** Opens the Edit Viewpoint dialog box, shown in Figure 3–5. The available options include changes to the camera, animation, saved attributes, and collision settings for the view.

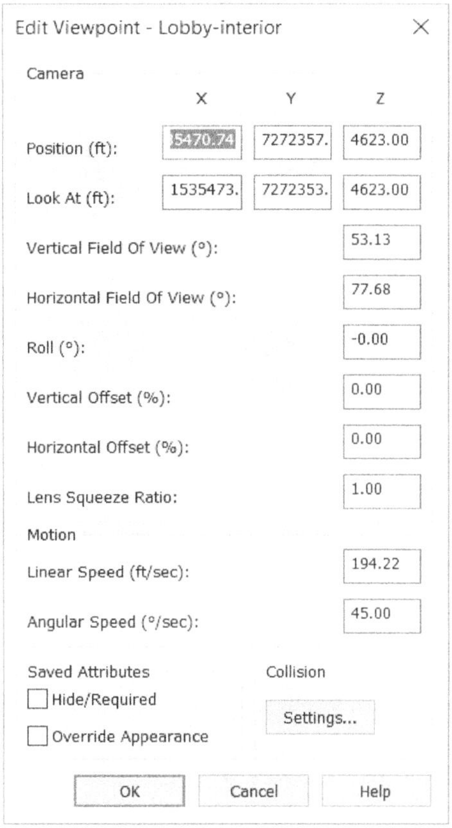

Figure 3–5

- **Update:** If you have made changes of any kind to the view, this option updates the saved viewpoint with those changes.

- **Transform:** Opens the Transform dialog box (shown in Figure 3–6), which enables you to specify X, Y, and Z values to move the entire view these distances.

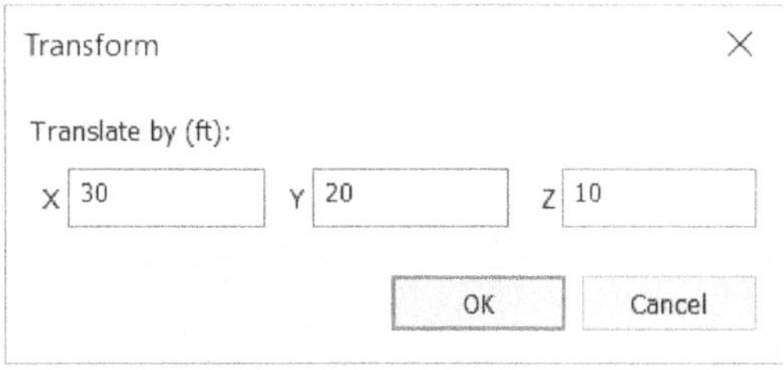

Figure 3–6

- **Delete:** Removes the view from the project.

- **Rename:** Enables you to type in a new name. You can also double-click on the name to do this.

Hint: Viewpoint Defaults

The viewpoint defaults impact all new viewpoints. To change the viewpoint defaults, proceed as follows:

1. Expand (Application Menu) and select **Options**.
2. In the Options Editor dialog box, do the following, as shown in Figure 3–7:
   - In the left pane, select **Interface>Viewpoint Defaults**.
   - In the right pane, select the Viewpoint settings required.
   - Click **OK**.

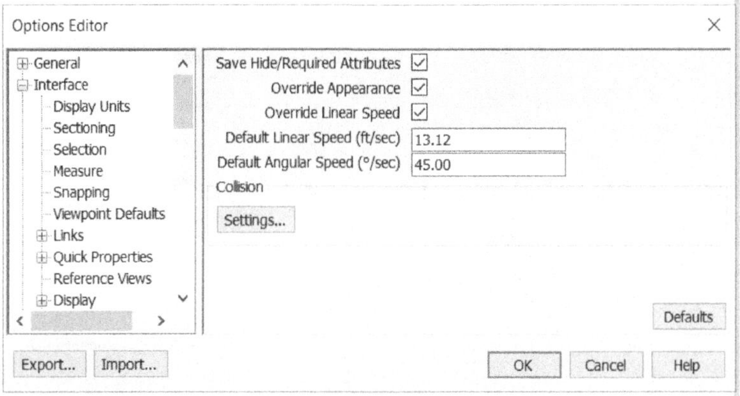

Figure 3–7

Organizing Viewpoints

You can sort viewpoints in the following ways:

- Alphanumerically
- Manually sorted into custom order
- Moved into folders which can also be sorted alphanumerically

How To: Organize Viewpoints into Folders

1. In the Saved Viewpoints window, right-click and select **New Folder**.
2. Type a name for the new folder and press <Enter>.
3. Drag and drop any saved views into the new folder.
4. In the Saved Viewpoints window, right-click and select **Sort** to sort the folders and views alphanumerically.

Practice 3a Save and Retrieve Viewpoints

Practice Objectives

- Restore existing saved viewpoints.
- Create new viewpoints.
- Modify a saved viewpoint.
- Organize saved viewpoints into folders.

In this practice, you will review several existing viewpoints, as shown in Figure 3–8. You will then create interior and exterior viewpoints and separate them into folders.

Figure 3–8

Task 1 - Restore viewpoints.

*If a Resolve dialog box opens that says that .PNG file cannot be found, click **Ignore All**.*

1. In the *Review* practice files folder, open **School-Viewpoints.nwf.**
2. In the *View* tab>Workspace panel, expand  (Windows) and select **Saved Viewpoints** to open the window (if not already visible; by default, it is usually in a hidden state in the top right corner of your screen).

3. In the Saved Viewpoints window, review several of the existing saved viewpoints. Some of the viewpoints were originally imported with the associated Autodesk Revit file.
4. Select the saved viewpoint **Front Entrance-Interior.**
5. Save the file.

Task 2 - Save new viewpoints.

1. From the front entrance area, use the viewing tools to look around the interior of the building.
2. When you see the angled front office, in the *Viewpoint* tab> Save, Load & Playback panel, click  (Save Viewpoint).
3. In the Saved Viewpoints window, enter the name **Office-Interior**, as shown in Figure 3–9.

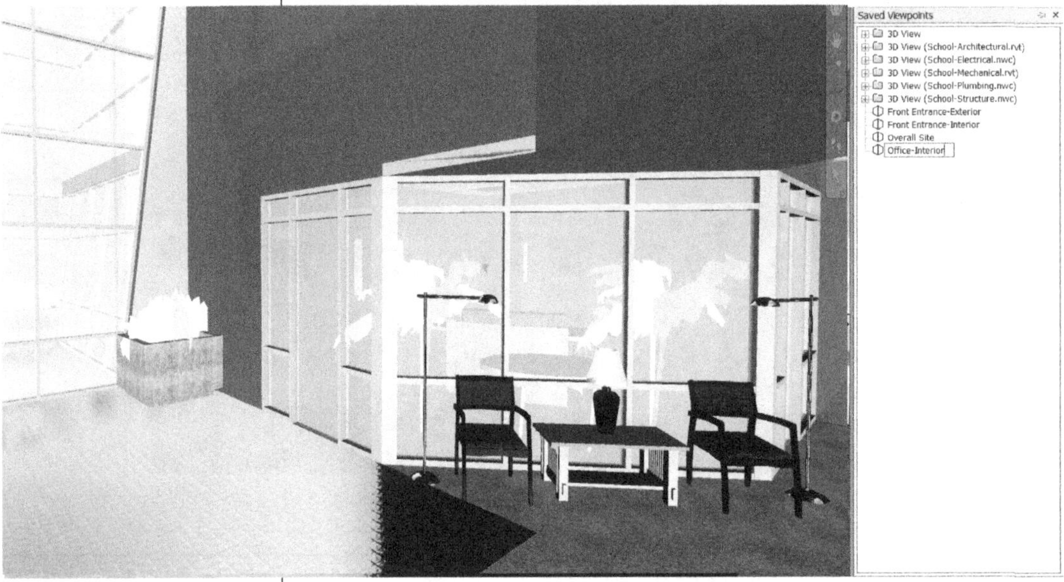

Figure 3–9

4. Continue viewing the interior of the building and make several additional viewpoints.
5. Save the file.

Task 3 - Edit a viewpoint.

1. In the Saved Viewpoints window, right-click on **Overall Site** and select **Add Copy**.
2. Click on the copy and rename it **Site Isometric Close-up**.
3. Zoom in on the building.
4. In the *Viewpoint* tab>Camera panel, expand (Perspective) and select (Orthographic).
5. In the Saved Viewpoints window, right-click on **Site Isometric Close-up** and select **Update**.
6. Switch between the two viewpoints and note the differences.
7. Save the file.

Task 4 - Organize the new viewpoints.

1. Open and pin the Saved Viewpoints window.
2. Right-click in the window and select **New Folder**. Do this again to add a second new folder.
3. Rename the new folders **Interior** and **Exterior**.
4. Drag and drop the viewpoints into the appropriate folder, as shown in Figure 3–10.

The exact names of your views might vary.

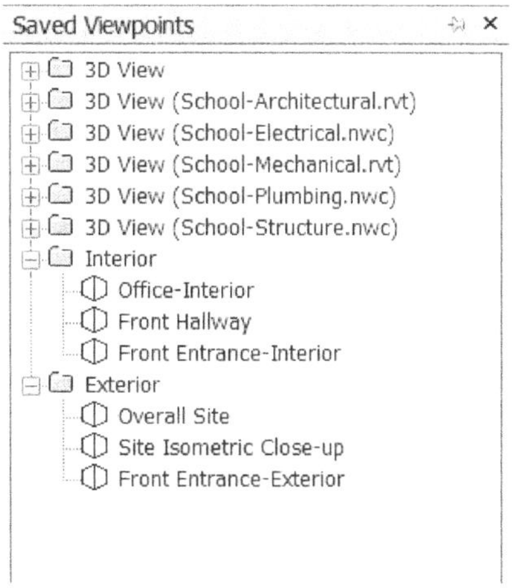

Figure 3–10

5. Save the file.

3.2 Sectioning the Model

A powerful way to view the model in the Autodesk Navisworks software is to create sections. When you enable sectioning, you can create and modify cut planes to customize the views you need. There are six, preset cut planes that correspond to the sides of a box that you can modify, as shown in Figure 3–11.

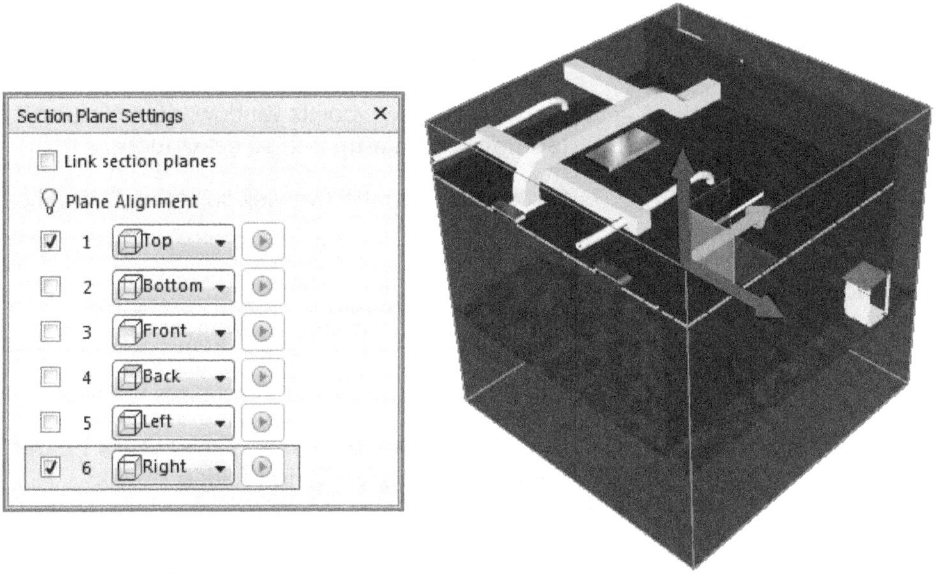

Figure 3–11

There are two modes used in sectioning:

- **(Planes):** Enables you to toggle and modify any of the six preset planes.
- **(Box):** Automatically cuts all six planes of the box.

How To: Modify Sections in Plane Mode

1. In the *Viewpoint* tab>Section panel, click (Enable Sectioning).
2. The first cut is made on the model and the *Sectioning Tools* tab displays, as shown in Figure 3–12.

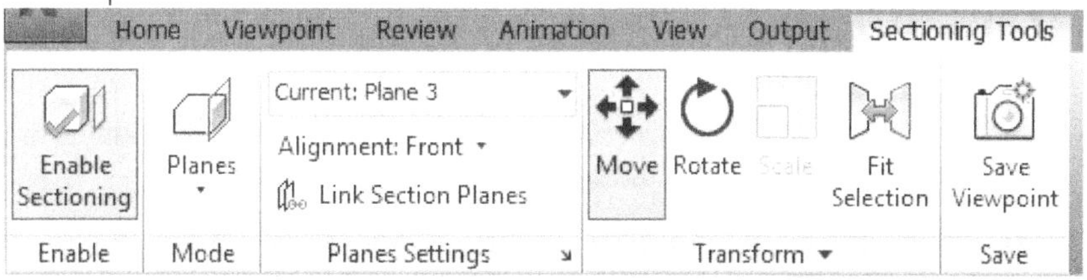

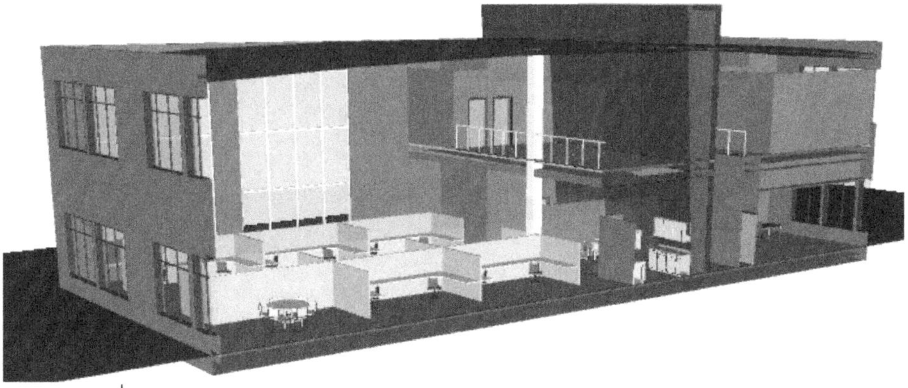

Figure 3–12

3. In the Planes Settings panel, expand the drop-down list shown in Figure 3–13 and click on a light bulb icon to toggle a plane on or off. Multiple planes can be displayed.
4. Click on the plane number to set the *Current Plane*.

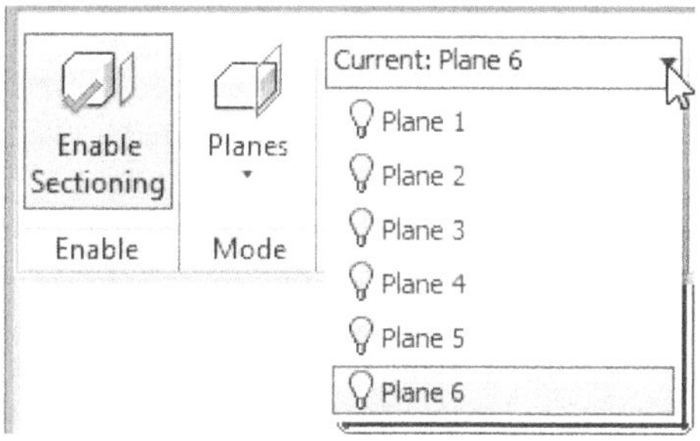

Figure 3–13

5. Use the tools on the *Sectioning Tools* tab>Transform panel to set the location of the current plane.

- When using Box mode, you modify all of the planes at the same time.

- Use the  (Save Viewpoint) command to save the location of the section planes.

Transforming Sections

The transform tools enable you to modify the location of the plane or box to create the exact section you need, such as the rotated plane shown in Figure 3–14. Each of the primary transform tools use the gizmo to modify the locations of the planes or box.

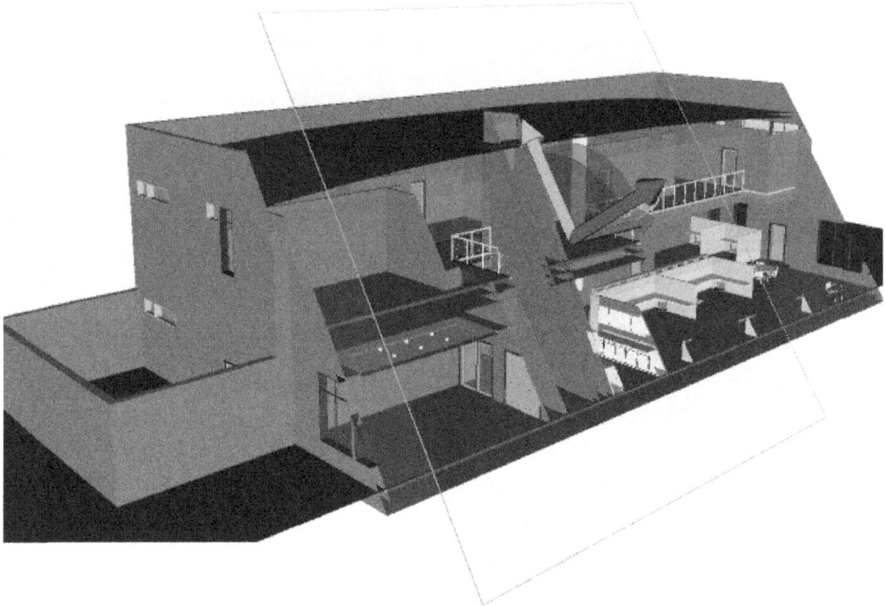

Figure 3–14

Each gizmo is based on the Cartesian coordinate system and has three directions and three planes that can be modified, as shown in Figure 3–15.

Red is the X-axis.
Green is the Y-axis.
Blue is the Z-axis.

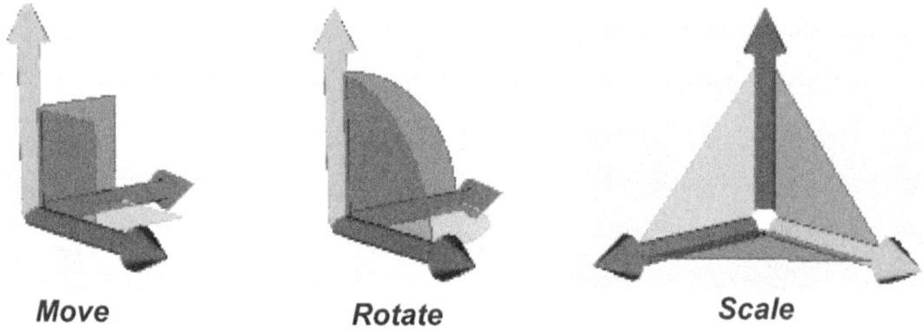

Figure 3–15

- In Planes mode, the gizmo is fixed on the current plane.
- In Box mode, the gizmo is fixed at the center of the box.

Transform Tools

- **(Move):** Moves the current plane or the entire box based on the arrow or plane you select.

- **(Rotate):** In plane mode, enables you to rotate the current plane. In Box mode, the tool rotates the entire box. You can only use the planes of the gizmo, not the arrows.

- **(Scale):** Available only in box mode, the tool enables you to move the opposing sides of the box to create a rectangle. In the example shown in Figure 3–16, the Y-axis arrow was used to create a cut on both the front and back of the building.

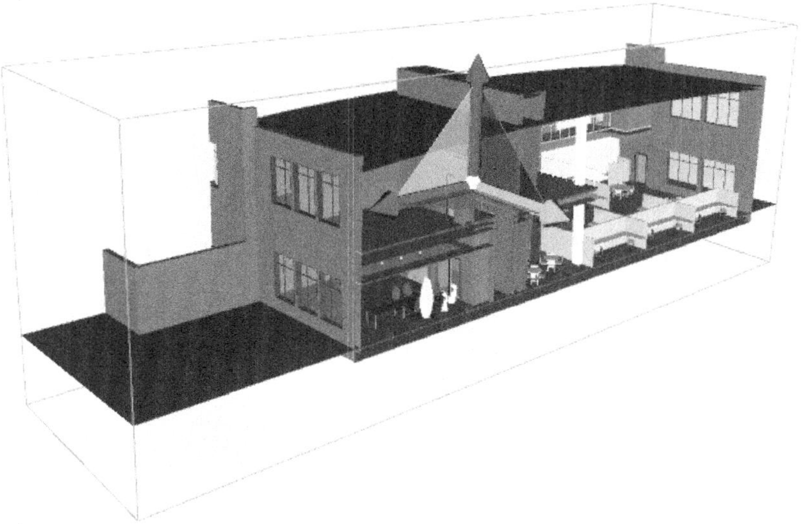

Figure 3–16

- **(Fit Selection):** In Plane mode, the tool moves the current plane so that the selected items are in the displayed area of the section. In box mode, the tool fits the box tightly around the selected items. This tool does not use a gizmo.

Additional Sectioning Tools

To display the Section Planes Setting dialog box, click the diagonal arrow in the right corner of the Planes Setting panel title.

Alignment: In the Planes Settings panel, you can use the drop-down list shown in Figure 3–17 to specify the alignment of the current plane. This changes the Section Plane Settings. For example, when the alignment for *Plane 1* is changed to **Front**, it displaces the original Top Alignment, as shown in Figure 3–18.

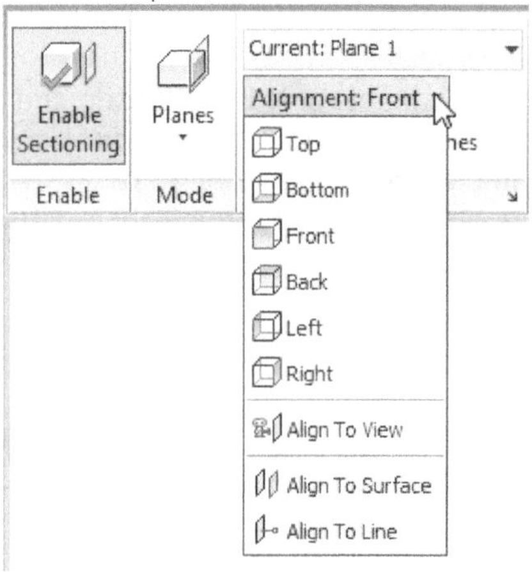

Figure 3–17

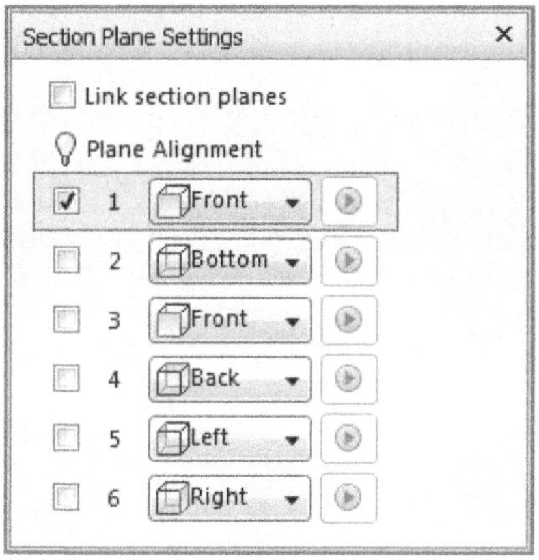

Figure 3–18

- The **Aligned to View** option orients the plane so that it is parallel to the plane of the monitor, as shown in Figure 3–19.

Figure 3–19

- The **Align to Surface** option orients the plane to a selected surface in a 3D model. To change the location, you can repeat the command or, in the Section Planes Settings dialog box, click  **Re-select** (as shown in Figure 3–20) and select a different surface.

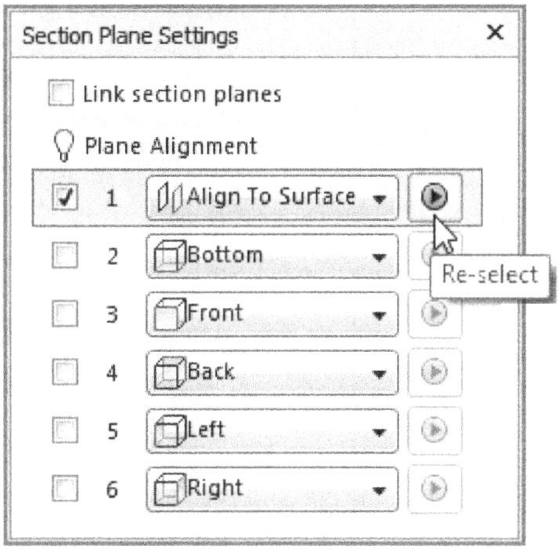

Figure 3–20

- The **Align to Line** option orients the plane to a selected line in a 2D drawing.

- The **Link Section Planes** option enables you to select several planes to move together. In the Section Plane Settings dialog box, select **Link section planes** and then place a checkmark in front of the planes that you want to link.

Hint: Reference Views

Reference views are like map keys in that they indicate where you are in the model. A triangular marker in the reference view enables you to navigate the scene by holding the left mouse button over it dragging the triangle to a new location. Reference Views are regular Navisworks windows that can be docked or floating.

In the *View* tab>Navigation Aids panel, expand  (Reference Views) and select **Plan View** or **Section View**.

- **Plan View** displays the entire model from the top by default, as shown in Figure 3–21.
- **Section View** displays the entire model from the front.

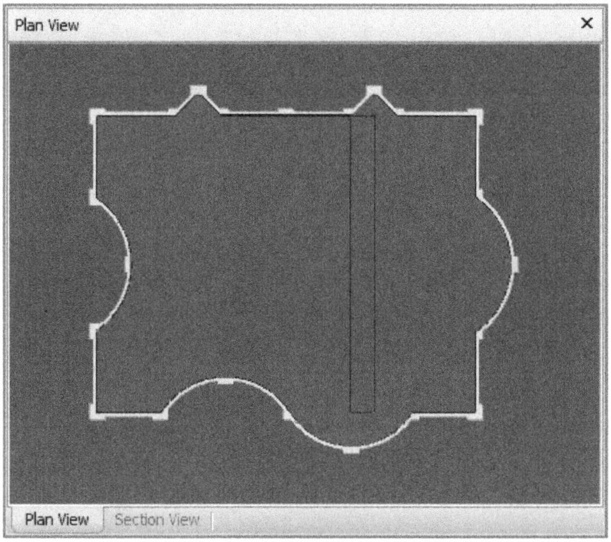

Figure 3–21

- Within the Reference View window, there are additional choices through the right-click menu, as shown in Figure 3–22.

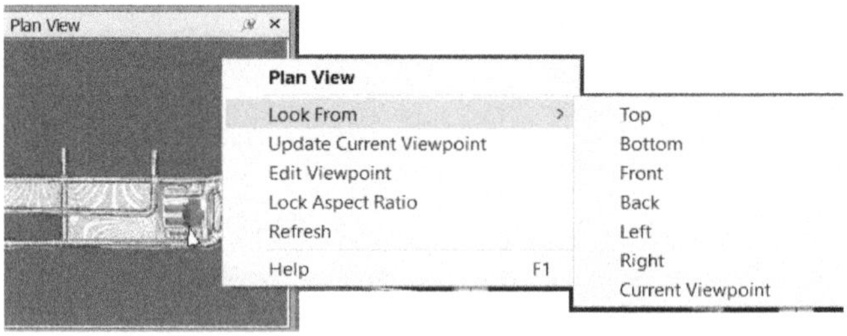

Figure 3–22

Practice 3b Section the Model

Practice Objective

- Create sections of a model.

In this practice, you will cut sections using individual planes and a box section, as shown in Figure 3–23. You will then modify the sections using the Transform tools.

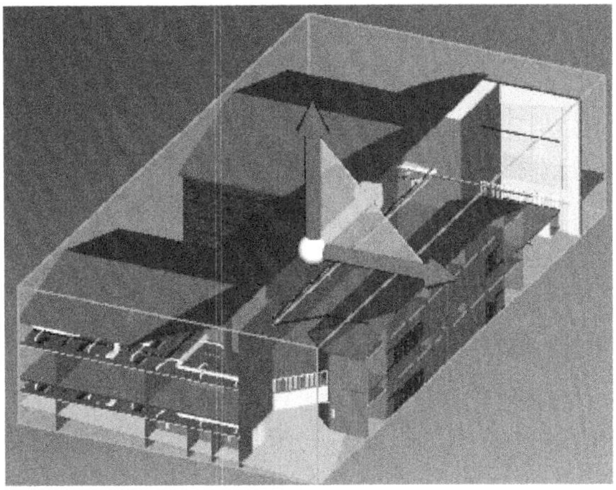

Figure 3–23

Task 1 - Create plane sections.

1. In the *Review* practice files folder, open **School-Sections.nwf**.
2. If the drawing displays only boxes where the surfaces and roads should be (as shown in Figure 3–24), you will need to install the Autodesk Civil 3D Object Enabler. Consult *B.3 Autodesk Civil 3D Object Enabler* to install this prior to proceeding.

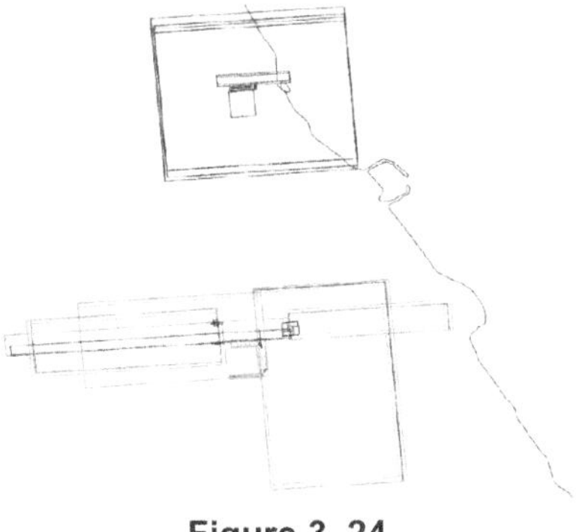

Figure 3–24

3. Open the Saved Viewpoint **Exterior for Sectioning**.

4. In the *Viewpoint* tab>Section panel, click (Enable Sectioning).

5. In the *Sectioning Tools* tab>Mode panel, select (Planes) from the drop-down list.

6. In the Planes Settings panel, expand the *Current Plane* drop-down list and click on the light bulb icon next to **Plane 3** to toggle the plane on. Select **Plane 3** to make it current, as shown in Figure 3–25.

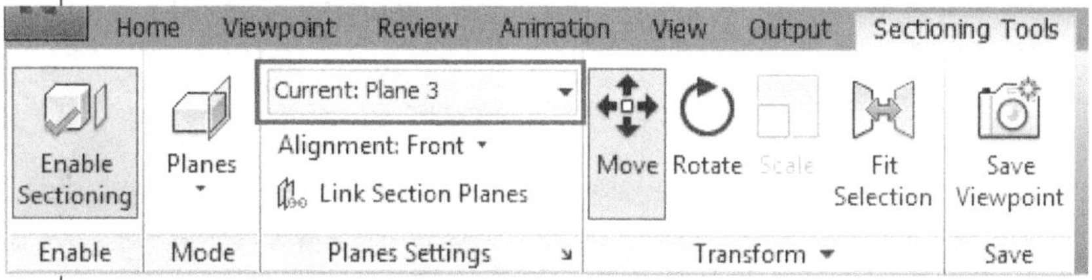

Figure 3–25

*If the gizmo does not display, toggle **Move** off and then on again.*

7. In the *Sectioning Tools* tab>Transform panel, click (Move). Click and drag the blue arrow of the gizmo forward to position the section as shown in Figure 3–26. The section should cut through the AC unit on the roof.

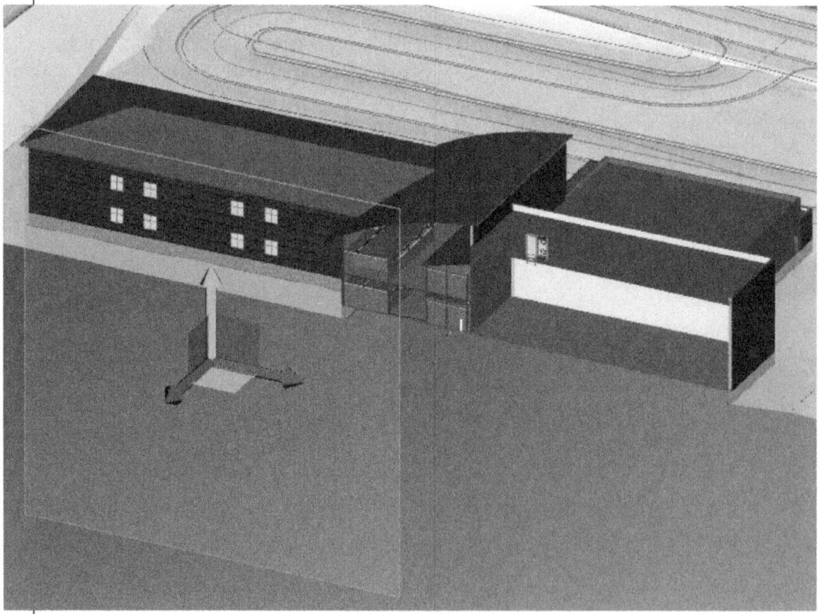

Figure 3–26

8. In the *Sectioning* Tools tab>Save panel, click (Save Viewpoint) to save the section position. Type **Section-North Wing** for the viewpoint name.

9. In the Current Plane drop-down list, click the Plane 4 light bulb icon to toggle the plane on. Then click the Plane 3 light bulb icon to toggle the plane off.

10. In the Planes Settings panel, make **Plane 4** current and set the *Alignment* to **Right**, as shown in Figure 3–27.

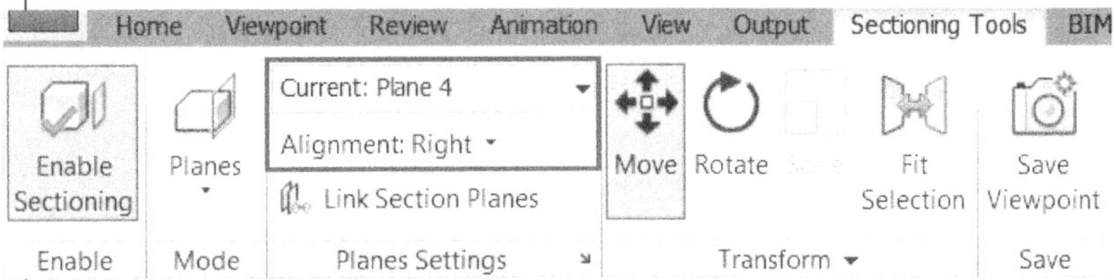

Figure 3–27

11. In the *Sectioning Tools* tab>Transform panel, click (Move). Click and drag the gizmo to position the section as shown in Figure 3–28 so that it cuts through the building entrance. Then, click (Move) again to toggle off the Move Gizmo.

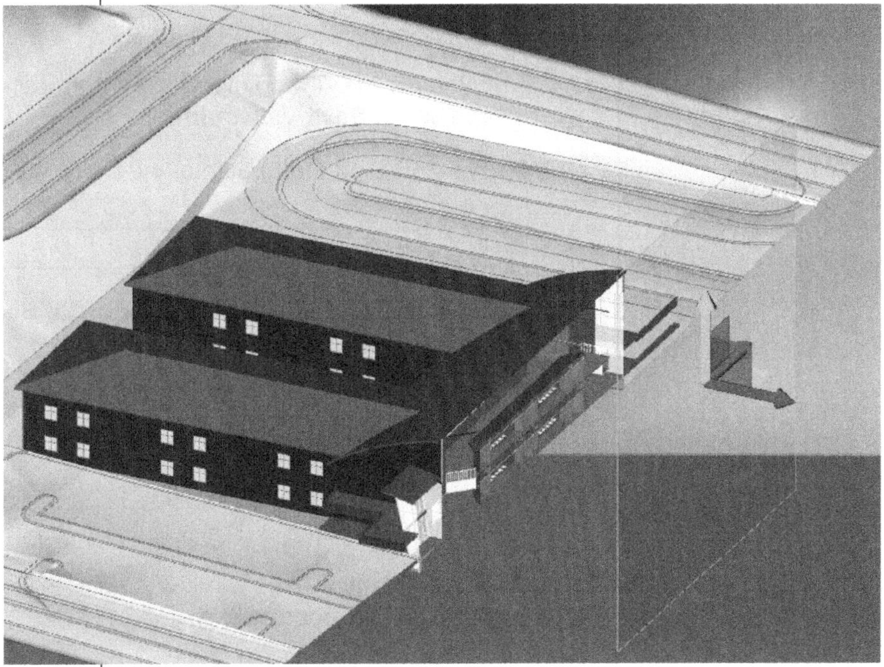

Figure 3–28

12. In the *Sectioning* Tools tab>Save panel, click (Save Viewpoint) to save the section position. For the viewpoint name, enter **Section-Entrance**.

Task 2 - Edit and save a viewpoint.

1. In the Saved Viewpoints window, click **Section-North Wing**.
2. Pan, zoom, and orbit to adjust the view for a closer look at the rooftop AC unit, as shown in Figure 3–29.

Figure 3–29

3. In the Saved Viewpoints window, right-click on a blank space and select **Save Viewpoint**.
4. Type **AC Unit** for the name and press <Enter>.

Task 3 - Create a box section.

1. Open the saved viewpoint **Exterior for Sectioning**.
2. In the *Viewpoint* tab>Section panel, click (Enable Sectioning).
3. In the *Sectioning Tools* tab>Mode panel, select (Box) in the **Planes** menu.
4. In the Selection Tree window, select **School-Architectural.rvt**.

5. In the *Sectioning Tools* tab>Transform panel, click (Fit Selection). The section box is created up close to the building, as shown in Figure 3–30.

Figure 3–30

6. Press <Esc> to release the selection.
7. In the *Sectioning Tools* tab>Transform panel, click (Scale).
8. Click and drag the Z-axis (blue arrow) on the gizmo to position the section so that the building roof and slab below are cut off, as shown in Figure 3–31.

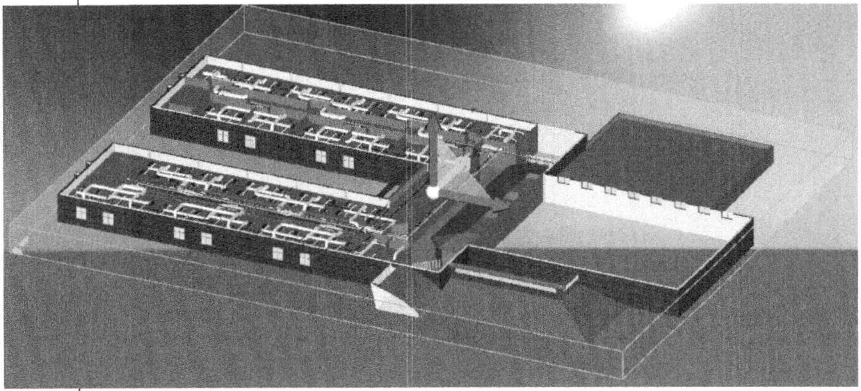

Figure 3–31

9. Save the viewpoint as **Section-Ductwork**.
10. Save the file.

3.3 Setting View Options

Controlling how a scene displays can help you see more clearly how things work together. You can change the way the view is rendered, and toggle the display of structural grids.

Render Style Modes

Each scene view has a render style which specifies the shading of the building model, such as the example shown in Figure 3–32 for the furnishings in the school lobby in Full Render mode.

Figure 3–32

The **Render Style** options are found in the *Viewpoint* tab> Render Style panel. These options apply to all types of views. For example, when the Render style is set to Full Render, you can see shadows, texture, reflections, and more.

The list below describes each type of render style mode available.

- **(Full Render):** Displays the materials and textures of items, including lights, reflections, and shadows. This is the default view type.

- **(Hidden Line):** Displays the lines, edges, and surfaces of the elements, but it does not display any colors.

- **(Wireframe):** Displays the lines and edges of elements, but hides the surfaces. This can be useful when you are dealing with complex intersections.

- **(Shaded):** Displays the surface color but not the textures of materials, as shown for the same school lobby scene in Figure 3–33.

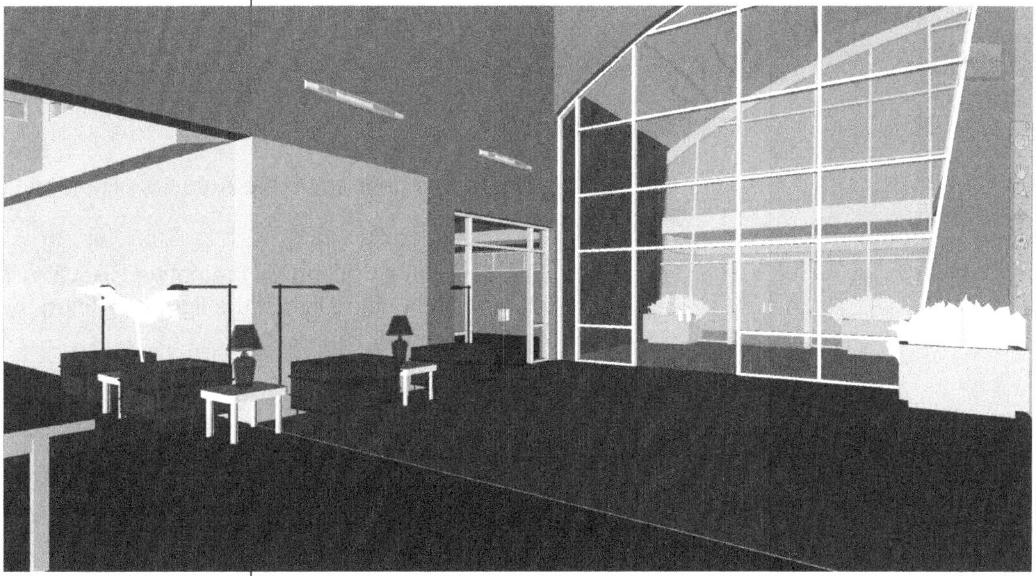

Figure 3–33

Photorealistic scenes can be created using the Autodesk Rendering system, as shown in Figure 3–34, which is included in Navisworks.

Figure 3–34

Hint: Lighting Modes

You can control how a 3D scene is lit using one of the following lighting modes:

- **Full Lights:** Lights defined by the Autodesk Rendering tool.
- **Scene Lights:** Lights defined by the native CAD file. If the original file did not include lights, the light is defined by two default opposing lights.
- **Head Light:** Single directional light positioned at the same location as the camera and pointing in the same direction as the camera.
- **No Lights:** All lights are switched off, leaving the scene shaded with flat rendering.

Displaying Grids

Autodesk Revit grids are available for display in the Autodesk Navisworks software, as shown in Figure 3–35. When working in a large project or when identifying a specific area, toggling on grids can help you describe feature locations in the model.

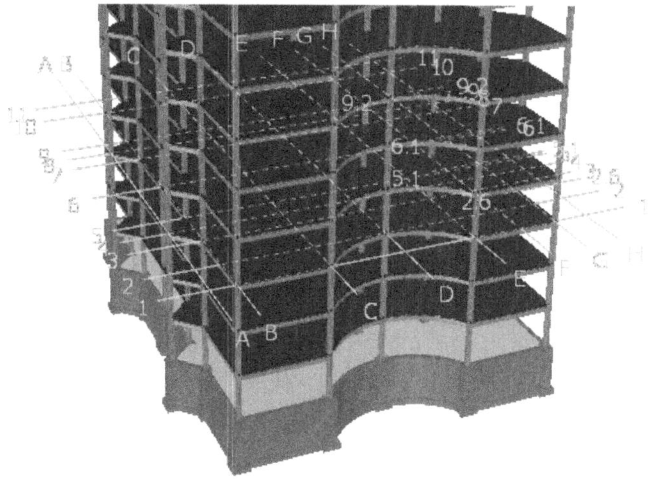

Figure 3–35

If a grid was not included in one of the Autodesk Revit models, the Show Grid tool is grayed out because it is unavailable.

- In the *View* tab>Grids & Levels panel, click (Show Grid).
- If you have multiple files, the (Active Grid) drop-down list enables you to specify the model whose grid you want to use.
- Grid Modes control the display of the grids in relation to the current camera position:
  - **(Above and Below):** Displays red grids above and green grids below.
  - **(Above):** Displays only red grids.
  - **(Below):** Displays only green grids.
  - **(All):** Displays red and green grids, as well as halftone images of all of the other grid locations.
  - **(Fixed):** Displays grids at the level specified in the drop-down list for the (Display Level). It does not change the location of the grid as you orbit around the model.

3.4 Setting Up Appearances

From time to time, an object might display in its wireframe color. This is because the material or texture for the object that was imported from the original model is unsupported. When this happens, you might have to override an object's appearance. You can do this in two ways:

- Individually
- Globally

How To: Override Appearances Individually

1. In the model, click on the objects that need to be changed to select them.
2. In the *Item Tools* contextual tab>Appearance panel, expand (Color) and select a color square, as shown in Figure 3–36.

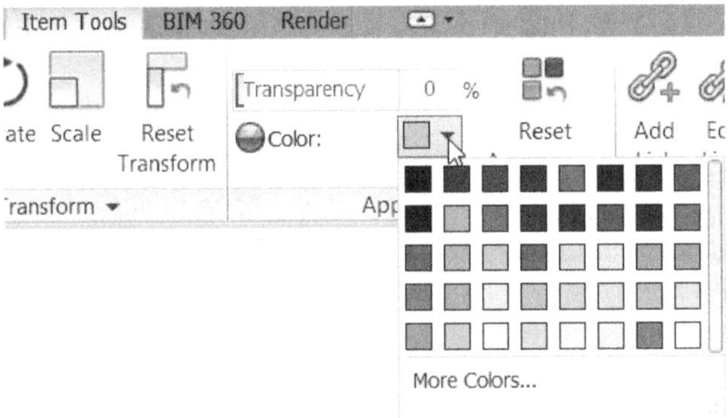

Figure 3–36

3. In the *Item Tools* contextual tab>Appearance panel, click and drag the *Transparency slider* to make the object more or less opaque, as required.
4. If the changes did not have the required results, or if you need to revert back to the original color or transparency, in the *Item Tools* contextual tab>Appearance panel, click (Reset Appearance).
5. Press <Esc> to clear the selection and view the changes.

Modify Appearances Globally

Materials can be edited in all new viewpoints globally. You can do this in the Options Editor dialog box.

How To: Override Appearances Globally

1. Expand (Application Menu) and select **Options**.
2. In the Options Editor dialog box, do the following, as shown in Figure 3–37:
   - In the left pane, expand *Interface* and select **Viewpoint Defaults**.
   - In the right pane, select **Override Appearance**.
   - Click **OK**.

Defaults affect all new Viewpoints.

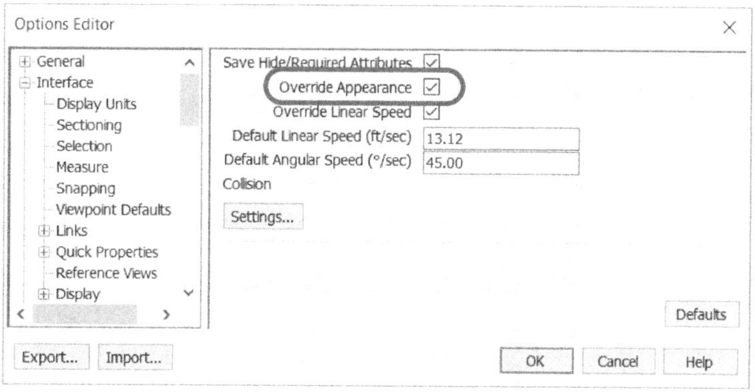

Figure 3–37

3. In the scene view, select the objects that need a material override.
4. In the *Item Tools* contextual tab>Appearance panel, expand (Color) and select a color square.
5. In the *Item Tools* contextual tab>Appearance panel, click and drag the *Transparency slider* to make the object more or less opaque.
6. Press <Esc> to clear the selection and view the changes.
7. In the Saved Viewpoints window, right-click on the viewpoint that you want to set to appearance override and select **Update**.

Practice 3c Set Up the Display

Practice Objectives

- Display a grid to help communicate where something is in the model.
- Set up appearances.

In this practice, you will turn on the grid that was imported with the Autodesk Revit model and change the display appearances for the site and the AC unit, as shown in Figure 3–38.

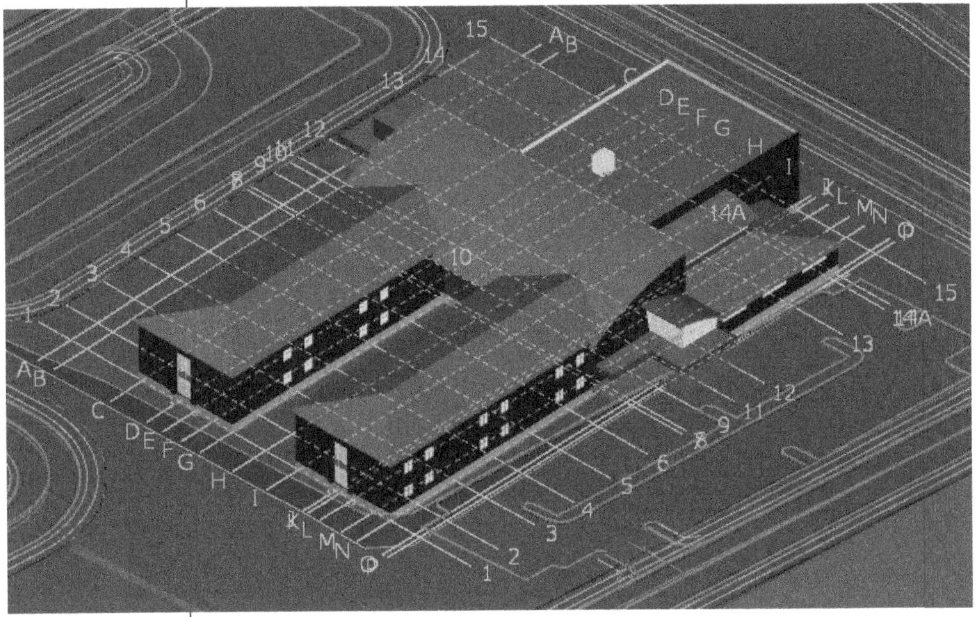

Figure 3–38

Task 1 - Display a grid.

1. In the *Review* practice files folder, open the file **School-Appearances.nwf**. In the Saved Viewpoints window, expand the *Exterior* folder and click **Site Isometric Close-up**.
2. In the *View* tab>Grids & Levels panel, click (Show Grid) to toggle it on and off a couple times. Note how the grid displays in the model. With the grid toggled on, continue to the next step.
3. Open another exterior viewpoint. Note that the grid displays in this view as well. Displaying the grid is a toggle and it affects all saved viewpoints.

4. In the Selection Tree, select the **Site Layout.dwg** model. Note that the grids are easier to see against the dark blue of the selection color.

5. Pan around the model and zoom in on the intersection of Grid P and Grid 14. Your display should be similar to that shown in Figure 3–39.

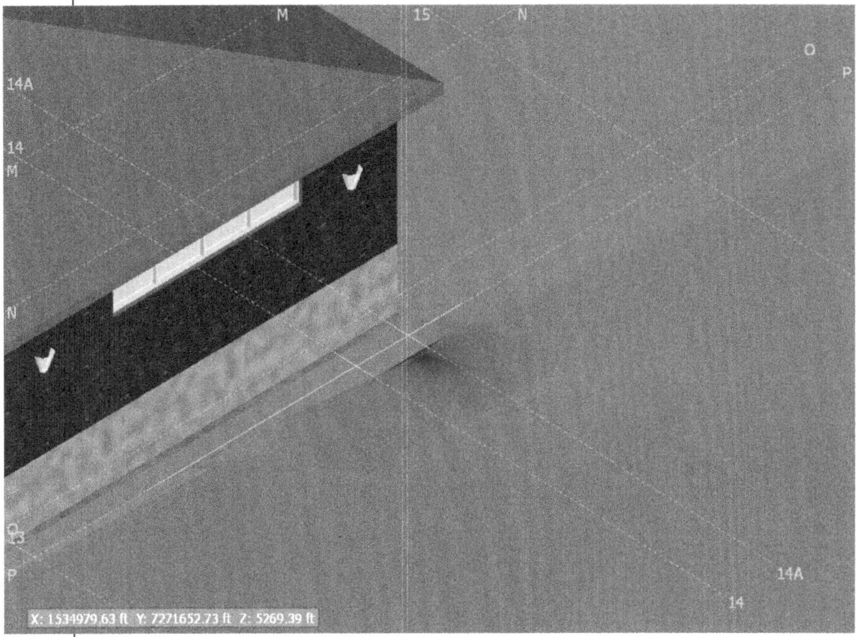

Figure 3–39

Task 2 - Change appearances.

1. With the site model still selected, in the *Item Tools* contextual tab>Appearance panel, expand (Color) and select the dark green color shown in Figure 3–40.

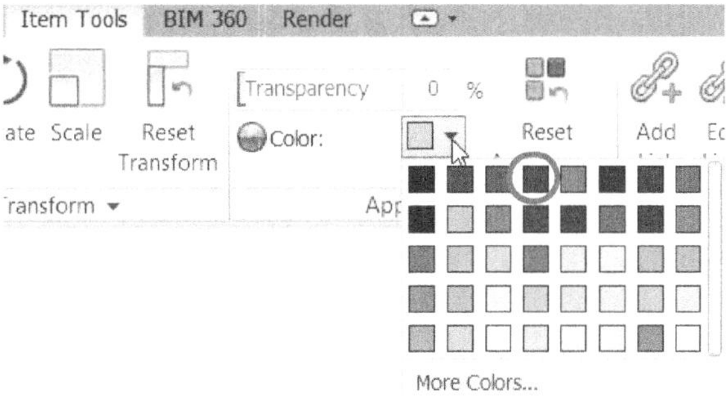

Figure 3–40

2. Press <Esc> to clear the selection and view the changes. Note that the site now displays in dark green.

3. Select the **Site Layout.dwg** again.

4. In the *Item Tools* contextual tab>Appearance panel, click and drag the *Transparency slider* near **80%** to make the surface more transparent.

5. Press <Esc> to clear the selection and view the changes.

6. Open the saved viewpoint **Section-AC Unit**.

7. In the *Home* tab>Select & Search panel, expand (Select) and click (Select Box) from the drop-down list.

8. Ensure that the *Selection Resolution* is set to **First Object**. Select the first part of the AC unit on top of the roof, hold <Ctrl> and select the second part, then release <Ctrl>, as shown in Figure 3–41.

Figure 3–41

9. In the *Item Tools* contextual tab>Appearance panel, expand (Color) and select the Cyan square shown in Figure 3–42.

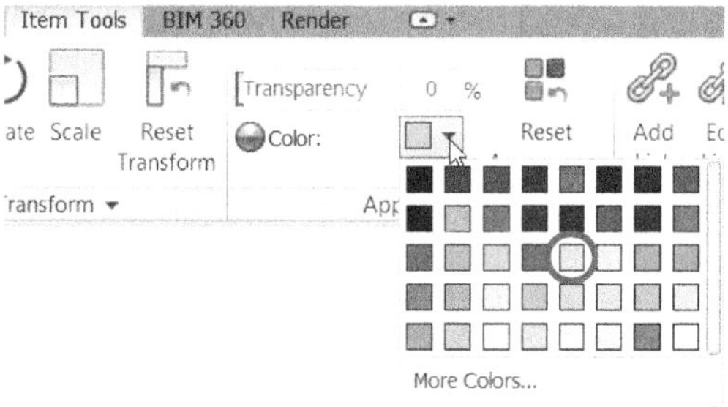

Figure 3–42

10. Press <Esc> to clear the selection of the AC unit. Note that it now displays in the cyan color.

11. Open the saved viewpoint **Exterior>Site Isometric Close-up**.

12. Zoom in on the AC unit.

13. Note that some of the unit is still gray, as shown in Figure 3–43. Select both parts of the unit again.

14. In the *Item Tools* tab>Appearance panel, select a different color. Press <Esc> and the full AC unit displays in the new color, as shown in Figure 3–44.

Figure 3–43

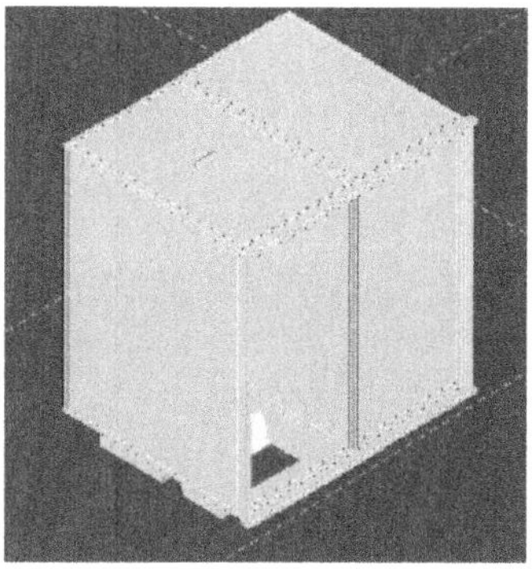

Figure 3–44

15. In the *View* tab>Grids & Levels panel, toggle off (Show Grid).

16. Save the file.

Chapter Review Questions

1. Which of the following can be edited for a saved viewpoint? (Select all that apply.)
   a. Position of the camera
   b. Focus point of the camera
   c. Sun settings
   d. Section planes
2. Viewpoints can be sorted alphanumerically on demand.
   a. True
   b. False
3. When creating a section with the Box option, how many section planes are cut at one time?
   a. 1
   b. 2
   c. 4
   d. 6
4. Which render style mode includes the materials and textures of items, including lights, reflections, and shadows?
   a. Full Render
   b. Hidden Line
   c. Wireframe
   d. Shaded
5. How do you create a grid in a scene to help you describe where something is in the model?
   a. In the *Home* tab>Visibility panel.
   b. In the *Viewpoint* tab>Navigate panel.
   c. You cannot create a grid in the Autodesk Navisworks software. It must be included in the original Autodesk Revit model.
   d. In the *View* tab>Grids & Levels panel.

6. Why would an object display in its wireframe color?
   a. The Render Style Mode is set wrong for the scene.
   b. The material or texture for the object that was imported from the original model is unsupported.
   c. The lighting mode is set wrong for the scene.
   d. Objects do not display in wireframe in the Autodesk Navisworks software.

Command Summary

Button	Command	Location
Viewpoints		
N/A	**Add Animation**	• **Right-Click:** in the Saved Viewpoints Window>**Save Viewpoint**
	**Animation Tools**	• **Ribbon:** *Viewpoint* tab>Save, Load & Playback panel
	**Edit Current Viewpoint**	• **Ribbon:** *Viewpoint* tab>Save, Load & Playback panel
	**Save Viewpoint**	• **Ribbon:** *Viewpoint* tab>Save, Load & Playback panel • **Right-Click:** in the Saved Viewpoints Window>**Save Viewpoint**
	**Saved Viewpoints Dialog Launcher**	• **Ribbon:** *Viewpoint* tab>Save, Load & Playback panel title
Sectioning		
	**Box**	• **Ribbon:** *Sectioning Tools* tab>Mode panel
	**Enable Sectioning**	• **Ribbon:** *Viewpoint* tab>Sectioning panel
	**Fit Selection**	• **Ribbon:** *Sectioning Tools* tab> Transform panel
	**Move**	• **Ribbon:** *Sectioning Tools* tab> Transform panel
	**Planes**	• **Ribbon:** *Sectioning Tools* tab>Mode panel
	**Rotate**	• **Ribbon:** *Sectioning Tools* tab> Transform panel
	**Scale**	• **Ribbon:** *Sectioning Tools* tab> Transform panel
Other Viewing Tools		
	**Full Render**	• **Ribbon:** *Views* tab>Render Style panel> expand Mode
	**Hidden Line**	• **Ribbon:** *Views* tab>Render Style panel> expand Mode
	**Reference View**	• **Ribbon:** *Views* tab>Navigation Aids panel

	**Shaded**	• **Ribbon:** *Views* tab>Render Style panel> expand Mode
	**Show Grid**	• **Ribbon:** *Views* tab>Grids & Levels panel
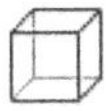	**Wireframe**	• **Ribbon:** *Views* tab>Render Style panel> expand Mode

Analyze Models

When you review a BIM model, you should also analyze the model at the same time. Performing a model analysis helps stakeholders predict the project outcome and reduce the number of requests for information (RFIs) and changes that are required during construction. In this chapter, you will learn how to select features to investigate their properties and save selection sets. You will also learn how to hide features to gain a clearer view of specific parts of the model.

Learning Objectives in This Chapter

- Select items in a model to evaluate their properties.
- Drill down into the content of a model using the Selection Tree.
- Save selections so that they can be retrieved later.
- Find items by using the selection filtering options.
- Hide items so they are not obstructing your view and unhide items when they need to be viewed again.

BIM Workflow: Analyze

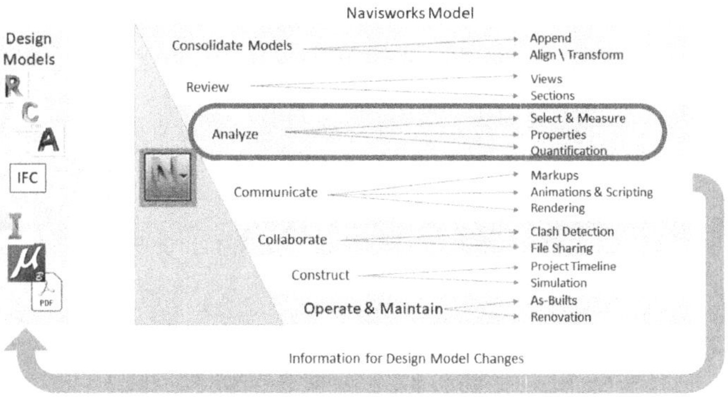

4.1 Selecting Items

A powerful part of using the Autodesk® Navisworks® software is selecting items and then discovering more about them, as shown in Figure 4–1. Selections can be grouped into sets that enable you to modify their visibility and reselect them when they are required again.

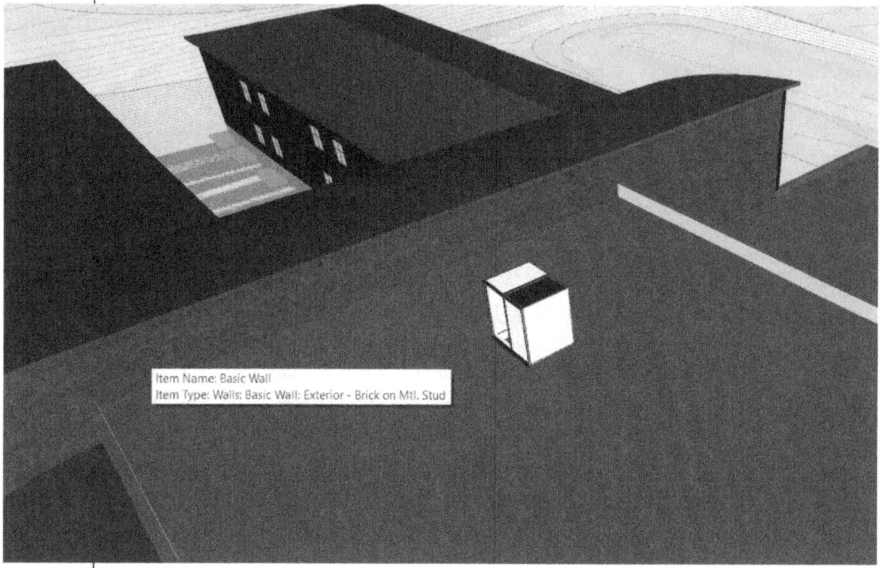

Figure 4–1

The (Select) tool is available in multiple locations, including the Quick Access Toolbar, the navigation bar, and the ribbon in the *Home* tab>Select & Search panel, as shown in Figure 4–2.

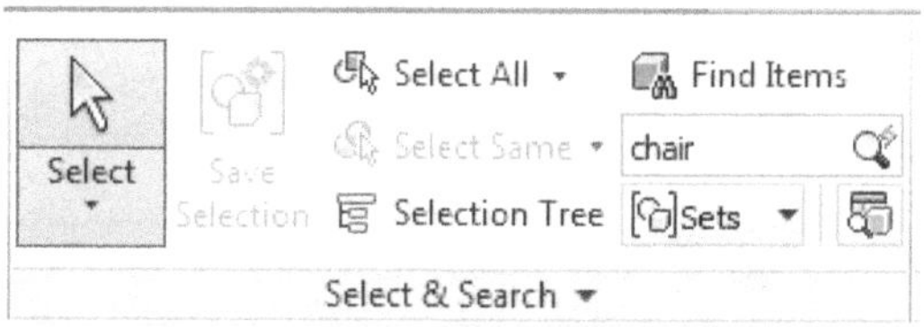

Figure 4–2

Additional options to select features are as follows:

- Press <Ctrl>+<1> to toggle on the (Select) tool.
- Hold <Ctrl> while selecting to add items to a selection.

- (Select Box) enables you to draw a window around groups of items. Only items that are totally inside the box are selected. Expand the **Select** tool for access.

- (Select All) selects everything in a project.

- (Select None) clears the selection. You can also press <Esc> to do this. Expand the **Select All** tool for access.

- (Invert Selection) switches the selection to everything that was not previously selected. Expand the **Select All** tool for access.

- With at least one items selected, the (Select Same) tool adds other similar items to the selection set. You can chose from a list of categories that match the selected item, as shown in Figure 4–3.

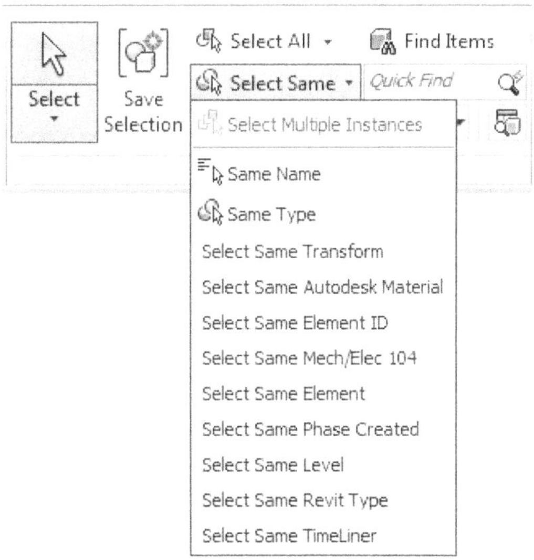

Figure 4–3

- When multiple items are selected, the list displays only the overlapping properties, such as **Same Name** and **Same Type**.

Selection Sets

If you need to select the same group of features frequently, you can save them as a selection set.

How To: Save Selections

1. Select the items you want to save in a selection set.
2. In the *Home* tab>Select & Search panel, click (Save Selection).
3. The Sets window displays with the new selection set, as shown in Figure 4–4. Type in a name for the selection set.

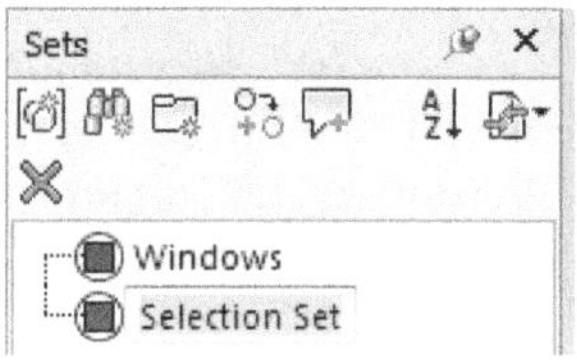

Figure 4–4

Using Saved Selections

- In the *Home* tab>Select & Search panel, expand the **Sets** drop-down list and select a set.
- To display the Sets window, expand the Sets drop-down list and select **Manage Sets**.
- The Sets window can be docked and set to auto-hide, similar to other windows.
- Several options are available in the Sets window:
  - **(Save Selection):** Saves the current selection.
  - **(Save Search):** Saves a search selection you made.
  - **(New Folder):** Adds a folder that you can name and use to organize sets.
  - **(Duplicate):** Duplicates an existing set
  - **(Add Comment):** Opens the Add Comment dialog box, where you can type in information about the set.
  - **(Sort):** Organizes the sets into alphabetical order.
  - **(Import/Export):** Enables you to import and export selection sets.

4.2 Investigating Properties

Selecting items enables you to review and add information to item properties. These properties include basic information, such as the *Item Name* and *Item Type,* as shown using the Quick Properties in Figure 4–5. The full list of properties displays in the Properties window.

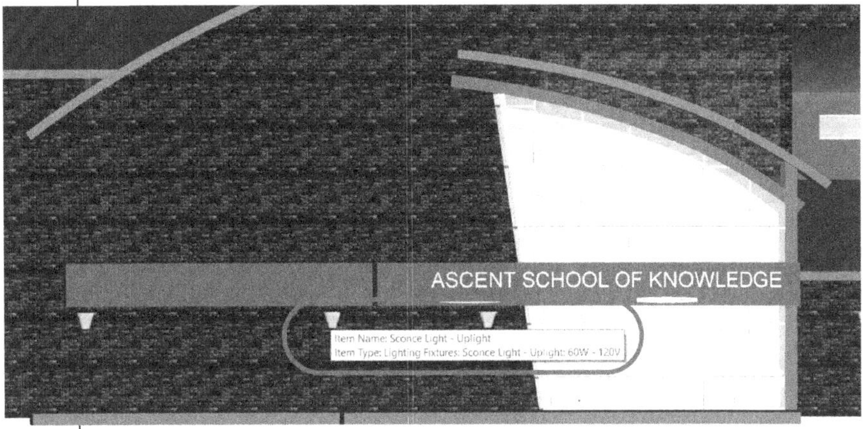

Figure 4–5

- To toggle the display tools on or off, in the *Home* tab>Display panel, click (Quick Properties) or (Properties).

Viewing Properties

In the Properties window, you can investigate the full range of properties for a selected item. They are divided by categories accessed through a series of tabs, as shown in Figure 4–6.

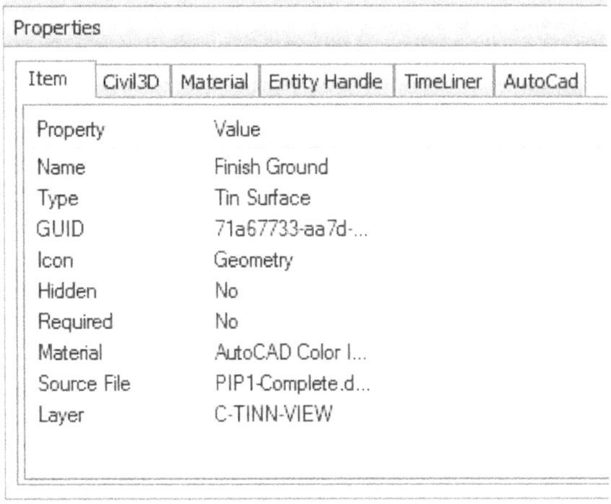

Figure 4–6

Depending on the authoring software of the original file, there could potentially be many properties. For example, an item from the Autodesk® Civil 3D® software might only have a few categories (as shown previously in Figure 4–6), while an Autodesk® Revit® model might have more, as shown in Figure 4–7.

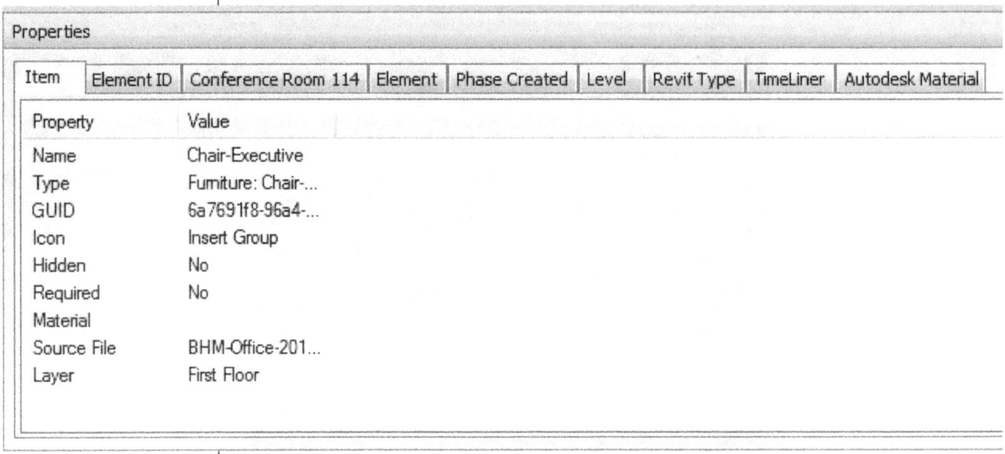

Figure 4–7

- Autodesk Revit items, such as walls, might have many more tabs, especially if rooms or spaces are assigned to the model, as shown in Figure 4–8.

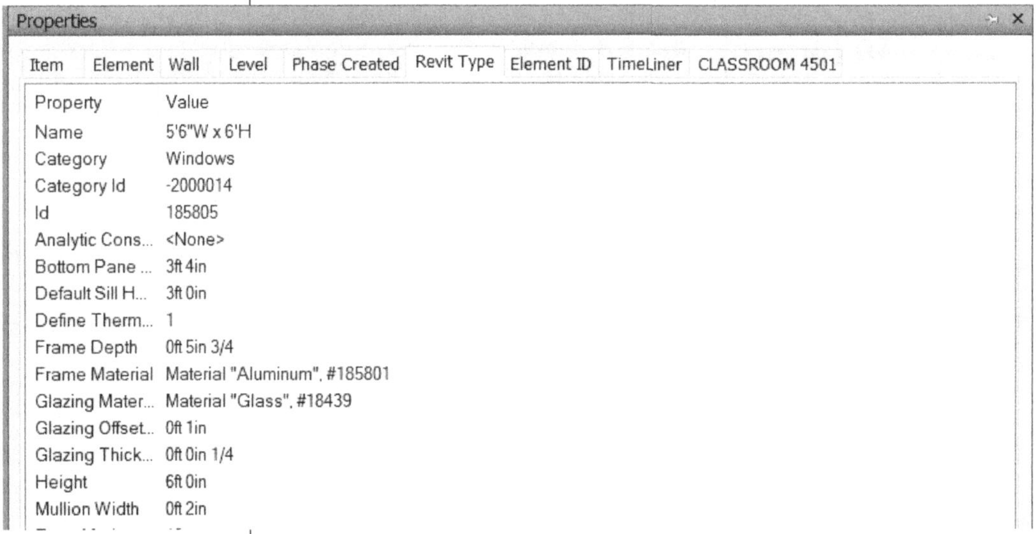

Figure 4–8

Hint: How to Create User Data

1. Right-click in the Properties dialog box and select **Add New User Data Tab**.
2. Select the new tab, right-click and select **Rename Tab** to type in a new name.
3. Right-click on the tab again, expand **Insert New Property**, and then select the type of data you want to add, as shown in Figure 4–9. The data types are as follows:
    - **String:** Alphanumeric characters
    - **Boolean:** Either Yes or No
    - **Float:** Decimal-based numbers
    - **Integer:** Numbers without any decimal

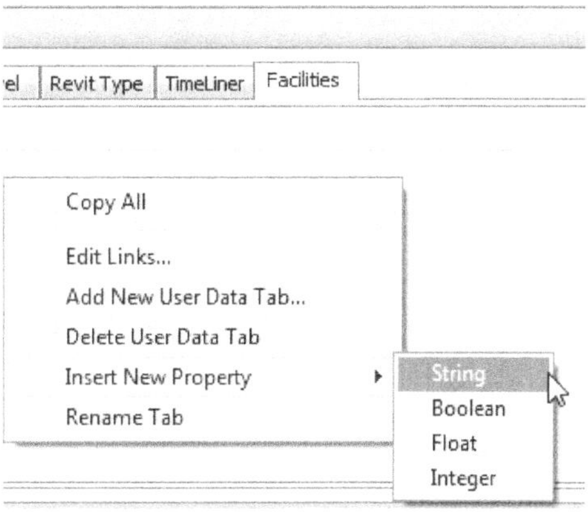

Figure 4–9

4. Once you have the new property in place, you can add a value. Select the property you want to modify, right-click, and select **Edit Property Value**.
5. In the Edit Property Value dialog box, add the required information and then click **OK**.
    - If you set up a Boolean option, you are prompted to select either Yes or No, as shown in Figure 4–10

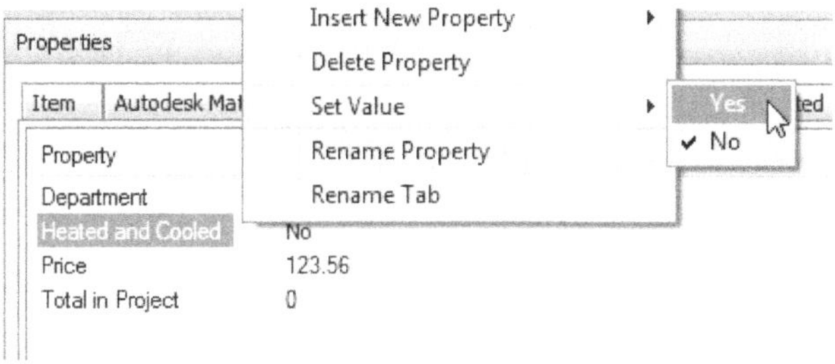

Figure 4–10

Selection Inspector

To view the properties of more than one element you need to use the Selection Inspector. In the *Home* tab>Select & Search panel, click (Selection Inspector). By default, Selection Inspector displays the same information as Quick Properties, as shown in Figure 4–11

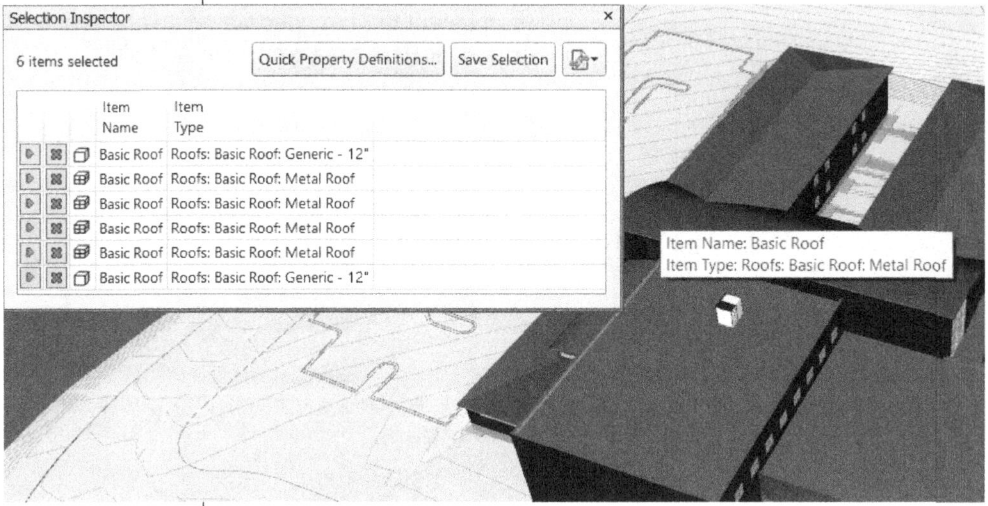

Figure 4–11

- **(Show Item):** Zooms in on the selected item in the view.
- **(Deselect):** Removes the item from the selection set.
- **(Export):** sends the information from the window to a .CSV file.

The next icon varies according to the item type, such as group, composite object, or surface.

- **Quick Property Definitions:** Enables you to add other properties to the list.
- **Save Selection:** Adds a list to a set.

Practice 4a Select and Investigate Items

Practice Objectives

- Select objects in the model.
- Save selection sets.
- Review object properties.

In this practice, you will select objects in the model and create selection sets, as shown in Figure 4–12. You will then review the properties of selected items.

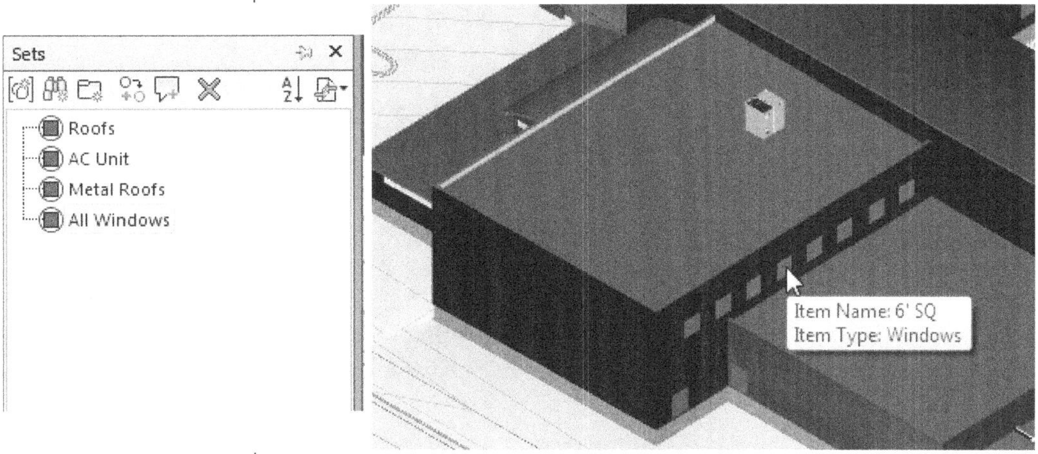

Figure 4–12

Task 1 - Use selection tools to select model features.

1. In the *Analyze* practice files folder, open **School-Select.nwf**.
2. In the Saved Viewpoints window, click **NE-View**.
3. Ensure that the *Selection Resolution* is set to **First Object**.
4. In the *Home* tab>Select & Search panel, click (Select).

Hold <Ctrl> to be able to select more than one rooftop.

5. In the scene view, select the rooftops shown in Figure 4–13.

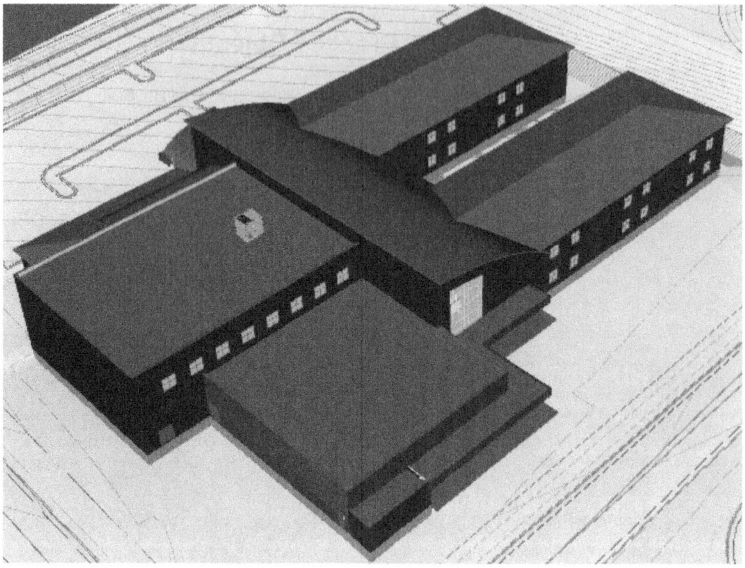

Figure 4–13

6. In the *Home* tab>Select & Search panel, click (Save Selection). Type **Roofs** for the name.

7. In the *Home* tab>Select & Search panel, expand (Select All) and click (Select None) to clear the selection of the roof tops. Recall that you can also press <Esc> to deselect everything.

8. Use the **Select Box** tool to select the AC unit sitting on top of the central flat roof.

9. Save the selection as **AC Unit**.

Task 2 - Investigate model feature properties.

1. In the *Home* tab>Select & Search panel, expand the Sets drop-down list and select **Roofs**.

2. In the *Home* tab>Display panel, click (Quick Properties) and (Properties) to toggle the tools on, if required.

3. Hover the cursor over one of the roofs to display the Quick Properties for the entire selection set, as shown in Figure 4–14.

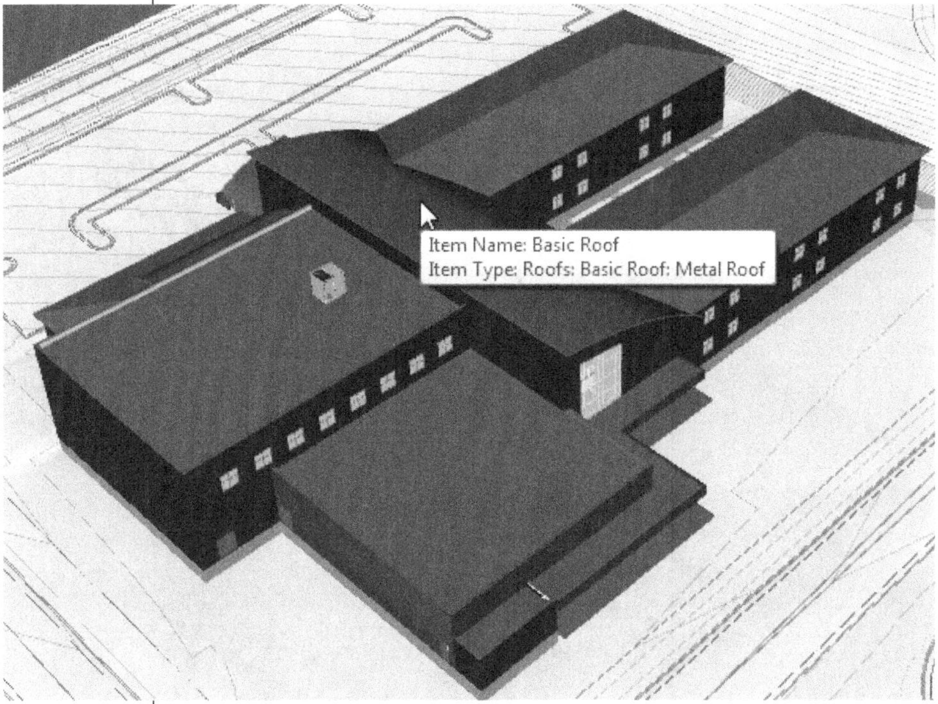

Figure 4–14

4. Expand the Properties window (which might be docked on the right-side of the window) and note that no properties display. This is because more than one item is selected.

5. In the *Home* tab>Select & Search panel, click  (Selection Inspector).

6. In the Selection Inspector window, click  (Show Item) next to each of the items in the list to zoom in on the selected item in the view.

7. In the Selection Inspector window, beside each of the **Generic - 12"** roofs, click (Deselect) to remove the items from the selection set, as shown in Figure 4–15.

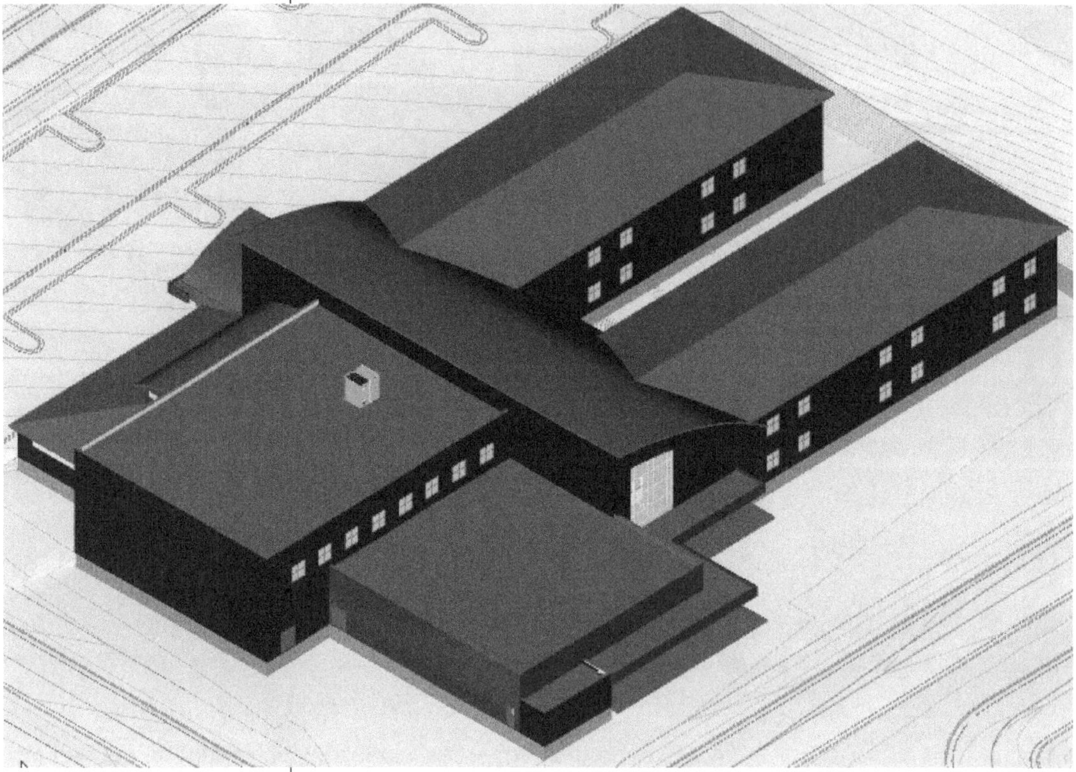

Figure 4–15

8. In the Selection Inspector window, click **Save Selection** and name the set **Metal Roofs**.
9. Close the Selection Inspector window.
10. Press <Esc> or, in the *Home* tab>Select & Search panel, click (Select None) to clear the selection of the rooftops.
11. In the *Home* tab>Select & Search panel, expand (Select Box) and click (Select).

12. In the scene view, click on the terrain surface surrounding the building. Then expand the Properties window to review the surface properties, as shown in Figure 4–16. Review each of the available tabs in the Properties window to review all of the surface properties.

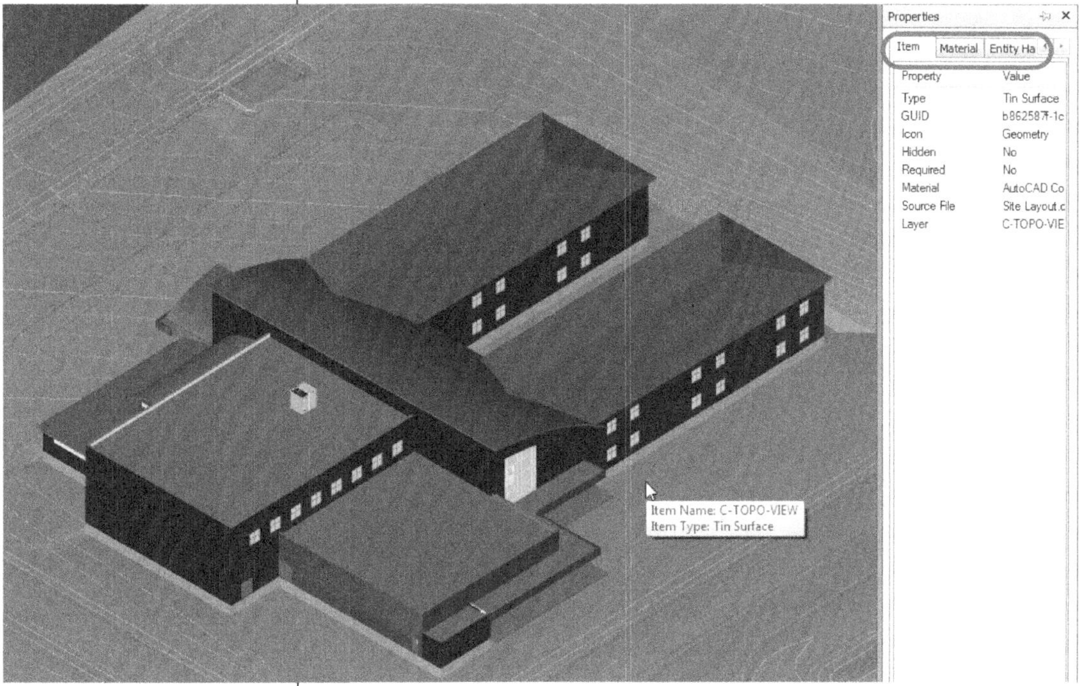

Figure 4–16

13. Press <Esc> to clear the surface selection.

14. In the *Home* tab>Select & Search panel, click (Select). In the model, select any one of the visible windows in the classroom wings, as shown in Figure 4–17.

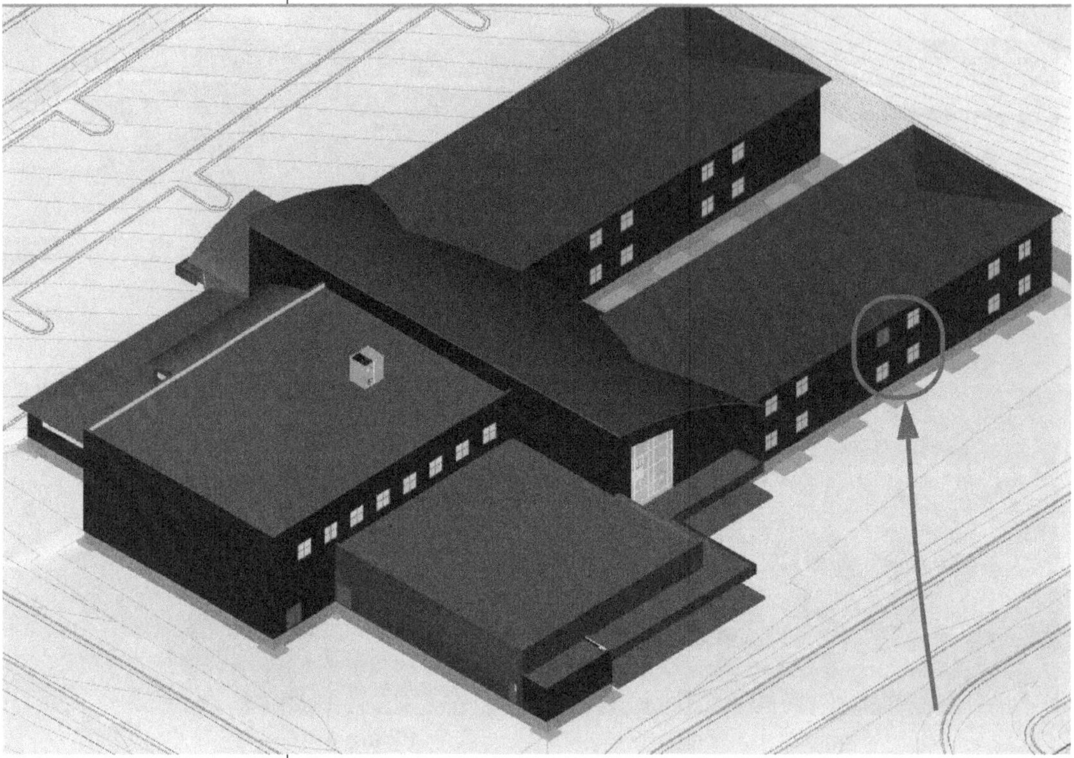

Figure 4–17

15. In the *Home* tab>Select & Search panel, click (Select Same) and select **Same Type** from the list.
16. Save the selection as **All Classroom Windows**.
17. Save the file.

4.3 Using the Selection Tree

The Selection Tree can be used to select very specific information in the model, right down to the material if required. The Selection Tree includes all of the models in the project and all of the geometry in every model, as shown in Figure 4–18.

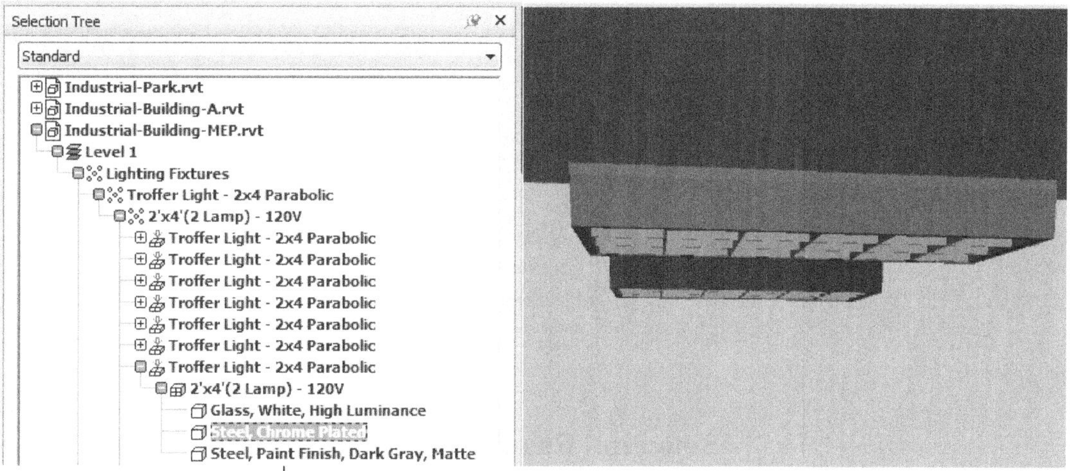

Figure 4–18

When you select items in the model, they display in the Selection Tree. Similarly, if you select items in the Selection Tree, they highlight in the model.

- In the *Home* tab>Select & Search panel, click (Selection Tree) or press <Ctrl>+<F12>.
- The Selection Tree is a window, and can therefore be docked and set to auto-hide.
- In the Selection Tree, hold <Ctrl> or <Shift> to select multiple items.
- To zoom in on a selected item, right-click on it in the Selection Tree and then select **Focus on Item**.
- You can save selections when they are highlighted in the Selection Tree. In the *Home* tab>Select & Search panel, click (Save Selection).
- Press <Esc> to clear the selection set.

Selection Resolution

To cycle through selection options, hold <Shift> and click on an item in the scene view to cycle through the resolutions. It helps to have the Selection Tree open to see how this works.

You can select items at the various levels of the hierarchy shown in the Selection Tree by setting the Selection Resolution. In the *Home* tab, expand the Select & Search panel title to display the drop-down list shown in Figure 4–19, or right-click on an item in the Selection Tree to select from the menu.

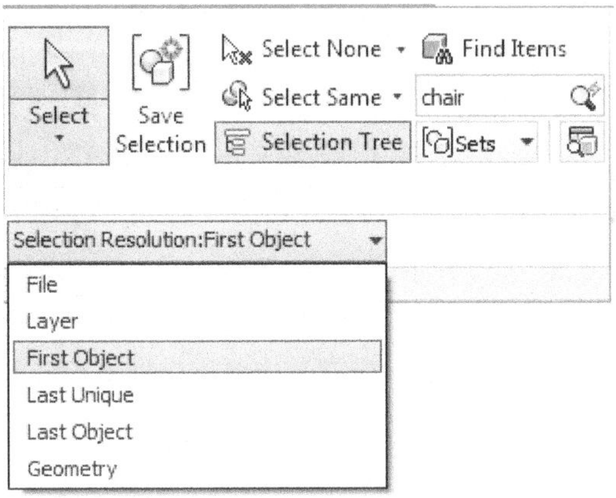

Figure 4–19

Selection Resolution Options

The Selection Resolution options (shown in Figure 4–20) are as follows:

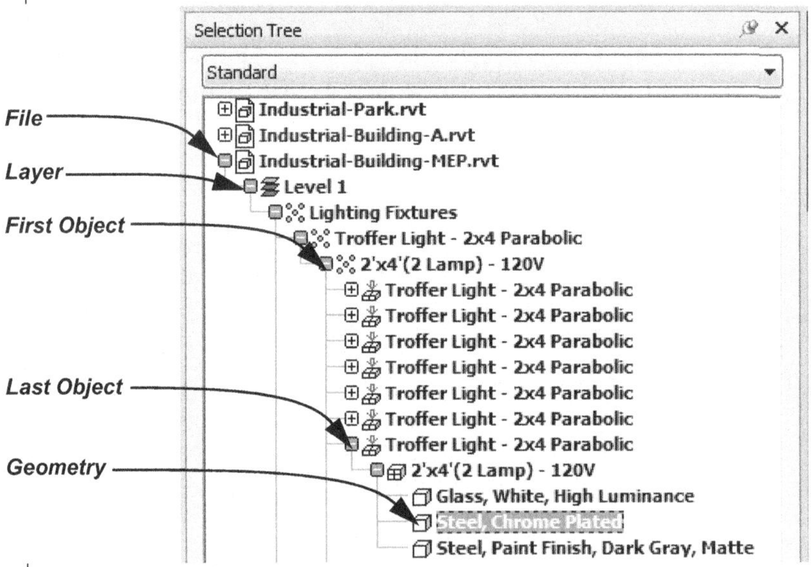

Figure 4–20

- **File:** Selects all of the elements in a file.

- **Layer:** Selects all of the elements on a specific layer. For the example shown in Figure 4–21, selecting the door on the first floor selects all of the other elements on that layer, in this case the windows and visible items such as the first floor interior walls.

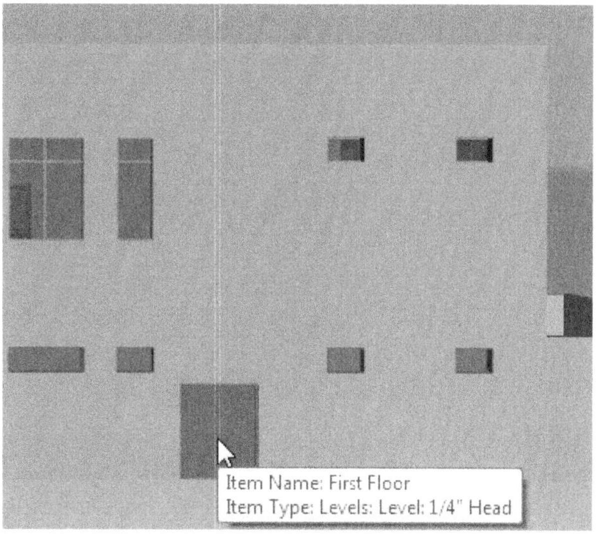

Figure 4–21

- **First Object, Last Object**, and **Last Unique** are based on their location below the level, but typically each option selects the exact item you pick, such as a specific wall, column, or lighting fixture in an Autodesk Revit model. AutoCAD-based models might be different because of the underlying geometry.

- **Geometry:** Selects the base geometry of the item, such as the material of a lighting fixture, or a line, polyline, or arc element in an AutoCAD project.

Hint: Selection Options

There are several options that can help you be more precise in selecting and viewing items. These are found in the Options Editor in the **Interface>Selection** pane, as shown in Figure 4–22.

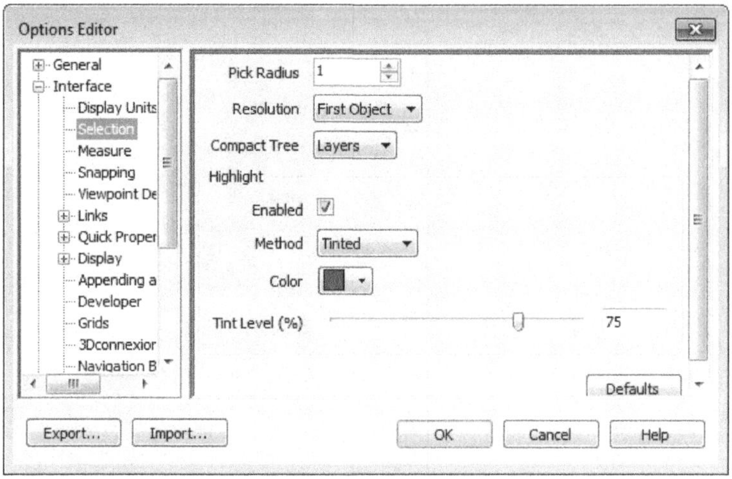

Figure 4–22

- **Pick Radius:** Sets the size (in pixels) of the point where you click the cursor to select an element.
- **Resolution:** Establishes the default pick order.
- **Compact Tree:** Establishes the default presentation of the Selection Tree.
- **Highlight:** Sets the method (Tinted, Shaded, Wireframe) and color of selected items.

Setting the Viewing Order

The Selection Tree can be very complex, depending on the number of models included in the project and the number of items within each model. There are at least three ways to view the information, as shown in Figure 4–23.

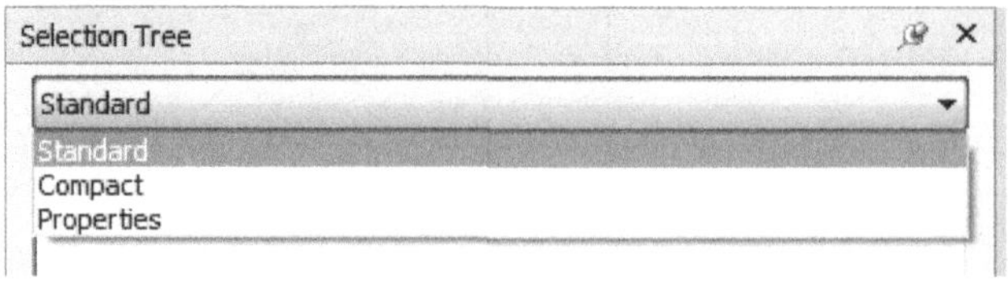

Figure 4–23

- **Standard:** Displays all of the nodes from *File* to *Geometry.*
- **Compact:** Displays only the nodes for *File* and *Layers.*
- **Properties:** Displays all of the properties of every item in the model by category. For example, in an Autodesk Revit model, each room is considered a category, and you can find properties such as the Area of the room. When you select the room, all of the related items (such as the exterior wall and windows) are selected, as shown in Figure 4–24.

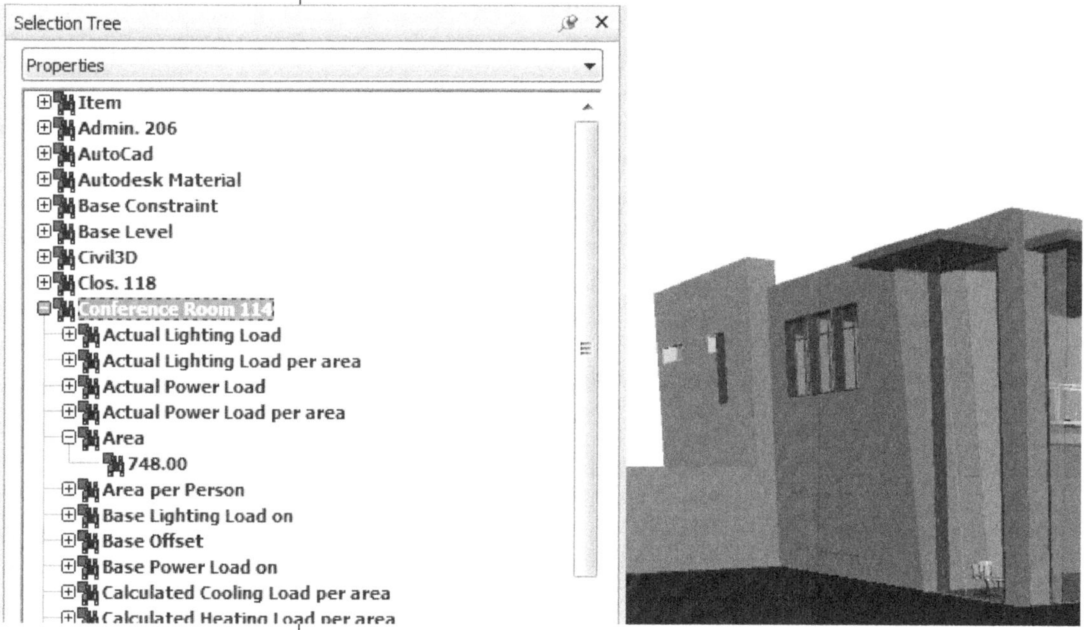

Figure 4–24

- **Sets:** Only available when you have saved selections in the project, and displays those sets.

Practice 4b Use the Selection Tree

Practice Objectives

- Change the selection resolution.
- Use the Selection Tree to familiarize yourself with the model.

In this practice, you will become more familiar with the model shown in Figure 4–25 by using the Selection Tree to select features and focus on them. You will also change the selection resolution to make selecting individual items much easier.

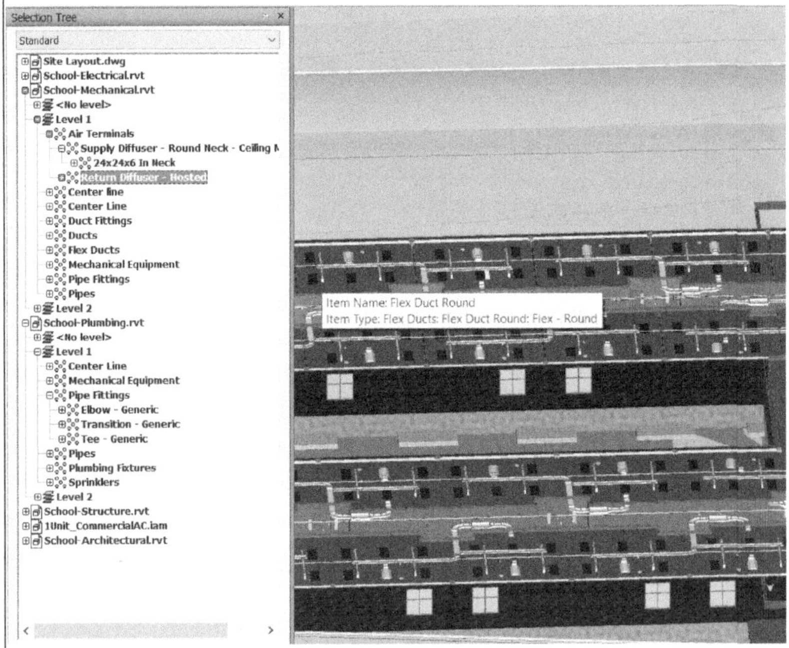

Figure 4–25

Task 1 - Change the selection resolution.

1. Continue working on the current file or open **School-Tree.nwf** in the *Analyze* practice files folder.
2. In the Saved Viewpoints window, click **NE-View**.
3. In the *Home* tab>Select & Search panel, ensure that your selection method is set to (Select) rather than (Select Box).

4. Ensure that the *Selection Resolution* is set to **First Object**. Then, pin the Selection Tree open.

5. In the scene view, click on the lower flat roof, as shown in Figure 4–26. Only that one roof should be selected.

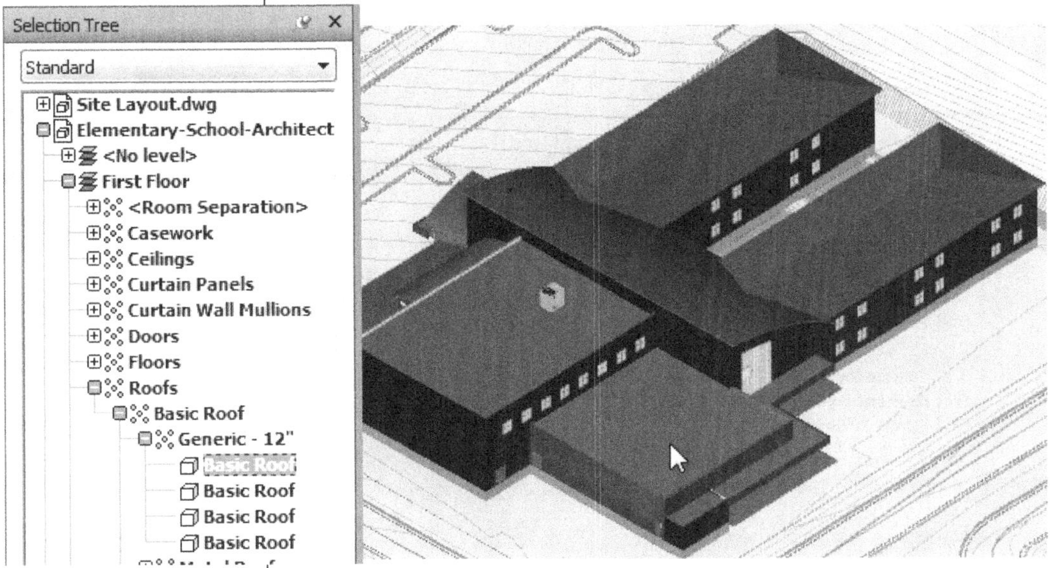

Figure 4–26

6. Click away from any elements or press <Esc> to clear the selection.

7. In the *Home* tab, expand the Select & Search panel title.

8. Expand the *Selection Resolution* drop-down list and note which method is selected.

9. Change *Selection Resolution* to **File**.

10. Select the same roof again and note how the entire building is now selected.

11. Clear the selection, change the *Selection Resolution* to **Layer**, and then reselect the same roof. Note that only the first floor elements are selected, as shown in Figure 4–27.

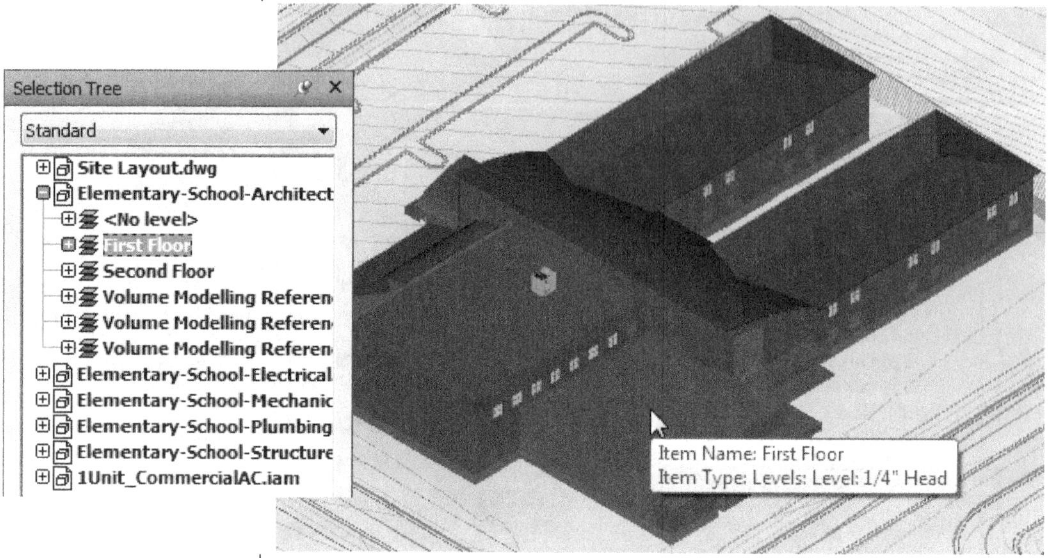

Figure 4–27

12. Once you have tested all of the selection resolution methods, reset the resolution to **First Object**.

13. Unpin the Selection Tree.

14. Save the file.

Task 2 - Fix a selection set.

1. In the *Home* tab>Select & Search panel, expand the Sets drop-down list and select **AC Unit**.

2. Hover the cursor over the Selection Tree. Note that some but not all of the elements in the AC unit are selected, as shown in Figure 4–28. Also note that other elements that are not in the AC Unit file were also selected. This occurs because the set was created using the Select Box tool.

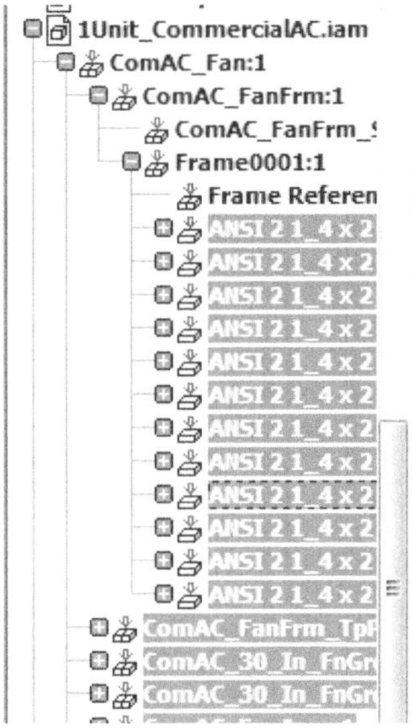

Figure 4–28

3. In the Selection Tree, select **1Unit_Commercial AC.iam** (the top level node).

4. In the Sets window, right-click on **AC Unit** and then select **Update**.

Task 3 - Use the Selection Tree to select objects.

1. Restore the **NE-View** viewpoint.

2. In the Selection Tree, expand *School-Architectural.rvt> First Floor* and select **Doors**. Note what is selected in the scene view.

3. Now expand **Doors** and select **Double Door**. Right-click and select **Focus on Item**.

4. In the Selection Tree, still in the **Doors** node, select **SINGLE**, right-click and select **Focus on Item**.

Note that the scene is panned to center the curtain wall in the view, but it is hidden.

5. Select **Curtain Wall Sgl Glass**, right-click and select **Focus on Item**.

6. With the **Curtain Wall Sgl Glass** item still selected, right-click and select **Selection Inspector** to make it visible.

7. In the Selection Inspector window, click (Show Item) next to **Curtain Wall Sgl Glass**. Note that the view zooms in and centers on the curtain wall, but that there is a brick wall in front of the window blocking your view.

8. Restore the Saved Viewpoint **Section-EntrancePlatform**.

9. Close the Selection Inspector window.

10. In the Saved Viewpoints window, click **Section-2ndFloorUtilities**.

11. In the Selection Tree window, click on **School- Electrical.rvt**, the electrical components display as shown in Figure 4–29. Then, click on **School- Mechanical.rvt** to display the mechanical ducts, as shown in Figure 4–30.

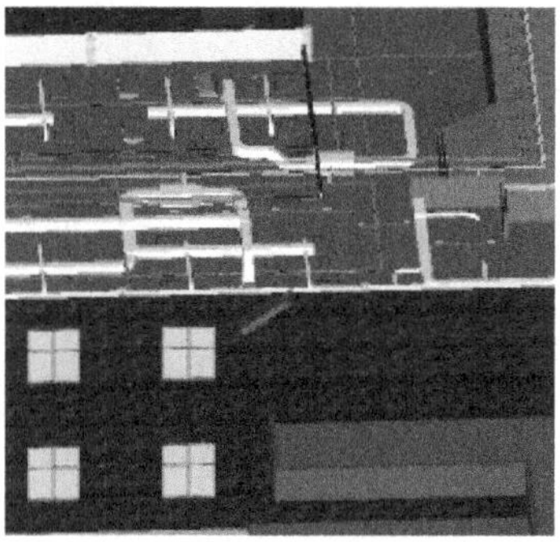

Figure 4–29

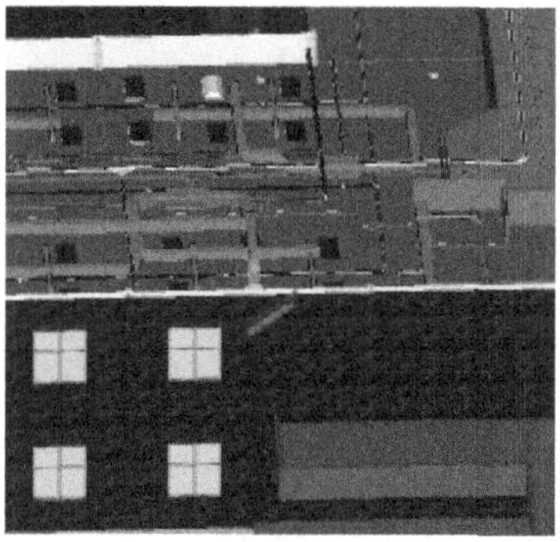

Figure 4–30

12. Continue selecting different items in the Selection Tree window to become more familiar with the model.

13. Press <Esc> to clear the selection.

14. In the Saved Viewpoints window, click **NE-View** to return to it.

15. In the Selection Tree, expand **School-Architectural.rvt>First Floor>Windows>4x4 Adjustable** and select **6' SQ**. Note that only one window is selected in the scene view.

16. In the *Home* tab>Select & Search panel, expand (Select Same) and select **Same Name**. All of the **4x4 Adjustable-6' SQ** windows are selected in the model.

17. In the *Home* tab>Select & Search panel, click (Save Selection). Enter **Gym Windows** for the name.

18. Save the file.

4.4 Finding Items and Saving Search Sets

Due to the large amount of information that can be stored in an Autodesk Navisworks project, the tools that help you find objects become very important. You can use Quick Find for simple searches or Find Items for more complex searches. The items you find can be saved to a search set.

The advantage of a search set over a saved set is that as new models are appended, the search set updates automatically to include new objects, while saved sets do not update automatically. Figure 4–31 shows an example of search sets.

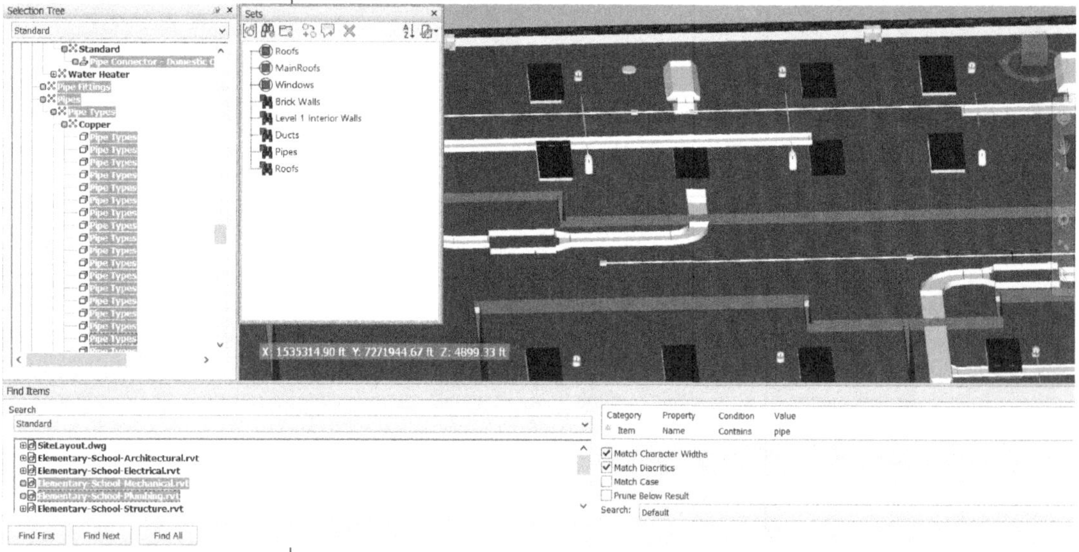

Figure 4–31

- Searches are based on information stored in item properties.

Using Quick Find

You can use Quick Find to do a search based on a text string. For example, in a Civil 3D model, type "road" (as shown in Figure 4–32) and press <Enter>, or click the (Quick Find) button. The first related item in the Selection Tree is highlighted, as shown in Figure 4–33.

Figure 4–32

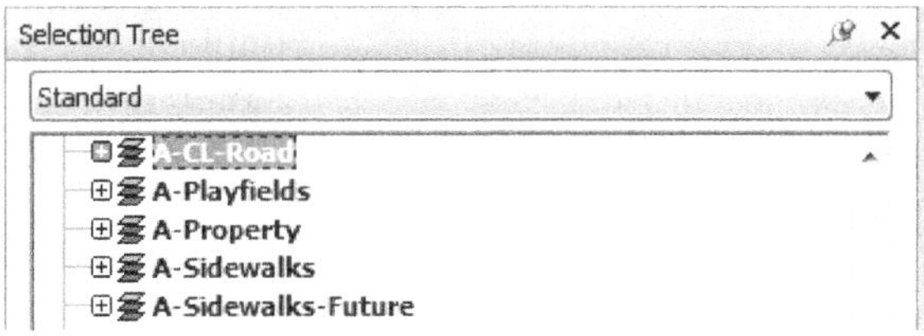

Figure 4–33

- Repeatedly pressing <Enter> or clicking the button will continue to the next item through the entire Selection Tree.
- Quick Find drills down to the geometry level with each click before moving to the top level of the next related item.

How To: Use the Find Item Dialog Box

1. In the *Home* tab>Select & Search panel, click  (Find Items).
2. In the Find Items dialog box, in the left pane, drill down to the level where you want to start searching. This list is the same as the Selection Tree.
3. In the right pane, expand each drop-down list and select the *Category*, *Property*, *Condition*, and *Value* to specify which rules you want active in the search, as shown in Figure 4–34.
    - **Category:** A list that corresponds to the tabs in Properties
    - **Property:** A list of properties within the selected category.
    - **Condition:** How you want to search.
    - **Value:** What you want to search for based on the condition.

The options available in each drop-down list depend on the items that you are investigating.

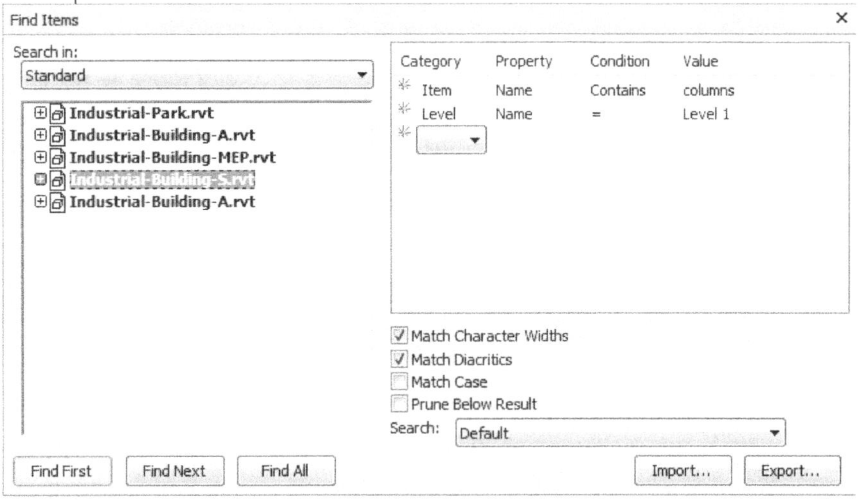

Figure 4–34

4. Select the Matching options below the right pane, or by right-clicking and selecting the appropriate **Ignore** statements.
5. Click **Find First**, **Find Next**, or **Find All**, as required.

Working with Conditions

The conditions that are available depend on whether the property you select is text based (as shown in Figure 4–35) or number based (as shown in Figure 4–36).

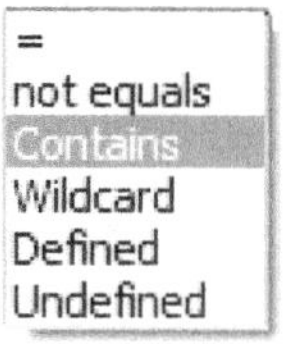

Figure 4–35

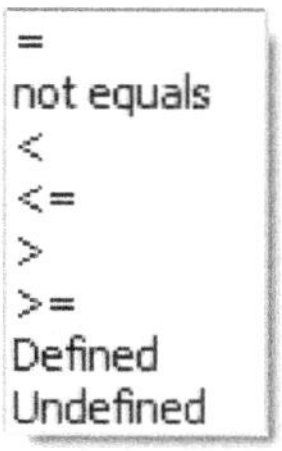

Figure 4–36

- Additional rows are automatically an "and" statement: both conditions must be matched to return any selections.

- If you want to change a row to an "or" statement, right-click on the row and select **Or Condition**. The row is distinguished by a **+** sign, as shown in Figure 4–37.

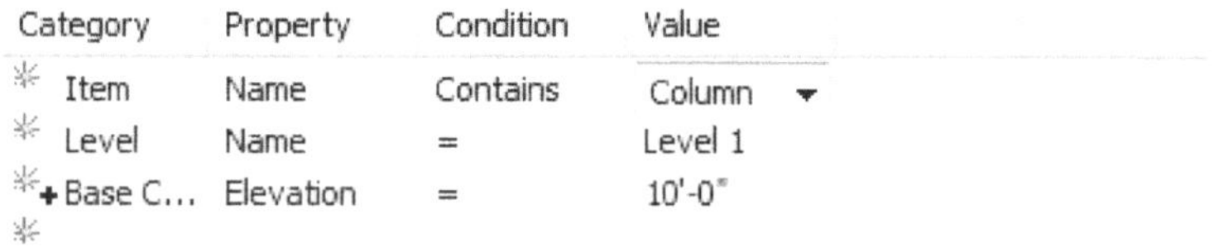

Figure 4–37

- To search for the opposite of a condition, right-click on the row and select **Negate Condition**.

- To remove a row from the list, right-click on it and select **Delete Condition**.

- You can also right-click and select **Delete All Conditions** to start over.

How To: Save Searches

1. In the Find Items window, create a search condition and click **Find All**.
2. In the Sets window, click  (Save Search), or right-click and select **Save Search**.
3. Type in a name for the search. The icon indicates that it is a search set, as shown in Figure 4–38.

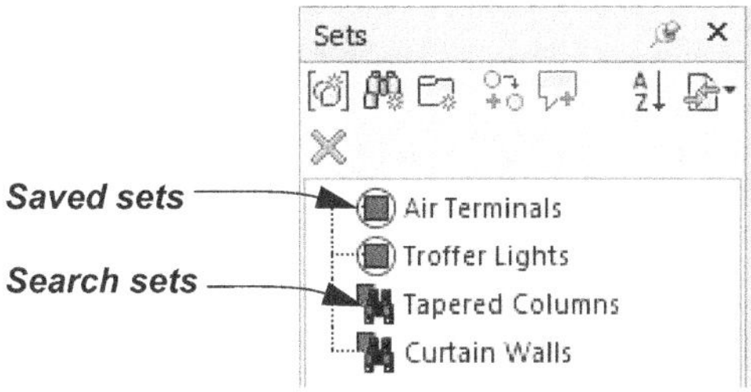

Figure 4–38

- Search sets update when new geometry is added to the model that matches the search.
- Click  (Duplicate) to make a copy of a search set to use as the base for another search set.

Practice 4c Find Items and Save Search Sets

Practice Objectives

- Create a search criteria.
- Save a search set for later use.

In this practice, you will run a quick search to find all of the HVAC ducts. Then, you will create a saved set based on the type of walls (interior vs. exterior) for use later, as shown in Figure 4–39.

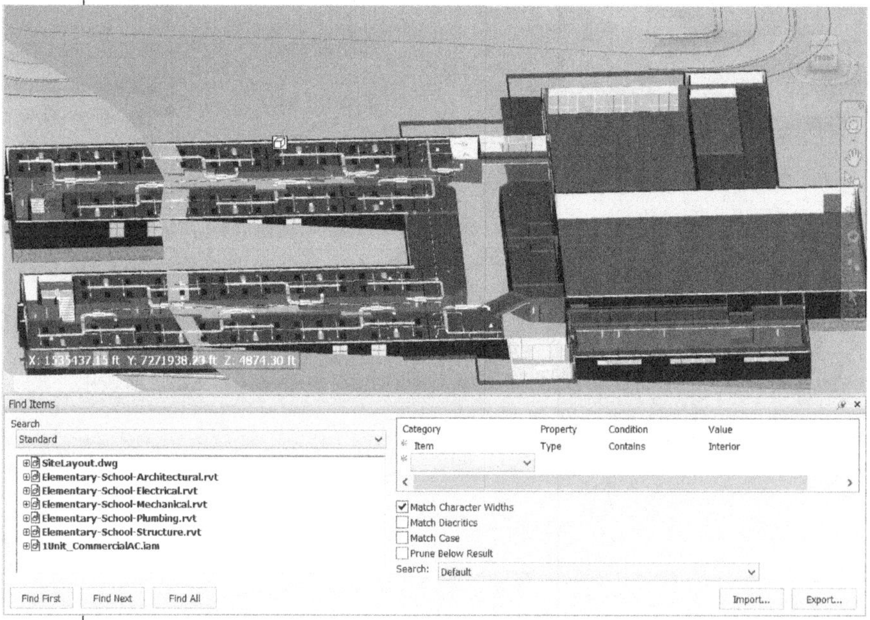

Figure 4–39

Task 1 - Do a quick search.

1. Continue working on the current file or open **School-Sets.nwf** in the *Analyze* practice files folder.

2. In the Saved Viewpoints window, click **Section-1stFloorUtilities**.

3. Pin the Properties window open so that it displays for the next step.

4. In the *Home* tab>Select & Search panel, next to the  (Quick Find) button, type **Ducts** and press <Enter>. Note that all of the ducts in the project are now selected.

5. Review the duct's properties in the Properties window, as shown in Figure 4–40.

6. Click the (Quick Find) button or press <Enter>. Only one duct is selected. Note that there are more properties for individual ducts than for the group of ducts as shown in Figure 4–41.

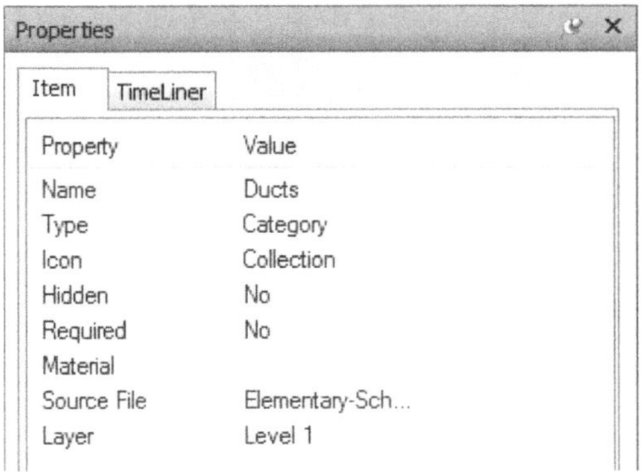

Figure 4–40

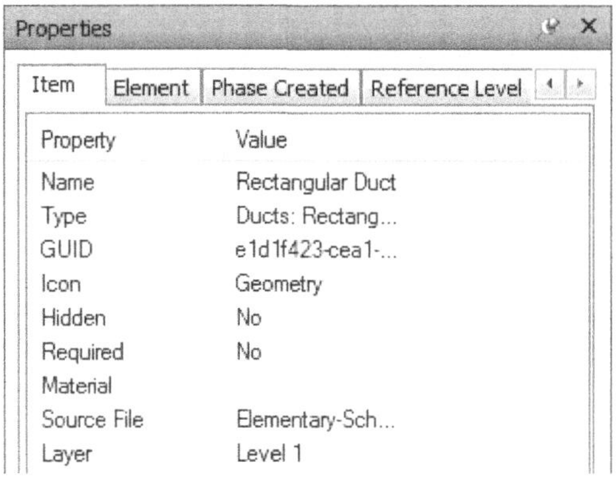

Figure 4–41

7. Continue to press <Enter> to cycle through the ducts in the model, reviewing each duct's properties.

Task 2 - Use the Find Items window for an advanced search.

1. Open and pin the Find Items window so that it is docked on the bottom of the screen.
   - If the Find Items window is not open, in the *Home* tab>Select & Search panel, click (Find Items).
2. In the Find Items window, in the left pane, click on **School-Architectural.rvt**.

Expand the width of the columns as required, to see the information.

3. In the right pane, do the following, as shown in Figure 4–42:
    - Under *Category*, select **Material**.
    - Under *Property*, select **Name**.
    - Under *Condition*, select **Contains**.
    - Under *Value*, type **Brick**.
      (Note: Ensure that you capitalize **Brick** or clear the checkmark from **Match Case**.)

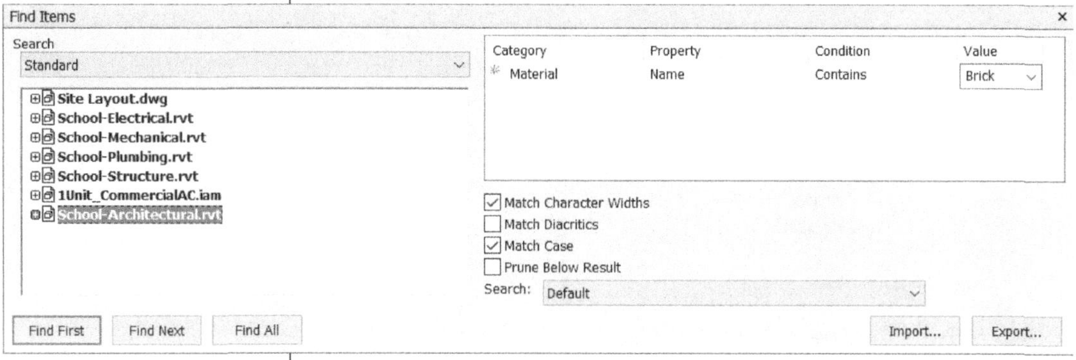

Figure 4–42

4. Leave the Matching options below the right pane set to the defaults.

5. Click **Find First**, **Find Next**, and then **Find All** and note what is selected in the model.

Task 3 - Save search sets.

1. In the Sets window, click (Save Search).

2. Type **Brick Wall** for the search. Note that the icon indicates that it is a search set, as shown in Figure 4–43.

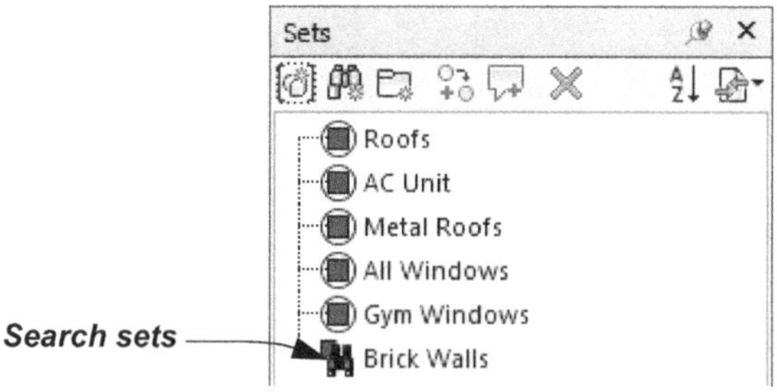

Figure 4–43

3. In the Find Items window, overwrite the information to create another search set with the criteria shown in Figure 4–44.

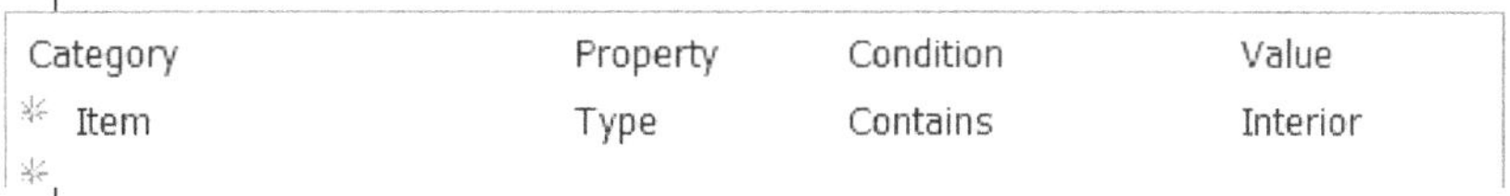

Figure 4–44

4. In the Sets window, save the search and name it **Interior Walls**.
5. In the Find Items window, create another search using the following criteria:
   - Under *Category*, select **Item**.
   - Under *Property*, select **Name**.
   - Under *Condition*, select **Contains**.
   - Under *Value*, type **Duct**.
6. Click **Find First**. A dialog box displays, as shown in Figure 4–45. Click **OK**.

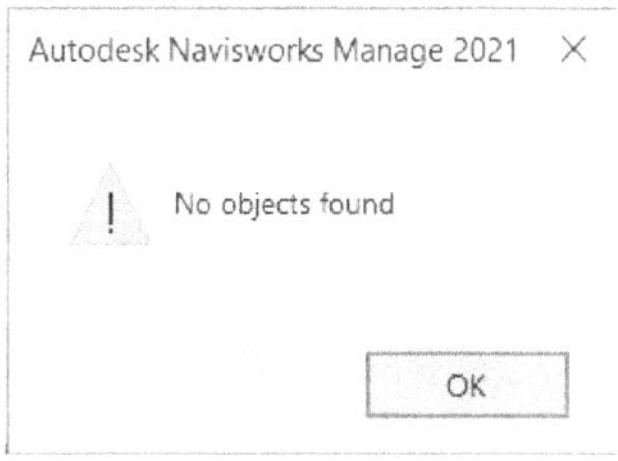

Figure 4–45

7. In the Find Items window, in the left pane, select **School-Mechanical.rvt** and then click **Find All**. The ducts now display as shown in Figure 4–46.

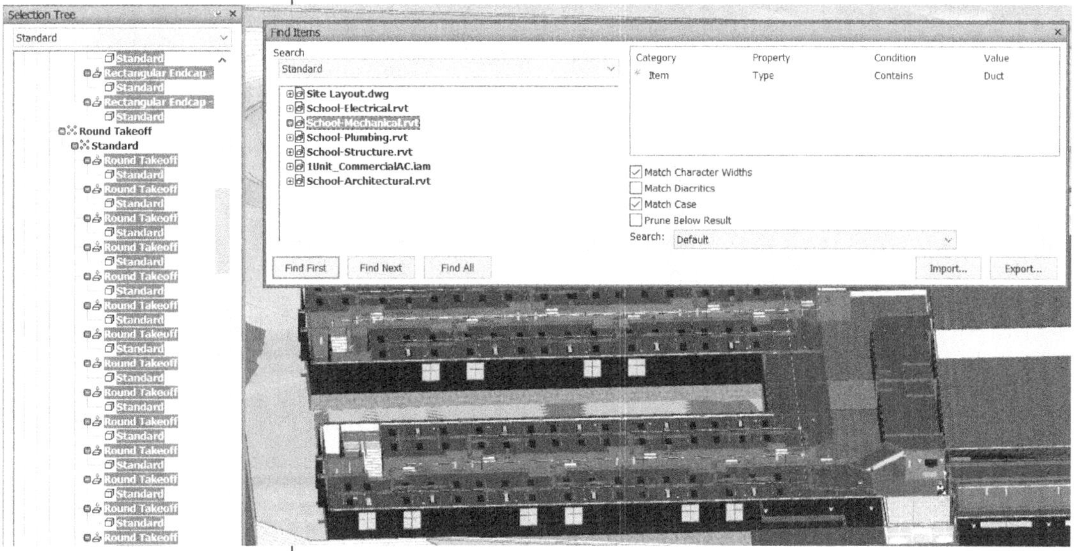

Figure 4–46

8. In the Sets window, click  (Save Search).
9. Type in **Ducts** for the search name.
10. Open the saved viewpoint **Section - 2ndFloorUtilities**.
11. Zoom in on the lower left corner of the building so that the pipes display as shown in Figure 4–47.

Figure 4–47

12. In the Find Items window, in the left pane, select the **School-Mechanical.rvt** and **School-Plumbing.rvt** files, using <Ctrl> to select the second one.

13. In the right pane, do the following, as shown in Figure 4–48:
    - Under *Category*, select **Item**.
    - Under *Property*, select **Name**.
    - Under *Condition*, select **Contains**.
    - Under *Value*, type **pipe**.
    - Clear the checkmark for **Match Case**.

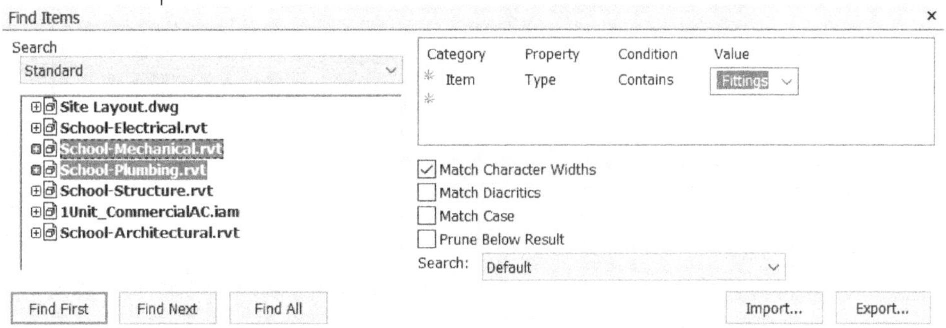

Figure 4–48

14. Click **Find All**. Pipes in both the mechanical and plumbing should highlight.

15. In the Sets window, click  (Save Search).

16. Type **Pipes** for the search name.

17. As you have time, create separate saved searches for piping in the mechanical and plumbing files.

18. Save the file.

4.5 Hiding and Unhiding Items

As you work in a model, it can help to hide items that are in the way or to isolate them so that you can investigate them more thoroughly. In the example shown in Figure 4–49, the brick walls are hidden to make viewing interior features easier.

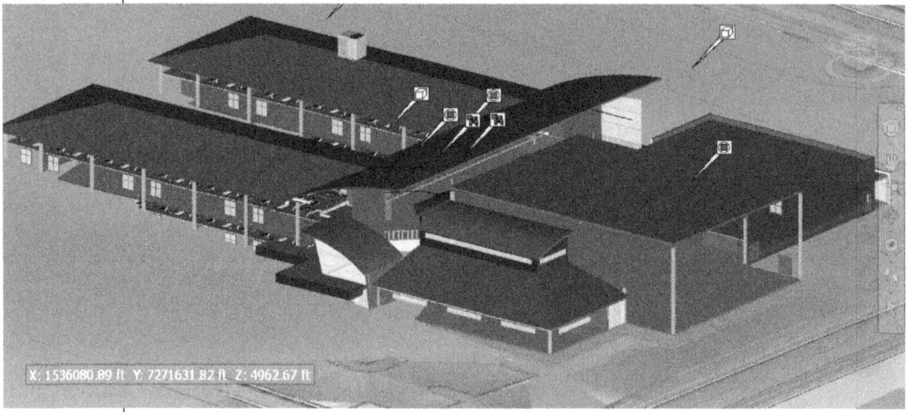

Figure 4–49

- Having saved sets and search sets can be very helpful when you want to hide and unhide elements.

How To: Hide Items

1. Select individual items in a scene or, in the Sets dialog box, click on a saved set or a search set.
2. In the *Home* tab>Visibility panel, click (Hide).
3. Note that the selected items are removed from the scene and are grayed out in the Selection Tree, as shown in Figure 4–50.

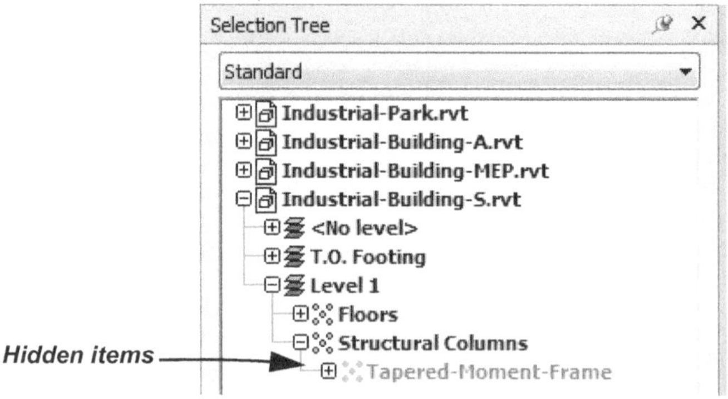

Figure 4–50

How To: Isolate Items

1. Select individual items in a scene or, in the Sets dialog box, click on a saved set or a search set.
2. In the *Home* tab>Visibility panel, click (Hide Unselected).
3. Any items that are not in the selection are hidden.

Unhiding Items

- To unhide everything in the project that has been hidden, in the *Home* tab>Visibility panel, click (Unhide All).
- To unhide only specific hidden items, select them in the Selection Tree, right-click and select **Hide**, as shown in Figure 4–51. This toggles off the checkmark and unhides the items.

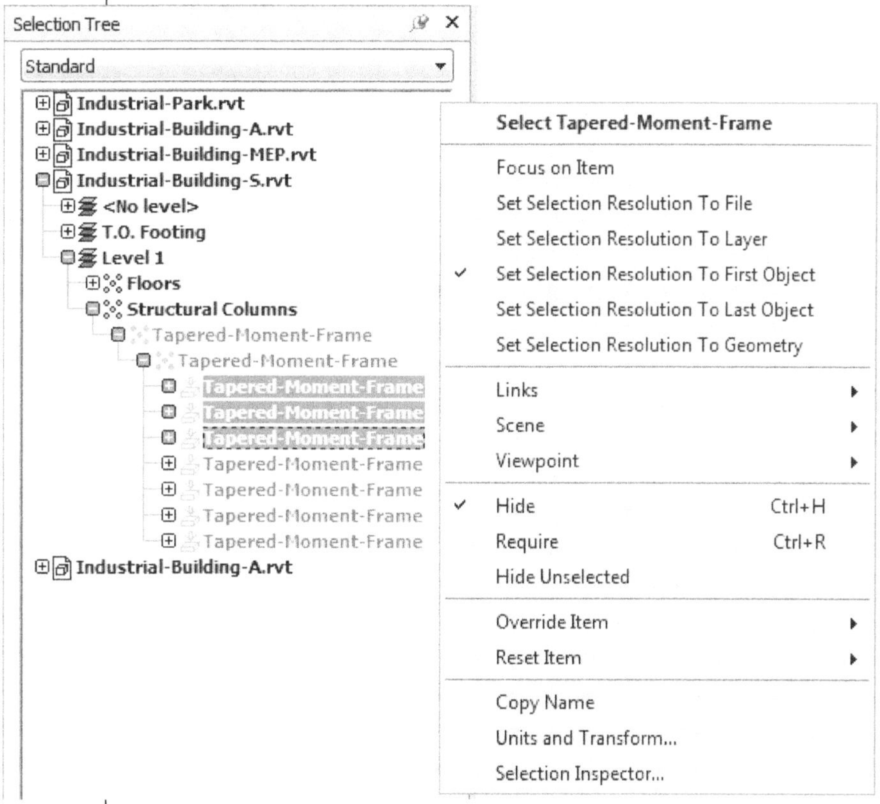

Figure 4–51

Hint: Required Items

To keep selected items displayed as you navigate through a model, you can select items and, in the *Home* tab>Visibility panel, click (Require). This can be helpful when you are using very complex models so you do not lose the items when the scene regenerates.

- To toggle this option off, expand (Unhide All) and select (Unrequire All).

Practice 4d Hide and Unhide Objects in a Model

Practice Objectives

- Hide objects in the scene.
- Unhide hidden objects.

In this practice, you will test out hiding sets of elements and use the Selection Tree to hide other elements as shown in Figure 4–52.

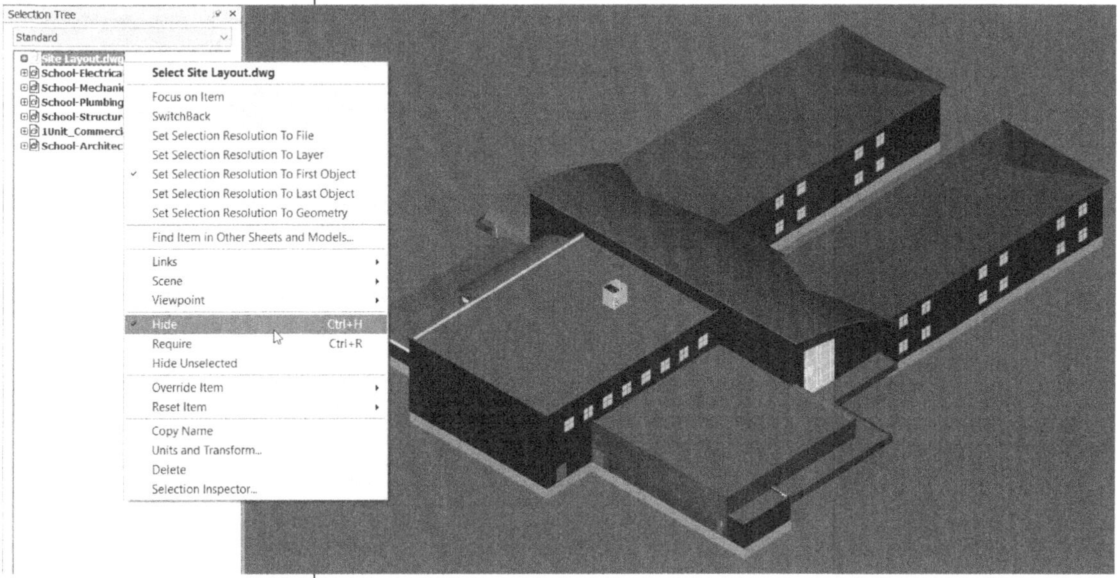

Figure 4–52

Task 1 - Hide walls.

1. Continue working on the current file or open **School-Hide.nwf** in the *Analyze* practice files folder.
2. Open the Saved Viewpoint **NE-View**.
3. In the Sets window, select **Brick Walls**.
4. In the *Home* tab>Visibility panel, click  (Hide)
5. In the Sets dialog box, select **Interior Walls**.

6. Note that the selected items are removed from the scene and grayed out in the Selection Tree as shown in Figure 4–53.

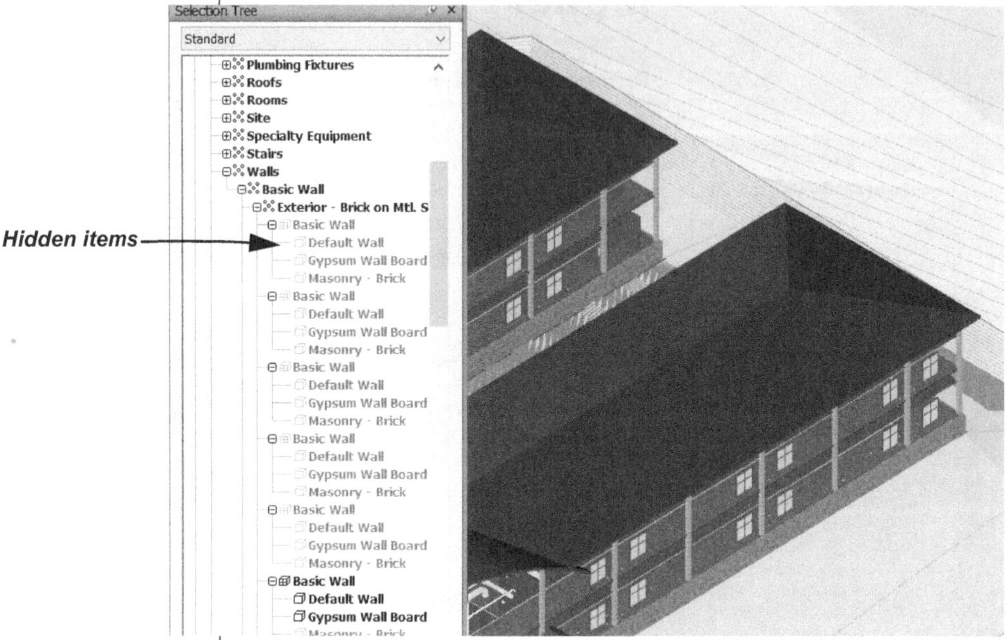

Figure 4–53

Task 2 - Hide site elements.

1. Select one of the site elements.
2. In the *Home* tab>Visibility panel, click (Hide Unselected). All of the building elements are hidden.
3. In the *Home* tab>Visibility panel, click (Unhide All).
4. With the site element still selected, in the *Home* tab>Visibility panel, click (Hide). Only the selected site element is hidden.
5. In the Selection Tree, select **Site Layout.dwg**. Right-click and select **Hide**. All of the site elements are hidden.
6. Save the file.

Chapter Review Questions

1. Which selection tool would you use to clear the current selection while simultaneously selecting everything that is not in the current selection?

   a. (Select All)

   b. (Select None)

   c. (Invert Selection)

   d. (Select Same)

2. Once a section set is saved, you cannot make any changes to it.

   a. True

   b. False

3. To view the properties of more than one element, which tool do you need to use?

   a. (Selection Inspector)

   b. (Quick Properties)

   c. (Properties)

4. Which Selection Resolution would you use to select the base geometry of an item, such as the material of a lighting fixture?

   a. File

   b. Layer

   c. First Object, Last Object, and Last Unique

   d. Geometry

5. How would you ensure that objects in the model that absolutely need to be visible do not disappear?

   a. Create a saved set.

   b. Create a search set.

   c. In the *Home* tab>Visibility panel, click (Require).

   d. You cannot make items remain visible.

Command Summary

Button	Command	Location
Selection Tools		
	**Invert Selection**	• **Ribbon:** *Home* tab>Select & Search panel>expand Select All
	**Manage Sets**	• **Ribbon:** *Home* tab>Select & Search panel
	**Save Selection**	• **Ribbon:** *Home* tab>Select & Search panel
	**Select**	• **Ribbon:** *Home* tab>Select & Search panel • **Quick Access Toolbar** • **Navigation Bar** • **Shortcut:** <Ctrl>+<1>
	**Select All**	• **Ribbon:** *Home* tab>Select & Search panel
	**Select Box**	• **Ribbon:** *Home* tab>Select & Search panel>expand Select
	**Select None**	• **Ribbon:** *Home* tab>Select & Search panel>expand Select All
	**Select Same**	• **Ribbon:** *Home* tab>Select & Search panel
	**Selection Inspector**	• **Ribbon:** *Home* tab>Select & Search panel
	**Selection Tree**	• **Ribbon:** *Home* tab>Select & Search panel • **Shortcut:** <Ctrl>+<F12>
Properties and Options		
Options	**Options**	• **Application Menu**
	**Properties**	• **Ribbon:** *Home* tab>Display panel
	**Quick Properties**	• **Ribbon:** *Home* tab>Display panel
Find Tools		
	**Find Items**	• **Ribbon:** *Home* tab>Select & Search panel

	Quick Find	• **Ribbon:** *Home* tab>Select & Search panel
	Save Search	• **Window:** *Sets*
Visibility Tools		
	Hide	• **Ribbon:** *Home* tab>Visibility panel
	Hide Unselected	• **Ribbon:** *Home* tab>Visibility panel
	Require	• **Ribbon:** *Home* tab>Visibility panel
	Select	• **Quick Access Toolbar** • Navigation Bar • **Ribbon:** *Home* tab>Select & Search panel
	Select Box	• **Quick Access Toolbar** • **Ribbon:** *Home* tab>Select & Search panel>expand Select
	Unhide All	• **Ribbon:** *Home* tab>Visibility panel
	Unrequire All	• **Ribbon:** *Home* tab>Visibility panel expand Unhide All

Chapter 5

Communication: Review and Mark Up a Model

The next step in the BIM workflow is communication. BIM was originally created as a way to increase communication and reduce RFIs. In this chapter, you will learn how to measure the model and turn those measurements into redlines to communicate to other team members what corrections need to be made. You will also learn how to mark up a scene using text, tags, and other drawing tools.

Learning Objectives in This Chapter

- Use measure tools to review information in the model and convert measurements to redline dimensions.
- Mark up scenes for review using text and drawing tools.
- Add tags and comments to elements in a model.

BIM Workflow: Communicate

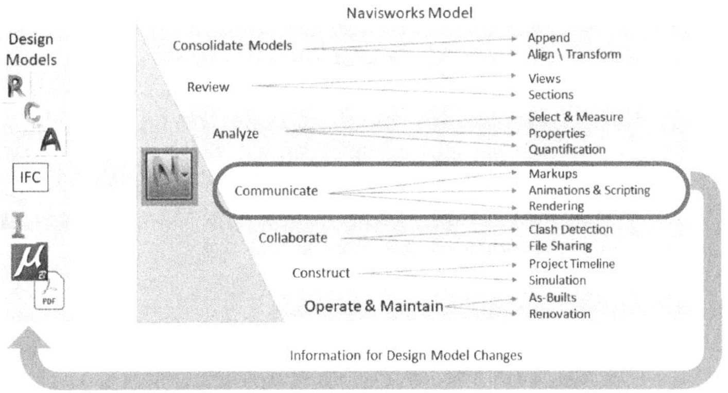

5.1 Using Measuring Tools

Measuring distances (as shown in Figure 5–1), angles, and areas in a model is a critical part of using the Autodesk® Navisworks® software. This information can be included in redline views sent to the architect or engineer as a request for information (known as an RFI), or to the construction superintendent to clarify a situation.

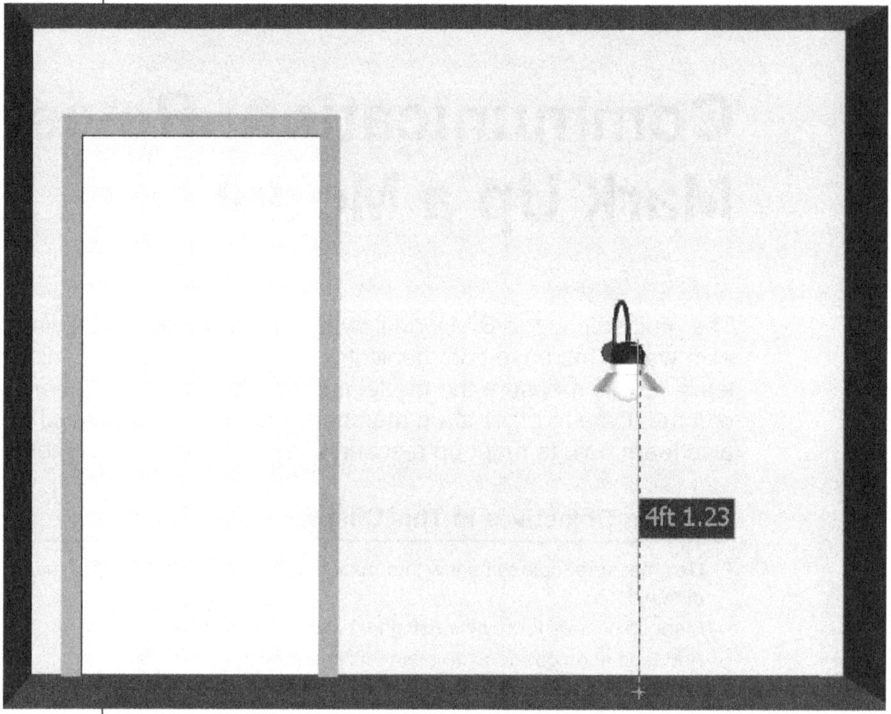

Figure 5–1

- There are a variety of measuring tools and options to help you get the most accurate measurements.
- All measurements are based on coordinate geometry. The actual distance and the X-, Y-, and Z-axis distances can be seen near the item measured, as shown in Figure 5–2. Additionally, you can open the Measure Tools window, shown in Figure 5–3.

Figure 5–2

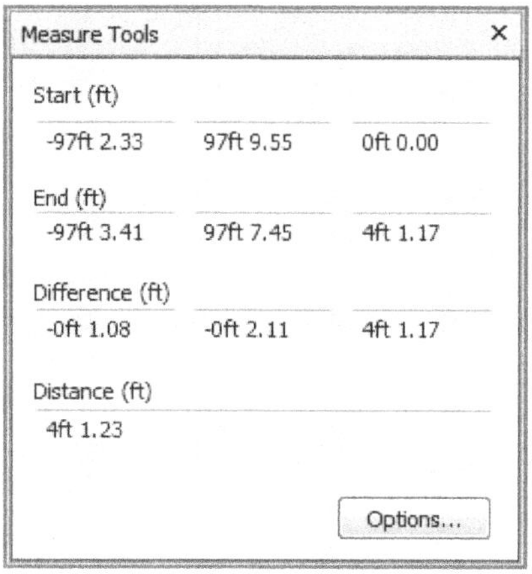

Figure 5–3

- To open the Measure Tools window, in the *Review* tab> Measure panel, in the panel title, click (Measure Options).

How To: Measure Distances

1. In the *Review* tab>Measure panel, expand (Measure) and click one of the measurement options.
2. Select the first point. The cursor displays a box that recognizes 3D surfaces (as shown in Figure 5–4 and Figure 5–5) and 2D lines and points.

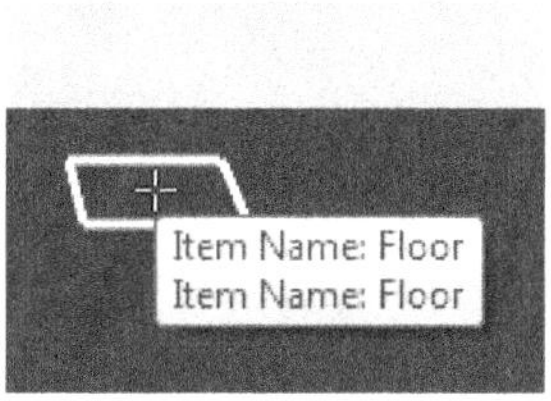

Figure 5–4

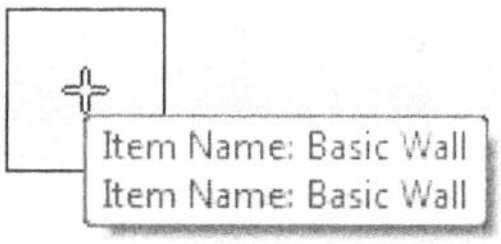

Figure 5–5

Measurement Options

- **(Point to Point):** Select two points to display the distance between them.

Point to Multiple Points is similar to using baseline dimensioning.

- **(Point to Multiple Points):** Select the first point and then a second point. Then select additional points and the measured distance of each point is based on the original first point.

- **(Point Line):** Select the first point and then additional points. The measured distance includes all selections along the path.
- **(Accumulate):** Select two points and then two more points, continuing as required. The measured distance of all of the sets of points are added together.
- Any time you want to clean up a view with measurements, in the *Review* tab>Measure panel, click (Clear).

How To: Measure Angles

1. In the *Review* tab>Measure panel, expand (Measure) and click (Angle).
2. For the first point, select the first plane of the angle.
3. For the second point, select a vertex point.
4. For the third point, select the second plane of the angle. The dimension displays as shown in Figure 5–6

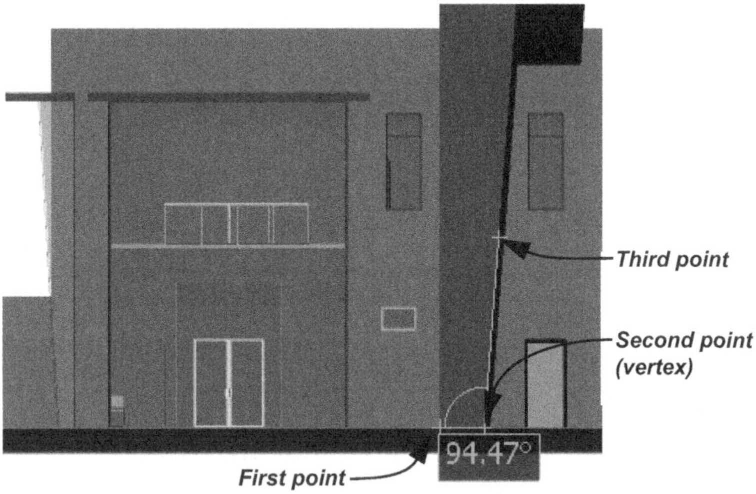

Figure 5–6

How To: Measure Areas

1. In the *Review* tab>Measure panel, expand (Measure) and click (Area)
2. Select at least three points to display the area.
3. Continue selecting points as required, as shown in Figure 5–7.

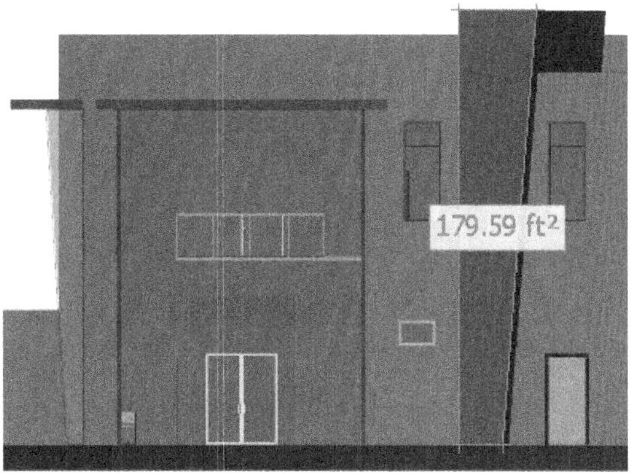

Figure 5–7

How To: Measure the Shortest Distance Between Two Items

1. Select an item, then hold <Ctrl> and select a second item.
2. In the *Review* tab>Measure panel, expand (Measure) and click (Shortest Distance).
3. The distance displays as shown in Figure 5–8.

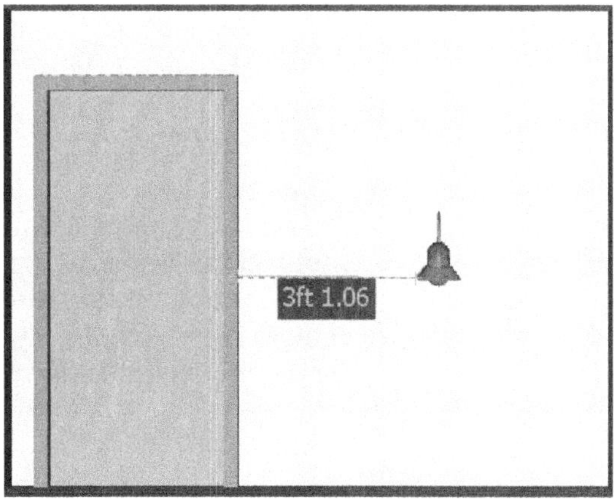

Figure 5–8

Working with the Locking Options

Many times you need to ensure that you are measuring exactly what you are expecting. The Lock options can help you focus the measuring tools to a specific plane. For example, in Figure 5–9, when measuring from the finish floor to the ceiling, toggle on the Z-axis lock so that the other axes are not included in the distance.

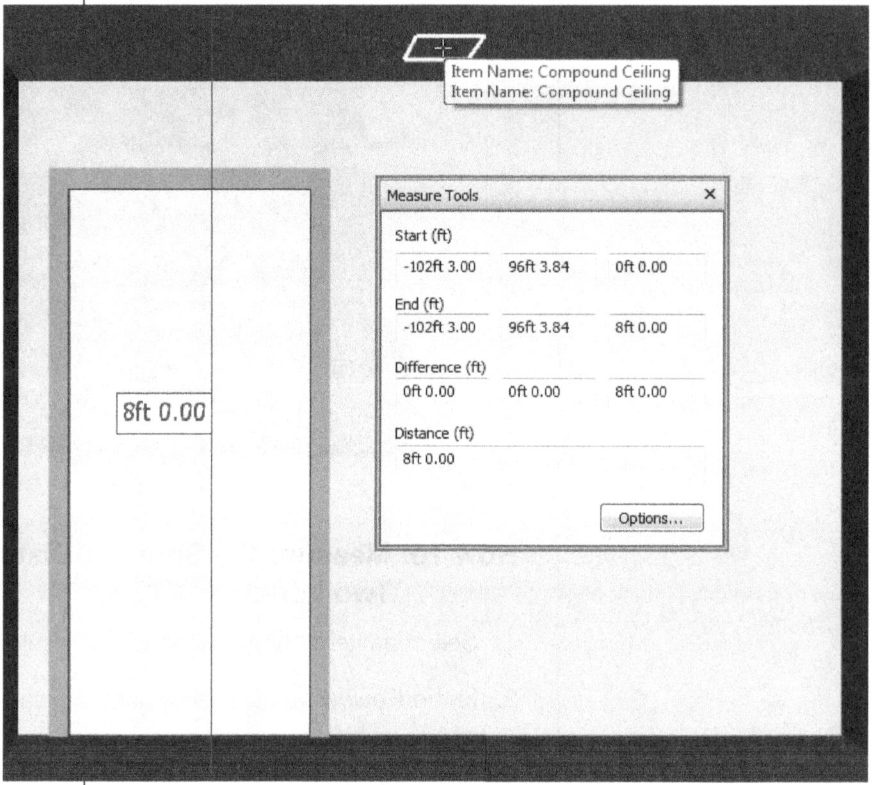

Figure 5–9

- The solid line indicates the locked measurement, while the dashed line is where the cursor is actually positioned.

Locking Options

To make the measurements as accurate as possible, it helps to set lock options in some circumstances. When you use any of the lock options, the measurement matches the specific lock colors. For example, if you use the Z-axis lock, the measurement lines are blue, as shown in Figure 5–9 (above).

In the *Review* tab>Measure panel, expand **Lock** and click an option from the list:

- **(None):** No lock is applied
- **(X Axis)**, **(Y Axis)**, **(Z Axis):** The measurement is locked to the specified axis. The color of each lock line matches the axis color shown in the gizmo, HUD icon, and other locations.
  - **Note:** When using the X-axis direction, the measurement is based on the rotation of the viewpoint and changes if you change the viewpoint.
- **(Perpendicular):** The measurement is locked to the plane of the first selected point, and moves perpendicular to that plane.
- **(Parallel):** The measurement is locked to the plane of the first selected point and moves parallel to it. This is most useful when using the Area tool.

Measurements of 3D models are based on the surface areas of the items. Sometimes, it can help to see these exact planes as you measure, as shown in Figure 5–10. In the *Viewpoint* tab>

Render Style panel, expand **Mode** and click (Hidden Line).

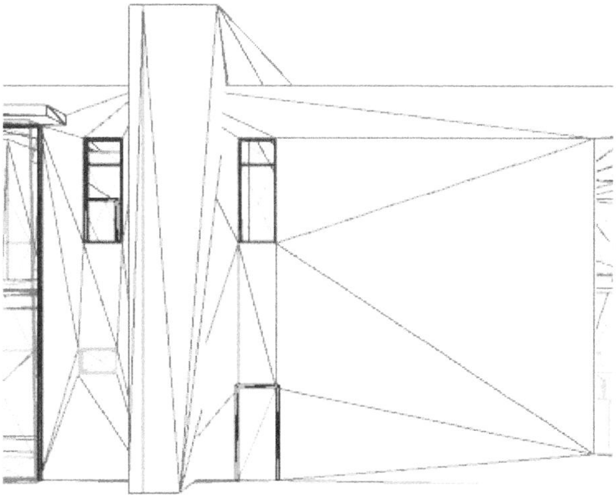

Figure 5–10

Hint: Measuring and Snapping Options

Many of the default options can be modified to fit your company standards or to help you get more precise measurements. These include setting up the color and thickness of the visual dimensions, as well as tools to clarify what you are measuring.

To open the Options Editor, in the Measure Tools window or Application Menu, click **Options**. In the Options Editor, expand **Interface** and select **Measure,** as shown in Figure 5–11.

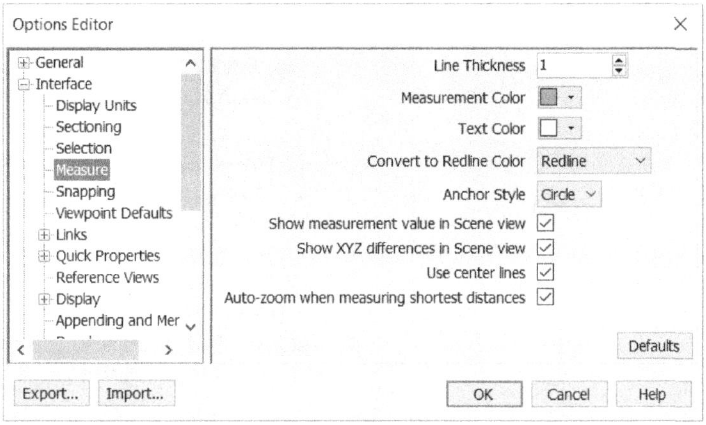

Figure 5–11

Snapping options are also important, especially the **Snap to Vertex** or **Snap to Edge** settings, as shown in Figure 5–12.

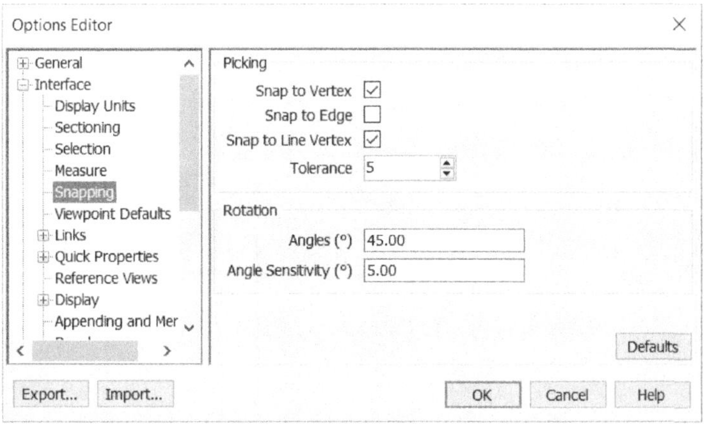

Figure 5–12

Converting Measurements to Redlines

As you are measuring items, you might want to use the measured distance as a redline dimension, as shown in Figure 5–13. To do this, in the Review tab>Measure panel, click (Convert to Redline).

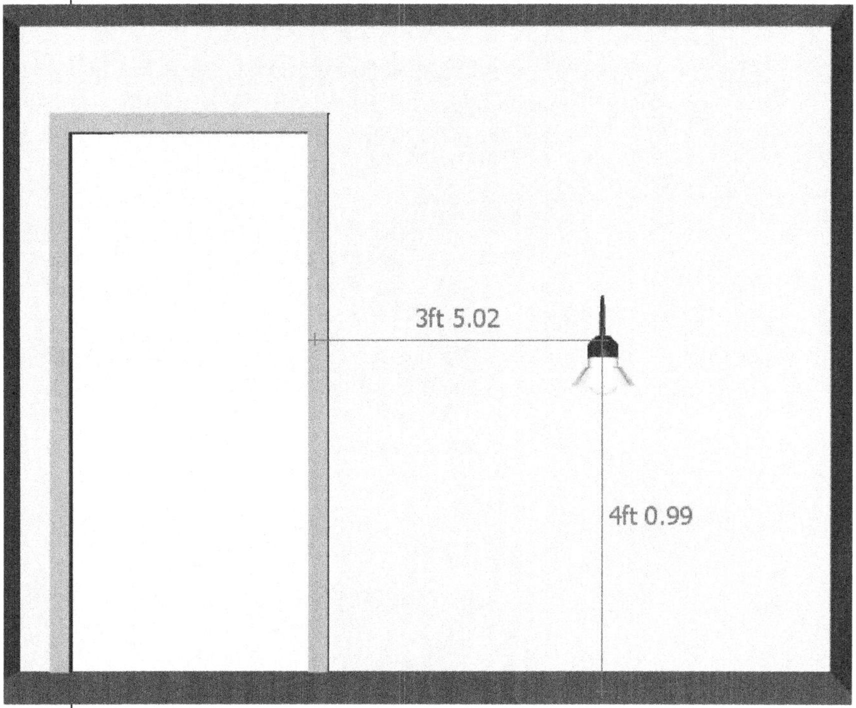

Figure 5–13

- Each measurement must be converted separately.
- When the first redline is added, a viewpoint is also automatically created in the Saved Viewpoints dialog box. Rename the view to help you retrieve it later.
- The view can be used with additional redline tools as well.

Practice 5a Use Measuring Tools

Practice Objectives

- Measure the model.
- Convert measurements into redlines.

In this practice, you will check the building model for accuracy. Then, you will turn those measurements into redlines to communicate any issues to the design team, as shown in Figure 5–14.

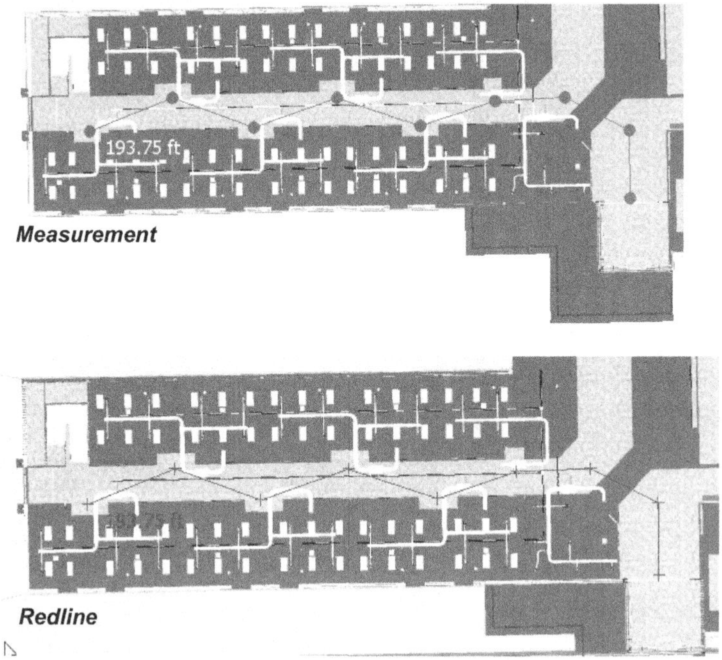

Figure 5–14

Task 1 - Measure distances.

1. In the *Markup* practice files folder, open **School-Measure.nwf**.
2. In the Saved Viewpoints window, click **AC Unit**.

If the units display in units that you are not expecting, in the Options Editor> Interface, check the Display Units option.

3. In the *Review* tab>Measure panel, expand (Measure) and click (Point to Point).

4. In the scene view, select the two points shown in Figure 5–15 to display the height of the AC unit.

Note that four distance values display: Actual (yellow), X (red), Y (green), and Z (blue).

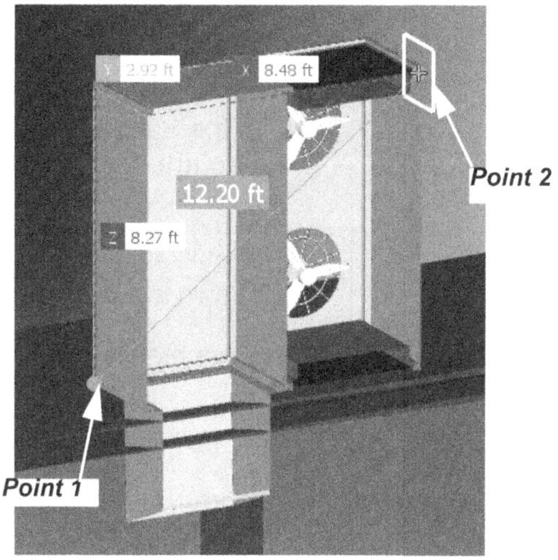

Figure 5–15

5. In the *Review* tab>Measure panel, expand (Lock) and click (X Axis).

6. In the scene view, select the same two points that you used in Step 4. Note that only the X (red) value displays this time, as shown in Figure 5–16.

***Note:** The dimensions will vary depending on the location of the points you pick.*

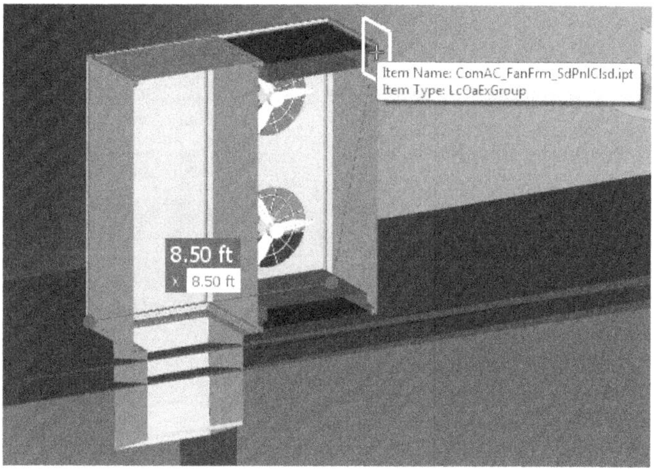

Figure 5–16

7. In the *Review* tab>Measure panel, click (Clear).
8. Return to the *Select* mode either by pressing <Ctrl>+<1> or by clicking (Select) in the Quick Access Toolbar.
9. In the Saved Viewpoints window, click **Section-1stFloorUtilities**.
10. In the scene view, click **Top** on the ViewCube to display a plan-like view, then zoom in to the lower classroom wing, as shown in Figure 5–17.
11. Save the viewpoint as **Egress Check**.
12. In the *Review* tab>Measure panel, expand (Measure) and click (Point to Multiple Points).
13. In the *Review* tab>Measure panel, expand (Lock) and click (Parallel).

Note: *The dimensions will vary depending on the location of the points you pick.*

14. Select a point near the entry doors, and then another point near one of the door setbacks on the hall, as shown in Figure 5–17.

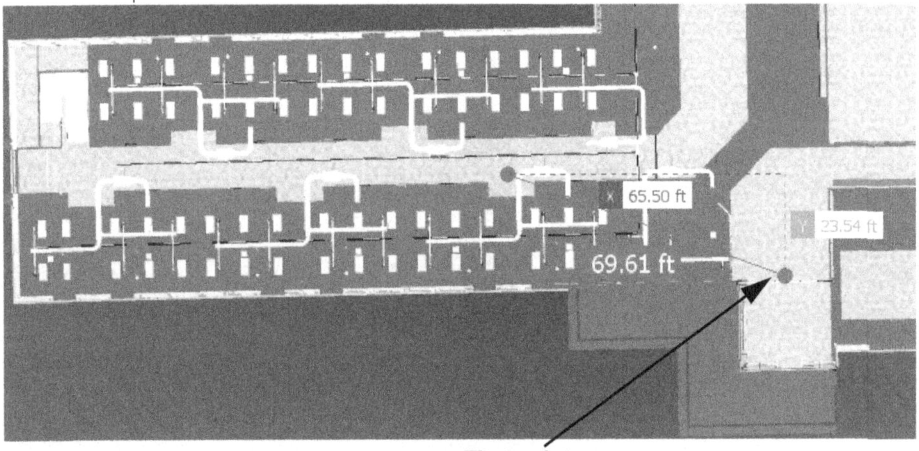

First point

Figure 5–17

15. Select another point on the next door setback, as shown in Figure 5–18. Note that the first point is remembered. Test the distances for the other door setbacks to check them against egress requirements as well.

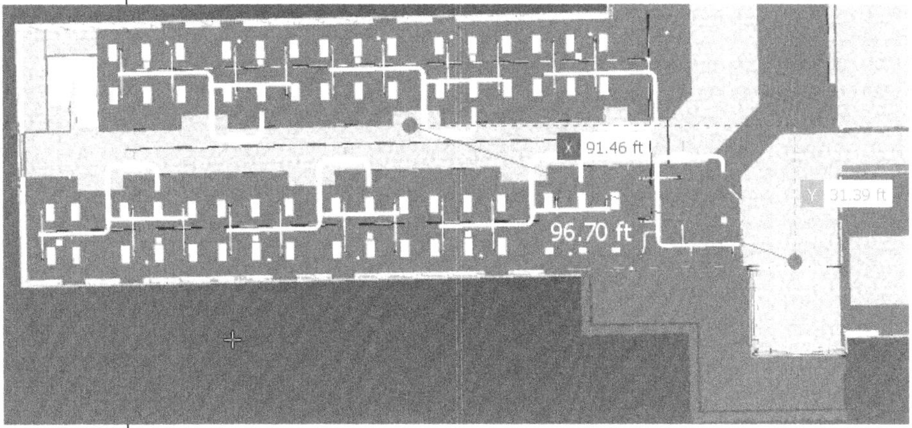

Figure 5–18

16. In the *Review* tab>Measure panel, click (Clear) to clean up the view measurements.

17. In the *Review* tab>Measure panel, expand (Measure) and select (Point Line).

18. Starting at the entry, select the points shown in Figure 5–19.

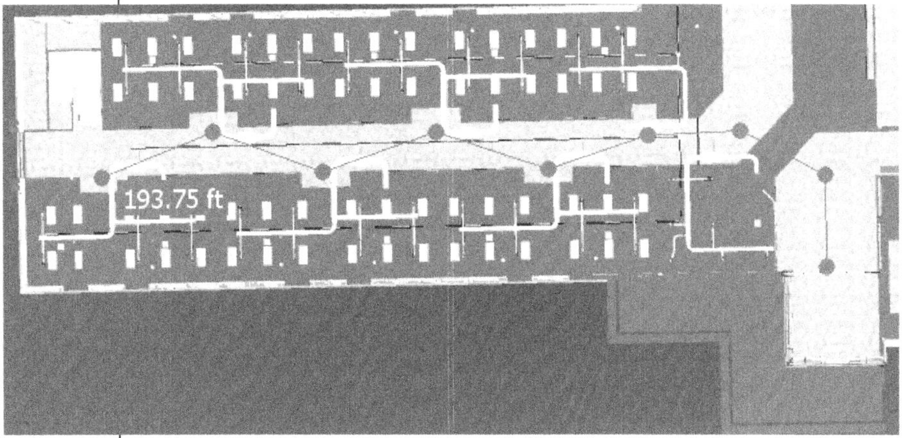

Figure 5–19

19. In the *Review* tab>Measure panel, click (Convert to Redline).

20. The view is saved with the redlines included.

21. Return to the *Select* mode either by pressing <Ctrl>+<1> or by clicking (Select) in the Quick Access Toolbar.

22. Save the file.

Task 2 - Convert measurements to redlines.

1. In the Saved Viewpoints window, click **Section-RetainingWall**.

2. In the *Review* tab>Measure panel, expand (Measure) and click (Point to Point).

3. In the *Review* tab>Measure panel, expand (Lock) and click (Z Axis).

4. In the scene view, select the two points shown in Figure 5–20 to display the height of the retaining wall.

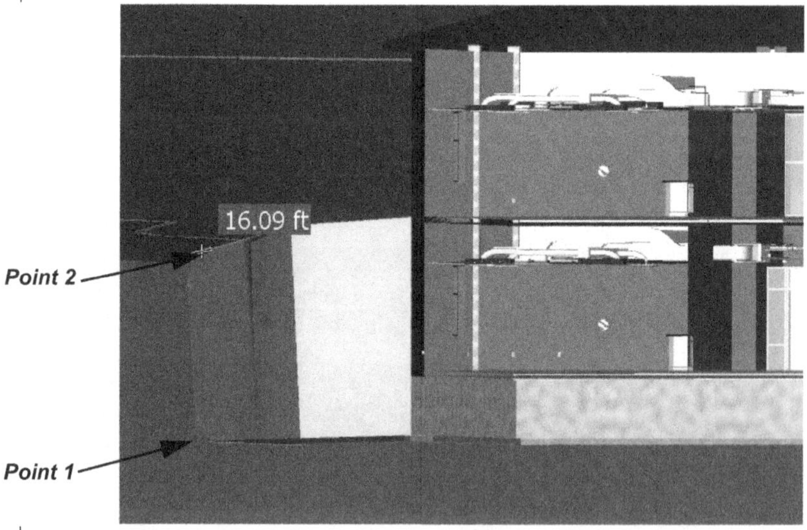

Figure 5–20

5. In the *Review* tab>Measure panel, click (Convert to Redline).

6. Add two more vertical dimensions at other heights along the retaining wall and covert them to redlines as well.

Task 3 - Measure areas and angles.

1. In the Saved Viewpoints window, click **Hallway**.

2. Set the measurement lock to **Parallel**.

3. In the *Review* tab>Measure panel, expand (Measure) and click (Area).

4. Click in the center of the hall to select the floor for the points to be parallel to. Then, select the points shown in Figure 5–21 to display the area.

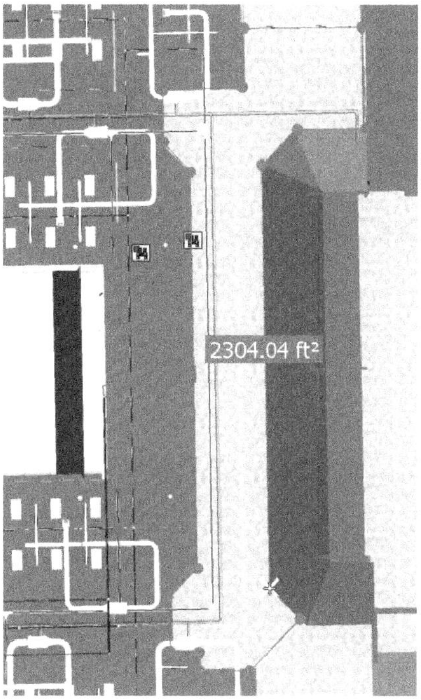

Figure 5–21

5. Convert the measurement to a redline.

6. If you have changed the zoom of the view, you are prompted to create a new saved viewpoint. Name it **Area of Hallway**.

7. In the *Review* tab>Measure panel, expand (Measure) and click (Angle).
8. In the scene view, select the points indicated in Figure 5–22.

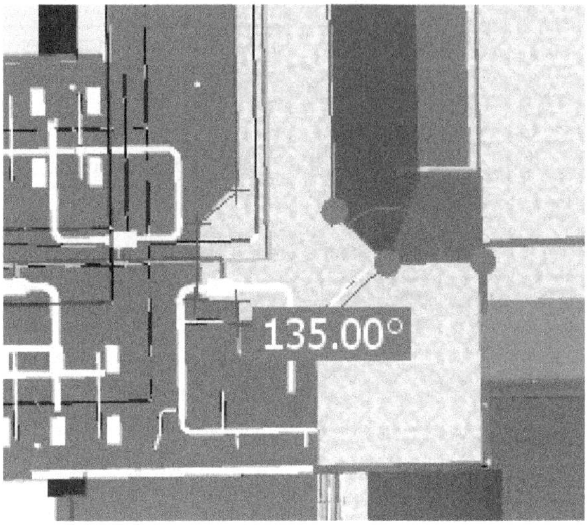

Figure 5–22

9. Click (Clear).
10. Save the file.

Task 4 - Measure shortest distances between two selections.

1. In the Saved Viewpoints window, click **Level2-Utilities**.
2. In the Quick Access Toolbar, click (Select).
3. In the *Home* tab>Select & Search panel, expand the panel title and set the *Selection Resolution* to **Last Unique**.

4. In the scene view, select the hall floor in the north wing. Then, hold <Ctrl> and select the hall floor in the south wing, as shown in Figure 5–23.

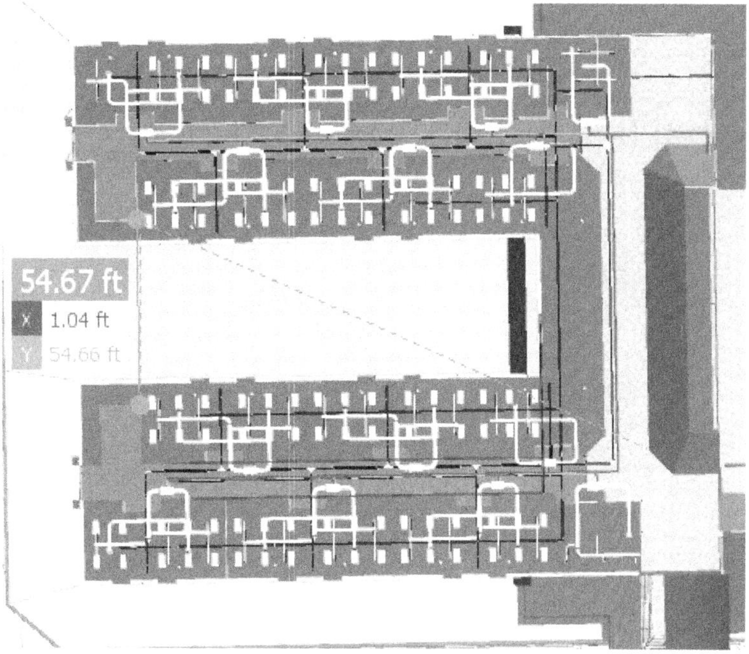

Figure 5–23

5. In the *Review* tab>Measure panel, click (Shortest Distance).

6. Select two other floors and test another shortest distance.

7. In the *Review* tab>Measure panel, click (Clear) to clean up the view measurements.

8. Save the file.

5.2 Marking Up Scenes for Review

Annotating Redline Views

Sometimes it is important to add comments or other geometry in addition to dimensions to fully communicate any questions you have regarding the design. In that case, you can mark up scenes for review using text, tags, and drawing tools, as shown in Figure 5–24.

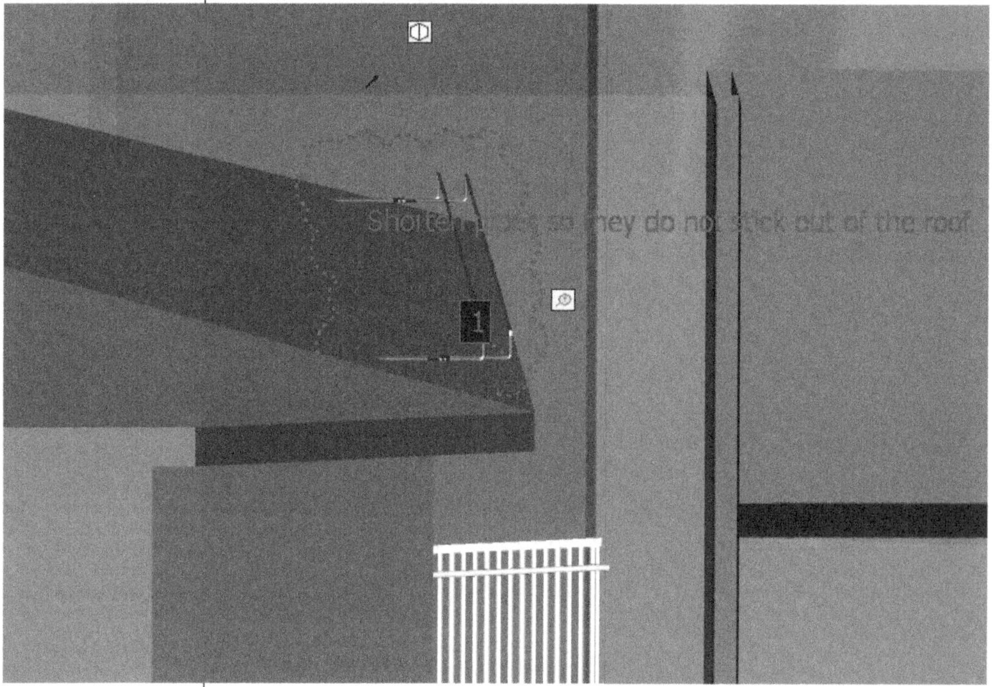

Figure 5–24

- Redlines are saved in a viewpoint.
- When you navigate away from the viewpoint the redlines disappear.
- A viewpoint is automatically added to the Saved Viewpoints window upon adding text or other redline geometry to the current view.
- If the viewpoint is deleted, the redline is lost with it.

How To: Add Text to a Viewpoint

1. Open the saved viewpoint where you want to add the text.
2. In the *Review* tab>Redline panel, click (Text).
3. In the dialog box, type the text you want to add (as shown in Figure 5–25) and click **OK**.

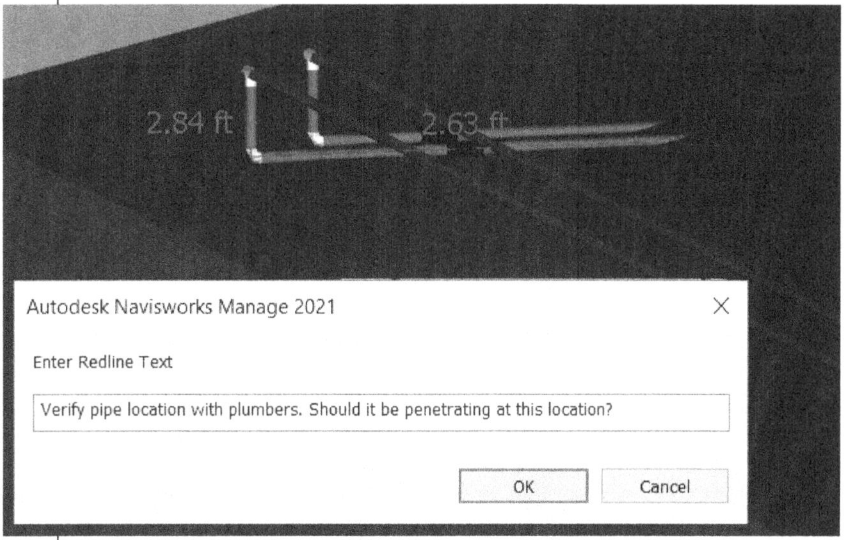

Figure 5–25

- Redline dimensions, text, and drawings cannot be moved, but they can be erased. To erase redlines, click (Erase) and draw a window around the entire redline item, as shown in Figure 5–26. If you select only part of the redline (as shown in Figure 5–27), the redline is not included in the deletion.

Figure 5–26

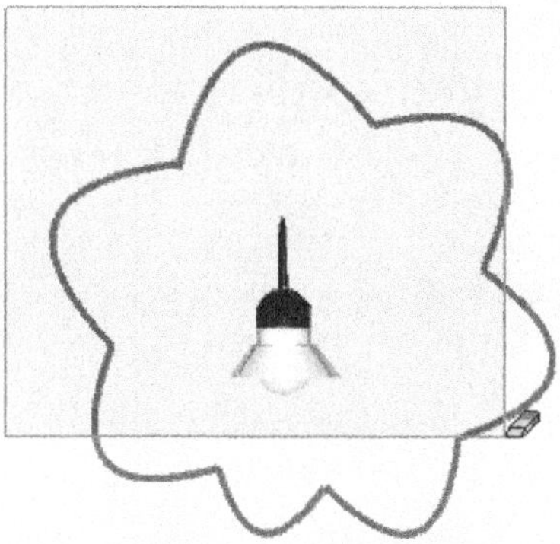

Figure 5–27

How To: Use the Draw Tools

The most recently-used tool remains on the top of the drop-down list.

1. Open the saved viewpoint where you want to add redlines.
2. In the *Review* tab>Redline panel, expand **Draw** and select the required tool:

    - **(Cloud):** Click two points to create each arc of the cloud. The distance between the clicks determines the size of the arc.
    - **(Ellipse):** Click and drag to create a bounding box. When you release the mouse button, the ellipse is created inside the bounding box you selected.
    - **(Freehand):** Click and drag the cursor around to create lines. Release the mouse button to stop drawing.
    - **(Line):** Click two points to place lines between them. The lines are individual, not connected.
    - **(Line String):** Click to place the first point and then as many other points as required. The lines are connected.
    - **(Arrow):** Click to place the end point for the arrow line, and then click again to place where you want the arrow pointing.

Hint: Set the Redline Tools' Color and Thickness

You can customize the Redline tools by changing the color and thickness in the *Review* tab>Redline panel, as shown in Figure 5–28.

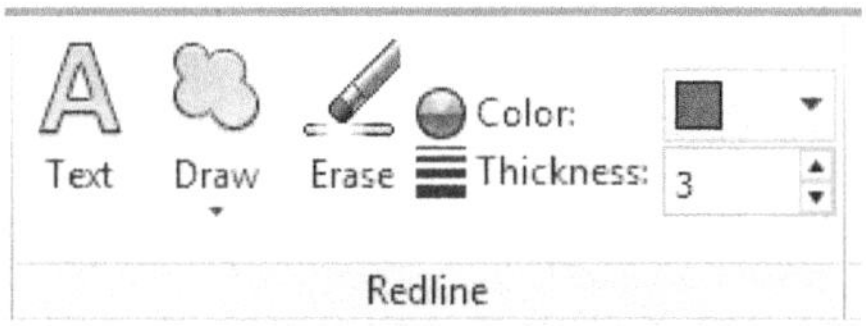

Figure 5–28

Adding Tags and Comments

The difference between adding text and a tag is that a tag places a marker in the scene view, rather than text. Once the tags are placed, you can review the comments added to tags in the order that they were added. In addition, tags enable you to see who added or edited a comment and the date that it was added.

How To: Add Tags

1. Open the saved viewpoint where you want to add a tag.
2. In the *Review* tab>Tags panel, click (Add Tag).
3. Click a point for the beginning of the line.
4. Click a point to place the tag.
5. In the Add Comments dialog box, type in the comment and click **OK**.

How To: Review Tags

1. In the *Review* tab>Comments panel, click (View Comments) to toggle the Comments window off and on. It can be resized or docked.
2. If there are a lot of comments, in the *Review* tab>Comments panel, type a search string in the Quick Find Comments area, as shown in Figure 5–29.

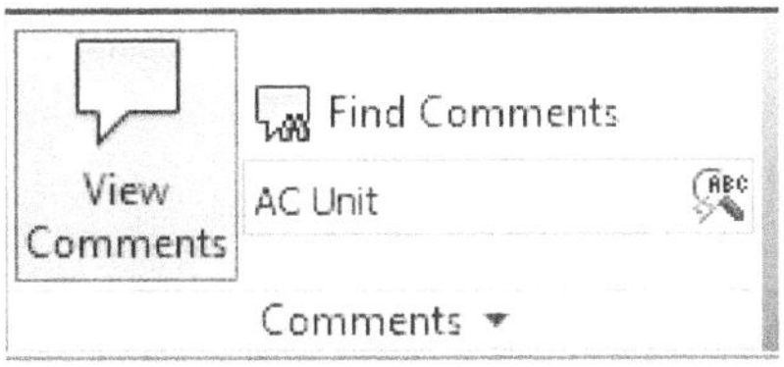

Figure 5–29

3. To step through the tags, in the *Review* tab>Tags panel, select the arrow buttons, or use one of the following keyboard shortcuts:

- **(First Tag):** <Ctrl>+<Shift>+<Up Arrow>
- **(Previous Tag):** <Ctrl>+<Shift>+<Left Arrow>
- **(Next Tag):** <Ctrl>+<Shift>+<Right Arrow>
- **(Last Tag):** <Ctrl>+<Shift>+<Down Arrow>

Hint: Merging Project Files

Since there might be multiple people reviewing and marking up the model, it might be necessary to merge redlines. When project files are merged, redlines from other users are copied into one file without creating duplicates.

You can use either of the following methods to merge redlines:

- In the *Home* Tab>Project panel, expand (Append) and click (Merge).
- In the Quick Access Toolbar, expand (Open) and click **Merge**.

Practice 5b Mark Up Scenes for Review

Practice Objectives

- Add text to communicate a question regarding the design.
- Create redline geometry to draw attention to specific parts of the design.
- Merge project files.

In this practice, you will redline the model to communicate questions and issues to the appropriate teams, as shown in Figure 5–30. You will then merge in another Autodesk Navisworks file and review additional markups.

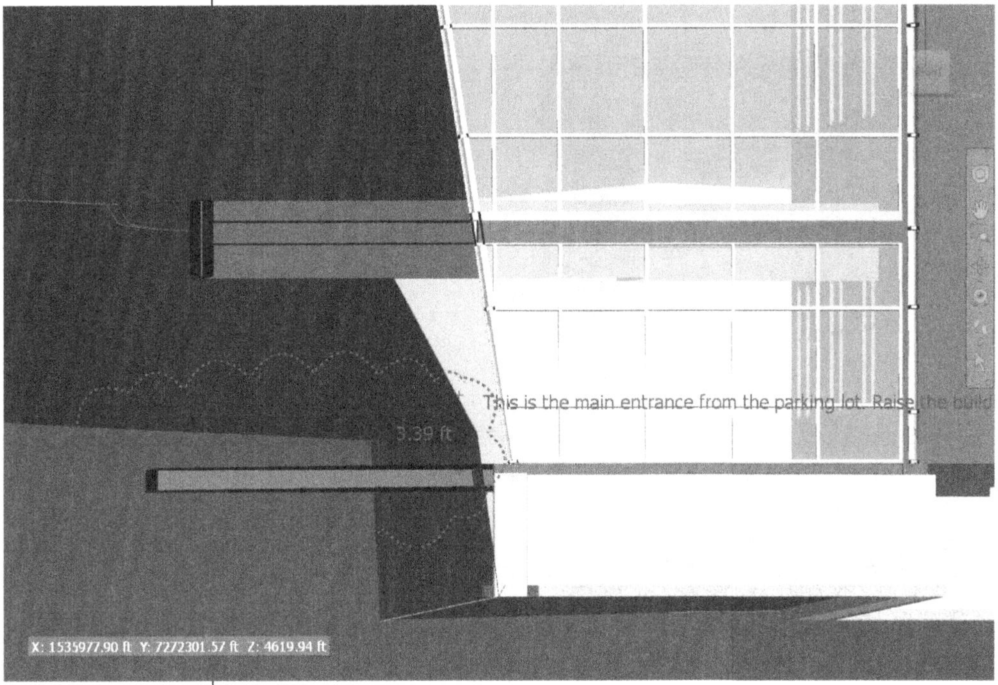

Figure 5–30

Task 1 - Add redline dimensions and text to the entrance section.

1. In the *Markup* practice files folder, open **School-Markup.nwf**.
2. In the Saved Viewpoints window, click **Section-EntrancePlatform**.

3. Add a point to point measurement from the base of the entrance floor to the cut of the topography and turn it into a redline, as shown in Figure 5–31.

4. The Saved Viewpoints window displays. Click on the new view and name it **Entrance Elevation Change Comments**.

5. In the *Review* tab>Redline panel, click (Text).

6. Click on the edge of the redline dimension.

7. In the dialog box, type in the comment **This is the main entrance from the parking lot. Raise the building elevation to accommodate surface elevations.** (as shown in Figure 5–31) and click **OK**.

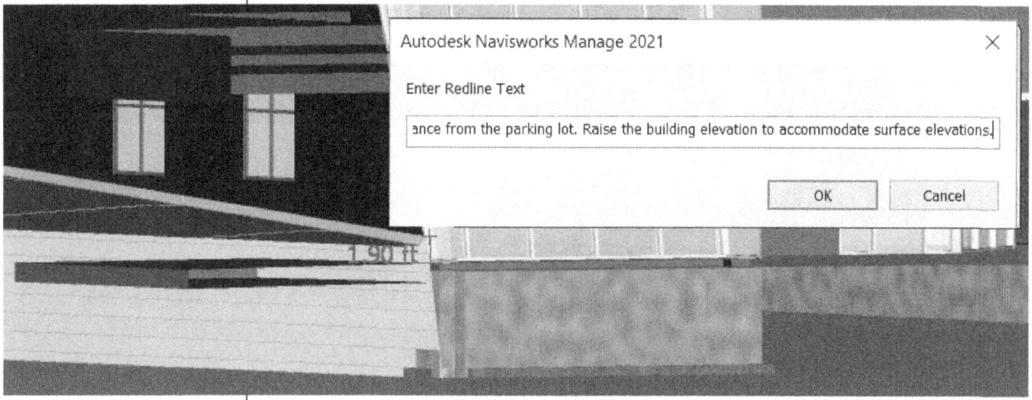

Figure 5–31

8. Without changing the viewpoint, in the *Review* tab>Redline panel, expand **Draw** and click (Cloud).

The distance between the clicks determines the size of the arc.

9. In the scene view, click points in a clockwise direction to create each arc of the cloud, as shown in Figure 5–32. The redline information is automatically saved with the viewpoint.

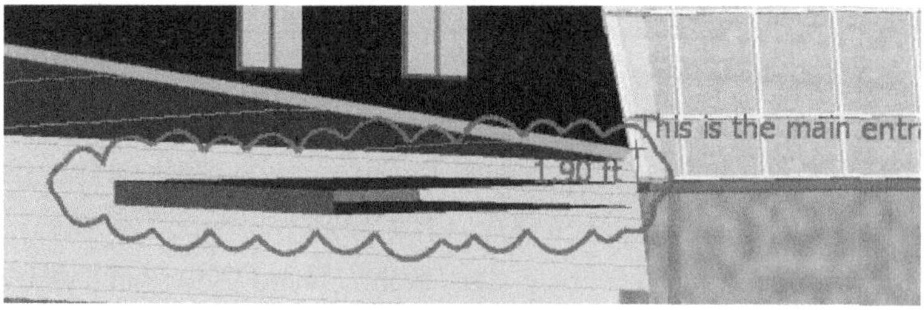

Figure 5–32

10. Save the file.

Task 2 - Use redline graphics and tags.

1. In the Saved Viewpoints window, click **NE-View**.
2. Save the viewpoint as **NE-View-Comments**.
3. In the *Review* tab>Redline panel, expand **Draw** and click  (Ellipse).
4. In the scene view, click and drag to draw the bounding box around the AC unit, as shown in Figure 5–33. When you release the mouse button, the ellipse is created inside the bounding box you selected, as shown in Figure 5–34.

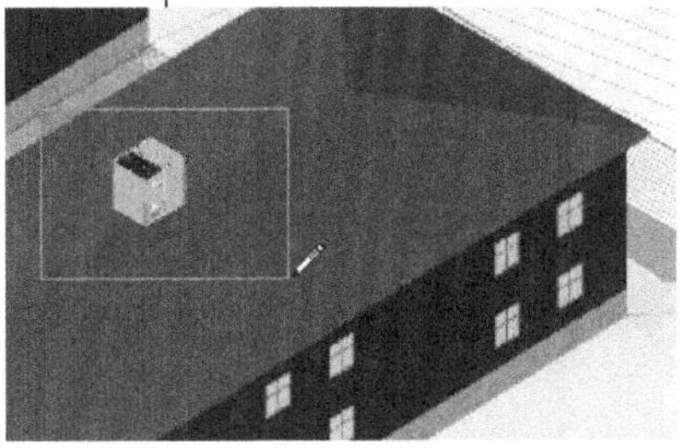

Figure 5–33

Figure 5–34

5. In the *Review* tab>Tags panel, click  (Add Tag).
6. Click a point on the AC unit for the beginning of the line.
7. Click a point on the ellipse to place the tag.
8. In the Add Comments dialog box, type in the comment **This is the worst place to put an AC Unit. Please move to flat roof.** (as shown in Figure 5–35) and click **OK**.

Figure 5–35

9. In the *Review* tab>Redline panel, expand **Draw** and click (Arrow).

10. In the scene view, click the AC unit for the start point, then click the center of the flat roof to place the arrow, as shown in Figure 5–36.

Figure 5–36

11. In the *Review* tab>Tags panel, click (Add Tag).

12. Click a point for the beginning of the line where you placed the arrow.

13. Click a point to place the tag, as shown in Figure 5–37.

14. In the Add Comments dialog box, type **New location of AC Unit** in the comment (as shown in Figure 5–37) and click **OK**.

Figure 5–37

15. Add an additional tag to the AC unit with the following comment: **AC Unit is much too small for building. Replace with larger unit.**

16. Open the Comments window.
    - The Comments window should display at the bottom of the screen. If it does not display, in the *Comments* tab>Tags panel, click (View Comments).

17. In the Comments window title bar, toggle off (Auto Hide) to force the window to always display.

18. Step through the tags in the *Review* tab>Tags panel by selecting the arrow buttons:
    - (First Tag)
    - (Previous Tag)
    - (Next Tag)
    - (Last Tag)

19. Save the file.

Task 3 - Merge files and review comments.

1. In the *Home* tab>Project panel, expand (Append) and click (Merge).
2. In the Merge dialog box, select **School-Markup-Mechanical.nwf** and then click Open.
3. In the Saved Viewpoints window, select **NE View-Mechanical Redline**.

4. Open the Comments window and review the comments in this viewpoint, as shown in Figure 5–38.

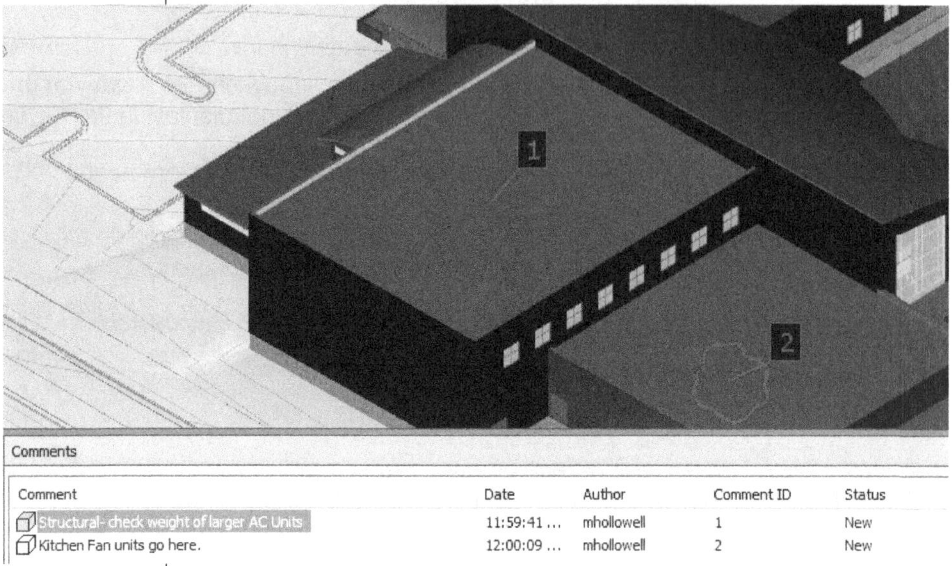

Figure 5–38

5. Save the file.

Chapter Review Questions

1. How do you make measurements as accurate as possible?
    a. Zoom in really close as you pick a point.
    b. Use one of the Lock options found in the *Review* tab>Measure panel.
    c. It is not possible to make measurements accurate in the Autodesk Navisworks software. You can only get them close to find an approximate dimension.
    d. Draw lines from the points you want to measure, and then dimension the lines.
2. How do you ensure that a measurement remains visible?
    a. In the *Review* tab>Measure panel, click  (Convert to Redline).
    b. Take a screen shot and add the image to the file.
    c. Put the dimension in a tag.
    d. Manually draw the dimension with the Draw and Text tools.
3. You can convert more than one measurement to a redline at a time.
    a. True
    b. False
4. What happens when you place a dimension, text, or some other redline geometry in the scene view, and then zoom in/out?
    a. The redlines seem to change size with the view.
    b. Nothing. The redline remains the same size (percentage of the screen) no matter how much you zoom in/out.
    c. The redline disappears if the view was not saved.
5. How do you move a redline?
    a. Select the redline and use the gizmo to move it.
    b. Select the redline and click **Move** on the *Redline* contextual tab.
    c. In the *Review* tab>Measure panel, click **Clear**.
    d. Redlines cannot be moved. They must be erased and redrawn in the new location.

Command Summary

Button	Command	Location
Measuring Tools		
	**Accumulate**	• **Ribbon:** *Review* tab>Measure panel> expand Measure
	**Angle**	• **Ribbon:** *Review* tab>Measure panel> expand Measure
	**Area**	• **Ribbon:** *Review* tab>Measure panel> expand Measure
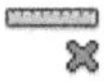	**Clear**	• **Ribbon:** *Review* tab>Measure panel
	**Convert to Redline**	• **Ribbon:** *Review* tab>Measure panel
	**None**	• **Ribbon:** *Review* tab>Measure panel> expand Lock
	**Parallel**	• **Ribbon:** *Review* tab>Measure panel> expand Lock
	**Perpendicular**	• **Ribbon:** *Review* tab>Measure panel> expand Lock
	**Point Line**	• **Ribbon:** *Review* tab>Measure panel> expand Measure
	**Point to Multiple Points**	• **Ribbon:** *Review* tab>Measure panel> expand Measure
	**Point to Point**	• **Ribbon:** *Review* tab>Measure panel> expand Measure
	**Shortest Distance**	• **Ribbon:** *Review* tab>Measure panel
	**X Axis**	• **Ribbon:** *Review* tab>Measure panel> expand Lock
	**Y Axis**	• **Ribbon:** *Review* tab>Measure panel> expand Lock
	**Z Axis**	• **Ribbon:** *Review* tab>Measure panel> expand Lock

Redline Tools		
	**Add Tag**	• **Ribbon:** *Review* tab>Redline panel
	**Arrow**	• **Ribbon:** *Review* tab>Redline panel, expand Draw
	**Cloud**	• **Ribbon:** *Review* tab>Redline panel, expand Draw
	**Color**	• **Ribbon:** *Review* tab>Redline panel
	**Ellipse**	• **Ribbon:** *Review* tab>Redline panel, expand Draw
	**Erase**	• **Ribbon:** *Review* tab>Redline panel
	**Find Comments**	• **Ribbon:** *Review* tab>Comments panel
	**Freehand**	• **Ribbon:** *Review* tab>Redline panel, expand Draw
	**Line**	• **Ribbon:** *Review* tab>Redline panel, expand Draw
	**Line String**	• **Ribbon:** *Review* tab>Redline panel, expand Draw
	**Text**	• **Ribbon:** *Review* tab>Redline panel
	**Thickness**	• **Ribbon:** *Review* tab>Redline panel
	**View Comments**	• **Ribbon:** *Review* tab>Comments panel

Chapter 6

Collaboration: Clash Detection

The collaboration stage of the BIM workflow is meant to ensure that all of the disciplines are on the same page. For example, it is important that HVAC ductwork does not interfere with the electrical or structural parts of the building, while at the same time, civil engineers need to be sure that they are bringing utilities into a building at the right location for interior connections to be made. In this chapter, you will learn how to run clash tests to ensure that everything is properly aligned. **Note:** Clash Detection is not available in Navisworks Simulate or Navisworks Freedom. It is only available in Navisworks Manage.

Learning Objectives in This Chapter

- Run a clash test and review clash test results.
- Fix clashes in the model.
- Communicate clash results using reports.

BIM Workflow: Collaborate

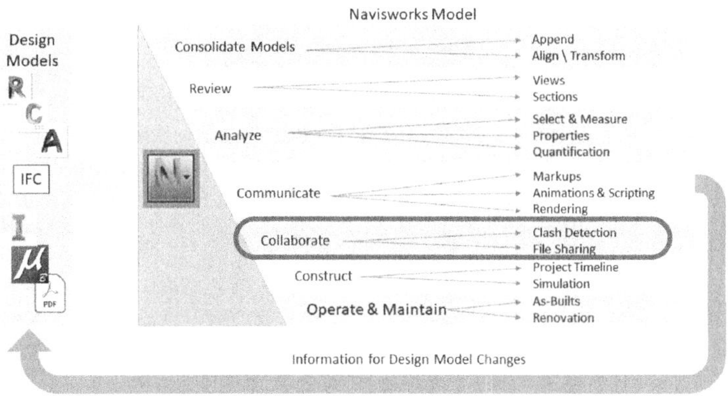

6.1 Overview of the Clash Detective

The Clash Detective eliminates the tedious manual process of inspecting and identifying interference clashes in a 3D project model. This process helps to keep construction costs down by reducing the number of change orders that are caused by objects occupying the same space. You can run clash tests using traditional 3D geometry, or using point clouds generated from laser scans. In addition, you can check stationary objects (buildings) against moving objects (cranes) to ensure that construction equipment does not collide with anything on the project site. When you are doing a clash test, consider the following:

- Always run a clash test on the most up-to-date 3D models.
- Rerun existing clash tests before creating a new test.
- Rules can be created to ignore certain clashes.
- You can minimize the number of clashes that must reviewed at a time by working with groups.
- Clash test parameters can be saved and used on other projects.

The Clash Detective Window is shown in Figure 6–1. The top pane is where you can manage all of the clash tests and displays a list of previously-created clash tests. The bottom pane includes four tabs, which are as follows:

- **Rules:** Configure the rules or list of items to be ignored when a clash test is run. You can create new rules, edit existing rules, or delete rules, as required.
- **Select:** Defines what items the test includes. The items selected in the Selection A pane are compared against the items selected in the Selection B pane, as shown in Figure 6–1. You can also set the clash type and tolerance here.

- **Results:** Shows a list of the clashes that were found. You can manage how clashes are handled in this tab.
- **Report:** Manage reports and what they include here.

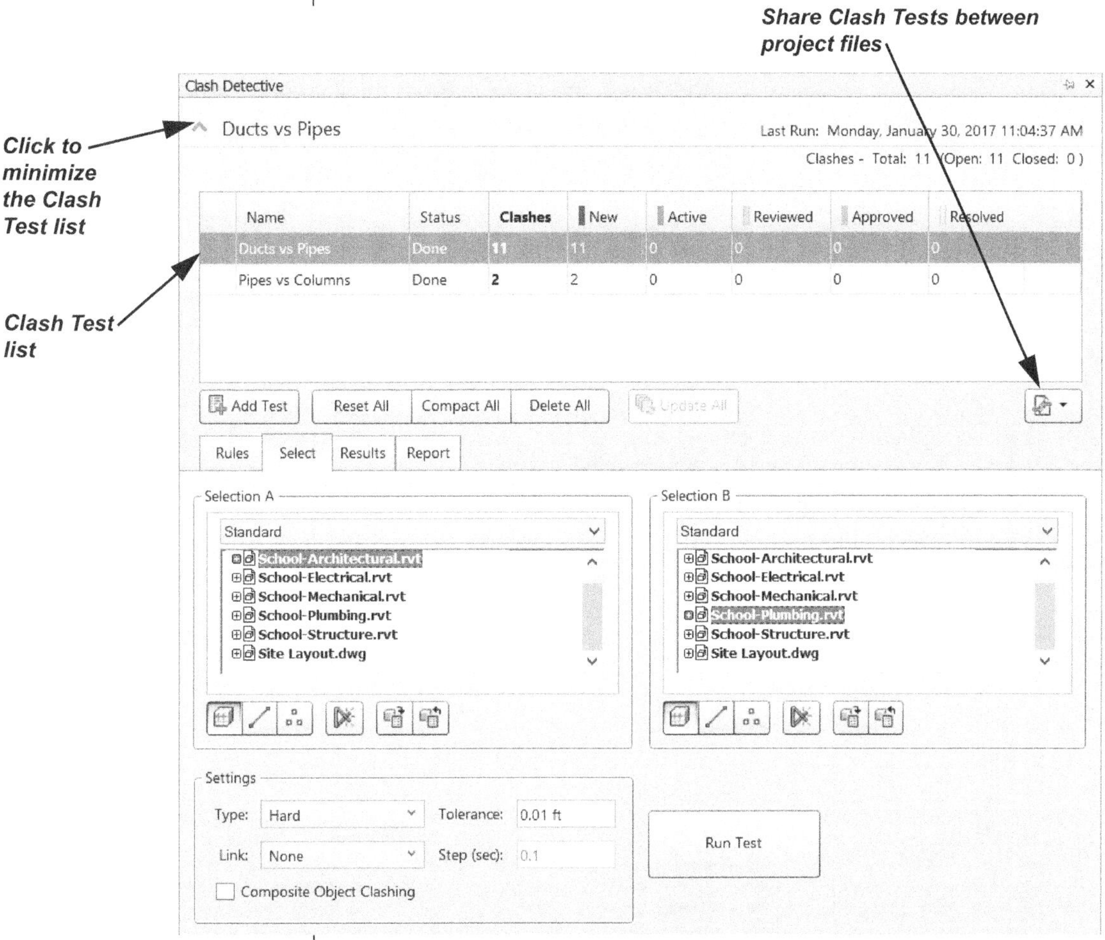

Figure 6–1

How To: Set Up and Run a Clash Test

1. In the *Home* tab>Tools panel, click (Clash Detective) or press <Ctrl>+<F2>.
2. In the Clash Detective window, click (Add Test). A new test is loaded in the top pane with tabs where you can set up the test in the lower panes, as shown in Figure 6–2.

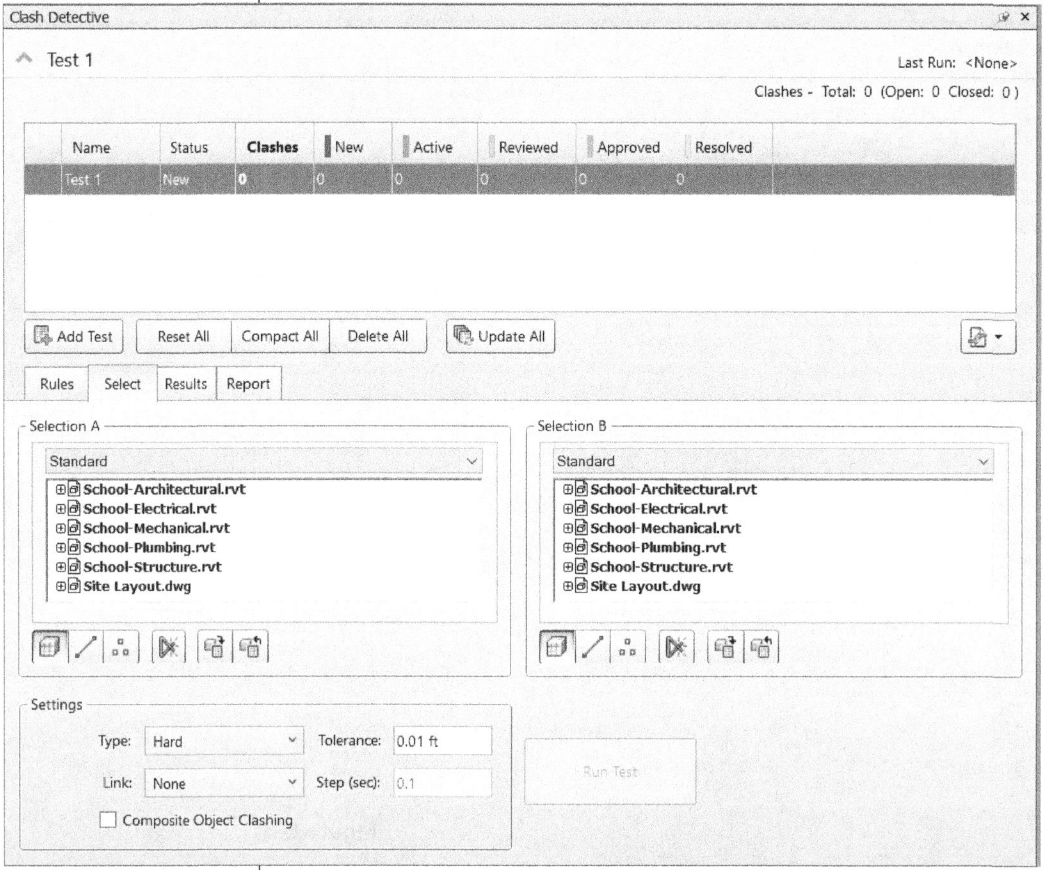

Figure 6–2

3. Type in a name for the new test. You can come back and rename the clash test later, if required.
4. Select the *Rules* tab and select any of the ignore clashes options, as shown in Figure 6–3.

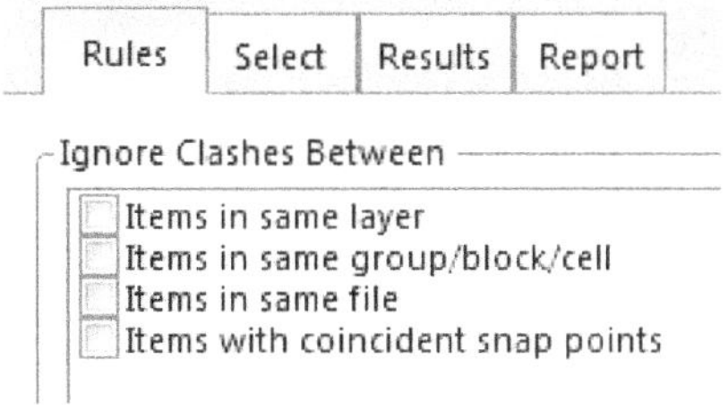

Figure 6–3

5. Select the *Select* tab to set up the clash criteria.
6. Click **Run Test**.
7. The *Results* tab opens displaying a list of clashes and the scene view zooms in on the first clash, as shown in Figure 6–4. Review the results.

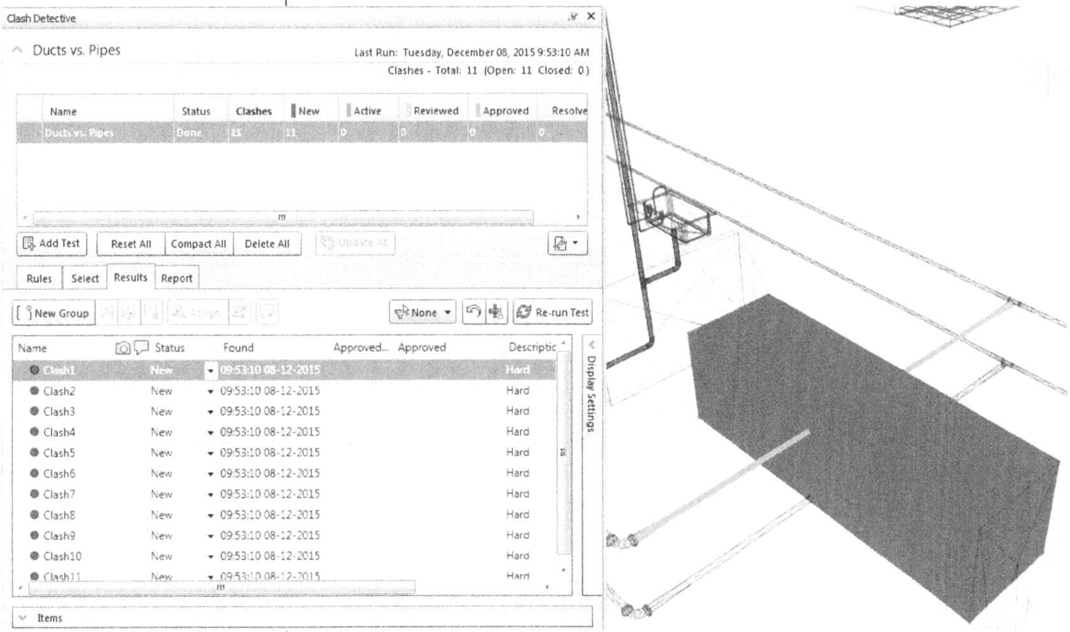

Figure 6–4

8. In the *Report* tab, create a report that can be viewed by others, as required.
9. After reloading files that have been modified, in the Clash Detective window, click **Update All** to re-run the clash test to ensure that everything has been corrected.

Importing and Exporting Clash Tests

Clash tests can be shared between project files. If you set up a clash test to check all of the objects on a specific layer against all of the objects on another layer, you can reuse that test on every project that uses the same standard layer names and definitions.

- Clash tests are saved as .XML files.

How To: Export Clash Tests

1. In the Clash Detective window, in the Test pane, expand  (Import/Export Clash Tests) and select **Export Clash Tests**.
2. In the Export dialog box, navigate to the location where you want to save the file.
3. Name the file and click **Save**.

- By default, the clash test is named the same as the Autodesk Navisworks file that you are working in. Rename it to fit a standard so that it can be used in other projects.

How To: Import Clash Tests

1. In the Clash Detective window, in the Test pane, expand  (Import/Export Clash Tests) and select **Import Clash Tests**.
2. In the Import dialog box, navigate to the location of the saved file.
3. Select the file you want to import and click **Open**.

> **Hint: Customizing Clash Tests**
>
> You can edit the .XML file to suit other projects. When you do this, using standard naming conventions for the clash test you are importing are the key to making them work.

6.2 Setting Up Clash Tests

Rules Tab

Use the *Rules* tab to filter out things that you do not want checked, as shown in Figure 6–5. This helps to eliminate false positives and makes the results more meaningful. For example, you might not want to check things that were originally created in the same file, as they are tested separately. For this example, in the *Ignore Clashes Between* pane, you would select the **Items in the same file** option.

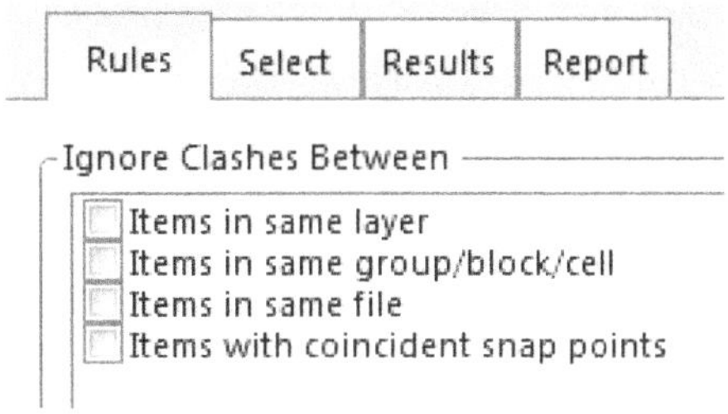

Figure 6–5

- Click **New** to add other options from the Rule Editor.
- Click **Edit** to modify an existing rule.
- Click **Delete** to remove the rule from the list.

Select Tab

The Selection A and Selection B panes enable you to select which items are compared against each other. The format drop-down list in each pane enables you to select the format in which the items are listed, as shown in Figure 6–6.

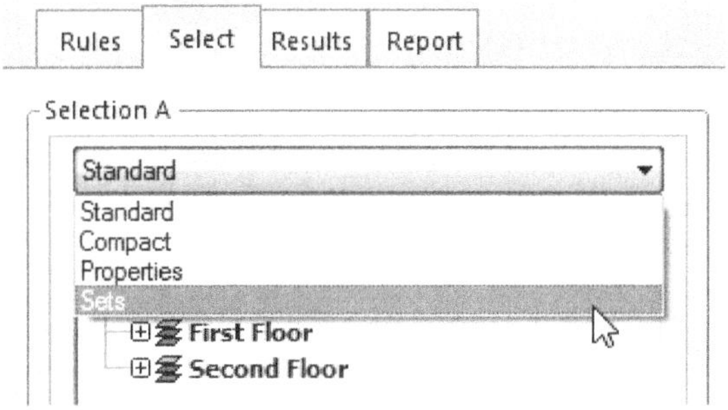

Figure 6–6

The formats are as follows:

- **Standard:** Provides the same list groups according to the appended files found in the Selection Tree.
- **Compact:** A simplified version of the Standard list.
- **Properties:** Lists objects according to their properties, such as the same name, material, area name, etc.

Using the Sets option makes clash tests easier to share and reuse.

- **Sets:** These are the sets that are listed in the Sets window, and can be either saved sets or search sets. Using a search set ensures that all of the objects in newly appended files are selected for the clash test.

Next you can select the types of geometry to compare. Select from the following geometry types, which are located below the selection panes, as shown in Figure 6–7:

*Surfaces refer to 3D planar objects, **NOT** to topo surfaces from Civil applications (such as Civil 3D).*

- **(Surfaces):** These are the 3D triangles most 3D objects are made out of. This is the default setting.
- **(Lines):** These represent linear objects that have centerlines, such as pipes.
- **(Points):** These are point clouds that are created using laser scan data.
- **(Self-Intersect):** Clash tests a selection against itself.

Hold <Ctrl> to select multiple items.

- **(Use Current Selection):** Selects anything in the selection list that is already selected in the scene view.
- **(Select in Scene):** Enables you to select items in the scene view to populate the selection list.

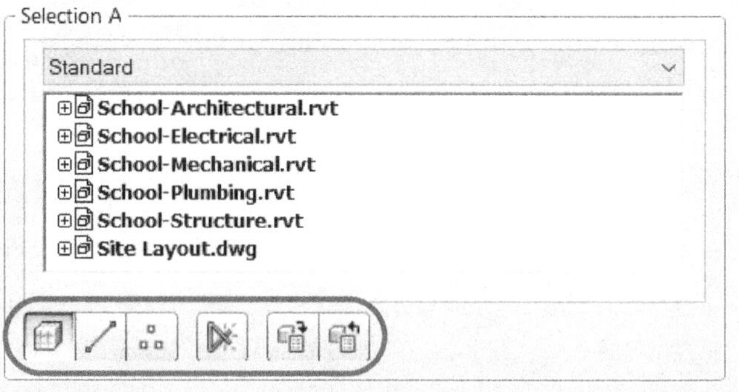

Figure 6–7

Clash Settings

Clash Settings are used to set the type of clash to run and the tolerance factor for the clash, as shown in Figure 6–8. There are four clash types, as follows:

- **Hard:** Two objects reside in the same space or intersect each other.
- **Hard (Conservative):** A more thorough method than Hard that returns two objects that might clash. You might receive false positives using this method, but it is a more thorough test.
- **Clearance:** Two objects are within the tolerance distance of each other. When using this method, hard clashes are also detected.
- **Duplicates:** Two objects are the same type and reside in the same position.

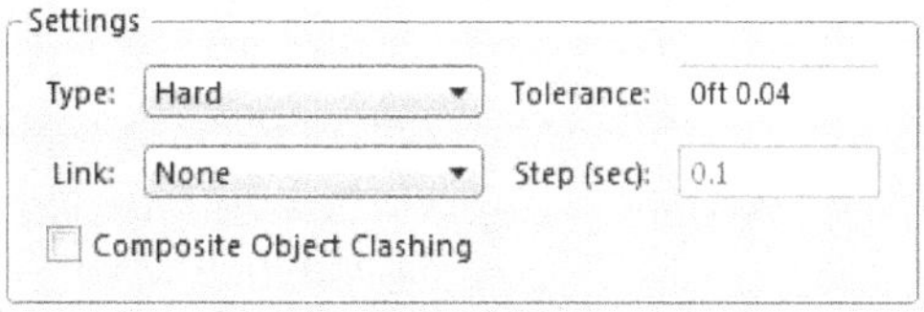

Figure 6–8

It is possible to run a clash test against construction equipment or other items that might move on site. To do this, link the clash test to a TimeLiner schedule or an object animation scene using the Settings area>Link drop-down list.

Then, set the period of time between clash tests in the *Step (sec)* field. Since multiple clash tests are run at set intervals throughout the simulation sequence, it does take more time to complete a clash test with a link.

If a clash test is taking too much time to finish, you can stop the test by clicking **Cancel** in the Working dialog box, as shown in Figure 6–9. The progress bar displays how much of the model was tested. All of the clashes that were found before the test was canceled are reported, and the test displays a *Partial* status in the Clash list, as shown in Figure 6–10.

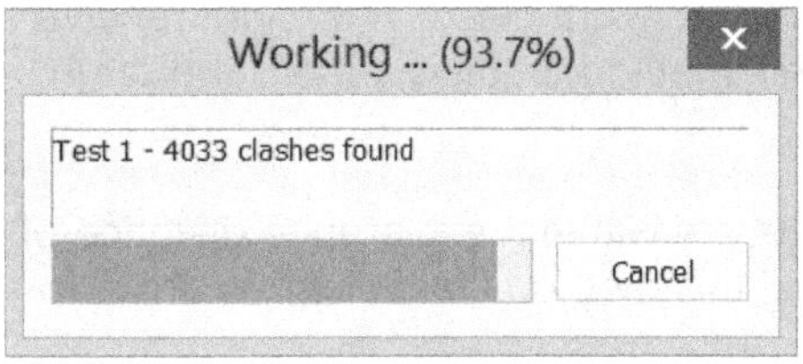

Figure 6–9

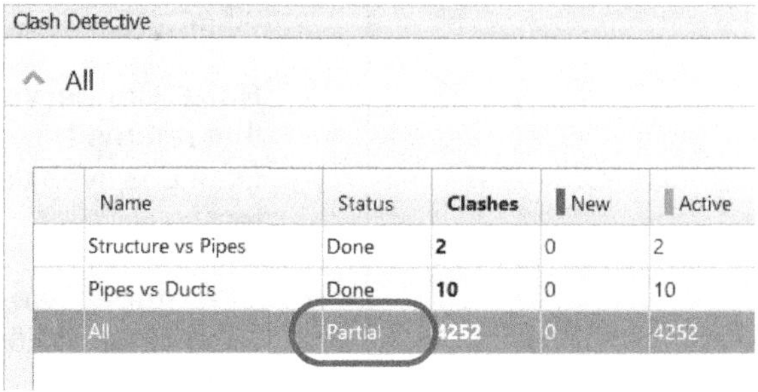

Figure 6–10

How To: Select Items to Test

1. In the *Selection A* column, expand the *Search in:* drop-down list and select the format of how you want to view the potential items, as shown in Figure 6–11.
   - Create and use sets if you expect to recheck the same clashes when models are updated.

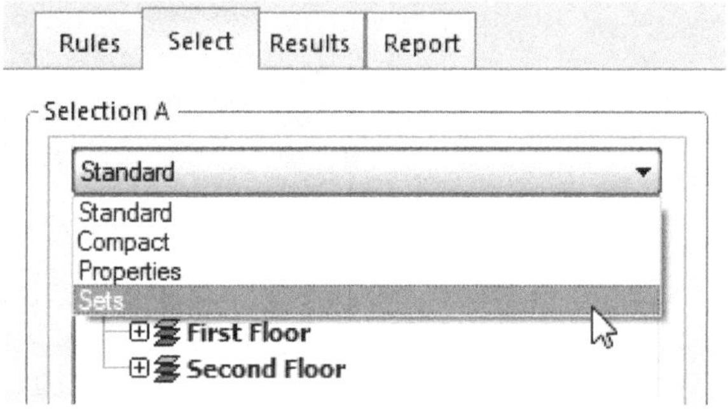

Figure 6–11

2. Select the items or sets you want to compare.
   - Hold <Ctrl> or <Shift> to select multiple options.
3. Repeat the process in the *Selection B* column.
4. Specify the geometry types and settings you want to use.

Practice 6a

Create Clash Tests

Practice Objective

- Check for clashes between objects.

Note: Clash Detection is only available in Navisworks Manage. It is not available in Navisworks Simulate or Navisworks Freedom.

In this practice, you will check the model for clashes against the structural columns and pipes, as shown in Figure 6–12.

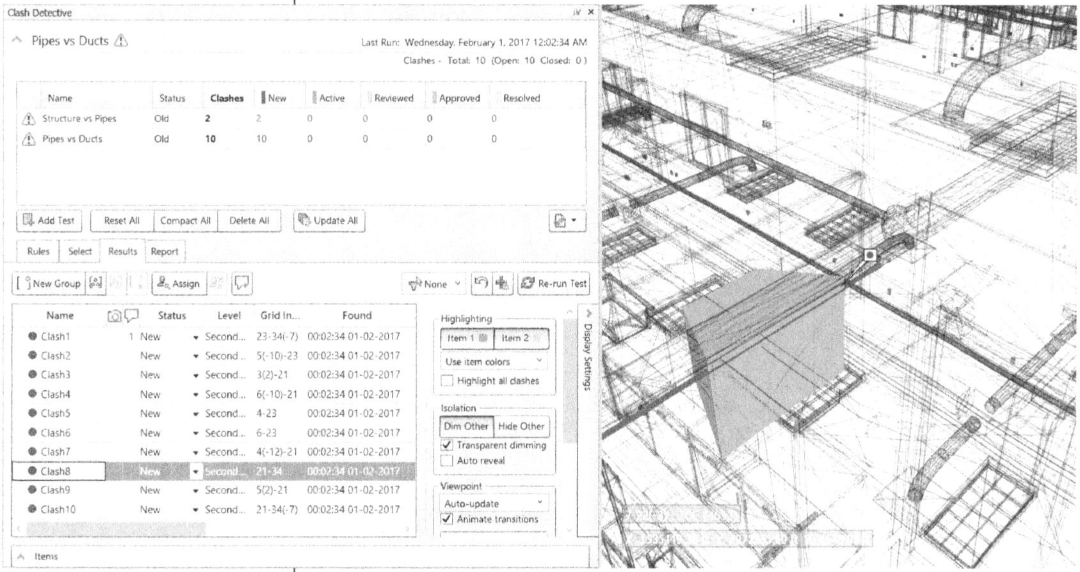

Figure 6–12

Task 1 - Create a simple clash test.

1. In the *Clash Detection* practice files folder, open **School-Simple.nwf**.

2. In the Saved Viewpoints window, click **SW Isometric**.

3. In the Home tab>Tools panel, click  (Clash Detective). if the Clash Detective is not already displayed. If the Clash Icon has a light blue sheen as a background, it is displayed and probably docked and retracted on the left hand side of the screen.

4. In the Clash Detective window, click the down arrow icon in the top left corner to reveal the Test area, as shown in Figure 6–13. Because no tests have yet been defined, this area is contracted.

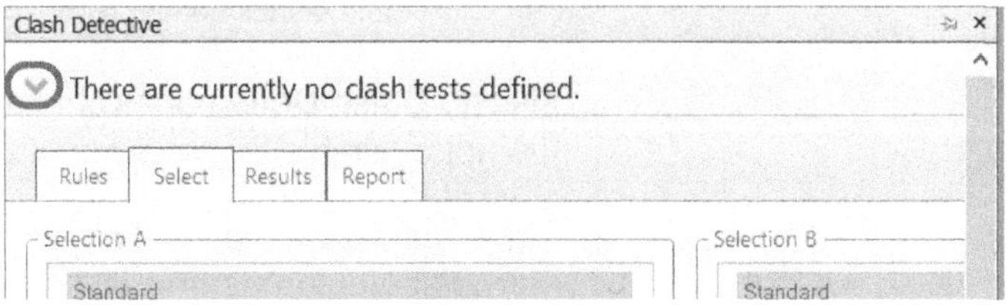

Figure 6–13

5. In the Test area, click (Add Test).

6. Select the name, and then click on it again to rename it. Type **Structure vs Pipes** for the name, as shown in Figure 6–14.

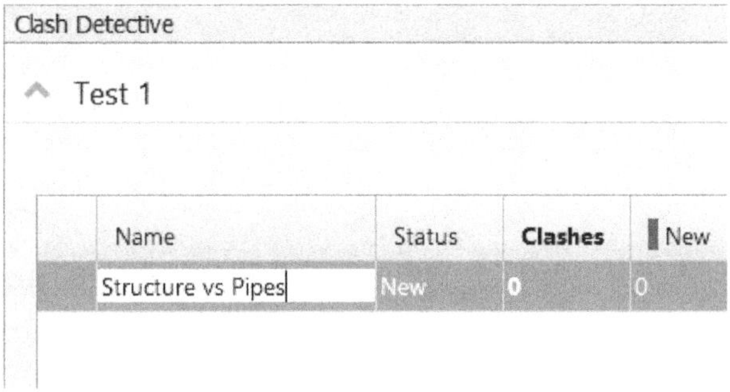

Figure 6–14

7. In the *Rules* tab, clear all of the *Ignore Clashes Between* options, as shown in Figure 6–15

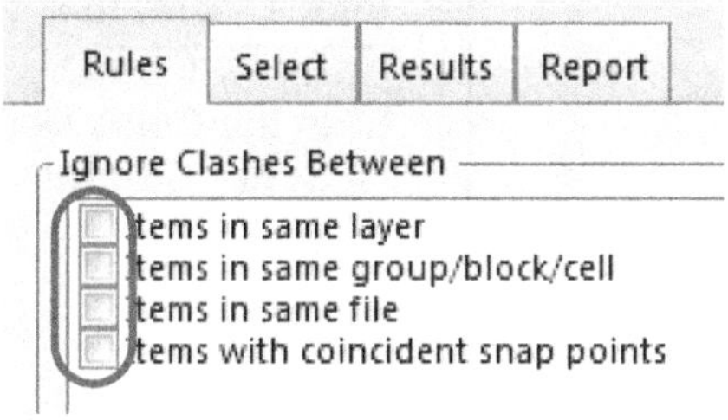

Figure 6–15

8. In the *Select* tab, set up the clash criteria.

9. In the Selection A pane, select **Standard** from the list format drop-down list. Then select **School-Structure.rvt**.

10. In the Selection B pane, select **Sets** from the list format drop-down list. Then select the **Pipes** search set.

11. Click **Run Test**.

12. The *Results* tab displays a list of clashes and the scene view zooms in on the first clash, as shown in Figure 6–16. Review the results.

Total number of clashes

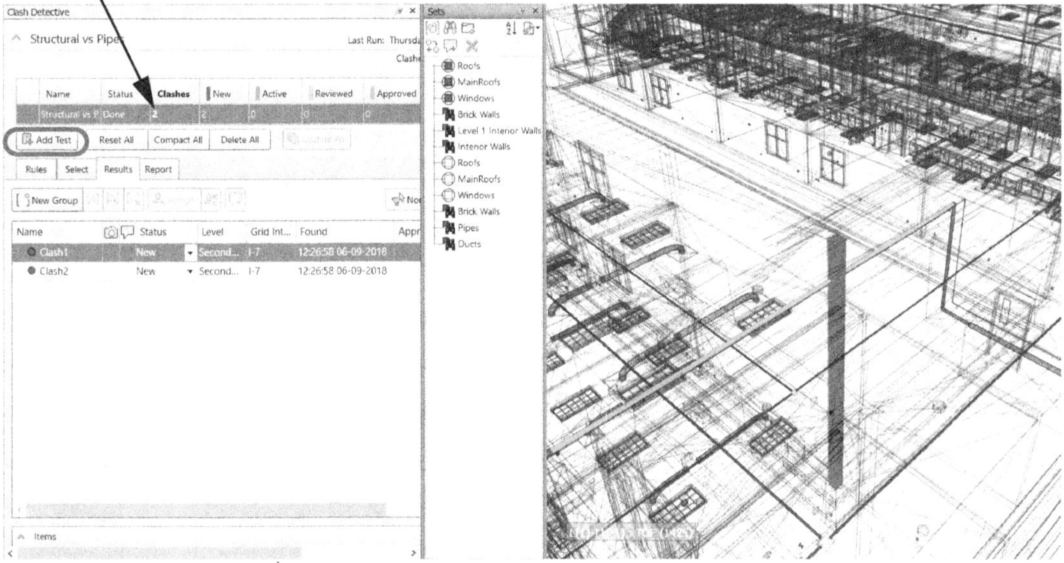

Figure 6–16

13. Save the file.

Task 2 - Run a clash test on pipes and ducts.

1. In the Clash Detective window, click (Add Test). Since there is already a test available, the location of this icon is now below the results window on the left-hand side of the Clash Detective window, as shown above in Figure 6–16.

2. Select the name, and then click on it again to rename it. Type **Pipes vs Ducts** for the name.

3. In the *Rules* tab, clear all of the *Ignore Clashes Between* options.

4. In the *Select* tab, set up the clash criteria.

5. In the *Selection A* pane, select **Sets** from the list format drop-down. Then select **Pipes** search set.

6. In the *Selection B* pane, select **Sets** from the list format drop-down. Then select the **Ducts** search set.

7. In the *Settings* area, change the Type to **Clearance** and set the *Tolerance* to **0.02 ft** so that you check for things that are less than a quarter of an inch part.

8. Click **Run Test**.

9. The *Results* tab displays a list of clashes and the scene view zooms in on the first clash, as shown in Figure 6–17. Review the results.

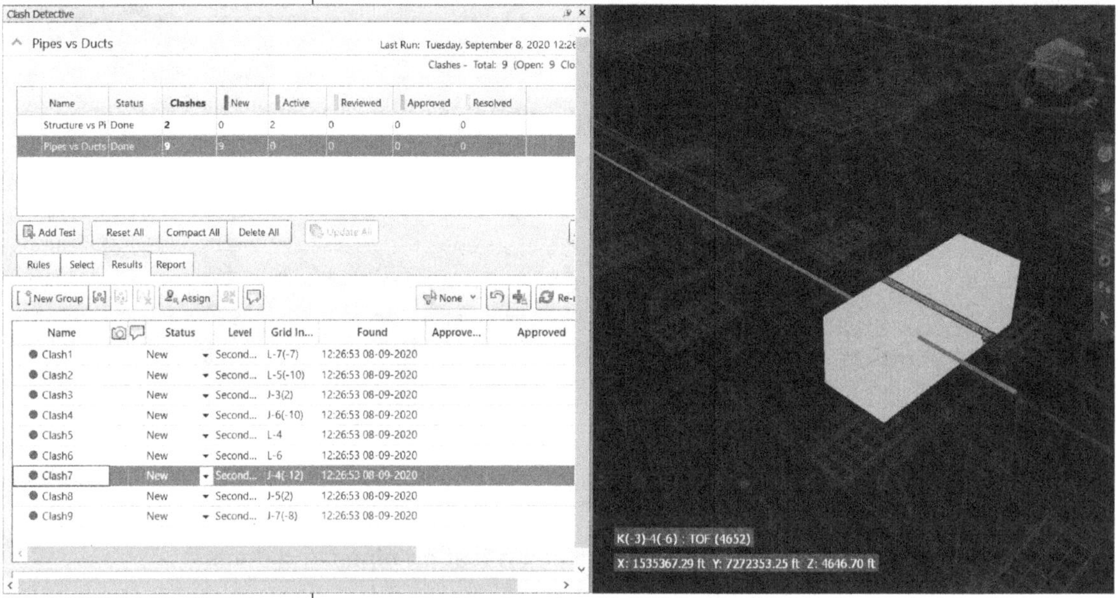

Figure 6–17

10. Save the file.

6.3 Reviewing Clash Results

The *Results* tab of the Clash Detective window enables you to review the clashes that were found during each clash test. Selecting a clash test in the top pane displays a list of clashes in the bottom pane, as shown in Figure 6–18. Use this pane to:

- View clash results and change how they display.
- Set the status of a clash.
- Add comments to each clash.

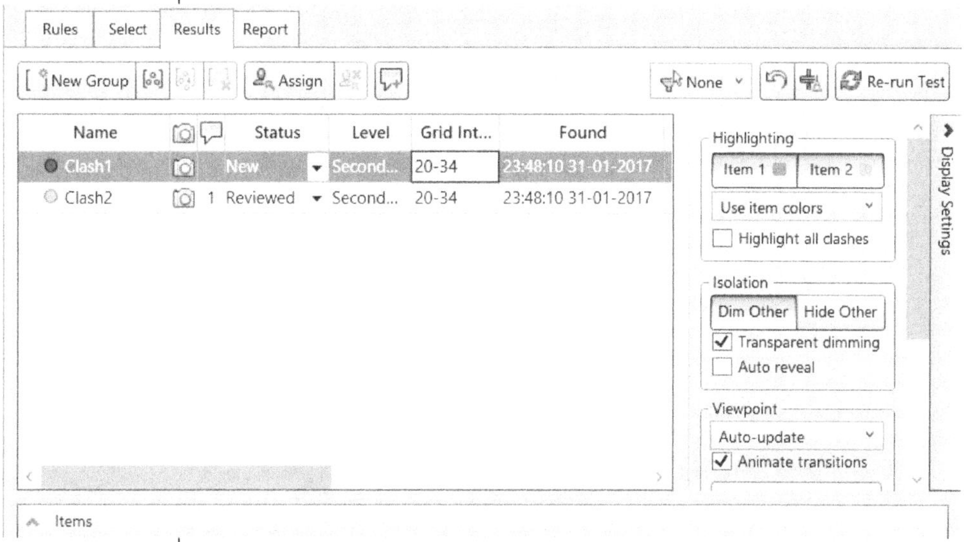

Figure 6–18

- Click the arrow next to the Items title to display or hide the tests at the top or the selected items at the bottom, as shown in Figure 6–19.

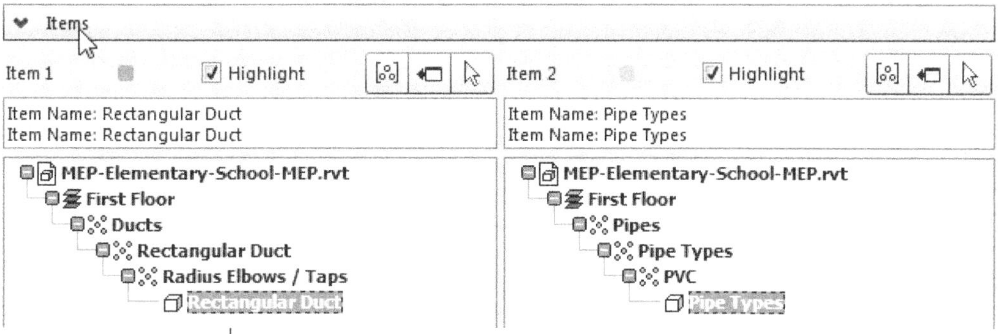

Figure 6–19

Viewing Clashes

Click on a clash to zoom to it in the scene view. If you Pan or Zoom the scene view while a clash is selected, the view is saved and the Camera icon displays (as shown in Figure 6–20) to indicate that there is a saved viewpoint available.

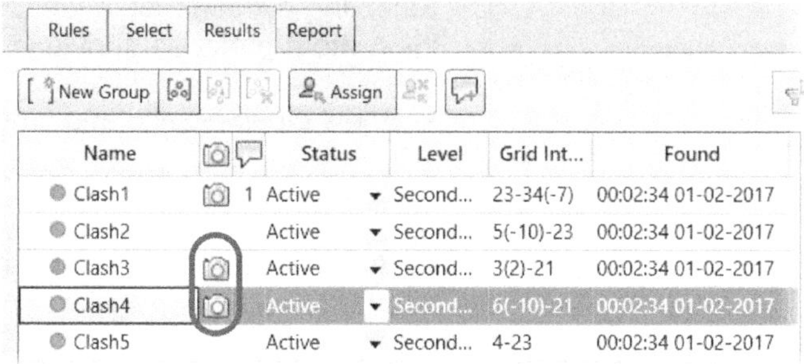

Figure 6–20

Display Settings

The Display Settings panel (shown in Figure 6–21) enables you to set how clashed items and other items display in the scene view. Each of the clash items can be set to its own color, and you can fade or completely hide everything else in the scene view. By isolating clashed items, you can get a cleaner picture of the corrections that need to be made.

- Click on the Display Settings title to open the panel.

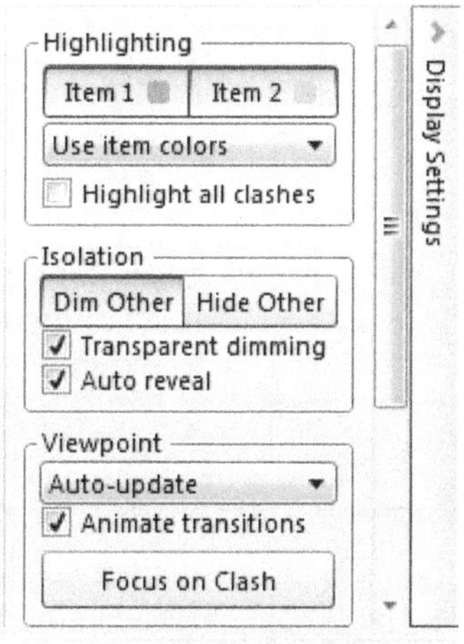

Figure 6–21

Highlighting

Highlighting can help you see which items are clashing, as shown in Figure 6–22.

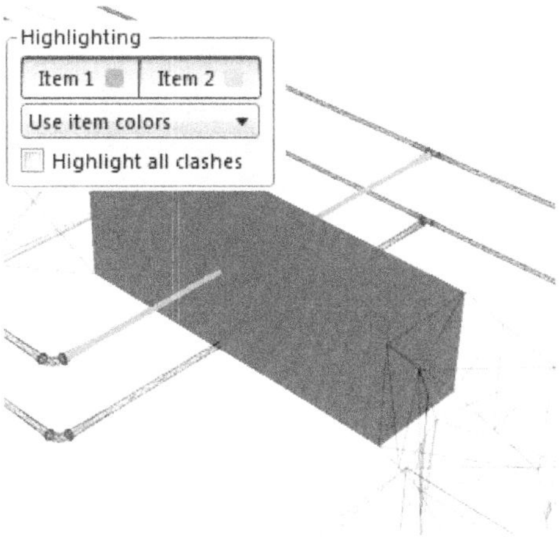

Figure 6–22

- Select the **Item 1** and **Item 2** buttons to toggle the highlighting on and off.
- In the drop-down list, use the **Use item colors** option to display the highlight colors, or use the **Use status color option** to display both items using the color defined for the status options.
- Select **Highlight all clashes** to display all clashes. This can be especially helpful if you have more than one item clashing with the same item (as shown in Figure 6–23), or if you want to see an overview of all of the clashed areas.

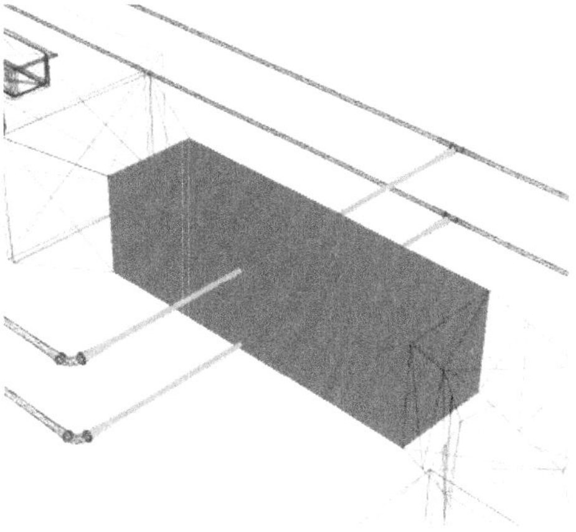

Figure 6–23

Isolation

By default, all of the other elements around the clashing elements are dimmed and display in wireframe (as shown previously in Figure 6–23). You can change this behavior in the Isolation area, shown in Figure 6–24. In the *Isolation* area, click **Hide Other** to display only the items in the current clash. This automatically toggles off the **Transparent dimming** option.

Figure 6–24

- If neither option is selected, the clash items are highlighted but the other elements display in the current Render Style Mode.
- **Auto reveal** temporarily hides any elements that might be obscuring the clash. It is a good idea to have this selected.

Viewpoint

In the *Viewpoint* area, you can specify how the viewpoint displays when you select clashes, as shown in Figure 6–25.

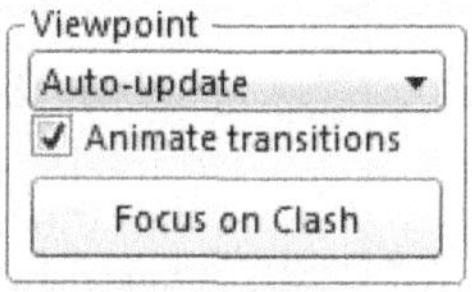

Figure 6–25

The *Viewpoint* area options are as follows:

- **Auto-update:** Automatically zooms in on an appropriate viewpoint and saves any changes you make to the viewpoint.
- **Auto-load:** Automatically zooms in on the default viewpoint, but does not save it as a new viewpoint if you navigate away.
- **Manual:** Does not change the viewpoint when you select clashes. You might want to use this option to display each clash in the context of the overall view.
- **Animate transitions:** Zooms out from the existing clash to the full model and then back in on the selected clash. This can help you locate a specific clash in the model.

- **Focus on Clash:** Zooms in on the clash again if you have moved away from it. This also turns on the **3rd Person** avatar by default.

You can right-click on a camera icon in the *Results* tab to load or save a viewpoint other than the automatic viewpoint. You can also specify **Focus on Clash** or delete the selected viewpoint or all viewpoints.

Hint: Clash Detective Options

You can specify how viewpoints display and animate when you select clashes, how clash tests are imported and exported, and set the default custom highlight colors.

To access these options, in the Application Menu, click **Options**. In the Options editor, expand **Tools>Clash Detective**, as shown in Figure 6–26.

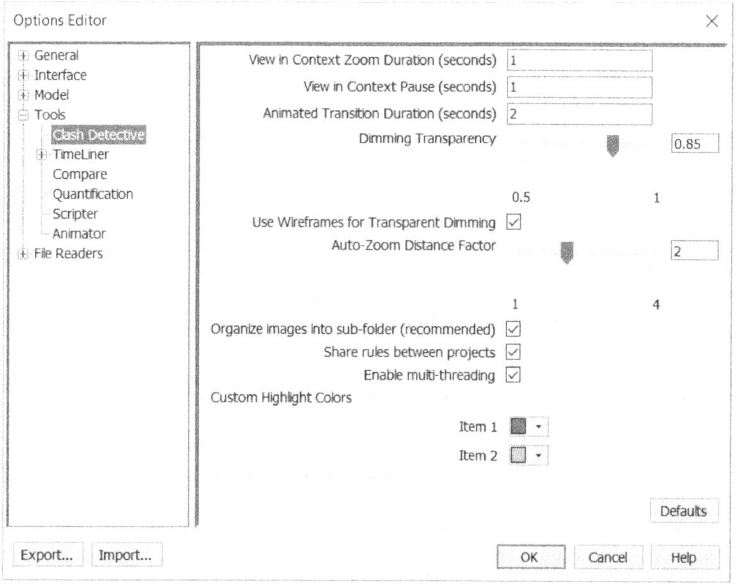

Figure 6–26

6.4 Assigning Clash Fixes

Assigning and Commenting

Clashes are most often found between different disciplines that do not work together. For example, electrical cable trays, plumbing pipes, and ducts are usually modeled by separate firms trying to occupy the same space in a plenum. You can assign responsibility for a clash (as shown in Figure 6–27) and add comments.

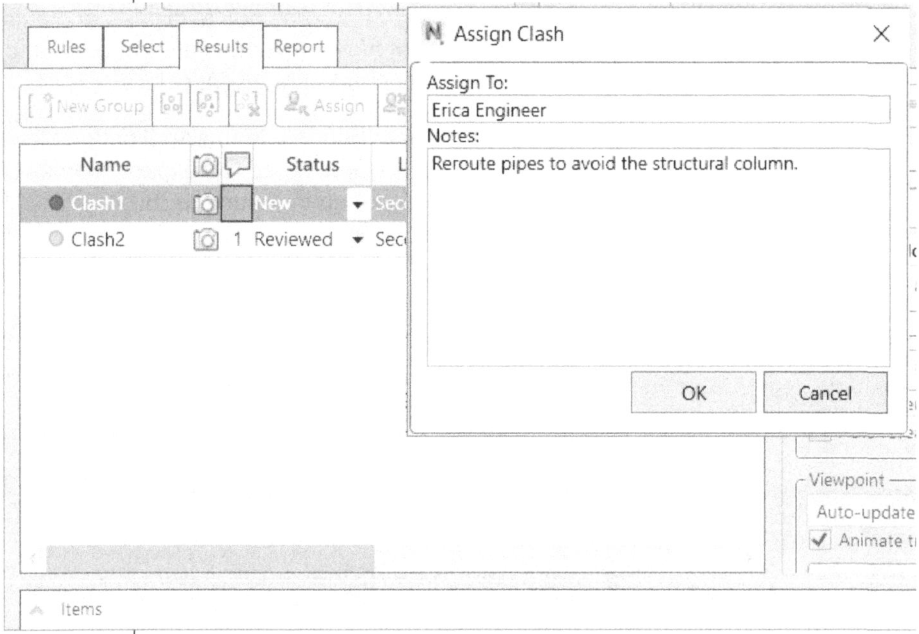

Figure 6–27

How To: Assign and Comment on Clashes

1. In the Clash Detective>*Results* tab, select a clash or clash group.
2. Click  (Assign) or  (Add Comment).

3. In the Assign Clash dialog box, enter a name in the *Assign To* field and add any notes (as shown previously in Figure 6–27).
   - Alternatively, in the Add Comment dialog box, type in the comment as shown in Figure 6–28.

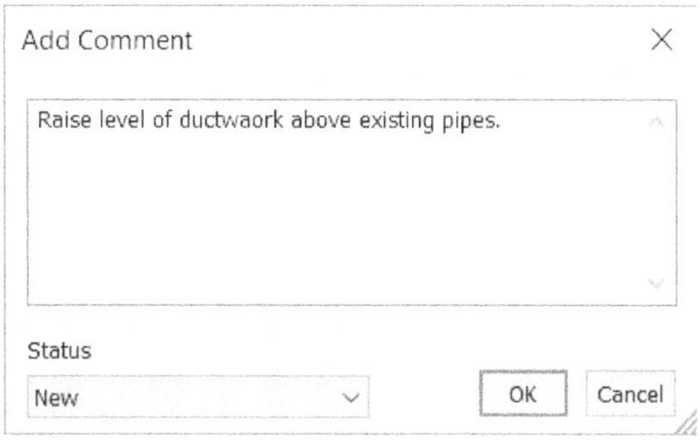

Figure 6–28

4. Click **OK**.

- To remove an assignment, select the clash and click (Unassign).
- Comments and assignments are typically included in any clash test reports.
- To view the comments in the Autodesk Navisworks software, in the *Review* tab>Comments panel, click (View Comments) to open the Comments window (shown in Figure 6–29).

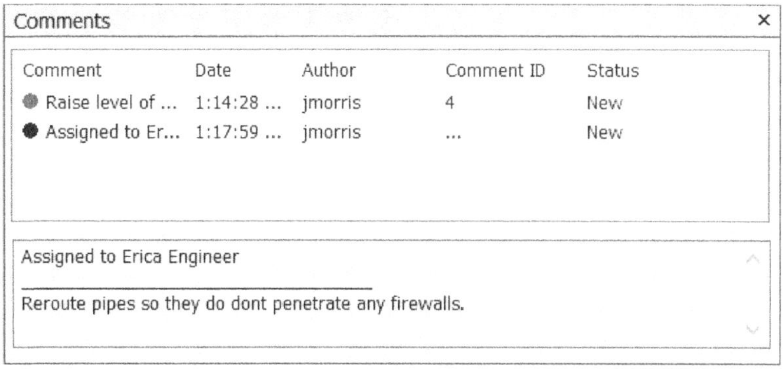

Figure 6–29

Setting the Clash Status

The Clash Status changes automatically as you work through the project. You can also manually apply a clash status, as shown in Figure 6–30.

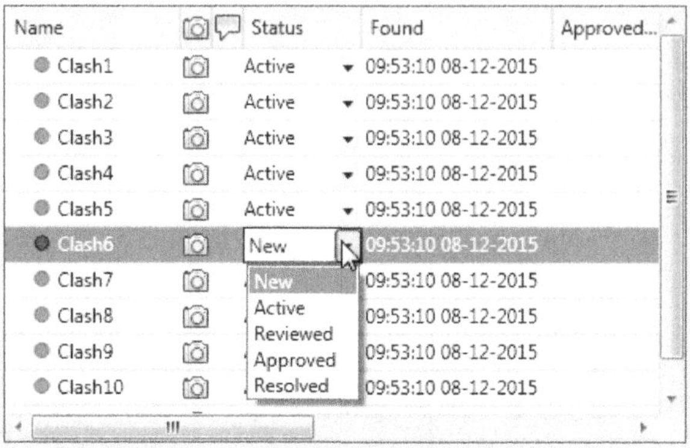

Figure 6–30

Each status displays a different color dot beside the name. The number of clashes for each status also displays in the Test pane, as shown in Figure 6–31.

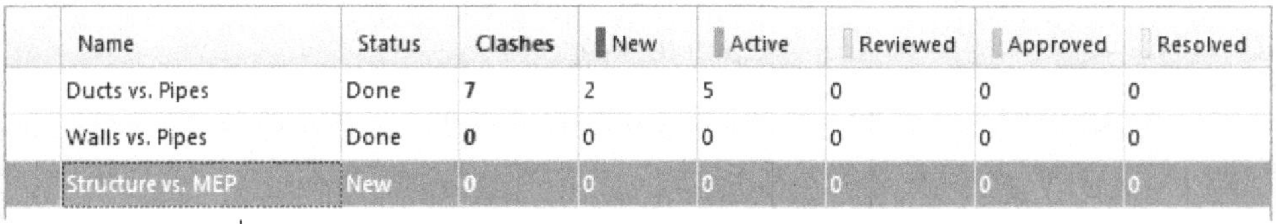

Name	Status	Clashes	New	Active	Reviewed	Approved	Resolved
Ducts vs. Pipes	Done	7	2	5	0	0	0
Walls vs. Pipes	Done	0	0	0	0	0	0
Structure vs. MEP	New	0	0	0	0	0	0

Figure 6–31

The clash statuses are as follows:

- **New:** The first time a clash has been detected.
- **Active:** A Clash test has been run again, and the clash is still unresolved.
- **Reviewed:** The clash has been reviewed, but not modified.
- **Approved:** The clash is approved to remain as is. The user who approved and the time of approval are logged.
- **Resolved:** The clash was in a previous run of the test, but is no longer found and is assumed to be resolved.
    - If a clash is manually changed to Resolved, when the test is run again and the clash still exists, the clash is assigned a New status.
- **Old:** When a model is updated since the test was run, this is a reminder that the current test does not reflect the information in the updated model. Clash tests show this status.

6.5 Clash Grouping

Grouping Clashes

Grouping related clashes together can save everyone time. For example, a series of pipes might be going through a fire-rated wall. Each intersection of pipe and wall is considered one clash. You can group these clashes together (as shown in Figure 6–32) so that they can all be addressed at the same time.

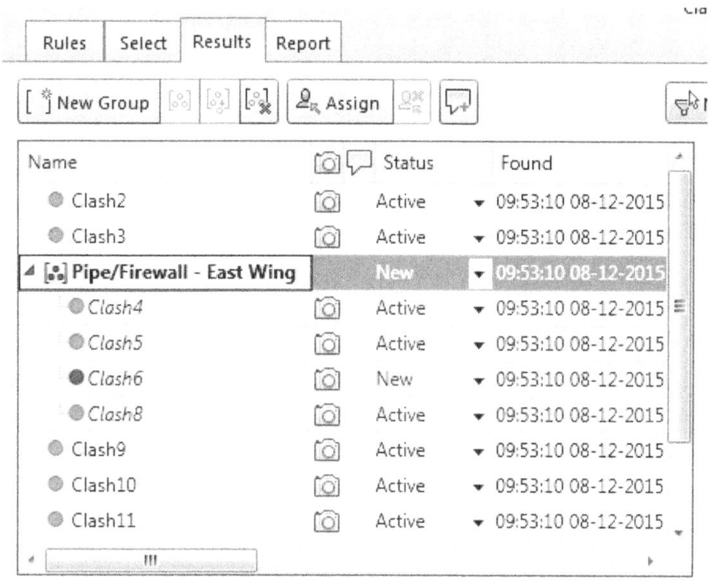

Figure 6–32

You can create groups in any of the following three ways:

- Click  (New Group) and then drag and drop clashes into the group.
- Select several clashes and click  (Group Selected Clashes).

- In the *Results* tab, select the clashes, right-click on them, and then select **Group,** as shown in Figure 6–33.

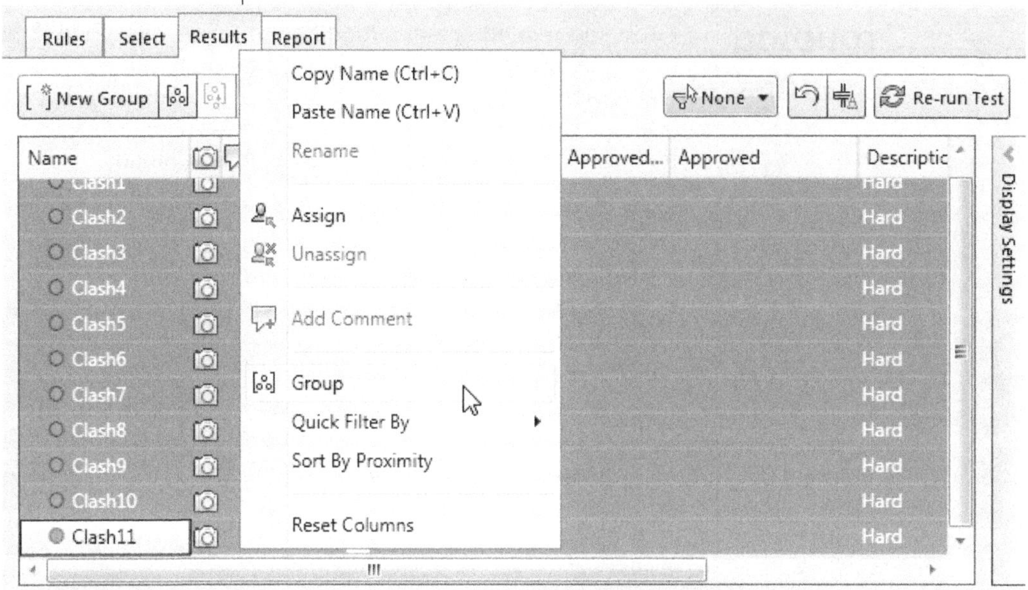

Figure 6–33

- Use <Ctrl> or <Shift> to select multiple names.
- You can rename the groups to make them easily recognizable. Click twice on the name or right-click and select **Rename**.
- To remove a clash from a group, select it and click (Remove from Group).
- To ungroup, select the group title and click (Explode Group).

6.6 Sharing Clash Test Results

The *Reports* tab of the Clash Detective window enables you to create a text file, HTML report, or XML report to communicate the details of the clash tests. You can also save a list of viewpoints for later review. The *Reports* tab is broken into the following three areas, as shown in Figure 6–34:

It is good practice to keep reports as short and as easy to read as possible, so only include succinct and necessary information in the report.

- **Contents:** Provides a list of selectable attributes that can be included in the report.
- **Include Clashes:** The clash status is used to select which clashes are included in the report. Groups can also be used to control the report contents.
- **Output Settings:** Sets the type and format of the report.

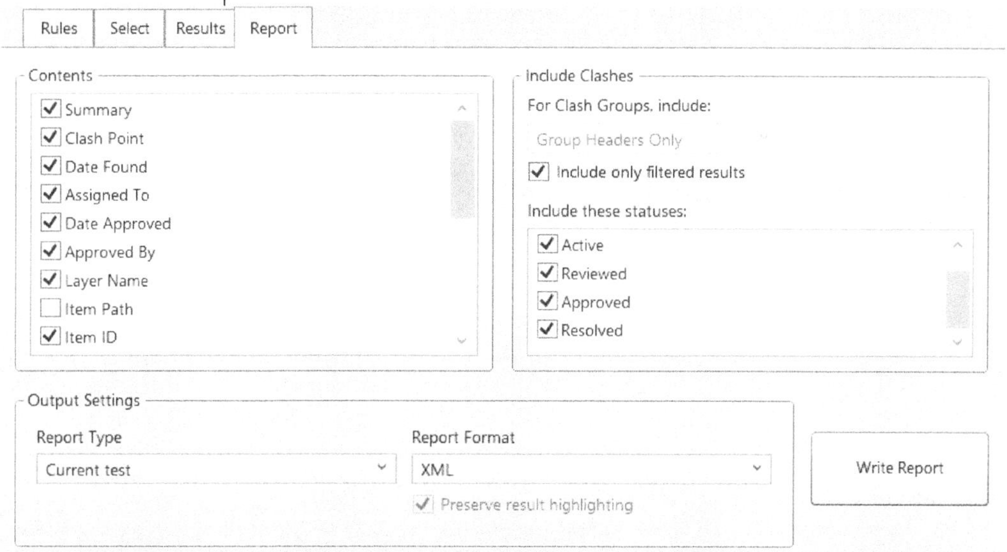

Figure 6–34

Output Settings

There are several types of reports and formats to chose from, as listed below:

Report Type

There are three report types, as shown in Figure 6–35:

- **Current test:** Run a report on the currently-selected clash test.
- **All tests (combined):** Combine all of the clash tests into a single report.
- **All tests (separate):** Create reports for all of the clash tests, with a separate report for each clash test.

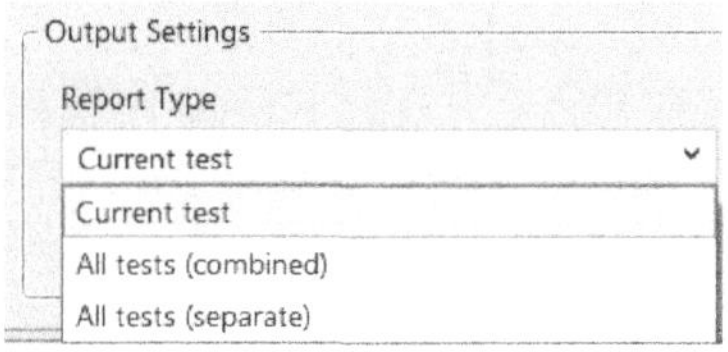

Figure 6–35

Report Format

There are several report formats available for the clash test results. When a report is written, an image file is created for each scene view that contains a clash. These image files are automatically saved to a folder located in the same directory as the report. The following report formats are available:

- **XML:** Includes images and details for clashes in an .XML file.
- **HTML:** Includes images and details for clashes in an .HTML file.
- **HTML (Tabular):** Includes details for clashes in a table which can be opened and edited in Microsoft Excel 2007 or later.
- **Text:** Includes the details for clashes in a text file with references to the image filenames.
- **As Viewpoint:** Creates a saved viewpoint for each clash and places all of the clash viewpoints within one folder in the Saved Viewpoints window. Comments containing the details of each clash are added to the viewpoint automatically.

This format option is helpful for sharing the clash results with anyone using the Autodesk Navisworks Freedom software.

How To: Write a Clash Test Report

1. Open the *Clash Detective* window.
2. Select the clash test you want to create a report for.
3. In the *Report* tab, do the following, as shown in Figure 6–36:
   - In the *Contents* area, select any information that you want to include in the report.
   - In the *Include Clashes area,* select the grouping level and statuses that you want to include in the report.
   - In the *Output Settings* area, select the type and format of the report that you need.

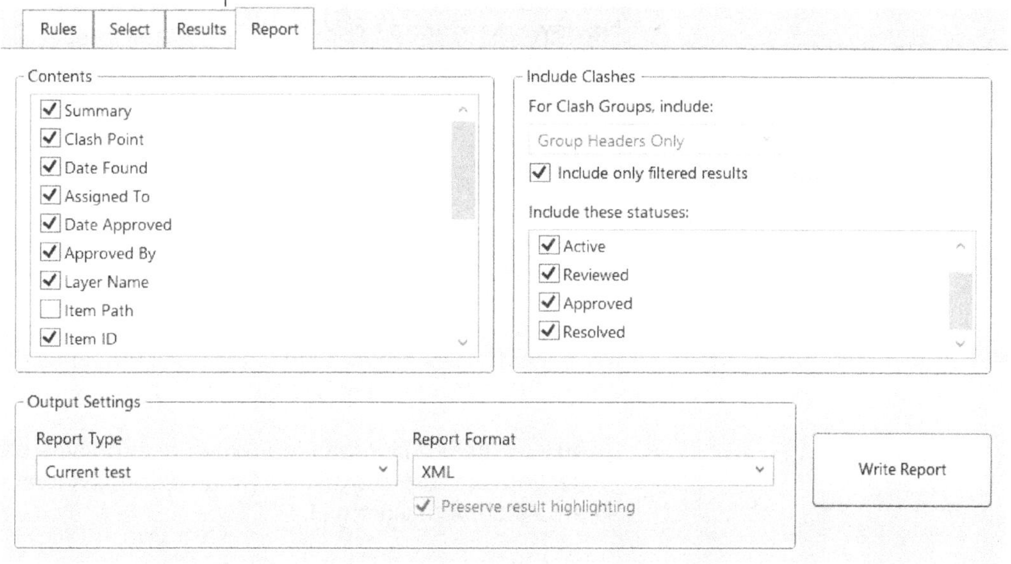

Figure 6–36

4. Click **Write Report**.

6.7 Incorporating Model Updates

Incorporating changes to the source models in the Autodesk Navisworks software can easily be done, depending on the file format you are using. Remember, the following file formats are used in the Autodesk Navisworks software:

- **Navisworks (.NWD):** The current state (or "snapshot") of a project, with all of the model geometry and redlines included.
- **Navisworks File Set (.NWF):** Includes links to the original files that form an Autodesk Navisworks model and redlines.
- **Navisworks Cache (.NWC):** Snapshots of each original file that are created automatically when you open or append files from other software.

The .NWF format are the files you should work with most often as updating this model is the easiest.

- Since the .NWF files include links to the source files, you can simply overwrite the original source file with the latest version of the source file.
- If the source files are on your server, you can chose to keep the .NWF file updated at all times.
- If you are sharing files with team members outside of your office, you can also copy files from an external server or send as an attachment via email.

How To: Incorporate Updated Models in Clash Tests

1. In Windows Explorer, navigate to the Project Files. Paste the updated models into the directory, overwriting the original source files.
2. In the Autodesk Navisworks software, on the *Home* Tab> Project panel, click (Refresh) to force a refresh of the model to the latest file version.
3. If the files do not update in the Autodesk Navisworks model, close the file, delete the corresponding (.NWC) file, and then re-open the Autodesk Navisworks model.
4. In the Clash Detective window, click Update All (Update All) to re-run all of the clash tests.

Practice 6b Review Clash Tests

Practice Objectives

- Review clash tests for clashes between objects.
- Assign clashes to individuals for correcting.

Note: Clash Detection is only available in Navisworks Manage. It is not available in Navisworks Simulate or Navisworks Freedom.

In this practice, you will review the clash tests ran in the previous practice. Then, you will assign clashes to specific team members for corrections, as shown in Figure 6–37. Finally, you will create reports to share the results with others.

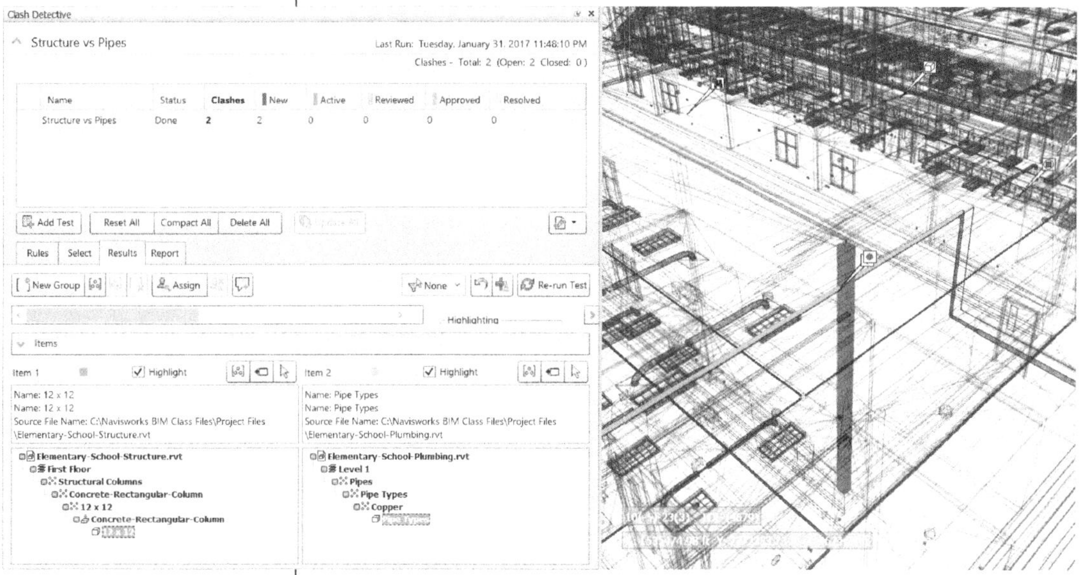

Figure 6–37

Task 1 - Review and group the results.

1. In the *Clash Detection* practice files folder, open **School-Review.nwf**.

2. In the Clash Detective window, notice the yellow alert triangle. As the tooltip explains, there have been changes to the models or the clash detective settings since the tests were run, as shown in Figure 6–38.

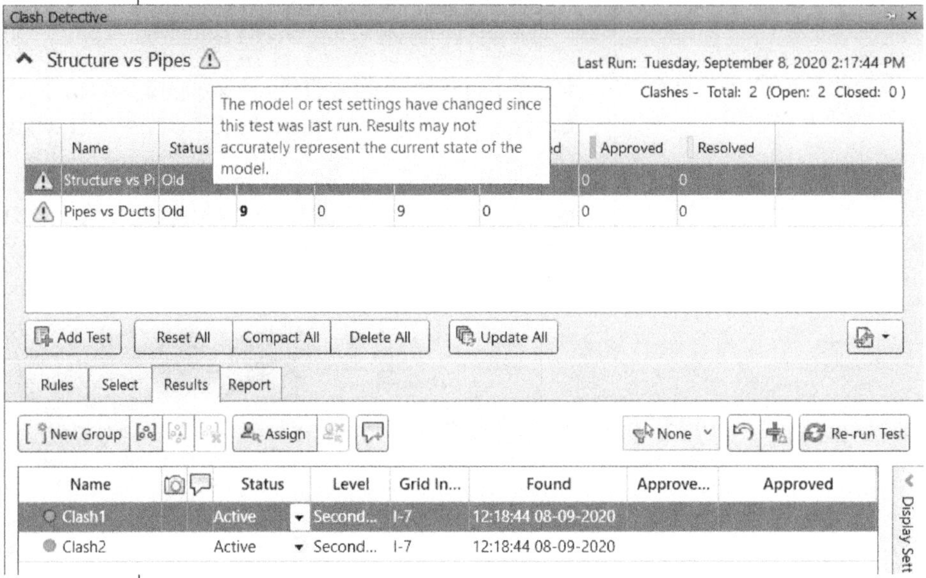

Figure 6–38

3. Select the **Pipes vs Ducts** clash test and click 

(Re-run Test) to update that test. While you're at it, also re-run the **Structures vs Pipes** clash test.

4. Select the *Results* tab. Review several of the clashes by clicking on them one at a time.

At first glance, all but one clash includes the same pipe.

5. In the *Results* tab, select **Clash1**. Hold <Shift> and select **Clash9** to select all of the clashes from 1 to 9. Hold <Ctrl> and select **Clash8** to clear it, as shown in Figure 6–39.

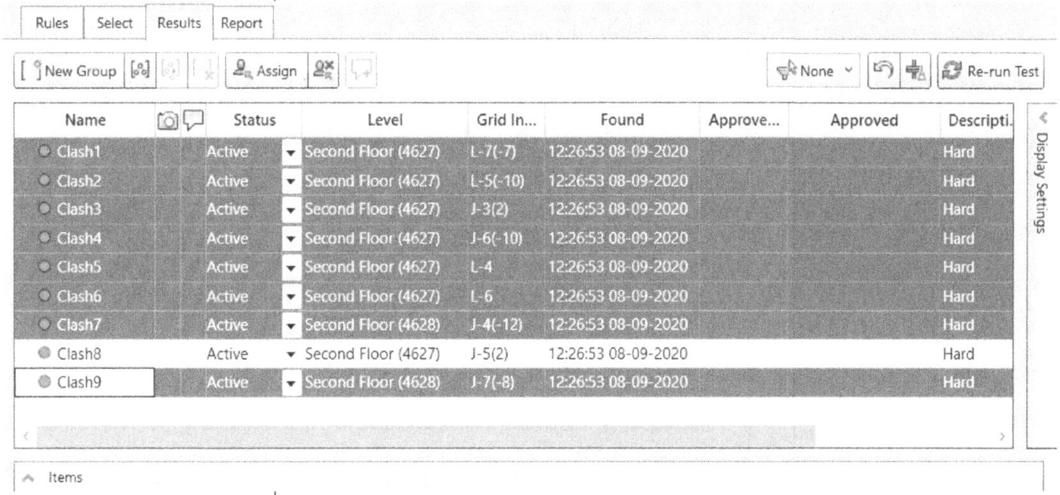

Figure 6–39

6. In the *Results* tab, click  (Group Selected Clashes). The results are shown in Figure 6–40. Note how the number of clashes in the clash list has been reduced to 2.

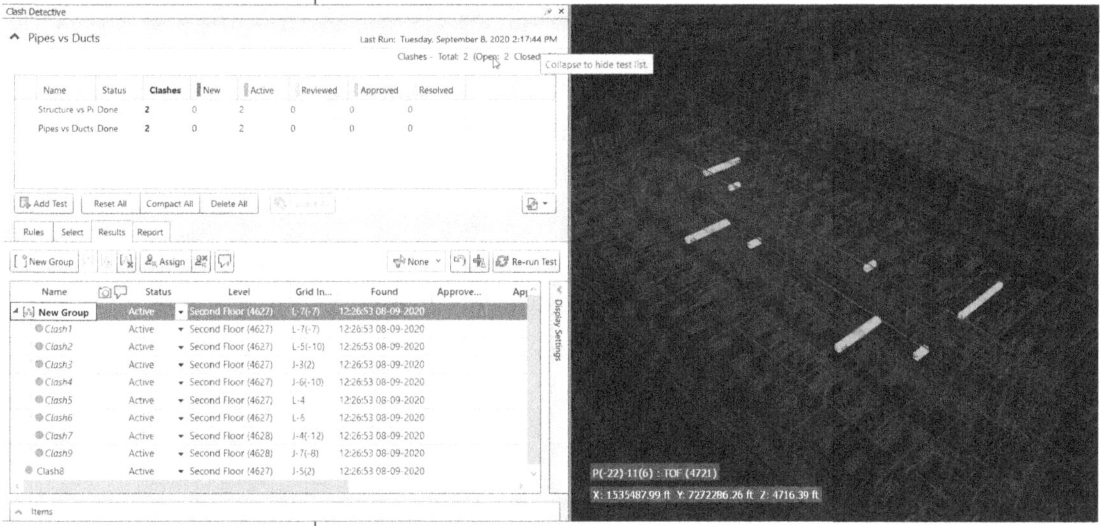

Figure 6–40

With the clashes grouped, note that the clashes do not all include the same pipe.

7. In the New Group, hold <Ctrl> and select Clashes 1, 2, 5, and 6. Note that the pipe penetrates the upper (northern) side of the highlighted ducts.

8. Click  (Remove from Group).

9. With Clashes 1, 2, 5, and 6 still selected, click  (Group Selected Clashes).

10. Right-click on the group containing Clashes 1, 2, 5, and 6 and select **Rename**. Type **South Pipe** for the name.

11. Right-click on the group containing Clashes 3, 4, 7, and 9 and select **Rename**. Type **North Pipe** for the name.

Task 2 - Assign clashes and add comments.

1. In the Clash Detective window, select the **Pipes vs Ducts** clash test.

2. In the *Results* tab, select the **South Pipe** group.

3. Click 

(Assign).

4. In the Assign Clash dialog box, in the *Assign To* field, type **Erica the Engineer**, and then enter **Reroute pipe above the ductwork and ensure a quarter inch clearance.** in the *Notes* field, as shown in Figure 6–41.

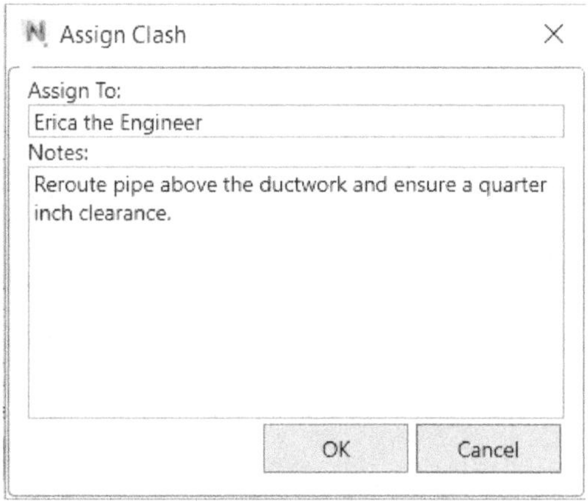

Figure 6–41

5. Click **OK**.

6. To the right of the **South Pipe** group, expand the Status drop-down list and select **Reviewed**. Note the change in color of the dot proceeding the clash name.

7. In the *Results* tab, select the **North Pipe** group.

8. Click Assign (Assign).

9. In the Assign Clash dialog box, in the *Assign To* field, type **Carl the Contractor**, and then enter **Ensure Pipe Insulation does not interfere with ducts.** in the *Notes* field, as shown in Figure 6–42.

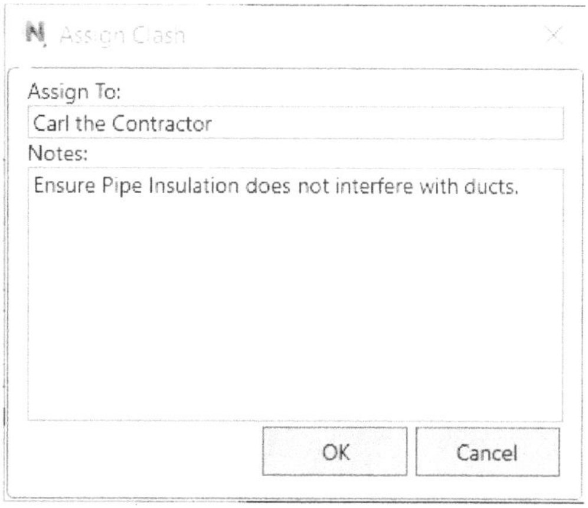

Figure 6–42

10. Click **OK**.

11. To the right of the ***North Pipe*** group, expand the Status drop-down list and select **Reviewed**.

12. In the *Results* tab, select **Clash8**. Upon review, this should be part of the *North Pipe* Clash Group. Click and drag it into the group, just above **Clash9**, and release it.

13. With **Clash8** still selected, click Assign (Assign).

14. In the Assign Clash dialog box, in the *Assign To* field, type **Carl the Contractor**, and then enter **Ensure this pipe insulation also clears the duct.** in the *Notes* field.

15. Click **OK**.
16. To the right of **Clash8**, expand the Status drop-down list and select **Reviewed**.
17. In the Clash Detective window, select the **Structure vs Pipes** clash test.
18. In the *Results* tab, select **Clash1**.
19. Click Assign (Assign).
20. In the Assign Clash dialog box, in the *Assign To* field, type **Pete Project**, and then enter **Reroute pipe to the left of the column and ensure a quarter inch clearance.** in the *Notes* field.
21. Click **OK**.
22. To the right of **Clash1**, expand the Status drop-down list and select **Reviewed**.
23. In the *Results* tab, select **Clash2**.
24. Click (Add Comment).
25. In the Add Comment dialog box, type **Is there enough room to bend this pipe or does it need elbows?**.
26. In the Status drop-down list, select **Active**, as shown in Figure 6–43.

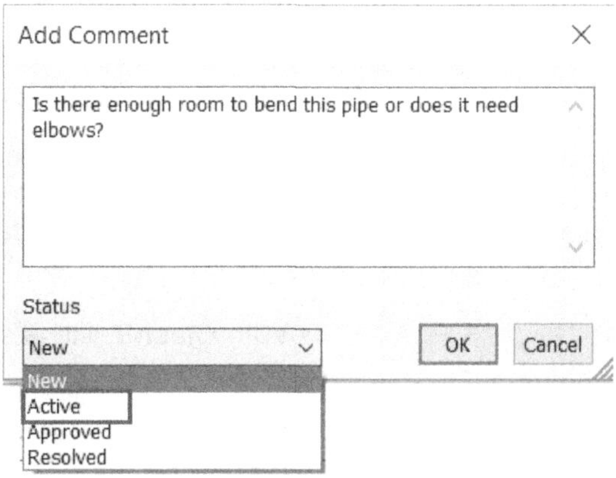

Figure 6–43

27. Click **OK**.

28. To see the comments in the Autodesk Navisworks software, in the *Review* tab>Comments panel, click (View Comments). The Comments window displays, as shown in Figure 6–44.

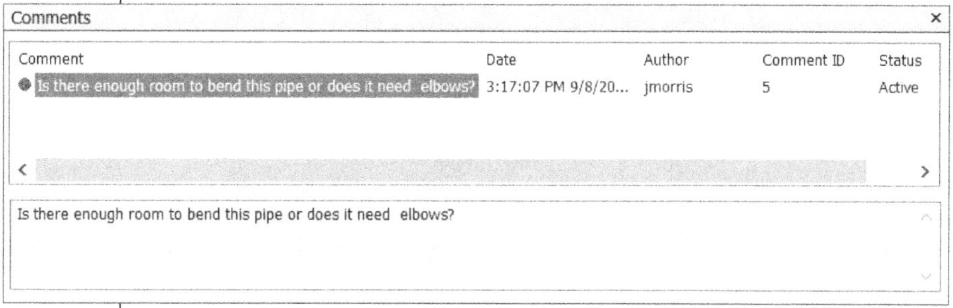

Figure 6–44

Task 3 - Create a clash report.

1. In the Clash Detective window, select the *Report* tab, as shown in Figure 6–45.

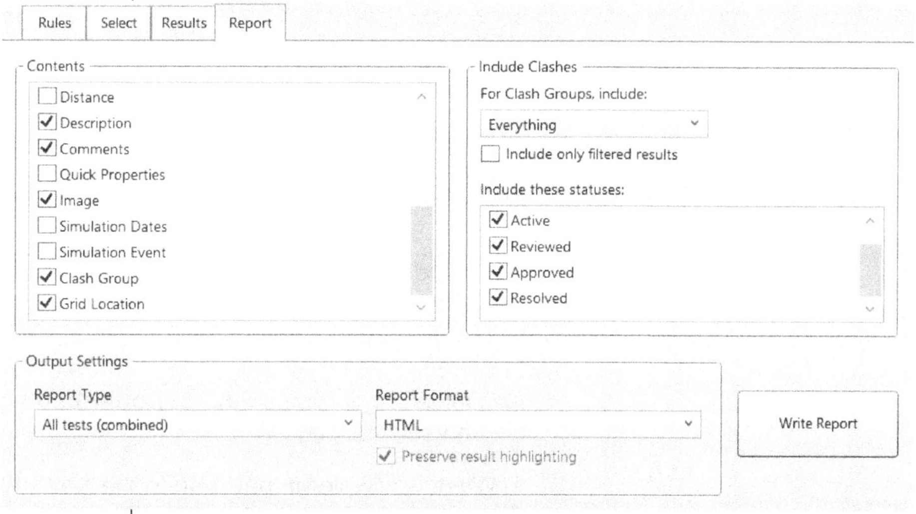

Figure 6–45

2. In the *Contents* area, select the following:
   - Summary
   - Clash Point
   - Assigned To
   - Status
   - Description
   - Comments
   - Image
   - Clash Group
   - Grid Location

3. In the *Include Clashes area,* uncheck the option to **Include only filtered results**. Ensure that all of the statuses are selected.

4. In the *Output Settings* area, for *Report Type,* select **All Tests (combined)**, and for *Report Format* select **HTML**.

5. Click **Write Report**.

6. In the Save As dialog box, navigate to the *Clash Detection* practice files folder and click **Save** to accept the default filename.

7. In Windows Explorer, note the folder containing the images for the report and the HTML file, as shown in Figure 6–46.

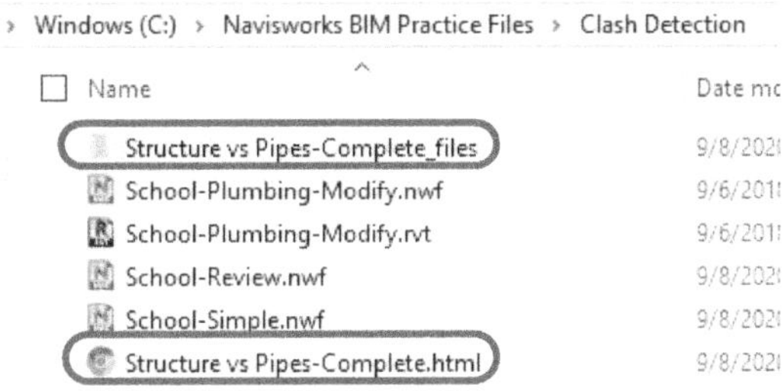

Figure 6–46

8. Open the HTML file to review the report.

9. Close the HTML file when done reviewing.

10. Keep the **School-Review.nwf**.file open.

Task 4 - Update the appended plumbing model and re-run the clash tests.

1. In Windows File Explorer, under the *Clash Detection* practice files folder, right-click on the **School-Plumbing-Modify.rvt** file and select **Copy**.

2. In Windows Explorer, navigate to the *Navisworks BIM Practice Files\Project Files\Revit Files* folder. Right-click in the folder window and select **Paste**.

3. Rename the *School-Plumbing.rvt* file to **School-Plumbing-Original.rvt**.

4. Rename the *School-Plumbing-Modify.rvt* file to **School-Plumbing.rvt**.

5. In the Autodesk Navisworks software, in the *Home* Tab> Project panel or in the Quick Access Toolbar, click  (Refresh). This can take some time, so be patient.

6. In the Clash Detective window, click 

(Update All) to re-run the clash tests.

7. Review the clashes individually. All of the clashes in the **Pipes vs Duct** clash test should display a status of **Resolved**. The clashes in the **Structure vs Pipes** clash test still need to be resolved.

8. Close the Clash Detective, but keep the **School-Review.nwf**.file open.

Task 5 - Update the Autodesk Civil 3D model.

In this task, you will update the Autodesk® Civil 3D® model to correct the elevation issues noted in the redlines. As the project base point was not updated in the Autodesk® Revit® models to accommodate the new building elevation, you will also modify the elevations of the Autodesk Revit models to match the new surface elevations.

1. In Windows File Explorer, navigate to the *Project Files\Civil Files\Source Drawings\Surfaces* practice files folder.

2. Rename *SiteLayout.dwg* to **SiteLayout-Original.dwg**.

3. Create a copy of *SiteLayout-Edited.dwg* and name it **SiteLayout.dwg**.

4. In the Autodesk Navisworks software, in the *Home* Tab> Project panel, click  (Refresh).

5. In the Saved Viewpoints window, click **Section-Entrance Platform**.
   - **Note:** If the surface does not change, it might be necessary to delete the .NWC file that was created when the original file was loaded into the model.

You should see that the surface has been updated so that the building pad is now at elevation 4615.2, with the entrance platform meeting the proposed finish ground. You will need to transform all of the Autodesk Revit and Autodesk® Inventor® files to adjust the elevation of the building to match.

6. In the Selection Tree window, select all of the files except **SiteLayout.dwg**.

7. Right-click on any one of the selected files and select **Override Item>Override Transform**.

8. In the Override Transform dialog box, enter **3.2** in the *Z value* and click **OK**.

9. Save the **School-Review.nwf**.file.

Chapter Review Questions

1. What are the different types of clashes that you can run? (Select all that apply.)
    a. Hard
    b. Soft
    c. Partial
    d. Clearance
2. Clash test parameters can be saved and used on other projects.
    a. True
    b. False
3. In the Clash Detective window, what would you use the *Rules* tab for?
    a. Use Rules to include the things you want to check.
    b. Use Rules to set the clearance tolerance.
    c. Use Rules to filter out things you do not want checked.
    d. Use Rules to change the colors of clashing items.
4. What is the purpose of Groups in the Clash Detective?
    a. To hide non-clashing items easily.
    b. To bring related clashes together.
    c. To run multiple clash tests at the same time.
    d. To view similar comments at the same time.
5. Where can you change the color of items that clash?
    a. In the Options dialog box.
    b. In the Clash Detective window, under Display Settings, in the *Isolation* Area.
    c. In the Clash Detective window, under Display Settings, in the *Highlighting* Area.
    d. In the Clash Detective window, in the Items pane.

Command Summary

Button	Command	Location
	**Add Comment**	• **Window:** Clash Detective>*Review* tab
	**Add Test**	• **Window:** Clash Detective
	**Assign**	• **Window:** Clash Detective>*Review* tab
	**Clash Detective**	• **Ribbon:** *Home* tab>Project Panel • **Hot Key:** <Ctrl>+<F2>
	**Explode Group**	• **Window:** Clash Detective>*Review* tab
	**Group Selected Clashes**	• **Window:** Clash Detective>*Review* tab
	**Import/Export Clash Tests**	• **Window:** Clash Detective
	**New Group**	• **Window:** Clash Detective>*Review* tab
	**Remove from Group**	• **Window:** Clash Detective>*Review* tab
	**Unassign**	• **Window:** Clash Detective>*Review* tab
	**View Comment**	• **Ribbon:** *Review* tab>Comments Panel

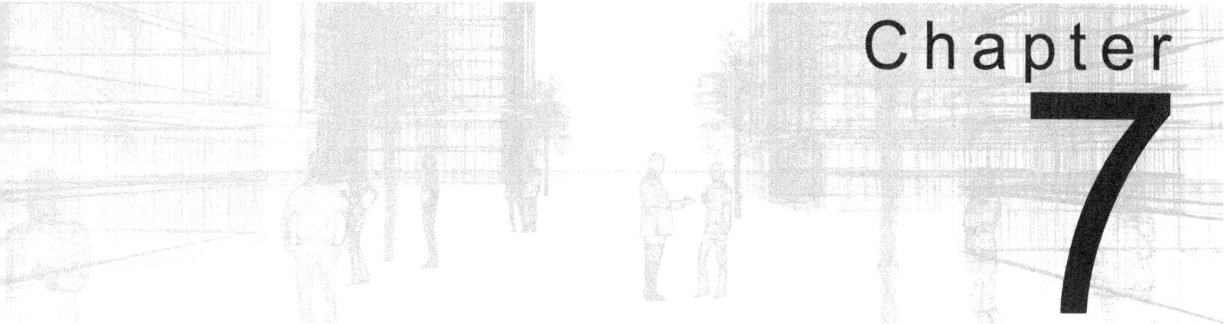

Chapter 7

Quantification

An important part of any construction project is estimating how much material is required. This quantification can occur in the authoring applications (such as Civil 3D and Revit), at later stages of design development, or at the tendering, pre-construction phase using Autodesk Navisworks. In this chapter, you will learn how to create material estimates, measure areas, count components, and perform various types of takeoffs on 2D plans. **Note:** Quantification is available for Navisworks Manage and Navisworks Simulate users.

Learning Objectives in This Chapter

- Set up a Quantification Workbook.
- Assign an Item Catalog to a project and create resources in the Resource Catalog.
- Conduct a model takeoff (3D).
- Conduct a takeoff from a DWF sheet (2D).
- Export takeoff data from a Quantification Workbook.

BIM Workflow: Quantification

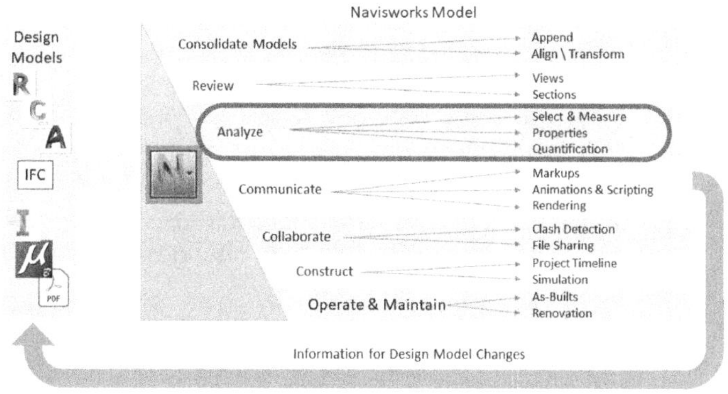

7.1 Quantification Overview

Navisworks Quantification is a feature that is available for both Navisworks Manage and Navisworks Simulate users. It enables you to measure material quantities, measure areas, and count components using data from your 3D models or your 2D drawing sheets. This process of measurement is called takeoff and it is an important part of providing accurate estimates for your construction and renovation projects.

Supported File Formats

For 2D takeoff, only .DWF and .DWFX file formats are supported. Consider converting 2D image files (e.g., PDFs) to .DWF using print driver software.

Navisworks Quantification supports the following multi-discipline Autodesk file types:

Publishing Application	File Format
AutoCAD Architecture	.DWF, .DWFX
AutoCAD MEP	.DWF, .DWFX
AutoCAD Plant 3D	.DWF, .DWFX
Autodesk Civil 3D	.DWF, .DWFX
Autodesk Inventor	.DWF, .DWFX
Autodesk Revit	.RVT, .NWC, .DWF, .DWFX
Adobe	.PDF

Quantification Workflow

The Quantification workflow begins with a design file (such as one of those listed above) that is brought into the Navisworks software. A typical workflow includes the following:

1. Open the file for which a Quantification project is to be created in the Navisworks software.
2. Set up a project in the Quantification tool.
3. Manage the Item and Resource Catalogs.
4. Create 3D model and virtual takeoffs, as required.
5. Create 2D takeoffs, as required.
6. Manage takeoff data, as required.
7. Review the takeoff data as changes are made to the source files.
8. Output the takeoff data, as required.

7.2 Setting Up a Quantification Project

The Quantification Workbook is your main workspace in a Quantification project. The first time the workbook is accessed in a Navisworks file, you must set up the project, which will consist of your model and any takeoff items that will be used to calculate material quantities. Once a project is created, you will import a catalog and specify project settings, then save it with the Navisworks file. It is accessed each time the Quantification feature is accessed.

How To: Set Up a Quantification Project

1. To access the Quantification Workbook, use one of the following methods:
    - On the ribbon, in the *Home* tab>Tools panel, click  (Quantification), as shown in Figure 7–1.

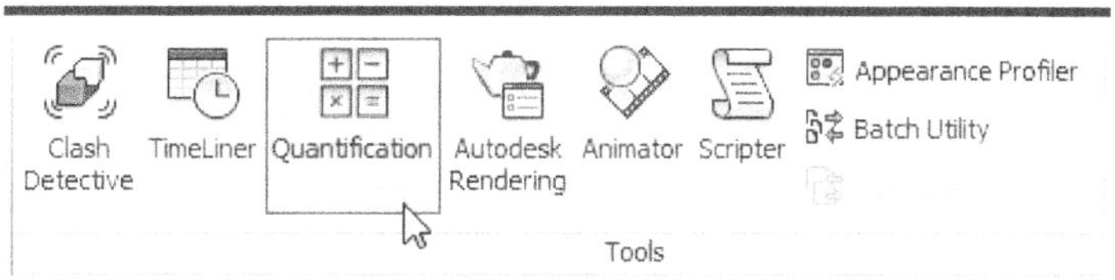

Figure 7–1

    - On the ribbon, in the *View* tab>Workspace panel, click the Windows drop-down list and select **Quantification Workbook**, as shown in Figure 7–2.

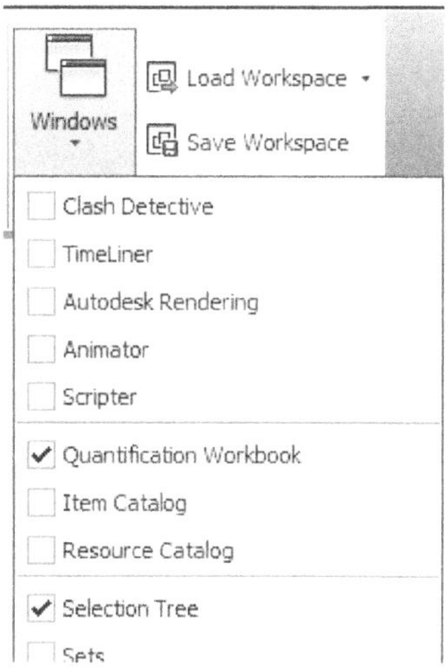

Figure 7–2

2. In the Quantification Workbook window, click  to access the Quantification Setup Wizard. If a project already exists in the Navisworks file, setup is not required.

3. Select an option in the Quantification Getting Started dialog box, as shown in Figure 7–3. This dialog box provides you with the opportunity to review help on Quantification.

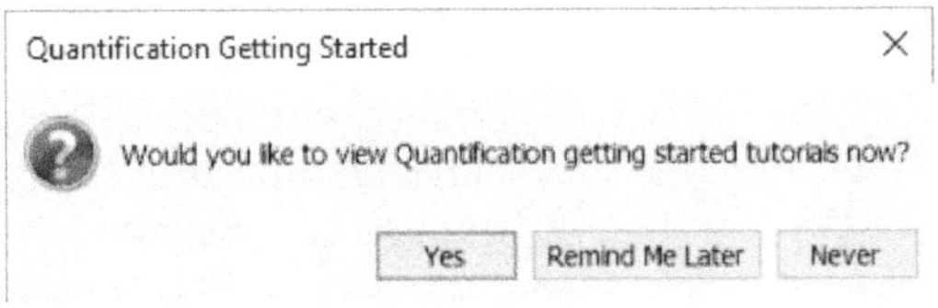

Figure 7–3

4. Select the item catalog that is to be used for the project. The Navisworks software provides a few default item catalogs or you can load any additional item catalog files (.XML). Browse to or select an existing catalog and click **Next**, as shown in Figure 7–4.

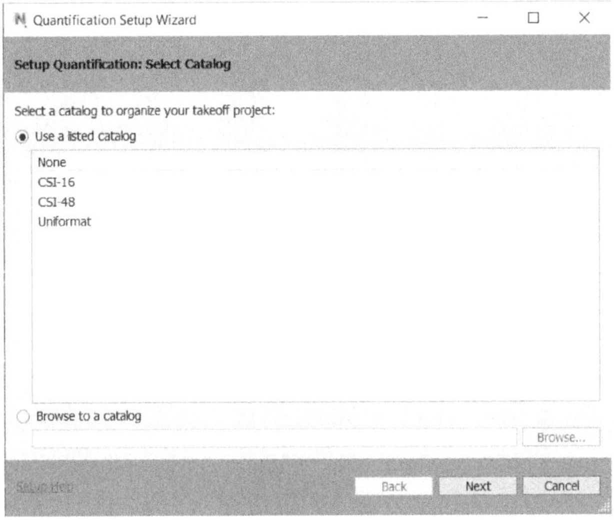

Figure 7–4

Note: The listed catalogs can also include company-specific catalogs that have been created. If you want to use a custom catalog for your project, it has to have the same units and properties.

5. Select the overall unit type to be used in the project and click **Next**, as shown in Figure 7–5. The options include:
   - **Imperial:** Units in the model are converted to imperial (e.g., feet, pounds, or gallons).

- **Metric:** Units in the model are converted to metric (e.g., meters, kilograms, or liters).
- **Variable:** Keeps the existing values for the model. The next wizard page will enable you to change each individual takeoff property's unit.

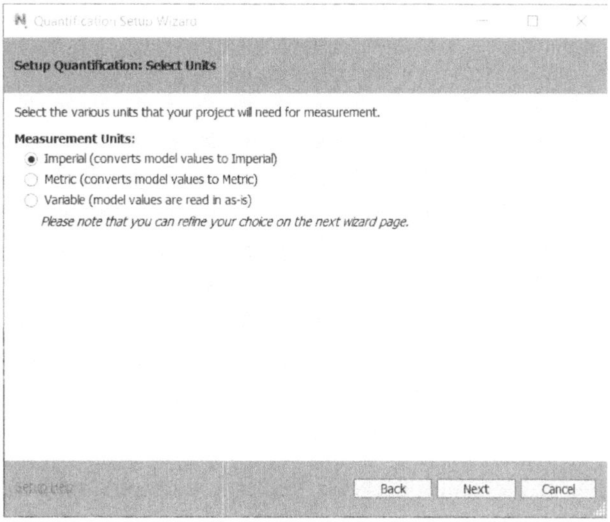

Figure 7–5

6. Refine the units for specific properties by selecting units in the drop-down lists adjacent to each property, as shown in Figure 7–6. Additionally, you can select the **Show Metric and Imperial units for each takeoff property** option, if required, to display both units. Click **Next**.

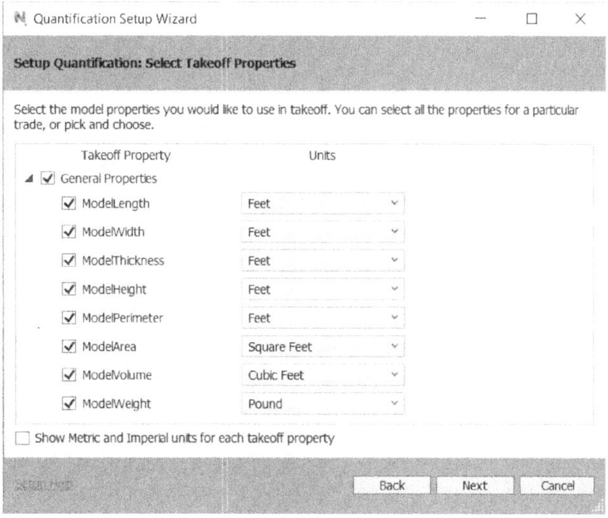

Figure 7–6

7. Click **Finish** to complete the project setup, as shown in Figure 7–7.

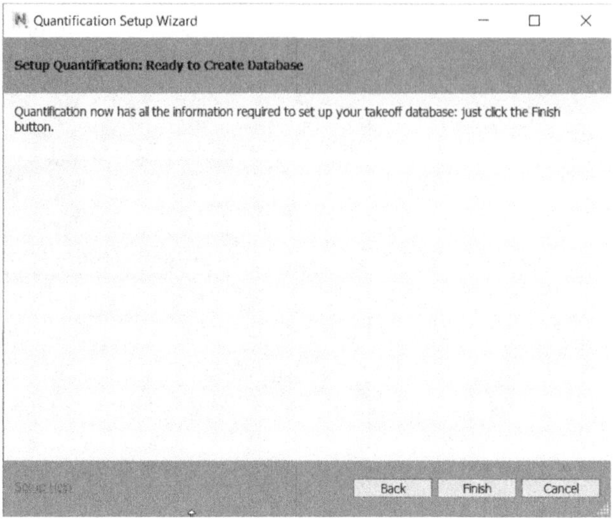

Figure 7–7

Once the project has been created, the Quantification Workbook updates to display the Item Catalog that was selected or imported, as shown in Figure 7–8.

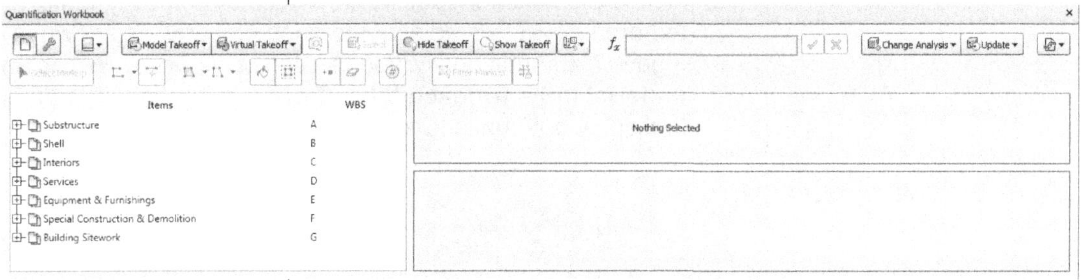

Figure 7–8

Hint: Quantification Catalogs

Quantification catalogs can be imported after the Quantification Workbook has been created. To import a catalog, click (Import/Export) in the Quantification Workbook, select **Import Catalog**, and browse to and open a new catalog. You are prompted if duplicate items are encountered.

Quantification Workbook

The Quantification Workbook consists of the following panes and a toolbar, as shown in Figure 7–9:

- **Navigation pane (1):** Contains a list of items or resources and their respective Work Breakdown Structure (WBS) codes. Click  in the toolbar to switch between the list of items (Item View) or resources (Resource View). If the Resource View is displayed, the Resource Breakdown Structure (RBS) codes are displayed.
- **Toolbar (2):** Contains the 2D and 3D Quantification commands.
- **Takeoff pane (3):** Contains a list of all takeoff items. Right-click a column header to change what is displayed in the pane.
- **Rollup pane (4):** Provides a takeoff summary. Right-click on the column headers in this pane to define what is displayed.

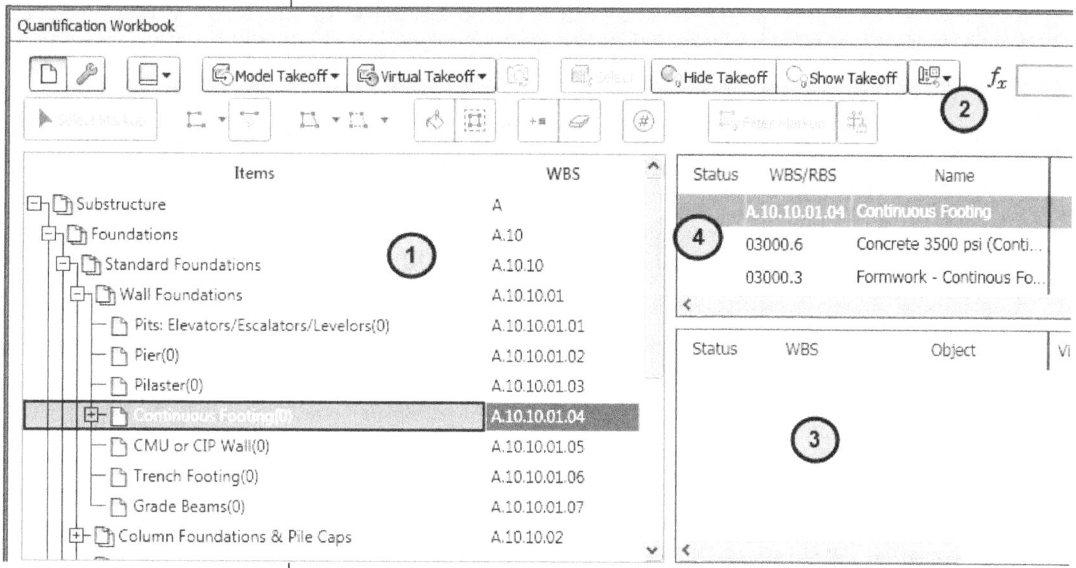

Figure 7–9

7.3 Item and Resource Management

The Item and Resource Catalog information is used to classify the elements. These catalogs enhance the model information to generate a more complete quantification/takeoff of the project, not just counts of objects. Basing a project on a catalog enables you to populate the workbook with the takeoff groups in these catalogs. If needed, you can also create additional groups and items by importing specific data from other catalogs or spreadsheets. Once catalogs are created in a project, consider exporting and reusing them in other projects.

Item and Resource Catalog Windows

By default, the Item and Resource Catalogs are nested together in the Quantification Workbook window. Each can be displayed by selecting their tab name along the bottom of the window. They can also be displayed as separate windows by double-clicking on their title bar and double-clicking again on the title bar to nest them. To toggle these windows on or off:

- In the *View* tab>Workspace panel, expand the Windows drop-down list and select **Item Catalog** or **Resource Catalog**, as required.
- On the toolbar in the Quantification Workbook, click and select **Item Catalog** or **Resource Catalog**, as required.
- With either the Item Catalog or Resource Catalog window active, you can click either **Resource Catalog** or **Item Catalog** to open the other window.

The Item Catalog consists of the following, as shown in Figure 7–10:

- **Items (1)**
- **Resources (2)**
- **Formulas (3):** The *Formula* area enables you to link variables with a formula to measure takeoff values.

Figure 7–10

The Resource Catalog consists of the following, as shown in Figure 7–11:

- **Resource Groups (1)**
- **Resources (2)**
- **Formulas (3):** The *Formula* area enables you to link variables with a formula to measure takeoff values.

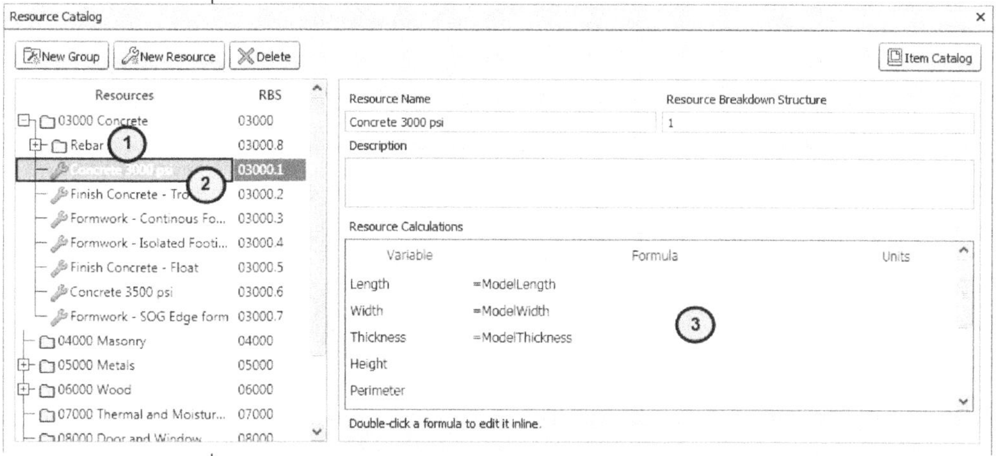

Figure 7–11

Items in the Item Catalog can be associated with an object in the model, such as a door or a wall, and can stand alone or contain resources. If resources exist, they are listed in the Resource Catalog, which is a database of your project resources.

Creating Groups and Items in the Item Catalog

In Quantification, takeoff data is organized in the following hierarchy in the Item Catalog:

- Work Breakdown Structure (WBS) groups ( )
- Items ( )
- Resources ( )

This hierarchy is shown in Figure 7–12 as navigation tree. There are multiple levels of WBS groups ( ) that contain items ( ), and the items contain resources ( ). This structure enables you to create the organizational structure required for your projects.

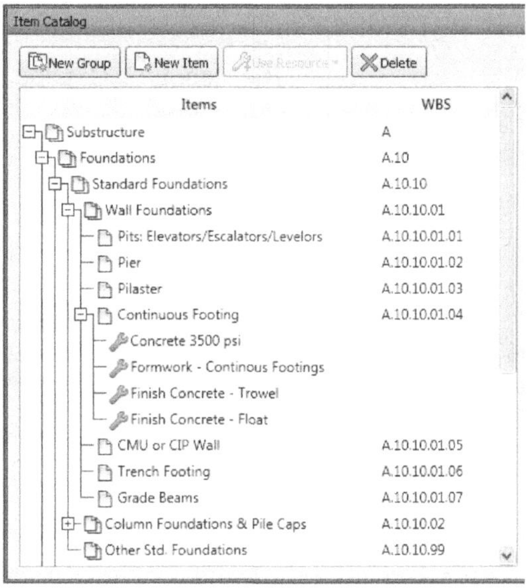

Figure 7–12

How To: Create a New Group

1. In the Item Catalog window, click **New Group**. If an existing group is selected, the new group is created in that group. To create a new group at the top of the hierarchy, ensure that no groups are currently selected.
   - Alternatively, you can right-click in the white space (nothing selected) and select **New Group** to create a new group at the top of the hierarchy, or right-click on an existing group and select **New Group** to create a new group within the selected group.
2. Enter a name for the group and press <Enter>.

How To: Create a New Item

1. In the Item Catalog window, expand and select the group in which you want to create the item. Once selected, click **New Item**. The item is created within the group. Items can also be created outside of groups by clearing all of the group selections in the item hierarchy before creating the item.
   - Alternatively, you can right-click in the white space (nothing selected) and select **New Item** to create a new item at the top of the hierarchy, or right-click on an existing group and select **New Item** to create a new item in the selected group.
2. Enter a name for the item and press <Enter>.

> **Hint: Copying Items and Groups**
>
> Items and groups can be copied to quickly add items in the Item Catalog. To copy, right-click the required item or group and select **Copy**. To paste, right-click the group in which you want the copied item or group to sit and select **Paste**.

Creating Resources in the Resource Catalog

In Quantification, takeoff data is organized in the following hierarchy in the Resource Catalog:

- Resource Breakdown Structure (RBS) groups ( )
- Resources ( )

This hierarchy is a navigation tree that supports multiple levels of RBS groups, enabling you to create the organizational structure required for your takeoff project, as shown in Figure 7–13.

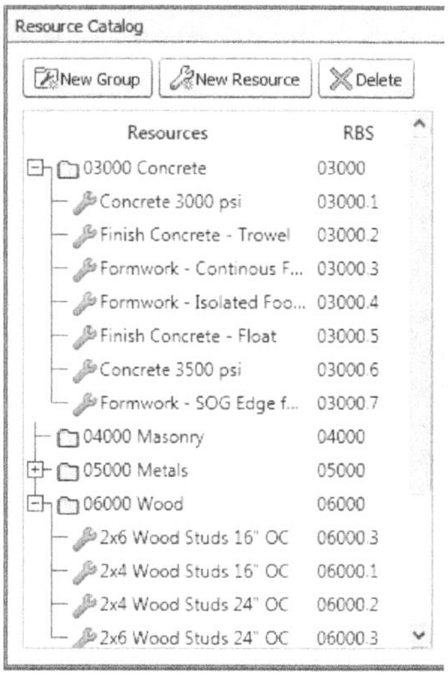

Figure 7–13

How To: Create a New Resource

1. In the Resource Catalog window, expand the resource grouping in which you want to create the resource.
    - To create a new group in the Resource Catalog, click **New Group**. Sub-groups can also be created to help further manage the resources required for a Quantification project.

    Note: Groups are only created and used in the Resource Catalog for resource management. The group headings are not used in the Quantification Workbook.

2. Once the required resource group has been selected, click **New Resource**. The resource is created within the group. Resources can also be created outside of groups by clearing all of the group selections in the Resource Catalog hierarchy before creating the resource.
    - Alternatively, you can right-click in the white space (with nothing selected) and select **New Resource** to create a new resource at the top of the hierarchy, or right-click on an existing group and select **New Resource** to create a new resource in a selected group.

Adding Resources to the Item Catalog

Resources that are created in the Resource Catalog are not automatically added to the Item Catalog. To be used in the project's Quantification Workbook, they must be copied into the Item Catalog.

How To: Copy a Resource to the Item Catalog

1. In the Item Catalog window, expand the item grouping in which to place the new resource.
2. In the Resource Catalog window, expand the resource grouping in which the required resource is located.

3. Select the resource to be copied, right-click, and select **Add To Selected Catalog Item**, as shown in Figure 7–14.

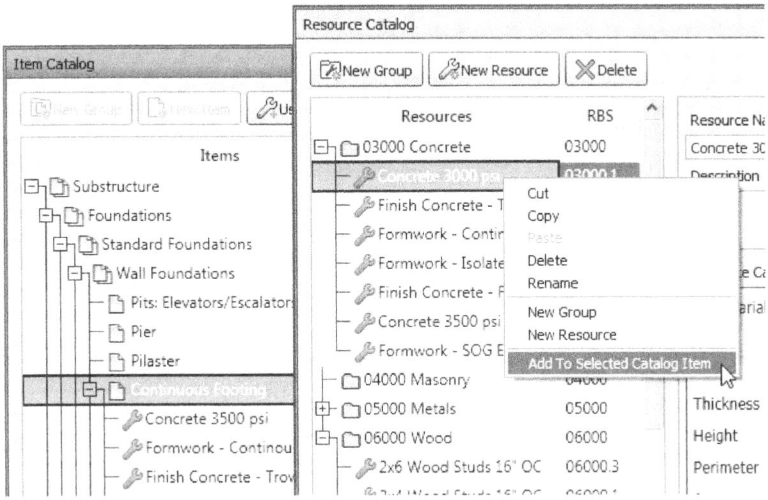

Figure 7–14

Copying Groups and Items in the Item Catalog

An existing group and item structure that is created in the Item Catalog can be duplicated as required to create another structure. When copied, all of the groups, items, and resources are also duplicated.

How To: Copy Groups in the Item Catalog

1. In the Item Catalog window, select the top level that you want to copy. It can contain groups, items, and resources.
2. Right-click and select **Copy**.
3. Select the level to which you want to paste.
4. Right-click and select **Paste**.
5. Right-click groups or items in the copied structure and select **Rename** to rename them.

Practice 7a Setting Up a Quantification Workbook

Practice Objectives

- Initialize the Quantification Workbook.
- Set up and review the Resource and Item Catalogs.

In this practice, you will begin the Quantification process by setting up the project, the Resource Catalog, and the Item Catalog. You will then review selected items.

Task 1 - Set up the Quantification project.

1. In the *Quantification* practice files folder, open **School-Takeoff-setup.nwf**.
2. In the *Home* tab>Tools panel, click  (Quantification) to open the Quantification Workbook, if not already open.
    - Alternatively, in the *View* tab>Workspace panel, you can select **Quantification Workbook** in the Windows drop-down list.
3. Dock the Quantification Workbook at the bottom of the Navisworks screen or on a second monitor, if available.
4. In the Quantification Workbook window, click **Project Setup**.
5. Select **Remind Me Later** from the Quantification Getting Started dialog box to continue to the Quantification Setup Wizard.
6. Select **Browse to a catalog** and click **Browse**. Navigate to the *Quantification* practice files folder and select **School-Quantification Catalog.xml**. This .XML file is the Item Catalog that will be used for this project.
7. Click **Open**.

8. In the Quantification Setup Wizard, click **Next**, then click **Finish** to complete the project setup. The Item Catalog has now been assigned to the file, as shown in Figure 7–15.

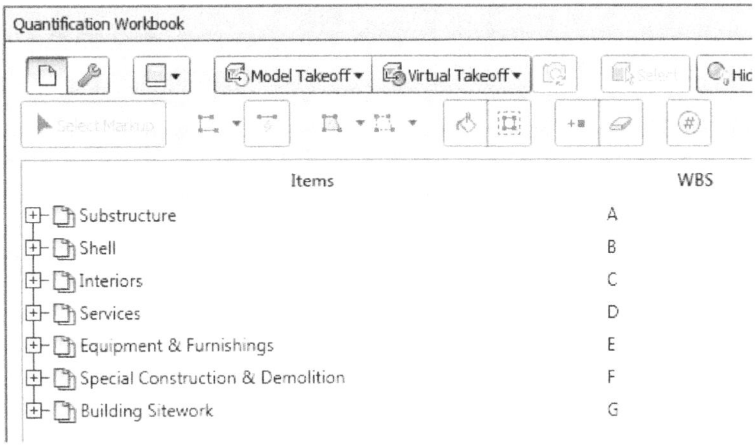

Figure 7–15

Note: If one of the default project types was selected, the wizard would prompt for additional unit measurement selections. Because an .XML file was selected, the unit definition has already been assigned.

Task 2 - Review the Item and Resource Catalogs and add items.

1. In the Quantification Workbook's toolbar, click  and ensure that the Item Catalog and Resource Catalog items are selected for display.
   - Alternatively, in the *View* tab>Workspace panel, you can select **Item Catalog** in the Windows drop-down list.
2. By default, the Quantification Workbook, Item Catalog, and Resource Catalog are all included in the window and are accessed by selecting the appropriate tab at the bottom of the window, when displayed. You can individually drag out any of the windows, as required, to display them separately.

   Note: Double-clicking on a title bar undocks a docked window.

3. Select the *Item Catalog* tab and browse the item collections showing the items in the list, the folder structure, and the WBS numbering, as shown in Figure 7–16.

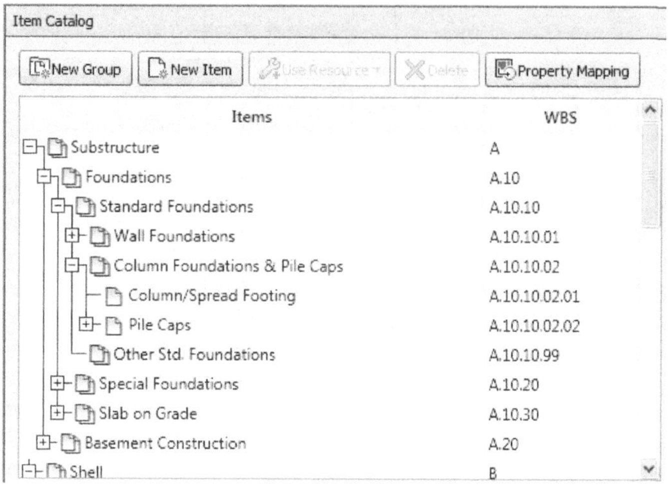

Figure 7–16

4. In the Item Catalog window, ensure that no groups are currently selected. This ensures that any new groups are added to the top level of the Item Catalog. Click **New Group**. Enter **Materials** as the name for the group and press <Enter>.

5. Ensure that the **Materials** group is selected. In the pane on the right, enter **H** as the *Work Breakdown Structure*.

6. With the Materials group still selected, click **New Group** again. Enter **Paint** as the name for the group and press <Enter>.

7. In the Item Catalog window, select the **Paint** group and click **New Item**. Enter **Blue Paint** as the name for the item and press <Enter>.

8. Select the **Paint** group and click **New Item**. Enter **Beige Paint** as the name for the item.

9. Add **White Paint** and **Red Paint** as two additional items in the Paint group, as shown in Figure 7–17.

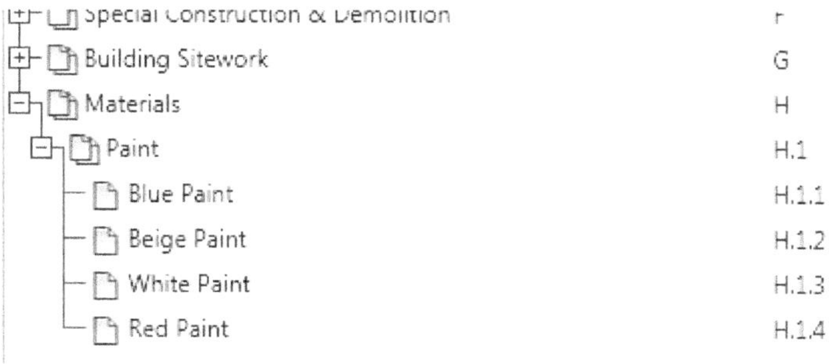

Figure 7–17

10. Return to the Quantification Workbook and note that the new groups and items are now available.

11. Select the *Resource Catalog* tab. If it is not a listed tab with the Quantification Workbook and Item Catalog, you must display it by clicking  in the Quantification Workbook and selecting **Resource Catalog**.

12. Browse the resource collections displaying the resources in the list, folder structure, and RBS numbering, as shown in Figure 7–18.

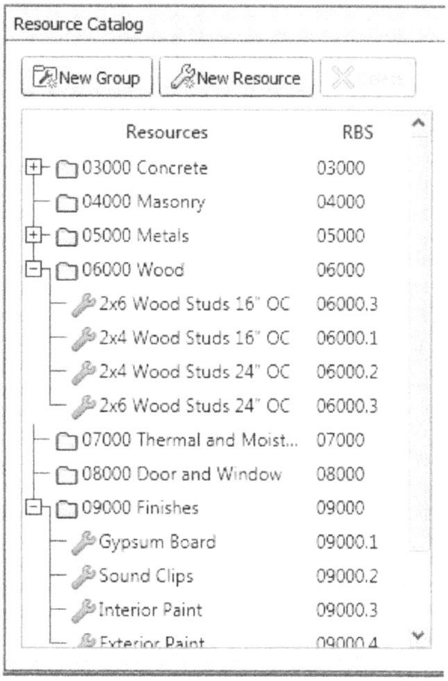

Figure 7–18

13. In the Resource Catalog window, expand the **03000 Concrete** resource grouping and ensure that it is selected. Click **New Group**. Enter **Rebar** as the name for the resource group and press <Enter>.

14. Ensure that the **Rebar** resource group is selected and click **New Resource**. Enter **Rebar #3** as the name for the resource and press <Enter>.

15. Ensure that the new resource is selected in the catalog. Note the default formulas in the Resource Calculations pane, as shown in Figure 7–19. They are used to calculate a takeoff value for this resource once it has been added to the workbook.

Resource Calculations

Variable	Formula	Units
Length	=ModelLength	Feet
Width	=ModelWidth	Feet
Thickness	=ModelThickness	Feet
Height	=ModelHeight	Feet
Perimeter	=ModelPerimeter	Feet
Area	=ModelArea	Square Feet

Figure 7–19

16. Return to the Item Catalog window. Expand the *Substructure>Foundations>Standard Foundations>Column Foundations & Pile Caps* group. Select the **Pile Caps** item as the location in which to place the new resource.

17. Return to the Resource Catalog window. Expand the *0300 Concrete>Rebar* resource group if not already done.

18. Select the **Rebar #3** resource, right-click, and select **Add To Selected Catalog Item**, as shown in Figure 7–20.

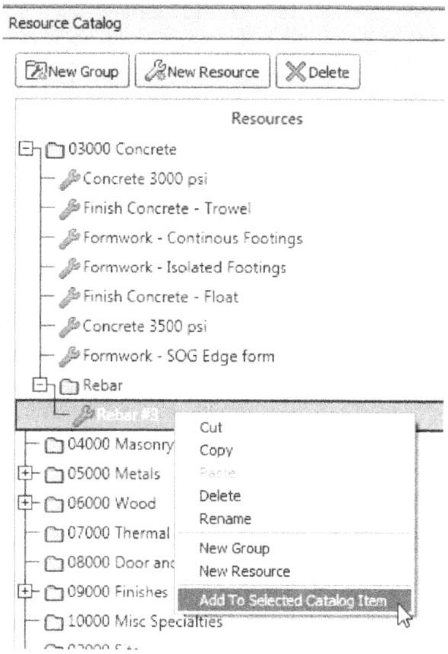

Figure 7–20

19. Return to the Quantification Workbook. Note that the Rebar #3 resource is now included in the Item Catalog for the Pile Caps item.

Task 3 - Duplicate items in the Item Catalog.

1. In the Item Catalog, select the **Pile Caps** item. Right-click and select **Copy**, as shown in Figure 7–21.

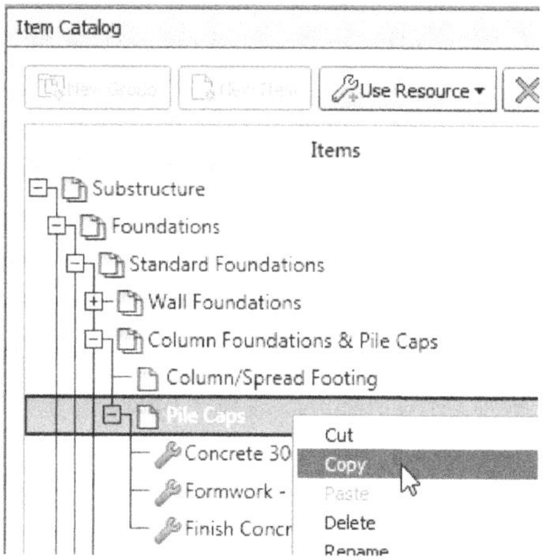

Figure 7–21

2. Select the parent **Column Foundations & Pile Caps** group. Right-click and select **Paste**.

3. Expand the copied Pile Caps item and note that all of the resources were copied with it.

4. Right-click on the first Pile Caps item and select **Rename**. Enter **Pile Caps-9 Pile** as the new name.

5. Rename the copied Pile Caps item as **Pile Caps-6 Pile.**

6. In the pane on the right, enter **03** as the *Work Breakdown Structure*, as shown in Figure 7–22, and press <Enter>.

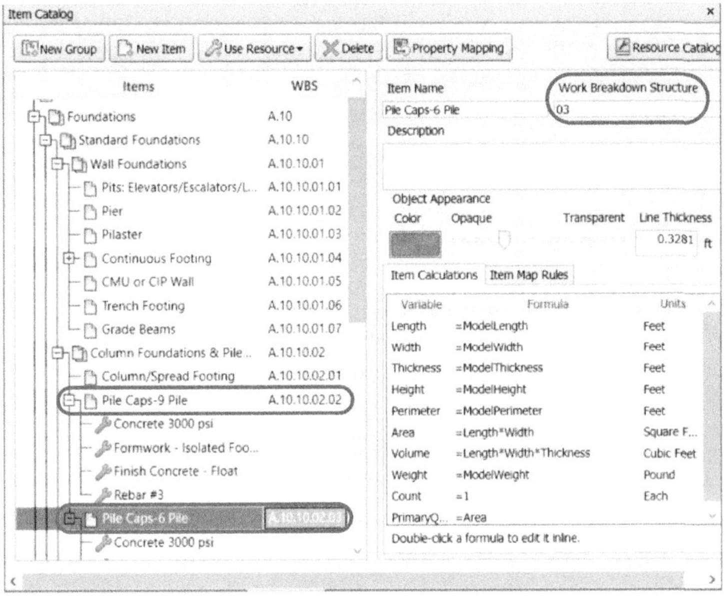

Figure 7–22

7. Return to the Quantification Workbook and note that the changes to the Pile Caps items are reflected in the Navigation pane.

8. Save the Navisworks file and leave it open. You will continue working on this file in the next practice.

7.4 3D Model and Virtual Takeoffs

Using the Quantification Workbook, you can perform a 3D model (automatic) takeoff or a virtual (manual) takeoff. The source model data determines if automatic model takeoff is possible. If your files retain their unique properties, including the globally unique identifier (GUID), from the original source software, you can perform model takeoff. A virtual takeoff can be used for items with no associated model geometry or properties.

- **Model takeoff** uses the data that has been exported from the design model (i.e., its properties) to derive the takeoff data for the report. Extracted objects are displayed as items in the Quantification Workbook.

- **Virtual takeoff** enables you to manually add takeoff items to the Quantification Workbook.

Object Selection for Takeoff

To conduct a model takeoff, you must select items in the scene. Selection can be accomplished using any of the following techniques:

- Select an object (group or above) directly in the scene view using your mouse.

- Expand items in the Selection Tree and click an object (group or above). Press and hold <Ctrl> to select multiple objects in the Selection Tree or <Shift> to select a range of objects.

  Note: If using the Selection Tree, ensure that the display is set to **Standard Tree**.

- Use the **Find Items** tool to find objects with the searched criteria. Once found, the objects are automatically selected.

  Note: Previously found items that were stored as sets can also be used to select objects.

- To select all of the objects that have the same name or type as an already selected object, you can use the **Select Same** tool. In the *Home* tab>Select & Search panel, expand the Select Same drop-down list and select **Same Name** or **Same Type**, as shown in Figure 7–23.

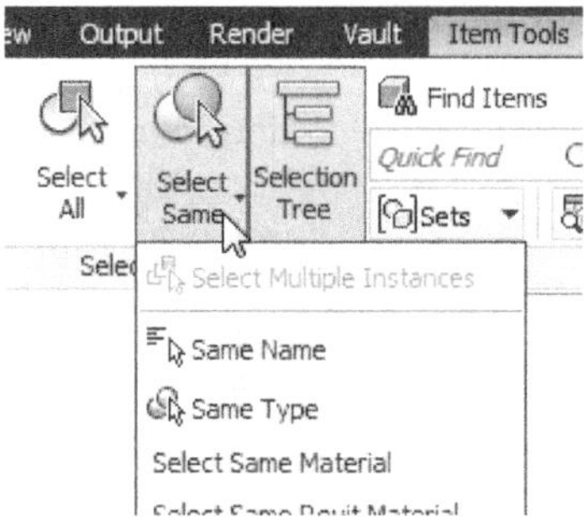

Figure 7–23

Model Takeoff

To conduct model takeoff, objects must be a group ( ) or instance (or). If you try to use an object that is a model ( ), layer ( ), collection ( ), or item ( ), or if it does not contain a GUID or properties, an error message displays (as shown in Figure 7–24). This indicates the object cannot be taken off.

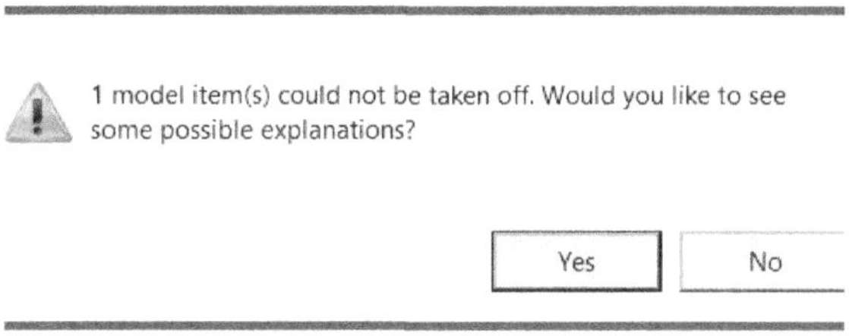

Figure 7–24

Note: Ensure that your workbook is in Item View before performing takeoff.

Globally Unique Identifier (GUID)

A globally unique identifier (GUID) is a unique value that is assigned to each object in a model. It is divided into several fields and written in groups of 8-4-4-4-12 hexadecimal characters (e.g., 71B923D4-ABCD-4BE4-861A-3A26146EF3F0).

When exporting files for use in Quantification, ensure that the export settings include object and GUID data.

Conducting a Model Takeoff

Once objects have been selected in the scene view, they can be taken off.

How To: Assign a Selected Scene Object to an Existing Workbook Item

1. In the Quantification Workbook, select the item to which you want to assign the scene object.
2. Add the selected object to the Quantification Workbook using one of the following:
   - Right-click in the Selection Tree and select **Quantification>Take off to: *<Name of Existing Item>*** (where *<Name of Existing Item>* represents the name of the item selected in the Quantification Workbook).
   - Right-click a selected object in the Selection Tree and select **Quantification>Select Corresponding Takeoff Objects**, as shown in Figure 7–25. The corresponding workbook item must be selected to assign the object(s).

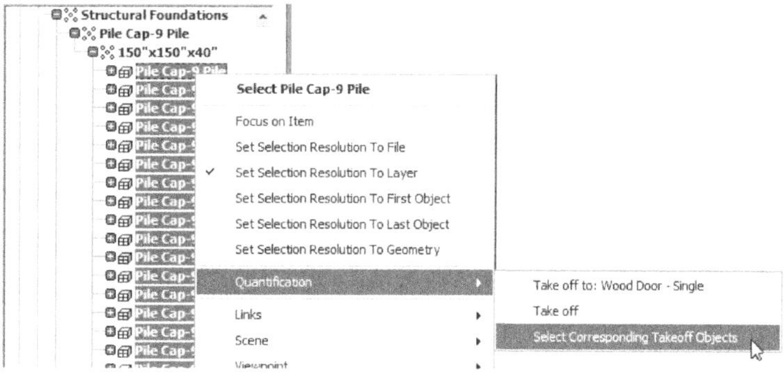

Figure 7–25

   - With the object(s) selected in the Selection Tree, in the Quantification Workbook, right-click the item to add the selected objects to and select **Take off Selected Model Items**, as shown in Figure 7–26.

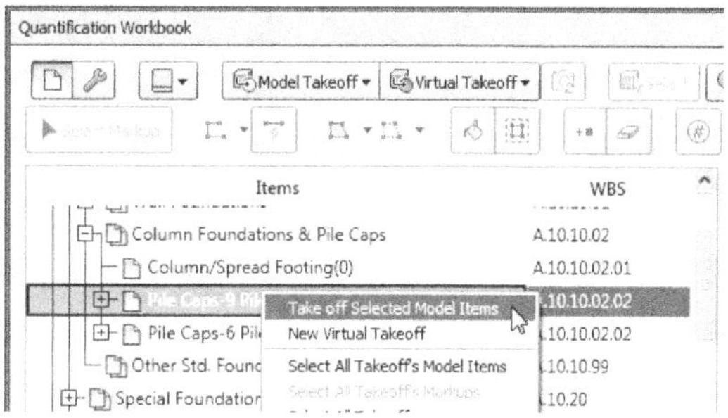

Figure 7–26

- With the object(s) selected in the Selection Tree, in the toolbar of the Quantification Workbook, click **Model Takeoff** and select **Take off to: *<Selected Item Name>***, as shown in Figure 7–27.

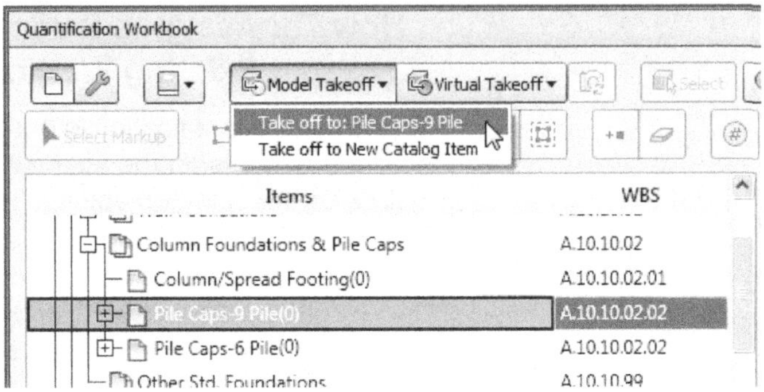

Figure 7–27

- Drag the selected object(s) into the Quantification Workbook's Navigation pane, as shown in Figure 7–28. When dragging to the Navigation pane, drop the object(s) by releasing the left mouse button on the item type. The item type does not need to be selected for this takeoff creation method.

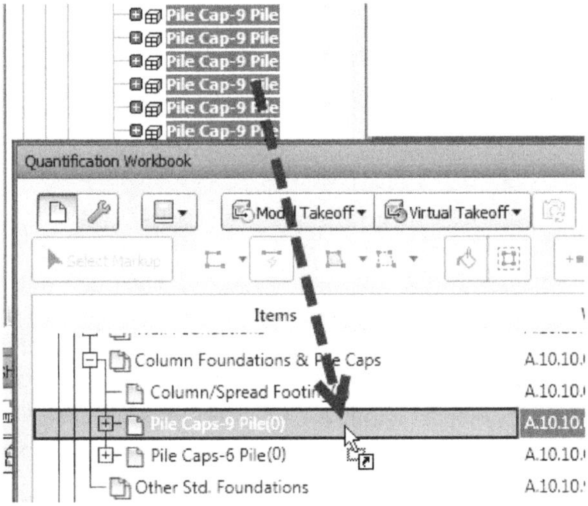

Figure 7–28

- Drag the selected object(s) into the Quantification Workbook's Takeoff pane, as shown in Figure 7–29.

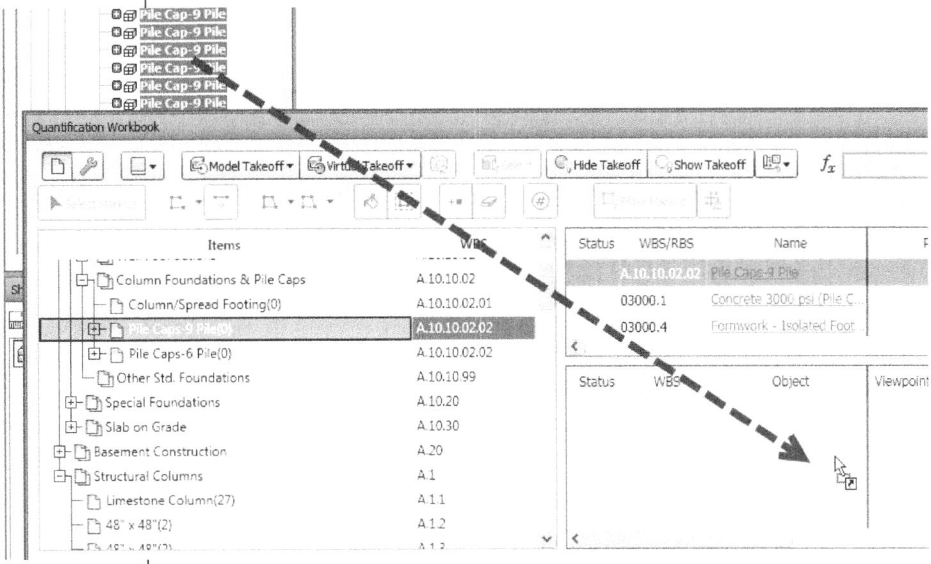

Figure 7–29

Workbook items might have been imported from an existing catalog as a starting point, or you might need to create items as you are generating the takeoff.

How To: Assign a Selected Scene Object to a New Workbook Item

1. Use any one of the techniques that were previously discussed to select objects in the scene.
2. Add the selected object to a new item using one of the following:
   - Right-click in the Selection Tree and select **Quantification>Take off to new catalog item**, as shown in Figure 7–30.

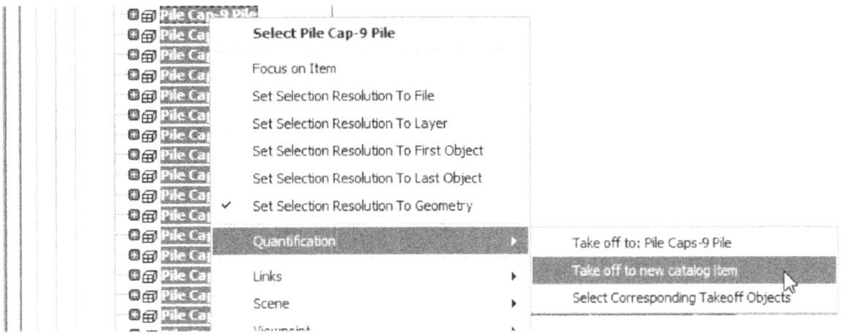

Figure 7–30

- With the object(s) selected in the Selection Tree, in the toolbar of the Quantification Workbook, click **Model Takeoff** and select **Take off to New Catalog Item**, as shown in Figure 7–31.

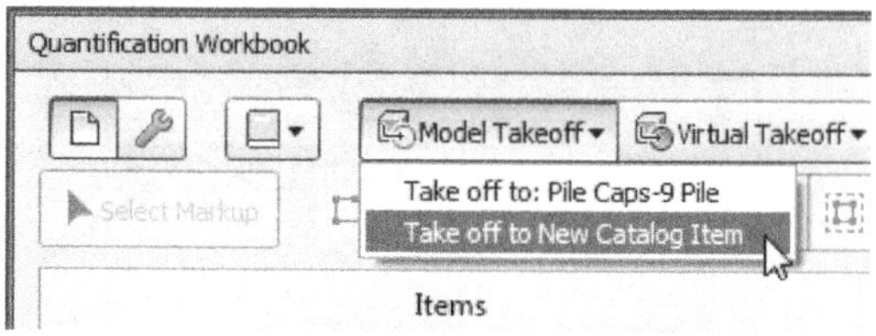

Figure 7–31

3. To rename the new item, double-click on its name in the Item Catalog, enter a new name, and press <Enter>.

How To: Use an Object Category to Create Items in a Workbook Group

1. In the Quantification Workbook, select the group you want to create new items in. Create a group, if required, using the Item Catalog.
2. At the top of the Selection Tree, expand the View Type drop-down list and select **Properties**. Expand *Category>Name Properties* to obtain a list of all the item types in the model.
3. Add the selected object to a new item using one of the following:
   - Right-click the property type to take off and select **Quantification>Take off to: *<Group to be added to>***, as shown in Figure 7–32.

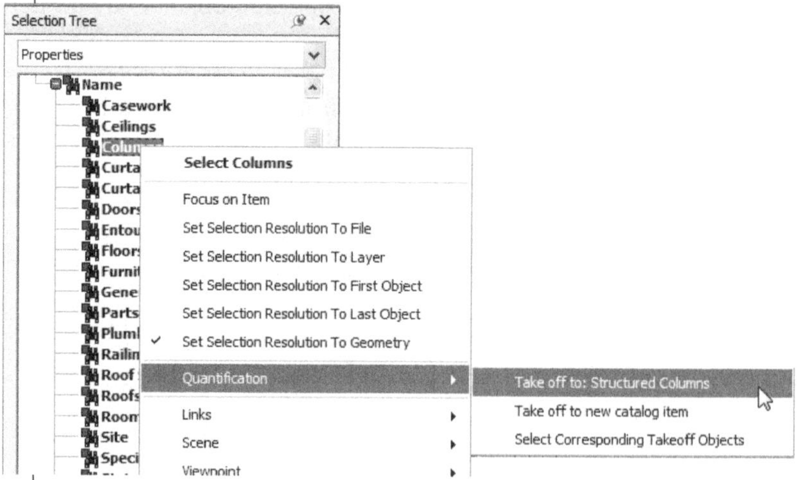

Figure 7–32

- Without any items selected in the Quantification Workbook, drag the selected property into the Quantification Workbook's Navigation pane, as shown in Figure 7–33. When dragging, drop the object(s) by releasing the left mouse button on the item type.

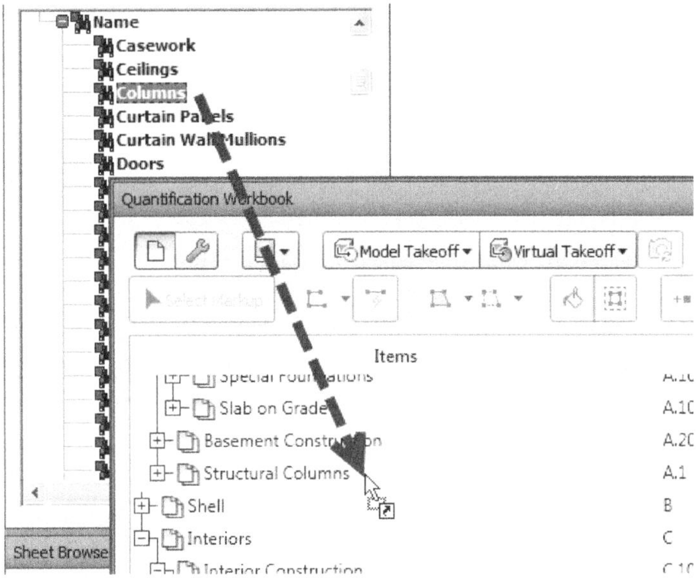

Figure 7–33

4. New item types are automatically added to the assigned group, and the takeoff data for each item is automatically populated, as shown in Figure 7–34.

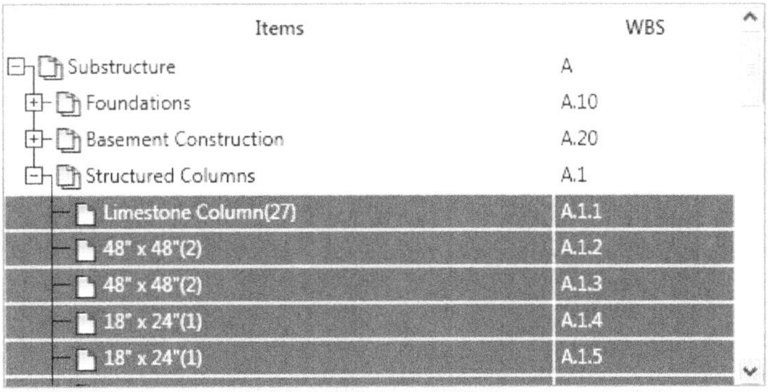

Figure 7–34

Virtual Takeoff

Virtual takeoffs are required when the object properties, whether the source includes geometry or not, cannot be used.

How To: Create a Virtual Takeoff

1. In the Quantification Workbook, click the item (🗋) that you want to contain the new virtual takeoff (e.g., Wood Door - Single).
2. To add a new virtual takeoff to the Quantification Workbook, use one of the following:
    - In the toolbar, click **Virtual Takeoff** and select **Create in: *<Selected Catalog Item>***, as shown in Figure 7–35.

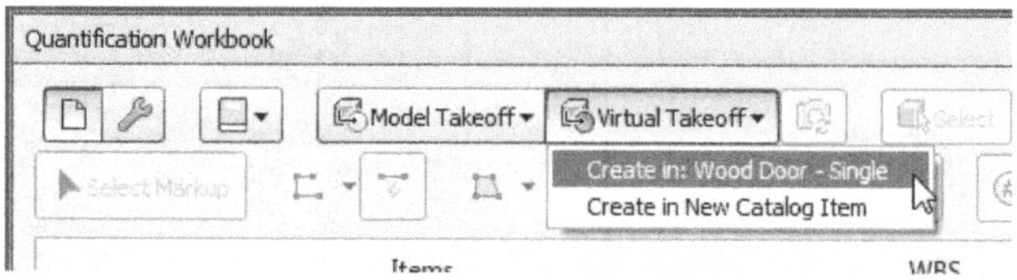

Figure 7–35

    - With the catalog item selected in the Quantification Workbook, right-click and select **New Virtual Takeoff**.
3. A new takeoff item is added to the Takeoff pane that includes the following:
    - The takeoff item with a default name.
    - A viewpoint based on the current model orientation.

   Note: Items added to the takeoff virtually are added one at a time.
4. To rename the new takeoff, select it in the Takeoff pane and enter a new name in the f_x field in the Quantification Workbook toolbar.
5. Use the Navisworks measurement tools as well as formulas to add property details, or enter values for those objects that might not be physically modeled in the scene. The takeoff fields may include *Length*, *Width*, *Thickness*, *Height*, *Perimeter*, *Area*, *Volume*, *Weight*, and *Count*.
6. In the Takeoff pane in the Quantification Workbook, navigate to the takeoff item you want to associate with the measurement. Double-click the takeoff formula cell that you want to change (e.g., *Height* or *Perimeter*) and enter the new measurement. Items that contain explicitly measured and entered values are identified with [icon] in the *Status* column of the Takeoff pane.

   Note: Items that are added to the Quantification Workbook using model takeoff can also have overwritten values and are identified with [icon] in the *Status* column of the Takeoff pane.

Working with Takeoff Viewpoints

A takeoff viewpoint is stored for a takeoff item that is created using Virtual Takeoff. The current orientation of the scene is the viewpoint that is stored when the Virtual Takeoff option is selected. This viewpoint is also stored in the Saved Viewpoints panel.

- To access the viewpoint for a takeoff item, click in the Takeoff pane in the Quantification Workbook or select the viewpoint in the Saved Viewpoints panel.
- To update the viewpoint associated with the virtual takeoff, right-click and select **Takeoff's Viewpoint>Add/Update**, or click (Add Viewpoint) in the Quantification Workbook toolbar.
- To remove the viewpoint associated with the virtual takeoff, right-click and select **Takeoff's Viewpoint>Remove**.

Although viewpoints are not automatically created using Model Takeoff, they can be added to the takeoff item.

- To create a viewpoint for a model takeoff item, select the item in the item list or in the Takeoff pane and click (Add Viewpoint) in the Quantification Workbook toolbar. If the item is selected in the item list, a viewpoint is created for all of its items, while selecting an item in the Takeoff pane enables you to select a single item. The icon is added to the *Viewpoint* column in the Takeoff pane and also to the Saved Viewpoints panel.

Redline markups can also be incorporated with the viewpoints that are stored with model and virtual takeoff data.

How To: Create a Redline in a Takeoff Viewpoint

1. Ensure that the viewpoint is active by clicking in the *Viewpoint* column associated with the takeoff.
2. Select the *Review* tab. Use the tools on the Redline panel to draw and add text as required and highlight areas in the viewpoint. The redline is only saved with the takeoff viewpoint.

Managing Takeoff Data

In the Quantification Workbook, there are a number of tools that you can use to manage and more efficiently create a takeoff report. You are able to:

- Change the columns that are displayed in the Quantification Workbook.
- Sort the column contents in the Quantification Workbook.
- Add comments to takeoff data.
- Change the appearance of the takeoff data.
- Control the display of items in the scene view based on whether they have been taken off or not.
- Delete the takeoff data.
- Remove overrides from the takeoff data.

Changing and Sorting Columns

The columns that are shown in the Takeoff or Rollup panes are assigned by default, but they can be customized for a project. Additionally, you can sort columns in ascending or descending order.

How To: Change the Columns Displayed in the Takeoff and Rollup Panes

1. In the Takeoff or Rollup pane of the Quantification Workbook, right-click a column header and select **Choose Columns**, as shown in Figure 7–36.

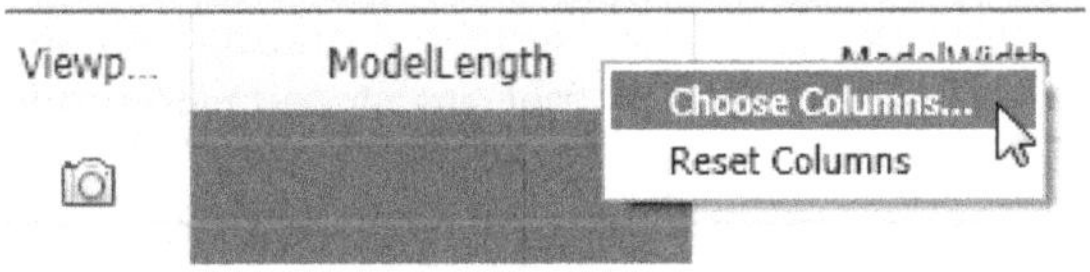

Figure 7–36

*Use **Show All** or **Hide All** to quickly display or suppress all of the columns.*

2. In the Choose Details Columns dialog box, select or clear the columns to be displayed and click **OK**, as shown in Figure 7–37.

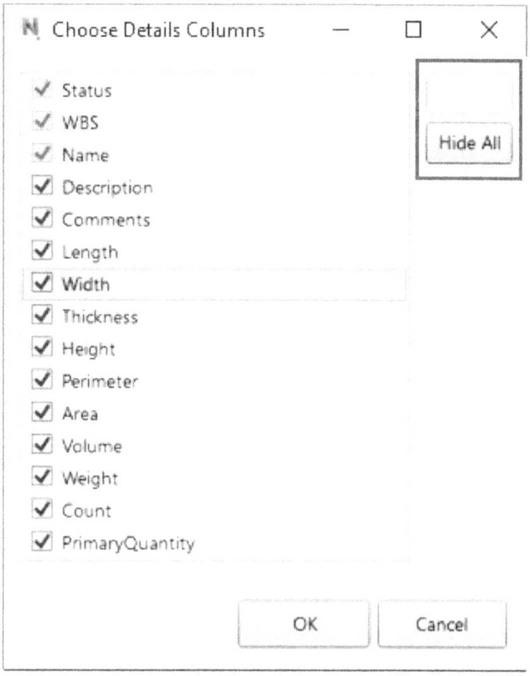

Figure 7–37

Columns can sorted by clicking on the column header. The ▲ icon indicates the column is sorted alphanumerically in ascending order, and the ▼ icon shows it is in descending order.

Adding Comments

Comments can be added to takeoff data to provide further annotation on takeoff information. A comment is given a number and is added to the Comments window with other comments. You can use the Find Comments tool to review any comments associated with the takeoff data.

How To: Add a Comment to Takeoff Data

1. In the Rollup pane in the Quantification Workbook, select a takeoff to display its information.
2. Right-click in the *Comments* field and click **Add Comment**, as shown in Figure 7–38. Alternatively, you can right-click a name in the Takeoff or Rollup pane and click **Add Comment**.

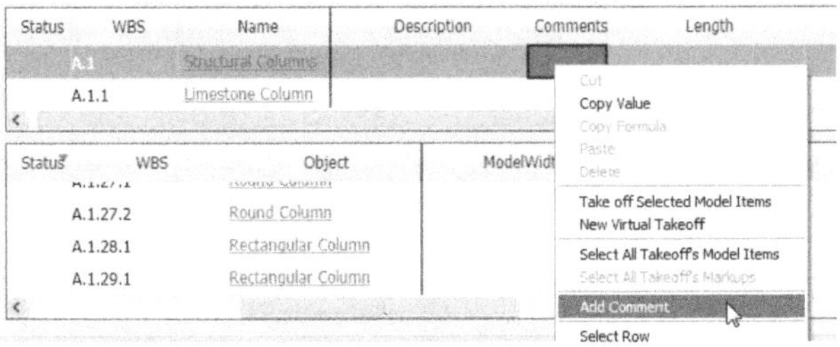

Figure 7–38

3. Type your comment in the Add Comment dialog box and click **OK**, as shown in Figure 7–39.

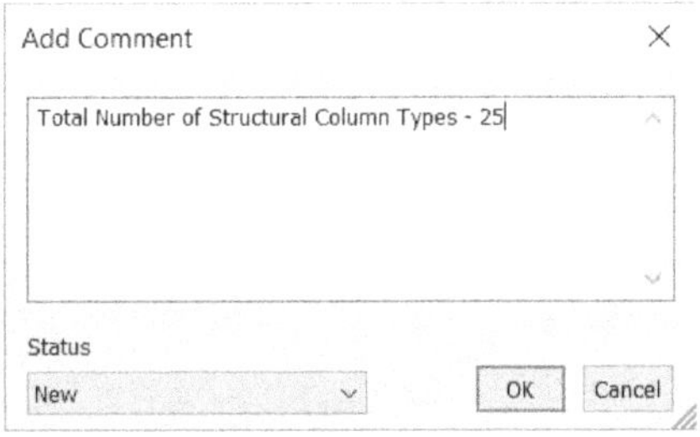

Figure 7–39

The comment number displays in the *Comments* cell in the Rollup pane and the comment is added to the Comments window, as shown in Figure 7–40.

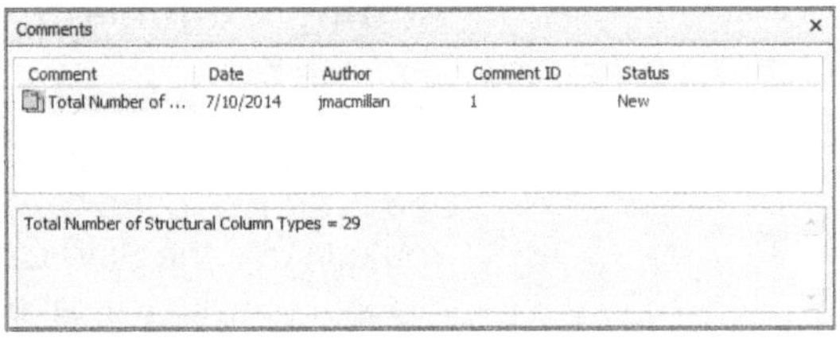

Figure 7–40

Controlling Takeoff Data Appearance

Once a scene item has been added to the Quantification Workbook, you can control its display appearance (color) in the scene based on the original model appearance or the takeoff appearance.

How To: Change the Takeoff Data Appearance

In the Quantification Workbook, click 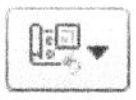 and select one of the following:

- **Reapply Quantification Appearance** sets the scene view to display the specific Item Catalog color for those items that have been taken off. All of the items that have been taken off are displayed with their assigned color and those not taken off remain with their original appearance.
- **Reapply Original Model Appearance** sets the scene view back to its original appearance (color).

Note: Controlling the appearance using the 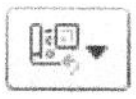 options is only available when the model is set to Shaded mode (not Full Render mode).

Controlling Item Display

When you add model items to the workbook, you can use tools in the Quantification Workbook toolbar to clear the display of items from the scene view as they are added, which enables you to ensure that all of the required items are added to the workbook and nothing is missed.

How To: Control the Scene Display Based on Taken Off Items

In the Quantification Workbook, use one of the following toolbar options:

- Click **Hide Takeoff** to hide all taken off model items and display all other model items.
- Click **Show Takeoff** to display only the taken off model items and hide the other model items.

Note: Click these icons a second time to clear the hide or show display option.

Deleting Takeoff Data

Model and virtual takeoff data can be deleted from the Quantification Workbook, if required.

How To: Delete a Takeoff Item

1. In the Quantification Workbook's Takeoff pane, select the takeoff that you want to delete.
2. In the toolbar, click **Update** and select **Delete Selected Takeoff**, as shown in Figure 7–41.

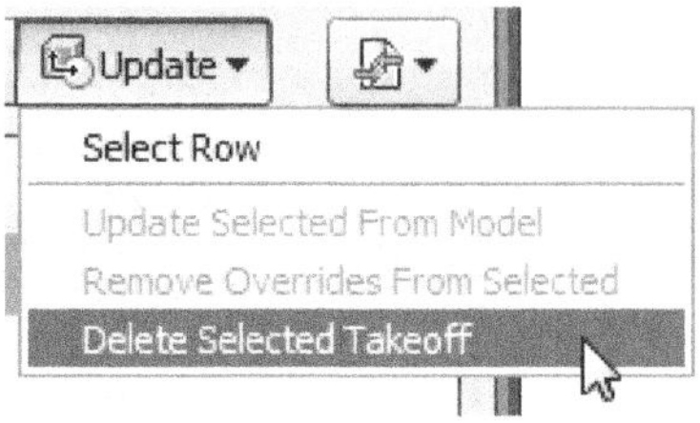

Figure 7–41

Resetting Takeoff Data

Overwritten model and virtual takeoff data can be reset from the Quantification Workbook, if required.

How To: Remove Overrides from a Takeoff Item

1. In the Quantification Workbook's Takeoff pane, select the takeoff that you want to reset.

   Hint: You can select individual cells in the Takeoff pane or you can select an entire row to clear all of the overrides in the row. To select an entire row, click **Update** and select **Select Row**.

2. In the toolbar, click **Update** and select **Remove Overrides From Selected**, as shown in Figure 7–42.

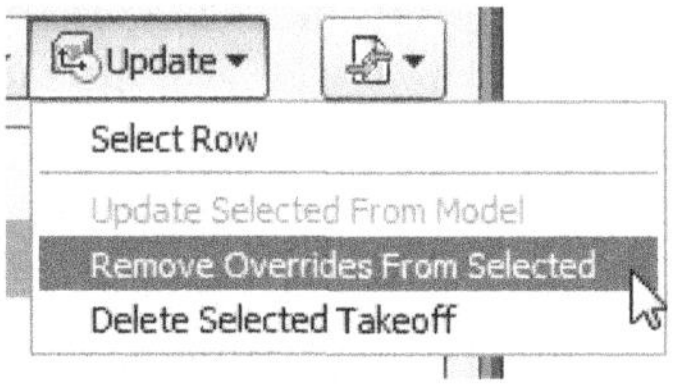

Figure 7–42

Note: This option is only available if there is an overwritten value for the item. Alternatively, you can right-click a cell and select **Remove Override**.

Practice 7b Creating and Working with 3D Model Takeoff Data

Practice Objectives

- Extract quantities from a model.
- Explore tools for managing the takeoff data.
- Perform a virtual takeoff.

In this practice, you will use the Quantification Workbook to extract quantities from the 3D Navisworks model. You will use tools to view the objects in your takeoffs, then conduct a virtual takeoff for objects not yet present in the model.

Task 1 - Conduct a model takeoff.

1. Continue to work on the file from the previous practice. If you did not complete that practice, open **School-Takeoff-3D.nwf** in the practice files *Quantification* folder.
2. In the Selection Tree, select **Site Layout-Edited.dwg**, right-click, and select **Hide** to hide the drawing.
3. In the Saved Viewpoints window, select **Structure** to change the viewpoint.
4. In the Quantification Workbook, expand the *Substructure>Foundations>Standard Foundations>Wall Foundations* group. Select the **Continuous Footing** item. This identifies the item to which the quantifications are going to be assigned.
5. Open the Sets window and select the **Continuous Footings** set at the bottom of the list. The Wall Foundation objects are selected in the Selection Tree.

6. Click and hold the left mouse button on the **Continuous Footing Selections** set in the Sets window. Drag the set to the Continuous Footing item in the Quantification Workbook and release the left mouse button on the Continuous Footing item to add the takeoff. Twenty Wall Foundation items should be added, as shown in Figure 7–43.

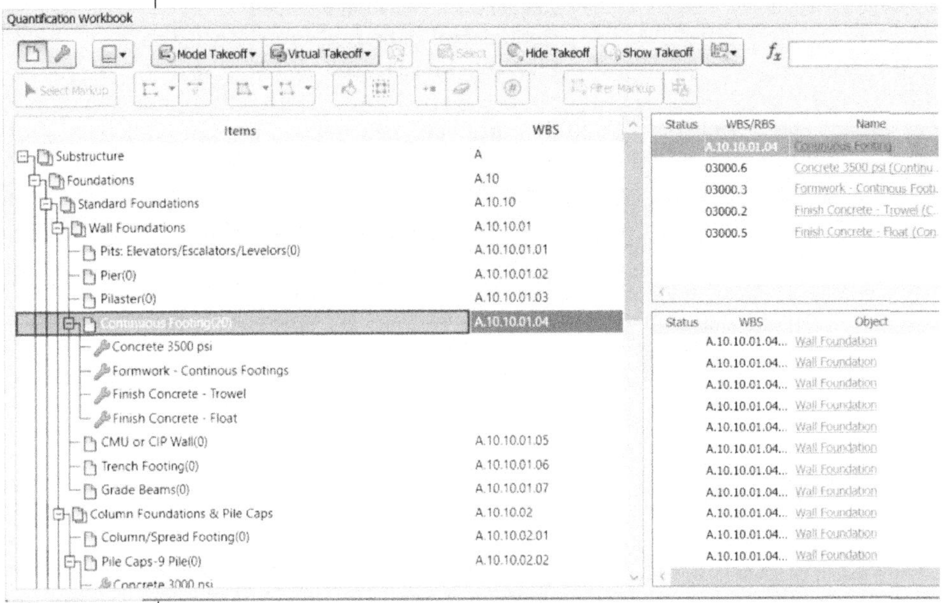

Figure 7–43

7. In the Rollup pane of the Quantification Workbook, scroll to the right to review the total volume of the Continuous Footing, as shown in Figure 7–44.

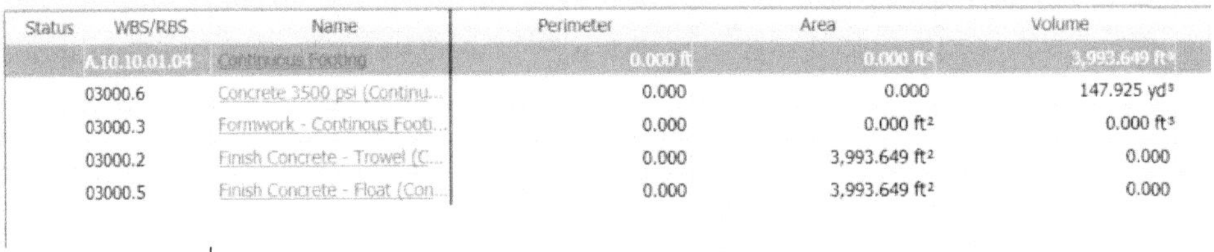

Figure 7–44

Note how the resources were automatically filled out for the Continuous Footing based on the element properties.

8. Close the Sets window.

9. In the Quantification Workbook, expand the *Substructure>Foundations>Standard Foundations>Column Foundations & Pile Caps* group. Select the **Pile Caps-9 Pile** item. This identifies the item to which the next quantification is going to be assigned.

10. In the *Home* tab, click **Find Items**. Conduct a search to locate all of the objects with the name Pile Cap-9, as shown in Figure 7–45, and click **Find All**.

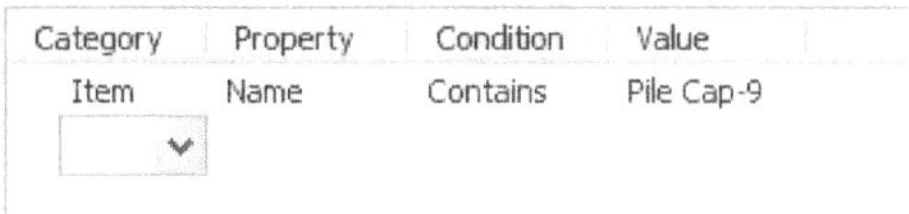

Figure 7–45

11. Once the items have been found, the Selection Tree files are expanded to display the selected items.

12. Return to the Quantification Workbook. Ensure that the **Pile Caps-9 Pile** item is still selected in the Navigation pane.

13. Right-click on any one of the selected Pile Cap-9 Pile objects in the Selection Tree and select **Quantification>Take off to: Pile Caps-9 Pile**, as shown in Figure 7–46.

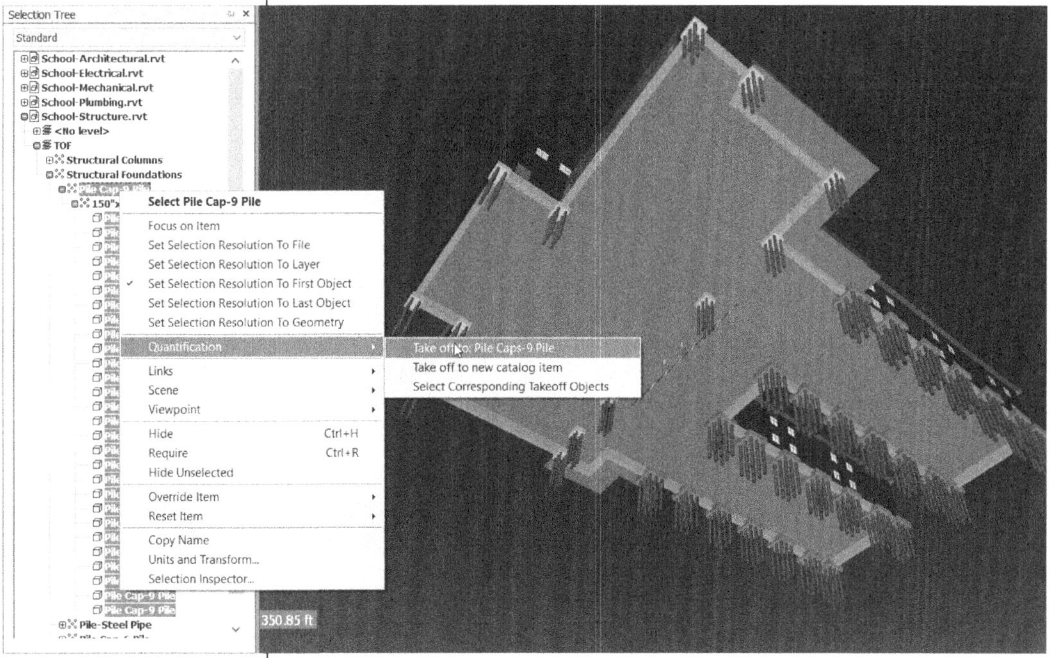

Figure 7–46

14. When prompted that one model item could not be taken off, click **No**. This prompt displays if any item is selected that cannot be taken off (e.g., Collections). This occurs if the Find Items tool is used and locates collection items that have the name that was being searched for but that cannot be taken off.

15. In the Selection Tree, press and hold <Ctrl> and click the **Pile Cap-9 Pile Collection** to clear it from the selection group.

16. In the Selection Tree, right-click on any one of the selected Pile Cap-9 Pile objects and select **Quantification>Take off to: Pile Caps-9 Pile**. Twenty-eight Pile Caps have been taken off.

17. Select all of the **Pile Cap-6 Pile** objects using any of the selection techniques.

18. Add the Pile Cap-6 Pile objects to their associated item in the Quantification Workbook. Thirteen Pile Caps have been taken off.

19. In the Quantification Workbook, expand the *Interiors>Interior Construction>Interior Doors>Standard Interior Doors* group. Select the **Wood Door - Single** item. This identifies the item to which the quantification is going to be assigned.

20. In the *Home* tab>Select & Search panel, enter **SINGLE** in the Quick Find field to search for a single-flush door, as shown in Figure 7–47.

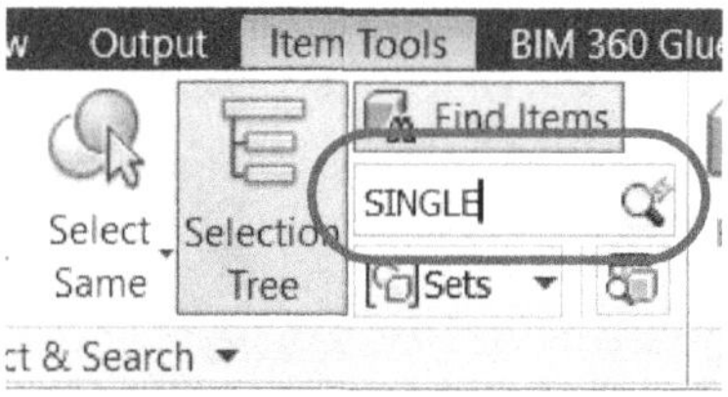

Figure 7–47

21. Once one of the Single-Flush doors has been selected in the Selection Tree, click the Select Same drop-down list in the Select & Search panel and select **Same Name**. All of the Single-Flush objects are selected in the Selection Tree.

22. With the objects selected in the Selection Tree, in the toolbar of the Quantification Workbook, click **Model Takeoff** and select **Take off to: Wood Door - Single**, as shown in Figure 7–48.

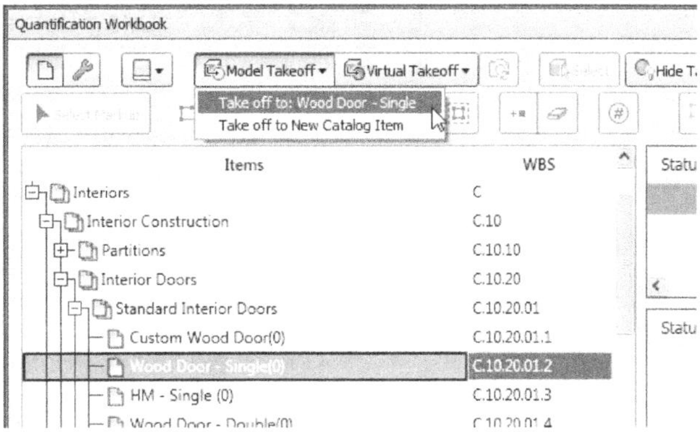

Figure 7–48

23. Click **No** when prompted that model items could not be taken off. As an alternative to clearing collections in the Selection Tree manually, you can run another search that only finds the required type. Clear all of the items from selection.

24. Open the Find Items window and add the criteria shown in Figure 7–49. Check the **Match Case** checkbox.

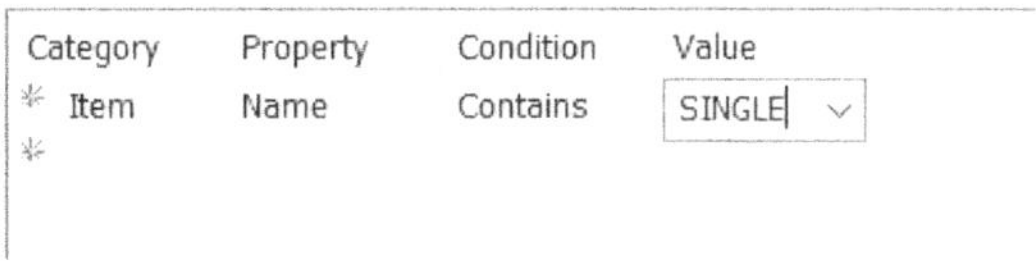

Figure 7–49

25. Conduct the search. As you did previously, in the Selection Tree, press and hold <Ctrl> and select the SINGLE collection to clear it from the selection group. There are two such collections, one for the first floor and one for the second floor.

26. Right-click one of the selected items in the Selection Tree and select **Quantification>Take off to: Wood Door - Single**. A total of 80 doors have now been added to the workbook, as shown in Figure 7–50.

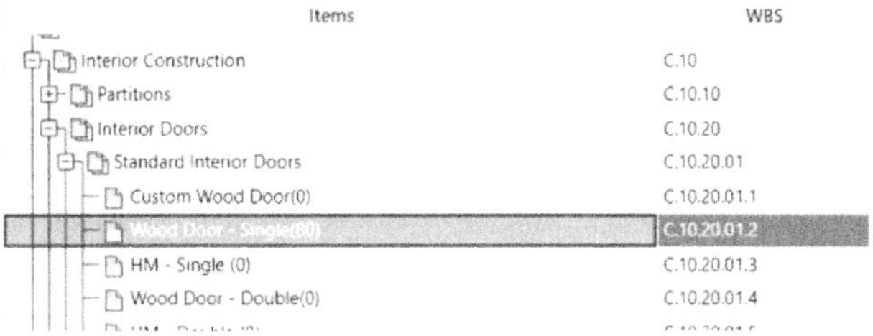

Figure 7–50

27. Close the Find Items window and save the Navisworks file.

Task 2 - Add catalog items directly from the model.

1. In the Item Catalog, select the **Substructure** group and click **New Group**. Enter **Structural Columns** as the name for the group and press <Enter>.
2. With the **Structural Columns** group selected, enter **30** as the *Work Breakdown Structure* in the pane on the right.
3. In the Selection Tree, expand *School-Structural.rvt>TOF*. TOF is the Top of Footing Revit level.
4. Select **Structural Columns**. Note that the structural columns in the model are now selected, just peeking out from over the pile caps. You will have to navigate around the model to see them, as shown in Figure 7–51.
5. Right-click the **Structural Columns** property and select **Quantification>Take off to: Structural Columns**, as shown in Figure 7–51.

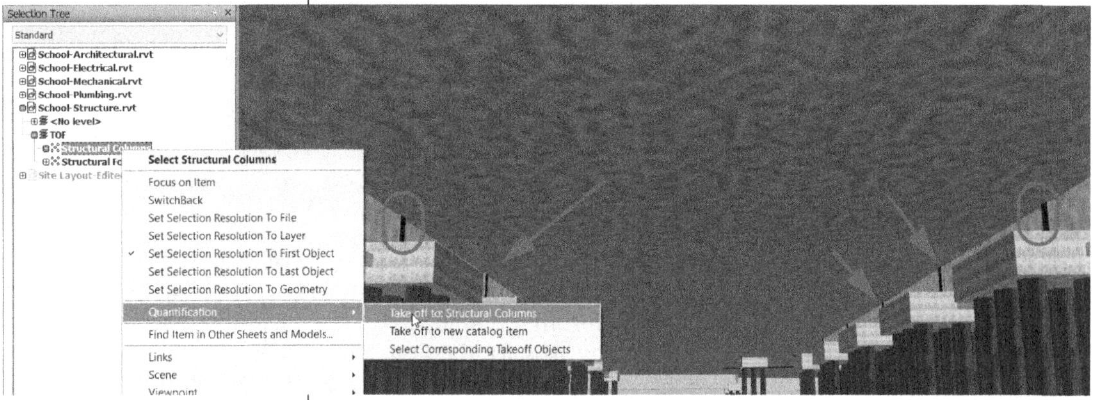

Figure 7–51

6. A total of 41 new item types have automatically been added to the item list and the takeoff data for each has been populated. This approach eliminates having to create the items individually.

Task 3 - Manage the quantification data.

1. Ensure that no objects are selected in the scene view.

2. In the Quantification Workbook, click (Hide Takeoff). All of the Pile Cap, Continuous Footing, Single-Flush Door, and Structural Column items are cleared from display in the scene view. This helps you to identify which scene objects are still left to take off.

   Note: This might be difficult to see without zooming into the model.

3. Click (Hide Takeoff) a second time to disable it and display all of the objects in the scene view.

4. Click (Show Takeoff) to display only the Pile Cap, Continuous Footing, Single-Flush Door, and Structural Column items in the scene view. This helps identify which items have already been taken off.

5. In the *Viewpoint* tab>Render Style panel, set the Mode to **Shaded**.

6. In the Quantification Workbook, click and select **Reapply Original Model Appearance** to set the scene view back to its original appearance (color).

   Note: Controlling the appearance using the options is only available when the model is set to Shaded mode (not Full Render mode).

7. Click and select **Reapply Quantification Appearance** to set the scene view to display the specific Item Catalog color for those items that have been taken off. All of the items that have been taken off are displayed with their assigned color (e.g., purple for Pile Caps) and those not taken off retain their original appearance.

8. Click (Show Takeoff) a second time to disable it.

9. In the Quantification Workbook, navigate to and select the **Pile Cap** items (*Substructure>Foundations>Standard Foundations>Column Foundations & Pile Caps*) in the Navigation pane. Select the **Pile Caps-9 Pile** item.

10. In the Takeoff pane, select the first Pile Cap item.

*<Page Down> is the keyboard shortcut for **Zoom Selected**.*

11. In the navigation bar, in the Zoom tools, click **Zoom Selected** to navigate to this item. Zoom out and reorient as required to obtain a good view of this first Pile Cap.

12. In the Quantification Workbook toolbar, click (Add Viewpoint) to save a viewpoint for this item. Note that a *Quantification Views* folder has been created in the Saved Viewpoints window.

13. Return to the **Structure** viewpoint. In the Quantification Workbook's Takeoff pane, click adjacent to the first Pile Cap-9 Pile item to change to the saved view, as shown in Figure 7–52. As an alternative, you can select the viewpoint in the Saved Viewpoints window in the *Quantification Views* folder.

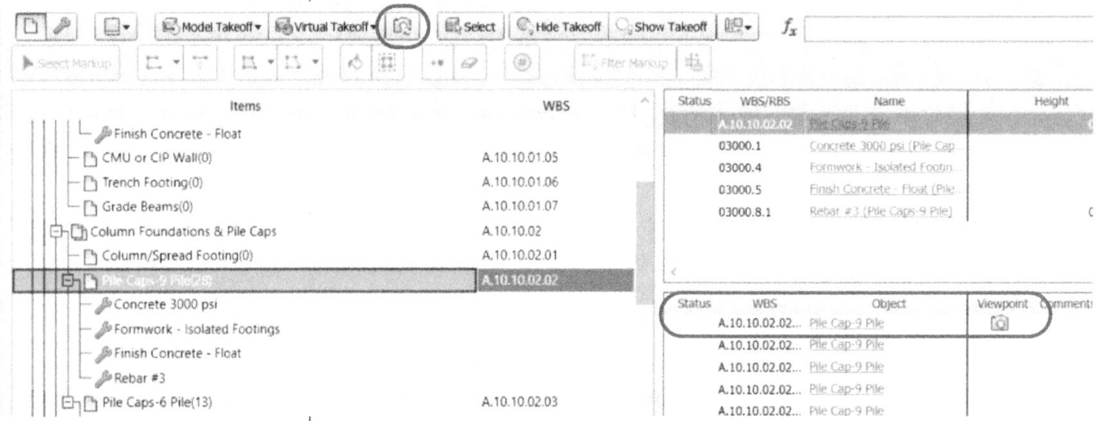

Figure 7–52

Hint: You can select multiple items and create the viewpoints at the same time.

Task 4 - Conduct a virtual takeoff.

1. In the Saved Viewpoints window, select **Turn2** to change the viewpoint.

2. In the Quantification Workbook, expand the *Interiors>Interior Construction>Interior Doors>Standard Interior Doors* group. Select the **Wood Door - Single** item.

   A number of doors have already been added using Model Takeoff. However, an office along this hallMway is missing a door, as shown in Figure 7–53. Because the door is not included in the source model, a virtual takeoff can be done to communicate this information.

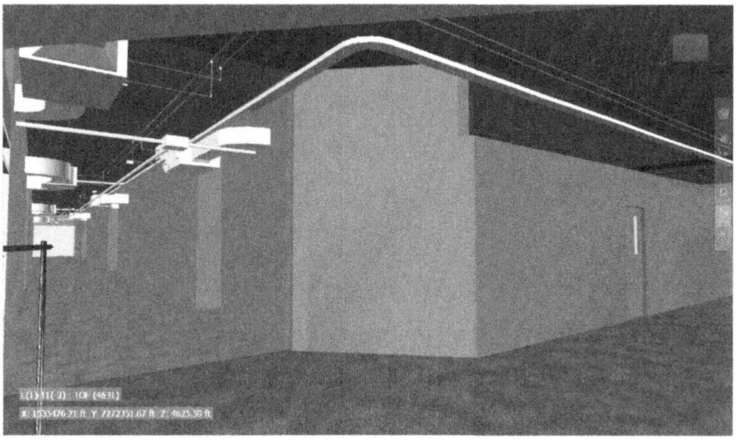

Figure 7–53

3. In the Quantification Workbook toolbar, click **Virtual Takeoff** and select **Create in: Wood Door - Single**, as shown in Figure 7–54.

Figure 7–54

4. A new takeoff item is added to the Takeoff pane that includes the following:
    - The takeoff item with a default name.
    - A viewpoint based on the current model orientation.

    Note: Items added to the takeoff virtually are added one at a time.

5. Select the *Name* cell for the virtual takeoff. Enter **Missing Door** in the f_x field in the Quantification Workbook toolbar.

6. In the Rollup pane, scroll and review the properties for the 81 doors. The quantity includes the virtual door. However, the model properties do not include the virtual property values as these fields are 0 by default.

7. In the columns for the Missing Door takeoff, enter the following property values:
    - ModelWidth = **3.000 ft**
    - ModelThickness = **0.167 ft**
    - ModelHeight = **7.00 ft**

    Note: Additional doors might be missing in this model, but you do not need to add any additional virtual takeoffs at this time.

8. In the Rollup pane, review the properties and note that the property values have been included in the totals for all doors.

9. Note that displays in the *Status* column. This indicates that fields in this item have been overwritten.

10. Click adjacent to the virtual takeoff item to activate it.

11. In the *Review* tab, select **Draw>Ellipse**.

12. Draw an ellipse on the office wall similar to the one shown in Figure 7–55. Select **Text** and pick a point inside the ellipse. Enter **Add Door** as a note in the viewpoint, as shown in Figure 7–55.

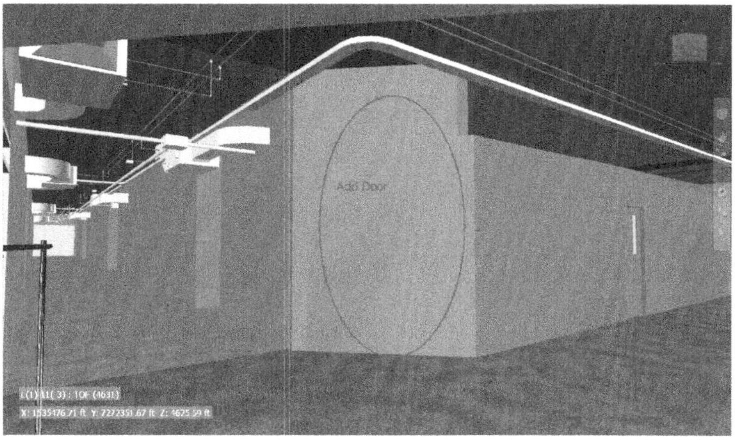

Figure 7–55

13. In the Saved Viewpoints window, select **Turn2** to change the viewpoint. Note that the redline is not included in this view.

14. Click adjacent to the virtual takeoff item and note that the redline is included in this view.

15. Save the Navisworks file and leave the file open. You will continue working on this file in the next practice.

7.5 2D Takeoffs

By using the 2D data in the project, you can measure and mark up geometry and perform accurate calculations for use in the Quantification Workbook. Both 2D and 3D quantification takeoffs can exist in the same workbook.

2D takeoff can be done using both native and scanned .DWF files. Non-native .DWF files (such as PDFs) can easily be converted to .DWF using print driver software for use in 2D takeoff or Autodesk TrueView. (See supported file formats in the Navisworks Help documentation.)

To conduct a 2D takeoff:

- 2D sheets must exist in the Navisworks project. Click  (Import Sheets & Models) in the Project Browser.
- The 2D sheets must be prepared/converted for use in the Navisworks project. Right-click a sheet name in the Project Browser and select **Prepare Sheet/Model** or **Prepare All Sheets/Models**.

Ensure the scale of the 2D sheets are the same as the 3D model.

Hint: Customizing Sheet Scale

When using 2D .DWFX data, it is important that the measurements taken are at the same scale as the data that is in the 3D model. To customize the sheet scale and display it in the Set Scale by Measurement window, complete the following:

1. Activate a 2D sheet.
2. In the *View* tab>Workspace panel, expand the Windows drop-down list and select **Set Scale by Measure**.
3. Click **New Measure**.
4. On the 2D sheet, trace a line that defines a length of geometry that has a length you already know.
5. In the Enter Value dialog box, type the known length and its unit and click **OK**. Once complete, the average scale displays.

To delete a measurement record, select a row, right-click, and select **Delete**. To delete a scale record, press <Delete> or right-click a row and select **Delete**.

2D Takeoff Tools

Similar to the 3D Takeoff tool, a Quantification project must be set up and the Item Catalog assigned in order to use 2D Takeoff. A 2D sheet must be activated in the Navisworks project using the Project Browser. By activating the 2D sheet, the 2D Takeoff tools are enabled. The tools are located in the second row of the Quantification Workbook's toolbar, as shown in Figure 7–56.

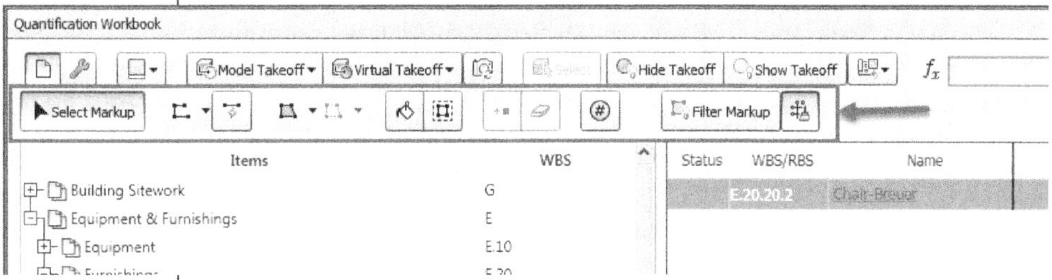

Figure 7–56

The following 2D takeoff types are discussed:

- Linear takeoffs
- Area takeoffs
- Count takeoffs

Linear Takeoffs

There are a number of commands in the 2D Takeoff toolbar that enable you to measure the length or perimeter of individual or multi-line geometry. The values obtained are added to the Quantification Workbook. The commands that can be used (shown in Figure 7–57) include:

- Polyline
- Rectangle Polyline
- Quick Line

Figure 7–57

How To: Conduct a Linear Takeoff

1. Activate the 2D sheet from which measurements will be taken to populate the takeoff data.
2. In the Item Catalog, select the item to which the 2D takeoff will be added.
3. Select a Linear measurement tool in the 2D Takeoff toolbar.
   - Click (Polyline) to measure single or multi-line segments when the length or perimeter is required and where the geometry is a non-standard shape.
   - Click (Rectangle Polyline) to measure perimeters. The tool creates a square or rectangular shape. Once drawn, you can move the vertices to create a different quadrilateral shape.
4. Conduct the measurement on the 2D sheet.
   - For a **Polyline** measurement, click on the sheet to position the start point for the measurement. As you move over existing geometry, the cursor changes to a snap (green vertex). Continue to select entities on the sheet to define the length or perimeter to be measured. To complete the polyline, select the start point a second time.
   - For a **Rectangle Polyline** measurement, click on the sheet to position the start point for the measurement. Select an entity in the opposite corner to define the rectangle.
5. The measurement is completed when:
   - the start point is selected a second time,
   - the second point in the Rectangular Polyline is selected, or
   - you press <Enter>.

   The takeoff item is added to the active item in the Item Catalog.

Hint: Draw Horizontal or Vertical Lines

When drawing a line using the (Polyline) tool, you can press and hold <Shift> to draw one that is perfectly horizontal or vertical.

The Quick Line tool in the 2D Takeoff toolbar is another measurement tool that can be used to obtain a linear takeoff on single or multi-line segments. To use this tool, click  (Quick Line) and click an entity on the sheet. Depending on the shape of the line, alternative Quick Line options may be available to more accurately define the measurement of the selected entity (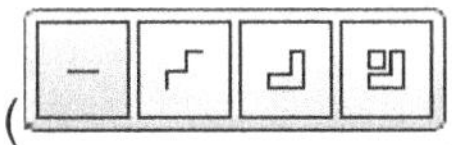). These options enable you to toggle between the selection of the selected single line segment, a polyline of lines connected to the selected line, a curve, or all connected curves.

Hint: Bucket Fill and Quick Box Tools

The Bucket Fill and Quick Box tools enable you to measure both linear and area takeoffs. These topics are discussed later in this section.

Area Takeoffs

Use the Area tools (shown in Figure 7–58) to build up multiple line segments of a polygon or trace a rectangle straight onto the sheet to obtain the area of the traced entities. Once the entities are traced, the area is automatically measured and a new takeoff item is added to the Quantification Workbook.

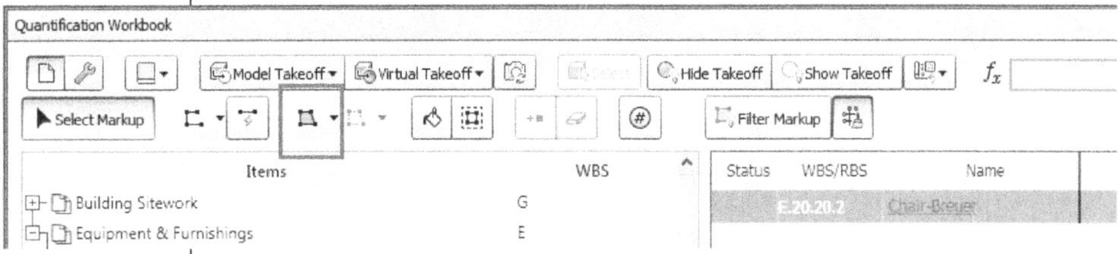

Figure 7–58

How To: Conduct an Area Takeoff

1. Activate the 2D sheet from which the measurements will be taken to populate the takeoff data.
2. In the Item Catalog, select the item to which the 2D takeoff will be added.
3. Select an Area measurement tool in the 2D Takeoff toolbar:
   - Click  (Area) to measure the size (area) of a non-rectangular area.
   - Click  (Rectangle Area) to measure the size (area) of a rectangular area.

4. Conduct the measurement on the 2D sheet.
   - Click on the sheet to position the start point for the **Area** measurement. Continue to select entities on the sheet to define the area to be measured. To complete the area, either select the start point a second time or right-click. As you select entities, a blue highlight displays, defining the area. Once drawn, you can move the vertices to create a different quadrilateral shape.
   - Click on the sheet to position the start point for the **Rectangle Area** measurement. Select an entity in the opposite corner to define the rectangle.
5. The measurement is completed when:
   - the start point is selected a second time,
   - you right-click to automatically close the area,
   - the second point in the Rectangle Area is selected, or
   - you press <Enter>.

   The takeoff item is added to the active item in the Item Catalog.

Backout Tools

When an area takeoff is conducted, there might be an area within the overall area that is not required in the takeoff value. For example, if an office has a column inside it, the column must be omitted to provide an accurate value for the available floor space, as shown in Figure 7–59. To remove a portion of an overall area, use the **Backout** commands.

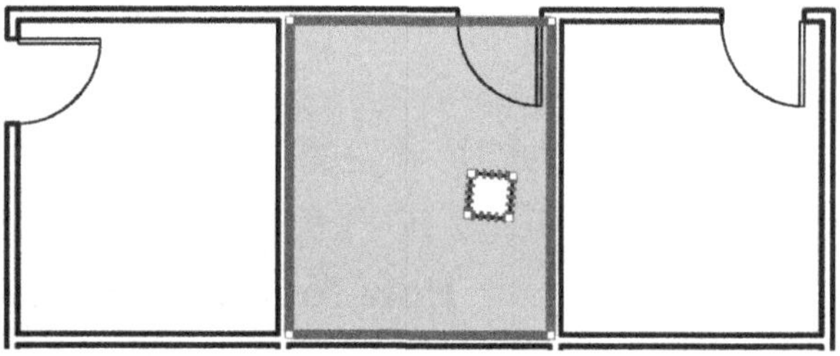

Figure 7–59

How To: Use Backout to Modify an Area Takeoff

1. Ensure that the area takeoff from which an area will be removed is selected in the Takeoff pane.
2. Select a Backout tool in the 2D Takeoff toolbar.
    - Click (Backout) to remove a non-rectangular area from a larger takeoff.
    - Click (Rectangle Backout) to remove a rectangular area from a larger takeoff.
3. Trace the area on the 2D sheet.
    - Click on the sheet to position the start point for the **Backout**. As you move over existing geometry, the cursor changes to a snap (green vertex). Continue to select entities on the sheet to define the length or perimeter to be measured. To complete the backout, either select the start point a second time or right-click. Once drawn, you can move the vertices to create a different quadrilateral shape.
    - Click on the sheet to position the start point for the **Rectangle Backout**. Select an entity in the opposite corner to define the rectangle.
4. The backout is completed when:
    - the start point is selected a second time,
    - you right-click to automatically close the area,
    - the second point in the Rectangle Backout is selected, or
    - you press <Enter>.

    The original takeoff item is updated to reflect the removal of the backout area.

Bucket Fill and Quick Box Tools

With the Bucket Fill and Quick Box tools in the 2D Takeoff toolbar, you can create either linear or area takeoff entries in the Quantification Workbook.

- The **Bucket Fill** tool selects within a geometry boundary to define the linear measurement or area for a takeoff item.

  Click (Bucket Fill) and click within an area to select all entities that are required to define a closed area. A linear measurement is identified (as shown on the left in Figure 7–60) with the first selection. Select again in the same area to obtain an area measurement (as shown on the right in Figure 7–60). While in the command, the last measurement type (linear or area) is used to define each successive selection. Press <Enter> to accept the measurement and add it to the selected item in the Quantification Workbook.

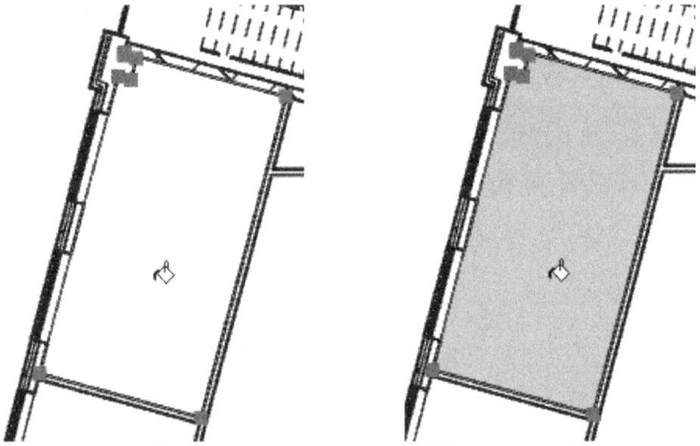

Figure 7–60

- The **Quick Box** tool enables you to efficiently drag a bounding box over existing geometry to select the length of multiple entities or an area for takeoff measurement. Click (Quick Box) and drag a bounding box over existing entities. Depending on the shape of the entities in the bounding box, Quick Box options appear to more accurately define the measurement ( ). These options enable you to toggle between multiple options. Hover over each item to preview its selection. Select the option to add the takeoff to the selected item in the Quantification Workbook. Similar to Bucket Fill, if you select within the enclosed area in the scene view (prior to finalizing the takeoff), it toggles the selection from a linear to an area measurement.

Count Takeoffs

A count takeoff is used to record the number of items. For example, it can be used to count the number of desks in an office. The process involves adding count pins to your 2D sheet. Each pin then becomes a takeoff value in the Quantification Workbook.

How To: Conduct a Count Takeoff

1. Activate the 2D sheet from which measurements will be taken to populate the count takeoff data.
2. In the Item Catalog, select the item to which the count takeoff will be added.
3. On the 2D Takeoff toolbar, click (Count) to position a count pin.
4. On the 2D sheet, click to position count pin(s). The Rollup pane displays the total count.

   Hint: To delete a count pin, select it and press <Delete>. As an alternative, you can use the Erase tool. Select the count pin so that it displays as blue, click (Erase), and select the pin again on the sheet to remove it. The takeoff value automatically updates.

Hint: Counting Items Using the Selection Tree

Similar to 3D quantification (in which you can select and use items directly from the 3D model's Selection Tree), when doing 2D quantification using a .DWFX file with properties, you can drag items into the Quantification Workbook to add a count takeoff. Linear and/or area measurements are not added to the object. This type of count takeoff can only be done on .DWFX files that were created with a source 3D CAD model, where the model's properties were maintained in the .DWFX file.

Additional 2D Takeoff Tools

The following additional 2D Takeoff tools can be used to efficiently work with 2D takeoffs.

- The **Select Markup** option enables you to activate the selection tool for selecting 2D takeoffs on a sheet. Once enabled, you can select single or multiple takeoffs. Multiple takeoffs can be selected by pressing and holding <Ctrl> and clicking the individual takeoffs on the sheet, or by dragging a box around the takeoffs.

- To edit the shape of a linear or area takeoff, you can select and drag any of the vertices that define the shape, or use the (Add Vertex) tool on the 2D Takeoff toolbar and select on an active entity to add additional vertices for dragging. Press <Enter> to update the takeoff values.

- The **Filter Markup** option enables you to clear unselected takeoffs from the display on the sheet. Select a takeoff in the Takeoff pane (not in the scene view) or select a category or item in the Quantification Workbook and use the command. To clear the filter, select the button again.
    - When an item is selected and the **Filter Markup** option is selected, all but the selected markup is removed from the sheet.
    - When a category is selected and the **Filter Markup** option is selected, all items in the selected category remain displayed, while any others outside of the category are removed from the sheet.

- The (Hide background and annotations) option can be used to help with visibility by toggling off the display of background images and annotations from a 2D worksheet.

  Once enabled, click a second time to toggle the background images and annotations on again. This tool will only clear backgrounds and annotations in files that were created with a source 3D CAD model where the backgrounds and annotations are identified as such.

- To quickly review a takeoff item in the Takeoff pane (when the item is not easily located), you can select the takeoff in the scene view, right-click, and select **Select Corresponding Takeoff Objects**.

- To temporarily zoom to a selected takeoff, select it in the scene view and press and hold the <Space Bar>. Once you release the <Space Bar>, the viewpoint returns to the previous zoom level and location.

Practice 7c Creating and Working with 2D Takeoff Data

Practice Objectives

- Take off linear 2D elements.
- Take off areas for quantification.
- Perform counting for individual takeoff elements.

In this practice, you will use the Quantification Workbook to add quantities by tracing over 2D geometry and by counting individual objects.

A new wing planned for the school is in its preliminary state and only 2D sketches are available. Initial quantities are required.

Task 1 - Conduct linear and area 2D takeoffs.

1. Continue to work on the file from the previous practice. Alternatively, if you did not complete that practice, open **School-Takeoff-2D.nwf** in your *Quantification* practice files folder.

2. In the *View* tab>Workspace panel, expand the Windows drop-down list and select **Sheet Browser** to display it, if not already displayed. In the Sheet Browser, click (Import Sheets & Models). Open **Proposed-School-Wing.dwfx** from your *Quantification* practice files folder. Four 2D sheets are added to the project.

3. If the four new sheets have the icon adjacent to them, they need to be prepared for use in Navisworks. Click on one of the sheets in the Sheet Browser, right-click, and select **Prepare All Sheets/Models**.

4. Double-click on the **Sheet: A103 - First Floor Plan** sheet in the Sheet Browser to activate it.

5. Navigate to the area shown in Figure 7–61.

Figure 7–61

6. In the Item Catalog, expand the *Interiors>Interior Finishes> Floor Finishes* group. Click **New Item**. Enter **Sheet Vinyl** as the name for the item and press <Enter>. Add **Office Carpet** and **Ceramic Floor** as additional items, as shown in Figure 7–62.

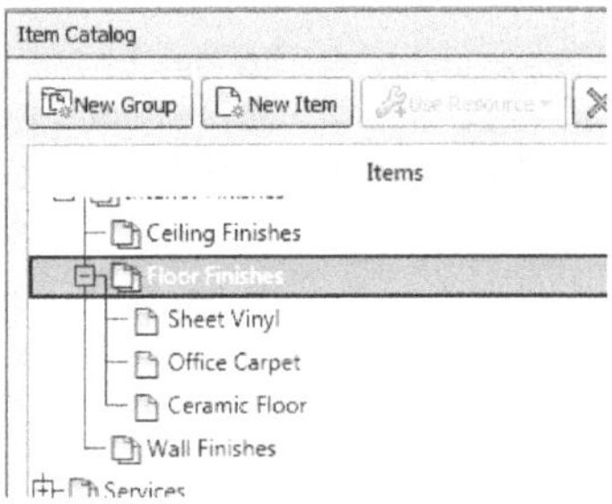

Figure 7–62

7. Return to the Quantification Workbook and select the **Office Carpet** item, if not already selected.

8. In the 2D Takeoff toolbar, click (Polyline) to measure the perimeter of a non-rectangular shape.

9. Click on the sheet to position the start point for the Polyline measurement, as shown at point 1 in Figure 7–63. Continue to select the points (2, 3, 4) that define the shape of this office. To complete the polyline, select the start point (1) a second time. The takeoff is added to the workbook.

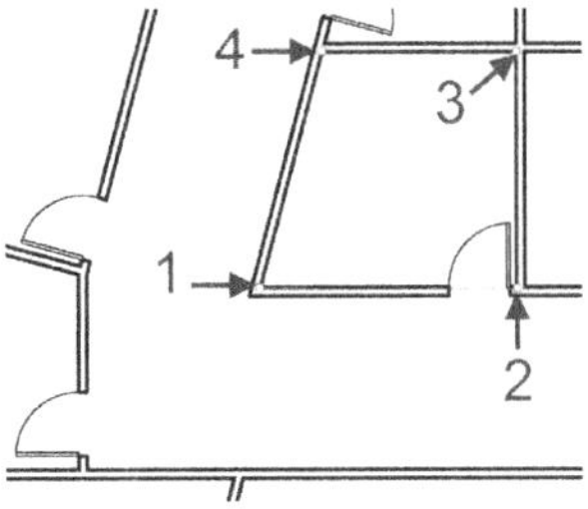

Figure 7–63

10. In the Quantification Workbook, review the Rollup and Takeoff panes for the newly added quantification data for the office, as shown in Figure 7–64. This quantification value measured the perimeter of the office and not the area that is required for a carpet measurement.

Status	WBS/RBS	Name	Length	Width	Thickness	Height	Perimeter	Area
	C.30.20.2	Office Carpet	44.520 ft	0.000 ft	0.000 ft	0.000 ft	44.520 ft	0.000 ft²

Status	WBS	Object	ModelLength	ModelWidth	ModelThickness	ModelHeight	ModelPerimeter
	C.30.20.2.1	Office Carpet 1	44.520 ft				44.520 ft

Figure 7–64

Note: It is always important to review the takeoff data to ensure that it is reporting the required information.

11. In the Takeoff pane, right-click **Office Carpet 1** and select **Delete Takeoff** to remove it from the workbook.

12. In the 2D Takeoff toolbar, click  (Area) to measure the area of a non-rectangular shape.

13. Click on the sheet to position the start point for the Area measurement, as shown at point 1 in Figure 7–65. Continue to select the points (2, 3, 4) that define the shape of this office. To complete the area measurement, either select the start point (1) a second time or right-click after making the fourth selection.

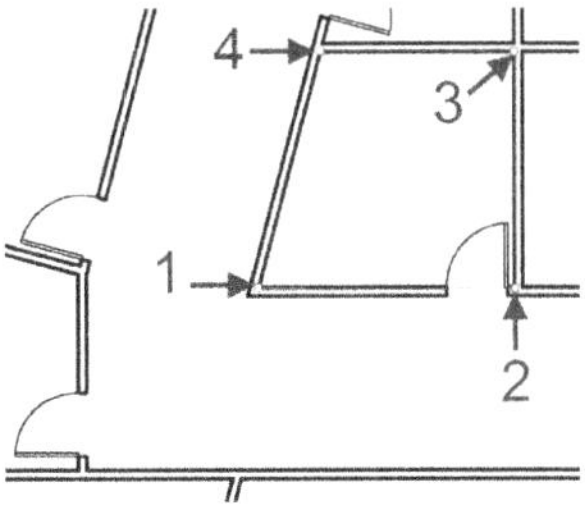

Figure 7–65

14. In the Quantification Workbook, review the Rollup and Takeoff panes for the required quantification data that measures the area of the office, as shown in Figure 7–66.

Status	WBS/RBS	Name	Length	Width	Thickness	Height	Perimeter	Area	Volume
	C.30.20.2	Office Carpet	0.000 ft	0.000 ft	0.000 ft	0.000 ft	44.523 ft	121.817 ft²	0.000 ft³

Status	WBS	Object	ModelLength	ModelWidth	ModelThickness	ModelHeight	ModelPerimeter	ModelArea
	C.30.20.2.1	Office Carpet 1					44.523 ft	121.817 ft²

Figure 7–66

Note: The (Polyline) and (Area) tools are measured in the same way; however, they provide different results. Polyline is for linear measurements and Area measures surface area. Ensure that you select the correct command for the required measurement. In a similar way, the

(Rectangle Polyline) and (Rectangle Area) tools produce linear and area measurements, respectively.

15. In the 2D Takeoff toolbar, click (Rectangle Area) to measure the area of the rectangular office to the right of the previously measured office. Ensure that the **Office Carpet** item is still selected. Select two opposing corners in the room to define the area.

16. Click on the sheet to position the start point for the Rectangle Area measurement. Select an entity in the opposite corner to define the rectangle. Review the Rollup and Takeoff panes. Note that two takeoffs now exist, as shown in Figure 7–67.

Status	WBS/RBS	Name	Length	Width	Thickness	Height	Perimeter	Area	Volume
	C.30.20.2	Office Carpet	0.000 ft	0.000 ft	0.000 ft	0.000 ft	85.764 ft	227.442 ft²	0.00

Status	WBS	Object	ModelLength	ModelWidth	ModelThickness	ModelHeight	ModelPerimeter	ModelArea
	C.30.20.2.1	Office Carpet 1					44.523 ft	121.817 ft²
	C.30.20.2.2	Office Carpet 2					41.241 ft	105.625 ft²

Figure 7–67

17. Pan upwards to one of the rectangular offices that have a column, as shown in Figure 7–68.

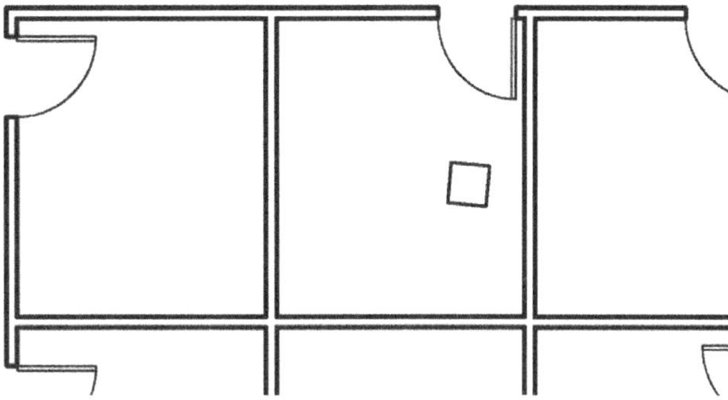

Figure 7–68

18. In the 2D Takeoff toolbar, click (Rectangle Area) and measure the area of the entire office. Review the area value in the Takeoff pane.
19. In the 2D Takeoff toolbar, click (Backout) and select the four vertices that define the outline of the column, as shown in Figure 7–69. Right-click to clear the selection once the fourth vertex is selected. Review the area in the Takeoff pane. The column's area has been removed.

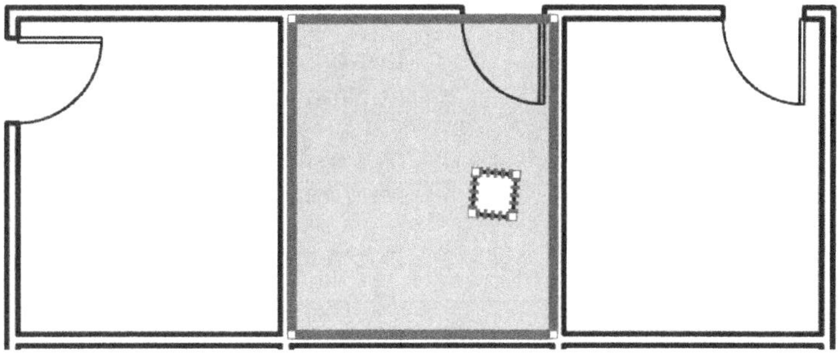

Figure 7–69

20. In the Quantification Workbook, select the **Ceramic Floor** item.

21. In the 2D Takeoff toolbar, click (Area) and measure the ceramic corridor flooring in the area shown in Figure 7–70. Zoom in and pan as you are selecting vertices for the takeoff to accurately make selections.

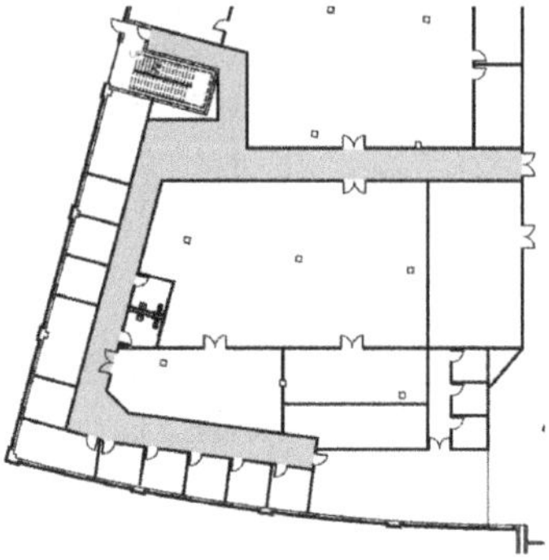

Figure 7–70

22. In the Quantification Workbook, return to one of the Office Carpet items and select it in the Takeoff pane. The sheet automatically reorients to show these takeoffs. This is a good way to quickly change the view to review the takeoffs.

23. In the scene view, select the takeoff that was done in the hallway (Ceramic), right-click, and select **Select Corresponding Takeoff Objects**. Note that the Quantification Workbook now displays the information on this takeoff. This is a good way to locate a takeoff when you do not know its category.

24. In the Quantification workbook, select the **Sheet Vinyl** item in the *Floor Finishes* group.

25. Zoom to the location shown in Figure 7–71 and use the (Area) command to measure the overall area of the room by defining the four corners. This room will be a kitchen with vinyl flooring.

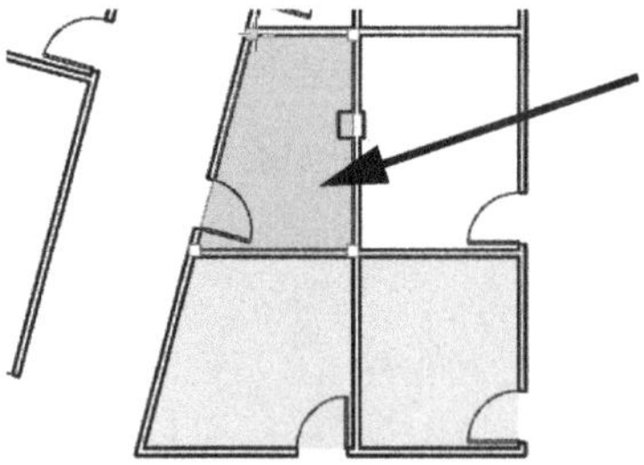

Figure 7–71

26. An area where the column comes into the room must be removed. This is not an enclosed area in the room so the Backout tool is not appropriate. With the takeoff still selected, in the 2D Takeoff toolbar, click  (Add Vertex) and make the four selections shown in Figure 7–72 to add four vertices near the column.

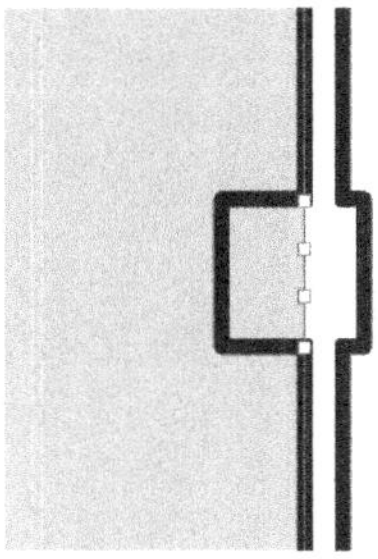

Figure 7–72

27. Press <Esc> to clear the **Add Vertex** command. Drag the two middle vertices to trace the shape of the column, as shown in Figure 7–73. Press <Enter> to complete the edit. The takeoff value updates to reflect the change.

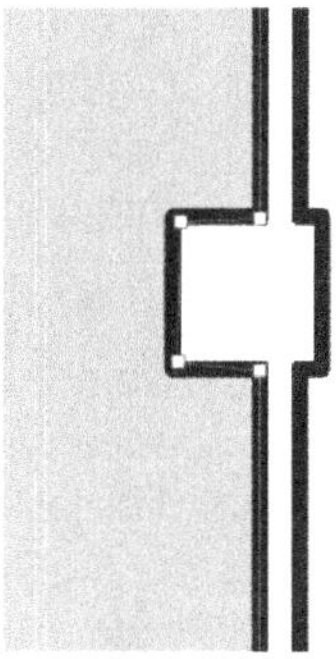

Figure 7–73

28. Zoom out on the drawing to see all five takeoffs. Note that the Carpet, Ceramic, and Vinyl flooring types have different colors. This is because of the color that was defined as the default when the item was created. This can be changed in the Item Catalog, if required.

29. In the Item Catalog, expand the *Interiors>Interior Construction* group. Click **New Item**. Enter **Column Closures** as the name for the item and press <Enter>.

30. Select the **Column Closures** item in the Quantification Workbook, if not already selected.

31. In the 2D Takeoff toolbar, click  (Quick Box) to quickly measure the perimeter of one of the columns in an office. Zoom to another office with a column.

32. Drag a selection box around the column, as shown in Figure 7–74.

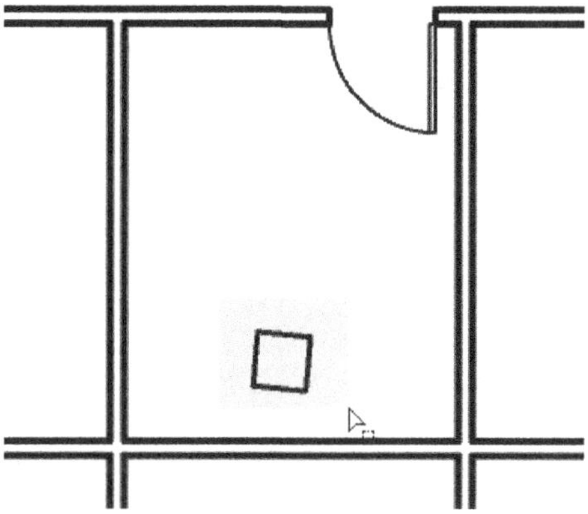

Figure 7–74

33. Once you complete the selection, the Quick Box tools appear. Note how the linear perimeter measurement is highlighting. Select again inside the selected area to convert to an Area measurement. The selection highlights in red indicating it is measuring area.

34. Select 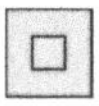 to select the area. It selects the largest boundary area with the least line segments, as shown in Figure 7–75. The area takeoff value is added to the workbook.

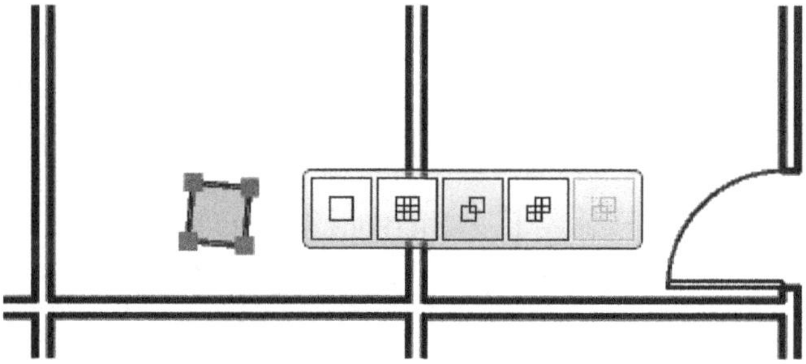

Figure 7–75

35. Zoom out and use the (Quick Box) command and the other options in the Quick Box set to select different entities in the selection box. Note the takeoff values that are added with each selection. Undo this action to clear the addition of these test takeoffs from the workbook.

    - As an alternative, you can use the (Bucket) tool to quickly select enclosed areas to take off their perimeters and areas.

    Note: Review the takeoffs that are created to ensure that they are reporting for the entities that are required. If a takeoff is added that is not required, select it in the Takeoff pane, click **Update**, and select **Delete Selected Takeoff**.

36. In the Item Catalog, expand the *Interiors>Interior Finishes>Wall Finishes* group. Click **New Item**. Enter **Beige Paint** as the name for the item and press <Enter>.

37. Zoom to the kitchen that was taken off using the Sheet Vinyl item, as shown in Figure 7–76. Ensure that the **Beige Paint** item is selected in the Quantification Workbook.

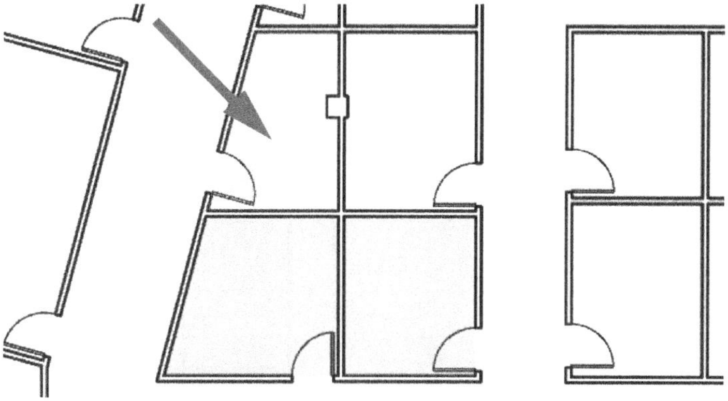

Figure 7–76

38. In the 2D Takeoff toolbar, click (Polyline). Trace the perimeter of the room to take off its perimeter. Ensure that you trace around the column.

39. In the Takeoff pane, scroll through the list of parameters for the new takeoff until you reach the *Height* parameter. Select it and enter **9.000 ft**, as shown in Figure 7–77. The icon in the *Status* cell indicates that this is an overwritten field.

Status	WBS	Object	Thickness	Height	Perimeter	Area
	C.30.10.1.1	Beige Paint 1	0.000 ft	9.000 ft	42.673 ft	0.000 ft²

Figure 7–77

40. Select the *Area* parameter field. In the equation field, enter **=Height*ModelPerimeter** to obtain the *Area* value for the paint takeoff, as shown in Figure 7–78.

f_x =Height*ModelPerimeter

Status	WBS	Object	Thickness	Height	Perimeter	Area
	C.30.10.1.1	Beige Paint 1	0.000 ft	9.000 ft	42.673 ft	384.060 ft²

Figure 7–78

Task 2 - Conduct a count takeoff.

1. Double-click on the **Sheet: A104 - Second Floor Plan** sheet in the Sheet Browser to activate it. On this sheet there are a number of tables that need to be counted. Zoom in to the tables, as shown in Figure 7–79.

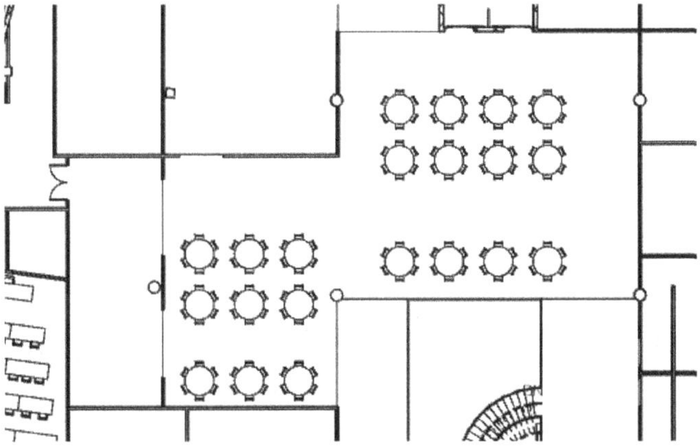

Figure 7–79

2. Add two new items to the *Equipment & Furnishings> Furnishings>Moveable Furnishings* group, one called **Round Table - Med** and the other called **Chair-Breuer**.

3. Select the **Round Table - Med** item in the Quantification Workbook.

4. In the 2D Takeoff toolbar, click  (Count). Select one of the tables on the sheet to position a count pin. Add a total of 21 pins, one on each table, as shown in Figure 7–80. Press <Esc> to disable the command.

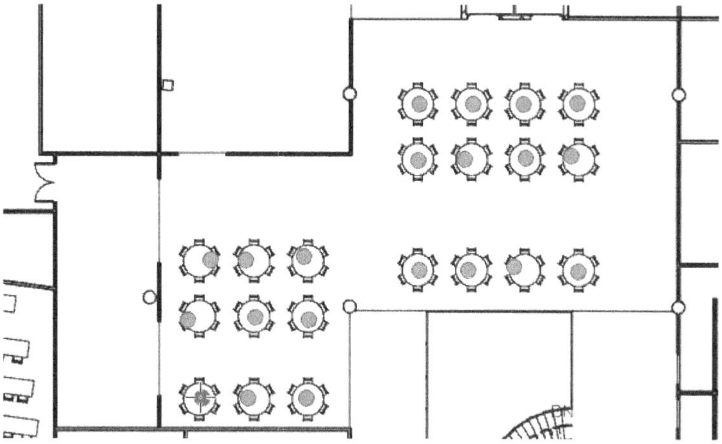

Figure 7–80

5. Review the Takeoff and Rollup panes to see the total count, as shown in Figure 7–81. There are 21 medium-sized round tables.

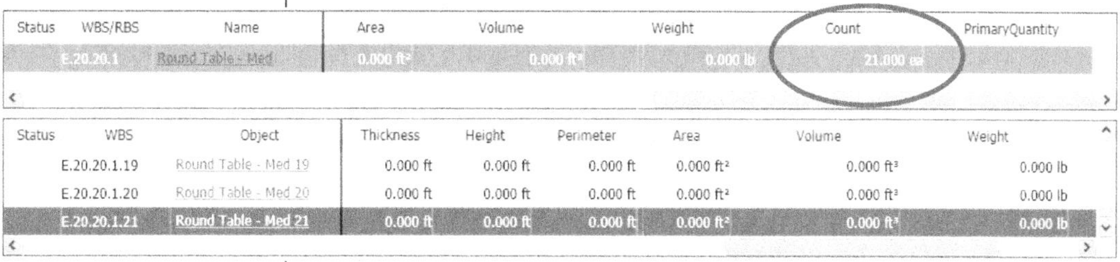

Status	WBS/RBS	Name	Area	Volume	Weight	Count	PrimaryQuantity
	E.20.20.1	Round Table - Med	0.000 ft²	0.000 ft³	0.000 lb	21.000 ea	

Status	WBS	Object	Thickness	Height	Perimeter	Area	Volume	Weight
	E.20.20.1.19	Round Table - Med 19	0.000 ft	0.000 ft	0.000 ft	0.000 ft²	0.000 ft³	0.000 lb
	E.20.20.1.20	Round Table - Med 20	0.000 ft	0.000 ft	0.000 ft	0.000 ft²	0.000 ft³	0.000 lb
	E.20.20.1.21	Round Table - Med 21	0.000 ft	0.000 ft	0.000 ft	0.000 ft²	0.000 ft³	0.000 lb

Figure 7–81

Note: To delete a count pin, select it so that the pin displays as blue and then press <Delete>. The takeoff value automatically updates.

6. Ensure that the Selection Tree is displaying the Standard view.

7. Open the Find Items window and conduct a search using the criteria shown in Figure 7–82. This represents the types of chairs used at the tables that were just counted. Find all instances of this chair: there should be 126 instances located.

Category	Property	Condition	Value
Item	Type	Contains	Chair-Breuer

Figure 7–82

8. Ensure that the **Chair-Breuer** item is selected in the Quantification Workbook.

9. Right-click on any of the selected items in the Selection Tree and select **Quantification>Take off to: Chair-Breuer**. Review the Rollup pane and note that all of these 2D items have been counted. If properties exist for items in the .DWFX file, this type of count takeoff can be done as an alternative to manually dropping pins.

Task 3 - Clear annotations from a sheet.

1. Double-click on the **Sheet: A101 - 4th Floor Wing A** sheet in the Sheet Browser to activate it. On this sheet, note that there are grid lines shown.

2. In the 2D Takeoff toolbar, click  (Hide background and annotations) to toggle off the display of the grid lines to clear the clutter from the sheet.

3. Save and close the file.

7.6 Takeoff Data

Analyzing Takeoff Data

With Change Analysis, you can compare changes to properties between different versions of a model. If differences are identified or there are changes to the takeoff data, status notifications in the Quantification Workbook will indicate what was changed.

The following are the types of notifications that can be presented:

- Warning flags ( ) appear adjacent to a changed item or resource in the Navigation pane.

- Green triangles appear in the corners of cells ( ) to indicate an overwritten value. Hover over the triangle to view a tooltip that shows the original and overridden value, as shown in Figure 7–83.

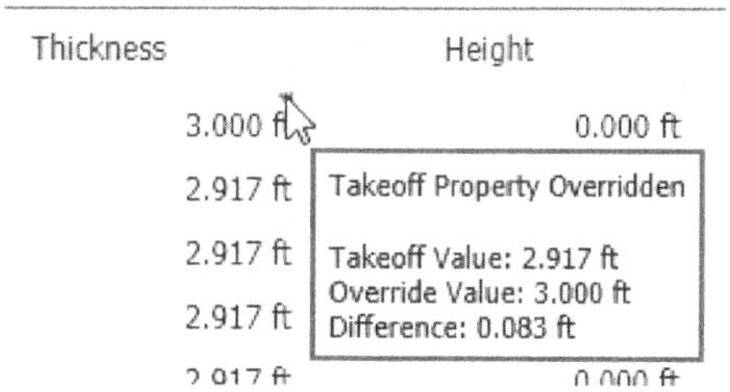

Figure 7–83

- Blue triangles appear in the corners of cells ( ) to indicate that a model property has changed. Hover over the triangle to display a tooltip showing the old and new values, as shown in Figure 7–84.

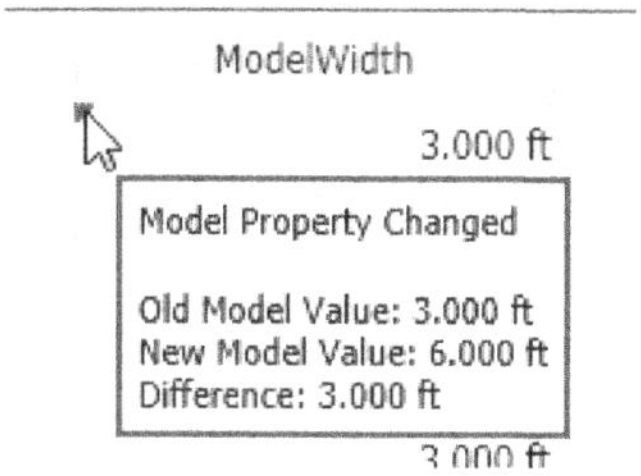

Figure 7–84

Multiple status notification "lights" might appear for one takeoff item.

- Icons in the *Status* column of the Quantification Workbook's Takeoff pane are described as follows. Hover over the icon to display the status in a tooltip.

Icon	Action	Description
	**Override** (Green)	This icon indicates that a formula has been overridden and Change Analysis is still required.
	**Change** (Blue)	This icon indicates that an object has changed and is different from the takeoff item in the workbook.
	**Error** (Red)	This icon indicates that there are errors with either the formula or the item.
	**Delete** (Black)	This icon indicates that a takeoff's item has been deleted.

- The formula bar displays with a red outline (vs. gray) in the Quantification Workbook if an invalid formula was entered. You are prevented from applying the formula.

How To: Analyze and Update Changes in the Quantification Workbook

1. In the Quantification Workbook, click **Change Analysis** and select **Analyze Changes**. Virtual takeoffs cannot be analyzed because they are not linked to the model.
2. Review the changes that are identified () in the Quantification window.
    - To update the Quantification Workbook with the new changes, select a cell in the row, click **Update**, and select **Update Selected from Model**. Items can be updated individually by selecting them in the Takeoff pane or you can select all of the items in a catalog item and update them at the same time.
    - For any takeoff item that indicates that the model item has been deleted (), select a cell in the row, click **Update**, and select **Delete Selected Takeoff**
    - Click **Change Analysis** and select **Clear Analyze Results** if you want to ignore the changes that have been identified.

Exporting Takeoff Data

Takeoff data can be exported from the Quantification Workbook for use in other applications using the .XML or Excel format.

How To: Export Takeoff Data

1. In the Quantification Workbook, click 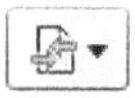.
2. In the drop-down list, select an export option. The available options include:
    - **Export Catalog to XML**
    - **Export Quantities to Excel**
    - **Export Selected Quantities to Excel**

    Note: The  drop-down list can also be used to import a catalog into the Quantification Workbook.
3. In the dialog box, navigate to the preferred save location. Enter a filename and save the data.

Practice 7d

Analyzing and Updating Takeoff Data

Practice Objectives

- Update the current Navisworks model with revised models.
- Export the Quantification Workbook.

In this practice, you will simulate a project's workflow. The Revit model has been updated to include the missing door that was noted in the previous practice. You will inspect the Quantification Workbook with the new changes, then you will export the workbook to a spreadsheet file.

Task 1 - Refresh the Navisworks files to reflect changes in the source model.

1. If necessary, close your current Navisworks file by clicking  in the Quick Access Toolbar.
2. Open Windows Explorer and navigate to the *Navisworks BIM Practice Files\Project Files\Revit Files* folder.
3. Delete the Navisworks cache file of the architectural model, which is **School-Architectural.nwc.** By deleting this file, Navisworks will open the **School-Architectural.rvt** file rather than the cache file.
4. Rename School-Architectural.rvt to **School-Architectural_OLD.rvt**.
5. Rename School-Architectural_Revised.rvt to **School-Architectural.rvt**.
6. Return to the Navisworks software and open the last file you worked on, from the previous practice. If you did not complete the previous practice, open the file **School-Takeoff-Export.nwf** instead.
    - Note that it now takes longer to load the School-Architectural file since you deleted the cache file and Navisworks has to import and process the Revit file.
7. If you are in a 2D DWF view from the last practice, in the Sheet Browser, return to the **SiteLayout.dwg** file, which is a component of your 3D Navisworks model.

8. Select the **Turn2** viewpoint. Note that a door has been added to the model.

   Note: The purpose of renaming the files was to simulate a design change in the Autodesk Revit model, as many training environments do not have access to this software. The **School-Architectural_Revised.nwc** file has had a design change. In a normal design environment, when a change is made to the Revit model, you can use the **Refresh** command to incorporate the changes from the source file into the Navisworks software.

9. In the upper right corner of the Quantification Workbook, click **Change Analysis** and select **Analyze Changes**, as shown in Figure 7–85.

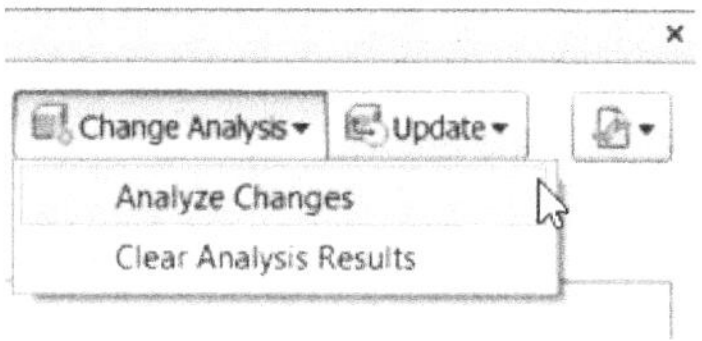

Figure 7–85

10. In the Quantification Workbook, expand the *Interiors>Interior Construction>Interior Doors>Standard Interior Doors* group.

    Note that  displays in the item list, helping you to determine where the differences have been found.

11. Select the **Wood Door - Single** item.

12. In the **School-Architectural_Revised.rvt** file, a door has been added where it was initially missing. The virtual takeoff is no longer required. In the Quantification Workbook's Takeoff pane, scroll to the bottom of the list and select the cell in the virtual takeoff row.

13. In the upper right corner of the toolbar, click **Update** and select **Delete Selected Takeoff,** as shown in Figure 7–86. Note that the quantity of Single-Flush doors is once again 80.

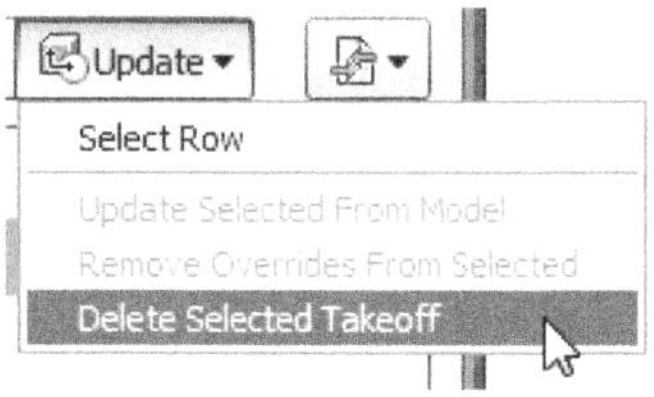

Figure 7–86

14. Select the *Status* column header in the Takeoff pane to sort the list. Select again, if required, so that the two changed items are listed at the top of the Takeoff pane, as shown in Figure 7–87. The **C.10.20.01.2.38** and **C.10.20.01.2.39** objects have been changed.

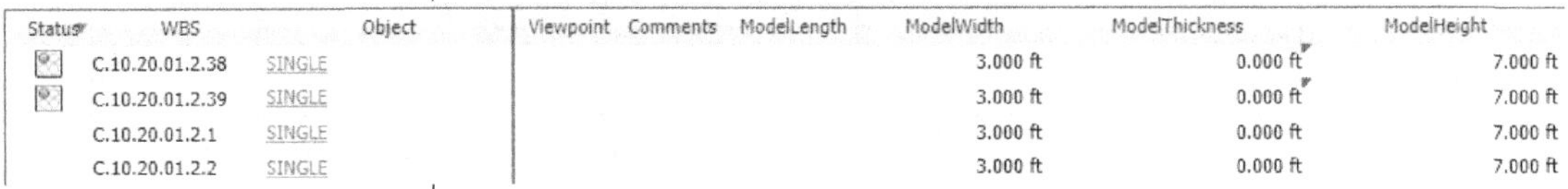

Figure 7–87

15. Roll the cursor over the blue triangular icon ( ) for both items and note that a model property for these objects has changed, as shown in Figure 7–88.

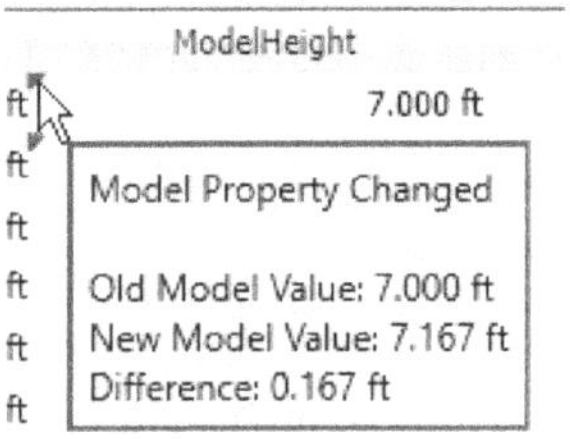

Figure 7–88

16. Select the *ModelHeight* cell for the C.10.20.01.2.38 object. Click **Update** and select **Select Row**.

17. In the toolbar, click **Update** and select **Update Selected From Model**. The C.10.20.01.2.39 object re-sorts in the list now that the data is no longer marked as changed.

18. Select the *ModelWidth* cell for the C.10.20.01.2.39 object. Click **Update** and select **Select Row**.

19. In the toolbar, click **Update** and select **Update Selected From Model**. It also re-sorts the list. Note that no longer displays in the item list because all of the changes have been updated.

20. It is good practice to review the changed objects to ensure that they should remain in the takeoff. Scroll to the C.10.20.01.2.38 object in the list. The door remains a Single-Flush door and only the height was changed.

21. Scroll to the C.10.20.01.2.39 object in the list.

22. The new door that was added to the revision of the model must be added to the takeoff. Select the **Turn2** viewpoint, if not already active.

*If the **Corridors 2011** Room is selected, use <Ctrl>+<H> to hide the room and reselect the door.*

23. Change the *Selection Priority* to **First Object** and select the new door in the scene view. The door highlights in the Selection Tree.

24. Drag the new door to the **Wood Door-Single (80)** item in the Quantification Workbook. The new door is added as the new C.10.20.01.2.81 item and the number of doors updates to 81.

Note: When updating and working with the Quantification Workbook, after objects have been added to a model, consider using the **Show Takeoff** and **Hide Takeoff** options to help identify the items that need to be added to the takeoff.

Task 2 - Export the Quantification Workbook.

1. In the Quantification Workbook, click [icon] and select **Export Catalog to XML**. This enables you to save the Item Catalog that was customized for use in another project.
2. In the Export Catalog to XML dialog box, browse to the *Navisworks BIM Practice Files\Quantification* folder, enter **Class Catalog.xml** as the name for the file, and save it.

   Note: Consider setting up and saving to a network location so that multiple Navisworks users can use the new catalog.

3. In the Quantification Workbook, click [icon] and select **Export Quantities to Excel**. This enables you to save all of the taken off quantities to an Excel spreadsheet.
4. In the Export Quantities to Excel dialog box, browse to the *Navisworks BIM Practice Files\Quantification* folder, enter **School Takeoff Report.xlsx** as the name for the file, and save it.
5. Click **Yes** to open the file once it has been created. This only opens if you have Excel on your computer.
6. Review the takeoff quantities that have been added to the file. Close the file.
7. Save and close the file.

Task 3 - Restore the original School-Architectural file.

1. Ensure that your current Navisworks file is closed by clicking  in the Quick Access Toolbar.
2. Open Windows Explorer and navigate to the *Navisworks BIM Practice Files\Project Files\Revit Files* folder.
3. Delete the Navisworks cache file of the architectural model, which is **School-Architectural.nwc**.
4. Rename School-Architectural.rvt to **School-Architectural_Revised.rvt**.
5. Rename School-Architectural_OLD.rvt to **School-Architectural.rvt**.

Chapter Review Questions

1. Which of the following is NOT part of the Quantification Workbook?
    a. Navigation pane
    b. Summary tab
    c. Toolbar
    d. Takeoff pane
2. Contents in the Resource Catalog can be edited.
    a. True
    b. False
3. What is a GUID?
    a. Graphical User Interface Dock
    b. Globally Unique Identifier
    c. User guide/manual
    d. General Unit Imperial Distance
4. What is a virtual takeoff used for? (Select all that apply.)
    a. Calculating quantities in the Autodesk Cloud.
    b. Objects planned for the model but not yet placed.
    c. Objects part of a future phase of the model but not yet placed.
    d. Objects that have been deleted from the model.
    e. Objects located only in certain viewpoints.
5. Which of the following is NOT part of the 2D Takeoff tools?
    a. Linear takeoff
    b. Area takeoff
    c. Volume takeoff
    d. Count takeoff

6. What formats can you export the quantification to? (Select all that apply.)
    a. .HTML
    b. .DBF
    c. .DWFX
    d. .XLSX

Command Summary

Button	Command	Location
	**Add Vertex**	• **Quantification Workbook:** 2D Takeoff toolbar
	**Add Viewpoint**	• **Quantification Workbook**
	**Appearance of items**	• **Quantification Workbook**
	**Area**	• **Quantification Workbook:** 2D Takeoff toolbar
	**Backout**	• **Quantification Workbook:** 2D Takeoff toolbar
	**Bucket Fill**	• **Quantification Workbook:** 2D Takeoff toolbar
	**Count**	• **Quantification Workbook:** 2D Takeoff toolbar
	**Erase**	• **Quantification Workbook:** 2D Takeoff toolbar
	**Find Items**	• **Ribbon:** *Home* tab
	**Formula Input**	• **Quantification Workbook**
	**Hide background and annotations**	• **Quantification Workbook:** 2D Takeoff toolbar
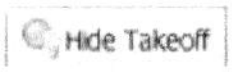	**Hide Takeoff**	• **Quantification Workbook**
	**Import/Export**	• **Quantification Workbook**
	**Import Sheets & Models**	• **Project Browser**
	**New Group**	• **Quantification Workbook>Item Catalog** • **Quantification Workbook>Resource Catalog**
	**New Item**	• **Quantification Workbook>Item Catalog**
	**New Resource**	• **Quantification Workbook>Resource Catalog**
	**Polyline**	• **Quantification Workbook:** 2D Takeoff toolbar

Project Setup...	**Project Setup**	• **Quantification Workbook**
	Quantification	• **Ribbon:** *Home* tab>Tools panel • **Ribbon:** *View* tab>Workspace panel> Windows drop-down list
	Quick Box	• **Quantification Workbook:** 2D Takeoff toolbar
	Quick Line	• **Quantification Workbook:** 2D Takeoff toolbar
	Rectangle Area	• **Quantification Workbook:** 2D Takeoff toolbar
	Rectangle Backout	• **Quantification Workbook:** 2D Takeoff toolbar
	Rectangle Polyline	• **Quantification Workbook:** 2D Takeoff toolbar
	Show/Hide catalogs	• **Quantification Workbook**
Show Takeoff	**Show Takeoff**	• **Quantification Workbook**

Communication: Animator

Communication is at the center of any efficient BIM workflow. Full communication ensures that all stakeholders fully understand how a project will look and function when it is complete. The Autodesk® Navisworks® Animator enables you to create movement in the model to show how objects interact with each other. In this chapter, you will learn how to animate objects and will create a simple animation to orbit a model. Then, you will learn how to animate a crane to ensure that it has a full range of motion on the project site. Finally, you will create .AVI movies to share with others.

Learning Objectives in This Chapter

- Create an animation to tour a model.
- Modify the position, rotation, size, color, and transparency of objects to animate them.
- Create .AVI files to share videos of a project with others.

BIM Workflow: Communicate

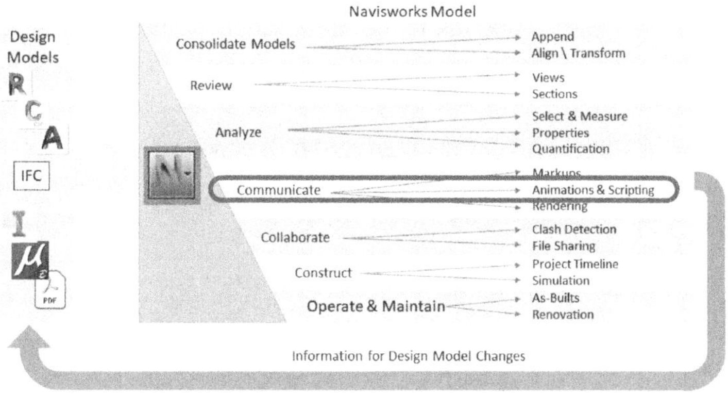

8.1 Creating Tours

You can create videos that simulate walking or flying through a model so that stakeholders can take a tour long before the structure is built.

Animator Window

Animator uses scenes along a timeline to create a slide show. The Animator window (shown in Figure 8–1) is broken into two key areas to reflect this: scenes display on the left in the Tree pane, while the scene's placement in the animation is shown in the Timeline pane on the right. The Animator toolbar sits above the Tree and Timeline panes.

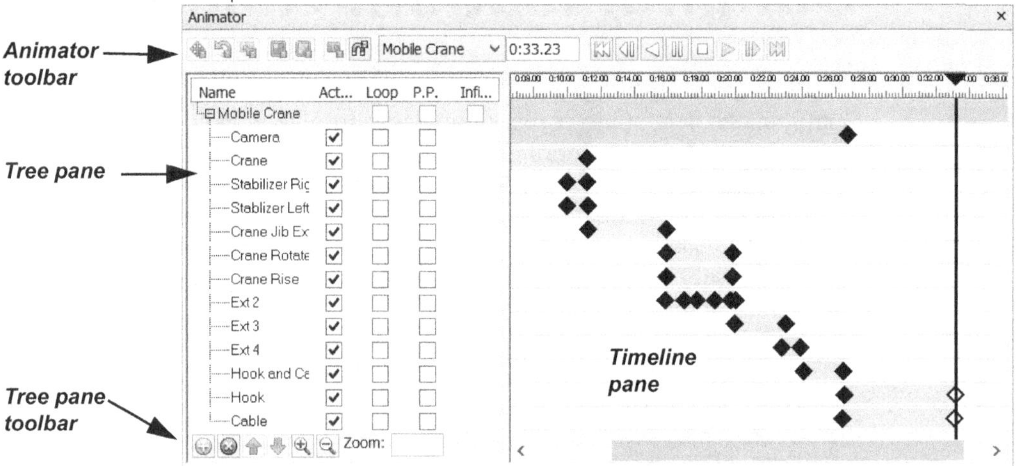

Figure 8–1

Tree Pane

You can add, view, and reorder scene components in the Tree pane. Scenes in the Tree pane can include:

- A camera
- Section planes for sectional views
- Animation sets of objects to be animated

Each scene can only contain one camera, but multiple scene views or viewpoints can be added to the camera.

- When using multiple viewpoints, the animation can jump from view to view or transition smoothly between views.
- When only one viewpoint is added to the animation, the scene continuously focuses on one spot as objects are animated.
- If no viewpoint is added to the camera, then the current view is used during the animation.

The Tree pane tools do the following:

- opens a menu that enables you to add a scene, animation set, section plane, folder, or scene folder, as shown in Figure 8–2. You can also access these tools by right-clicking on a scene in the Tree pane, as shown in Figure 8–3.

Figure 8–2

Figure 8–3

- deletes a scene or scene component.
- / changes the order of the scenes and scene components by moving them up or down in the Tree pane.
- / zooms in or out on the Timeline to make it easier to see the start, end, and duration of each item in the Tree pane.
- Zoom: 1/2 sets how many seconds display in the Timeline.

Timeline Pane

The Timeline pane is used to set when each keyframe is displayed in the animation and the length of the keyframe. A keyframe is a snapshot of a change to the model or the camera viewpoint. The animation bar indicates where on the Timeline the current keyframe falls. As the animation bar is moved, the scene view is updated.The start and end diamonds can be dragged to a new location on the Timeline to change when a keyframe displays in the scene view and the duration of the keyframe, as shown in Figure 8–4.

- In the Animator toolbar, click  (Capture Keyframe) to add the current viewpoint of the camera to the animation.

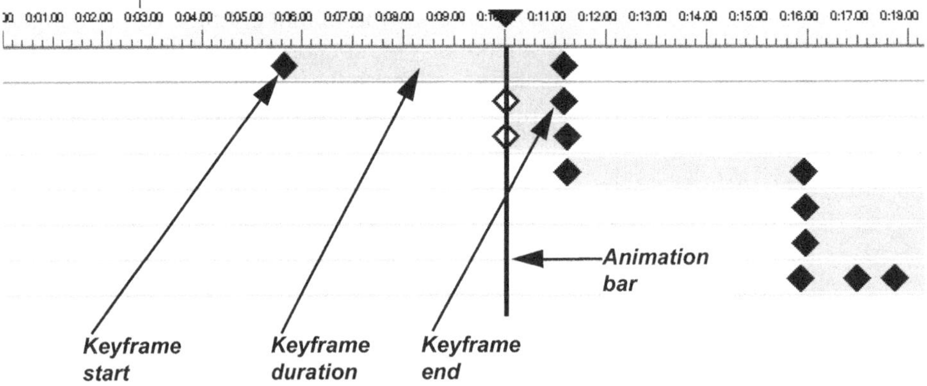

Figure 8–4

- Right-click on a keyframe to display additional tools, as shown in Figure 8–5.
    - **Edit:** Opens the Edit Key Frame dialog box (shown in Figure 8–6), which enables you to modify the keyframe focus, similar to modifying a viewpoint.

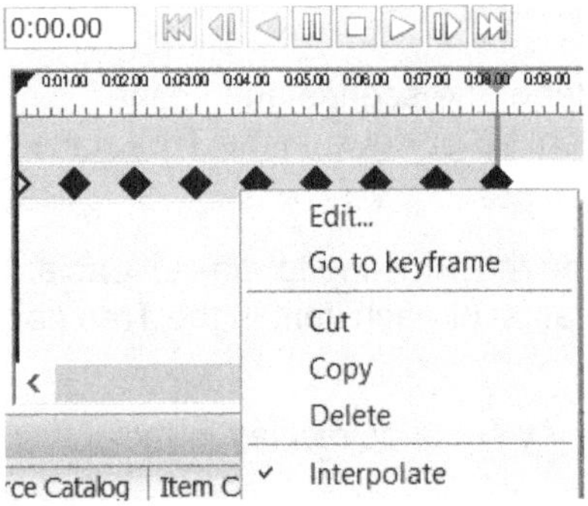

Figure 8–5

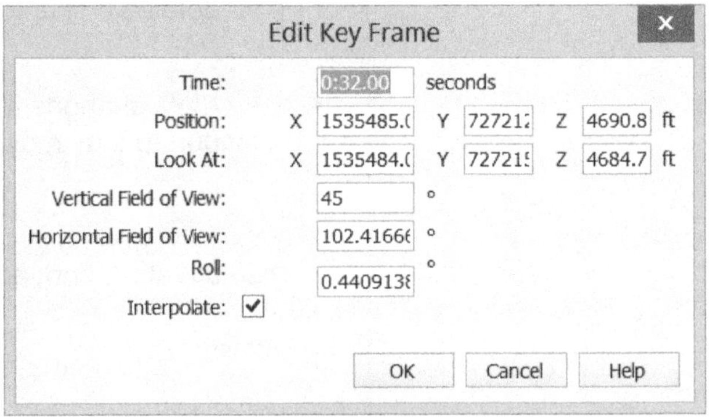

Figure 8–6

If Cut or Copy are selected, right-clicking anywhere on the Timeline provides a Paste option. ***Paste*** *enables you to place the last keyframe saved to the clipboard at the location where you right-click.*

- **Cut:** Removes a keyframe from the Timeline and saves it in a clipboard for later use.
- **Copy:** Saves a keyframe to the clipboard for later use without changing the original keyframe.
- **Delete:** Removes the keyframe.
- **Go to keyframe:** Moves the animation bar to the selected keyframe, and changes the scene view to that keyframe's view.
- **Interpolate:** Creates a smooth transition between keyframes, as if panning or zooming in real-time.

How To: Create a Simple Animation to Display the Model

1. In the *Home* tab>Tools panel, click (Animator) to open the Animator window.
2. In the Animator window>Tree pane, click (Add Scene).
3. Type a name for the scene.
4. In the scene view, set the current view as it is expected to display in the keyframe, using saved viewpoints as required.
5. Move the animation bar to the time that you want the scene to start.
6. Right-click on the scene name and select **Add Camera> Blank Camera**.
7. In the Animator toolbar, click (Capture Keyframe). A black diamond displays in the Timeline to indicate the start of the keyframe.
8. Use the viewing tools (e.g., Pan, Orbit, Saved Viewpoints, etc.) to change the scene view to a new camera position.
9. Move the animation bar to where you want the scene to end.

Multiple keyframes can be added to the same camera.

10. In the Animator toolbar, click (Capture Keyframe). This sets the end of the keyframe and its duration, as shown previously in Figure 8–4.
11. Repeat Steps 2 to 10 until all of the required scenes are added to the Timeline.

Play Animations

The Animator toolbar contains a variety of tools. The tools found on the right of the Animator toolbar helps you review the animations, as follows:

- (Scene Picker): Displays the active scene. Expanding this drop-down list provides a list of the available scenes.
- (Time Position): Displays the current position of the black animation bar in the Timeline pane. You can type a time to jump to that location in the Timeline.
- (Rewind): Moves the animation bar to the beginning of the animation and changes the scene view to match.
- (Step Back): Rewinds the animation one keyframe at a time.
- (Reverse Play): Plays the animation in reverse.
- (Pause): Pauses the animation.
- (Stop): Stops the animation, moves the animation bar back to the beginning of the Timeline, and changes the scene view to match.
- (Play): Starts the animation from the current position of the animation bar.
- (Step Forward): Moves forward in the animation, one keyframe at a time.
- (To End): Fast forwards to the end of the animation.

In addition to the tools in the Animator toolbar, there are four columns in the Tree pane that set the play options, as shown in Figure 8–7.

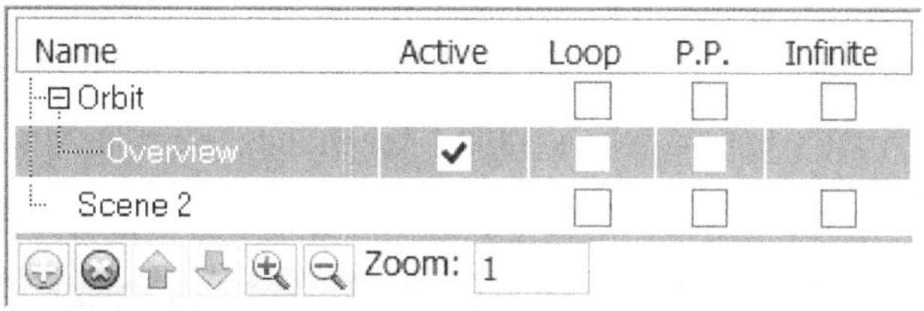

Figure 8–7

- **Active:** When checked, a scene component is active and is used in the animation. Clear the checkmark to make a scene component inactive.

- **Loop:** Causes the animation to automatically play again from the beginning once it reaches the end of the animation.

- **Ping-Pong (P.P.):** As the name implies, Ping-Pong causes the animation to play normally from beginning to end, and then plays it in reverse until it returns to the beginning again.

- **Infinite:** Makes the scene play indefinitely, or until you click  (Stop).

Practice 8a

Create a Simple Animation

Practice Objective

- Create a tour of the model using Animator.

In this practice, you will create an animation to tour the model, as shown in Figure 8–8.

Figure 8–8

Task 1 - Create an animation that orbits around the model.

1. In the *Animator* practice files folder, open **School-Orbit.nwf**.
2. If the drawing displays only boxes where the surfaces and roads should be (as shown in Figure 8–9), you will need to install the Autodesk Civil 3D Object Enabler. Consult *B.3 Autodesk Civil 3D Object Enabler* to install this prior to proceeding.

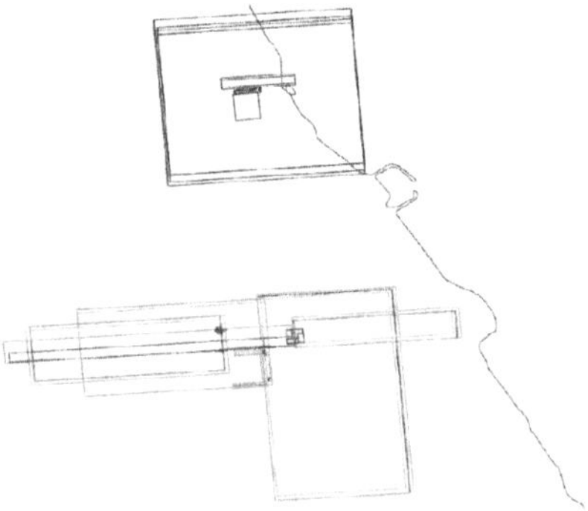

Figure 8–9

3. In the Saved Viewpoints window, in the **Animator** folder, click **Overview**.

4. In the *Home* tab>Tools panel, click (Animator) to display the Animator window. Pin the window open to make it easier to work with it.

5. In the Animator window>Tree pane, click (Add Scene).

6. Click on the scene name and type **Orbit** for the name.

7. Ensure that the animation bar is at 0 on the Timeline. If it is not, drag the animation bar to 0.

8. Right-click on the scene name and select **Add Camera> Blank Camera**.

9. Type **Overview** for the camera name.

10. In the Animator toolbar, click (Capture Keyframe). A black diamond is added to the Timeline at 0 to indicate the start of the keyframe.

11. Right-click on the new keyframe and ensure that **Interpolate** is checked. If it is not, select it to toggle it on.

12. Move the animation bar to **4** seconds on the Timeline, or type **4** in the *Time Position* field.

13. In the Saved Viewpoints window, select the **SE-Isometric** viewpoint.

14. In the Animator toolbar, click (Capture Keyframe).

*All these viewpoints are in the **Animator** folder.*

15. Repeat Steps 11 to 13 to create additional keyframes at the following times and viewpoints:
    - At **8** seconds, capture the **East Side** viewpoint.
    - At **12** seconds, capture the **NE-Isometric** viewpoint.
    - At **16** seconds, capture the **North Side** viewpoint.
    - At **20** seconds, capture the **NW-Isometric** viewpoint.
    - At **24** seconds, capture the **West Side** viewpoint.
    - At **28** seconds, capture the **SW-Isometric** viewpoint.
    - At **32** seconds, capture the **Overview** viewpoint.

16. In the Animator toolbar, click (Stop), and then click (Play) to play the animation from the beginning. Note how the animation moves through each of the viewpoints that you selected.

Task 2 - Create an animation that walks into the model.

1. Continue working in the same animation that was created in the last task.
2. Move the animation bar to **36** seconds on the Timeline.
3. In the Saved Viewpoints window, in the **Animator** folder, select **Front Entry**.
4. In the Animator toolbar, click (Capture Keyframe).

*These viewpoints are in the **Animator** folder.*

5. Repeat Steps 2 to 4 to create additional keyframes at the following times and viewpoints:
   - At **40** seconds, capture the **Turn1** viewpoint.
   - At **42** seconds, capture the **Turn2** viewpoint.
6. In the Animator toolbar, click (Stop), and then click (Play) to play the animation from the beginning. Note how the animation moves through each of the viewpoints that you selected.

8.2 Animating Objects

Touring a model is a great way to demonstrate to stakeholders the design intent and gain their buy-in. Being able to show how objects move and interact within the model helps stakeholders delve deeper into the project. Objects can be animated using a variety of tools found in the Animator toolbar.

- (Translate Animation Set): Provides a gizmo tool to modify the position of geometry objects.
- (Rotate Animation Set): Provides a gizmo tool to rotate geometry objects.
- (Scale Animation Set): Provides a gizmo tool to resize geometry objects.
- (Change Color of Animation Set): Displays the color palette in the Manual Entry bar, enabling you to modify the color of geometry objects.
- (Change Transparency of Animation Set): Displays the transparency slider in the Manual Entry bar, enabling you to modify the transparency of geometry objects.

Note that Capture Keyframe also adds viewpoints to the camera.

- (Capture Keyframe): Adds the current objects' position to an animation set.
- (Toggle Snapping): Toggles snap on and off, enabling you to control whether you snap to other animation sets (translate, rotate, or scale).

How To: Animate Objects

1. In the Sets window, create a selection set or saved set that contains the objects that you want to move.
2. In the Animator window, create a scene and add any required cameras.
3. In the Sets window, select the selection set you created.
4. In the Animator window>Tree pane, right-click on the desired scene and select either of the following options:
   - **Add Animation Set>From current selection**
   - **Add Animation Set>From current search/selection**

The advantage of using a search set is that it automatically updates if the source file changes.

5. Type a name for the animation set.
6. Move the animation bar to the location on the Timeline where you want the animation to start.
7. In the Animator toolbar, click (Capture Keyframe). Note that this captures the current location, rotation, or scale of the animation set.
8. Move the animation bar to the location on the Timeline where you want the animation to end.
9. In the Animator toolbar, click (Translate Animation Set), (Rotate Animation Set), or (Scale Animation Set).
10. Click and drag the center of the gizmo to move the origin point.
    - When (Rotate Animation Set) is selected, the pivot point for all of the selected objects is set.
    - When (Scale Animation Set) or (Translate Animation Set) is selected, you must hold <Ctrl> as you drag the gizmo to change the center of translation.
11. Use the appropriate gizmo shown in Figure 8–10 to translate (move), rotate, or scale the selection set, as required.
    - Red makes changes along the X-axis or in the X-plane.
    - Green makes changes along the Y-axis or in the Y-plane.
    - Blue makes changes along the Z-axis or in the Z-plane.

Translate ***Rotate*** ***Scale***

Figure 8–10

12. In the Animator toolbar, click (Capture Keyframe). This captures the new location of the animation set.

Hint: Translation Errors

When a non-Autodesk file is appended in the Autodesk Navisworks software, a translation error might occur. A warning of the error does not display, but the error causes the X-, Y-, or Z-axis to be incorrect.

If an error occurs, when you try to transpose objects along one gizmo axis (e.g., the X-axis), the objects instead move along a different axis (e.g., the Y-axis), as shown in Figure 8–11. This is a known issue and has no resolution at the time of publication of this guide.

As the error cannot be fixed, you will have to select another axis on the gizmo to translate the objects until you find the axis that causes the objects to move in the required direction.

Figure 8–11

Practice 8b Create a Complex Animation

Practice Objective

- Animate objects and note how they move in the model.

In this practice, you will animate the crane and note how it moves in the model, as shown in Figure 8–12. The specific sets of the crane to move and rotate were already created for you. See **Appendix A "Practices to Prepare for Animator"** for instructions to create the sets.

Figure 8–12

Task 1 - Add views to the animation.

If the Animator window is not displayed, in the Home tab>Tools panel, click (Animator) to open it. Then, pin it open to make it easier to access.

1. In the *Animator* practice files folder, open **School-Crane.nwf**.
2. In the Animator window, uncheck the **Active** option next to **Overview**, thus making it inactive.
3. In the Saved Viewpoints window, **Animator** folder, click **Overview**.
4. In the Animator window>Tree pane, click (Add Scene).
5. Click on the scene name and type **Mobile Crane** for the name.
6. Ensure that the animation bar is at 0 on the Timeline.
7. Right-click on **Mobile Crane** and select **Add Camera>Blank Camera**. For the camera name, accept the default name of **Camera**.

8. In the Animator toolbar, click  (Capture Keyframe). A black diamond displays in the Timeline at 0 to indicate the start of the keyframe.

Interpolate should be on by default. This is just a verification step.

9. Right-click on the keyframe and ensure that **Interpolate** is checked.

10. Move the animation bar to **4** seconds on the Timeline.

11. Pan and orbit the model so that the crane displays similar to the view shown in Figure 8–13.

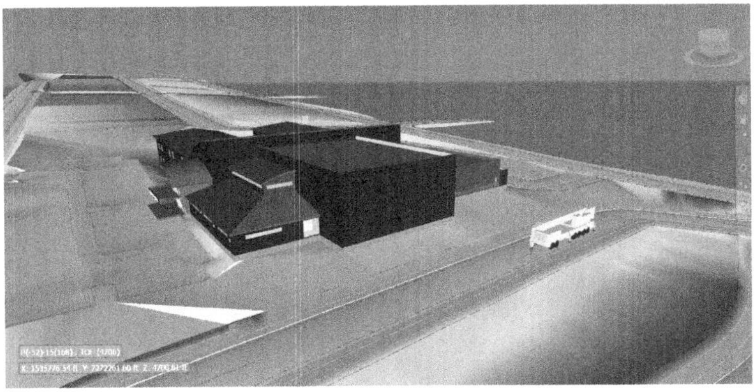

Figure 8–13

12. In the Animator toolbar, click  (Capture Keyframe).

13. In the Animator toolbar, click  (Stop), and then click  (Play) to play the animation from the beginning.

14. Save the file.

Task 2 - Add a transition animation.

*If the Sets window is not displayed, in the View tab>Workspace panel, expand **Windows** and select **Sets**.*

1. Open the Sets window and pin it open to make it easy to access.

2. In the Sets window, select **Crane**. Note that the entire crane is selected in the model.

3. In the Animator window>Tree pane, right-click on the **Mobile Crane** scene and select **Add Animation Set>From current selection**.

4. Type **Crane** for the animation set name.

5. Move the animation bar to **4** seconds on the Timeline.

6. In the Animator toolbar, click (Capture Keyframe).
7. Move the animation bar to **8** seconds on the Timeline.
8. In the Animator toolbar, click (Translate Animation Set).
9. Use the Y-axis (green arrow) on the translate gizmo to move the crane forward, similar to what is shown in Figure 8–14.

Figure 8–14

10. In the Animator toolbar, click (Capture Keyframe).
11. In the Animator toolbar, click (Stop), and then click (Play) to play the animation from the beginning.
12. Save the file.

Task 3 - Add rotation animations.

1. In the Sets window, select **Crane Rise**.
2. In the Animator window>Tree pane, right-click on the **Mobile Crane** scene and select **Add Animation Set>From current selection**.
3. Type **Rise** for the animation name.
4. Move the animation bar to **8** seconds on the Timeline.
5. In the Animator toolbar, click (Capture Keyframe).
6. Move the animation bar to **12** seconds on the Timeline.

7. In the Animator toolbar, click  (Rotate Animation Set).

8. In the Animator toolbar, click  (Toggle Snapping).

9. Click and drag the center of the rotate gizmo to the center of the hinge pin shown in Figure 8–15. Orbit and zoom the scene as required to display the pin better. With snapping toggled on, you should be able to snap to the center of the circle.

   - **Note:** If you hold <Ctrl> when moving the gizmo, only the gizmo moves and not the selected objects.

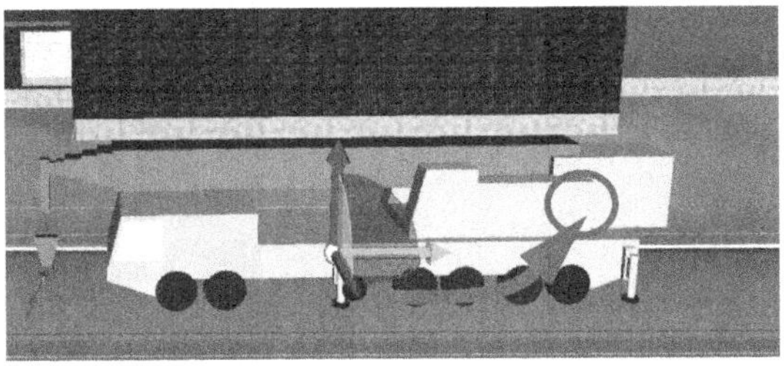

Figure 8–15

10. Use the X-axis (red) plane of the gizmo to rotate the jib **30°** around the X-axis, as shown in Figure 8–16.

Figure 8–16

11. In the Animator toolbar, click  (Capture Keyframe). This captures the new rotation of the animation set.

12. In the Sets window, select **Hook and Cable**.

13. In the Animator window>Tree pane, right-click on the **Mobile Crane** scene and select **Add Animation Set>From current selection**.

14. Type **Gravity** for the animation name.

15. Move the animation bar to **8** seconds on the Timeline.

16. In the Animator toolbar, click (Capture Keyframe).

17. Move the animation bar to **12** seconds on the Timeline.

18. In the Animator toolbar, click (Rotate Animation Set).

19. Click and drag the center of the rotate gizmo to the top of the cable, as shown in Figure 8–17

Figure 8–17

20. Use the X-axis (red) plane of the gizmo to rotate the cable **30°** around the X-axis so that it is perpendicular to the ground as if gravity is pulling on it, as shown in Figure 8–18.

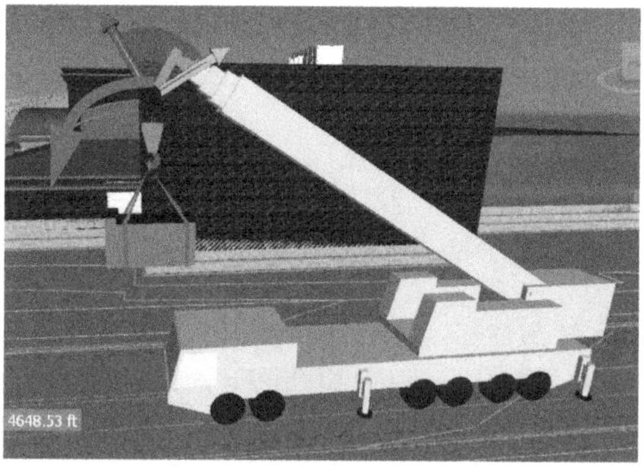

Figure 8–18

21. In the Animator toolbar, click (Capture Keyframe).

22. In the Sets window, select **Crane Rotate**.

23. In the Animator window>Tree pane, right-click on the **Mobile Crane** scene and select **Add Animation Set>From current selection**.

24. Type **Rotate** for the animation name.

25. Move the animation bar to **12** seconds on the Timeline.

26. In the Animator toolbar, click (Capture Keyframe).

27. Move the animation bar to **16** seconds on the Timeline.

28. In the Animator toolbar, click (Rotate Animation Set).

29. Click and drag the center of the rotate gizmo to the center of the truck below the jib, as shown in Figure 8–19

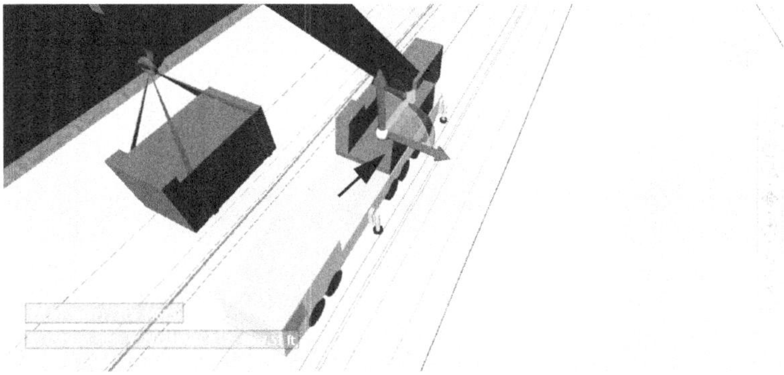

Figure 8–19

30. Use the Z-axis (blue) plane of the gizmo to rotate the jib **90°** around the Z-axis so that it is pointing at the building and the X-axis lines up with the truck, as shown in Figure 8–20.

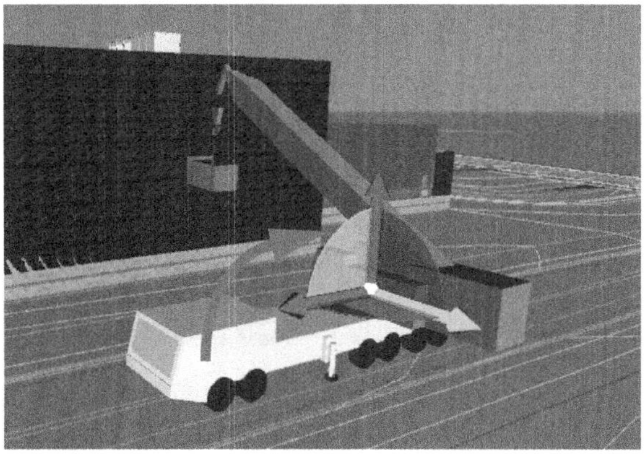

Figure 8–20

31. In the Animator toolbar, click (Capture Keyframe).

32. In the Animator toolbar, click (Stop), and then click (Play) to play the animation from the beginning.

33. Save the file.

Task 4 - Extend the jib.

1. In the Sets window, select **Crane Jib Ext 4**.
2. In the Animator window>Tree pane, right-click on the **Mobile Crane** scene and select **Add Animation Set>From current selection**.
3. Type **Etx-1** for the animation set name.
4. Move the animation bar to **16** seconds on the Timeline.
5. In the Animator toolbar, click (Capture Keyframe).
6. Move the animation bar to **20** seconds on the Timeline.
7. In the Animator toolbar, click (Translate Animation Set).
8. Use the X-axis (red arrow) and Z-axis (blue arrow) on the gizmo to extend the jib the full length of the smallest extension, similar to what is shown in Figure 8–21.

It might be necessary to orbit the model after each move to ensure that the jib moves in the correct direction.

Figure 8–21

9. In the Animator toolbar, click (Capture Keyframe).

10. In the Animator toolbar, click  (Stop), and then click  (Play) to play the animation from the beginning.
11. Save the file.

8.3 Animation and Scripts

Animation is great to demonstrate your ideas, both in time and space, as you can give a tour of your BIM project. You can also introduce movement into your tour as cranes arrive on site or extend their booms.

You can even go one step further in realism to have animations occur within certain areas. For example, rather than simply walking *through* a closed door, have the door open as you approach, and then have the door close once you have passed through. Such actions can be done with Autodesk Navisworks by using scripts. This topic is covered extensively in the next chapter, but this section will cover the animations for doors opening and closing.

Similarly to the previous practice, you will create scenes, cameras, selections for the camera, and keyframes for the animations to follow. You will then add some movement for the doors: the outer set will pivot on their hinges and the inner doors will slide open. Finally, as an introduction to scripts, you will create small animation snippets of opening doors, sliding doors, and wilting plants.

Practice 8c

Create Animation Snippets for Scripting

Practice Objective

- Create simple animations of objects to be used in interactive scripts.

In this practice, you will animate the action of a door opening, as shown in Figure 8–22. You will also create animations of a door sliding open and a plant changing size to emulate growth.

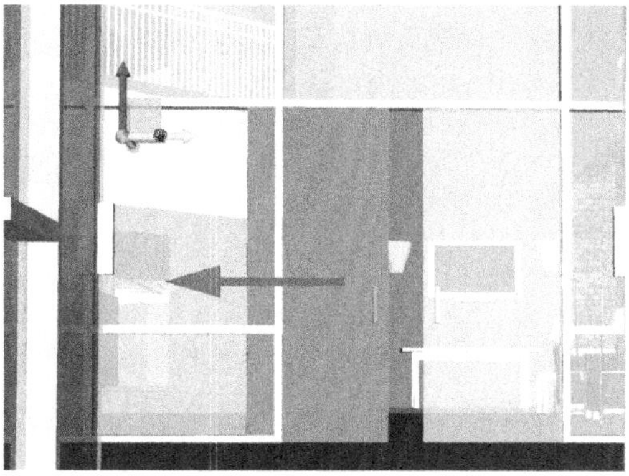

Figure 8–22

Task 1 - Create an animation of the doors opening when walking through.

If the Animator window is not displayed, in the Home tab>Tools panel, click (Animator) to open it. Then, pin it open to make it easier to access.

1. In the *Animator* practice files folder, open **School-Animation.nwf**.
2. In the Saved Viewpoints window, **Animator** folder, click **Front Entry**.
3. Set the *Selection Resolution* to **First Object**.

4. Select one of the front doors and wait until the tooltip appears. Note that the tooltip lists the *Item Type* as **Rooms**, as shown in Figure 8–23.

Figure 8–23

5. *Rooms* are special organizational objects used in Autodesk Revit that have little to no value in Navisworks. Therefore, you can hide all the rooms. In the Selection Tree window, go to the top of the branch of the selected object and right-click on **Rooms**.

6. In the shortcut menu, select **Hide** to hide all of the rooms in the model, as shown in Figure 8–24. You could also use the **<Ctrl>+<H>** keyboard shortcut to hide them.

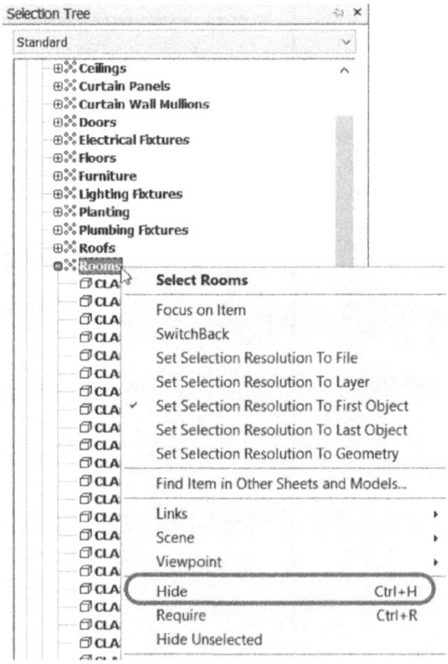

Figure 8–24

7. Now when you select the door, the tooltip tells you it is a **Curtain Wall Single Glazed Door**.

8. In the Animator window>Tree pane, click  (Add Scene).

9. Click on the scene name and type **Entrance Doors** for the name.

10. Ensure that the animation bar is at 0 on the Timeline. If it is not, drag the animation bar to 0.

11. Right-click on the **Entrance Doors** scene and select **Add Camera>Blank Camera**.

12. Type **Entering** for the camera name (to distinguish it as a pivoting door compared to a sliding door).

13. Select the **Entering** camera entry. Ensure that the view does not change as you are selecting the camera entry. Selecting the entry in a column other than the *Name* column helps, as shown in Figure 8–25.

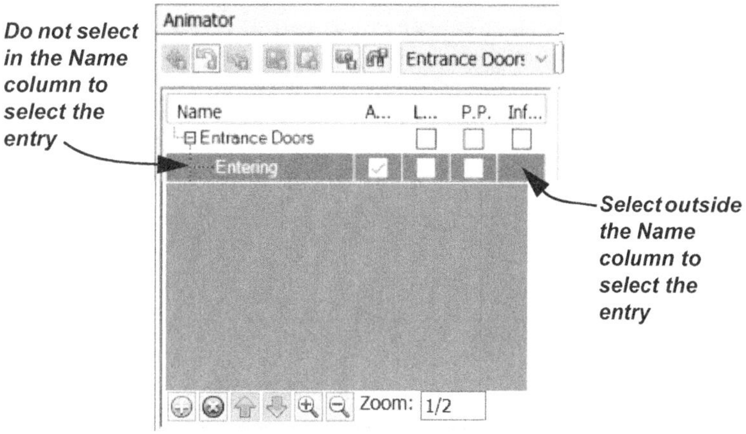

Figure 8–25

14. If you did accidentally move the viewpoint (it can happen easily!), you can restore the **Front Entrance** saved viewpoint.

15. In the Animator toolbar, click  (Capture Keyframe). This captures a keyframe of the current view and places it at the beginning of the camera timeline.

16. In the scene view, select the left door.

17. In the Animator window, right-click on the **Entering** scene and click **Add>Add Animation Set>From current selection**.

18. Click the new animation set and rename it **Hinge Outer Left**.

19. Repeat Steps 16 and 17 to add another animation set by selecting the right door and naming the animation set **Hinge Outer Right**.

20. Repeat Steps 17 to 19 for the vestibule doors, as follows:

    - In the Saved Viewpoints window, **Animator** folder, click **Front Vestibule**.
    - Name the two animation sets (one for each door) **Slide Inner Right** and **Slide Inner Left**, respectively.

If you select the scene name when making the animation sets rather than picking another column, the viewpoint will revert to the starting position and you will need to restore the ***Front Vestibule*** *viewpoint again.*

21. Figure 8–26 shows the final layout of the scenes, cameras, and animation sets.

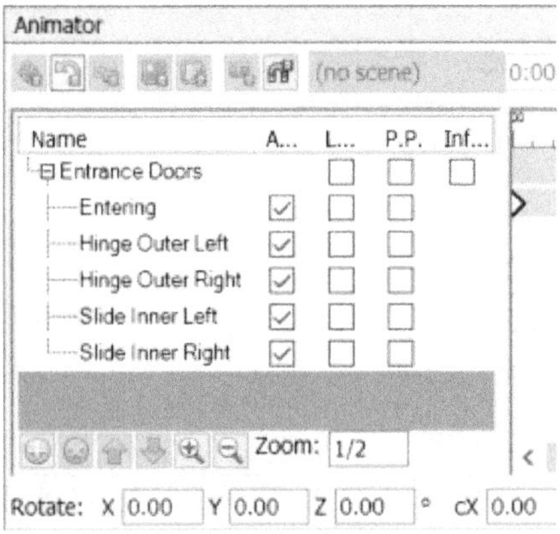

Figure 8–26

22. Save the file.

Task 2 - Add cameras and keyframes.

1. An initial keyframe was created for the **Hinge** camera using the **Front Entry** saved viewpoint.

2. Select the **Entering** camera entry. In the Timeline pane, drag the animation bar to **8**.

3. Using the  (Walk) navigation tool, walk towards the entrance doors and proceed until you are between the outer and inner doors.

4. In the Animator toolbar, click (Capture Keyframe). This captures a keyframe of the current view and places it at the current camera timeline at the 8-second mark.

5. In the Timeline pane, drag the animation bar to **13** or enter the value in the *Time Position* field.

6. Using the (Walk) navigation tool, walk into the center of the foyer, then click (Capture Keyframe).

7. In the Timeline pane, drag the animation bar to **18**.

8. Using the (Look Around) navigation tool, turn around to see the doors you have just walked through and capture this keyframe.

9. In the Timeline pane, drag the animation bar to **22**.

10. Using the (Walk) navigation tool, walk backwards from the entrance doors a few paces and then capture the keyframe. It should look like Figure 8–27.

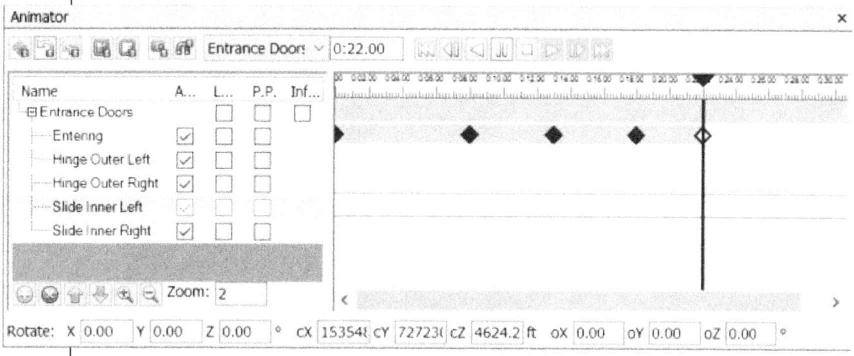

Figure 8–27

11. Click (Stop), then click (Play) in the Animator toolbar to view your newly created animation. The animation should walk through the doors, turn around to view the doors, then move backwards away from the doors.

12. Note how the doors were not animated. Only the camera has been animated.

13. Save the file.

Task 3 - Open and close the hinged doors.

1. In the **Entrance Doors** scene, select the **Hinge Outer Left** animation set.
2. In the Timeline pane, drag the animation bar to **4** or enter the value in the *Time Position* field.
3. In the Animator toolbar, click  (Capture Keyframe). This captures a keyframe of the current view and places it at the current position of the Timeline for the **Hinge Outer Left** set.
4. In the Timeline pane, drag the animation bar to **6** or enter the value in the *Time Position* field.
5. Save this viewpoint in the **Animator** folder, and name it **6 sec**, so you can return to this viewpoint later.
6. In the Animator toolbar, click  (Rotate Animation Set). The translation handles should be displayed near the center of selected door. Click and drag the gizmo to the left frame of the door by selecting the X-axis (red horizontal arrow), which turns yellow, and dragging it to the edge of the highlighted door, as shown in Figure 8–28.

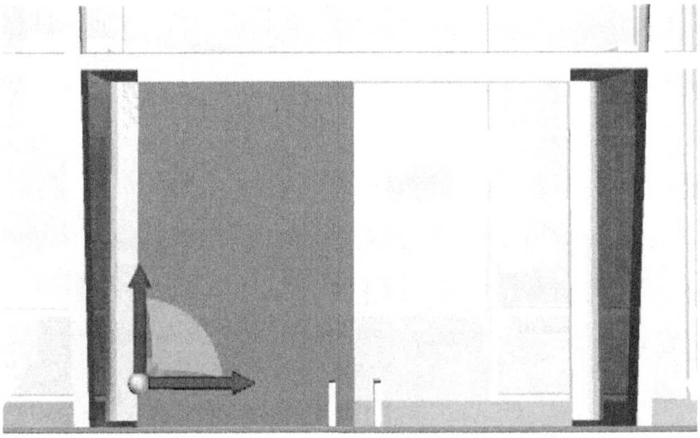

Figure 8–28

7. Use the Orbit and Pan navigation tools to get a top view of the door. If you are having trouble, you can restore the **Door Hinged Top** viewpoint in the **Animator** folder. Hover over the blue arc, which will turn yellow. Swing the door inward by about 90°, as shown in Figure 8–29.

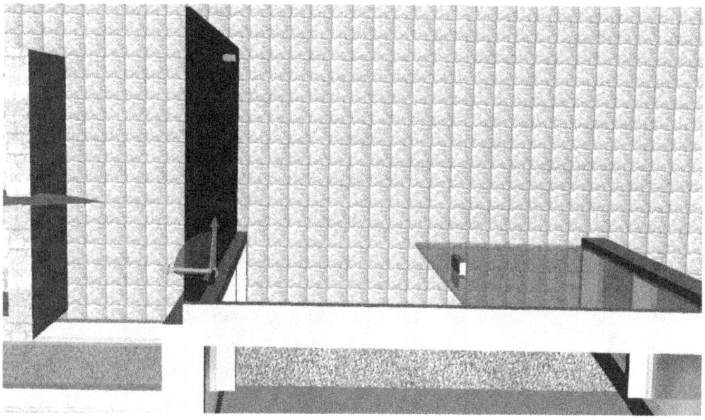

Figure 8–29

8. Restore the **6 sec** viewpoint.

9. In the Animator toolbar, click (Capture Keyframe). This captures a keyframe of the current view and places it at the current position of the Timeline for the outer left door.

10. Right-click this new keyframe and select **Copy**, as shown in Figure 8–30.

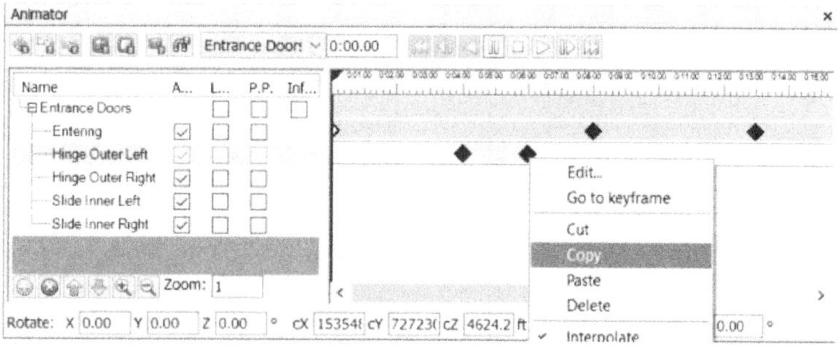

Figure 8–30

11. Drag the animation bar to **18** (or enter the value), then right-click and select **Paste**. This pastes a copy of the last keyframe at 18, which means the door remains open between 6 and 18.

12. Right-click the first keyframe at 4 and select **Copy**. Drag the animation bar to **21**, then right-click and select **Paste**. This pastes a copy of the first keyframe at 21.

13. Click (Stop), then click (Play). As the entrance is approached, the left door should swing open, then the door should close as you move away from it at the end of the animation.

14. Repeat Steps 4 to 13 to animate the right outer door.
    - Remember to orbit into a top view of the door prior to rotating it.
    - It will be tricky to get the correct hinge point. You will need to move it in both the X- and Y-axis directions to get to the frame, as shown in Figure 8–31.

Figure 8–31

    - Remember to restore the **6 sec** viewpoint prior to capturing the keyframe.

Task 4 - Open and close the sliding doors.

1. In the **Entrance Doors** scene, select the **Slide Inner Left** animation set.
2. In the Timeline pane, drag the animation bar to **6** or enter the value in the *Time Position* field.
3. You may need to pan a bit to get the camera centered on the sliding doors.
4. In the Animator toolbar, click  (Capture Keyframe). This captures a keyframe of the current view and places it at the current position of the Timeline for the **Slide Inner Left** set.
5. While you are here, select the **Slide Inner Right** set and click  (Capture Keyframe).
6. Select the **Slide Inner Left** animation set again.
7. In the Timeline pane, drag the animation bar to **8** or enter the value in the *Time Position* field. Using the Pan tool, center the camera once again, if necessary.

8. Save this viewpoint in the **Animator** folder, and name it **8 sec**, so you can return to this viewpoint later.

9. Zoom back so you see the frame of the first (hinged) doors.

10. In the Animator toolbar, click (Translate Animation Set). The translation handles should be displayed near the hinged door, as shown in Figure 8–32. Select the red X-axis, which turns yellow, and slide the door all the way open.

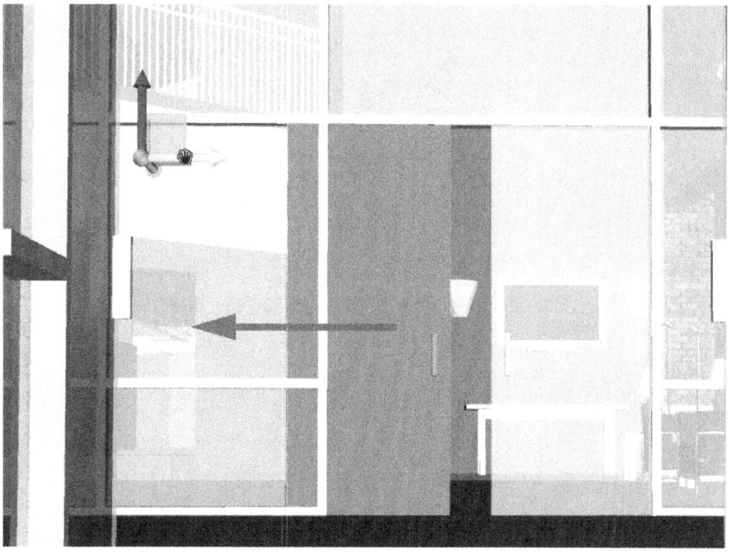

Figure 8–32

11. Restore the **8 sec** viewpoint.

12. In the Animator toolbar, click (Capture Keyframe). This captures a keyframe of the current view and places it at the current position of the Timeline for the **Slide Inner Left** set.

13. Right-click this new keyframe and select **Copy**.

14. Drag the animation bar to **18** (or enter the value), then right-click and select **Paste**. This pastes a copy of the last keyframe at 18, which means the sliding door remains open between 8 and 18.

15. Right-click the first keyframe at 6 and select **Copy**. Drag the animation bar to **21**, then right-click and select **Paste**. This pastes a copy of the first keyframe at 21.

16. Click (Stop), then click (Play). As the entrance is approached, the two front doors should swing open, then the left inner door should slide open, then as you move away from the door at the end of the animation, the left inner door and both front doors should close.

17. Repeat Steps 9 to 15 to animate the right inner door.
    - Remember to restore the **8 sec** viewpoint prior to capturing the keyframe.

18. Play the animation to ensure all is good.

19. Save the file.

Task 5 - (Optional) Create snippet animations for the Scripter.

Most the steps listed below have already been done in the previous tasks, albeit in a different order.

1. In the Animator window>Tree pane, click (Add Scene).
2. Click on the scene name and type **Opening Doors** for the name.
3. Ensure that the animation bar is at 0 on the Timeline. If it is not, drag the animation bar to 0.
4. In the Animator toolbar, click (Capture Keyframe). This captures a keyframe of the current view and places it at the beginning of the camera timeline.
5. In the Navisworks scene view, select the left door.
6. In the Animator window, right-click on the **Opening Doors** scene and click **Add>Add Animation Set>From current selection**.

A camera is not required since you are only recording the movement of the door. A camera would pre-determine the vantage point.

7. Click the new animation set and rename it **Hinge Left.**
8. Add another animation set by selecting the right door and naming the animation set **Hinge Right.**
9. Restore the **Front Vestibule** viewpoint from the **Animator** folder.

If the order of the animation sets is different, you can drag and drop them to rearrange them.

10. Repeat the Steps 1 to 9 for the vestibule doors, as follows:
    - Name the scene **Sliding Doors**.
    - Name the two animation sets **Sliding Left** and **Sliding Right** accordingly.

11. To check that the sets are correct, highlight each animation set and see if the corresponding door is selected, as shown in Figure 8–33.

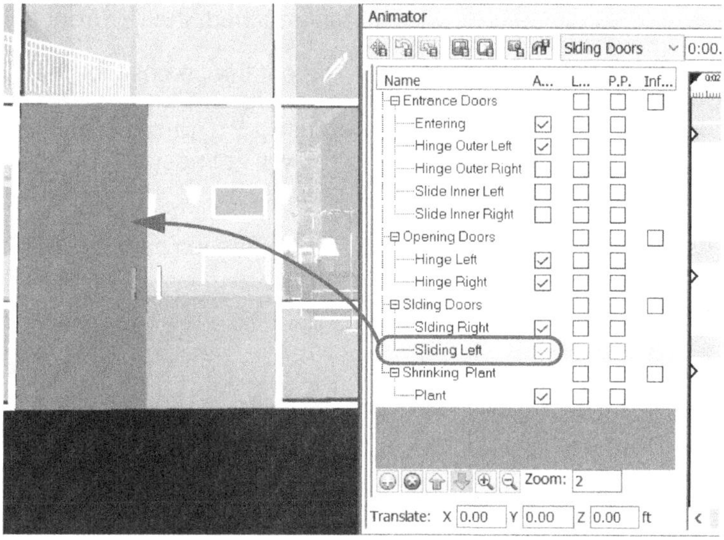

Figure 8–33

12. Select the **Hinge Left** animation set by name. This will also change your viewpoint.

13. In the Animator toolbar, click  (Capture Keyframe) to save the left door in a closed position at the beginning of the animation.

14. In the Timeline pane, drag the animation bar to **3** or enter the value in the *Time Position* field.

15. In the Animator toolbar, click  (Rotate Animation Set).

16. Restore the **Door Hinged Top** viewpoint from the **Animator** folder.

17. Hover over the blue arc, which will turn yellow. Swing the door inward by about 90°.

18. In the Animator toolbar, click (Capture Keyframe). This restores the view and captures the keyframe for the **Hinge Left** set.

19. Repeat the process for the **Hinge Right** animation set.

20. Select the **Opening Doors** scene.

21. Click (Stop), then click (Play). As the entrance is approached, the two front doors should swing open.

22. Repeat the process for the **Sliding Door** scene. Remember to use (Translate Animation Set) in the Animator toolbar. You will not need to change your viewpoint to slide the doors open.

23. The Animation pane should look like Figure 8–34.

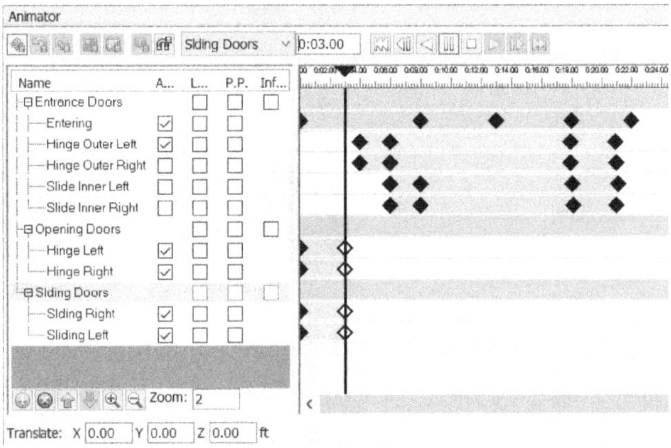

Figure 8–34

24. Restore the **Shrinking Plant** viewpoint from the **Animator** folder.

25. Add one more scene and name it **Shrinking Plant**.

26. Select the plant that is sitting on the table between the chairs and add it to the **Shrinking Plant** scene as an animation set named **Plant**.

27. In the Timeline pane, drag the animation bar to **4** or enter the value in the *Time Position* field.

28. In the Animator toolbar, click (Capture Keyframe) to save the size of the plant at the end of the animation.

29. In the Timeline pane, drag the animation bar back to 0 or enter the value in the *Time Position* field.

30. In the Animator toolbar, click (Scale Animation Set).

31. You have a few choices for how you want your plant to shrink. If you select the small white sphere at the intersection of the three axes, it will scale uniformly, as shown in Figure 8–35. If you select a triangular plane between two axes, it will scale in those two directions. If you select an individual axis, it will scale in that direction.

Figure 8–35

32. In the Animator toolbar, click (Translate Animation Set).

33. Select the blue Z-axis arrow to lower the plant to the table, then the green Y-axis arrow to move the plant back towards the wall.

34. In the Animator toolbar, click (Capture Keyframe) to save the size of the plant at the beginning of the animation.

35. Play the animation.

36. Save and close the file.

Chapter Review Questions

1. In the Animator toolbar, what happens when you click  (Capture Keyframe)? (Select all that apply.)
    a. Captures a snapshot of the currently appended files.
    b. Captures a snapshot of the current viewpoint.
    c. Captures a snapshot of the current object positions.
    d. Captures key elements for later use.
2. What does the **Ping Pong (P.P.)** option do?
    a. Causes an animation to play in reverse when it reaches the end.
    b. Causes animations to randomly shuffle in the Timeline.
    c. Causes an animation to replay once when it reaches the end.
    d. Causes an animation to replay continuously when it reaches the end.
3. Using the Timeline, how do you change the length of time an animation plays?
    a. Select the animation set, right-click, and select **Set Duration**.
    b. Select the animation set and type a duration in the *Time Position* field.
    c. Select the animation set and drag the animation bar in the Timeline to set the length.
    d. Drag the diamonds in the Timeline to lengthen or shorten the duration.
4. How many cameras can you have in a scene?
    a. 1
    b. 2
    c. 3
    d. Infinite

5. How can you move the point of translation when moving, rotating, or scaling an animation set?
   a. The point of translation cannot be changed.
   b. In the *Item Tools* tab>Transform panel, click **Move**.
   c. In the *Item Tools* tab>Look At panel, click **Focus on Item**.
   d. Hold <Ctrl> as you drag the center point of the gizmo.

Command Summary

Button	Command	Location
	**Add Scene**	• **Window:** Animator
	**Animator**	• **Ribbon:** *Home* tab>Tools panel
	**Capture Keyframe**	• **Window:** Animator
	**Change Color of Animation Set**	• **Window:** Animator
	**Change Transparency of Animation Set**	• **Window:** Animator
	**Delete**	• **Window:** Animator
	**Move Down**	• **Window:** Animator
	**Move Up**	• **Window:** Animator
	**Pause**	• **Window:** Animator
	**Play**	• **Window:** Animator
	**Reverse Play**	• **Window:** Animator
	**Rewind**	• **Window:** Animator
	**Rotate Animation Set**	• **Window:** Animator
	**Scale Animation Set**	• **Window:** Animator
	**Scene Picker**	• **Window:** Animator
	**Step Back**	• **Window:** Animator
	**Step Forward**	• **Window:** Animator

	**Stop**	• **Window:** Animator
0:36.25	**Time Position**	• **Window:** Animator
	**To End**	• **Window:** Animator
	**Toggle Snapping**	• **Window:** Animator
	**Translate Animation Set**	• **Window:** Animator
	**Zoom In**	• **Window:** Animator
	**Zoom Out**	• **Window:** Animator

Communication: Scripter

For communication to be effective, it needs to be interactive. The ability to record actions and validate different aspects of a model can be quite informative. To build such interactions with a model, scripts are required that allow for parts of the model to move on demand, messages to be exported to text files, the condition of properties to be recorded, events to happen upon collision, etc. In this chapter, you will learn how to use the Autodesk® Navisworks® Scripter to create such scripts. You will create a simple script invoking animations developed in another chapter. You will also examine how to create scripts based on certain keystrokes.

Learning Objectives in This Chapter

- Create a hotspot script and a keystroke script.
- Examine a message output file.

BIM Workflow: Communicate

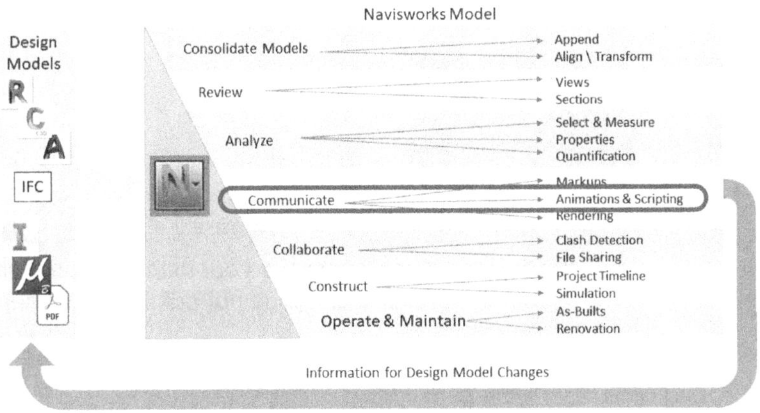

9.1 Scripter

Animation is good, but interactivity with your model is better. The Navisworks Scripter is designed to add events to the animation based on triggers. By combining scripts with animations created in Animator, an animation can be triggered by an event created in Scripter. For example, doors open (animation) as you approach them (script) in your model. You could animate how a crane moves around a site or how a car is assembled or dismantled. You can also create interaction scripts, which link your animations to specific events.

Scripting

You need to create at least one animation scene to add interactivity to your model. Within this animation, certain events and actions must be created (scripted) that are carried out when those events are activated.

Each script can contain these two components:

- Events
- Actions

To open the Scripter window, in the *Home* tab>Tools panel or in the *Animation* tab>Script panel, click (Scripter). The Scripter window displays at the bottom of the Autodesk Navisworks window. The Scripter window consists of four panes, as shown in Figure 9–1.

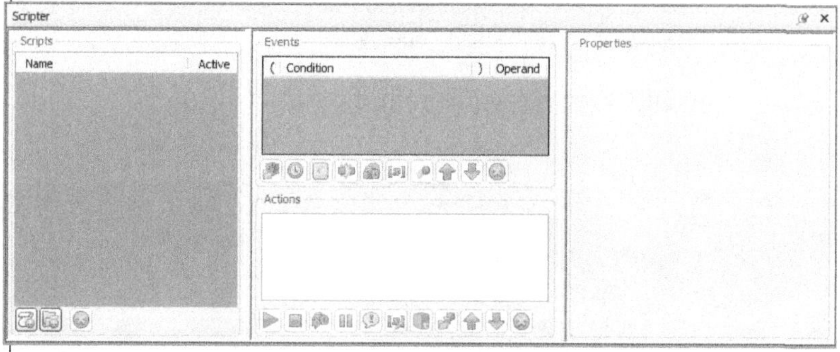

Figure 9–1

Note: If the icons are grayed out in the Scripts pane, it means scripts are enabled and thus not editable. To disable scripts, go to the *Animation* tab of the main ribbon and deselect (Enable Scripts), as shown in Figure 9–2.

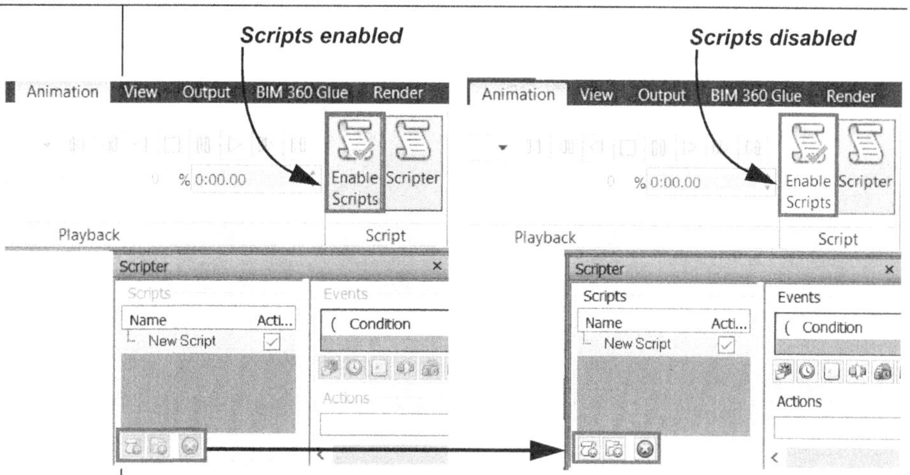

Figure 9–2

Scripts

The left pane of the Scripter window lists the available scripts and is where new scripts are added. If necessary, folders can be set up to house the various scripts. The Scripts pane also includes controls to add new scripts and folders or delete them.

Events

The center top pane lists the events for the script. New event types can be added, edited, and reordered using buttons located at the bottom of the pane.

Actions

The center lower pane lists the actions for the script. The Action pane also includes playback icons, action types, and reorder buttons located at the bottom to manage new and existing actions.

Properties

The right pane displays the properties of the selected event or action. This pane displays the properties and options used to configure events and actions that were added in the central panes.

Creating/ Managing Scripts

To add interactivity to your model, you first create a script. Events and actions are added to that script, and each event and action is configured for the desired interactivity. The scripts are then set up to work with the animations that have been created in Animator.

How To: Create Scripts

1. To add a new script, click (Add New Script) in the Scripts pane or right-click in the Scripts pane and select **Add New Script**.
    - If scripts are enabled, (Add New Script) will be grayed out in the Scripter window.

When scripts are enabled, you cannot create or edit scripts in the Scripter window. To disable scripting, in the Animation tab>Script panel, click (Enable Scripts) to clear the option.

2. Enter a new descriptive name for the script to help identify it and press <Enter>.
3. To delete a script, select it and click (Delete Item) or right-click the script and select **Delete Item**.

How To: Organize Scripts

1. To add a new folder, click (Add New Folder) in the Scripts pane or right-click in the Scripts pane and select **Add New Folder**.
2. Enter a new descriptive name for the folder and press <Enter>. The folder will be added to the Scripts pane, as shown in Figure 9–3.

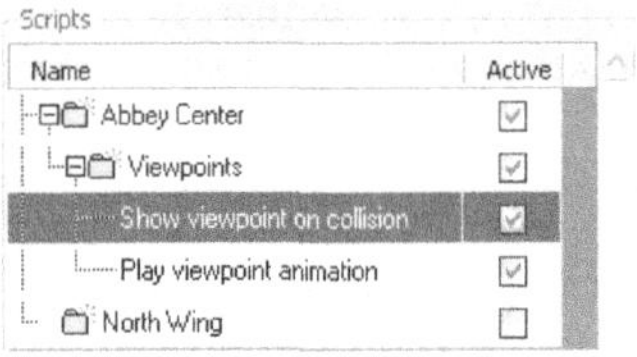

Figure 9–3

3. To move a script into a folder, drag the script using the left mouse button and drop it in the destination folder so that the black arrow head is displayed on the folder.

Practice 9a Create a Script

Practice Objectives

- Add a script to open doors as one approaches.
- Organize scripts in folders.

In this practice, you will add a script to open doors as one approaches, as shown in Figure 9–4. The events and actions will be added later.

Figure 9–4

1. In the *Animator* practice files folder, open **School-Script.nwf**.
2. In the *Home* tab>Tools panel, click (Scripter) to display the Scripter window. Pin the window open to make it easier to work with.
3. In the Saved Viewpoints window, **Animator** folder, click **Front Entry**.
4. Check to ensure that the *Selection Resolution* is set to **First Object**.
5. Select one of the front doors and wait until the tooltip appears. If the tooltip tells you it is a **Curtain Wall Single Glazed Door**, you can proceed; otherwise, you will have to hide the Revit Rooms, as follows:
   - In the Selection Tree window, go to the top of the branch of the selected object and right-click on **Rooms**.

- In the shortcut menu, select **Hide** to hide all rooms in the model, as shown in Figure 9–5. You could also use the <Ctrl>+<H> shortcut to hide them all.

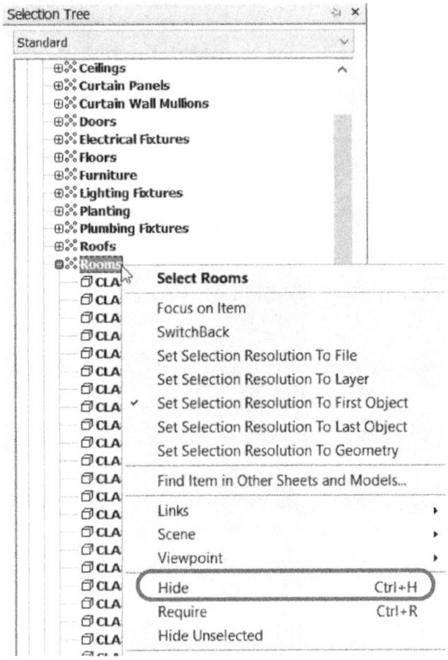

Figure 9–5

6. In the Scripter window>Scripts pane, click (Add New Script).

   - If the icons are grayed out in the Scripter window, it means scripts are enabled and thus not editable. To disable scripts, go to the *Animation* tab of the main ribbon and deselect (Enable Scripts), as shown in Figure 9–6.

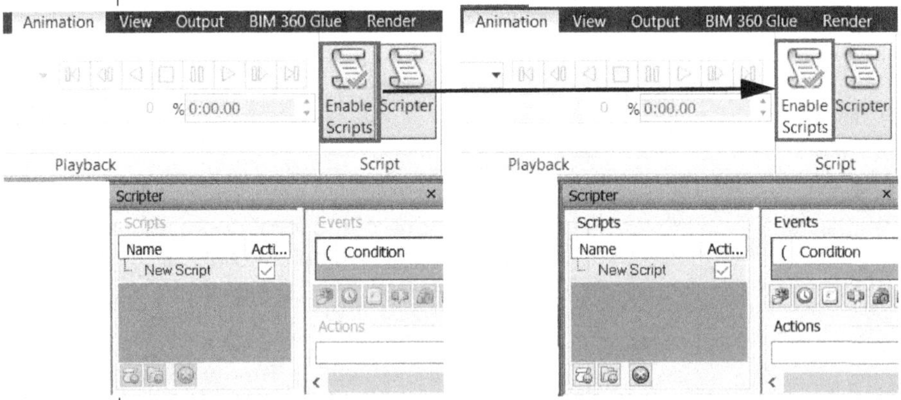

Figure 9–6

7. Click on the new script and name it **Open Exterior Doors**.

8. Repeat Steps 6 and 7 to add a new script and name it **Close Exterior Doors**.

9. In the Scripter window>Scripts pane, click (Add New Folder) and name it **Exterior Vestibule Doors**.

10. Click and hold the left mouse button on the **Open Exterior Doors** script and drag it to the *Exterior Vestibule Doors* folder so the arrow head is on the folder. Release the mouse to move the script into the folder.

11. Repeat Step 10 to move the **Close Exterior Doors** script to the same folder.

12. Follow the same process to create two new scripts and name them **Open Interior Doors** and **Close Interior Doors**.

13. Create a new folder and name it **Interior Vestibule Doors**, then drag and drop the **Open Interior Doors** and **Close Interior Doors** scripts into the new folder.

14. The script structure should look like the one shown in Figure 9–7.

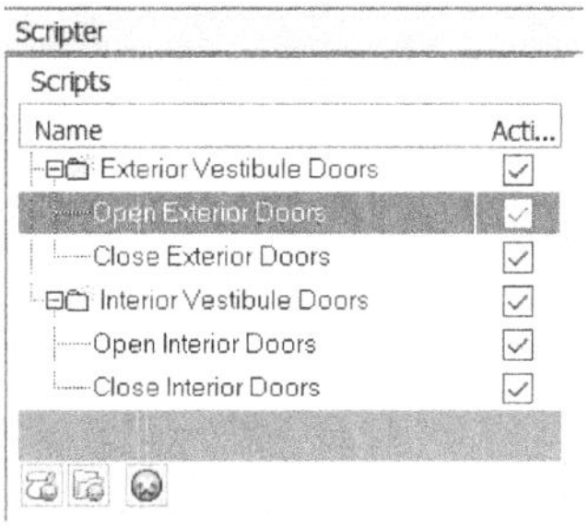

Figure 9–7

15. Save the file.

9.2 Creating and Managing Events

An event is created with certain actions, such as a mouse click, a pressed key, or a collision, which determine whether your script is activated or deactivated. Your script can have multiple events in it.

When you use several events in the same script, the event sequence becomes very important. You need to ensure the proper steps and logic make sense, the brackets are correctly closed, etc. Additionally, until the combination of all event conditions in the script is properly established, your script will not be able to run.

Event Types

There are seven event types available, which are displayed at the bottom of the Events pane, as shown in Figure 9–8. When an event is added, the Properties pane shows the properties for that event type. These properties may be configured at this time or can be deferred to a later time.

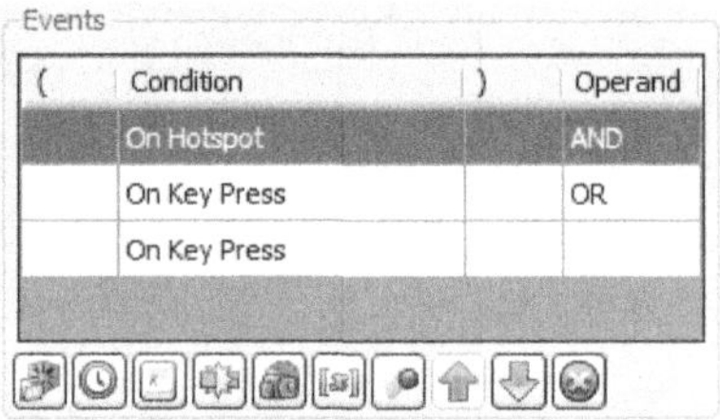

Figure 9–8

How To: Create an Event

1. In the Scripts pane, select the script you want to add an event to.
2. At the bottom of the Events pane, click an event type button (as described below) to define the event.
3. Review the properties in the Properties pane and change the property values, as required.

On Start Event

(On Start Event) triggers a script when scripting is enabled. If scripting is enabled when a file is loaded, then any start events in the file are triggered, similarly to auto-executable commands or batch files. For example, On Start events can set initial conditions of your script, giving default values to variables or repositioning a camera to a proper vantage point. You do not need to configure any properties for this event type.

On Timer Event

(On Timer Event) triggers a script at predefined time intervals. You can specify the following properties for this event type:

- **Interval:** Enter the length of time in seconds between timer triggering.
- **Regularity:** Select the event frequency.
    - *Once After*: An event happens once only. Use this option when you want to have an event that starts after a certain length of time.
    - *Continuous*: An event is continuously repeated at specified time intervals. You can use this to simulate cyclic work on an assembly floor.

On Key Press Event

(On Key Press Event) triggers a script with a specific key on the keyboard. You can specify the following properties for this event type:

- **Key:** This is a read-only box showing the currently selected key.
- **Trigger On:** Select how the event is triggered.
    - *Key Up*: An event is triggered after you press and release the key.
    - *Key Down*: An event is triggered the moment you press the key.
    - *Key Pressed*: An event is triggered while the key is pressed. This option enables you to use a key press event together with Boolean operators such as AND, which would allow you to chain it with an On Timer event.

On Collision Event

 (On Collision Event) triggers a script when your pointing device (such as a mouse) collides with a certain object. You can specify the following properties for this event type:

- **Selection to collide with:** Click the set and use the shortcut menu to define the collision objects.
    - *Clear*: Clears your currently selected collision objects.
    - *Set From Current Selection*: Sets the collision objects to your current object selection in the scene view.
    - *Set From Current Selection Set*: Sets the collision objects to your current search set or selection set.
- **Show:** This is a read-only box showing the number of geometry objects selected as collision objects.
- **Include the effects of gravity:** Select this option if you want to include gravity in collision detection. The event is triggered when you hit the floor.

On Hotspot Event

 (On Hotspot Event) triggers a script when your pointing device (such as a mouse) is within a certain radius of a hotspot. You can specify the following properties for this event type:

- **Hotspot:** Select the hotspot type.
    - *Sphere*: A sphere from a given point in space.
    - *Sphere on selection*: A sphere around a given selection. This option does not require you to define the given point in space as the hotspot moves with the selected objects in the model.
- **Trigger When:** Select how the event is triggered.
    - *Entering*: An event is triggered when you cross into the sphere of the hotspot. This is useful for opening doors, for example.
    - *Leaving*: An event is triggered when you exit the sphere of the hotspot. This is useful for closing doors.
    - *In Range*: An event is triggered when you are inside the hotspot. This option enables you to use a hotspot event together with Boolean operators. For example, you can use AND to connect this event to an On Timer event.

The remaining options are valid depending on which hotspot option is selected.

- **Position:** Specify the position of the hotspot point in your model's units. If the hotspot type you select is *Sphere on selection*, this field is not available.
- **Pick:** Pick the position of the hotspot point. If the hotspot type you select is *Sphere on selection*, this button is not available. Click this button and then click a point for the hotspot in the main Navisworks window.
- **Set:** Select the hotspot objects. If the hotspot type you select is *Sphere*, this button is not available. Click **Set** and select an option.
  - *Clear*: Clears the current selection.
  - *Set From Current Selection*: Sets the hotspot to your current object selection in the main Navisworks window.
  - *Set From Current Selection Set*: Sets the hotspot to your current search set or selection set.
- **Show:** Displays the number of geometry objects linked to the hotspot. If the hotspot type you select is *Sphere*, this field is not available.This is a read-only field.
- **Radius:** Set the radius of the hotspot in your model's units.

On Variable Event

 (On Variable Event) triggers a script when a variable meets a predefined criterion. You can specify the following properties for this event type:

- **Variable:** Specify the name of the variable to be evaluated.
- **Value:** Enter a value or a name of another variable to be tested against the value in your variable.
  - If you enter a number, the value is treated as a numeric value. If it has a decimal place, the floating-point formatting is preserved up to the user-defined decimal places.
  - If you enter an alphanumeric string between single or double quote marks, the value is treated as a string.
  - If you enter an alphanumeric string without single or double quote marks, the value is treated as the name of another variable. If this variable has never been used before, it is assigned a numerical value of 0.
  - If you enter the words **true** or **false** without any quotes, the value is treated as a Boolean (true = 1, false = 0).

- **Evaluation:** Enter an operator used for variable comparison. You can use the following operators with numbers and Boolean values, whereas when comparing strings, only the *Equal to* and *Not equal to* operators can be used.
  - *Equal to*
  - *Not Equal to*
  - *Greater than*
  - *Less than*
  - *Greater than or equal to*
  - *Less than or equal to*

On Animation Event

 (On Animation Event) triggers a script when a certain animation starts or stops. You can specify the following properties for this event type:

- **Animation:** Select an animation that triggers the event.
- **Trigger On:** Select how the event is triggered.
  - *Starting*: An event is triggered when the animation starts.
  - *Ending*: An event is triggered when the animation ends. This is useful for chaining animations together.

9.3 Creating and Configuring Actions

An action is triggered by an event. Your script can have one or multiple actions in it. Actions are sequentially executed so it is important to get the order of the actions right. Scripter does not wait for the current action to be completed before moving on to the next action unless specifically scripted.

Action Types

There are eight action types available, which are displayed at the bottom of the Actions pane, as shown in Figure 9–9. When an action is added, the Properties pane shows the properties for that action type. These properties may be configured at this time or can be deferred to a later time.

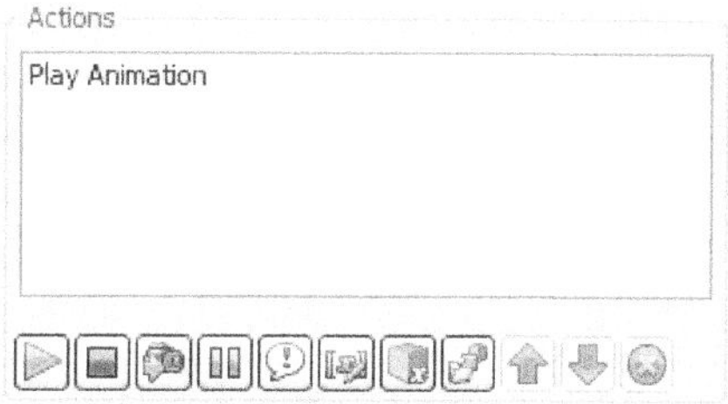

Figure 9–9

How To: Add an Action to an Event

1. In the Scripts pane, select the script to be modified.
2. In the Events pane, select the event requiring a specific action (or more).
3. At the bottom of the Actions pane, click an action type button to define the action, as described below.
4. Review the properties in the Properties pane and change any of the property values, as required.

Play Animation Action

 (Play Animation Action) specifies which animation to play back when a script is triggered. You can specify the following properties for this action type:

- **Animation:** Select the animation to play. If you do not have any object animations in your Navisworks file, this field is unavailable.

- **Pause at End:** Select this checkbox if you want the animation to stop at the end. If not selected, the animation snaps back to the starting point when it ends.

- **Starting at:** Select where the playback starts.
  - *Start*: The animation plays forwards from the beginning.
  - *End*: The animation plays backwards from the end.
  - *Current Position*: The animation plays from its current position if the playback has already started; otherwise, the animation plays from the beginning.
  - *Specified Time*: The animation plays from the segment defined in the *Specific Start Time* field.

- **Ending at:** Select when the playback will end from the drop-down list.
  - *Start*: The playback ends at the beginning of the animation.
  - *End*: The playback ends at the end of the animation.
  - *Specified Time*: The playback ends at the segment defined in the *Specific End Time* field.

- **Specific Start Time:** Specify the start point of a playback segment.

- **Specific End Time:** Specify the end point of a playback segment.

Stop Animation Action

 (Stop Animation Action) specifies which animation is to stop when a script is triggered. The animation needs to be playing for it to be able to stop. You can specify the following properties for this action type:

- **Animation:** Select the animation to stop. If you do not have any object animation in your Navisworks file, this field is unavailable.

- **Reset To:** Select the position of the stopped animation:
  - *Default Position*: The animation returns to its starting point.
  - *Current Position*: The animation remains at its existing position.

Show Viewpoint Action

 (Show Viewpoint Action) specifies which viewpoint to use when a script is triggered. You can specify the following property for this action type:

- **Viewpoint:** Select the viewpoint to show. If you do not have any viewpoints in your Navisworks file, this field is unavailable.

Pause Script Action

Actions are executed one after another in a script, but Scripter does not wait for the current action to be completed before moving on to the next. With  (Pause Action), you can interrupt the script for a specified amount of time before the next action is run. Alternatively, you can create several scripts to execute actions individually.

You can specify the following property for this action type:

- **Delay:** Enter the time period in seconds.

Send Message Action

 (Send Message Action) outputs a text string to an external text file when a script is triggered. This can be useful in debugging when creating multiple interactive scripts. You can specify the following property for this action type:

- **Message:** Enter the text string to be sent to a text file. The location of the text file can be configured in the Options Editor, under Tools>Scripter, as shown in Figure 9–10.

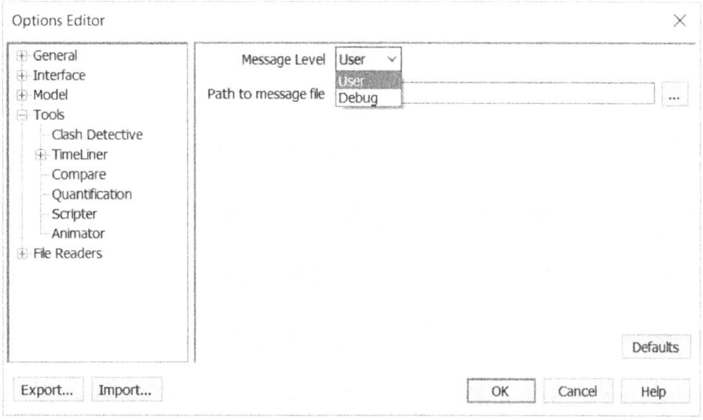

Figure 9–10

- For the *Path to message file*, enter a file location or click on the ellipses (...) to browse to a location
- In the Message Level drop-down list, select the contents of the message file:
  - *User*: The message file only contains user messages (text strings generated by message actions).
  - *Debug*: The message file contains both user messages and debug messages (text strings generated internally by Scripter). Debugging enables you to see what is going on in more complex scripts.
- When a script is triggered, the Send Message action sends the message to the location as configured.

Set Variable Action

 (Set Variable Action) assigns, increases, or decreases a variable value when a script is triggered. You can specify the following properties for this action type:

- **Variable Name:** Specify the name for the variable.
- **Value:** Enter a value to assign.
  - If you enter a number, the value is treated as a numeric value. If it has a decimal place, the floating-point formatting is preserved up to the user-defined decimal places.
  - If you enter a string between single or double quote marks, the value is treated as a string.
  - If you enter the words **true** or **false** without any quotes, the value is treated as a Boolean (true = 1, false = 0).
- **Modifier:** Enter assignment operators for your variable. You can use any of the following operators with numbers and Boolean values. However, using strings is limited to the *Set equal to* operator only.
  - *Set equal to*
  - *Increment by*
  - *Decrement by*

Store Property Action

 (Store Property Action) stores an object property in a variable when a script is triggered. This can be useful if you need to trigger events based on embedded object properties or data in an external database link. You can specify the following properties for this action type:

- **Selection to get property from:** Click **Set** and use the shortcut menu to define the objects, which are used to get the property.
    - *Clear*: Clears the current selection.
    - *Set From Current Selection*: Sets the objects to your current object selection in the main Navisworks window.
    - *Set From Current Selection Set*: Sets the objects to your current search set or selection set.

  Note: If your selection contains a hierarchy of objects, the top-level object is used to get the property.
- **Variable to set:** The name of the variable to receive the property.
- **Category:** The values in this drop-down list depend on the selected objects.
- **Property:** The values in this drop-down list depend on the chosen property category.

Practice 9b Create and Configure the Events

Practice Objective

- Create and configure events in a script.

In this practice, you will add to the script so that first the outer doors pivot open when one approaches and then the inner doors slide open. Finally, you will create a magical plant that grows and shrinks when pressing certain keys on the keyboard.

Task 1 - Create and configure the events.

1. In the Scripter window, in the Scripts pane, select the **Open Exterior Doors** script (in the *Exterior Vestibule Doors* folder).
2. In the Events pane, select  (On Hotspot).
3. In the scene view of Navisworks, select both of the exterior doors.
4. In the Properties pane of the Scripter window, select **Sphere on selection** in the *Hotspot* drop-down list.
5. Click **Set** and select **Set From Current Selection** to attach the hotspot to both doors.
6. In the *Trigger when* drop-down list, select **Entering**, as shown in Figure 9–11.

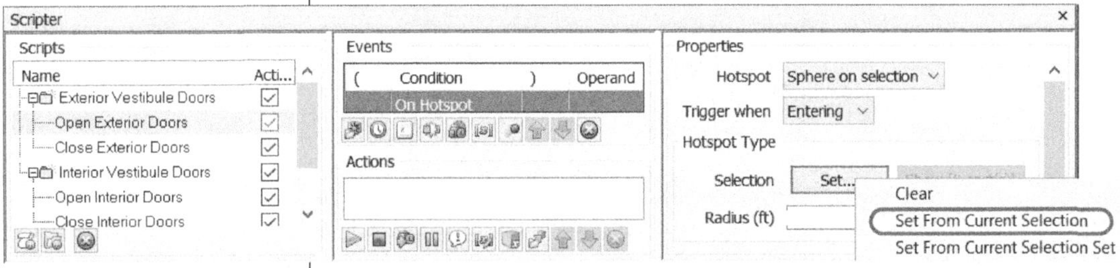

Figure 9–11

7. In the *Radius (ft)* field, enter **35.0**.
8. Repeat Steps 1 to 7 with the following differences:
   - Select the **Close Exterior Doors** script (in the *Exterior Vestibule Doors* folder).
   - In the Properties pane, in the *Trigger when* drop-down list, select **Leaving**.

9. In the Saved Viewpoints window, **Animator** folder, click **Front Vestibule**.

10. Repeat Steps 1 to 7 for the two scripts contained within the *Interior Vestibule Doors* folder.

11. Save the file.

Task 2 - Create and configure the actions required.

1. In the Scripter window, in the Scripts pane, select the **Open Exterior Doors** script (in the *Exterior Vestibule Doors* folder).

2. In the Actions pane, click (Play Animation) to add a play animation action.

*The **Hinged** animation was created in a previous chapter.*

3. In the Properties pane, click on the drop-down arrow in the *Animation* field, then expand the **Opening Doors** branch and select **Hinged**, as shown in Figure 9–12.

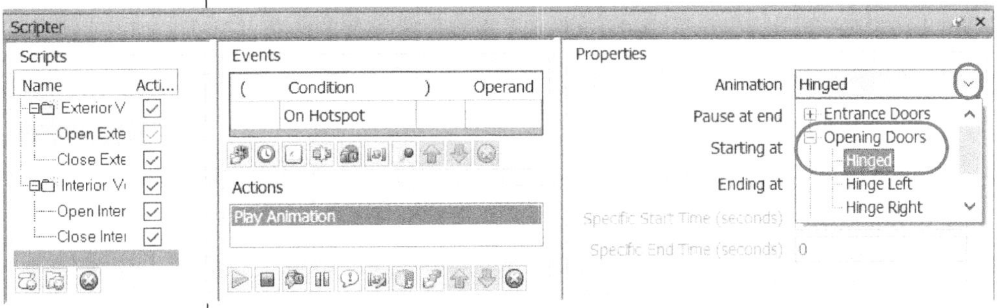

Figure 9–12

4. Check the *Pause at end* checkbox.

5. In the *Starting at* drop-down list, select **Start**.

6. In the *Ending at* drop-down list, select **End**.

7. In the Scripts pane, select the **Close Exterior Doors** script.

8. In the Events pane, select the On Hotspot event.

9. In the Actions pane, click (Play Animation) to add a play animation action.

10. As you did above, in the Properties pane, click on the drop-down arrow in the *Animation* field, then expand the **Opening Doors** branch and select **Hinged**.

11. Once again, check the *Pause at end* checkbox.

By reversing Start and End, the animation will play backwards (and close the doors).

12. In the *Starting at* drop-down list, select **End** (NOT Start).
13. In the *Ending At* drop-down list, select **Start** (NOT End).
14. Repeat the process to apply actions to the two scripts within the *Interior Vestibule Doors* folder, using the **Sliding** animation in the **Sliding Doors** branch for the proper animation.
15. Save the file.

Task 3 - Test out the interactive animations.

Now that you have added and configured actions to the hotspots in the scripts, you are ready to see the interactive animations. The created scripts need to be enabled to work with the navigation tools.

1. To enable scripts, go to the *Animation* tab of the main ribbon and select  (Enable Scripts), as shown in Figure 9–13.

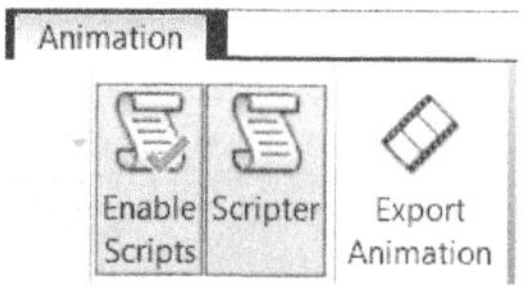

Figure 9–13

2. Note how the Events, Actions, and Properties panes are all disabled.
3. Select the **Front Entrance** saved viewpoint from the **Animator** folder.
4. Use the navigation bar to interact with your model. When navigating towards the entrance doors, they should open and then close behind you as you proceed into the building.

Task 4 - (Optional) Create the wilting plant script.

To review all the steps, you will create another script for a plant that wilts when you press <S>. When you press <R>, the plant will return to its original size. A message will also be written to a specified file.

Although this example is a bit whimsical, it demonstrates the power of scripting by assigning certain keystrokes to actions and also having Navisworks report on the state of the model by writing messages to an external file.

1. Restore the **Shrinking Plant** viewpoint from the **Animator** folder.
2. In the Scripter window>Scripts pane, click (Add New Folder) and name it **Plants**.
3. Select the newly created folder.
4. In the Scripter window>Scripts pane, click (Add New Script) to create a new script. Name it **Wilting Tree**.
5. Create another script and name it **Resurrecting Tree**.
6. Select the **Wilting Tree** script.
7. In the Actions pane, click (On Key Press) to add a trigger when a specific key is pressed.
8. In the Properties pane, click in the *Key* field, then press <S>. Use the drop-down list to select **Key Pressed** in the *Trigger on* field, as shown in Figure 9–14.

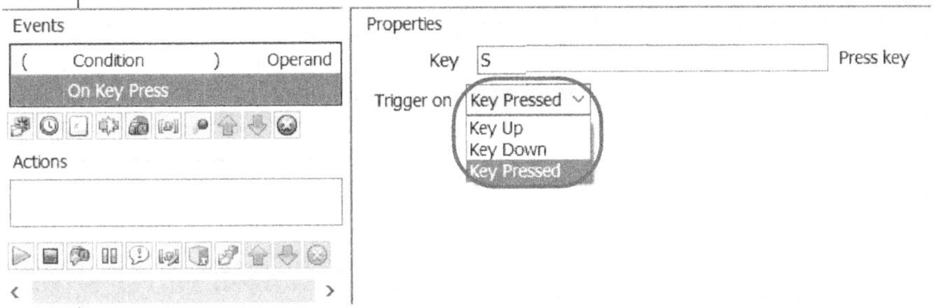

Figure 9–14

9. In the Actions pane, click (Send Message) to write a text string to an external file.

10. In the Properties pane, click in the *Message* field and type **Plant Wilting** as the text to be exported, as shown in Figure 9–15.

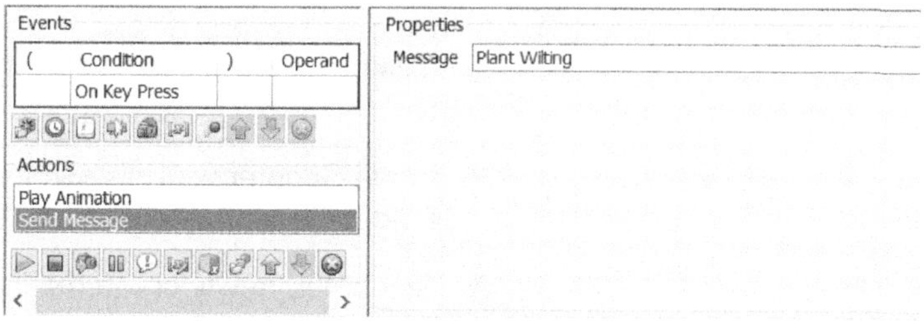

Figure 9–15

11. In the Actions pane, click (Play Animation) to add a play animation action.

*The **Shrinking Plant** animation was created in a previous chapter.*

12. In the Properties pane, click on the drop-down arrow in the *Animation* field, then expand the **Shrinking Plant** branch and select **Plant**, as shown in Figure 9–16.

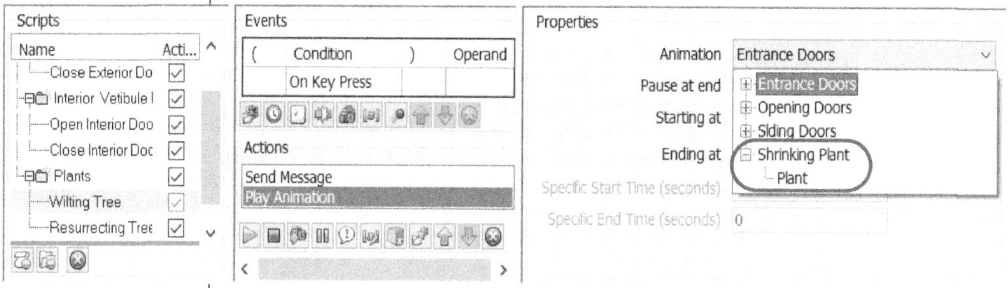

Figure 9–16

13. Check the *Pause at end* checkbox.

By reversing Start and End, the animation will play backwards (and the plant will shrink).

14. In the *Starting at* drop-down list, select **End** (NOT Start).
15. In the *Ending at* drop-down list, select **Start** (NOT End).
16. Repeat Steps 6 to 14 for the **Resurrecting Plant** script, but with the following differences:
    - For the *Key*, press <R>.
    - For the *Message,* type **Plant Resurrecting**.
    - For the *Starting at* option, select **Start**.
    - For the *Ending at* option, select **End**.

17. For the location of the text file, you need to configure Navisworks by going to the Options Editor, under Tools>Scripter, click on the ellipses (...) and browse to the *Navisworks BIM Practice Files\Animator* folder, as shown in Figure 9–17. Type **Plants.txt** as the file name and click **OK**.

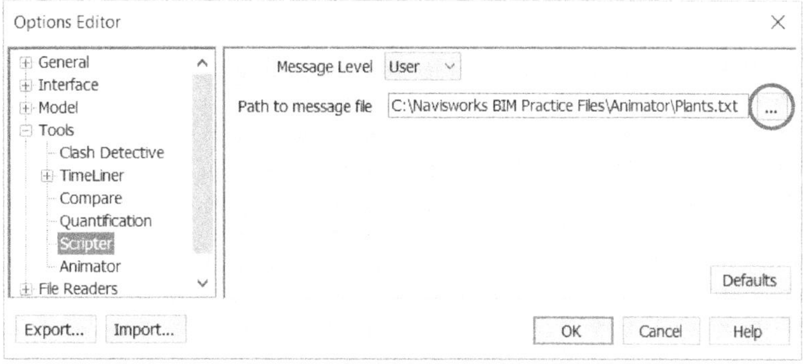

Figure 9–17

18. Save the file.

19. To enable scripts, go to the *Animation* tab of the main ribbon and select  (Enable Scripts).

20. If need be, restore the **Shrinking Plant** viewpoint from the **Animator** folder.

21. Press <S> and the plant should diminish in size.

22. Press <R> and the plant should return to its prior size.

23. In the Windows File Explorer, browse to the *Navisworks BIM Practice Files\Animator* folder and double-click on the **Plants.txt** file.

24. Every time you pressed <S> and <R>, a line was recorded in this file, as seen in Figure 9–18.

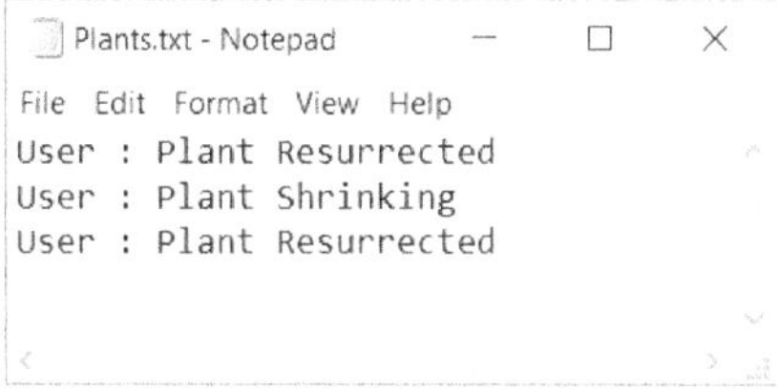

Figure 9–18

25. Save and close the file.

Chapter Review Questions

1. Which of the following is NOT part of the Scripter window?
    a. Properties pane
    b. File pane
    c. Actions pane
    d. Events pane
2. Which of the following options are available for the On Key Press event? (Select all that apply.)
    a. Key Double Tap
    b. Key Pressed
    c. Key Held
    d. Key Up
3. Which of the following is NOT a Scripter event?
    a. On Collision
    b. On Timer
    c. On Hotspot
    d. On Saving
4. What is the issue when elements in the Scripter window are grayed out and cannot be edited?
    a. The script has not been saved.
    b. Scripts are enabled.
    c. The script is in read-only mode.
    d. There is an error in the script.
5. Can you specify the output file for exporting text strings?
    a. Yes
    b. No
    c. It depends on the script.
    d. You cannot export test strings.

Command Summary

Button	Command	Location
	**Add Folder**	• **Ribbon:** *Home* tab>Tools panel
	**Add Script**	• **Window: Scripter**
	**Delete Item**	• **Window: Scripter**
	**Enable/ Disable Scripts**	• **Ribbon:** *Animation* tab>Script panel
	**Load Model**	• **Window: Scripter**
	**On Animation**	• **Window: Scripter**
	**On Collision**	• **Window: Scripter**
	**On Hotspot**	• **Window: Scripter**
	**On Key Press**	• **Window: Scripter**
	**On Start**	• **Window: Scripter**
	**On Timer**	• **Window: Scripter**
	**On Variable**	• **Window: Scripter**
	**Play Animation**	• **Window: Scripter**
	**Send Message**	• **Window: Scripter**
	**Set Variable**	• **Window: Scripter**
	**Show/Hide Scripter Window**	• **Ribbon:** *Home* tab>Tools panel • **Ribbon:** *Animation* tab>Script panel
	**Show Viewpoint**	• **Window: Scripter**

	**Stop Animation**	• **Window: Scripter**
	**Store Property**	• **Window: Scripter**

Chapter 10

Construct: Project Scheduling

The next step in the BIM workflow is to construct the project. Creating a 4D simulation connects a 3D model to a construction schedule, which gives it that fourth dimension (time). This helps users better understand errors in the schedule or safety issues that need to be addressed.

In this chapter, you will learn how to create and import a Gantt chart. Then, you will connect model elements to the Gantt chart to create a construction simulation.

Learning Objectives in This Chapter

- Create a construction timeline.
- Import a construction timeline created in an external project management application.
- Run a time-based clash test.

BIM Workflow: Construct

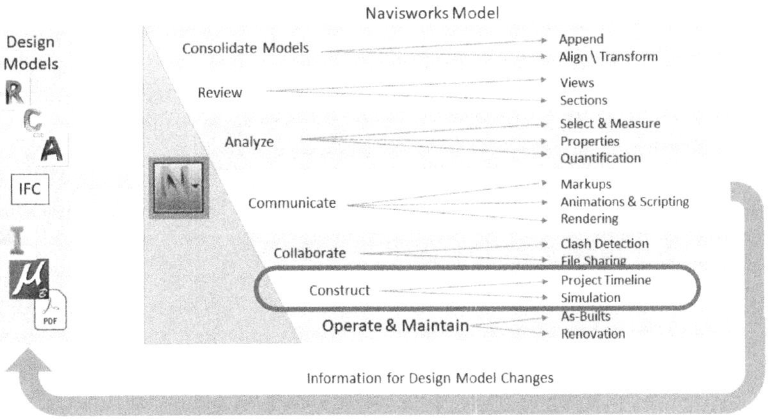

10.1 Introduction to TimeLiner

4D models visually communicate the relationships between model elements and the construction schedule. This can help stakeholders better understand any issues that might arise during the construction phase. The TimeLiner window (shown in Figure 10–1) is used to connect tasks in the Gantt chart with elements in the model to simulate construction.

You can create a Gantt chart in the Autodesk® Navisworks® software in two ways:

- Create a new chart from scratch.
- Import an existing chart from a project management software application.

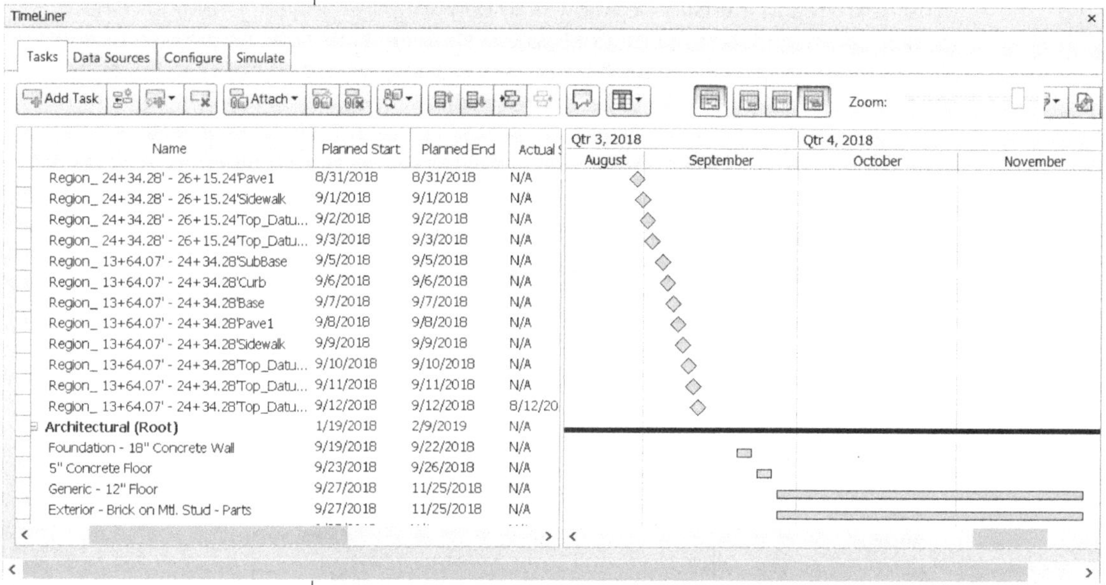

Figure 10–1

The TimeLiner window has four tabs, as shown above in Figure 10–1. Most of the work is completed in the *Tasks* tab.

Tasks Tab

The *Tasks* tab contains a list of all of the active tasks in the left pane and a Gantt chart in the right pane. Several columns are available in the task list pane that include information about each task. The columns can be reordered as required by dragging the column heading to a new location. The following information can be found in each column:

- **Active:** Displays a checkmark if the task is active and included in the simulation.
- **Status:** Displays two bars, as shown in Figure 10–2. The top bar represents the planned dates, while the bottom bar represents the actual dates. When the planned and actual dates match, the bars display in green. When they do not match, they display in red. If the date field is empty, the bar displays as clear.

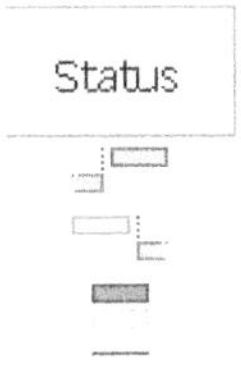

Figure 10–2

- **Name:** Displays the task name.
- **Planned Start/End Dates:** Displays the planned start and planned end dates of the task.
- **Actual Start/End Dates:** Displays the actual start and actual end dates of the task.
- **Task Type:** Displays the types of tasks that can be assigned, which determine the objects' appearance. The task types are set up in the *Configure* tab.
- **Attached:** Lists the objects attached to the task from the model.
- **Total Cost:** Displays a monetary ($) amount connected to the task.

Data Sources Tab

The *Data Sources* tab is used to connect to external project management software. There are multiple project management databases that can be connected, as shown in Figure 10–3. A database can be connected for each discipline or each model attached to the project, if required.

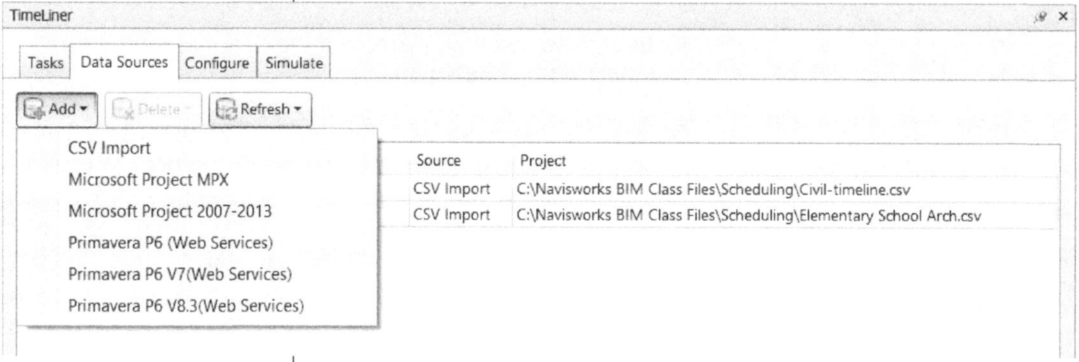

Figure 10–3

Configure Tab

The *Configure* tab enables you to set how you want objects to display at key times during a simulation. By default, there are three options, as shown in Figure 10–4:

- Construct
- Demolish
- Temporary (Constructed and demolished within the same key time)

Figure 10–4

Simulate Tab

The *Simulate* tab enables you to play, stop, and go to any point in the simulation. Similar to the *Tasks* tab, it contains two panes: the task list is on the left and the Gantt chart is on the right, as shown in Figure 10–5.

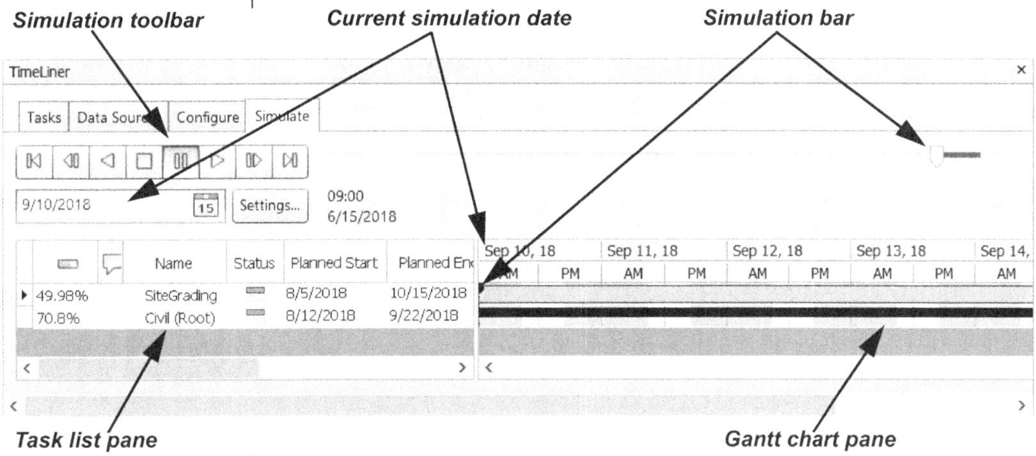

Figure 10–5

Task List Pane

The columns in the task list pane include information about each task. The columns can be reordered as required by dragging the column heading to a new location. The following information is found in each column:

- (Simulation Progress): Displays a percentage for how much of a specific task is complete in the simulation.
- (Comments): Lists the number of comments applied to a specific task.
- **Name:** Displays the task name.
- **Planned Start/End Dates:** Displays the planned start and planned end dates of the task.
- **Actual Start/End Dates:** Displays the actual start and actual end dates of the task.
- **Total Cost:** Displays a monetary ($) amount connected to the task.
- **Task Type:** Displays the task type that is assigned, which determines the objects' appearance.

Gantt Chart Pane

In the Gantt chart pane, columns list dates, while bars show each task's duration in the schedule. The beginning of the bar is located at the start date, and the end of the bar is located at the end date. Depending on the zoom level, the dates might display as months and days, months and weeks, or quarters and months, as shown in Figure 10–6.

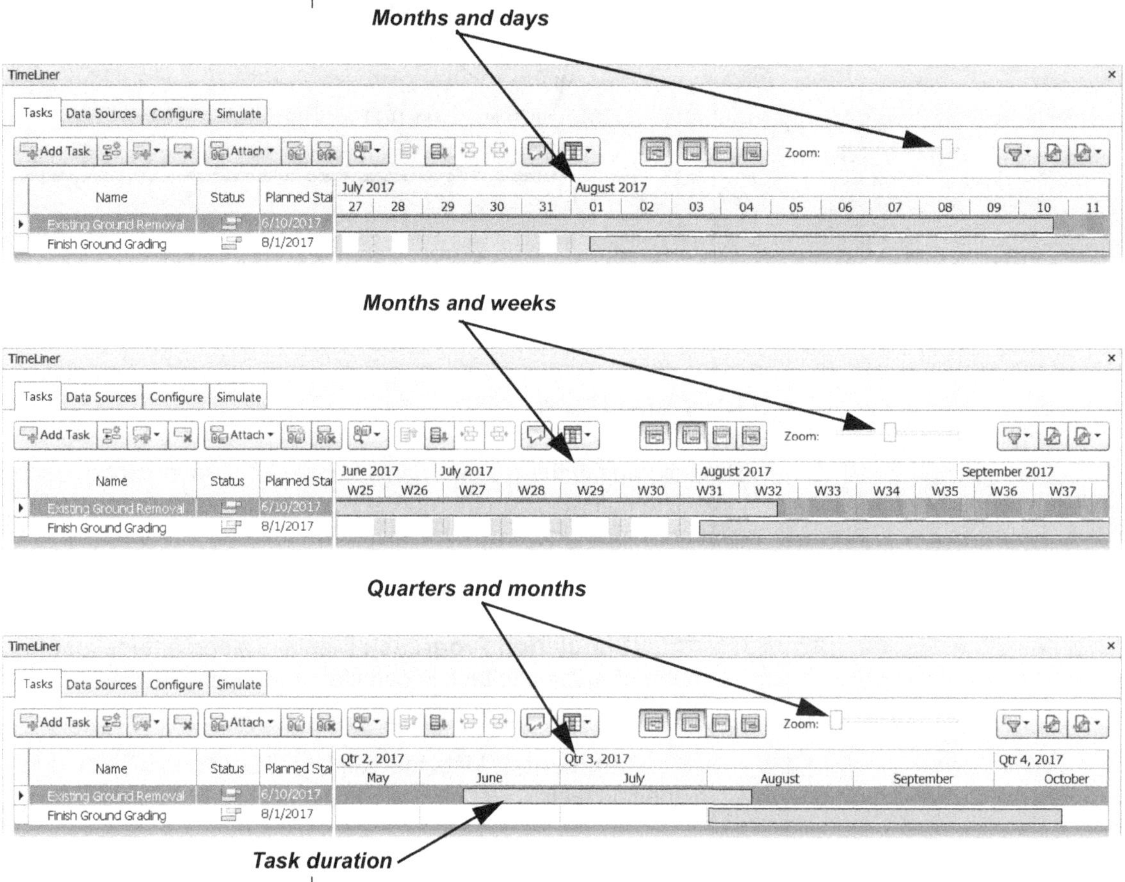

Figure 10–6

10.2 Manually Creating a Construction Simulation

Creating a construction simulation requires preparation. The models have to be created and then merged together. Next, the task list and Gantt chart must be created. Finally, the tasks must be connected to the task list.

General Steps

Use the following general steps to create a construction simulation:

1. Prepare the models.
2. Create saved sets and search sets.
3. Add tasks to the Gantt chart.
4. Configure how objects display during the simulation.
5. Link the simulation to any previously created animations.
6. Play the simulation.
7. Make any required changes.

Step 1 - Prepare the models.

In the Autodesk® Revit® software and the Autodesk® Civil 3D® software, multiple parts form one object in the model. For example, Figure 10–7 shows the parts that form a wall, while Figure 10–8 shows the parts that form a corridor model.

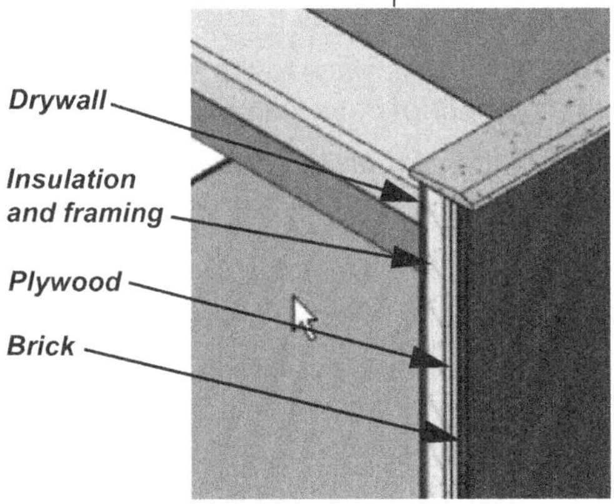

Figure 10–7

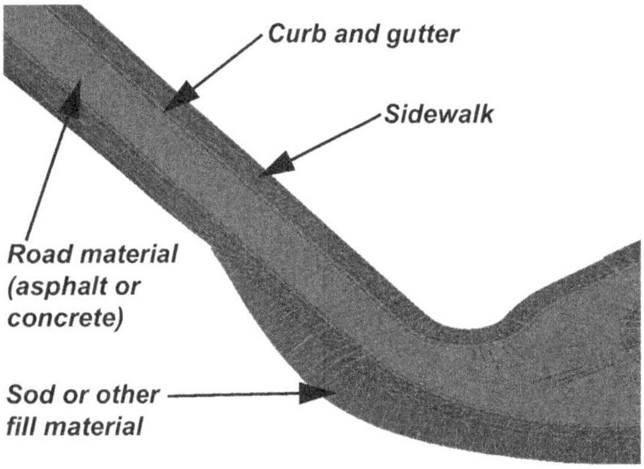

Figure 10–8

During construction, an entire road would not be built at once. First, grading would set the datum elevation, then the sub-base and base would be laid down. Next would come the sidewalks, curb, and gutter. Finally, the asphalt or concrete would be poured for the wearing course of the road.

When creating a construction animation using TimeLiner, you can create a simulation to match a real construction schedule. In order to do this, you must separate objects into parts in the Autodesk Civil 3D software and the Autodesk Revit software before importing the model into the Autodesk Navisworks software.

For more information on separating objects, see *Coordination Tools*.

Step 2 - Create saved sets and search sets.

Saved sets and search sets make connecting objects to the construction schedule much easier. You should use saved searches whenever possible to ensure that the sets are updated automatically whenever new or updated models are appended in the Autodesk Navisworks software.

For more information on creating saved sets and search sets, see *Chapter 4: Analyze Models*.

Step 3 - Add tasks to the Gantt chart.

To manually create tasks in the Autodesk Navisworks software, you must be on the *Tasks* tab of the TimeLiner window. Using this method, each task is created one line item at a time.

- Start and end dates must be manually input for each line item.
- You cannot set the end date in reference to the start date (i.e., you cannot set the number of days to complete).
- You cannot set the start of the next task to automatically follow the end of a previous task.

Hint: Date Standards

This guide uses the North American date standard of MM/DD/YYYY. If you are working in a region with a different date format, you will need to configure Navisworks to work with the MM/DD/YYYY date format for this course. In actual practice, you can configure Navisworks to work in your date format of choice.

To change the date format, go to the Application Menu 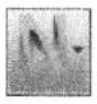 > Options Editor>Tools>TimeLiner and change the *Date Format* to **7/26/2010**, which is the MM/DD/YYYY format, as shown in Figure 10–9.

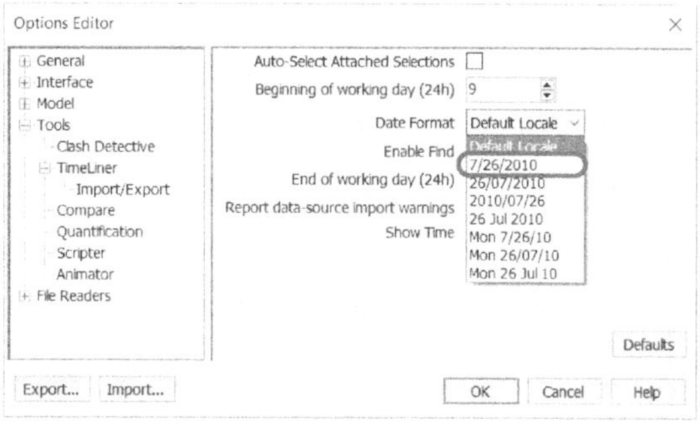

Figure 10–9

The **Default Locale** format is your system's format, controlled by your operating system and based on your location's standard.

How To: Manually Add Tasks to the Construction Simulation

1. In the TimeLiner window>*Tasks* tab, click (Add Task).
2. In the task's data fields, do the following:
   - *Name:* Type a name.
   - *Planned Start Date:* Set the date (MM/DD/YYYY format).
   - *Planned End Date:* Set the date (MM/DD/YYYY format).
   - *Actual Start Date:* Set the date (MM/DD/YYYY format).
   - *Actual End Date:* Set the date (MM/DD/YYYY format).
   - *Task Type:* Expand the list and select a task type. Task types are defined in the *Configure* tab.
   - *Attached:* There are several options for attaching objects. Right-click on the field and select one of the options shown in Figure 10–10.

It is recommended to use search sets whenever possible to ensure that new items connect to the construction schedule.

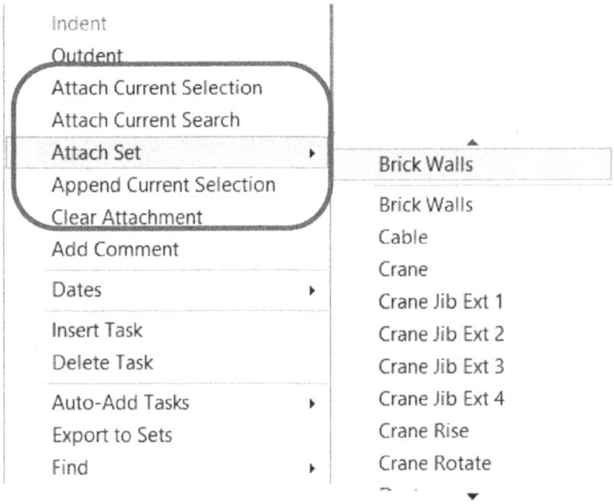

Figure 10–10

Step 4 - Configure how objects display during the simulation.

The *Configure* tab enables you to set how you want objects to display at key times during the simulation.

- You can remove options by clicking Delete (Delete), which deletes the selected row.
- You can create additional options by clicking Add (Add), which creates a new row. You can then use the down arrows in each column to select how you want objects to display.
- Additional appearance definitions can be created by clicking **Appearance Definitions**.

How To: Create a New Appearance Definition

1. In the TimeLiner window>*Configure* tab, click **Appearance Definitions**.
2. In the Appearance Definitions dialog box, click **Add**. A new row is added at the bottom of the list.
3. Select the new row and click on the **Name** field to change the name.
4. Double-click on the **Color** field to select a color from the color palette. Click **OK**.
5. Slide the **Transparency** slider to set the amount of transparency/opacity, as shown in Figure 10–11.

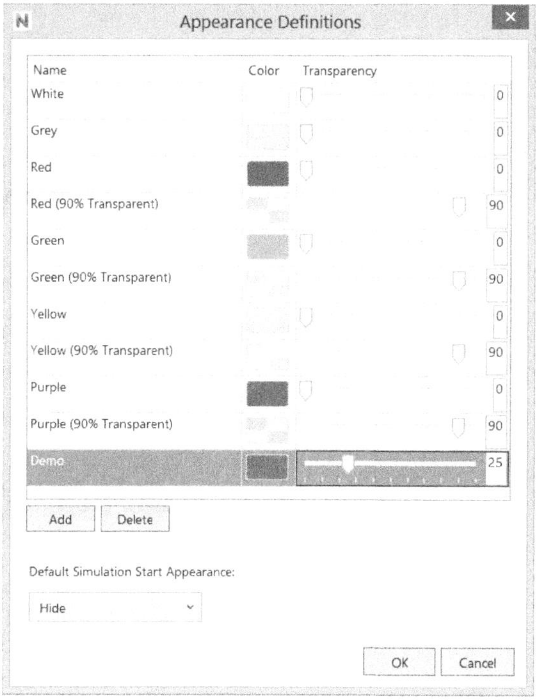

Figure 10–11

6. Expand the Default Simulation Start Appearance drop-down list and select the appearance you plan to use routinely at the start of the simulation.
7. Click **OK**.

Step 5 - Link the simulation to any previously created animations.

Simulations can be linked to any previously created animations to demonstrate how the project develops on the site as construction proceeds.

Step 6 - Play the simulation.

Tools at the top of the *Simulate* tab enable you to navigate the simulation. The tools are as follows:

- **(Rewind):** Moves the simulation bar to the beginning and changes the scene view to match.
- **(Step Back):** Rewinds the simulation a frame at a time.
- **(Reverse Play):** Plays the simulation in reverse.
- **(Pause):** Pauses the simulation, enabling you to resume play from the same spot by clicking (Play).
- **(Stop):** Stops the simulation, moves the simulation bar to the beginning, and changes the scene view to match.
- **(Play):** Starts the simulation from the current position of the simulation bar.
- **(Step Forward):** Moves forward a frame at a time.
- **(Forward):** Fast forwards the simulation to the end.

Step 7 - Make any required changes.

It is easier to make construction timeline adjustments before scheduling all of the sub-contractors due to complex project schedules. Being able to watch the construction virtually before breaking ground helps you to predict any issues that might occur during construction. Once an issue is discovered, you can go back to the TimeLiner window>*Tasks* tab to make any required adjustments to the construction timeline.

Scripter

By linking TimeLiner and scripted object animation together, you can trigger and schedule object movement based on start time and duration of project tasks. This can help you with workspace and process planning. For example, a TimeLiner sequence might indicate that when a particular site crane moves from its start to end point on a particular afternoon, a work group causes an obstruction along its route.

Practice 10a Manually Create a Construction Simulation

Practice Objectives

- Consolidate models from multiple software sources.
- Align the models with each other.

In this practice, you will manually add tasks to the TimeLiner window and attach them to objects in the model, as shown in Figure 10–12.

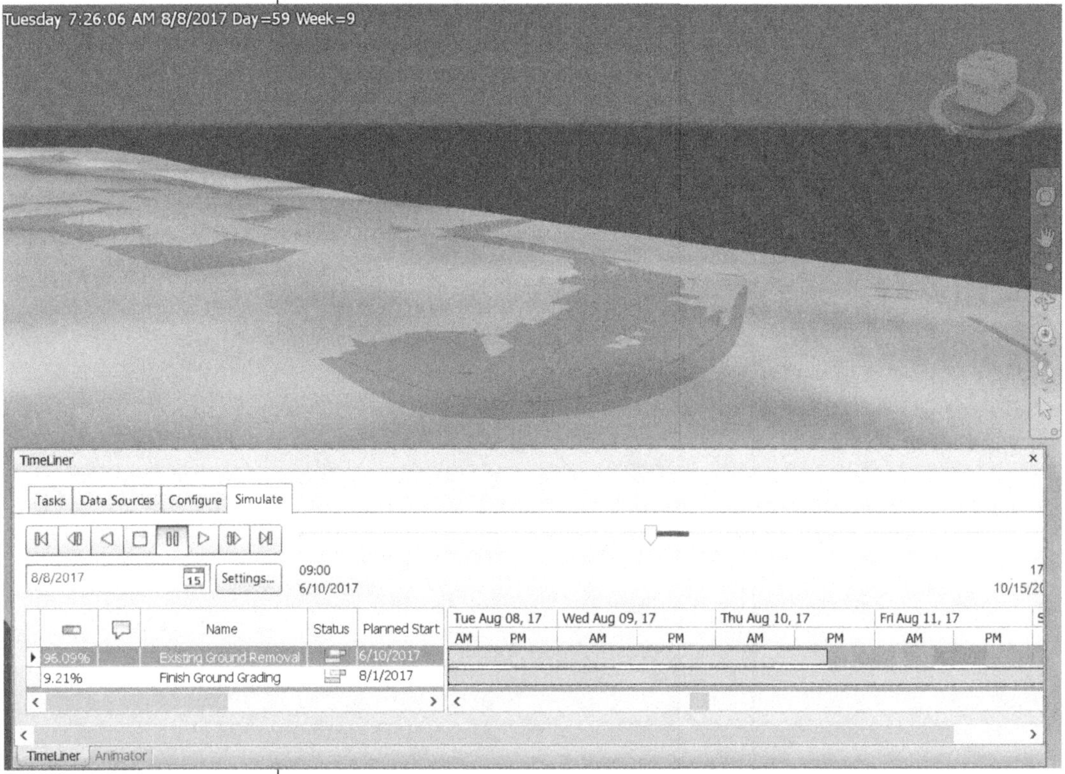

Figure 10–12

Task 1 - Append the parts models.

For TimeLiner to work properly, the original files must be correctly organized and objects should be separated into parts. In *Coordination Tools*, you will learn how to set up the Autodesk Revit file and the Autodesk Civil 3D corridor model for use in TimeLiner. In this task, you will attach new models that have already been separated into parts for the simulation.

1. In the *Scheduling* practice files folder, open **New-School-Prep.nwf**.

2. If the drawing displays only boxes where the surfaces and roads should be (as shown in Figure 10–13), you will need to install the Autodesk Civil 3D Object Enabler. Consult *B.3 Autodesk Civil 3D Object Enabler* to install this prior to proceeding.

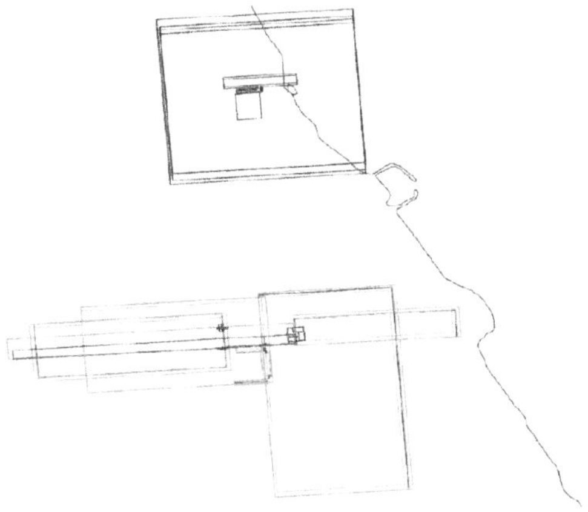

Figure 10–13

3. In the *Home* tab>Project panel, click (Append).

4. In the Append dialog box, expand the Files of type drop-down list and select **Autodesk DWG/DXF (*.dwg, *.dxf)**.

5. Navigate to the *Scheduling* practice files folder, select **CorridorSolids.dwg**, and click **Open**.

6. In the Selection Tree window, right-click on **CorridorSolids.dwg** and select **Units and Transform**.

7. In the Units and Transform dialog box, set the *Origin* values as: *X:* **0**, *Y:* **0**, *Z:* **0.15**.

    - **Note:** You are only doing this transformation for visual purposes. The finished ground surface included the corridor model, which ends up hiding the corridor. Therefore, you are raising the corridor to ensure that the corridor model is not hidden by the surface during the simulation.

8. In the *Home* tab>Project panel, click (Append).

9. In the Append dialog box, expand the Files of type drop-down list and select **Revit (*.rvt, *.rfa, *.rte)**.

10. Navigate to the *Scheduling* practice files folder, select **School-Architectural TimeLiner.rvt**, and click **Open**.

11. You can now hide the School-Architectural.rvt file from your model since the School-Architectural TimeLiner.rvt file supersedes it. Right-click on **School-Architectural.rvt** in the Selection Tree window and select **Hide**, or use the **<Ctrl>+<H>** keyboard shortcut.

This task can be skipped if you are short on time. If skipped, ensure that you open the indicated file in the next task so that the TimeLiner will work properly.

Task 2 - (Optional) Create selection sets within the file.

To make the connection between parts in the model and the Gantt chart, it is important to create saved sets and saved searches within the file. In this task, you will create saved sets for the Autodesk Revit model parts.

1. Continue working in the same file as the previous task.

Pin the Selection Tree open to make it easier to access since you will be using it repeatedly for this task (as shown in Figure 10–14).

2. In the Selection Tree, expand *School- Architectural TimeLiner.rvt>First Floor>Doors* and select the following, as shown in Figure 10–14:
    - **Double Door**
    - **SINGLE**
    - **DOUBLE**

    Use <Ctrl> to select multiple items after you select the first one.

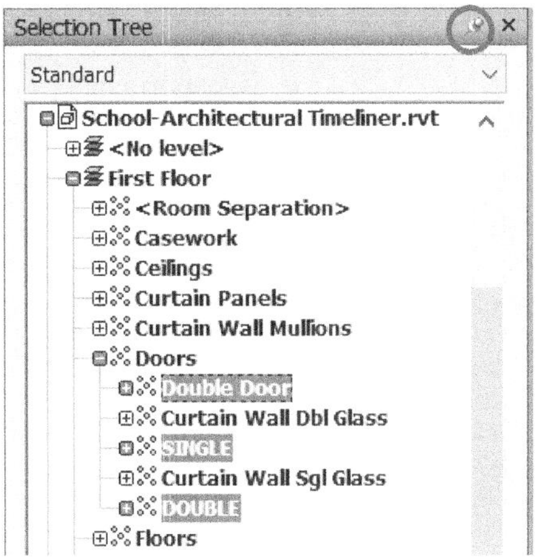

Figure 10–14

3. In the *Home* tab>Select & Search panel, click (Save Selection). Type **1st Floor Doors** for the name.

4. Collapse the **Doors** branch.

5. Expand *School-Architectural TimeLiner.rvt>First Floor> Walls>Basic Wall* and select the following, as shown in Figure 10–15:
   - **Interior 6" Metal Stud**
   - **Interior 4" Metal Stud**
   - **Interior - 4 1/4" Chase Partition**
   - **Interior 4" Metal Stud - Chase**

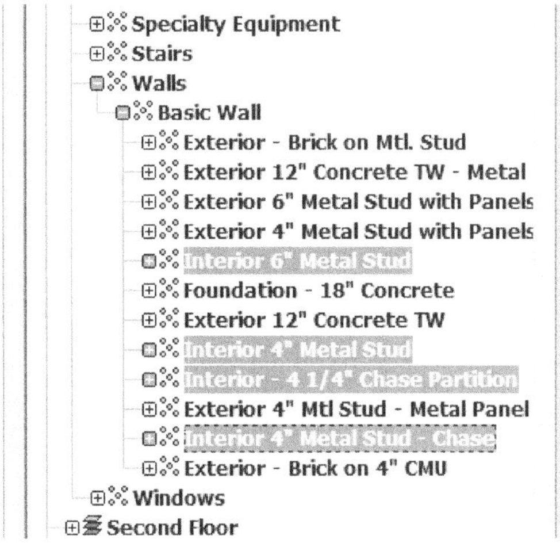

Figure 10–15

6. Save the selection as **1st Floor Interior Walls**.

7. Collapse the **Walls** branch.

8. Expand *School-Architectural TimeLiner.rvt>First Floor* and select **Windows**, as shown in Figure 10–16.

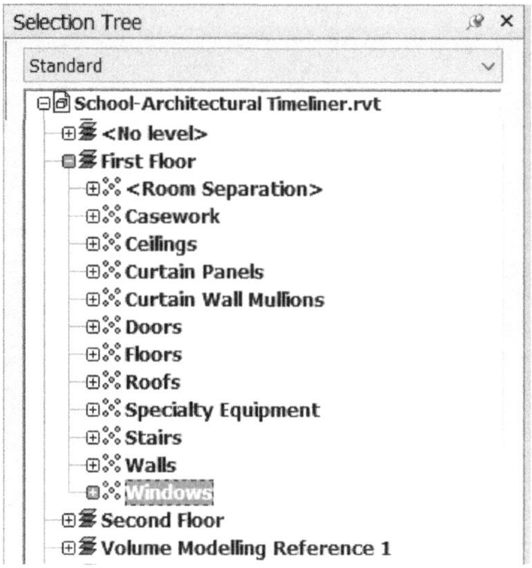

Figure 10–16

9. Save the selection as **1st Floor Windows**.

10. Collapse the **First Floor** branch.

11. Expand *School-Architectural TimeLiner.rvt>Second Floor>Doors* and select **SINGLE**, as shown in Figure 10–17.

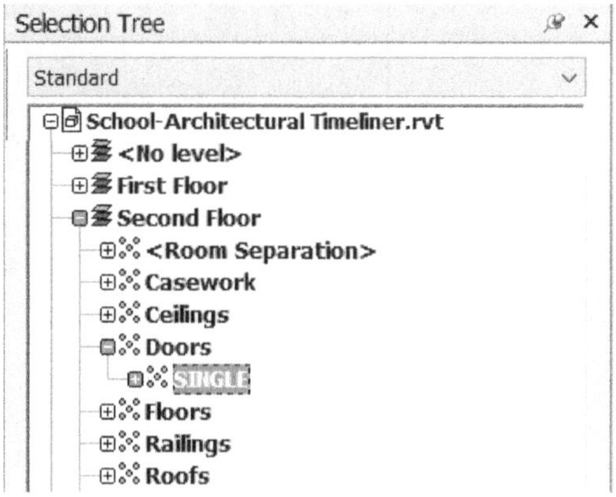

Figure 10–17

12. Save the selection as **2nd Floor Doors**.

13. Collapse the **Doors** branch.

*Since these two are the only Basic Walls on the second floor, you could simply select **Basic Wall**.*

14. Expand *School-Architectural TimeLiner.rvt>Second Floor> Walls>Basic Wall* and select the following, as shown in Figure 10–18:
    - **Interior 6" Metal Stud**
    - **Interior 4" Metal Stud**

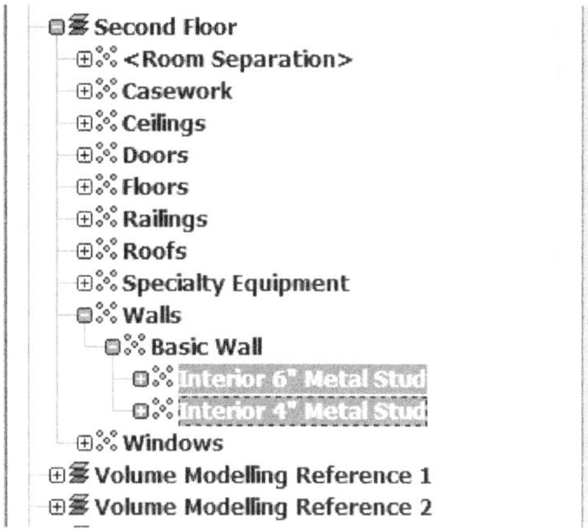

Figure 10–18

15. Save the selection as **2nd Floor Interior Walls**.

16. Collapse the **Walls** branch.

17. Expand *School-Architectural TimeLiner.rvt>Second Floor* and select **Windows**, as shown in Figure 10–19.

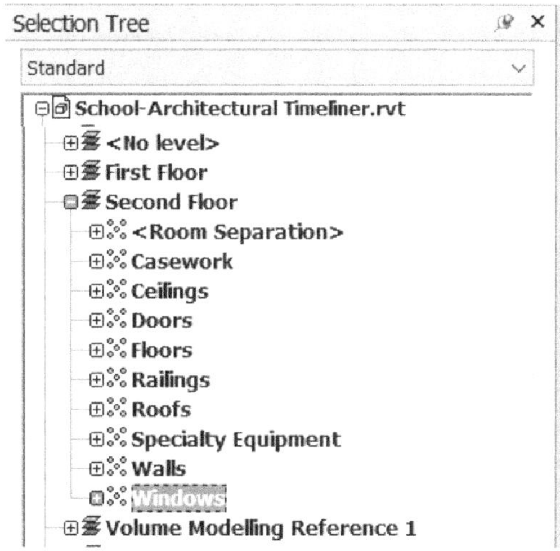

Figure 10–19

18. Save the selection as **2nd Floor Windows**.

19. Collapse the **Second Floor** branch.

20. Expand *School-Architectural TimeLiner.rvt><No level>* and select the following, as shown in Figure 10–20:
    - **Curtain Panels**
    - **Curtain Wall Mullions**

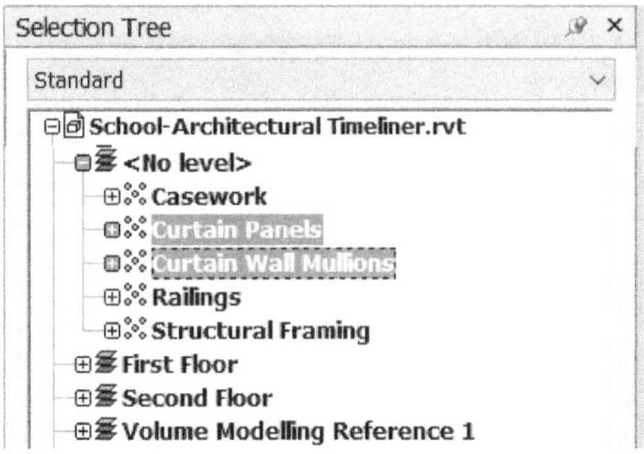

Figure 10–20

21. Save the selection as **Curtain Panels and Mullions**.

22. Collapse the **<No level>** branch.

23. Expand *School-Architectural TimeLiner.rvt>First Floor* and select the following, as shown in Figure 10–21:
    - **Curtain Panels**
    - **Curtain Wall Mullions**
    - *Doors*>**Curtain Wall Dbl Glass**
    - *Doors*>**Curtain Wall Sgl Glass**

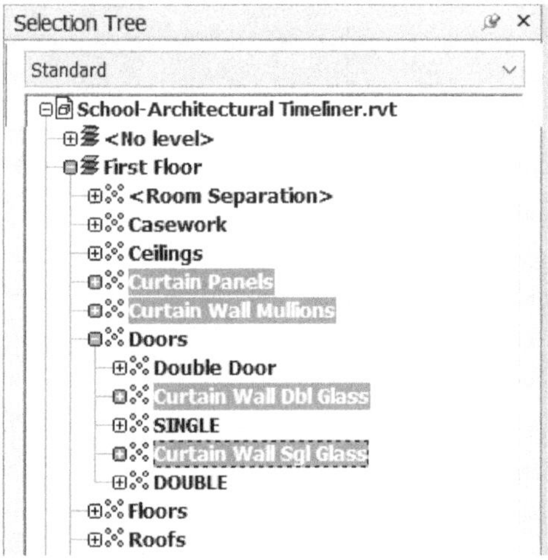

Figure 10–21

24. Save the selection as **Curtain Walls**.

25. Collapse the **Doors** branch and expand the **Second Floor** branch.

26. Expand *School-Architectural TimeLiner.rvt* and select the following, as shown in Figure 10–22:
    - *First Floor*>**Roofs**
    - *Second Floor*>**Roofs**

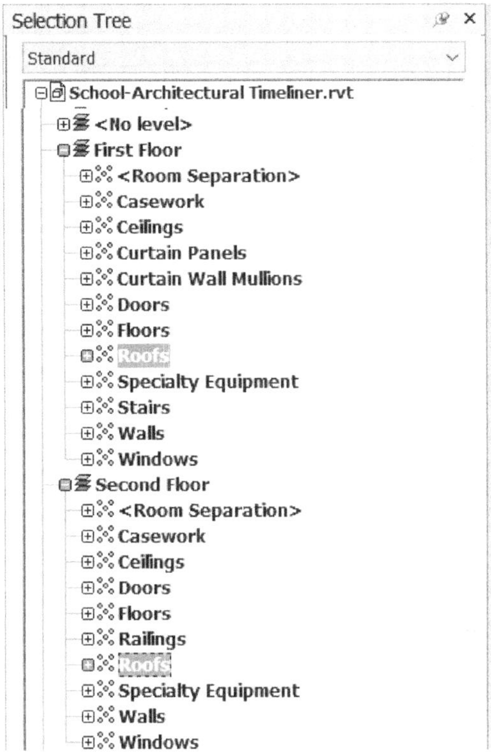

Figure 10–22

27. Save the selection set. Type **Roofs 1 and 2** for the name.

28. Collapse the **First Floor** and **Second Floor** branches.

29. Expand *School-Architectural TimeLiner.rvt>Volume Modeling Reference 1* and select **Roofs**, as shown in Figure 10–23.

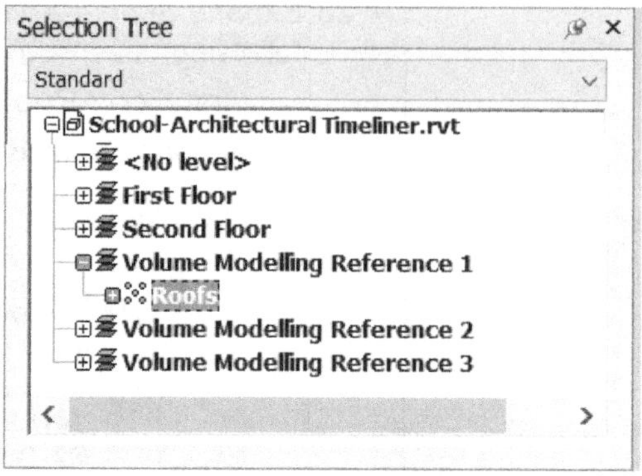

Figure 10–23

30. Save the selection as **Roofs Reference 2**.

31. Expand *School-Architectural TimeLiner.rvt>Volume Modeling Reference 3* and select **Roofs**, as shown in Figure 10–24.

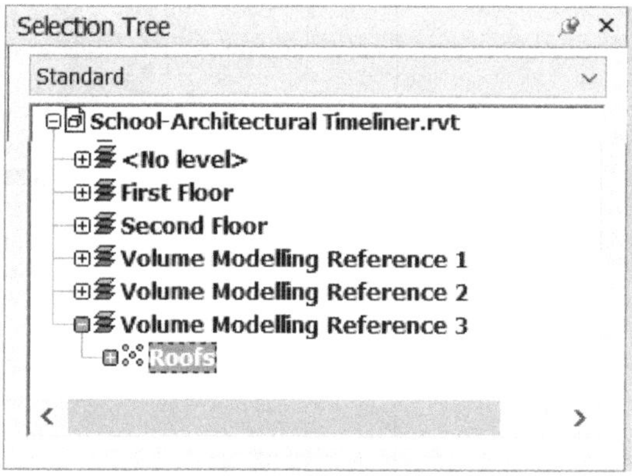

Figure 10–24

32. Save the selection as **Roofs Reference 3**.

33. Expand *School-Architectural TimeLiner.rvt>Second Floor>Floors>Floor* and select **Concrete on Metal Deck**, as shown in Figure 10–25.

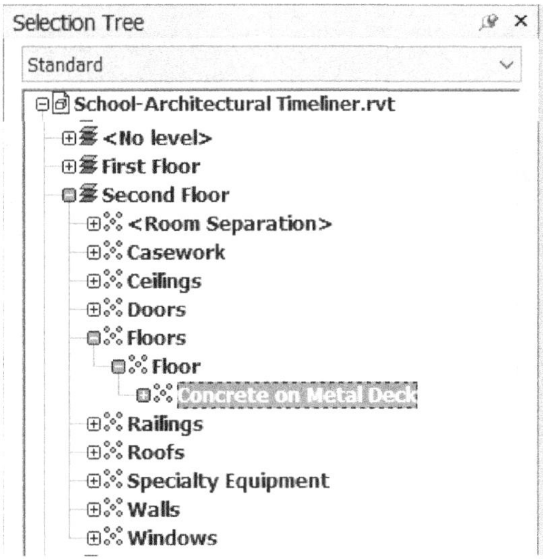

Figure 10–25

34. Save the selection as **Concrete on Metal Deck - 2nd Floor**.

35. Collapse the **Second Floor** branch.

36. Expand *School-Architectural TimeLiner.rvt>First Floor>Floors>Floor* and select **Generic - 12"**, as shown in Figure 10–26.

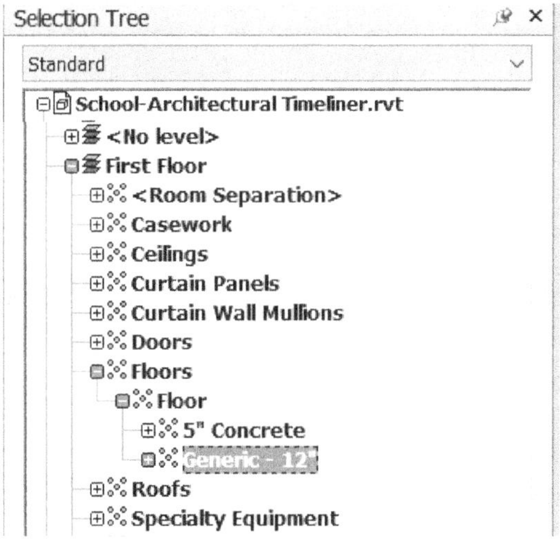

Figure 10–26

37. Save the selection as **Generic - 12" Floor**.

38. Expand *School-Architectural TimeLiner.rvt>First Floor>Floors>Floor* and select **5" Concrete**, as shown in Figure 10–27.

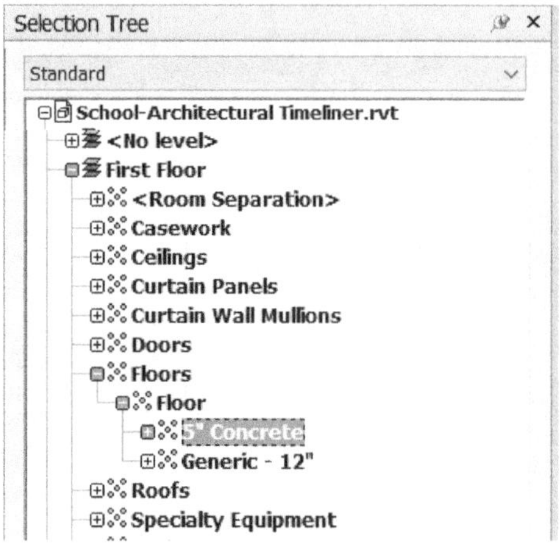

Figure 10–27

39. Save the selection as **5" Concrete Floor**.

40. Collapse the **Floors** branch.

41. Expand *School-Architectural TimeLiner.rvt>First Floor>Walls>Basic Wall* and select **Foundation - 18" Concrete**, as shown in Figure 10–28.

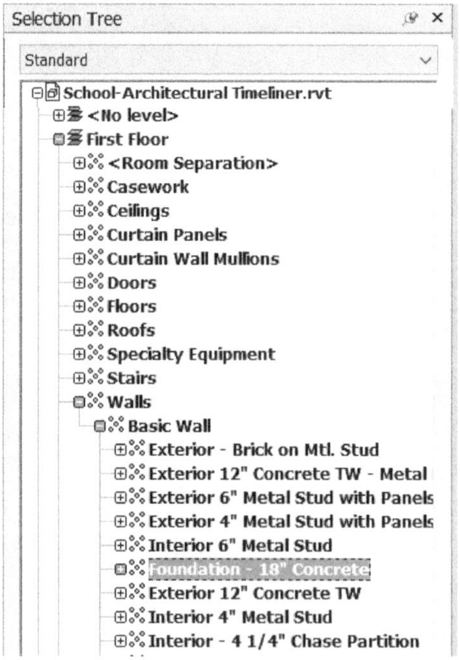

Figure 10–28

42. Save the selection as **Foundation - 18" Concrete Wall**.

43. Save the file.

Task 3 - Create tasks manually.

In this task, you will add the existing ground to finish ground grading to the Gantt chart using the task pane.

1. Continue working with the same file from the last task. If you skipped the last task, you will need to open **New-School-Manual.nwf** in the *Scheduling* practice files folder.

2. In the *Home* tab>Tools panel, click (TimeLiner) to open the TimeLiner window.

3. In the TimeLiner window>*Tasks* tab, click (Add Task).

4. In the task's data fields, enter the following, as shown in Figure 10–29:
    - *Name:* **Existing Ground Removal**.
    - *Planned Start Date:* **6/10/2022**
    - *Planned End Date:* **8/10/2022**
    - *Actual Start Date:* **7/01/2022**
    - *Actual End Date:* **8/31/2022**
    - *Task Type:* **Demolish**

    Note: You can highlight the first cell and use the keyboard to type in the data, then use <Tab> to jump to the next cell and keep typing. For the *Task Type*, you can type the first letter and it will fill in. You do not need to use the mouse for the data entry as using the keyboard is more efficient.

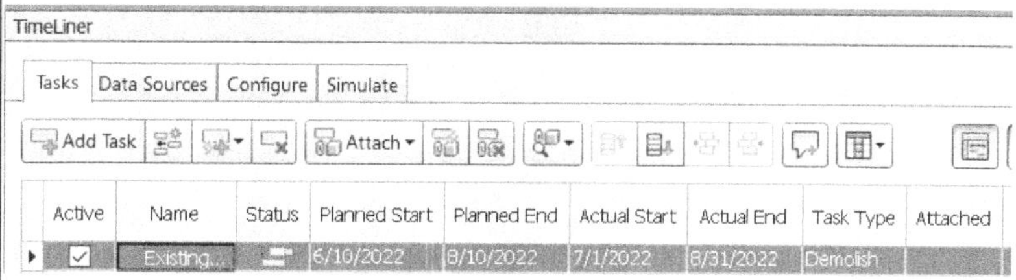

Figure 10–29

5. In the TimeLiner window>*Tasks* tab, click (Add Task).

6. In the task's data fields, enter the following:
   - *Name:* **Finish Ground Grading**.
   - *Planned Start Date:* **8/01/2022**
   - *Planned End Date:* **10/15/2022**
   - *Actual Start Date:* **9/10/2022**
   - *Actual End Date:* **11/21/2022**
   - *Task Type:* **Construct**
7. Save the file.

Task 4 - Connect objects in the model to tasks.

In order to review the grading change from the existing ground to the finish ground, you must attach the objects to the tasks. In this task, you attach the existing ground to the first task and the proposed ground to the second task in TimeLiner.

1. Continue working with the same file from the last task.
2. In the Selection Tree window, expand *Site Layout-Edited.dwg>C-TOPO-VIEW* and select **AIW_Existing_Ground**, as shown in Figure 10–30. Unhide the surface with the **<Ctrl>+<H>** keyboard shortcut.
3. In the TimeLiner window, right-click on the **Existing Ground Removal** task in the *Attached* column and select **Attach Current Selection**, as shown in Figure 10–30.

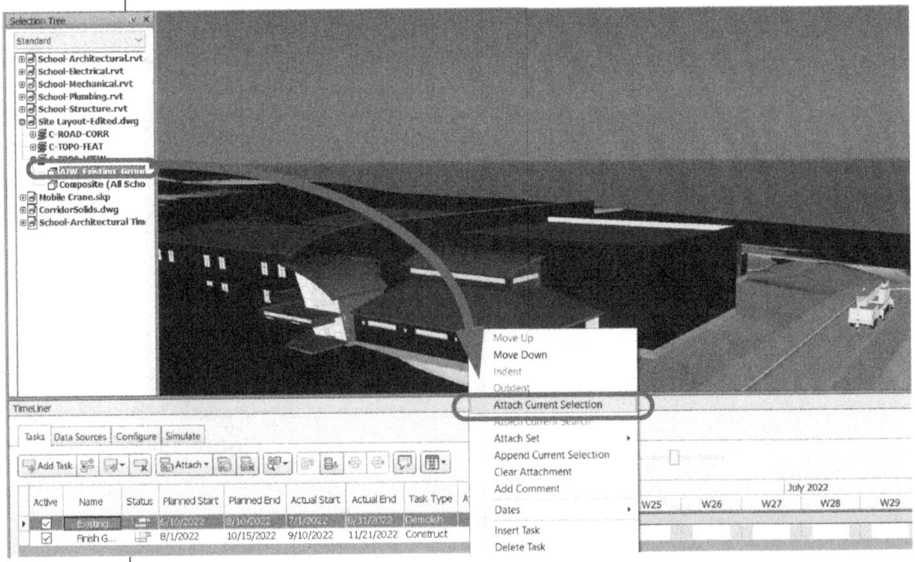

Figure 10–30

4. In the Selection Tree window, expand *Site Layout.dwg> C-TOPO-VIEW* and select **Composite (All School Site FG Surfaces)**.

5. In the TimeLiner window, right-click on the **Finish Ground Grading** task in the *Attached* column and select **Attach Current Selection**.

6. In the TimeLiner window, open the *Configure* tab.

7. Set the following parameters for the Appearance Definitions, as shown in Figure 10–31.

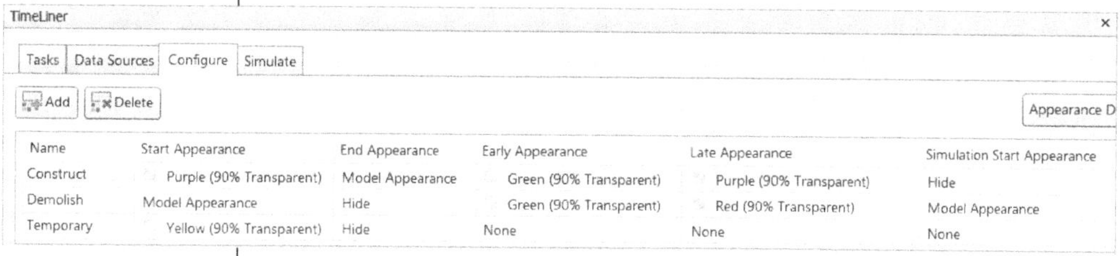

Figure 10–31

Construct:

- *Start Appearance:* **Purple (90% Transparent)**
- *End Appearance:* **Model Appearance**
- *Early Appearance:* **Green (90% Transparent)**
- *Late Appearance:* **Purple (90% Transparent)**
- *Simulation Start Appearance:* **Hide**

Demolish:

- *Start Appearance:* **Model Appearance**
- *End Appearance:* **Hide**
- *Early Appearance:* **Green (90% Transparent)**
- *Late Appearance:* **Red (90% Transparent)**
- *Simulation Start Appearance:* **Model Appearance**

Temporary:

- *Start Appearance:* **Yellow (90% Transparent)**
- *End Appearance:* **Hide**
- *Early Appearance:* **None**
- *Late Appearance:* **None**
- *Simulation Start Appearance:* **None**

8. Press <Esc> to deselect everything, or click *Select None* on the **Select All** dropdown menu in the *Select & Search* panel of the *Home* tab, as shown in Figure 10–32 (so that nothing is highlighted in blue).

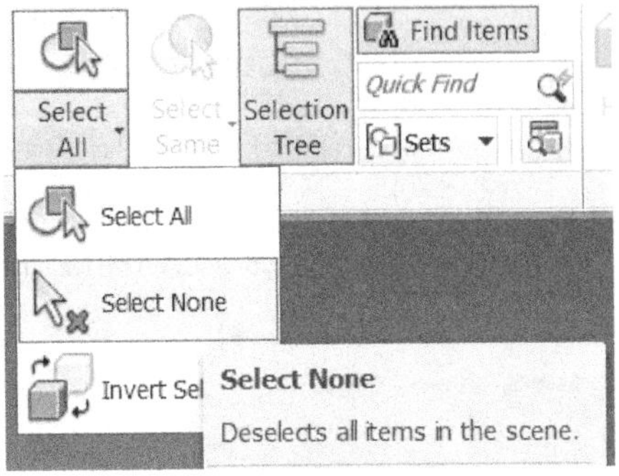

Figure 10–32

9. In the TimeLiner window, open the *Simulate* tab. Notice that the school disappears when you do.

10. Click  (Play) to run the simulation. Depending on your start date, it may take a while for anything to happen.

11. When done, return to the *Tasks* tab in the TimeLiner window (to restore the model to its finished state).

12. In the Selection Tree window, expand *Site Layout-Edited.dwg>C-TOPO-VIEW* and select **AIW_Existing_Ground**. Hide the surface using the <Ctrl>+<H> keyboard shortcut.

13. Save the file.

10.3 Importing an External Task List

Most architecture, engineering, and construction firms use project management software to manage their project schedules. These programs make it easier to set dates based on the start or completion dates of an earlier task.

You can use TimeLiner to import project schedules from a variety of external data sources. Once imported, a task list can be created and automatically connected to model objects. The key to ensuring this information is correct is using saved sets and saved searches whose names match the task names in the project management database.

The following project management databases can be imported:

- .CSV files
- Microsoft Project MPX
- Microsoft Project 2007-2013
- Primavera P6 (Web Services)
- Primavera P6 V7 (Web Services)
- Primavera P6 V8.3 (Web Services)

TimeLiner Rules

TimeLiner rules assist in connecting tasks with items in the scene view. There are three rules available, as shown in Figure 10–33. In all cases, the name cases must match.

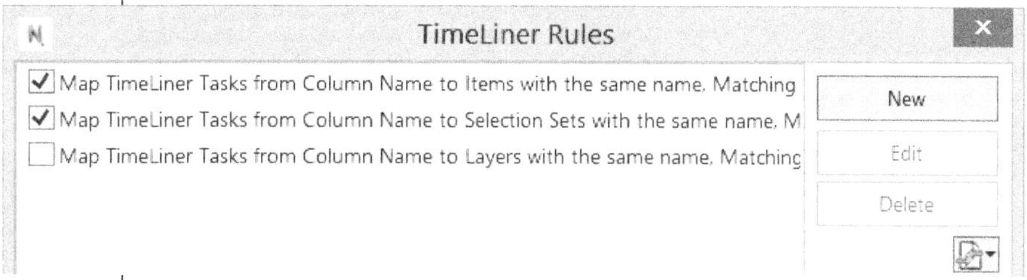

Figure 10–33

- Use the first rule when the item names in the Selection Tree match the task names in the project schedule.
- Use the second rule when the selection set names match the task names in the project schedule.
- Use the third rule when the layer names in the original file match the task names in the project schedule.

The first two rules are most often used with Autodesk Revit files, while the third rule is most often used to connect AutoCAD layers or Autodesk Civil 3D corridor shapes.

How To: Import a Task List

1. In the TimeLiner>*Data Sources* tab, expand (Add) and select the source database.
2. In the Open files dialog box, navigate to the file and select it.
3. Click **Open**.
4. In the Field Selector dialog box, map the TimeLiner column names to the external database fields, as shown in Figure 10–34.

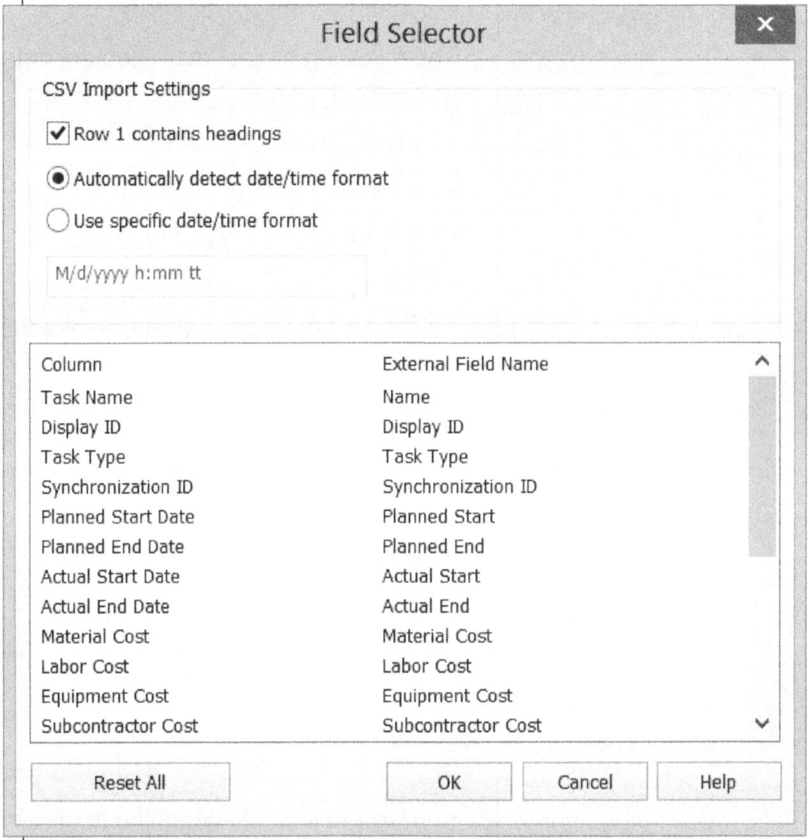

Figure 10–34

5. Click **OK**.
6. In the TimeLiner>*Data Sources* tab, right-click on the new data source and select **Rename**.
7. Type an appropriate name. The name you use displays in the task pane.

8. In the TimeLiner>*Data Sources* tab, right-click on the new data source and select **Rebuild Task Hierarchy**.
9. If any fields are missing information, you might get an error message. Click **OK**.
10. In the TimeLiner>*Tasks* tab, click  (Auto-Attach Using Rules).
11. In the TimeLiner Rules dialog box, select the required rules and click **Apply Rules**, as shown in Figure 10–35.

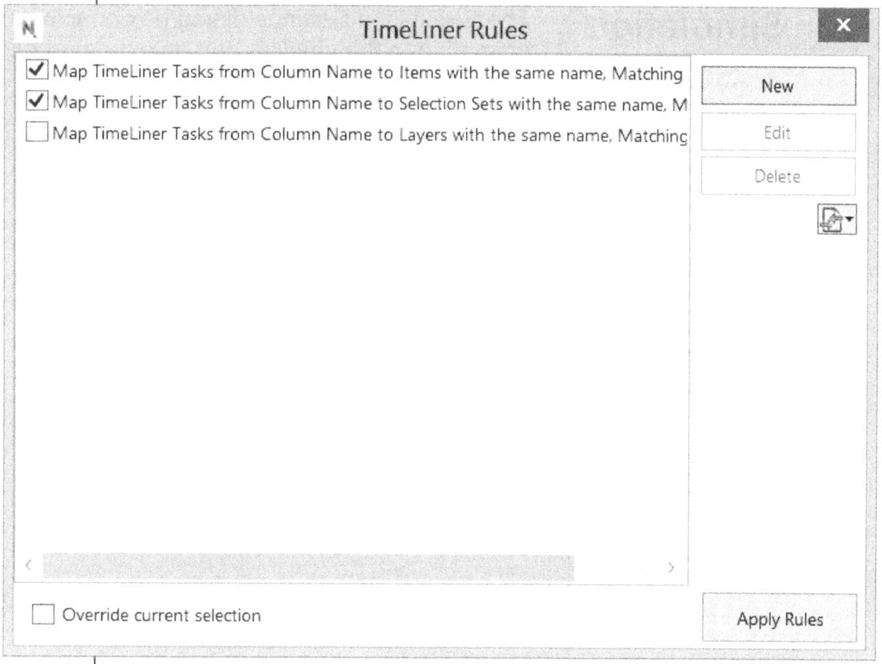

Figure 10–35

12. Ensure that all of the tasks have objects attached to them. If any are missing, manually attach the objects.
13. Play the simulation.

10.4 Combining TimeLiner and Animator

During a construction simulation, it can be helpful to view the model from multiple angles to understand how everything comes together. You can do this by setting up an animation first, and then connecting the animation to the project schedule.

Simulation Settings

The Simulation Settings dialog box enables you to connect an animation to the timeline and adjust a number of settings, as shown in Figure 10–36.

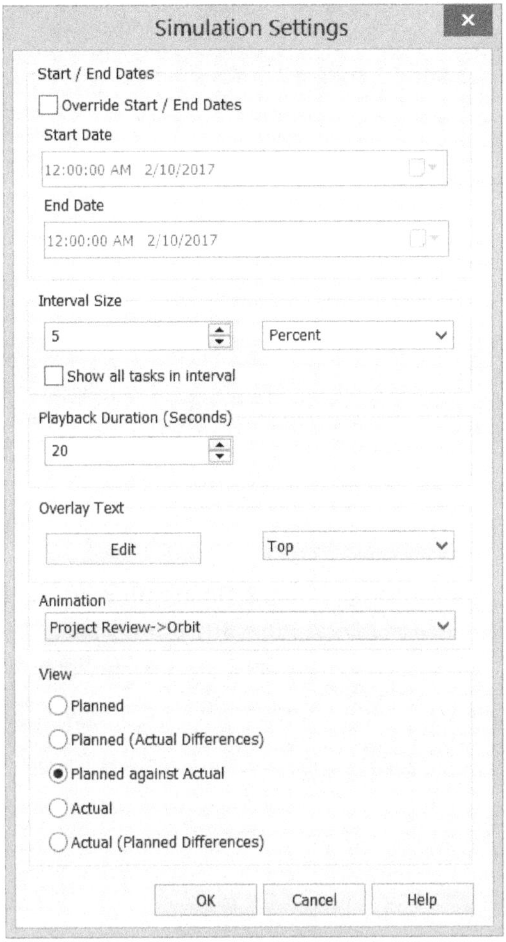

Figure 10–36

Start/End Dates

You can override the start and end dates for the animation, but this only changes what date the animation of the simulation starts. It does not automatically change the dates of the tasks according to the override start date. This means that if an override start date is selected that is the mid-point of the construction timeline, then half of the simulation shows as already being complete when you run the simulation.

Interval Size

The *Interval Size* determines how much of the Timeline plays at once. A numeric value, combined with one of the following, determine the interval:

- Percent
- Weeks
- Days
- Hours
- Minutes
- Seconds

Playback Duration (Seconds)

You can set the playback duration to control how long it takes to play the entire animation. The duration units are in seconds.

Overlay Text

Text can be added to the scene view to communicate information about the simulation. The text can be placed at the top or the bottom of the scene view.

Animation

The Animation drop-down list provides a list of previously created animations. By default, it is set to **No Link**. TimeLiner only uses the camera viewpoints from the animation to tour the model while the TimeLiner simulation plays.

View

The dates that are used to animate the simulation are selected in the *View* area. You have the following options to choose from:

- Planned
- Planned (Actual Differences)
- Planned against Actual
- Actual
- Actual (Planned Differences)

How To: Add an Animation to TimeLiner

Only animations that were previously created display in the list. You cannot create an animation at this point.

1. Create an animation with the required camera viewpoints. **Note:** Object animations are ignored unless they are added to the task list.
2. In the TimeLiner window>*Simulate* tab, click **Settings**.
3. In the Simulation Settings dialog box, expand the Animation drop-down list and select the animation with the required viewpoints, as shown in Figure 10–37.

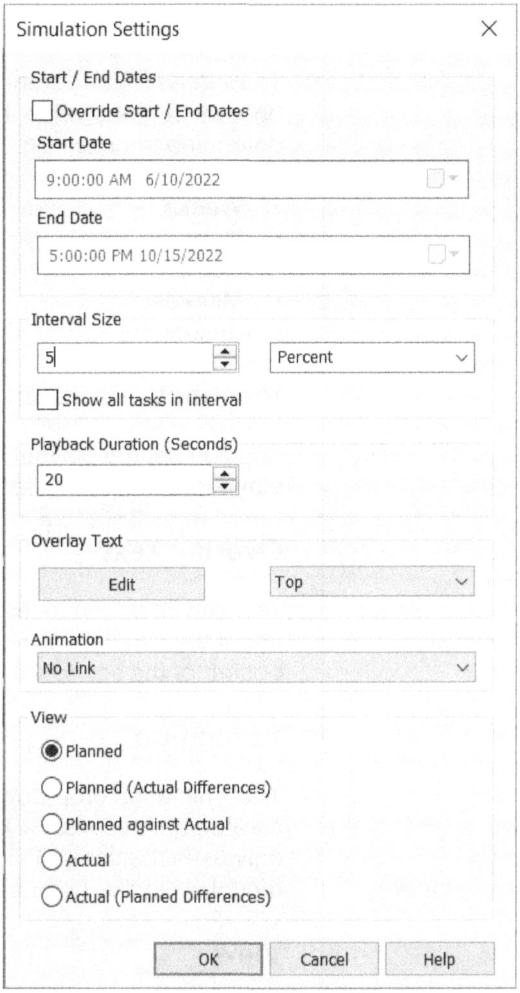

Figure 10–37

4. Click **OK**.
5. In the *Simulate* tab, click  (Play) to run the simulation.

Practice 10b Import an External Project Schedule

Practice Objectives

- Import an external project management database to populate the TimeLiner task list.
- Connect objects to tasks automatically using rules.

In this practice, you will connect an external project management database to automatically populate TimeLiner tasks. Then, you will use rules to connect the tasks to the model automatically before running the simulation, as shown in Figure 10–38.

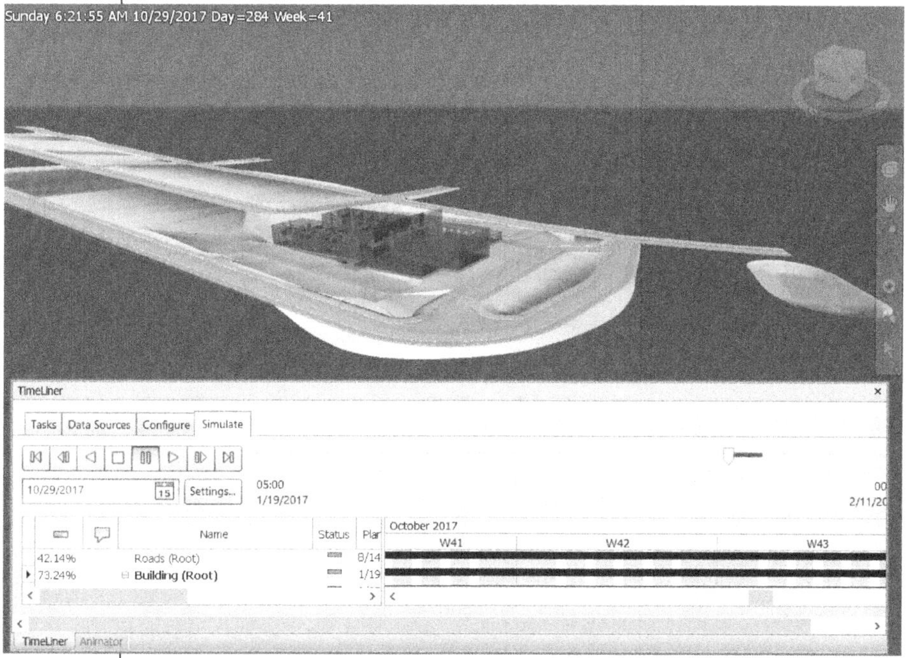

Figure 10–38

Task 1 - Connect the corridor schedule.

In this task, you will connect a .CSV file to import the tasks for the road construction schedule.

Do not continue with the previous files. More sets have been set up in the New-School-Import.nwc file in order for TimeLiner to sequence properly.

1. In the Quick Access Toolbar, click (Open).
2. In the *Scheduling* practice files folder, open **New-School-Import.nwf**.
3. In the TimeLiner window>*Data Sources* tab, expand (Add) and select **CSV Import**.
4. In the Open files dialog box, navigate to the *Scheduling* practice files folder and select **Civil-timeline.csv**.
5. Click **Open**.
6. In the Field Selector dialog box, map the TimeLiner column names to the external database fields, as shown in Figure 10–39.

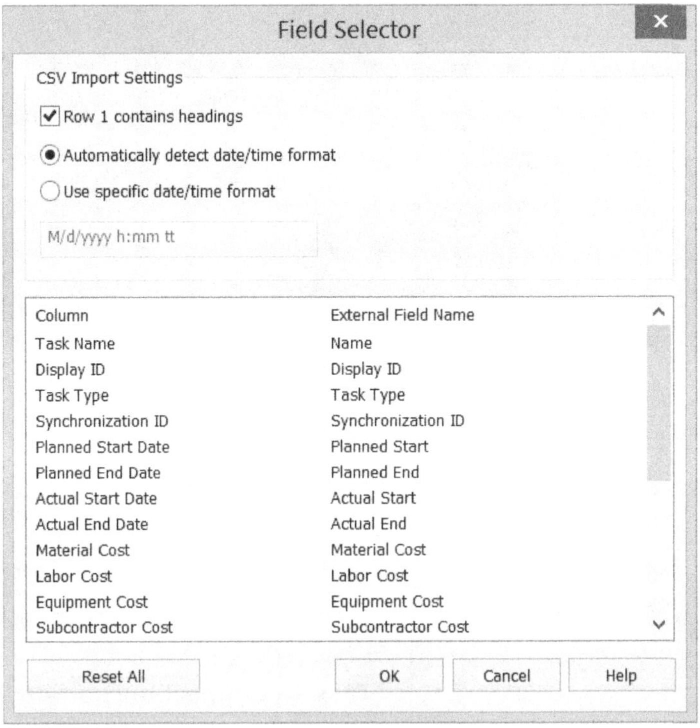

Figure 10–39

7. Click **OK**.

8. In the TimeLiner window>*Data Sources* tab, right-click on the **New Data Source** and select **Rename**, as shown in Figure 10–40.

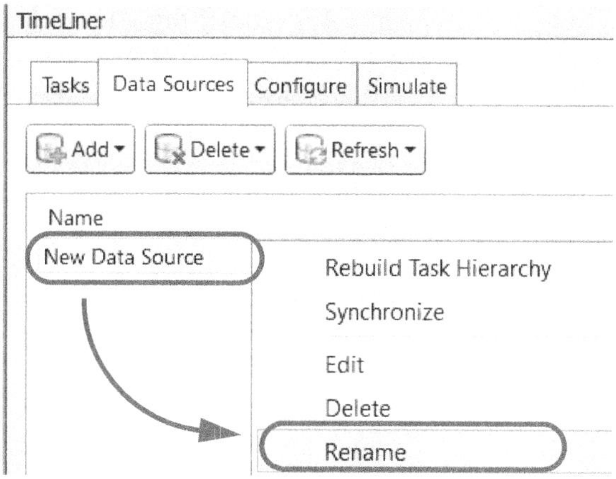

Figure 10–40

9. Type **Roads** for the name and press <Enter>.

10. In the TimeLiner window>*Data Sources* tab, right-click on thenewly renamed **Roads** data source and select **Rebuild Task Hierarchy**.

11. The Problems in imported data dialog box displays noting that some fields are missing information, as shown in Figure 10–41. For example, not all of the Actual Start and Actual End dates are entered in the spreadsheet. Click **OK**.

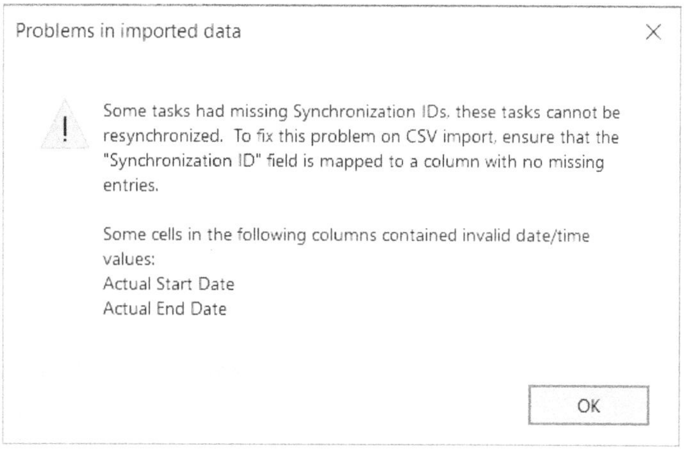

Figure 10–41

12. In the TimeLiner window>*Tasks* tab, click (Auto-Attach Using Rules).

13. In the TimeLiner Rules dialog box, ensure that **(A)** only the last rule, **Map TimeLiner Tasks from Column Name to Layers with the same name, Matching case**, is selected. Click **(B) Apply Rules**, as shown in Figure 10–42.

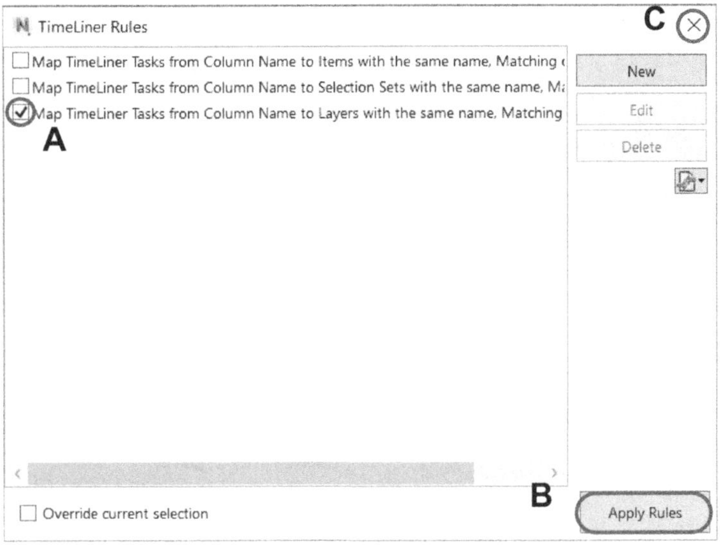

Figure 10–42

14. Close the TimeLiner Rules dialog box by clicking **(C)** the **X** in the upper right corner.

15. Ensure that all of the tasks have objects attached to them. In the *Attached* column, there should be an **Explicit Selection** text entry in blue. This means that the layer name in the Civil 3D drawing file matches the task name imported through the spreadsheet.

16. In the TimeLiner window, open the *Simulate* tab.

17. In the Saved Viewpoints window, click **NE-Isometric** to restore that viewpoint.

18. In the TimeLiner window, open the *Simulate* tab. Notice that the school and site disappear when you do.

19. Click (Play) to run the simulation. Depending on your start date, it may take a while for anything to happen.

20. When done, return to the *Tasks* tab in the TimeLiner window (to restore the model to its finished state).

21. Save the file.

Task 2 - Connect the building schedule.

In this task, you will import the project schedule for the building components. Since not all of the object and set names match the task names, they do not all connect automatically. Therefore, some tasks must be connected manually.

1. In the TimeLiner window>*Data Sources* tab, expand  (Add) and select **CSV Import**.
2. In the Open files dialog box, navigate to the *Scheduling* practice files folder and select **School Arch-timeline.csv**.
3. Click **Open**.
4. In the Field Selector dialog box, ensure that the TimeLiner column names are still mapped to the external database fields and click **OK**.
5. In the TimeLiner window>*Data Sources* tab, right-click on the new data source and select **Rename**.
6. Type **Building** for the name and press <Enter>.
7. In the TimeLiner window>*Data Sources* tab, right-click on the **Building** data source and select **Rebuild Task Hierarchy**.
8. Note that some of the fields are missing information. Click **OK** in the Problems in imported data dialog box.
9. In the TimeLiner window>*Tasks* tab, click  (Auto-Attach Using Rules).

10. In the TimeLiner Rules dialog box, select the first two rules and click **Apply Rules**, as shown in Figure 10–43.

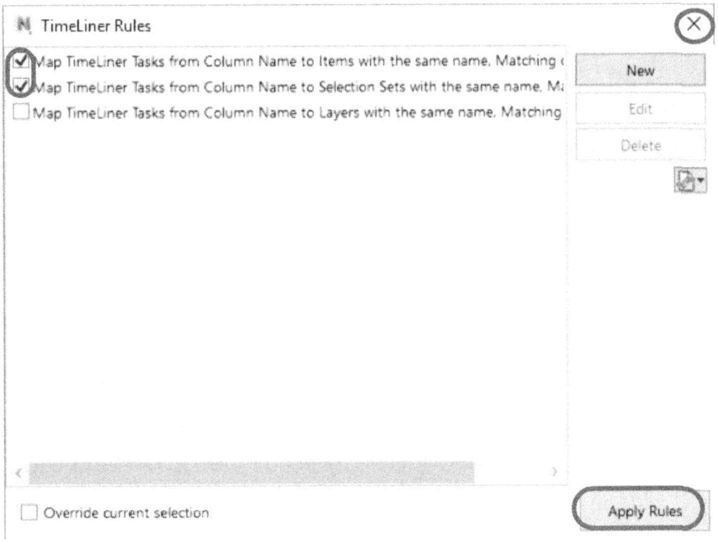

Figure 10–43

11. Close the TimeLiner Rules dialog box by clicking the **X** in the upper right corner.

12. Review the tasks and note that not all of the tasks have objects attached to them (an **Explicit Selection** or **Sets** text entry in blue), as shown in Figure 10–44.

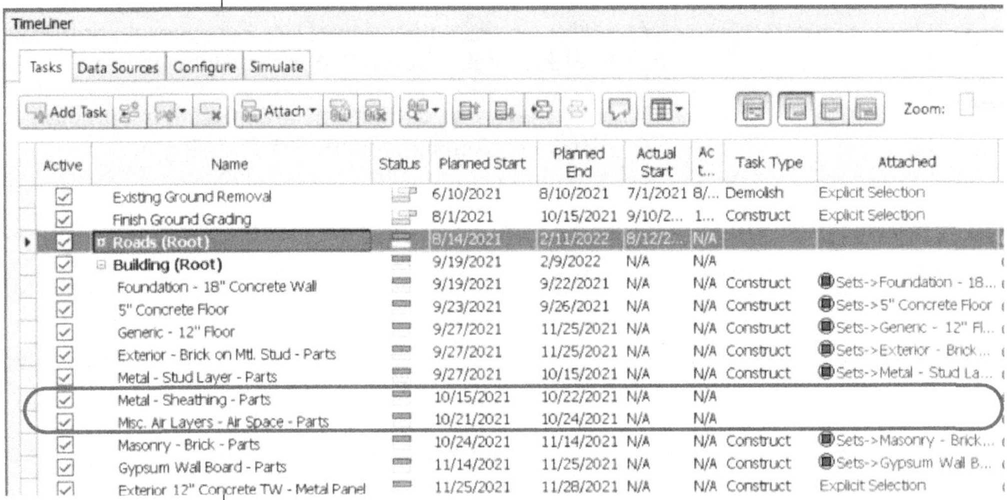

Figure 10–44

13. In the task pane, scroll down to *Metal - Sheathing - Parts*. Right-click in the **Attached** field and select **Attach Set>Panels - Parts** to connect the paneling to this task. Set the *Task Type* to **Construct**, as shown in .Figure 10–45 You will have to scroll down to find the **Panels - Parts set.**

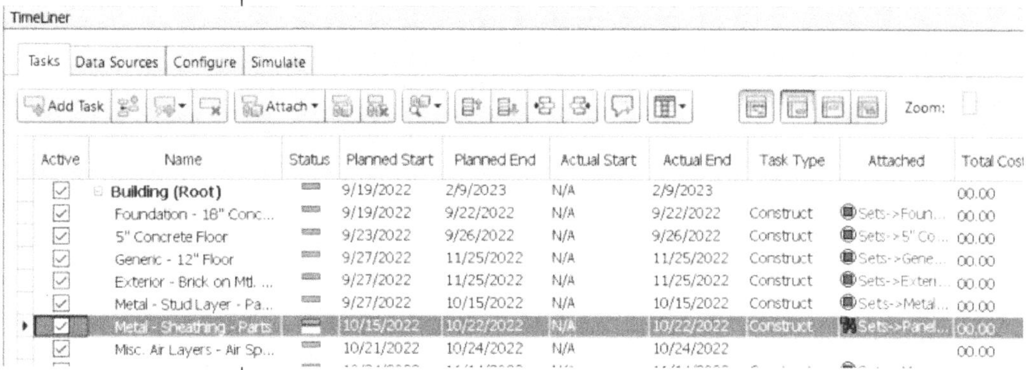

Figure 10–45

14. You do not need to attach anything for the air layer because there is nothing to install for this layer.

15. In the TimeLiner window, open the *Simulate* tab.

16. Click (Play) to run the simulation. Depending on your start date, it may take a while for anything to happen.

17. When done, return to the *Tasks* tab in the TimeLiner window (to restore the model to its finished state).

18. Save the file.

Task 3 - Orbit the model as you play the simulation.

In this task, you connect an animation to the simulation to orbit the model as the simulation plays.

1. In the TimeLiner window>*Simulate* tab, click **Settings**.

2. In the Simulation Settings dialog box, expand the Animation drop-down list and select **Orbit>Overview**. Then, in the *View* area, select **Planned against Actual**, as shown in Figure 10–46.

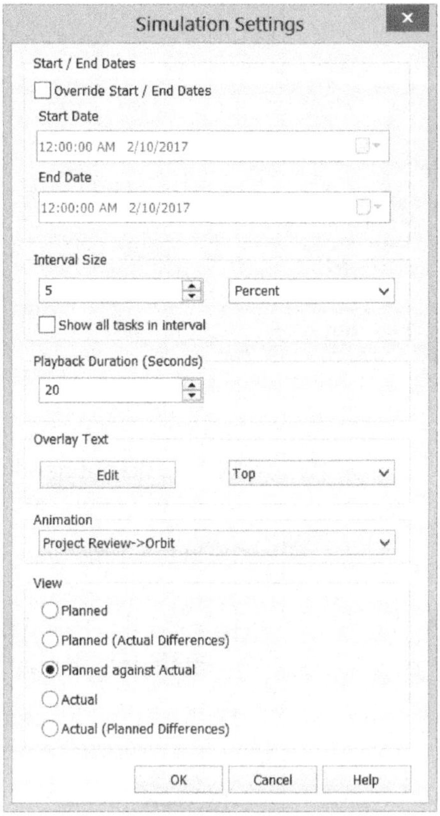

Figure 10–46

3. Click **OK**.

4. In the *Simulate* tab, click  (Play) to run the simulation. Depending on your start date, it may take a while for anything to happen.

5. This time the camera orbits during the simulation and ends with a eye-level view of the site with the earthwork completed (but no school yet constructed).

6. When done, return to the *Tasks* tab in the TimeLiner window (to restore the model to its finished state).

7. Save the file.

10.5 Time-Based Clashes

A very costly and time-consuming situation may occur in construction when things fit together within the BIM model but do not fit together in the field. Construction simulations help you discover when a piece of equipment does not have the necessary room to maneuver on a job site. Combining TimeLiner, Animator, and Clash Detective, you can run a time-based clash test, as shown in Figure 10–47.

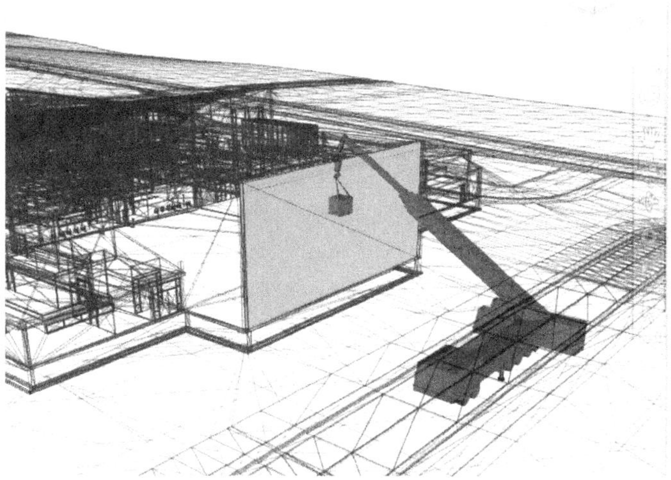

Figure 10–47

How To: Set Up a Time-Based Clash Test

1. In the Clash Detective window, click (Add Test). Rename the test as required.
2. In the Clash Detective window, open the *Select* tab.
3. In the *Selection A* area, select the first item to compare.
4. In the *Selection B* area, select the second item to compare.
5. In the *Settings* area, expand the Link drop-down list and select either an animation or TimeLiner.
6. Click **Run Test**.

Hint: TimeLiner could interfere

If you have recently run a TimeLiner simulation, the model might still be displaying the ending scene view. This can interfere with the true results of a time-based clash test.

If you suspect that clashes should have occurred, but the result showed 0 clashes, go into the TimeLiner window, activate the *Tasks* tab, and then re-run the clash test.

Practice 10c Conduct a Time-Based Clash Test

Practice Objective

- Run a clash test.

In this practice, you will use a combination of TimeLiner, Animator, and Clash Detective to create a time-based clash test, as shown in Figure 10–48.

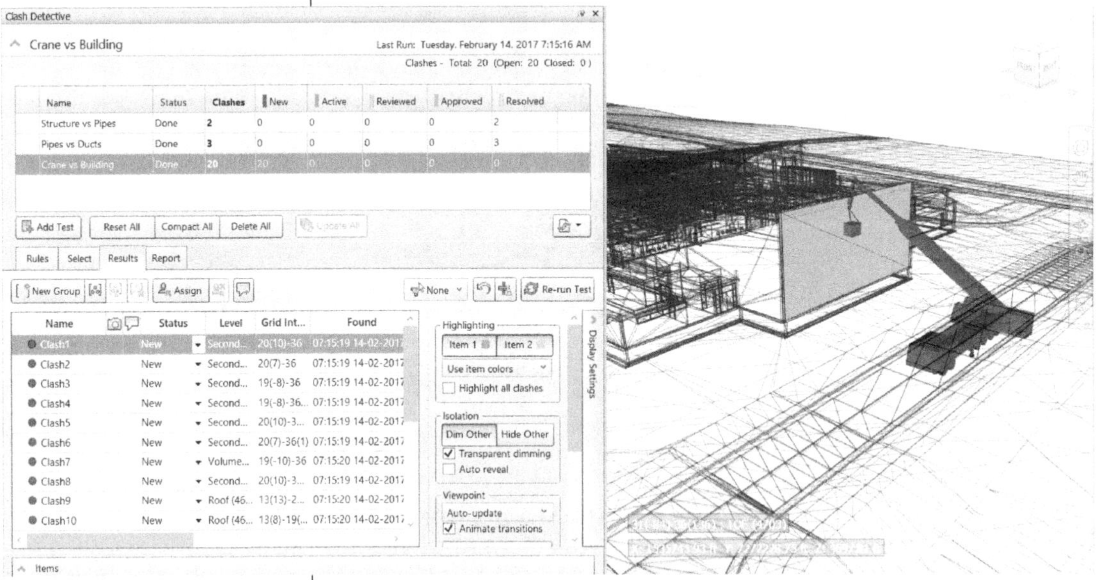

Figure 10–48

Task 1 - Combine Clash Detective and Animator.

In this task, you will run a clash detection with a link to an animation to ensure that the crane does not clash with the building.

*Do not continue with the previous files. The animation required for the clash is set up in the **New-School-Clash.nwc** file.*

1. In the *Scheduling* practice files folder, open **New-School-Clash.nwf**.

If the Clash Detective window is not displayed, toggle it on in the Home tab>Tools panel.

2. In the Clash Detective window, notice the yellow alert triangle. As the tooltip explains, there have been changes to the models or the clash detective settings since the tests were run, as shown in Figure 10–49.

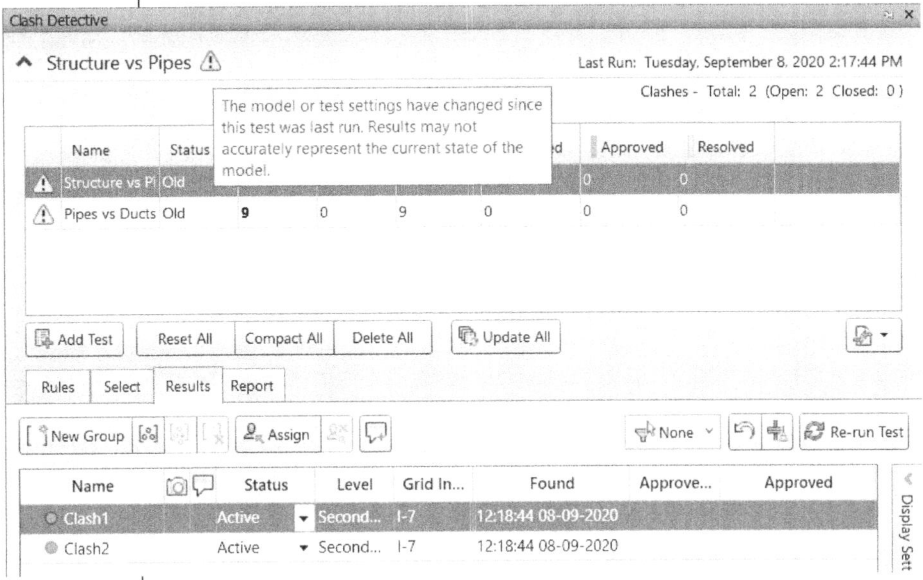

Figure 10–49new

3. Select the **Pipes vs Ducts** clash test and click 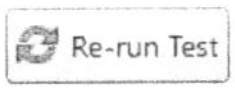 (Re-run Test) to update that test. While you're at it, also re-run the **Structures vs Pipes** clash test.

4. In the Clash Detective window, open the *Select* tab.

5. In the Clash Detective window, click  (Add Test).

6. Select the name and rename it to **Crane vs Building**.

7. In the *Selection A* pane, select **Mobile Crane.skp**.

8. In the *Selection B* pane, select **School-Architectural Timeliner.rvt**.

9. In the *Settings* area, expand the Link drop-down list and select **Mobile Crane** to link the crane animation to the test.

10. Click **Run Test**.

11. If you come up with **0** clashes, ensure that you make the *Tasks* tab active in the TimeLiner window, then re-run the clash test. Figure 10–50 shows the results. Yours might be slightly different if you used an animation you created.

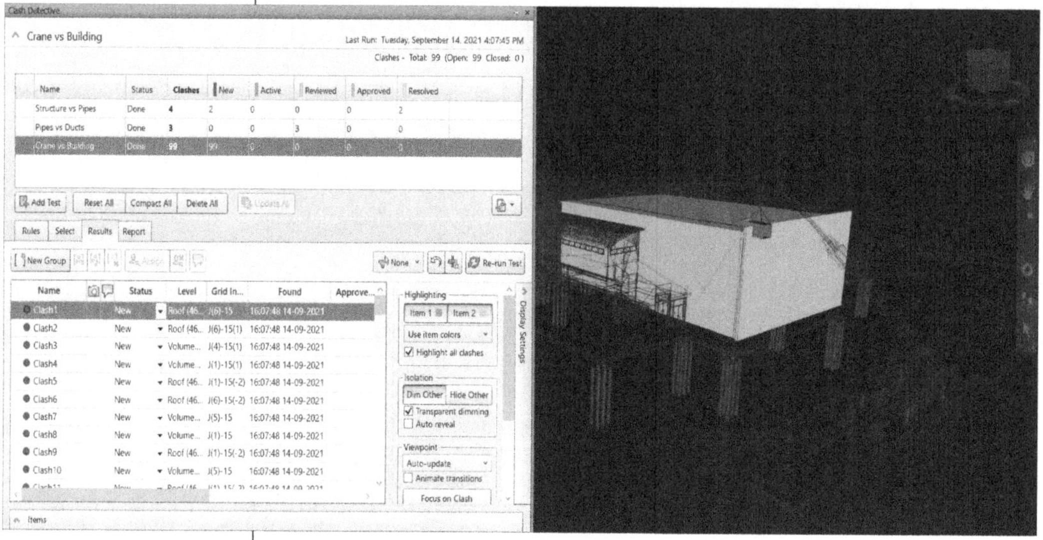

Figure 10–50

Chapter Review Questions

1. What tab in the TimeLiner window would you use to manually create a Gantt chart?
   a. *Tasks* tab
   b. *Data Sources* tab
   c. *Configure* tab
   d. *Simulate* tab
2. What tab in the TimeLiner window would you use to set up how items display during the simulation?
   a. *Tasks* tab
   b. *Data Sources* tab
   c. *Configure* tab
   d. *Simulate* tab
3. Put the following general steps in the correct order for creating a construction simulation:
   a. Configure how objects display during the simulation.
   b. Prepare the models.
   c. Make any required changes.
   d. Create saved sets and search sets.
   e. Link the simulation to any previously created animations.
   f. Play the simulation.
   g. Add tasks to the Gantt chart.
4. Which rule would you most likely use to connect Autodesk Civil 3D corridor shapes to the task list?
   a. Map TimeLiner Tasks from Column Name to Items with the same name, Matching case
   b. Map TimeLiner Tasks from Column Name to Selection Sets with the same name, Matching case
   c. Map TimeLiner Tasks from Column Name to Layers with the same name, Matching case

5. Which window would you use to run a time-based clash detection?
   a. Selection Tree
   b. Animator
   c. TimeLiner
   d. Clash Detective

Command Summary

Button	Command	Location
	**Add Comment**	• **Window:** TimeLiner>*Tasks* tab
	**Add Configuration**	• **Window:** TimeLiner>*Configure* tab
	**Add Data Source**	• **Window:** TimeLiner>*Data Sources* tab
	**Add Task**	• **Window:** TimeLiner>*Tasks* tab
	**Attach**	• **Window:** TimeLiner>*Tasks* tab
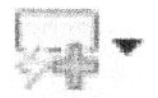	**Auto-Add Tasks**	• **Window:** TimeLiner>*Tasks* tab
	**Auto-Attach Using Rules**	• **Window:** TimeLiner>*Tasks* tab
	**Clear Attachment**	• **Window:** TimeLiner>*Tasks* tab
	**Columns**	• **Window:** TimeLiner>*Tasks* tab
	**Delete Configuration**	• **Window:** TimeLiner>*Configure* tab
	**Delete Data Source**	• **Window:** TimeLiner>*Data Sources* tab
	**Delete Task**	• **Window:** TimeLiner>*Tasks* tab
	**Export to Schedule**	• **Window:** TimeLiner>*Tasks* tab
	**Export to Sets**	• **Window:** TimeLiner>*Tasks* tab
	**Filter by Status**	• **Window:** TimeLiner>*Tasks* tab
	**Find Items**	• **Window:** TimeLiner>*Tasks* tab
	**Forward**	• **Window:** TimeLiner>*Simulate* tab

	Indent	• **Window:** TimeLiner>*Tasks* tab
	Insert Task	• **Window:** TimeLiner>*Tasks* tab
	Move Down	• **Window:** TimeLiner>*Tasks* tab
	Move Up	• **Window:** TimeLiner>*Tasks* tab
	Outdent	• **Window:** TimeLiner>*Tasks* tab
	Pause	• **Window:** TimeLiner>*Simulate* tab
	Play	• **Window:** TimeLiner>*Simulate* tab
	Play Backwards	• **Window:** TimeLiner>*Simulate* tab
	Refresh Data Source	• **Window:** TimeLiner>*Data Sources* tab
	Rewind	• **Window:** TimeLiner>*Simulate* tab
	Show Actual Dates	• **Window:** TimeLiner>*Tasks* tab
	Show Planned Dates	• **Window:** TimeLiner>*Tasks* tab
	Show Planned vs Actual Dates	• **Window:** TimeLiner>*Tasks* tab
	Show/Hide Gantt Chart	• **Window:** TimeLiner>*Tasks* tab
	Step Back	• **Window:** TimeLiner>*Simulate* tab
	Step Forward	• **Window:** TimeLiner>*Simulate* tab
	Stop	• **Window:** TimeLiner>*Simulate* tab
	TimeLiner	• **Ribbon:** *Home* tab>Tools panel

Chapter 11

Communication: Rendering

Autodesk® Rendering is an integral part of Autodesk® Navisworks®. It is a general-purpose rendering tool that enables you to customize a model to create physically correct renderings. Rendering uses the lighting, materials, and sun and sky settings in a model to shade the model's geometry.

Learning Objectives in This Chapter

- Open the Autodesk Rendering window and understand its interface.
- Select materials from the Autodesk Material Libraries and add them to the document library.
- Edit a material using the Material Editor and edit material mapping values for a material.
- Create and edit lights in an Autodesk Navisworks scene.
- Enable the use and display of the sun and sky lighting effects in the scene view.
- Understand the purpose of the fields in the Environment tab that deal with exposure.
- Render and save photorealistic images using the Autodesk Rendering tool in both Autodesk Navisworks and Autodesk Rendering.

BIM Workflow: Rendering

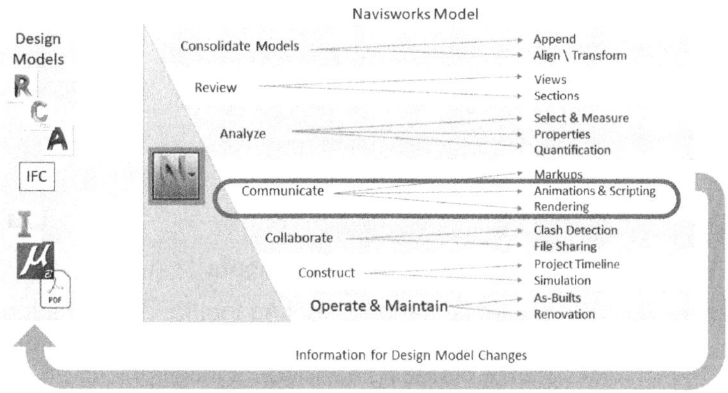

11.1 Autodesk Rendering Overview

Overview of the Autodesk Rendering Environment

The Autodesk Rendering window enables you to create, edit, and apply materials, lights, and environments to your Autodesk Navisworks files. To open the Autodesk Rendering window, in the *Home* tab>Tools panel, click (Autodesk Rendering). Alternatively, in the *View* tab, expand the Windows options and click **Autodesk Rendering** in the drop-down list. You can also select the *Render* tab>System panel and click (Autodesk Rendering). The Autodesk Rendering window contains multiple commands and tabs. Each tab is broken into areas, as shown in Figure 11–1 for the *Materials* tab.

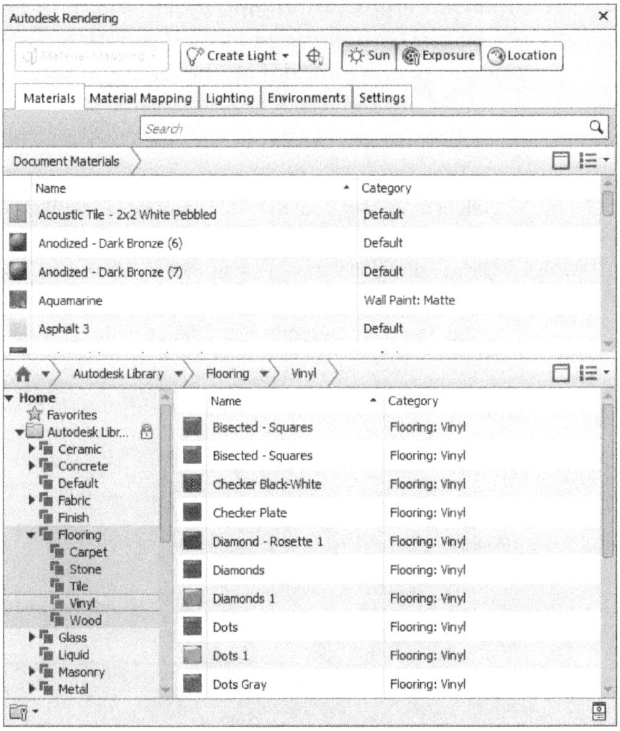

Figure 11–1

The buttons in the Rendering toolbar along the top of the Autodesk Rendering window enable you to define material mapping, create lights, toggle light glyphs, or enable/disable sun, exposure, and location settings. Selecting any of these options directly activates the appropriate tab for the button.

Overview of the Rendering Workflow

Using the Autodesk Rendering tools available in the Navisworks software enables you to create highly detailed and photorealistic images.

How To: Render a Navisworks Scene

1. Open the Autodesk Rendering window.
2. Set up the model geometry for the scene.
    - Apply materials and material mappings. You can apply materials to objects selected in the scene view.
    - Add artificial and natural lights. Photometric lights (artificial lighting) accurately define lights in a scene. Sun and Sky lighting simulates the effect of sunlight and sky illumination (natural lighting).
    - Define the exposure settings to control how real-world luminance values are converted into an image.
    - Orient the scene view with the required orientation and zoom level.
3. Select the rendering method (cloud or local).
4. Select the rendering quality.
5. Render the image.
6. Save (or download) the rendered image.

Hint: Navisworks Presenter Assigned Materials

In earlier versions of the Navisworks software, there was a rendering environment called Presenter. This tool has been removed from the software. Any materials that were assigned using the Presenter tool will have to be reassigned using the current Autodesk materials.

11.2 Materials

Materials are available in the Navisworks material libraries to enable you to assign real-world materials, such as plastic, wood, and glass, to objects in a model to give it a more realistic appearance.

Materials Tab

In the Autodesk Rendering window, select the *Materials* tab, as shown in Figure 11–2. The *Materials* tab provides access to the Library panel and the Document Materials panel.

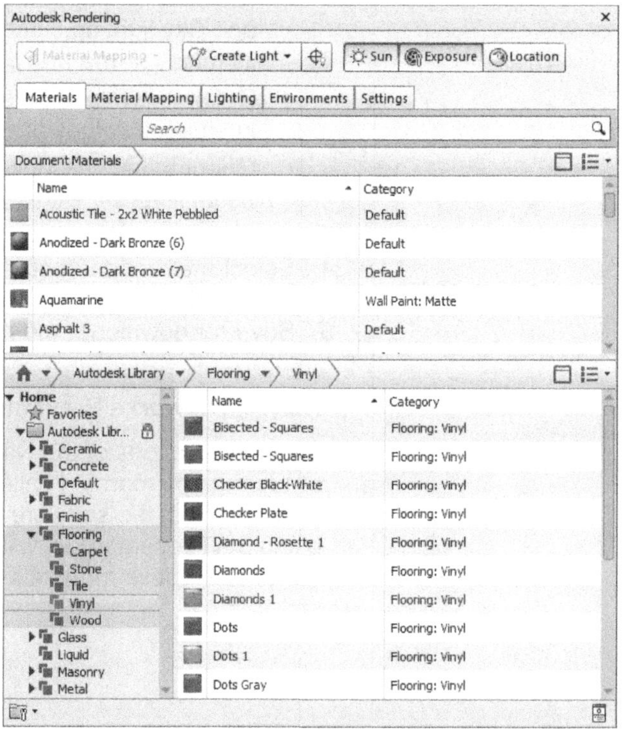

Figure 11–2

Library Panel

The Library panel is located in the lower half of the Autodesk Rendering dialog box, as shown in Figure 11–3. It provides access to the library of materials (standard and advanced) that are provided with the Navisworks software. Materials are selected in the library and then added to the current model for use.

To navigate the Library panel, expand the *Autodesk Library* folder in the left pane and then further expand any required nodes to find the required material categories. Select the category in the left pane to display its list of materials. Once a material has been located, select it in the pane on the right. When you hover your cursor over the material swatch, the buttons for applying or editing the material will display. The list of materials can be sorted by selecting the column headers in this panel.

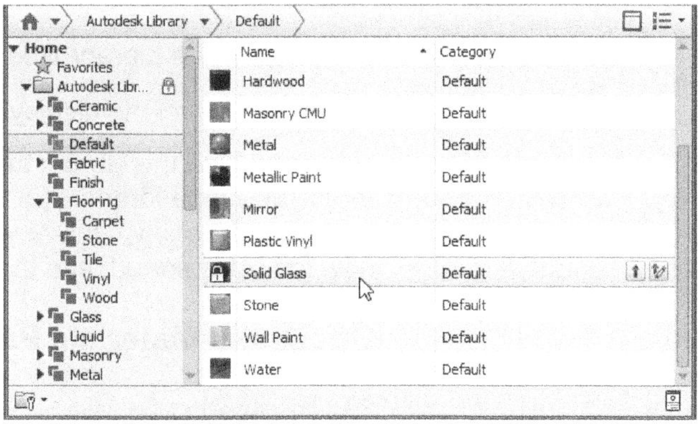

Figure 11–3

As you navigate through the nodes, the path is displayed at the top of the Library panel. You can use the drop-down arrows in the components of this path as another means of navigation, as shown in Figure 11–4.

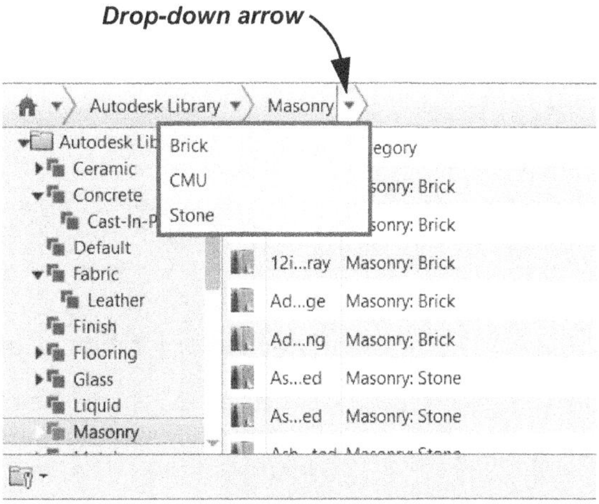

Figure 11–4

The following libraries are available in the Library panel:

- The Autodesk Library, which contains read-only materials provided by Autodesk.
- The User Library, which contains your own custom materials that you have modified and saved based on Autodesk materials or that you have created yourself.

The header for the Library panel lists the full path to the selected material category. Additionally, the header provides the (Show/Hide Library Tree) and (Display Options) icons to filter or control the display of the panel. enables you to show and hide the Library tree. enables you to customize the display type for materials. For example, you can control the library that is shown, the type of view (thumbnail, list, or text), how the list is sorted, and the thumbnail size.

Document Materials Panel

The Document Materials panel (shown in Figure 11–5) is located in the upper portion of the Autodesk Rendering dialog box and lists the materials that have been included for use in the document. These materials can consist of materials that have been applied or that have not yet been applied. Library materials must be added to the Document Materials panel if they are to be used in the model.

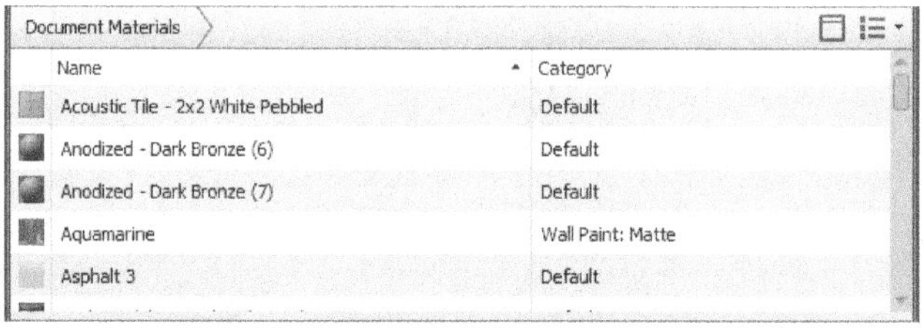

Figure 11–5

The header for the Document Materials panel also contains the and icons. These icons enable you to show or hide the Document Materials panel and customize the display type for the document materials, respectively.

Adding Materials to the Document

When a model is first created in the Navisworks software, it does not contain any materials unless they are brought in with the source CAD or BIM file. To assign materials to objects in the model, materials must be selected from a library and added to the document.

How To: Add Materials to the Document Materials Panel

1. Browse to the required material in the Library panel.
   - Consider using the **Search** field at the top of the *Materials* tab to locate specific materials in the library.
2. Select the material in the pane on the right and click  to add the material to the current document. Alternatively, right-click the material and select **Add to>Document Materials**. A copy of this material is now available in the Document Materials panel for use in the current model.
   - **Note:** If an object has been preselected in the scene, the material is also assigned to that object.
   - Click  to add the material to the current document and immediately open the material in the Material Editor. If an object is selected, it also applies the material to that object.

Applying Materials to Model Objects

Once a model has been brought into the Navisworks software and materials have been added to the document, you can add materials to the objects in the model. You can apply materials to objects that have been selected in the scene view or in the Selection Tree. Materials are applied to an item, layer, etc., depending on the resolution setting of the Selection tool.

How To: Apply a Material to Items in the Scene

1. Select items in the scene using any of the following techniques:
   - Select individual items directly in the scene view or press and hold <Ctrl> to select multiple files.
   - Select individual items directly in the Selection Tree or press and hold <Ctrl> to select multiple items in the Selection Tree. To select a range of files, press and hold <Shift> while selecting two items to also select all of the items listed between them.
   - Select all of the items included in a selection or search set by selecting a name in the Sets window.

Using search sets has the added benefit of materials being easily applied to items that are added to the model at a later stage.

2. In the Autodesk Rendering window, use any of the following techniques:
   - In the Document Materials panel, right-click the required material and click **Apply to Selection**.
   - In the Library panel, navigate to and select the required material and click . Once selected, the material is copied to the Document Materials panel and assigned to an object if it is selected in the model.
   - Click and drag the required material directly onto an item from either the Document Materials panel or the Library panel. If you click and drag from the Library panel, the material is also added to the Document Materials panel.
3. Press <Esc> to clear item selection and view the item(s) with the applied materials.

Once a model has had a material assigned to it, that material can be overwritten with another material by selecting the object again and assigning a new material. Alternatively, you can remove the material that was previously assigned by selecting the object, right-clicking, and selecting **Reset Item>Reset Appearance**.

Rename and Manage Materials

Materials that are copied from the Library panel to the Document Materials panel have the same name as the one in the library by default. Once the material is copied to the document, you can maintain this name or rename it for easy reference, reuse, and management. Renaming materials is recommended if a library material is edited to help identify that it is different than the material in the library. Once materials have been customized in the Document Materials panel, they can be saved for reuse in other documents using the Favorites library.

How To: Rename a Material

1. Right-click the material in the Document Materials panel and select **Rename**.
2. Enter a descriptive name and press <Enter>.
3. It is useful to prefix the new material name with your company's initials for easy identification of a customized material.

How To: Manage Materials in the Favorites Library

1. Right-click the material in the Document Materials panel and select **Add to>Favorites**.
2. Navigate to the top of the Library tree and select the **Favorites** library node. The added document material displays in the pane on the right.
3. To further organize materials in the Favorites library, right-click the **Favorites** node and select **Create Category** to create a new category. Right-click the category, select **Rename**, and enter a new descriptive name for the category. Sub-categories can also be created. Materials can be dragged and dropped between categories, as required.
    - Once a category has been added to the Favorites library, you can add materials either to the top level or to a category when you use the **Add** option in the Document Materials panel.

Note: Materials that are deleted from the Document Materials panel are also cleared from any object they have previously been assigned to.

Material Editor

A material is defined by its properties. The available properties depend on the selected material type. Use the Material Editor to review and edit the properties of a material. Materials in the Autodesk materials library cannot be modified, but they can be used to create new materials.

To open the Material Editor, use one of the following techniques:

- Double-click a material in the Document Materials panel.
- Right-click a material in the Document Materials panel and select **Edit**.
- Select a material in the Autodesk Library and click . This option adds the material to the Document Materials panel and opens the Material Editor at the same time. If an object is selected, it also assigns the material to the model.

Other Autodesk programs have more tabs when editing materials, such as Graphics, Physical Properties, and Thermal Properties.

The Material Editor contains two tabs: the *Appearance* tab and the *Information* tab.

Appearance Tab

The *Appearance* tab is used to change how a material will display, as shown in Figure 11–6. The options available in this tab change depending on which material type is selected.

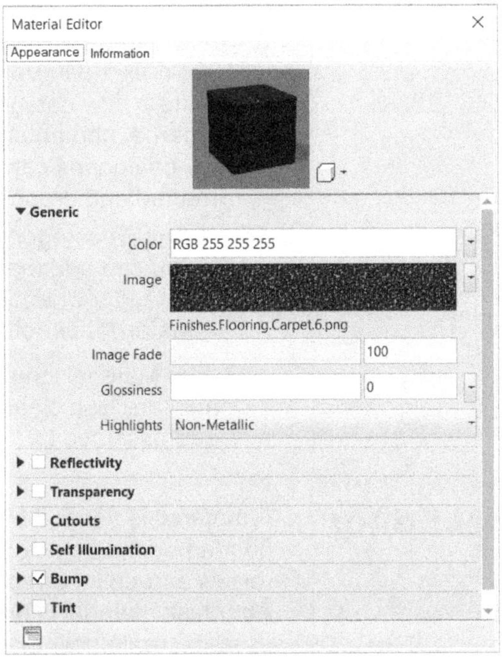

Figure 11–6

The following are consistent tools that are available for all material types when using the Materials Editor:

- Click  next to the lower right corner of the thumbnail image to access a list of display options for the thumbnail.
-  at the bottom of the Material Editor enables you to toggle the display of the Autodesk Rendering window on and off.

The following categories can be customized to define a material's properties.

When creating or editing materials other than the Generic type, the list of available options for customizing the material might vary slightly.

- **Generic:** The Generic category is required for all materials.
  - **Color:** Assigns the color of the material.
  - **Image:** Assigns textures to a material's color. The texture would display on the assigned material color. Two types of textures can be used: image (1) and procedural-based (2), as shown in Figure 11–7.

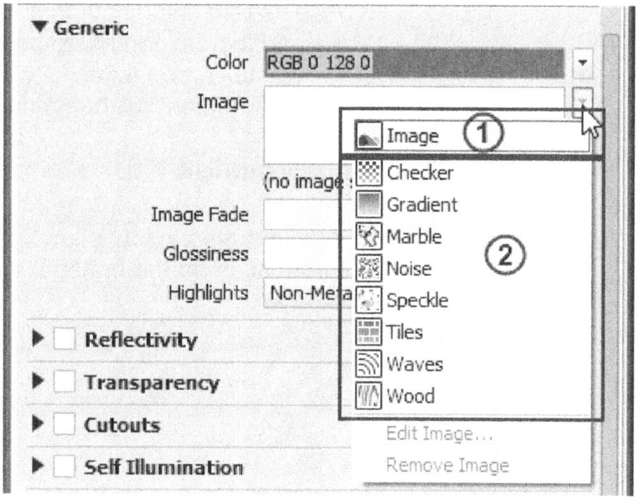

Figure 11–7

Image textures (1) are assigned using the **Image** option and use an image representing a certain texture. For example, you can use an image representing wood, concrete, brass, or weave.

Procedural-based textures (2) are selected from the predefined list and represent repetitive texture patterns, as shown in Figure 11–8.

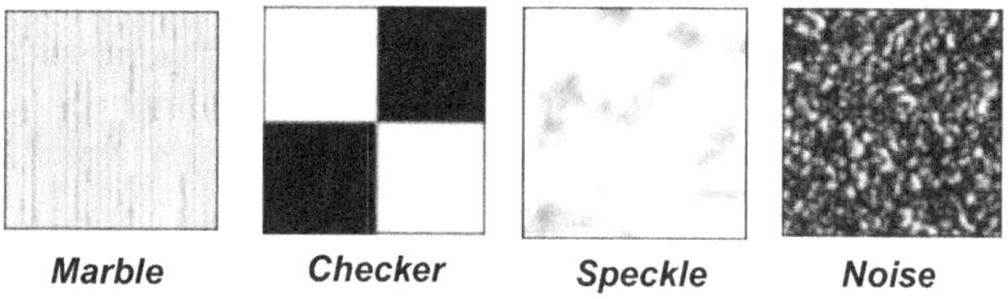

Figure 11–8

Hint: Texture Editor

The Navisworks software has a Texture Editor that can be used to edit either image or procedural-based textures. To open the Texture Editor, double-click the image field when a texture has been assigned. Refer to Texture Editor in the Navisworks Help documentation for more information on using the Texture Editor.

- **Image Fade**
- **Glossiness**
- **Highlights**

- The remaining categories can be selected to activate them and then expanded to assign values for them. These enable you to control reflectivity, transparency, cutouts, self-illumination, bump maps, and tint.

Information Tab

The *Information* tab, shown in Figure 11–9, contains general information on the material and its type.

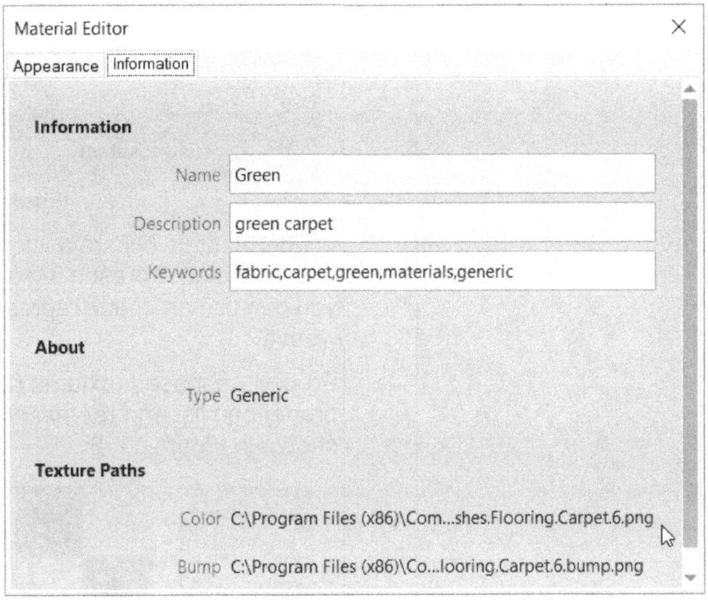

Figure 11–9

Creating Materials

You can also create your own custom materials for your project.

How To: Create a New Material

1. To create a new material, select an existing material from a library and add it to the Document Materials list using one of the following techniques:
   - Select the material in the pane on the right and click to add the material to the current document.
   - Select the material in the pane on the right and click to add it to the current document and immediately open it in the Material Editor.
   - Right-click the material and select **Add to>Document Materials**.

2. Double-click on the material in the Document Materials list to open the Material Editor. If you used the  icon to add the material, the Material Editor will already be open.
3. Click the *Appearance* tab and modify the options in all of the required categories.
4. In the Material Editor, click the *Information* tab and enter a name, description, and any required keywords for the material.
5. Close the Material Editor to save the material to the Document Materials panel

Consider copying the material to a Favorites library for easy retrieval and reuse in other documents.

Editing Materials

Materials can be edited once they have been added to the Document Materials panel. Editing materials enables you to adjust the properties of any Autodesk Library materials or any of the custom materials that have been created to improve or enhance their appearance.

How To: Edit an Applied Material

1. To open the Material Editor, do one of the following:
   - Double-click a material in the Document Materials panel.
   - Right-click a material in the Document Materials panel and select **Edit**.
2. Using the Material Editor, make the required changes to the options available in the *Appearance* and *Information* tabs.
3. Close the Material Editor to save the material to the Document Materials panel.
   - If the material has been assigned to the model, its appearance updates to reflect the changes.

11.3 Material Mapping

When mapping a material to an item, Navisworks initially determines the best mapping solution using one of the following options (shown in Figure 11–10). Each option will shrink-wrap the material texture to the geometry boundary as accurately as possible.

- **Planar mapping**
- **Box mapping**
- **Spherical mapping**
- **Cylindrical mapping**
- **Explicit mapping**

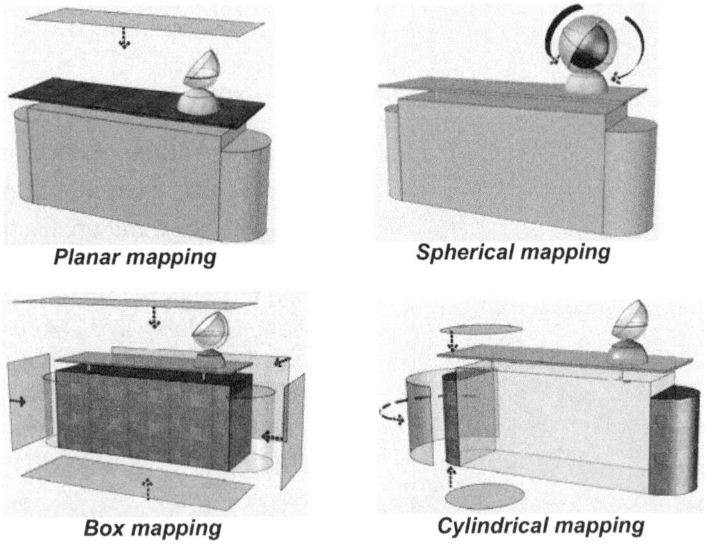

Figure 11–10

If the resulting mapping is not how you intended it, you can edit the texture space using the options in the *Material Mapping* tab.

Material Mapping Tab

The *Material Mapping* tab controls the texture spacing and proportions used when a textured material is assigned to an object. To change the type of texture spacing used, you select the object in the scene and then use the mapping type drop-down list. To edit the assigned texture space's settings, use the options in the *Material Mapping* tab, as shown in Figure 11–11.

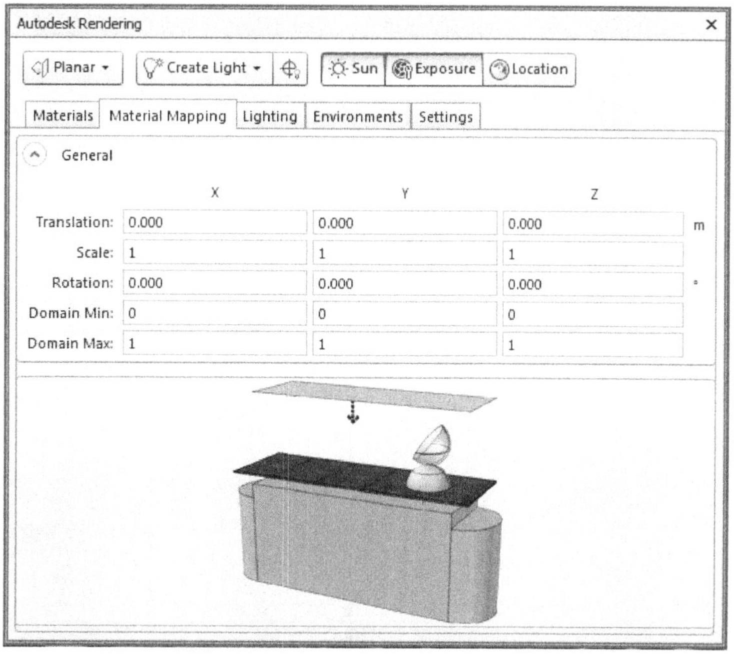

Figure 11–11

Material Mapping Drop-Down List

The Material Mapping drop-down list, shown in Figure 11–12, identifies the current texture space setting used on the object and can be used to assign a new type. Select the drop-down list to access and select another type.

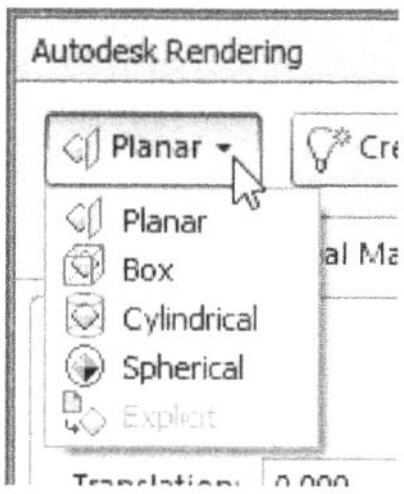

Figure 11–12

Material Mapping Settings

The *Material Mapping* tab provides fields that can be customized to refine the mapping settings, as shown in Figure 11–13. The fields are dependent on the active texture space setting.

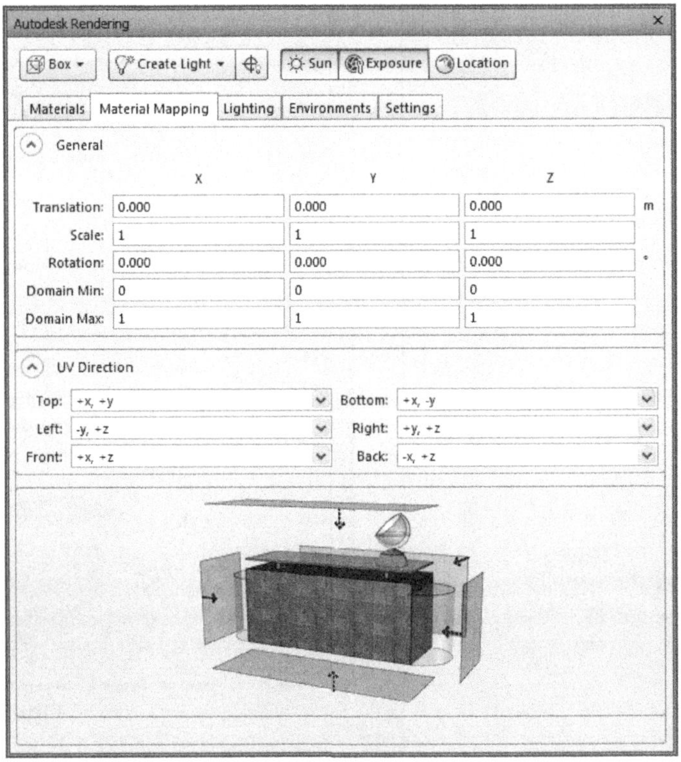

Figure 11–13

Adjusting Material Mapping

You can change the texture space setting in the Rendering toolbar by selecting a new option in the Material Mapping drop-down list. You can also adjust the fields that define the current mapping to adjust how a material map is placed, oriented, and scaled.

How To: Adjust the Material Mapping Settings

1. Select an object in the scene view or in the Selection Tree that you want to work with.
2. If no material has been previously added to the object, select the *Materials* tab, right-click on a material, and select **Assign to Selection**. Alternatively, you can click and drag the required material onto the object.

3. The current texture space setting is listed in the Rendering toolbar (e.g., Box, Cylindrical, Spherical, Planar, or Explicit). If this current setting is not appropriate, select a new type that is appropriate for the object.
4. Use the fields in the *Material Mapping* tab to adjust the mapping setting, as required. A preview of the result is shown in the scene view in real time.

Practice 11a Adding and Mapping Materials

Practice Objectives

- Navigate around the Autodesk Rendering window.
- Apply materials to objects.
- Apply material mapping to objects.

In this practice, you will study the Autodesk Rendering window, apply materials to objects, create a new material from a copy of an existing material, and map materials to better fit the object.

Task 1 - Add materials.

1. In the *Rendering* practice files folder, open **School-Lobby-Materials.nwf**.
2. In the *Home* tab>Tools panel, click  (Autodesk Rendering) to open the Autodesk Rendering window.
3. In the Saved Viewpoints window, select **Lobby** to change the viewpoint to an internal view of the entrance lobby of the school.
4. In the *Viewpoint* tab>Render Style panel, expand **Lighting** and select **Scene Lights**. The Scene Lights option uses the lights that were defined in the source BIM model. The difference is noticeable, which means there are light sources imported from Autodesk Revit.
5. In the *Viewpoint* tab>Render Style panel, expand **Lighting** and select **Head Light**. This mode will make selecting objects easier.
6. In the Render Style panel, expand **Mode** and select **Full Render** to ensure a smooth rendering that includes all of the materials.
7. Change the Lighting style back to **Head Light.**
8. In the Autodesk Rendering window, select the *Materials* tab. The Document Materials panel is populated with the materials that have been brought in from the source Autodesk Revit model.
9. In the scene view, select a wall on the left side of the lobby. and wait until the tooltip appears. If the tooltip lists the *Item Type* as **Rooms**, as shown in Figure 11–14, then proceed to the next step. If the tooltip lists a Basic Wall, then you should still proceed with the next steps of hiding the Revit Rooms.

Figure 11–14

10. *Rooms* are special organizational objects used in Autodesk Revit that have little to no value in Navisworks. Therefore, you can hide all the rooms. In the Selection Tree window, go to the top of the branch of the selected object and right-click on **Rooms**.

11. In the shortcut menu, select **Hide** to hide all of the rooms in the model, as shown in Figure 11–15. You could also use the <Ctrl>+<H> keyboard shortcut to hide them.

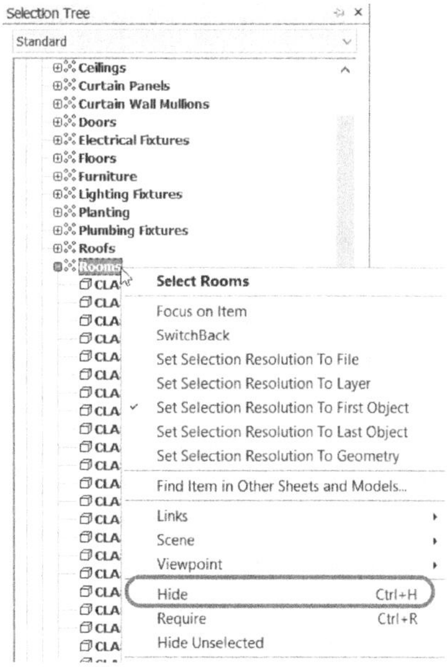

Figure 11–15

Remember to hold <Ctrl> when selecting the second wall in order to select both walls.

12. In the scene view, select the two walls on the left side of the lobby. Ensure that the *Selection Resolution* is set to **Geometry** so that only the two walls are selected, as shown in Figure 11–16.

Figure 11–16

13. In the Library panel of the *Materials* tab, expand the Autodesk Library and select the **Wall Paint** category. In the pane on the right, right-click the **Aquamarine** color and select **Assign to Selection**, as shown in Figure 11–17.

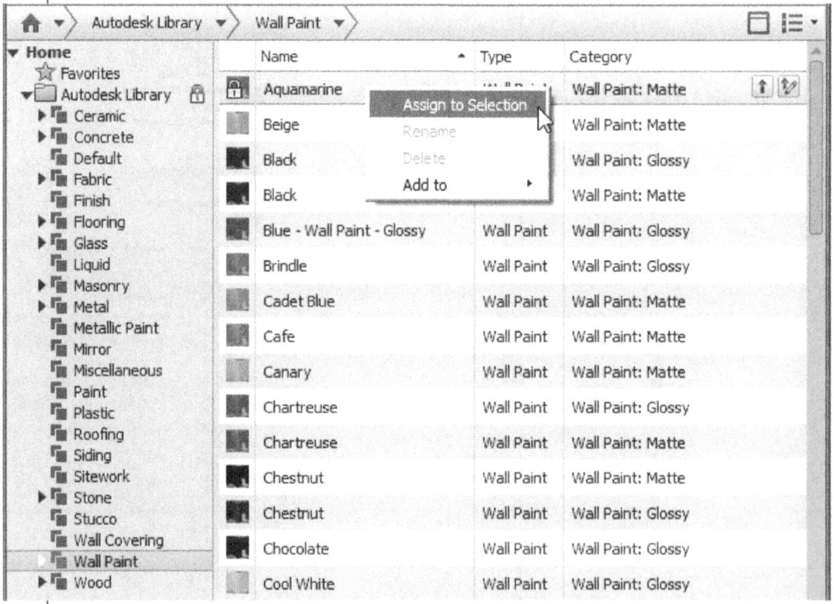

Figure 11–17

14. Clear the selection in the scene view by pressing <Esc> or clicking  (Select None) in the *Home* tab>Select & Search panel, and note that the Aquamarine Wall Paint material has been added to the wall. It has also been added to the Document Materials list near the top of the *Materials* tab.

15. In the Selection Tree, expand *School-Architectural.rvt>First Floor>Generic Models* and select the **Porcelain, Navy Blue** object in one of the **Table-Lamp** objects, as shown in Figure 11–18.

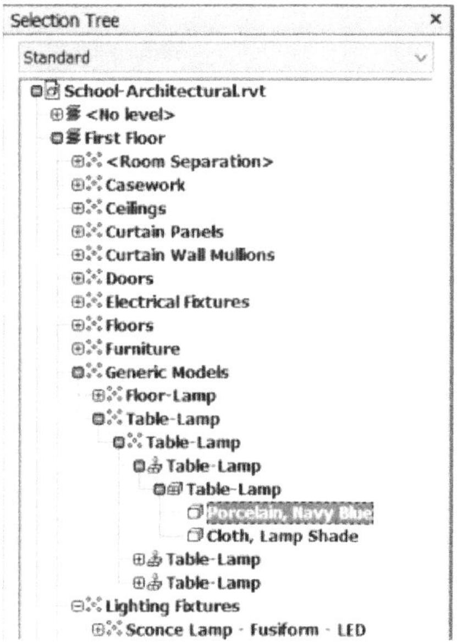

Figure 11–18

16. In the *Home* tab>Select & Search panel, expand **Select Same** and select **Same Name**. All three of the table lamp bases in the lobby are selected.

17. In the Material Library, expand the *Stone>Marble* category. In the pane on the right, right-click the **Coarse Polished-White** material and select **Assign to Selection**.

18. In the scene view, select the ceiling, which is at the top of the scene.

19. In the Material Library, select the **Stucco** category. In the pane on the right, right-click the **Exterior-Beige** material and select **Assign to Selection**.

20. Clear the selection.

21. In the Document Materials panel, scroll to the **Metal - Aluminum (1)** material. Right-click on this material and select **Select Object Applied To**. All of the curtain wall mullions and door handles are selected in the scene view.

22. Double-click the **Metal - Aluminum (1)** material in the list to open the Material Editor, as shown in Figure 11–19. Note that this material is Satin Aluminum, which is a matte material. Close the Material Editor.

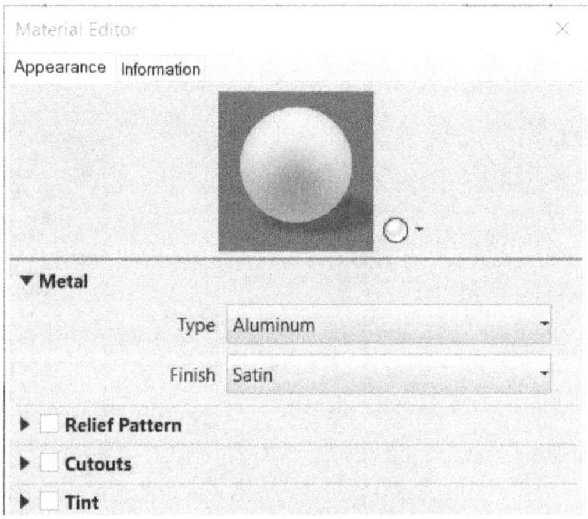

Figure 11–19

23. In the Material Library, select the **Metal** category. In the pane on the right, double-click the **Bronze-Satin Hammered** material to open the Material Editor, as shown in Figure 11–20. Note that this material is not a reflective material. Close the Material Editor.

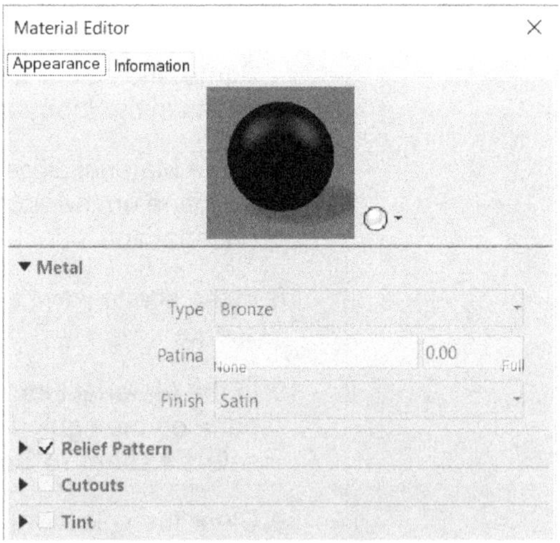

Figure 11–20

24. Ensure that all the mullions are still selected in the Selection Tree. In the Material Library, right-click the **Bronze-Satin Hammered** material and select **Assign to Selection**.

Task 2 - Map materials.

1. In the scene view, select the gray floor of the lobby and hallways (not the shiny entrance tile).
2. In the Material Library, expand the *Flooring>Vinyl* category. In the pane on the right, right-click the **Checker Black-White** material and select **Assign to Selection**.
3. Clear the selection of the floor in the scene view. Note that the checked pattern is too small for the model.
4. Select the floor again. Verify in the Selection Tree that the **5" Concrete Floor** object is selected.
5. In the Autodesk Rendering window, select the *Material Mapping* tab.
6. In the Material Mapping drop-down list, select **Planar** to change the mapping type for the floor, as shown in Figure 11–21.

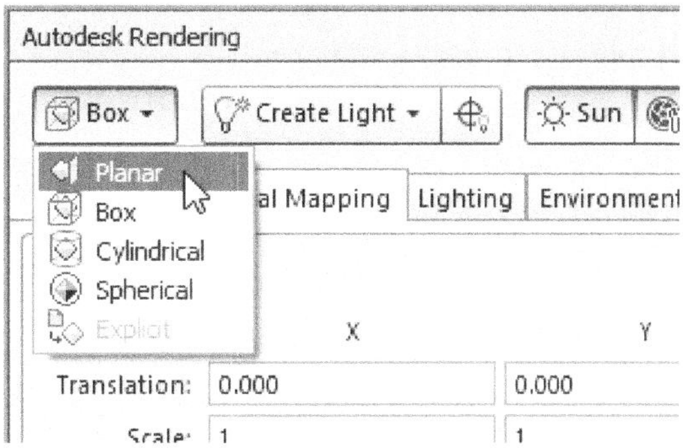

Figure 11–21

7. In the Material Mapping settings, change the scale values in the *General* settings to **0.2** for the X-, Y-, and Z-directions, as shown in Figure 11–22. This produces less tiling and a larger pattern.

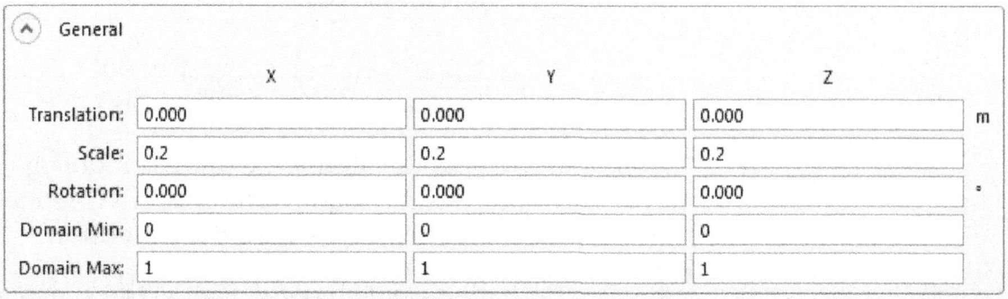

Figure 11–22

8. Clear the selection of the floor and note the larger checkered pattern.

9. Save the file and leave it open. You will continue working on this file in the next practice.

11.4 Lighting

Lighting is used in models to further customize a more realistic rendering then what materials alone can provide. Lighting also enhances the overall scene in which the model is presented. There are multiple types of lights that can be incorporated into a scene, including artificial lights and natural lights.

Artificial Lights

Scenes illuminated with point, spot, distant, or web lights are using artificially illuminated light sources. Artificial lights are subdivided into two types: photometric and standard.

Photometric lights provide lighting options as they would be in the real world. Point, spot, and web lights are photometric lights.

- **Point Light:** A point light illuminates everything around it.
- **Spot Light:** A spot light has a hotspot and falloff cone area that are defined by an angular value that radiates from the source.
    - The hotspot is the brightest area of the light beam.
    - The falloff defines the full cone of light.
    - The difference between the hotspot and falloff angles determines the sharpness of the edge of the light beam. Angles that are near equal will produce a sharp edge while angles with a greater difference will produce a softer edge. These values can be adjusted directly using the light's gizmo.
- **Web Light:** A web light can use data provided by manufacturers of real-world lights to represent irregular light distributions, giving the light a more precise representation when rendered versus using spot or point lights.

Using the light gizmos, you can adjust the sharpness or softness of the light by adjusting the hotspot and falloff angles.

You can set a light's distribution, intensity, color, and other characteristics, such as IES standard file format.

Standard lights are objects that mimic lights in a rendered image. The distant light type is a standard light. You can set its intensity and color values.

- **Distant Light:** A distant light shines uniform parallel light rays in a single direction. The light's intensity does not diminish and it is generally used to illuminate objects or uniformly illuminate a backdrop.

Use standard lights when you want to create and control a required effect in rendering and use photometric lights to enable the scene to render based on how the lights would look in the real world.

Natural Light

Natural light includes the Sun and Sky lighting system. Once enabled, the options for this are controlled in the *Environments* tab and the Rendering toolbar. Natural light does not use light glyphs because the sun lights up an entire scene.

Lighting Units

Both international (SI) and American lighting units are available.

Lighting Tab

The *Lighting* tab of the Autodesk Rendering window, shown in Figure 11–23, enables you to manage lights. The creation, use, and settings for those lights are managed using the following interface items:

- Rendering toolbar
- Lights panel
- Properties panel

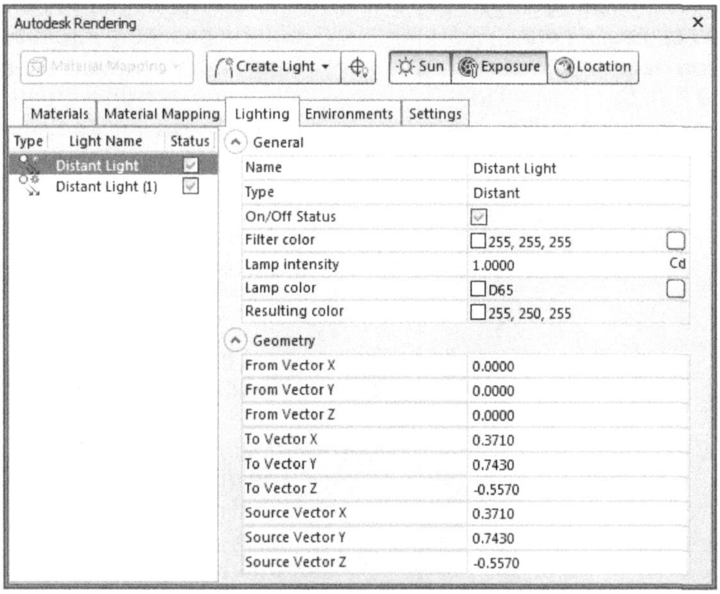

Figure 11–23

Rendering Toolbar

The Create Light drop-down list, located in the Rendering toolbar, enables you to create light sources in the scene view. The available light types are:

- **Point**
- **Spot**
- **Distant**
- **Web**

Once lights are placed in a model, they are represented by unique light glyphs indicating their location and type (point, spot, distant, or web). You can toggle the display of light glyphs on or off while you work by using (Light Glyphs) in the Rendering toolbar to control the display of the glyphs in the current viewpoint. **Note:** This does not toggle the light sources on or off.

Lights Panel

The sun and sky light is not included in the Lights panel.

The Lights panel is on the left side of the *Lights* tab. Use the **Status** checkbox to toggle the lights on and off, as needed. To display the light's properties, select it in the list. Selecting a light in the Lights panel also highlights it in the model (if the glyphs are displayed).

- An unlimited number of lights can be used in your model. To limit the lights used to eight lights, click Application Menu >Options>Interface>Display>Autodesk page and clear the **Use Unlimited Lights** option.

Properties Panel

The Properties panel displays the properties of the selected light. These can be modified as needed to update the lighting for the scene. The effects of changes are visible in the scene view in real time. The following general properties are available for artificial light types.

- **General Properties**
  - Name
  - Type
  - On/Off Status
  - Filter color
  - Lamp intensity
  - Lamp color
  - Resulting color
  - Hotspot and Falloff angle (spot light only)
  - IES filename and location (web light only)
- **Geometry:** Geometry properties enable you to enter specific values to control the light's location in the scene.

Creating Lights

The procedure for creating the four types of artificial lights is similar and involves the initial use of the Create Light drop-down list in the Rendering toolbar, as shown in Figure 11–24.

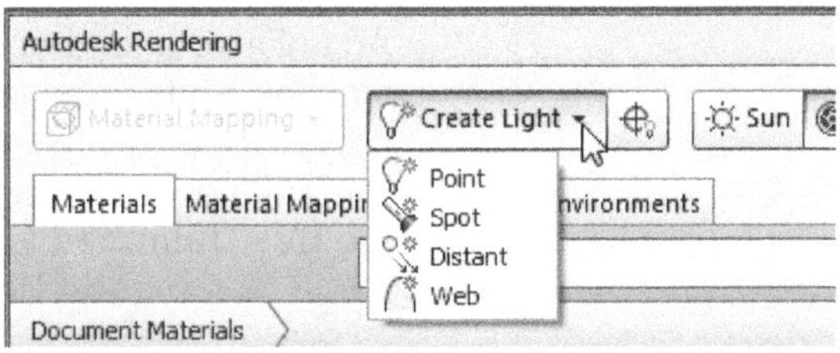

Figure 11–24

How To: Add a Point Light

1. In the Autodesk Rendering window>Rendering toolbar> Create Light drop-down list, click (Point).
2. Click in the scene view to locate the light. Adjust the light gizmo as needed to control the light's position in the model.
3. Use the Properties panel in the *Lighting* tab to adjust the light's properties, if required.

How To: Add a Spot Light

1. In the Autodesk Rendering window>Rendering toolbar> Create Light drop-down list, click (Spot).
2. Click in the scene view to locate the light.
3. Click to specify a target for the spot light. Adjust the light gizmo as needed to control the light's location and direction.
4. Use the Properties panel in the *Lighting* tab to adjust the light's properties, if required.

How To: Add a Distant Light

1. In the Autodesk Rendering window>Rendering toolbar> Create Light drop-down list, click (Distant).
2. Click in the scene view to locate the light.
3. Click to specify a direction. Adjust the light gizmo as needed to control the light's position and target.
4. Use the Properties panel in the *Lighting* tab to adjust the light's properties, if required.

How To: Add a Web Light with a Manufacturer's IES File

1. In the Autodesk Rendering window>Rendering toolbar> Create Light drop-down list, click (Web).
2. Click in the scene view to locate the light.
3. Click to specify a direction. Adjust the light gizmo as needed to control the light's position and target.
4. In the Autodesk Rendering window, in the *Lighting* tab, click in the *Web file* field. Browse to and open an IES file. The light properties update using the IES file data.
5. Use the Properties panel in the *Lighting* tab to adjust the light's properties, if required.

Autodesk Revit Lights

If the Autodesk Revit model contains lights, you can use them as light sources in Navisworks. In Revit, there are architectural and MEP lighting fixture families. The MEP lighting fixtures contain more BIM information for circuitry, switch networks, electrical panel identification, etc.

Consult the Revit Help documentation about placing and managing light sources in Revit.

Both Revit lighting types can be imported into Navisworks. First, you need to configure Navisworks to accept the Revit lights, which are disabled by default. Go to the Navisworks Options Editor>File Readers>Revit page and check **Convert lights**, as shown in Figure 11–25. By default, this setting is off.

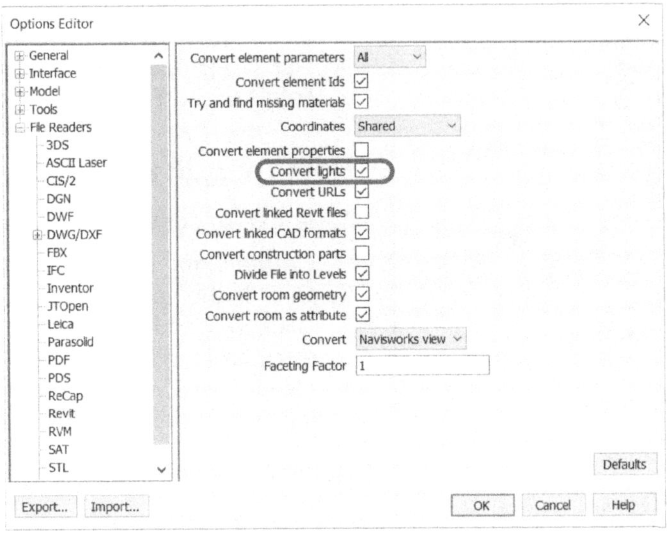

Figure 11–25

When the Revit file is appended, the lights and their properties will be extracted and defined as Navisworks light sources. They will automatically be assigned the proper lighting type (as defined in Revit), such as point light, spot light, or web light.

The *marks* (unique ID number in Revit) of the lighting fixture or the lighting groups established in Revit are **not** used in Navisworks. Instead, Navisworks assigns sequential numbers to the three light types. This makes it rather difficult to identify the individual light in the Lights panel, as shown in Figure 11–26.

Figure 11–26

However, using Revit lights can save a lot of time, since no Navisworks lights need to be created. The output is very acceptable, as shown in Figure 11–27.

Figure 11–27

Note: If a Revit file has been appended to the Navisworks model prior to the **Convert lights** checkbox being checked in the Navisworks Options Editor, you will need to delete the Revit file from the Navisworks model (through the Selection Tree window) and add the Revit file again for the lights to be imported. Of course, you will need to check the **Convert lights** checkbox first.

Editing Lights

Lights can be edited directly in the scene view or by using the Properties panel in the *Lighting* tab. When a light is selected in the model or in the Lights panel, a triad displays on the light's glyph, as shown in Figure 11–28. In the case of a spot light, hotspot and falloff cones also appear. Additional property modification is done using the General properties in the *Lighting* tab. As you change the properties of a light, you will see the effect on the model.

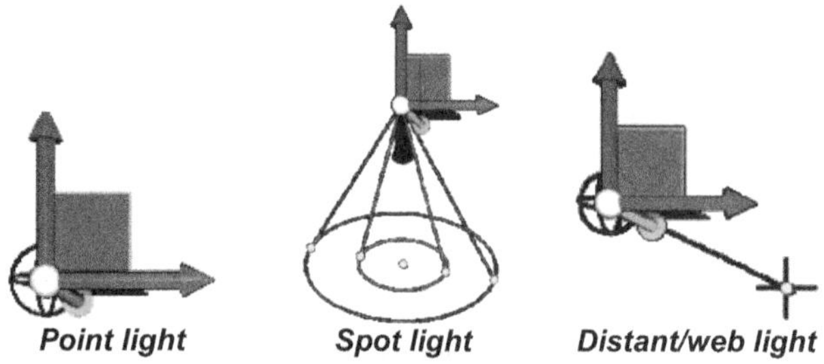

Figure 11–28

- Select any of the direction arrows on the triad to translate the glyph (light) in that direction.
- Select the planar rectangle between arrows to move the glyph (light) in a plane.
- Select and drag the center of the triad to freely move the glyph (light) in the scene.
- Select the yellow dots that lie on the perimeter of the hotspot (inner) and falloff (outer) cones for a spot light and drag them to adjust their angle.
- Select the yellow dot that lies at the center of the cone for a spot light to relocate the target location. If the yellow dot is not visible, ensure that the **Targeted** option is enabled in the *Geometry properties* area.
- For distant and web lights, enter values in the *Geometry properties* area to change the location of the target.

You can also adjust a light's location and light's hotspot and falloff angle settings in the Properties view.

Filter Color

The filter color defines the color of the light that is being emitted.

The default color is white. To modify this color, click and change the color using the Color dialog box that displays, as shown in Figure 11–29. Click **OK** to confirm and assign the new color for the light.

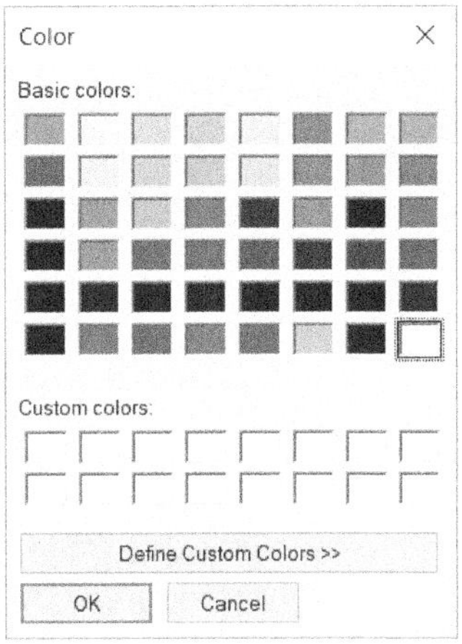

Figure 11–29

Lamp Settings

A lamp's intensity and color can be modified from its default values to customize the light's appearance.

- Clicking (...) adjacent to the *Lamp Intensity* field in the *General properties* area activates the Lamp Intensity dialog box.
- Lamp color can also be specified by clicking (...) adjacent to the *Lamp Color* field in the *General properties* area. Use the Lamp Color dialog box to modify the lamp color.

Deleting Lights

To delete an existing light in a Navisworks scene, right-click the light's name in the Lights panel and select **Delete**.

Controlling Lights in the Scene View

Lights in the scene view can be controlled in the Autodesk Rendering window or controlled globally.

Disabling Lights in the Autodesk Rendering Window

As an alternative to deleting lights from the scene, you can selectively disable lights that are not required. Disabling a light enables it to remain in the file, but temporarily removes it from use in the scene. To disable an existing light, in the Lights panel, clear the checkbox in the *Status* column, as shown for the Spot Light in Figure 11–30.

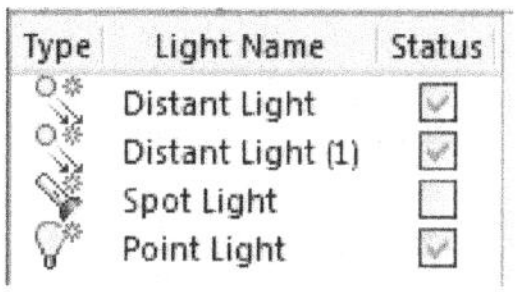

Figure 11–30

Controlling Lights for the Scene

The lights in the scene view can also be controlled using the **Lighting** options in the *Viewpoint* tab>Render Style panel, as shown in Figure 11–31. A scene consists of lights imported from the source CAD file and any lights that are created in the Autodesk Rendering environment.

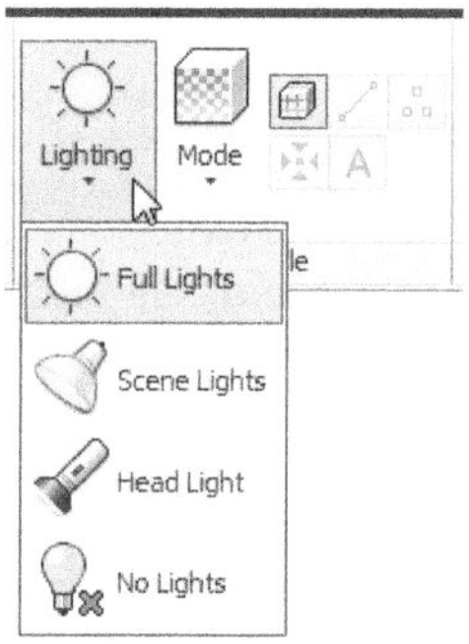

Figure 11–31

The following controls can be used to achieve the required lighting appearance.

Icon	Name	Description
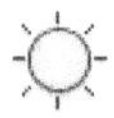	**Full Lights**	This mode takes into account the lights that are enabled in the *Lighting* tab of the Autodesk Rendering window (i.e., defined with Navisworks).
	**Scene Lights**	Uses the lights defined and imported from the source CAD model. If there are none available, two default opposing lights are used.

	**Head Lights**	Uses a single directional light located at the camera (viewer) in addition to an ambient light.
	**No Lights**	Disables the use of all lights, including any defined in the model.

Environments Tab

The *Environments* tab in the Autodesk Rendering window, shown in Figure 11–32, enables you to manage sunlight and sky illumination in a model. The settings are saved per file.

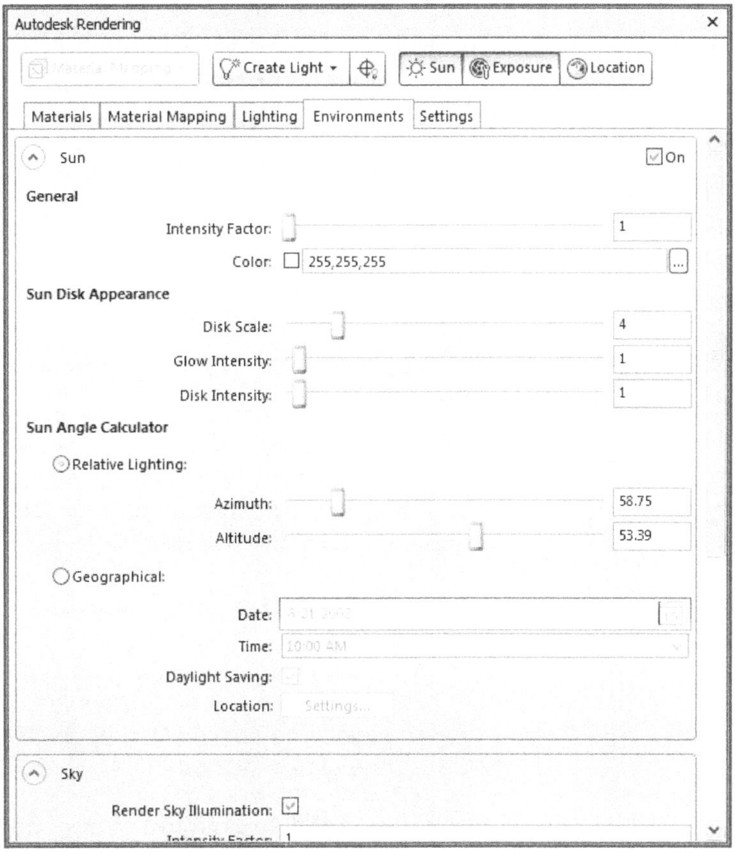

Figure 11–32

The options in the Sun and Sky panels enable you to modify the effect that these systems have in the scene.

Working with the Sun and Sky Environments

To add the sun and sky light to your model, use the following overall workflow:

1. Toggle on the sun light environment in the scene view.
2. Set the location of the sun.
3. Adjust the Sun properties, as required.
4. Adjust the Sky properties, as required.

Enabling the Sun Light System

Enabling the sun light environment in the scene requires you to toggle on the sun and then enable sky illumination.

How To: Enable the Sun Light System in the Scene View

1. In the Autodesk Rendering window>Rendering toolbar, click 

(Sun). Alternatively, you can select the **Sun** checkbox in the Sun panel in the *Environments* tab.
2. By default, the sun light effect is visible in the scene view. The sun's display in the scene view can be enabled/disabled as required.
3. The sun and sky effects are only visible in the scene view if the exposure is toggled on. By default, the exposure is enabled when the sun light is enabled, but it can also be disabled independently by clearing the **Exposure** option in the Exposure panel. If disabled, the background in the scene view displays as white.

Setting the Sun Location

Setting the sun location is done using the Geographic Location dialog box and the *Sun Angle Calculator* settings in the Sun panel. The position and angle of the sun can be defined using one of two methods:

- **Relative Lighting**
- **Geographical**

How To: Set the Geographic Position

1. In the Autodesk Rendering window, in the *Environments* tab, select **Geographical** in the *Sun Angle Calculator* area.
2. Click **Settings** in the *Geographical* area, or in the Autodesk Rendering window>Rendering toolbar, click **Location**.
3. In the *Latitude & Longitude* area, select a measurement type and enter the coordinates to locate the sun in the scene, as shown in Figure 11–33.

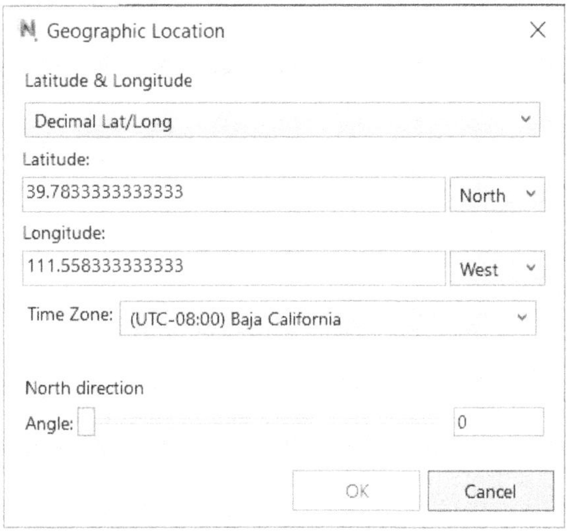

Figure 11–33

4. In the Time Zone drop-down list, set the time zone.
5. In the *North direction* area of the dialog box, move the **Angle** slider to define the angle of the position of the sun in the scene view.
   - **Note:** This setting does not have any effect on the model's coordinate system or the ViewCube compass direction.
6. Click **OK** to close the Geographic Location dialog box.
7. In the *Geographical* area, enter a *Date* and *Time* value for the sun, as shown in Figure 11–34.

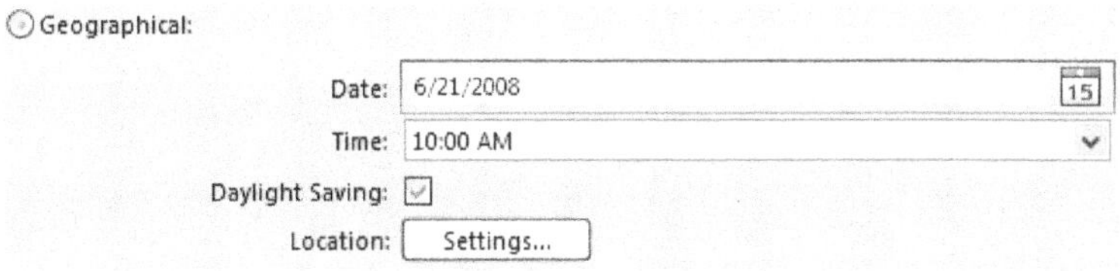

Figure 11–34

Adjusting the Sun Properties

You can further customize the default settings that are assigned for the sun using the *General* and *Sun Disk Appearance* options in the Sun panel, as shown in Figure 11–35.

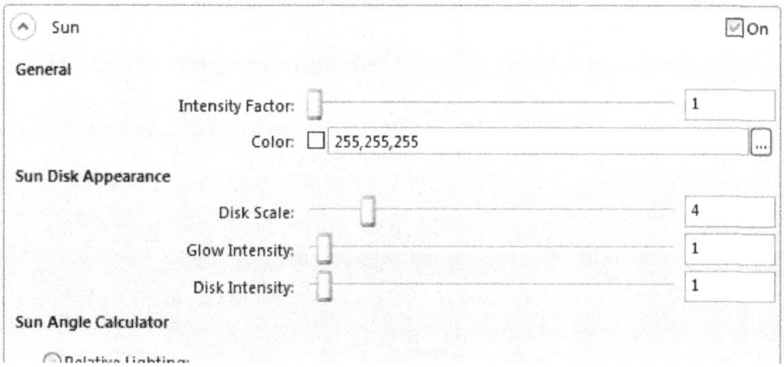

Figure 11–35

Adjusting the Sky Properties

The actual effect that all of the specified sun properties has on the scene can be further adjusted with the properties that are available in the Sky panel, as shown in Figure 11–36.

*The **Render Sky Illumination** option can be disabled, as required, to toggle off the sun light effect in the scene view.*

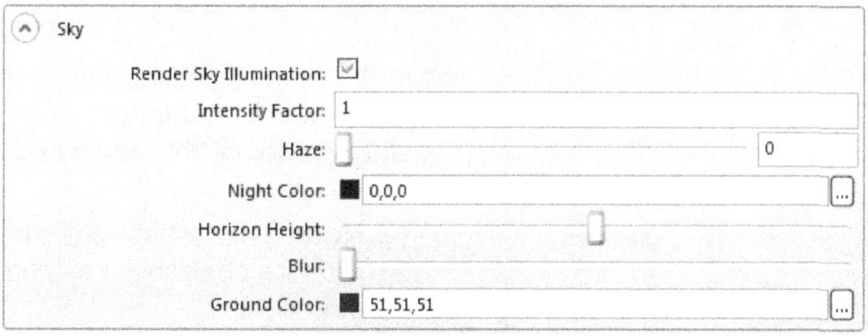

Figure 11–36

Practice 11b Adding Lights to a Model

Practice Objectives

- Place point lights and spot lights in the model.
- Adjust the lights.

In this practice, you will place lights strategically on walls and within light fixtures. Then, you will adjust the various settings of the lights and study the results. Finally, you will add some exterior lights.

There are light fixtures in the appended Revit file that have been imported. For this practice, the freestanding fixtures in the lobby have been disabled, whereas the ones attached to the wall and the exterior lights are enabled.

Task 1 - Add point lights.

1. Continue to work on the file from the previous practice. If you did not complete that practice, in the *Rendering* practice files folder, open **School-Lobby-Lights.nwf**.
2. Go to the Navisworks Options Editor>File Readers>Revit page and set the **Convert lights** to checked, if required, as shown in Figure 11–37. Click **OK** to dismiss the *Navisworks Options Editor* window.

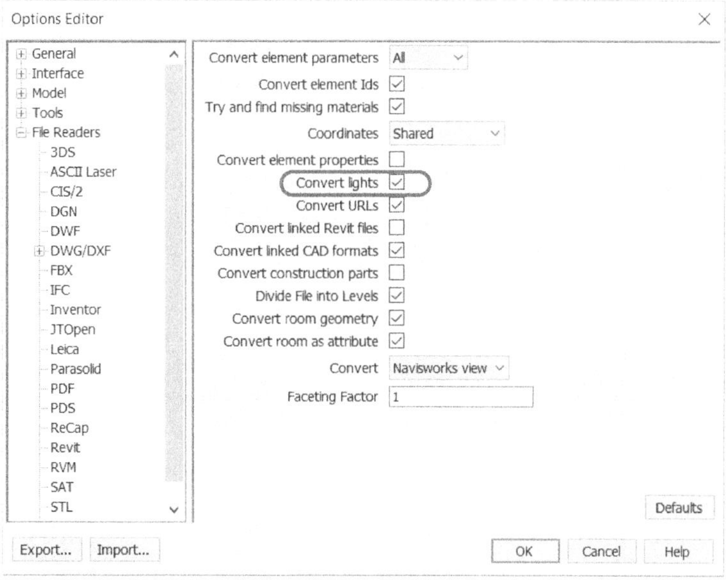

Figure 11–37

3. If the Convert lights needed to be checked, you will need to refresh the models by clicking on Refresh (Refresh) in the *Home* tab>Project panel. This can take some time since it has to convert the lights from the Revit model.

4. In the *Home* tab>Tools panel, click (Autodesk Rendering) to open the Autodesk Rendering window, if not already open.

5. In the Saved Viewpoints window, select **Lobby**, if necessary.

6. In the lobby and on the exterior are light sources from the Autodesk Revit model. The freestanding table lamps and floor lamps are not Autodesk Revit light sources, so these need to be supplied Navisworks light sources.

7. In the Autodesk Rendering window, select the *Lighting* tab. Note that there are two distant lights and multiple other lights in the scene, as shown in Figure 11–38. These lights were brought in from the source Autodesk Revit model.

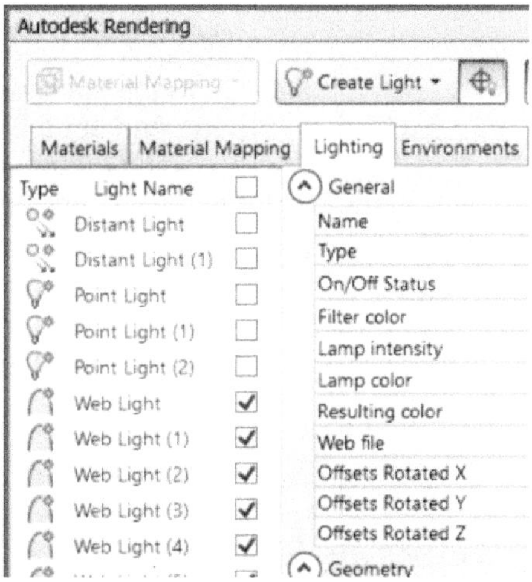

Figure 11–38

8. In the Autodesk Rendering window>Rendering toolbar> Create Light drop-down list, click (Point), as shown in Figure 11–39.

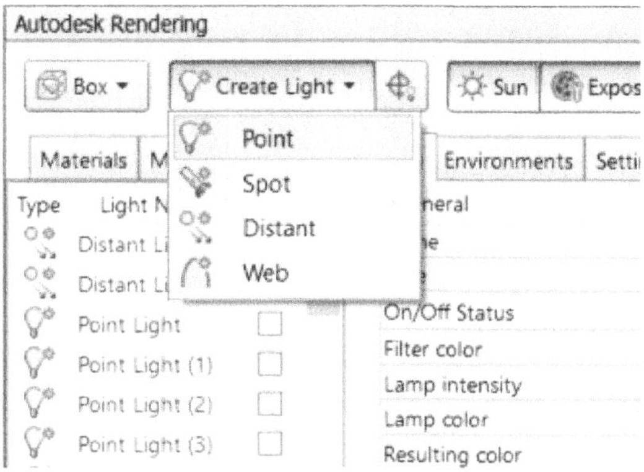

Figure 11–39

9. In the scene view, select the light shade of the table lamps to the right to place the point light, as shown in Figure 11–40.

Figure 11–40

10. When you create a new light source in Navisworks, the scene is fully rendered immediately. The glyphs of any other light sources are also revealed.

11. For the General properties of the point light, enter the following, as shown in Figure 11–41:
    - *Name*: **Table Lamp 1**
    - *Lamp intensity - Intensity*: **60**
    - *Lamp intensity - Unit*: **Wattage (watt)** (pick from the drop-down list)

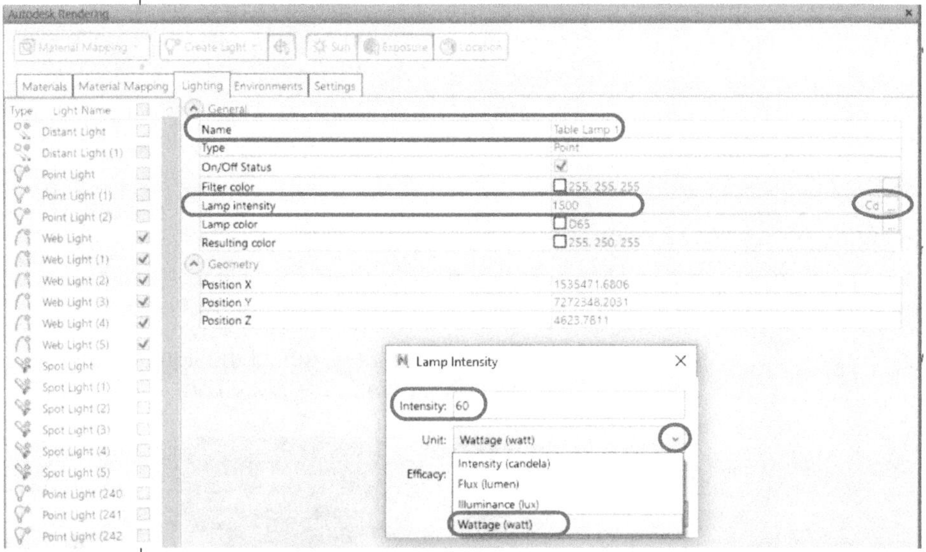

Figure 11–41

12. Select the red axis on the gizmo for the point light and drag the light toward the entrance doors, as shown in Figure 11–42. Note that the cursor displays as a hand when moving a light and the scene updates the lighting as the light moves.

Figure 11–42

13. Return the point light back to the lamp shade. These two steps are simply to demonstrate the lighting effects when a light source is moved.

You cannot select multiple light sources to edit in the General properties; they have to be edited one by one.

14. Create two more point lights for the other two table lamps along the far wall, rename them to **Table Lamp 2** and **Table Lamp 3** respectively, and change their intensity to **60 watts** as you did previously.

15. Save the Navisworks file.

Task 2 - Add spot lights.

1. In the Create Light drop-down list, click (Spot).

2. In the scene view, select the floor lamp nearest you (in the right side of the view) to place the spot light and select the black chair near it as the target, as shown in Figure 11–43.

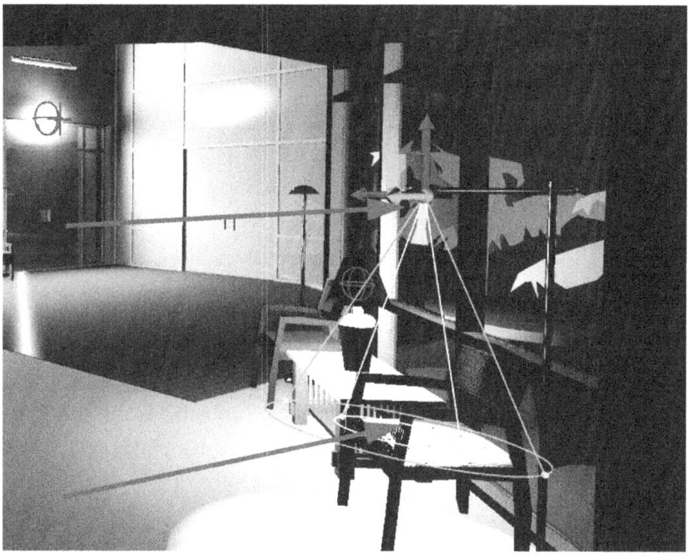

Figure 11–43

3. For the General properties of the spot light, enter the following, as shown in Figure 11–44:

   - *Name*: **Floor Lamp 1**
   - *Filter color*: Salmon (click the ellipsis to select a color)

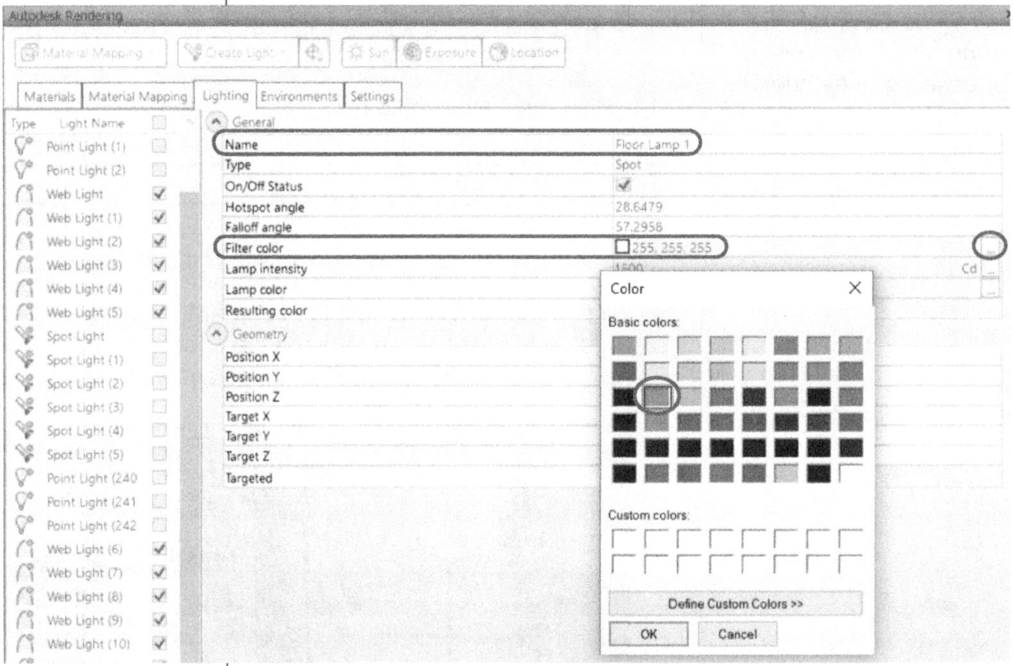

Figure 11–44

4. Select the yellow dot on the outside of the inner ring that is centered on the target and drag by selecting the arrow to make it smaller, as shown in Figure 11–45. This is the hotspot angle. Note how the *Hotspot angle* changes in the General properties for this light.

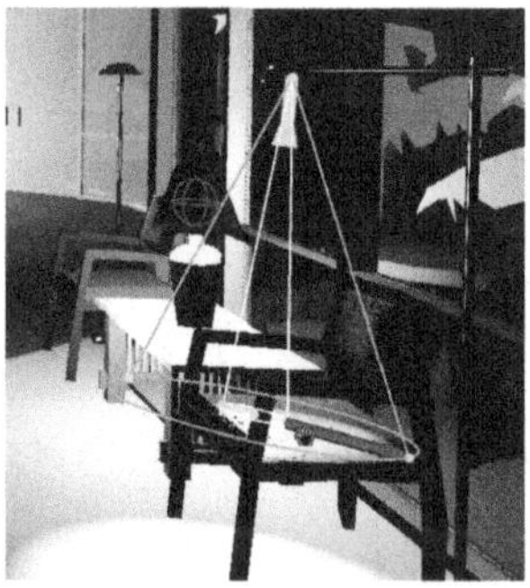

Figure 11–45

5. Select the yellow dot on the outside of the outer ring that is centered on the target and drag by selecting the arrow to make it smaller, as shown in Figure 11–46. This is the falloff angle. Note how the *Falloff angle* changes in the General properties for this light.

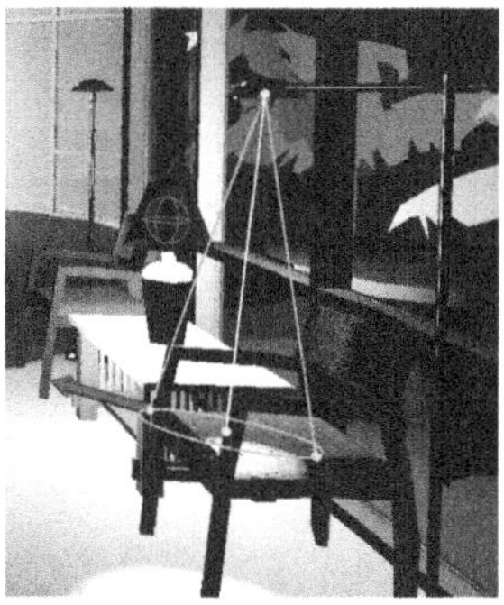

Figure 11–46

6. Adjust the values for the *Hotspot angle* and *Falloff angle* in the General properties for the spot light. Enter **17** as the hotspot value and **36** as the falloff value, as shown in Figure 11–47.

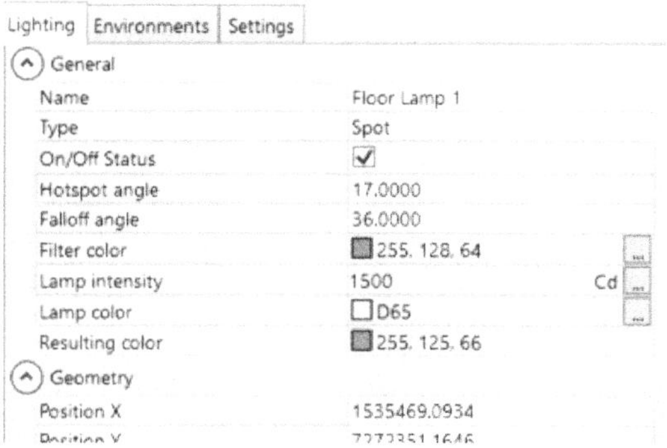

Figure 11–47

If the scene view goes black, you need to restore a viewpoint to resume.

7. Create five more spot lights for the other floor lamps in the scene, aiming them onto the chairs nearest to them. You can zoom and pan within the scene for easier placement, if necessary.

8. The fifth one is behind the plant, so you will need to navigate carefully to see it. The **Shrinking Plant** viewpoint can get you into the vicinity. You may have to reset the **Lighting** in the *Viewpoint* tab>Render Style panel to **Full Lights**.

9. Adjust the *Hotspot angle* and *Falloff angle* and change the names of the spot lights in the General properties. Keep the *Filter color* as the default.

10. Save the Navisworks file.

Task 3 - Add a web light.

1. In the Saved Viewpoints window, select **8 sec** to move into the foyer. Use the Look Around (and perhaps Orbit) tool to get a vantage point similar to the one in Figure 11–48. You will need to increase the **F.O.V.** value in the *Viewpoint* tab>Camera panel.

2. Save the viewpoint as **Foyer-Ceiling**.

3. In the Create Light drop-down list, click (Web).

4. In the scene view, select the brick area above the curtain wall to place the web light and select the gray wall to the right as the direction reference, as shown in Figure 11–48.

Figure 11–48

5. Name the light **High Foyer** in the General properties.

6. For the *Web file*, click on the ellipses (as shown in Figure 11–49), browse to the *Navisworks BIM Practice Files\Project Files\Lighting* folder, and select the **482T12.ies** file.

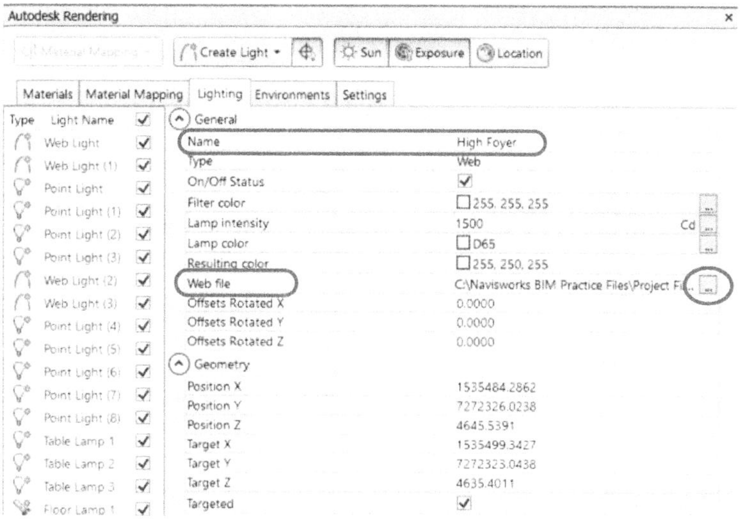

Figure 11–49

7. In the Rendering toolbar, click  (Light Glyphs). This turns off the display of glyphs representing the light sources in the current viewpoint only; it does not toggle the light sources on or off.

8. In the Saved Viewpoints window, select **Lobby**.

9. In the *Viewpoint* tab>Render Style panel, expand **Lighting** and note that **Full Lights** is now active. The Full Lights option uses the lights that were defined in the Autodesk Rendering environment. As soon as new lights are created, this option is enabled.

   - **Note:** Disabling the Full Lights option and returning to Scene Lights temporarily eliminates the use of the lights created in the Rendering environment of the scene.

10. Save the file.

11.5 Exposure Control

The sun and sky effects are only visible when the exposure is toggled on; otherwise, the background in the scene view becomes white.

Exposure settings enable you to control how the lights that have been defined in the scene are processed in a the final rendered image, providing real-world characteristics to the scene's lighting.

Environments Tab

The use and settings for exposure control are managed using the Exposure panel in the *Environments* tab, as shown in Figure 11–50. As settings are specified, their effects are immediate in the scene view.

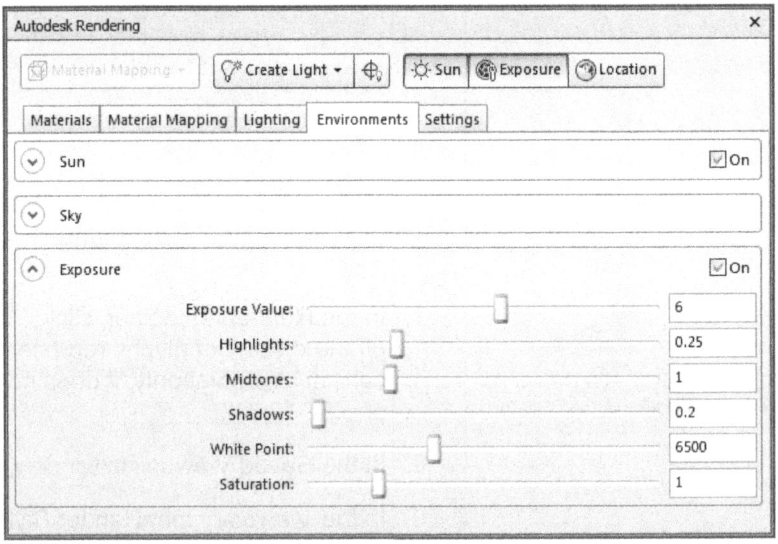

Figure 11–50

The options in the Exposure panel allow you to enable or disable the use of exposure and customize the effect that it has in the scene.

Enabling and Adjusting Exposure

Adjusting the exposure of the scene enables you to refine the results of the rendering to obtain a more real-world effect.

How To: Adjust the Exposure in a Scene

1. In the Autodesk Rendering window>Rendering toolbar, click **Exposure**.
    - Alternatively, in the *Environments* tab>Exposure panel, you can select **On**.

2. Refine the exposure controls using the sliders for the following options:
   - **Exposure Value:** Controls brightness (range is between -6 (brighter) and 16 (darker)).
   - **Highlights:** Adjusts the light level for the brightest area of the image (range is between 0 (darker) and 1 (brighter)).
   - **Midtones:** Adjusts the light level for areas between the highlights and shadows (range is between 0.1 (darker) and 4 (brighter)).
   - **Shadows:** Adjust the light levels for the darkest areas (range is between 0.1 (lighter) and 4 (darker)).
   - **White Point:** Controls the color of the light source.
   - **Saturation:** Controls the intensity of the colors (range is between 0 (gray/black/white) and 5 (more intense colors)).

11.6 Photorealistic Rendering

Rendering creates highly detailed and photorealistic images in the Navisworks software, as shown in Figure 11–51. The renderings are created using all of the materials, lights, and environments that were applied to the scene view using the Autodesk Rendering window. Rendering can be run in the Navisworks software (Autodesk Rendering) or it can be done using Autodesk Rendering (Render in Cloud). Rendering involves complex calculations that can occupy your computer for an extended time, which may help you decide which render location is best.

Once the scene is rendered, small changes to the scene might be required to further refine it, which requires re-rendering the scene. Thus, creating photorealistic images can be quite time-consuming.

Figure 11–51

Autodesk Rendering

When the **Autodesk Rendering** option is enabled in the *Render* tab, the viewpoint is rendered directly in the Navisworks software. During rendering, the output displays directly in the scene view, along with a progress indicator showing the completed rendering percentage.

Rendering in the Cloud

When the **Render in Cloud** option is enabled in the *Render* tab, Autodesk Rendering is used to create photorealistic images and panoramic renderings without using the resources on your system, enabling you to continue working in your local software. To render using Autodesk Rendering, Navisworks creates a version of the project containing just the information required to render and then transmits it to the rendering service. By accessing the online render gallery, you can access your renderings, re-render images as panoramas, or re-render with other settings. Additionally, you can preview and download the rendered image.

Once a rendering is complete, you can save it as an image.

Defining the Render Style

When rendering in the Navisworks software, you must define the render style that is to be used. There are six default styles available for use.

- **Low Quality**
- **Medium Quality**
- **High Quality**
- **Coffee Break Rendering**
- **Lunch Break Rendering**
- **Overnight Rendering**

The higher quality rendered images take more time to render. For the final photorealistic finish, you can select a high-quality rendering style to create the final image, but consider using a lower quality to initially test the rendering settings.

Custom Render Settings

The six render styles that are provided in the Navisworks software may not provide the exact rendering settings that you require. For these situations, you can customize the settings using the *Settings* tab in the Autodesk Rendering window, as shown in Figure 11–52.

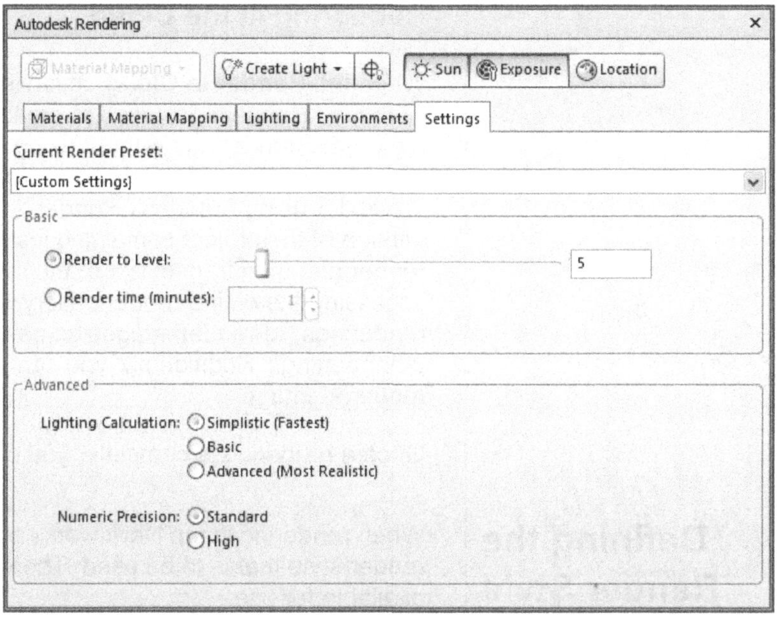

Figure 11–52

When rendering, the computer system slows down considerably and may appear to become unresponsive. Patience is required. During the rendering process, a status of the rendering is tracked in the lower left corner (below the HUD), as shown in Figure 11–53.

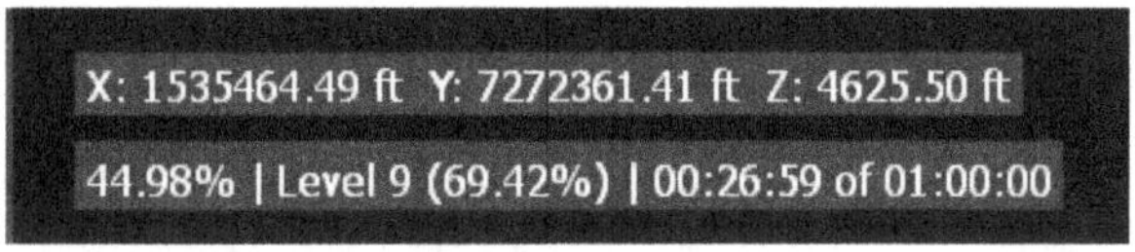

Figure 11–53

Rendering Workflows

The process for rendering directly in the Navisworks software or using the Autodesk Rendering cloud service are slightly different. To access either rendering method, use the *Render* tab in the Navisworks ribbon, as shown in Figure 11–54.

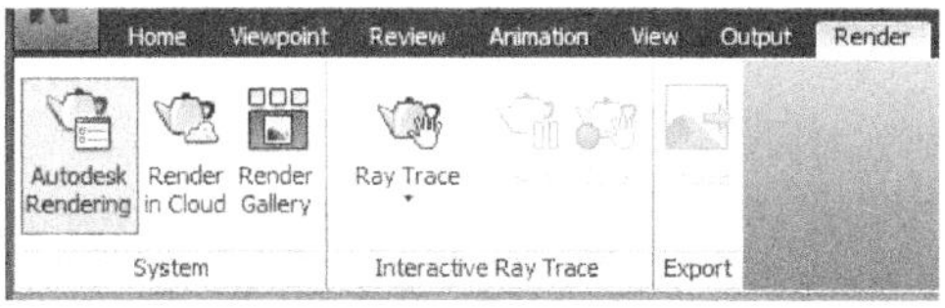

Figure 11–54

How To: Render a Scene in the Autodesk Software

1. Open the Autodesk Rendering window using one of the following options:
   - In the *Render* tab>System panel, click  (Autodesk Rendering).
   - In the *Home* tab>Tools panel, click  (Autodesk Rendering).
2. Set up the scene using the Autodesk Rendering window. This includes materials, material mapping, lighting, environments, and creating the viewpoint (orientation and zoom level).
   - **Note:** You can change the size of the rendered image by resizing the scene view before rendering.
3. Select the rendering quality. In the *Render* tab>Render panel, expand the **Ray Trace** option to provide the list of available render styles, as shown in Figure 11–55.

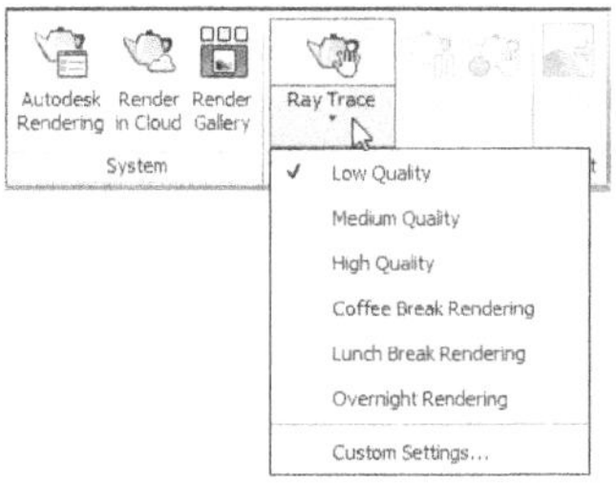

Figure 11–55

Real-time navigation during rendering causes the process to restart from the beginning.

4. In the *Render* tab>Render panel, click  (Start) to start rendering. Click  (Pause) to temporarily pause the process.

5. Save the rendered image. When the scene is rendered, click (Save) in the *Render* tab. In the Save As dialog box, select the required file format, browse to a storage location, and enter a name for the file. Click **Save**.

To stop a rendering and return to the scene, click (Stop).

How To: Render a Scene Using Cloud Rendering

1. Set up the scene using the Autodesk Rendering window. In the *Render* tab>Render panel, click (Render in Cloud) to access Autodesk Rendering.
2. In the Render in Cloud window, define the render settings and click **Start Rendering**, as shown in Figure 11–56. If you want the system to email you when the rendering is complete, select **Email me when complete**. The file is uploaded to the cloud where the rendering process is completed.

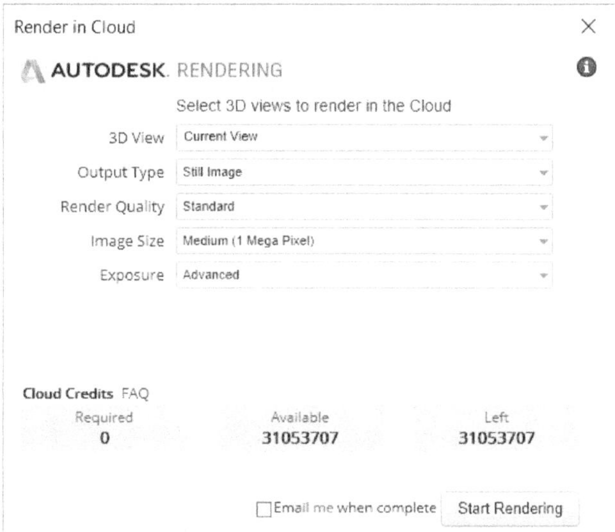

Figure 11–56

- Autodesk Rendering renders the Navisworks viewpoint in a project by making it the current view before starting the **Render in Cloud** command.
- Autodesk Rendering is a highly optimized engine. It is not the same as the rendering engine used in Navisworks.
- Autodesk Rendering automatically applies advanced exposure controls to simulate real-world lighting conditions.

3. Click (Render Gallery) in the *Render* tab to review the file in Autodesk Rendering once it has been rendered, as shown in Figure 11–57.

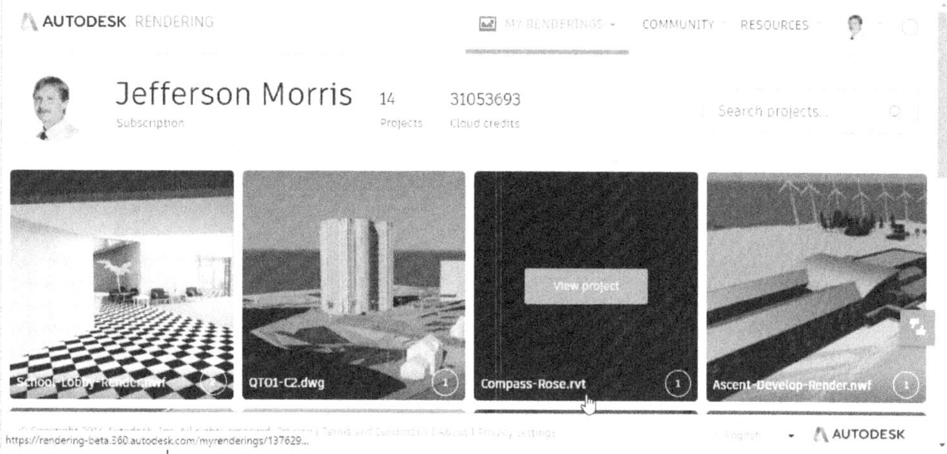

Figure 11–57

The following describes what can be done with the file.

- Select **Re-render using new settings** to define new render settings and re-render the file.
- Select a **Render As** setting.
  - Create panoramas of your scene.
  - Perform solar studies of designs in progress during the day.
  - Perform illuminance simulations of scenes.
- Show or hide the preview image.
- Download the image.
- Delete the image from Autodesk Rendering.

- Adjust the exposure settings using the **Adjust Exposure** option, as shown in Figure 11–58.

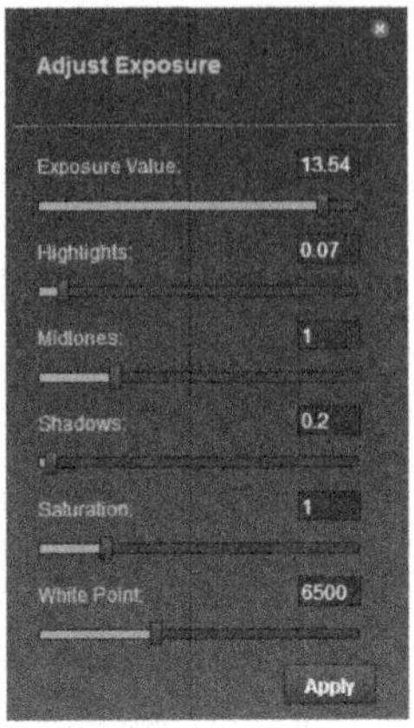

Figure 11–58

Ground Planes

Ground planes provide a visual base for the model. They can also hide the foundation geometry of a model.

You can append the ground planes that have been created in CAD software to the model files in the Navisworks software.

How To: Add a Ground Plane

1. In the *Home* tab>Project panel, click (Append). Browse, select, and open the required ground plane file.
2. In the scene view, right-click the ground plane and select **Override Item>Override Transform**. The Override Transform dialog box displays, as shown in Figure 11–59.

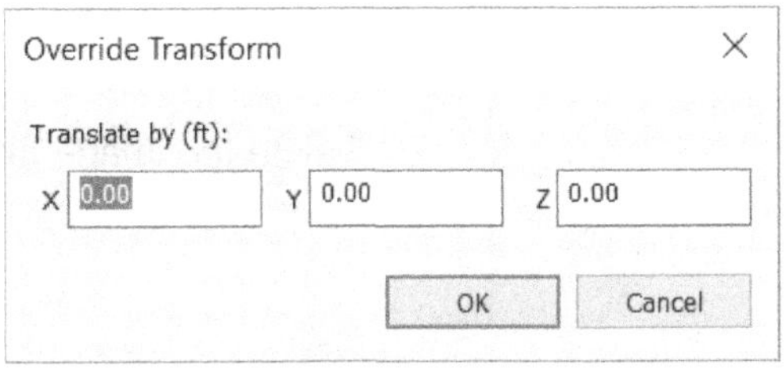

Figure 11–59

   - You can move the ground plane by selecting it, right-clicking, and selecting **File Units and Transform**.
3. In the Override Transform dialog box, change the *X*, *Y*, and *Z* dimensions, as required.
4. Click **OK** to save the changes and close the dialog box.

Practice 11c Render a Model

Practice Objectives

- Render an interior scene.
- Render an exterior scene.

Now that the materials are properly mapped and adjusted and the light sources placed and modified to suite the scene, it is time for action. In this practice, you will render an interior scene and an exterior scene and study the results. If you have access to an Autodesk Rendering account, you will also send the interior scene to the cloud for expedient rendering.

Task 1 - Render the scene and make adjustments.

1. Continue to work on the file from the previous practice. If you did not complete that practice, in the *Rendering* practice files folder, open **School-Lobby-Render.nwf**.

2. If necessary, restore the **Lobby** viewpoint.

3. In the *Viewpoint* tab>Render Style panel, expand **Lighting** and select **Full Lights** if not already set.

4. In the Render Style panel, expand **Mode** and select **Full Render** if not already set.

5. Select the *Render* tab in the ribbon to access the rendering tools.

6. In the Interactive Ray Trace panel, expand the **Ray Trace** option and select **Medium Quality**, as shown in Figure 11–60. This sets the rendering quality as medium.

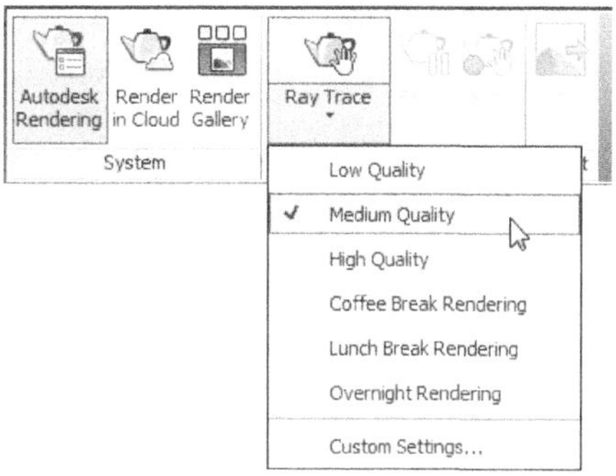

Figure 11–60

- **Note:** The **Low Quality** style is the fastest to render and the **High Quality** style is the slowest to render. It is recommended that you begin rendering using a lower quality as you are developing appropriate material and lighting settings and then render at the higher quality once done. Consider using the other options for specific rendering settings based on time.

7. In the Interactive Ray Trace panel, click (Start) to start rendering.
8. As the rendering is progressing, note that the lighting is displaying as too white. In the Interactive Ray Trace panel, click (Stop) to return to the realistic visual style.
9. In the *Lighting* tab in the Autodesk Rendering window, select the **Table Lamp** lights to access their properties. This has to be done one at a time.
10. Click (...) adjacent to the *Lamp color* property. In the Lamp Color dialog box, select **Quartz Cool** in the Standard colors drop-down list, as shown in Figure 11–61. Click **OK**.

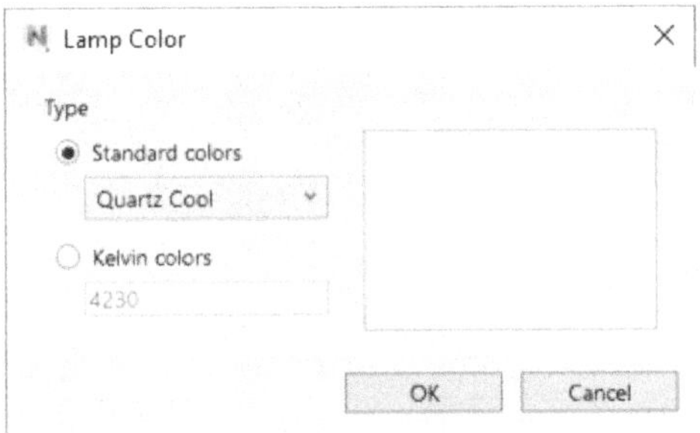

Figure 11–61

11. In the *Lighting* tab in the Autodesk Rendering window, select **Floor Lamp 3** to access its properties.
12. Click (...) adjacent to the *Lamp color* property. In the Lamp Color dialog box, select **Quartz Cool** in the Standard colors drop-down list. Click **OK**.

13. In the Render panel, click (Start) to start the render. Depending on your system, this rendering might take anywhere from 20 to 60 minutes to render. Figure 11–62 is provided to show you a final rendering of this scene. Yours might vary slightly depending on the placement of your lights.

Figure 11–62

14. Stop the rendering to continue with the practice. To review a saved image of this final rendering, navigate to the *Navisworks BIM Practice Files\Rendering\Images* folder and open **Lobby-3-hour.png**.

- During rendering, you can **Pause** and save the current rendering using the **Image** option in the Export panel. This enables you to create an image file mid-way through rendering instead of using the **Stop** option, which returns you to the original visual style.

- Rendering using Autodesk Rendering enables you to take advantage of its powerful rendering engine and tools. To review an image of the lobby rendered using the cloud and some of its settings, navigate to the *Navisworks BIM Practice Files\Rendering\Images* folder and open **Lobby_Cloud_Rendering.jpg**.

Task 2 - Navigate to an exterior viewpoint and prepare the scene.

1. In the Saved Viewpoints window, select **Front Entry** to change the viewpoint to an external view of the model. Zoom, orbit, and pan so you have a vantage point similar to the one shown in Figure 11–63.

Figure 11–63

2. Save the viewpoint as **Rendering-Exterior**.

3. In the Autodesk Rendering window>Rendering toolbar, click **Location**. In the Geographic Location dialog box, set the *Time Zone* to **(UTC-05:00) Eastern Time (US & Canada)**, as shown in Figure 11–64. Click **OK**.

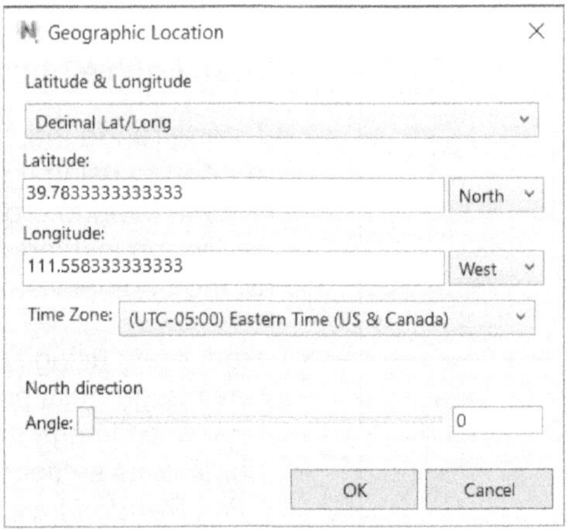

Figure 11–64

4. In the Autodesk Rendering window>Rendering toolbar, ensure that the  (Sun) option is enabled so that the sun is toggled on in the scene view.

5. In the Autodesk Rendering window, select the *Environments* tab. Make the following changes to the Sun properties, as shown in Figure 11–65:

   - Enter **4** as the *Intensity Factor*.
   - Select the **Geographical** option and enter the current date in the *Date* field.
   - Enter **1:45 PM** as the *Time*.

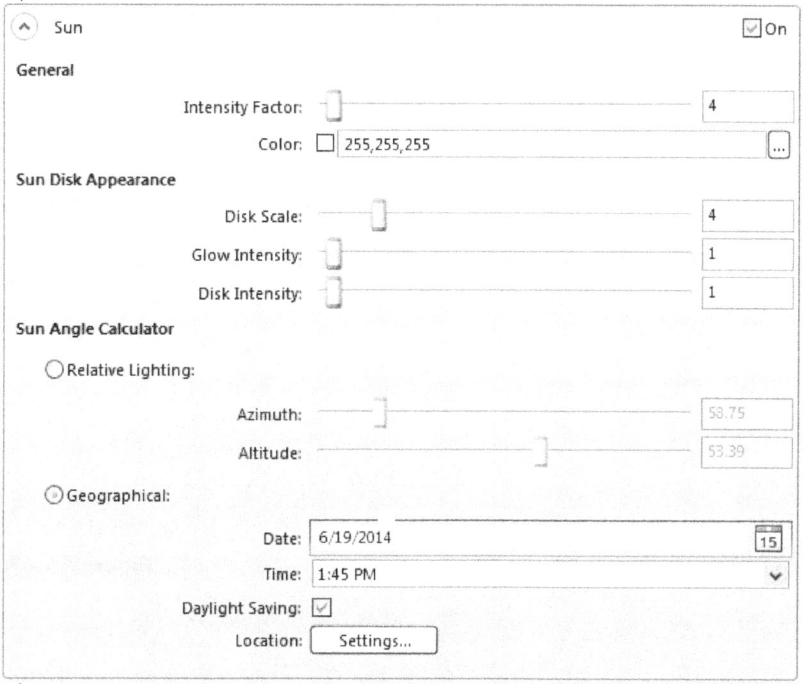

Figure 11–65

6. In the *Environments* tab, make the following changes to the Sky properties, as shown in Figure 11–66:

   - Enter **2** as the *Haze* factor.
   - Lower the *Horizon Height* using the slider.
   - Increase the *Blur* using the slider.
   - Change the *Ground Color* to a dark green.

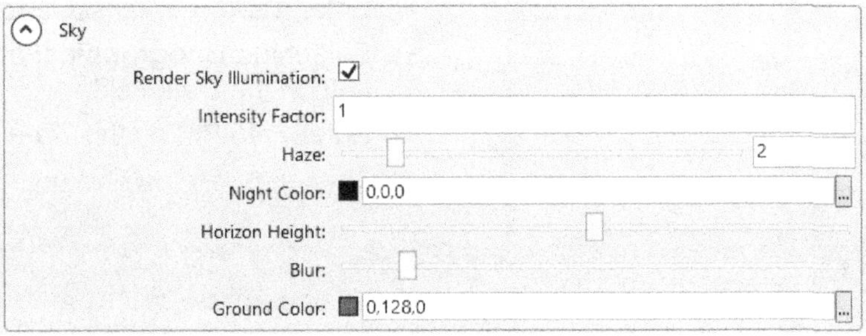

Figure 11–66

7. In the *Environments* tab, in the Exposure properties, enter **4** as the *Exposure Value,* as shown in Figure 11–67.

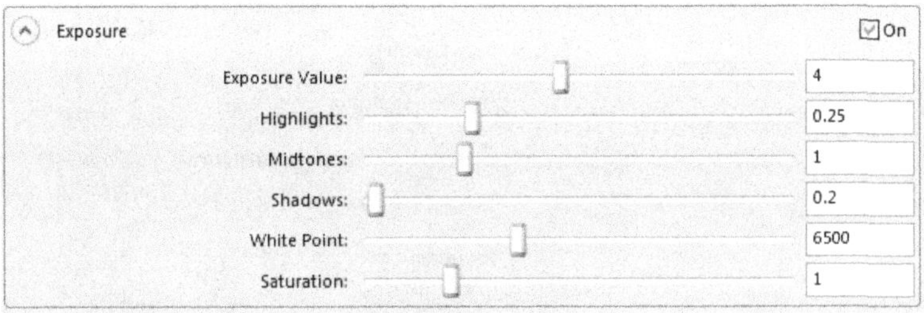

Figure 11–67

8. Save the Navisworks file.

9. In the Rendering toolbar, toggle the  (Sun) and  (Exposure) options on and off and note the differences in the scene view.

10. In the *Render* tab>Render panel, click (Start) to start rendering. A sample of the final rendering (rendered in the cloud) displays similar to the one shown in Figure 11–68. To review saved images of this final rendering, navigate to the *Navisworks BIM Practice Files\Rendering\Images* folder and open **School_Rendering_Ext-Cloud.jpg** and **School_Rendering Ext-Local.png**.

Figure 11–68

- In this exterior view, the default materials that existed in the model, lighting sources, and ground plane were used and only the Sky and Environment settings were customized. To further refine the scene, you can manipulate the materials, as required.

11. When the scene is rendered, click (Save) in the *Render* tab. In the Save As dialog box, select **.PNG** in the Type drop-down list, browse to the *Navisworks BIM Practice Files\Rendering\Images* folder, and enter **School Rendering-Ext-Day.png** as the name for the file. Click **Save**.
12. In the Autodesk Rendering window>Rendering toolbar, click (Sun) to disable the sun to simulate a night scene.
13. Re-render the scene. In the Save As dialog box, select **.PNG** in the Type drop-down list, browse to the *Navisworks BIM Practice Files\Rendering\Images* folder, and enter **School Rendering-Ext-Night.png** as the name for the file. Click **Save**.
14. Save and close the Navisworks file.

Chapter Review Questions

1. Which of the following are Navisworks lights? (Select all that apply.)
   a. Spot light
   b. Distant light
   c. Sun light
   d. Web light
2. You can select multiple lights and edit them in the Lighting panel.
   a. True
   b. False
3. Which render style mode includes the materials and textures of items, including lights, reflections, and shadows?
   a. Full Render
   b. Hidden Line
   c. Wireframe
   d. Shaded
4. Which of the following is NOT an option for mapping materials in Navisworks?
   a. Planar
   b. Box
   c. Surface
   d. Cylindrical
5. Which of the following is NOT an option for rendering styles in Navisworks?
   a. Coffee Break
   b. Full Day
   c. High Quality
   d. Overnight

Command Summary

Button	Command	Location
	**Append**	• **Ribbon:** *Home* tab>Project panel
	**Autodesk Rendering**	• **Ribbon:** *Home* tab>Tools panel • **Ribbon:** *View* tab>Workspace panel> Windows drop-down list • **Ribbon:** *Render* tab>System panel
	**Distant Light**	• **Autodesk Rendering window:** Rendering toolbar>Create Light drop-down list
	**File Options**	• **Ribbon:** *Home* tab>Project panel
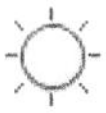	**Full Lights**	• **Ribbon:** *Viewpoint* tab>Render Style panel>Lighting drop-down list
	**Head Lights**	• **Ribbon:** *Viewpoint* tab>Render Style panel>Lighting drop-down list
	**Light Glyphs**	• **Autodesk Rendering window:** Rendering toolbar
	**No Lights**	• **Ribbon:** *Viewpoint* tab>Render Style panel>Lighting drop-down list
	**Pause**	• **Ribbon:** *Render* tab>Render panel
	**Point Light**	• **Autodesk Rendering window:** Rendering toolbar>Create Light drop-down list
	**Ray Trace**	• **Ribbon:** *Render* tab>Render panel
	**Render Gallery**	• **Ribbon:** *Render* tab>Render panel
	**Render in Cloud**	• **Ribbon:** *Render* tab>System panel
	**Save**	• **Ribbon:** *Render* tab>Render panel
	**Scene Lights**	• **Ribbon:** *Viewpoint* tab>Render Style panel>Lighting drop-down list
	**Select None**	• **Ribbon:** *Home* tab>Select & Search panel
	**Show Grid**	• **Ribbon:** *View* tab>Grids& Levels panel

	**Spot Light**	• **Autodesk Rendering window:** Rendering toolbar>Create Light drop-down list
	**Start**	• **Ribbon:** *Render* tab>Render panel
	**Stop**	• **Ribbon:** *Render* tab>Render panel
	**Sun**	• **Autodesk Rendering window:** Rendering toolbar
	**Web Light**	• **Autodesk Rendering window:** Rendering toolbar>Create Light drop-down list

Appendix A

Practices to Prepare for Animator

There is a lot of work that goes into a project. In a classroom environment, you might not have time to create all of the viewpoints, sets, or search sets required for the class project. This appendix provides extra practice to help you test your skills. If you cannot complete a practice, you can move on to the next practice; however, it is recommended that you still review the referenced appendices to refresh your memory on how to complete the tasks.

Learning Objectives in This Appendix

- Append a model.
- Transform a model.
- Create a viewpoint.
- Create a selection set.
- Create a search set.

Practice A1 Append Models

Practice Objectives

- Append a crane to the model.
- Transform the crane to the correct location.

This practice is a review of *2.1Consolidating the Model* and *2.2Aligning Models*. You will add a crane for later use, as shown in Figure A–1.

Figure A–1

Task 1 - Append a new model to the project.

1. In the *Extra Practice* practice files folder, open **School-Append.nwf**.
2. If the drawing displays only boxes where the surfaces and roads should be (as shown in Figure A–2), you will need to install the Autodesk Civil 3D Object Enabler. Consult *B.3: Autodesk Civil 3D Object Enabler* to install this prior to proceeding.

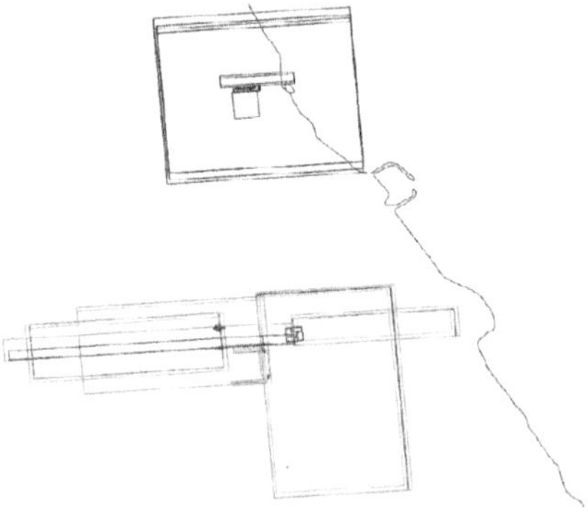

Figure A–2

3. Ensure that you are in the **NE-View** viewpoint.
4. In the *Home* tab>Project panel, click (Append).
5. In the Append dialog box, expand the Files of type drop-down list and set the file type to **SketchUp (*.skp)**.
6. Navigate to the *Animator* practice files folder, select **Mobile Crane.skp**, and click **Open**.

Task 2 - Transform the new model so it lines up.

You might not see the crane because it was imported at the wrong location.

1. In the Selection Tree window, right-click on the newly appended SketchUp file and select **Units and Transform**.
2. In the Units and Transform dialog box, set the following values, as shown in Figure A–3:
   - *Units:* **Centimeters**
   - *Origin (ft): X:* ***1535779***, *Y:* ***7272131***, *Z:* ***4615***
   - Rotation: **76.5**

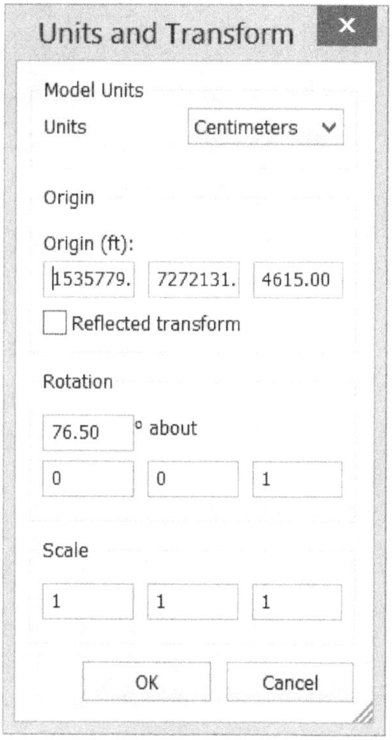

Figure A–3

3. Click **OK** and save the file.

Practice A2 Save Viewpoints

Practice Objective

- Save viewpoints for easy navigation and communication.

This practice is a review of *3.1Saving and Retrieving Views*. In the model shown in Figure A–4, you will create additional viewpoints and save them for later use.

Figure A–4

Task 1 - Create a series of views around the building.

1. In the *Extra Practice* practice files folder, open **School-Views.nwf**.
2. In the *Viewpoint* tab>Camera panel, ensure that the **Perspective** view is selected.
3. Open the Saved Viewpoints window, if it is not already open.
4. Create a folder in the *Viewpoints* window (using the right-click menu) and name it **Animator**.
5. Pan and orbit the model until the scene view displays similar to that shown in Figure A–5.

Figure A–5

6. In the *Viewpoint* tab>Save, Load & Playback panel, click  (Save Viewpoint).
7. In the Saved Viewpoints window, *Animator* folder, type **Overview** for the name.
8. Repeat Steps 4 to 6 to create the following saved viewpoints, using the names and figure references provided.
   - Save the view shown in Figure A–6 as **SE-Isometric**.

Save all viewpoints to the Animator *folder.*

Figure A–6

- Save the view shown in Figure A–7 as **East Side**.

Figure A–7

- Save the view shown in Figure A–8 as **NE-Isometric**.

Figure A–8

- Save the view shown in Figure A–9 as **North Side**.

Figure A–9

- Save the view shown in Figure A–10 as **NW-Isometric**.

Figure A–10

- Save the view shown in Figure A–11 as **West Side**.

Figure A–11

- Save the view shown in Figure A–12 as **SW-Isometric**.

Figure A–12

Task 2 - Create a series of views to walk into the building.

1. Pan and orbit the model until the scene view displays similar to that shown in Figure A–13.

Figure A–13

2. In the *Viewpoint* tab>Save, Load & Playback panel, click (Save Viewpoint).
3. In the Saved Viewpoints window, *Animator* folder, type **Front Entry** for the name.
4. In the navigation bar, click (Walk).
5. Click and drag the mouse forward until the scene view displays similar to that shown in Figure A–14.

Figure A–14

6. In the *Viewpoint* tab>Save, Load & Playback panel, click (Save Viewpoint).

7. In the Saved Viewpoints window, *Animator* folder, type **Turn1** for the name.

8. Pan and orbit the model until the scene view displays similar to that shown in Figure A–15.

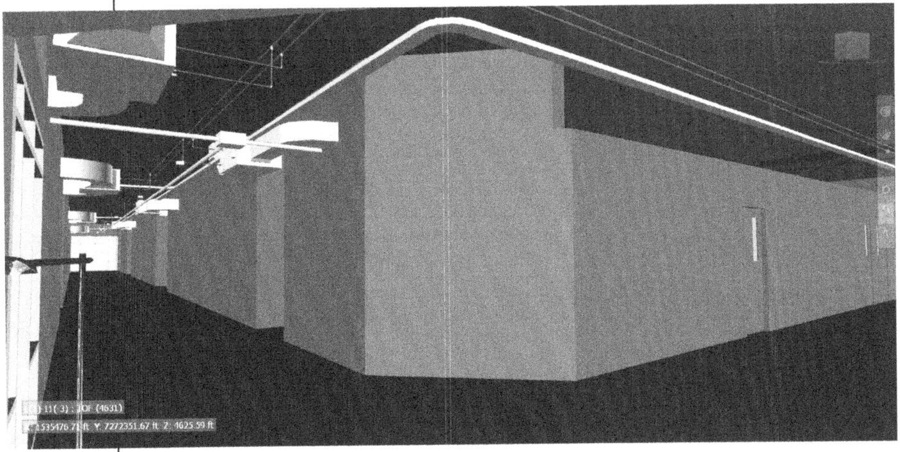

Figure A–15

9. In the *Viewpoint* tab>Save, Load & Playback panel, click (Save Viewpoint).

10. In the Saved Viewpoints window, *Animator* folder, type **Turn2** for the name and save the file.

Practice A3 Save Selection Sets

Practice Objectives

- Select items using the Selection Tree.
- Save selection sets for later use.

This practice is a review of *4.1Selecting Items*. You will create additional selection sets for later use using the model shown in Figure A–16.

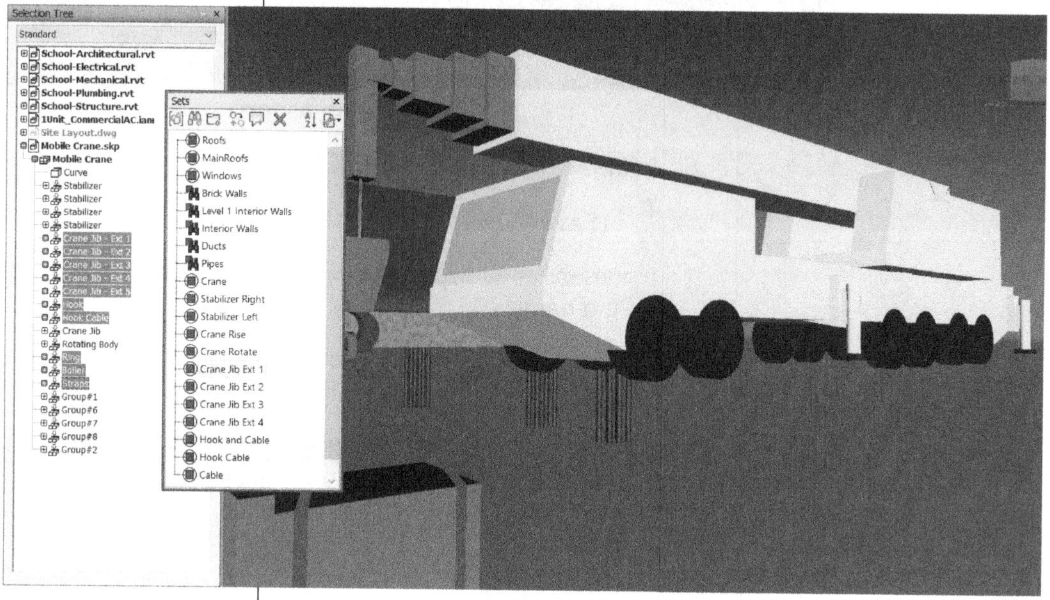

Figure A–16

Task 1 - Select the crane.

1. In the *Extra Practice* practice files folder, open **School-Select.nwf**.
2. In the *Home* tab, expand the Select & Search panel title to display the Selection Resolution drop-down list. Expand it and select **First Object**.
3. In the Selection Tree, select **Mobile Crane.skp**.
4. In the *Home* tab>Select & Search panel, click (Save Selection). Type **Crane** for the name.

Task 2 - Create selection sets for the crane stabilizers.

1. In the Selection Tree, expand **Mobile Crane.skp>Mobile Crane** and select the first two **Stabilizer** items, as shown in Figure A–17. These are the right stabilizers.

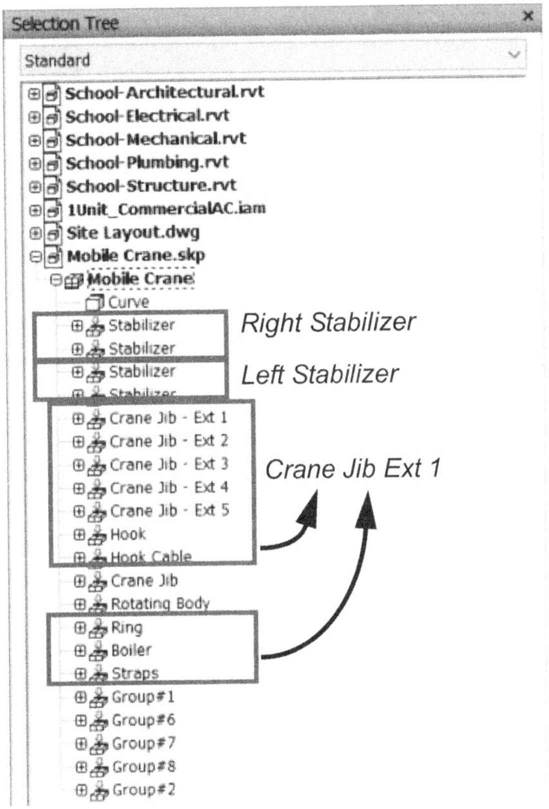

Figure A–17

2. In the *Home* tab>Select & Search panel, click  (Save Selection). Type **Stabilizer Right** for the name.

3. In the Selection Tree, expand **Mobile Crane.skp>Mobile Crane** and select the third and forth **Stabilizer** items, as shown in Figure A–17. These are the left stabilizers.

4. In the *Home* tab>Select & Search panel, click  (Save Selection). Type **Stabilizer Left** for the name.

Task 3 - Create selection sets for animations.

1. In the Selection Tree, expand **Mobile Crane.skp>Mobile Crane**. Select all of the items from the boiler to the first extender for the crane, as shown in Figure A–18 and listed below. These will all move together.

- Crane Jib - Ext 1
- Crane Jib - Ext 2
- Crane Jib - Ext 3
- Crane Jib - Ext 4
- Crane Jib - Ext 5
- Hook
- Hook Cable
- Ring
- Boiler
- Straps

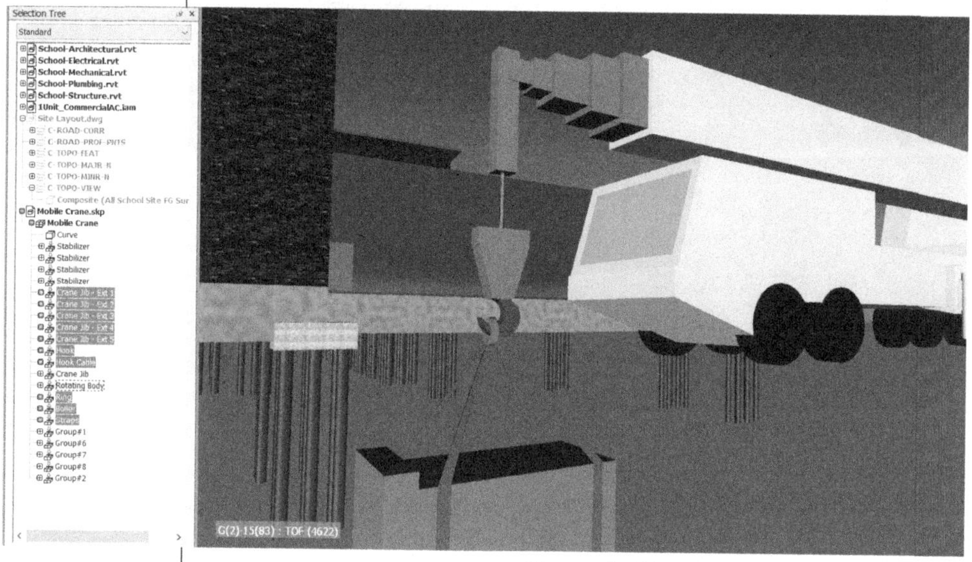

Figure A–18

2. In the *Home* tab>Select & Search panel, click  (Save Selection). Type **Crane Jib Ext 1** for the name.

3. In the Sets window, select **Crane Jib Ext 1**.

4. In the Selection Tree, hold <Ctrl> and select **Crane Jib** to add it to the selection, as shown in Figure A–19 and listed below. These will all move together.

- Crane Jib - Ext 1
- Crane Jib - Ext 2
- Crane Jib - Ext 3
- Crane Jib - Ext 4
- Crane Jib - Ext 5
- Hook
- Hook Cable
- Crane Jib
- Ring
- Boiler
- Straps

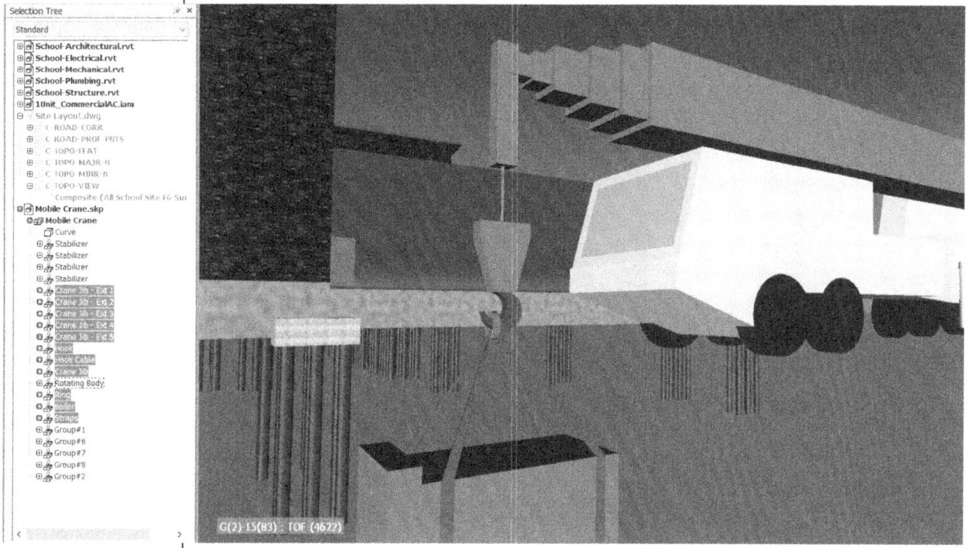

Figure A–19

5. In the *Home* tab>Select & Search panel, click (Save Selection). Type **Crane Rise** for the name.

6. In the Sets window, select **Crane Rise**.

7. In the Selection Tree, hold <Ctrl> and select **Rotating Body** to add it to the selection, as shown in Figure A–20 and listed below. These will all move together.

- Crane Jib - Ext 1
- Crane Jib - Ext 2
- Crane Jib - Ext 3
- Crane Jib - Ext 4
- Crane Jib - Ext 5
- Hook
- Hook Cable
- Crane Jib
- Rotating Body
- Ring
- Boiler
- Straps

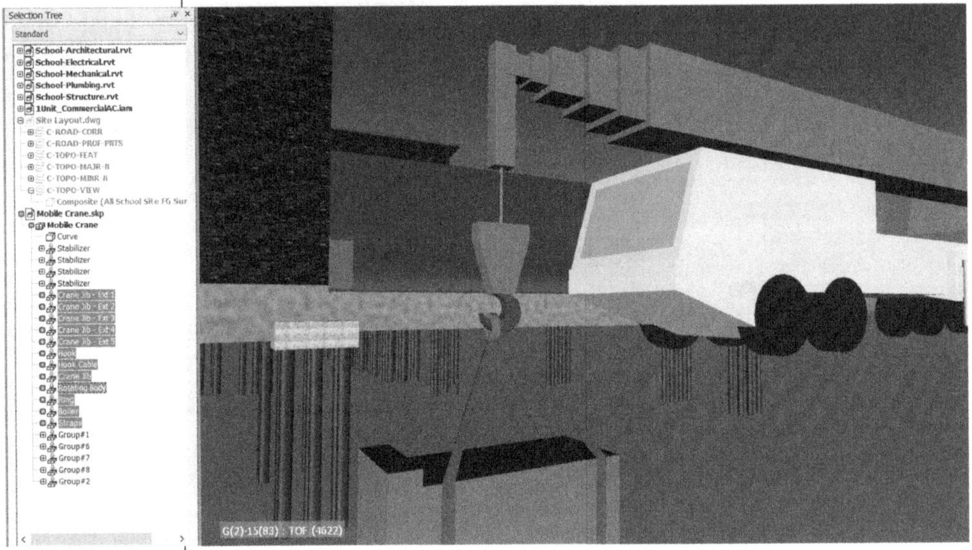

Figure A–20

8. In the *Home* tab>Select & Search panel, click (Save Selection). Type **Crane Rotate** for the name.

9. In the Sets window, select **Crane Jib Ext 1**.

10. In the Selection Tree, hold <Ctrl> and clear the selection of **Crane Jib - Ext 1**, so that all that is selected are the parts listed below. These will all move together.

- Crane Jib - Ext 2
- Crane Jib - Ext 3
- Crane Jib - Ext 4
- Crane Jib - Ext 5
- Hook
- Hook Cable
- Ring
- Boiler
- Straps

11. In the Sets window, click (Save Selection). Type **Crane Jib Ext 2** for the name.

12. In the Sets window, select **Crane Jib Ext 2**.

13. In the Selection Tree, hold <Ctrl> and clear the selection of **Crane Jib - Ext 2** so that all that is selected are the parts and listed below. These will all move together.

    - Crane Jib - Ext 3
    - Crane Jib - Ext 4
    - Crane Jib - Ext 5
    - Hook
    - Hook Cable
    - Ring
    - Boiler
    - Straps

14. In the Sets window, click (Save Selection). Type **Crane Jib Ext 3** for the name.

15. In the Sets window, select **Crane Jib Ext 3**.

16. In the Selection Tree, hold <Ctrl> and clear the selection of **Crane Jib - Ext 3** so that all that is selected are the parts shown in Figure A–21 and listed below. These will all move together.

    - Crane Jib - Ext 4
    - Crane Jib - Ext 5
    - Hook
    - Hook Cable
    - Ring
    - Boiler
    - Straps

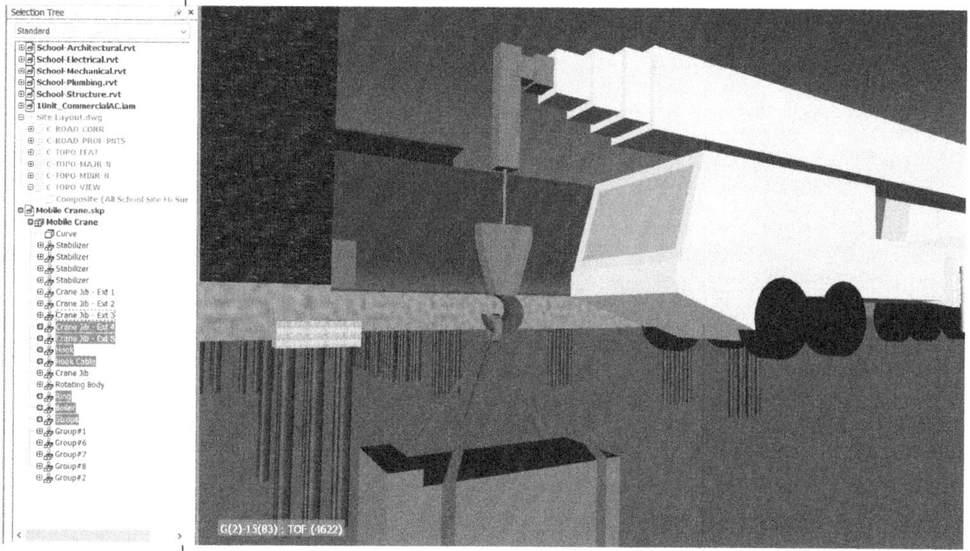

Figure A–21

17. In the Sets window, click (Save Selection). Type **Crane Jib Ext 4** for the name.

18. In the Selection Tree, hold <Ctrl> and clear the selection of **Crane Jib - Ext 4** and **Crane Jib - Ext 5** so that all that is selected are the parts shown in Figure A–23 and listed below. These will all move together.

    - Hook
    - Hook Cable
    - Ring
    - Boiler
    - Straps

19. In the *Home* tab>Select & Search panel, click (Save Selection). Type **Hook and Cable** for the name.

20. In the Sets window, select **Hook and Cable**.

21. In the Selection Tree, hold <Ctrl> and clear the selection of **Hook Cable** so that all that is selected are the parts shown in Figure A–24 and listed below. These will all move together.

    - Hook
    - Ring
    - Boiler
    - Straps

22. In the Sets window, click (Save Selection). Type **Hook** for the name.

23. In the Selection Tree, select **Hook Cable**, as shown in Figure A–22

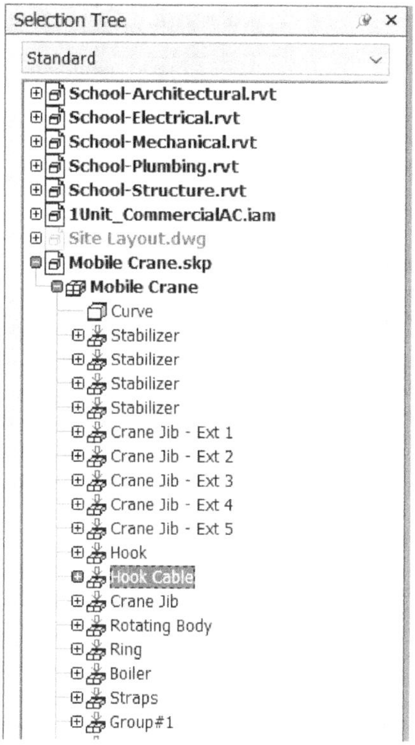

Figure A–22

24. In the Sets window, click (Save Selection). Type **Cable** for the name.

Practice A4 Save Search Sets

Practice Objective

- Create a search set for easy selection of items with similar properties.

This practice is a review of *4.4Finding Items and Saving Search Sets*. You will create additional search sets for later use, as shown in Figure A–23.

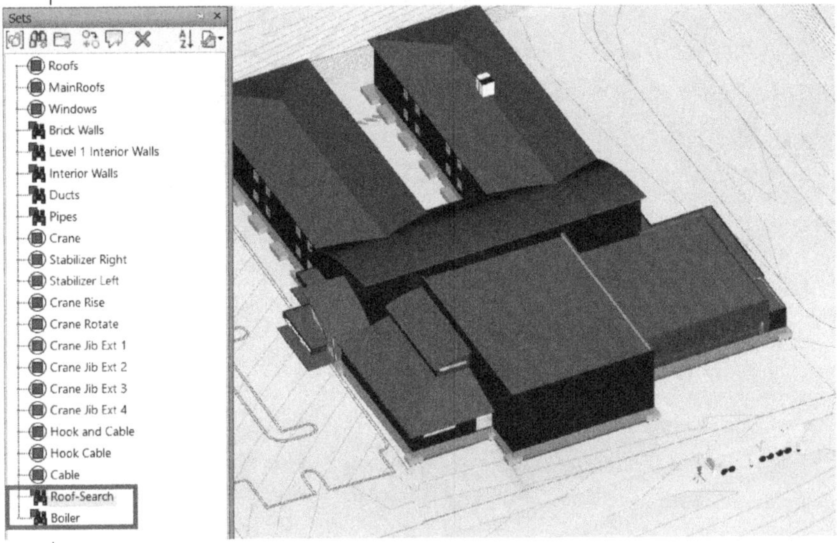

Figure A–23

Task 1 - Create a search set for roofs.

1. In the *Extra Practice* practice files folder, open **School-Search.nwf**.

2. In the *Home* tab>Select & Search panel, click (Find Items).

3. In the Find Items dialog box, in the left pane, do not select anything. This is the same as a select all on the files.

4. In the right pane, do the following, as shown in Figure A–24:
   - Under *Category*, select **Item**.
   - Under *Property*, select **Name**.
   - Under *Condition*, select **Contains**.
   - Under *Value*, type **Roof**.
   - Clear all of the Match options below the right pane.

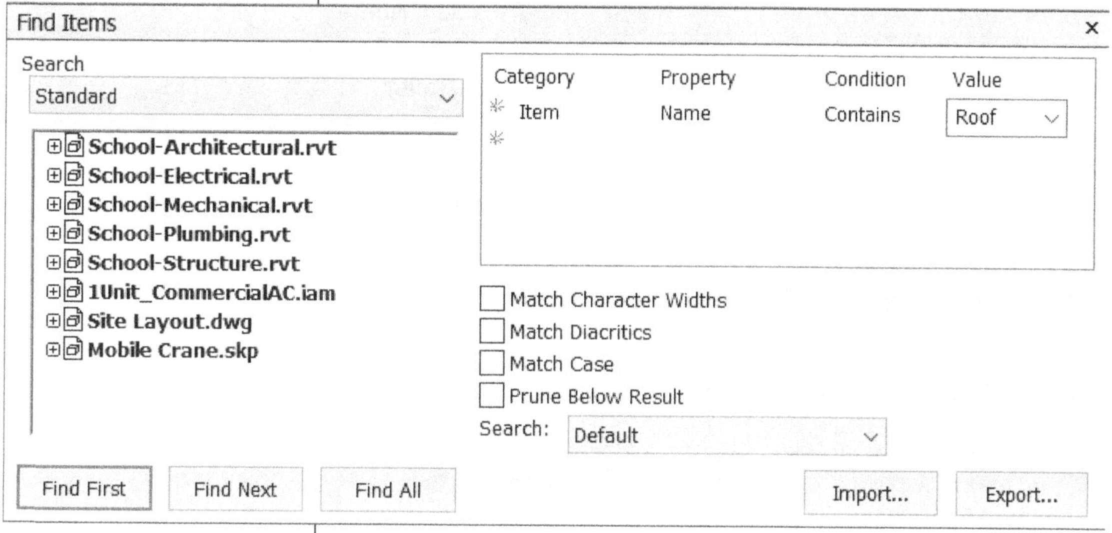

Figure A–24

5. Click **Find All** and note what is selected in the model.
6. In the Sets window, click  (Save Search).
7. Type in **Roof-Search** for the search.

Task 2 - Create a search set for boilers.

1. In the Find Items dialog box, in the left pane, click on a blank space to clear any selections.
2. In the right pane, do the following, as shown in Figure A–25:
   - Under *Category*, select **Item**.
   - Under *Property*, select **Name**.
   - Under *Condition*, select **Contains**.
   - Under *Value*, type **Boiler**.
   - Clear all of the Match options below the right pane.

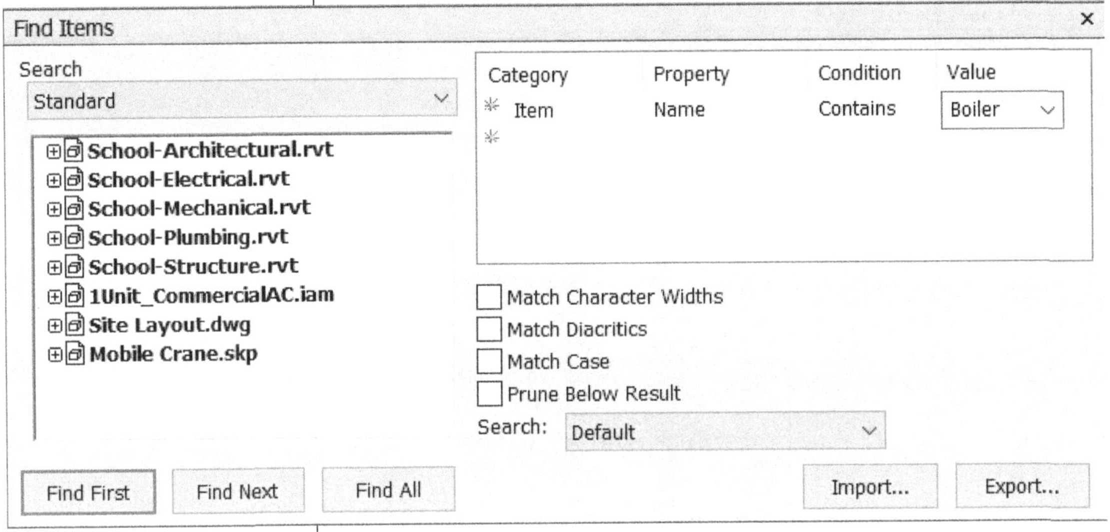

Figure A–25

3. Click **Find All** to see what is selected in the model.
4. In the Sets window, click  (Save Search).
5. Type in **Boiler** for the search.
6. Save the file.

Appendix B

Coordination Tools

When you are working in multiple software packages, it is often necessary to prepare your models before providing them to the BIM coordinator. This appendix introduces some of the best practices for Autodesk® software users who plan to share their models in the Autodesk® Navisworks® software.

Learning Objectives in This Appendix

- Create views in the Autodesk® Revit® software.
- Add a real-world coordinate to an Autodesk Revit model.
- Install the Autodesk® Civil 3D® Object Enabler.
- Share an Autodesk® InfraWorks® model with the Autodesk Navisworks software.
- Prepare an Autodesk Civil 3D corridor model for use in the Autodesk Navisworks TimeLiner.
- Prepare an Autodesk Revit model for use in the Autodesk Navisworks TimeLiner.

B.1 Creating a View in Autodesk Revit

When you append or open an Autodesk Revit model in the Autodesk Navisworks software, the display matches what was toggled on in the Autodesk Revit view when the model was saved. In order to ensure that unnecessary items (such as masses) do not display and that other necessary items (such as walls) display in the Autodesk Navisworks software, you should create a view in the Autodesk Revit software.

There are a couple of key things to keep in mind when creating the view, which are:

- You must start with a 3D view.
- The view must have "Navis" in its name for the Autodesk Navisworks software to recognize it.

How To: Create a Revit View

1. In the Autodesk Revit software, set the view to a 3D view.
2. In the Project Browser, right-click on the view, expand **Duplicate View**, and select **Duplicate**, as shown in Figure B–1.

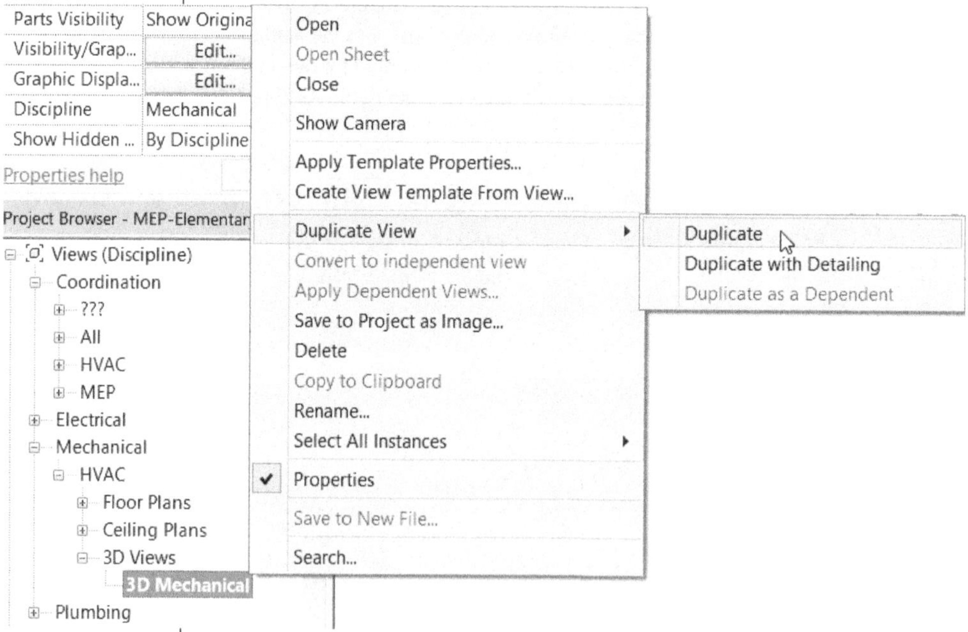

Figure B–1

3. In the Project Browser, right-click on the duplicated view and select **Rename**, as shown in Figure B–2.

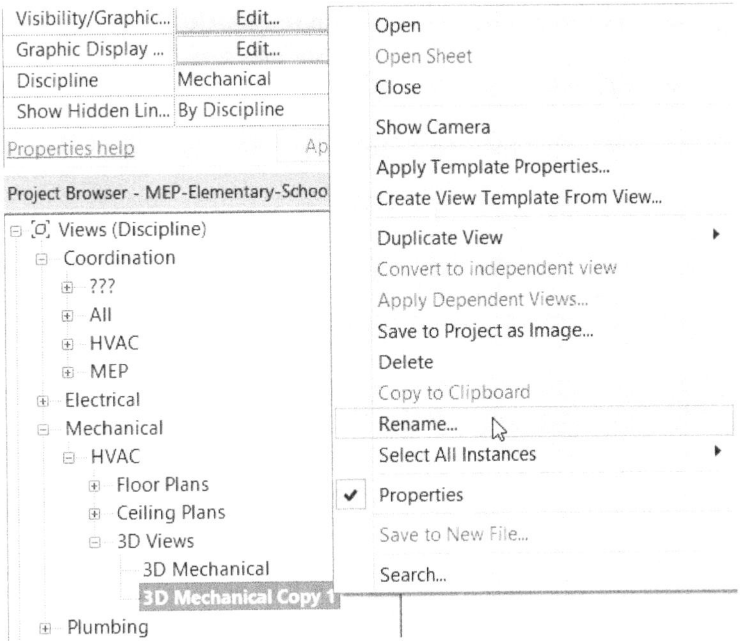

Figure B–2

4. In the Rename View dialog box, type **Navis** for the name and click **OK**. This step is important to ensure that the Autodesk Navisworks software recognizes the view.
5. In the Properties palette, next to *Visibility/Graphic Overrides*, click **Edit**, as shown in Figure B–3.

*Alternatively, you can type **VV**.*

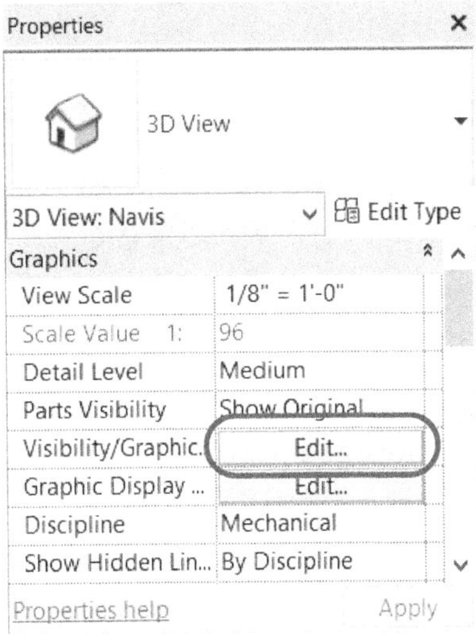

Figure B–3

Toggle off items such as masses, areas, and lighting. Toggling off lights ensures that there is no duplication from the electrical model.

6. In the Visibility/Graphic Overrides dialog box, in the *Model Categories* tab, clear the selection of any items that are not required, and select all of the items that need to be displayed in the Autodesk Navisworks software, as shown in Figure B–4.

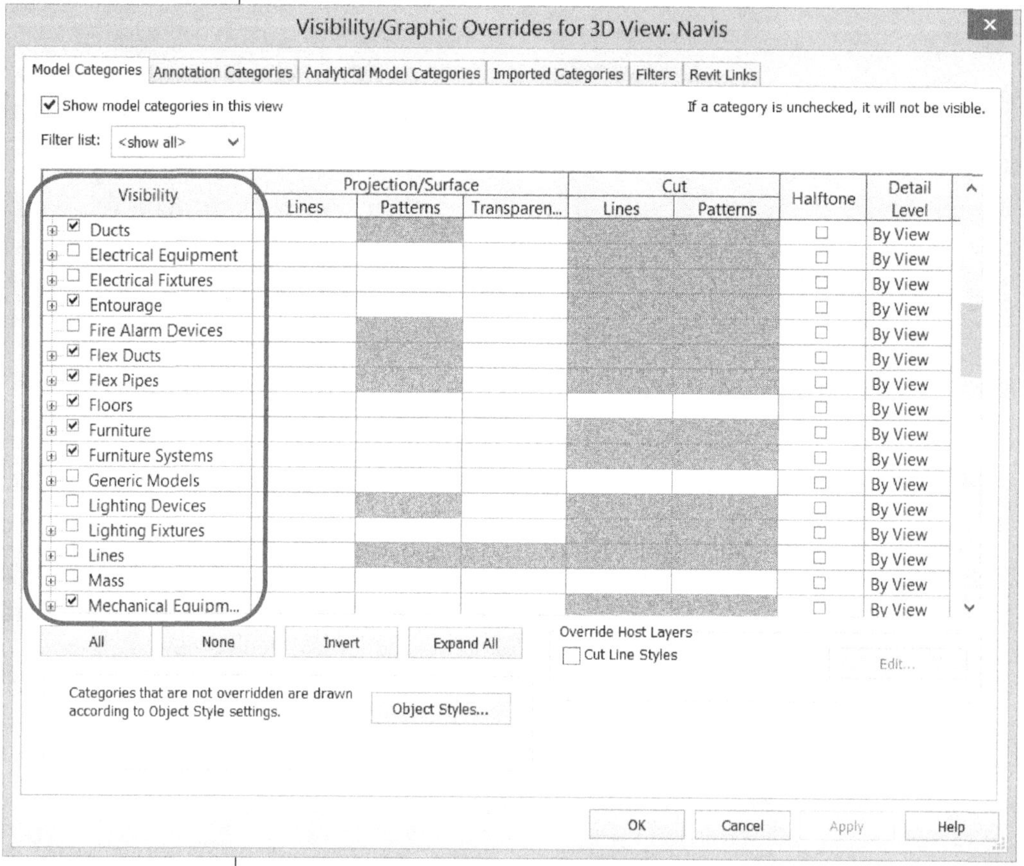

Figure B–4

7. Click **OK**.

8. Save the file and close the Autodesk Revit software.

9. In the Autodesk Navisworks software, ensure that you set the options as shown in Figure B–5 before appending the Autodesk Revit model to ensure that the view is recognized.

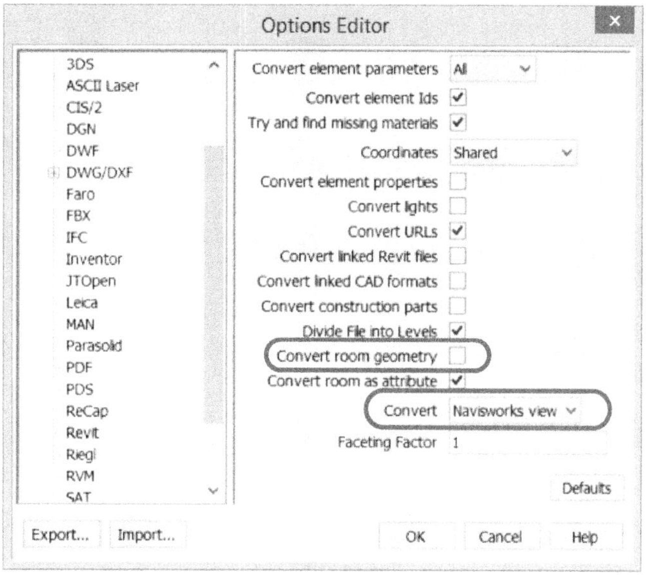

Figure B–5

B.2 Setting a Project Point in Autodesk Revit

Architectural models often have a base point of 0,0,0. However, when you import that model into the Autodesk Navisworks software and combine it with other files that use real-world coordinates for their base point, the models do not line up. To fix this, you need to move and rotate the architectural model manually using the Units and Transform dialog box in the Autodesk Navisworks software, as shown in Figure B–6.

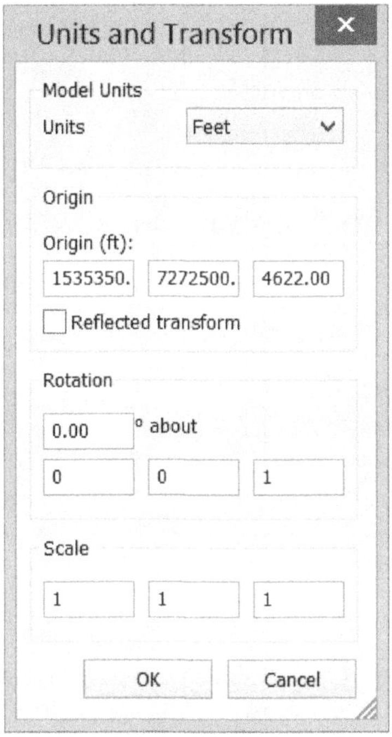

Figure B–6

The coordinates used for the transformation process is the centroid of the Autodesk Revit model. Because of this, figuring out the correct coordinates to enter can be challenging. Additionally, if there are multiple Autodesk Revit models, you will need to move and rotate each model individually.

In order to avoid this, Autodesk Revit users can include a project point in their model. The project point can be a point of their choosing. This makes it much easier to coordinate a building's location with other team members that are using different software.

Before you can set a project point, you must:

- Communicate with the civil team members (engineers or surveyors) to know what coordinates to use.
- Use a 3D view in the Autodesk Revit software to pick a point.

How To: Set a Revit Project Point

1. In the Autodesk Revit software, open the model that needs a project point.
2. Ensure that you are in a 3D view.
3. In the *Manage* tab>Project Location panel, expand the coordinates tool and click (Specify Coordinates at Point).
4. In the Autodesk Revit model, click the point on the building where you want the reference point to sit. Ensure that you use the snap option appropriate for the selected point, as shown in Figure B–7.

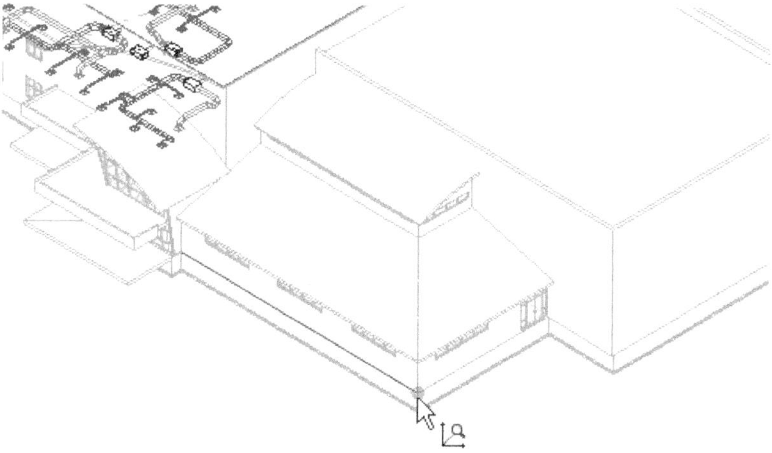

Figure B–7

5. In the Specify Shared Coordinates dialog box, type in the *North/South*, *East/West*, *Elevation*, and *Angle from Project North to True North* values, as shown in Figure B–8.

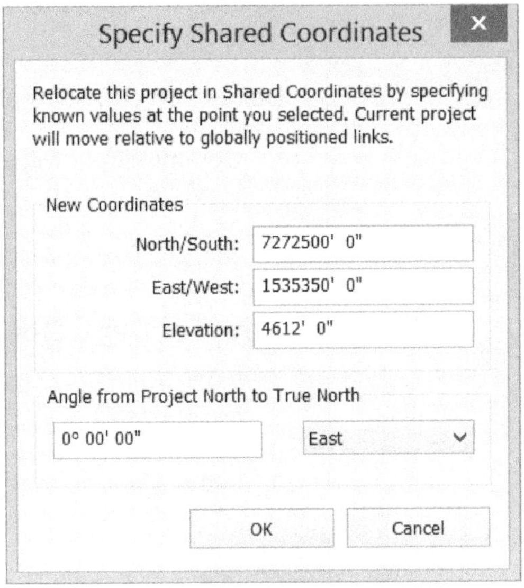

Figure B–8

Hint: The Autodesk Shared Reference Point Extension

There are two separate installations for this extension, one for Autodesk Civil 3D and one for Autodesk Revit.

It provides functionality to export a point with known coordinates and north direction from Civil 3D via an .XML file, which can be imported into Revit. This facilitates collaboration between Revit and Civil 3D. Navisworks will be able to read these shared coordinates as well.

The location of these extensions is shown in Figure B–9.

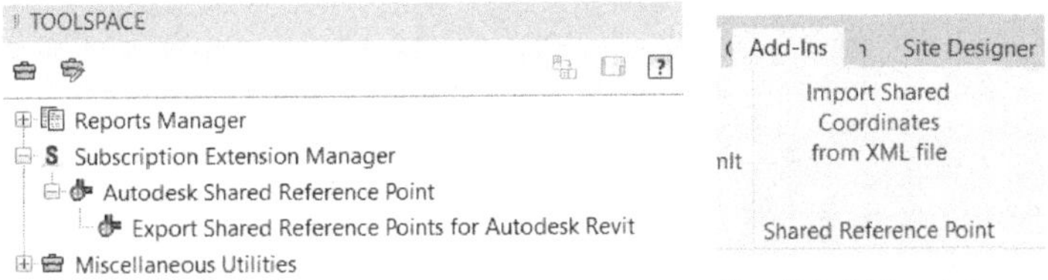

Civil 3D Toolspace ***Revit Add-ins tab***

Figure B–9

B.3 Autodesk Civil 3D Object Enabler

If you open or append an Autodesk Civil 3D drawing in the Autodesk Navisworks software and boxes display where surfaces and roads should be (as shown in Figure B–10), then you need to install the Autodesk Civil 3D Object Enabler. The Object Enabler ensures that objects that are created in the Autodesk Civil 3D software can be used outside of the Autodesk Civil 3D software.

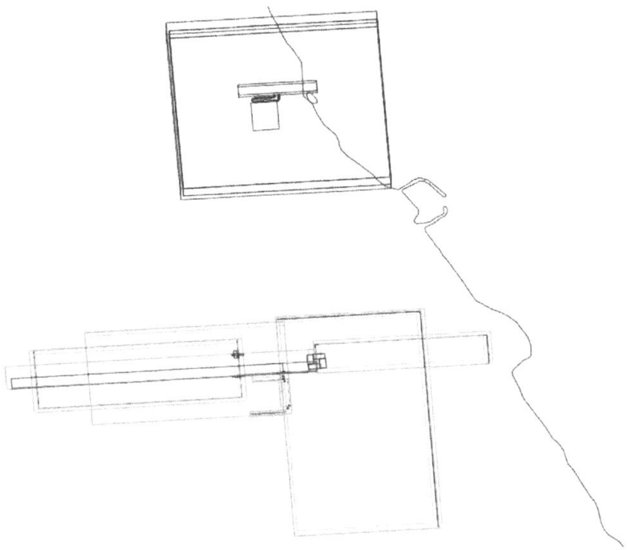

Figure B–10

An update for the Object Enabler is released with each new release of the Autodesk Civil 3D software. The newest version is available for download from the Autodesk Knowledge Network (https://knowledge.autodesk.com) and can be found by searching for Civil 3D Object Enabler.

There are usually two Object Enablers available: one for 32-bit operating systems and one for 64-bit operating systems. Ensure that you download and install the correct .EXE file for your specific computer. For more information on the Object Enabler or how to install it, read the help document provided on the download page.

B.4 Creating an .FBX File in Autodesk InfraWorks

The best BIM workflows take full advantage of any software that adds value to the project. The photorealistic 3D models created in the Autodesk InfraWorks software provide a way to display designs in context with their surrounding areas. For infrastructure projects, the ideal workflow looks similar to the one outlined in Figure B–11. The software recommendations listed at the left of each phase provide the highest benefit to the project.

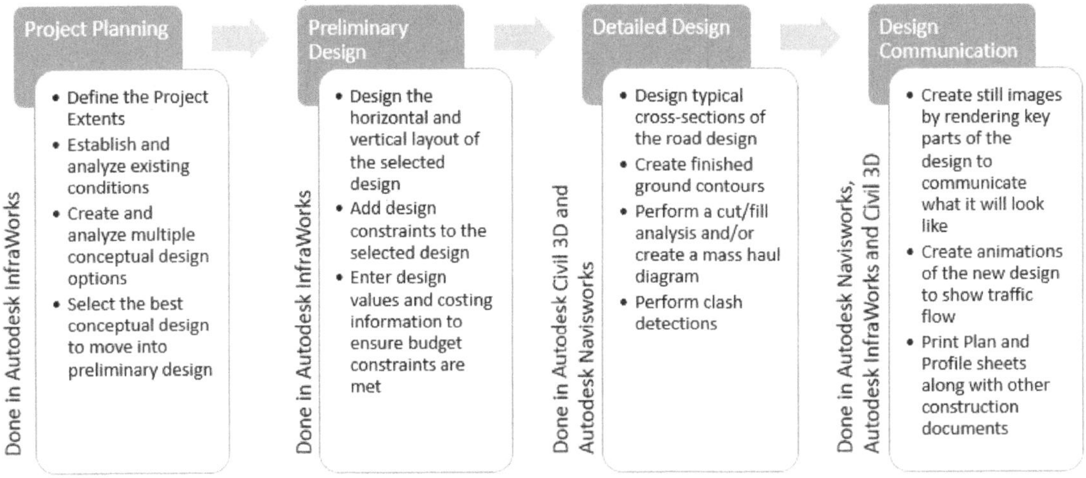

Figure B–11

If you follow this workflow, you can take advantage of using an early stage Autodesk InfraWorks model inside the Autodesk Navisworks software to uncover design problems and constructibility issues more effectively. In the Autodesk InfraWorks software, you can export the model as a single file or multiple files. By using multiple files, you can select specific features in the model to export.

How To: Export an Autodesk InfraWorks Model to the Autodesk Navisworks Software

1. In the Autodesk InfraWorks software, open the model you want to import into the Autodesk Navisworks software.
2. In the In Canvas Tools, click (Settings and Utilities)> (Export 3D Model).

3. In the Export to 3D Model File dialog box, do the following, as shown in Figure B–12:
   - Define the area to export.
   - Set the *Target Coordinate System*.
   - Determine if you want one file or several files.
   - Click **Export**.

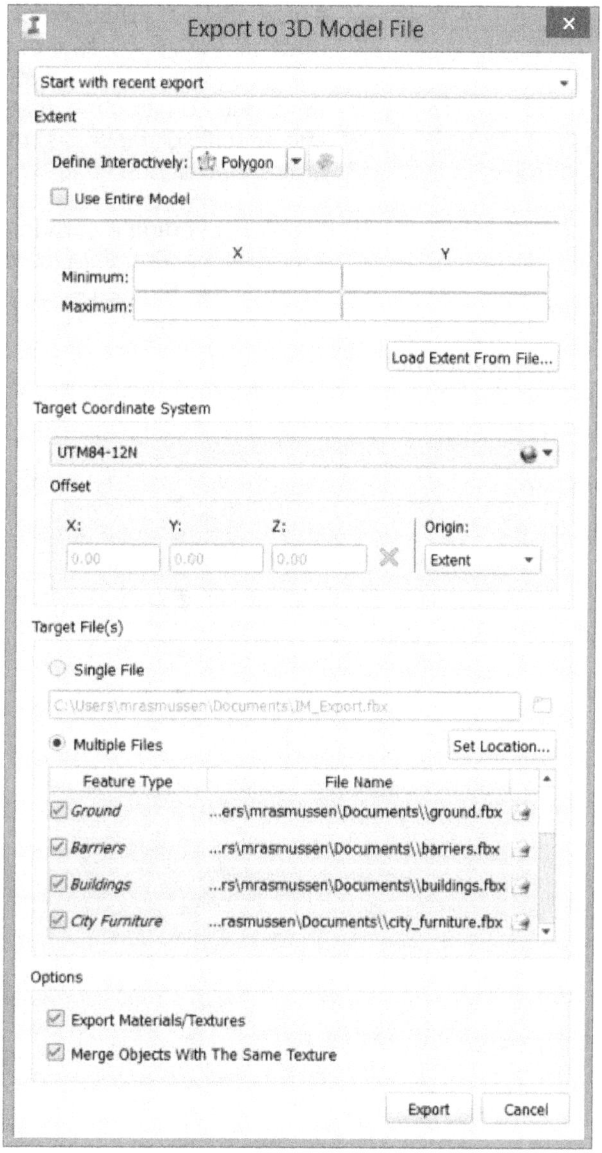

Figure B–12

4. In the Autodesk Navisworks software, you can open the .FBX file or append it to an existing Autodesk Navisworks model.

B.5 Preparing a Corridor Model for TimeLiner

In order to use the Autodesk Navisworks TimeLiner to display a simulation of a road being constructed, you must turn the corridor model into solid parts. This conversion is done in the Autodesk Civil 3D software. By creating separate parts for each material (e.g, sub-base, base, sidewalk, etc.), you can animate the road being constructed one layer at a time, just like it would be during construction. It also enables you to break the road up into specific distances, since the contractor does not build the entire road at one time.

When converting a corridor to solids, it is important that the *Layer Name Template* match the item names in the Gantt chart, as shown in Figure B–13.

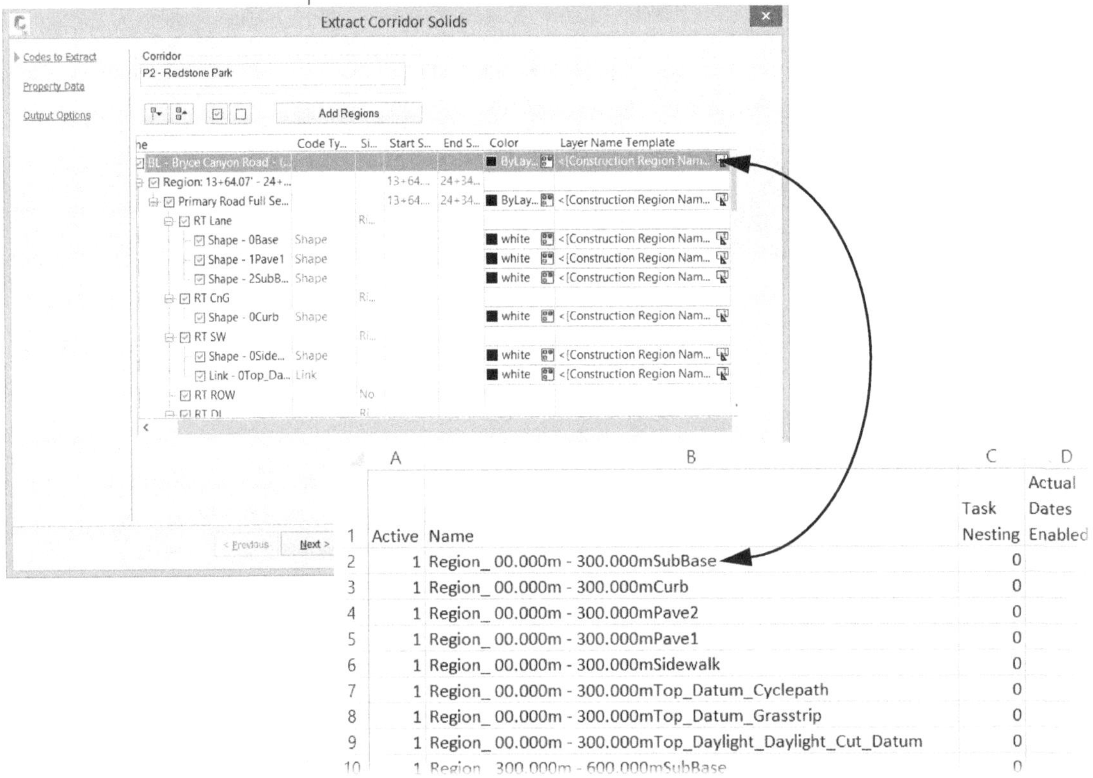

Figure B–13

How To: Extract Corridor Solids

1. In the Autodesk Civil 3D software, select the corridor.
2. In the *Corridor* contextual tab>Corridor Tools panel, click (Extract Corridor Solids).
3. In the model, select only the regions for the area you want to extract. The options include:

*Type **S**, **P**, or **A** in the command line to select the associated option.*

   - **Station Range (S):** Select a region first, and then you are prompted to specify the start station. You can use the cursor to select it or you can type a start station in the command line. After setting the start station, you are prompted to set the end station.
   - **Within Polygon (P):** Enables you to select a previously created polygon.
   - **All Regions (A):** Selects the entire corridor model.
4. In the Extract Corridor Solids dialog box, ensure that the *Layer Name Template* matches the item names in the Gantt chart. If you are using the Gantt chart (.CSV file) included in this guide, do the following to ensure the names match:

- In the *Layer Name Template* column, click (Modify Name Template) next to the **Baseline**, as shown in Figure B–14.

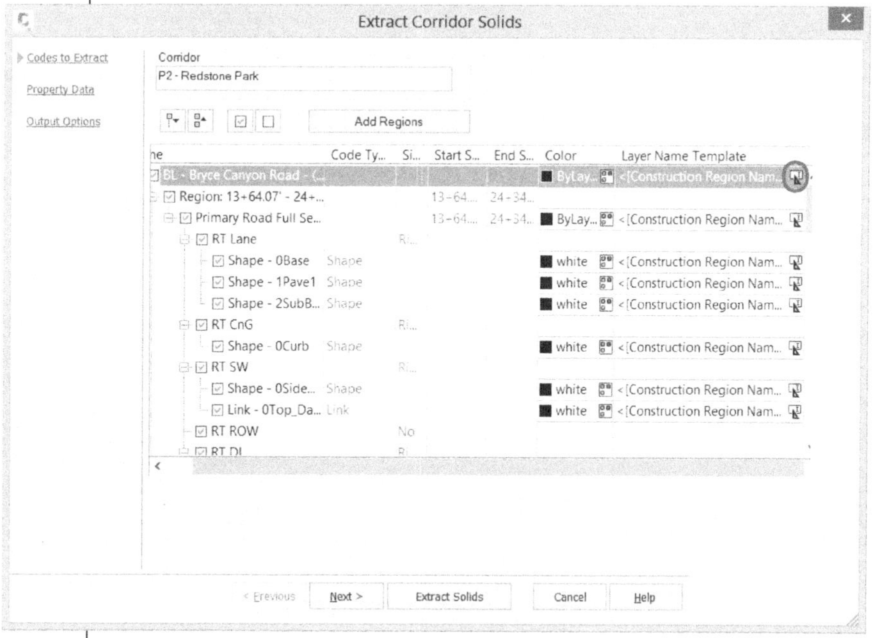

Figure B–14

Selecting the name template for the baseline ensures that all of the regions are updated to the new name template.

You must do this for each baseline listed in the Extract Corridor Solids dialog box.

- In the Name Template dialog box, do the following, as shown in Figure B–15:
    - In the Property fields drop-down list, select **Construction Region Name**.
    - In the *Name* field, highlight everything and click **Insert**.
    - In the Property fields drop-down list, select **Codes**.
    - In the *Name* field, place the cursor at the end and click **Insert**.
    - Click **OK**.

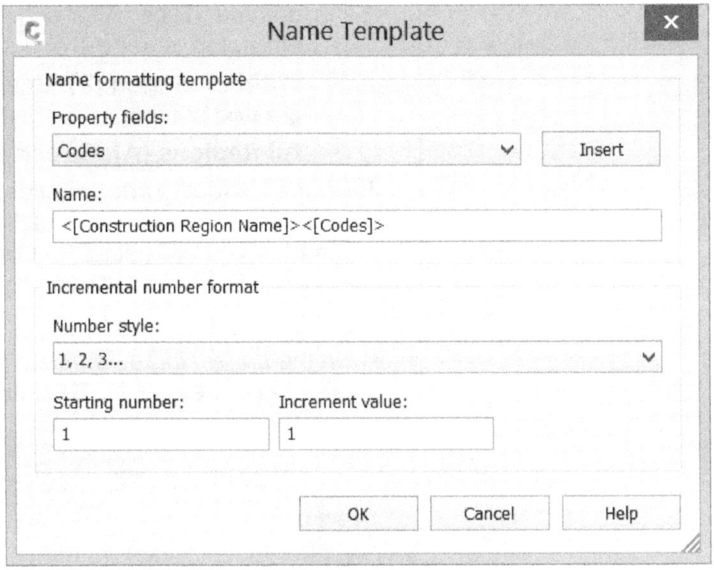

Figure B–15

5. In the Extract Corridor Solids dialog box, click **Next** twice.

6. In the Extract Corridor Solids dialog box>Output Options page (shown in Figure B–16), ensure that **AutoCAD 3D Solids (based on corridor sampling)** is selected, then select where you would like the solids stored:
    - Insert into current drawing
    - Add to an existing drawing
    - Add to a new drawing

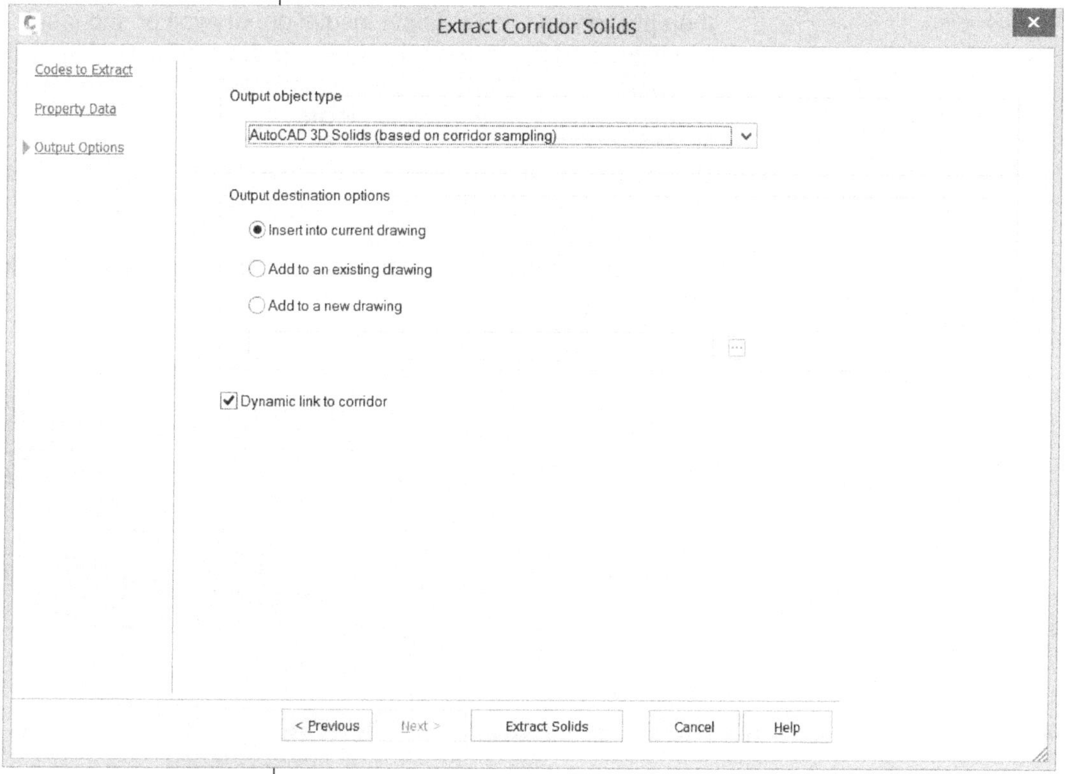

Figure B–16

7. Click **Extract Solids**.

B.6 Preparing an Autodesk Revit Model for TimeLiner

In the Autodesk Revit software, multiple parts form a single object. For example, Figure B–17 shows the parts that form a wall. However, during construction, a wall is built in parts, rather than as a single piece. Framing might be the first thing to go up, then plywood on the outside, insulation, drywall on the inside, windows, and finally the brick on the outermost part of the wall. These Revit parts can be selected in Navisworks when the *Selection Resolution* is set to **Geometry**.

When creating a construction animation using TimeLiner, you want to simulate as closely as possible the construction schedule as laid out in the Gantt chart. In order to do this, you must separate all of the walls, ceilings, floors, etc. into parts in the Autodesk Revit software before importing the model into the Autodesk Navisworks software.

Figure B–17

How To: Separate Objects into Parts

Hint: It is helpful to use selection sets for this.

1. In the Autodesk Revit software, select the objects (all exterior walls, all interior walls, etc.) you want to separate into parts.
2. In the *Modify (Object)* contextual tab>Create panel, click  (Create Parts).
3. Save the file.

Index

S

T

U

V

W

Made in the USA
Las Vegas, NV
01 June 2025

22994889R10293